PC
Help Desk
in a Book

The Do-It-Yourself Guide
to PC Troubleshooting and Repair

Mark Edward Soper

201 West 103rd Street,
Indianapolis, Indiana 46290

PC Help Desk in a Book: The Do-It-Yourself Guide to PC Troubleshooting and Repairing Your PC

International Standard Book Number: 0-7897-2756-0

Library of Congress Catalog Card Number: 2002103977

Printed in the United States of America

First Printing: November 2002

05   04   03   02   4   3   2   1

Trademarks

Warning and Disclaimer

Associate Publisher
Greg Wiegand

Executive Editor
Rick Kughen

Development Editor
Todd Brakke

Managing Editor
Thomas F. Hayes

Project Editor
Tonya Simpson

Production Editor
Benjamin Berg

Indexer
Heather McNeill

Proofreaders
Abby VanHuss
Katie Robinson

Technical Editor
Mark Reddin

Team Coordinator
Sharry Lee Gregory

Interior Designers
Gary Adair
Anne Jones

Cover Designer
Anne Jones

Page Layout
Ayanna Lacey
Stacey Richwine-DeRome

Contents at a Glance

Table of Contents

About the Author

Mark Edward Soper is president of Select Systems and Associates, Inc., a technical writing and training organization.

Mark has taught computer troubleshooting and other technical subjects to thousands of students from Maine to Hawaii since 1992. He is an A+ Certified hardware technician and a Microsoft Certified Professional. He has been writing technical documents since the mid-1980s and has contributed to several other Que books, including *Upgrading and Repairing PCs, 11th, 12th, 13th*, and *14th Editions*; *Upgrading and Repairing Networks, Second Edition*; *Special Edition Using Windows XP, Home Edition*; *Special Edition Using Windows XP, Professional Edition*; and *Special Edition Using Microsoft Windows Millennium Edition*. Mark coauthored *Upgrading and Repairing PCs, Technician's Portable Reference*; *Upgrading and Repairing PCs Field Guide*; and *Upgrading and Repairing PCs: A+ Study Certification Guide, Second Edition*. He is the author of *The Complete Idiot's Guide to High-Speed Internet Connections* and *Absolute Beginner's Guide to Cable Internet Connections* and is coauthor of *TechTV's Upgrading Your PC*.

Mark has been writing for major computer magazines since 1990, with more than 125 articles in publications such as *SmartComputing, PCNovice, PCNovice Guides*, and the *PCNovice Learning Series*. His early work was published in *WordPerfect Magazine, The WordPerfectionist*, and *PCToday*. Many of Mark's articles are available in back issues or electronically via the World Wide Web at www.smartcomputing.com. Select Systems maintains a subject index of all Mark's articles at http://www.selectsystems.com.

Mark welcomes comments at mesoper@selectsystems.com.

Dedication

This book is dedicated to Mayer and Naomi Rubin, who taught me a lot about computer troubleshooting and provided the opportunity for me to teach computer troubleshooting to thousands of others across the country.

Acknowledgments

First of all, as always, I thank God for the ability to write and communicate with you, my readers.

I am deeply grateful to my family for their love and support: Cheryl, whose encouragement and counsel helps improve this book and everything I do. To our children, Kate and her husband Hugh; Edward and his wife Erin; Ian; and Jeremy: Thanks for all the computer questions and problems we've discussed, argued over, and solved together. You've helped keep me on my toes. To my father, Stuart; stepmother, Elaine; and mother-in-law, Alice: Thanks for your love and support and for the opportunity to diagnose your computers in person and remotely.

I also want to thank the publishing and editing team at Que for all the help and support they've provided with this book as with my previous book projects. Whenever I stop by the Que offices, it's like a family reunion.

In particular, I want to thank

David Culverwell, who keeps everyone at Que going in the right direction.

Greg Wiegand, who provides the resources the editors need and answers your questions and comments.

Rick Kughen, whose vision inspired this book.

Todd Brakke, whose sharp eye for structure helped improve the book's organization.

Mark Reddin, whose questions and comments help improve the content.

Tonya Simpson, who keeps every element of the development process going to the right people at the right time.

Sharry Lee Gregory, who keeps those payments coming.

Benjamin Berg, who makes sure that the words and pictures line up properly and that no grammatical rules were broken during the production of this book.

Anne Jones, Gary Adair, Laura Robbins, Tammy Graham, Oliver Jackson, Ayanna Lacey and Stacey Richwine-DeRome (the design, illustration, and layout team), who turn my rough sketches and photos into finished artwork and incorporate them into a coherent design.

Abby VanHuss and Katie Robinson, the proofreaders, who catch any spelling errors that survived my edits.

We Want to Hear from You!

As the reader of this book, *you* are our most important critic and commentator. We value your opinion and want to know what we're doing right, what we could do better, what areas you'd like to see us publish in, and any other words of wisdom you're willing to pass our way.

As an associate publisher for Que, I welcome your comments. You can email or write me directly to let me know what you did or didn't like about this book—as well as what we can do to make our books better.

Please note that I cannot help you with technical problems related to the *topic* of this book. We do have a User Services group, however, where I will forward specific technical questions related to the book.

When you write, please be sure to include this book's title and author as well as your name, email address, and phone number. I will carefully review your comments and share them with the author and editors who worked on the book.

Email: feedback@quepublishing.com

Mail: Greg Wiegand
            Que
            201 West 103rd Street
            Indianapolis, IN 46290 USA

For more information about this book or another Que title, visit our Web site at www.quepublishing.com. Type the ISBN (excluding hyphens) or the title of a book in the Search field to find the page you're looking for.

Introduction

Why You Need This Book

I wrote *PC Help Desk in a Book* for the many computer users who need fast and authoritative solutions to hardware, Windows, application, and Internet problems. Whether you are a home computer user, the designated expert in your office, or working at a computer help desk, when things go wrong for you or the people you support, you need fast answers that work.

Computer problems can be divided into three categories:

- Hardware problems
- Software problems
- Internet/networking problems

To make matters worse, a lot of computer problems involve two or even all three of these areas. Fortunately, *PC Help Desk in a Book* is designed to solve the most common problems you'll encounter in all three areas, even if a combination of hardware, software, and Internet or network problems are plaguing you.

You've probably read troubleshooting books that were all about hardware or all about Windows or application software. These books can be helpful if you're sure which type of problem you're having, but what if you're not sure? The source of a PC problem can be both elusive and misleading. After all, just because your PC crashes on bootup doesn't necessarily mean your problem is with Windows. *PC Help Desk in a Book* is the book you need. You might know that a balky piece of hardware could be malfunctioning because of driver problems, or your software could be broken because of some other problem in your system. With *PC Help Desk in a Book* you can quickly find the solution to your "pure" hardware, "pure" software, or the increasingly common combination hardware-software problems in your system.

What about Internet and network problems? Since the answers to so many computer problems often involve using the Internet to download a new driver, install a service pack, or locate detailed system documentation, you need a working Internet connection to solve problems. If your Internet connection is broken, your ability to solve other types of computer problems is severely limited. *PC Help Desk in a Book* can help, whether your Internet connection is a direct or shared connection. Even if you don't use your network for Internet access, you depend upon it for printer or storage sharing, and *PC Help Desk in a Book*, once again, is the book you need.

Finally, although this book makes every effort to avoid this scenario, no troubleshooting book can solve every problem. Sometimes, you need to call a professional, and this book tells you when you've reached that time. However, I'm confident that *PC Help Desk in a Book* will save you time, money, and effort by helping you diagnose and solve most computer problems yourself. At the very least, you'll have eliminated enough of the possibilities that any qualified tech support professional won't waste your time on "obvious" solutions that run up your long-distance bill!

With this book in hand, you have a total solution for most computer problems. It's a total solution you can trust because it's based on my 18 years of experience with Windows and Intel-compatible computers, 7 years of teaching computer troubleshooting to thousands of students across the country, extensive research, and field testing. During the writing of this book, I added, removed, configured, and reconfigured countless hardware and software combinations on my trusty laboratory computer FRANKENPC and its office mates to develop and test most of the solutions in this book, and Que's terrific team of editors provided additional insight and suggestions during the development process. As a result, *PC Help Desk in a Book* provides real solutions for real problems.

How to Use This Book

Some books are designed to be read from cover to cover. *PC Help Desk in a Book* is different. It's designed to provide you with fast access to technical solutions you can apply right away. Someday, I hope to write the type of book the critics will describe as "a book you can't put down." Frankly, I'd be disappointed if you don't put this book down as soon as you find the solution to your computer problem.

Some books are designed to be read just once; again, *PC Help Desk in a Book* is different. Because of its broad and deep coverage of computer problems and solutions, you'll turn to it as a valuable reference again and again to solve computer problems at home, at the office, or at the corporate help desk.

Here's how to get the most from this book:

1. Start with the Symptoms tables to point you toward underlying problems and their solutions. This is the place to start when you need help fast. Each of the six tables lists symptoms common to parts of your computer, such as display problems, printer or scanner problems, or problems with Windows or its applications.

2. Once at your table, look up the symptom. Each symptom sends you directly to a troubleshooting flowchart that dissects your problem step-by-step until it uncovers the root cause of your problem or to a section in the book that has the solution.

3. Each flowchart provides ample cross-references to the text that provide detailed information about the problem and how to effect a solution. The text, screen shots, and equipment photos found in this book work together to help you learn more about how your hardware and software work and to show you how to solve your problem.

4. Use the special elements in each chapter to find valuable tips and shortcuts, discover useful Web sites, and avoid potential dangers.

As you use this book, you'll no doubt notice that the primary version of Windows used for screen shots is Windows XP. If you're a Windows 9x or Me user, worry not. Other Windows versions are illustrated and discussed when their operation differs greatly from Windows XP. Whether you use Windows XP, Windows Me, Windows 9x, or even Windows 2000, you will find the Windows discussions useful.

Here's an example of how to use this book to solve your problems:

Assume that the onscreen pointer for your mouse or other pointing device, such as a touchpad or trackball, won't move. Consult the Peripherals symptoms table to find the location of a flowchart that has the symptom "Pointing Device Pointer Won't Move." As you go through the flowchart, follow the solutions given in order. For example, in this flowchart, the first question is "Has more than one pointing device been installed on this computer?" If the answer is Yes, use the keyboard to select the correct pointing device or disconnect the pointing device you don't want to use. If the answer is No, the next question is, "How is the device connected to the computer?" If the device is built into your portable computer, you need to be sure the pointing device is enabled in your computer's BIOS setup. I provide a cross-reference to the section of the book that describes how to access the BIOS. Continue through the flowchart until you find the solution that matches your hardware and situation.

Although this might seem a little complicated, it'll become second nature when you start using these flowcharts to find the solution to a PC problem. Troubleshooting PCs is a very complex process, and PC professionals earn very good salaries for their ability to determine why, for example, a display device has failed. This book puts that power in your hands.

How This Book Is Organized

PC Help Desk in a Book includes the following sections:

- Symptoms Tables
- Problem and Solution Flowcharts
- PC Anatomy
- Eleven chapters covering all the important hardware and software components of your computer, their potential problems, and how to fix them

- Appendix A, which covers various Windows utilities and tools that you'll likely use throughout the troubleshooting process
- Appendix B, which helps you develop your troubleshooting philosophy and build your hardware and software toolkit

Each of these parts serves a unique role in helping you fix almost any common PC problem. The following sections explain these roles in greater detail.

Symptoms Tables

When you have a problem with your PC, it's very likely you're not going to know exactly what the source of the problem is. Like a doctor trying to diagnose a sickness, all you have to go on are symptoms. No matter how obscure the problem, these symptoms are clues that you can use to get things running again. So, ask yourself, where does the problem show itself? A Windows error? Your printer won't print? You can't connect to the Internet? The Symptoms Tables provided here are divided into six key areas you are likely to see symptoms of a computer problem:

- Internet and Networking Problems
- Display Problems
- Printer and Scanner Problems
- Windows and Application Problems
- Storage Media and Device Problems
- Peripherals Problems (Mouse/Keyboard/and so on)

To use the Symptoms Tables, select the category associated with your problem, read through the list of symptoms, and go to the flowchart or book section that provides the solutions for your problem.

Problems and Solutions Flowcharts

The "Problem and Solution Flowcharts" section includes dozens of flowcharts covering the most common computer problems you are likely to encounter. Some flowcharts are self-contained, whereas others refer you to additional flowcharts to help further isolate the problem. These flowcharts are easy to read and are extensively cross-referenced to the book sections that provide more detailed background information and solutions.

PC Anatomy 101

The "PC Anatomy 101" section provides a detailed look at what makes your computer work inside and out. It features a tour of the exterior and interior components of typical desktop and notebook computers, focusing on the major points of failure in each area. It also features an extensive tour of the BIOS setup program to help you discover how to configure, enable, or disable particular built-in hardware features. "PC Anatomy 101" also includes a discussion of hardware resources, Power-on Self-Test error codes, and details about the major I/O port types built into typical computers. All of these tools and resources can be valuable allies in diagnosing and fixing a problem. Because you need to be careful when you work inside your computer, "PC Anatomy 101" also provides instructions on how to avoid damage from electrostatic discharge (ESD).

Book Chapters

The main text of this book is divided into 11 chapters. Each chapter focuses on a particular area of troubleshooting, covering both the cause and resolution of common PC problems.

Chapter 1, "Troubleshooting a Windows Installation," provides you with methods to determine whether startup or system hard disk configuration problems are preventing you from starting Windows successfully. This chapter also covers the special startup options available in different versions of Windows, helps you troubleshoot shutdown problems, helps you troubleshoot programs that won't run, and provides help with popular Windows troubleshooting tools and Windows Update.

Chapter 2, "Internet and Online Problems," covers problems with ISP setup software, browser encryption, plug-ins and spyware, Web site viewing, dial-up and broadband Internet connections, and TCP/IP configurations. If you're having problems with your Internet or network connection, this is the chapter for you!

Chapter 3, "Troubleshooting Storage Devices," solves problems with the processes used to install and prepare hard, optical (CD/DVD), and removable-media drives for use with Windows. Interface-specific sections on ATA/IDE, IEEE-1394, USB, SCSI, PC Card, and parallel port drives help you solve problems with all types of drive interfacing. Use the optical drives section to troubleshoot writeable DVD and CD drives and media.

Chapter 4, "Troubleshooting Your Printer," provides solutions for printer recognition, port, and print quality problems. This chapter also teaches you how to use the printer properties sheets and status lights to troubleshoot and control print functions and make use of cleaning utilities.

Chapter 5, "Troubleshooting Display, Audio, and Multimedia Problems," helps you diagnose problems with your monitor, display adapter, sound card, and multimedia playback features.

Chapter 6, "Troubleshooting Input Devices," provides solutions to problems with keyboards, mice and other pointing devices, and scanners. Separate sections on each device and interface type help you deal with the unique challenges of PS/2, USB, wireless, parallel-port, SCSI, and IEEE-1394 devices.

Chapter 7, "Troubleshooting Your Network," provides methods for fixing common network types, and helps you solve problems with Internet sharing, router and client configuration, and the Home Networking Wizard.

Chapter 8, "Troubleshooting Memory Problems," solves problems with virtual memory configuration, system optimization, and physical memory installation.

Chapter 9, "Troubleshooting Processors and Motherboards," tracks down the reasons for processor and motherboard failures, solves upgrade and installation issues, and outlines cures for system cooling issues.

Chapter 10, "Troubleshooting Power Supplies," provides solutions for common problems with power supplies, and demonstrates how to test power supplies, how to replace a power supply with a new one of the correct type and size, and how to protect your system against overvoltages, brownouts, and blackouts.

Chapter 11, "Solving Application Software Problems," helps you overcome problems with application compatibility with Windows XP, how and where to search for solutions, how to update programs with vendor-supplied patch files, and how to cope with file-format problems and other miscellaneous application irritants.

Clear, concise step-by-step instructions, extensively annotated screen shots and equipment photos, and cross-references to related material make each chapter a powerful troubleshooting tool.

Appendixes

PC Help Desk in a Book also features two appendixes designed to help you master the tools, techniques, and philosophy of computer troubleshooting:

- Appendix A, "Using Windows Diagnostic Tools," shows you how to use the Control Panel, Device Manager, System Information, DirectX Diagnostics, Remote Assistance, and other built-in Windows tools to troubleshoot and control your system.
- Appendix B, "The Philosophy of Troubleshooting," provides guidelines and basic methods for troubleshooting your system.

Special Elements in This Book

In addition to extensive cross-referencing, screen shots, and equipment photos, you will also find several special elements in this book to help you with particular troubleshooting issues:

Fast Track to Success

Shortcuts and tips help you learn more about the current topic.

On the Web

Web sites that have more information about the current topic.

Cautions and Warnings

Information you should read and digest before attempting operations that can be hazardous to you, your data, or your computer.

Symptom Tables

Use the tables in this section to find your problem and locate a solution. Cross-references listed here point to various troubleshooting flowcharts and chapter sections, sidebars, and tables that can help identify and resolve your PC's problem.

DISPLAY AND AUDIO PROBLEMS

Symptom	Flowchart or Book Section	Page Number
I'm having display quality problems while running 3D games.	Flowchart: 3D Gaming Display Quality Problems	32
I'm having display speed problems while playing 3D games.	Flowchart: 3D Gaming Display Speed Problems	33
I'm having problems seeing the display when I start my computer.	Flowchart: The Computer Starts but the Screen Is Blank	27
My CRT display is flickering.	Flowchart: CRT Display Is Flickering	31
Photos and graphics look distorted; there aren't enough colors.	Flowchart: Display Has Too Few Colors	29
My display has wavy lines.	Flowchart: Display Has Wavy Lines	30
My display is too dark.	Section: The Text Is Too Dim or Too Bright	283
I can't see part of the screen image.	Flowchart: Part of the Screen Image Is Missing	28
The cursor is hard to see.	Section: Display	474
I don't have any tabs for adjusting 3D modes on my display driver.	Sidebar: Fast Track to Success	303
The text and fonts onscreen are too small.	Sidebar: Fast Track to Success	474
The screen keeps blanking out on a computer I want to keep running all the time.	Section: Power Options Section: Display	479 474

Continues...

TROUBLESHOOTING

DISPLAY AND AUDIO PROBLEMS, *Continued*

Symptom	Flowchart or Book Section	Page Number
I need to disable the screen saver.	Section: Power Options Section: Display	479 474
The display is blank after I install a new ATA/IDE drive.	Section: Checking the Drive and Host Adapter Connection to the Data Cable	196
Some Web sites are very hard to read.	Section: Troubleshooting Problems with Viewing Certain Web Sites	162
The edges of the CRT monitor display are distorted.	Section: The Edges of the Windows Desktop Are Curved	283
I can't select the color setting I prefer on my system with integrated graphics.	Section: Increasing Available Display Memory on Systems with Integrated Video	296
The computer starts only if I choose VGA mode or Safe Mode.	Section: Can't Start the Computer Using Normal Display Drivers	299
My computer starts, but locks up frequently.	Section: Computer Locks Up Frequently or Has Display Quality Problems	300
My computer's display gets corrupted when I move the mouse.	Section: Computer Locks Up Frequently or Has Display Quality Problems	300
My computer's display gets corrupted when I play 3D games.	Section: Computer Locks Up Frequently or Has Display Quality Problems	300
My secondary display isn't working.	Section: Troubleshooting Multiple Displays	305
I think my monitor is damaged.	Section: Troubleshooting Damaged or Defective Displays or Display Adapters	311
I can't replace the built-in sound on my motherboard with a sound card.	Section: Troubleshooting Problems with Sound Card Installation and Drivers	312

TROUBLESHOOTING

DISPLAY AND AUDIO PROBLEMS, *Continued*

Symptom	Flowchart or Book Section	Page Number
My sound hardware doesn't seem to be working.	Flowchart: Audio Hardware Problems	34
I can't hear anything coming from my speakers.	Flowchart: Speaker and Volume Control Problems	35
I'm having problems playing music CDs.	Section: Troubleshooting Playback Problems with Music CDs	319
I've replaced my stereo speakers with a set with additional speakers, but the new speakers don't work.	Section: Can't Hear Sound from Additional Speakers	316
I don't know what volume controls to adjust when I play different types of sounds or music.	Table: Refer to Table 5.7	316
I need to update DirectX to fix problems with my sound card.	Sidebar: On the Web	318

INTERNET AND NETWORKING PROBLEMS

Symptom	Flowchart or Book Section	Page Number
Can't connect to Internet using a dial-up modem.	Flowchart: Can't Connect to Internet via a Dial-Up Connection	36
Can't connect to Internet using a broadband or PPPoE connection (cable, DSL, etc.).	Flowchart: Can't Connect to Internet via a Broadband or PPPoE Connection	37
Network users can't change or copy files to a shared folder.	Flowchart: Can't Access Shared Files	41
Some users on the network can't access shared resources.	Flowchart: Shared Resource Troubleshooting	42
I can't download a file from a Web site.	Flowchart: File Download Problems	40

Continues...

TROUBLESHOOTING

INTERNET AND NETWORKING PROBLEMS, *Continued*

Symptom	Flowchart or Book Section	Page Number
I can't open or view a particular Web page, although other pages open properly.	Flowchart: Web Page Problems	39
I can't use email.	Flowchart: Email Problems	38
I can't open a secured Web site.	Section: Troubleshooting Problems with Secure Web Sites	158
I need to find out what the encryption strength of my browser is.	Section: Troubleshooting Problems with Secure Web Sites	158
Some of my favorite Web sites use Java, but my copy of Internet Explorer doesn't include Java.	Sidebar: Fast Track to Success	161
The colors used on some Web pages are hard to read.	Section: Troubleshooting Problems with Viewing Certain Web Sites	162
I want to save a Web page as a document so that I can view it or email it at a later time.	Sidebar: Fast Track to Success	163
I've just moved, and I need to change the dial-up number I use to connect to the Internet.	Section: The Dial-Up Networking General Tab	165
I use a dial-up Internet connection in various locations, and I don't want to keep entering the dial-up number every time.	Section: The Dial-Up Networking General Tab	165
I can't connect to the Internet Connection Sharing host after I enabled an Internet firewall on that computer.	Section: The Advanced Tab	168
I need to configure my dial-up or PPPoE Internet connection to use a fixed IP address.	Section: Using a Fixed IP Address with a Dial-Up or PPPoE Broadband Connection in Windows XP/2000	169
	Section: Using a Fixed IP Address with a Dial-Up Connection in Windows 9x/Me	170

Continues...

TROUBLESHOOTING

INTERNET AND NETWORKING PROBLEMS, *Continued*

Symptom	Flowchart or Book Section	Page Number
I need to configure my cable modem or wireless Internet connection with a fixed IP address.	Section: Using a Fixed IP Address with a LAN, Cable Modem, or Fixed Wireless Connection in Windows XP/2000	171
	Section: Using a Fixed IP Address with a Cable Modem, Fixed Wireless, or Internet Connection in Windows 9x/Me	171
I need to configure a computer on the network with a fixed IP address.	Section: Using a Fixed IP Address with a LAN, Cable Modem, or Fixed Wireless Connection in Windows XP/2000	171
	Section: Using a Fixed IP Address with a Cable Modem, Fixed Wireless, or Internet Connection in Windows 9x/Me	171
When I try to connect to the Internet with my modem, there's no dial tone.	Section: Modem Has No Dial Tone	173
My computer dials, but I never connect with the remote computer.	Section: PC Can Dial but Does Not Connect	174
I get a "port already open" error when I try to connect to the Internet with my modem.	Section: Port Already Open	175
I'm not sure whether my modem is working.	Section: Using Analog Modem Diagnostics	176
I'm not sure my network cables are plugged in properly.	Section: Troubleshooting a Broadband Internet Connection	177
I'm not sure the connections to my cable modem are working.	Section: Troubleshooting a Cable Modem Connection	178
I'm having problems with my DSL connection to the Internet.	Section: Troubleshooting a DSL Connection	179

Continues...

TROUBLESHOOTING

INTERNET AND NETWORKING PROBLEMS, *Continued*

Symptom	Flowchart or Book Section	Page Number
I'm having problems with my DirecWAY, Starband, or other satellite Internet connection.	Section: Troubleshooting a Satellite Connection	181
The signal lights on my broadband Internet modem don't look right.	Section: Using Signal Lights to Troubleshoot Your Connection	182
I connect to the Internet through a router, and I've lost my connection.	Section: Troubleshooting a Router	183
I need to find out what Internet settings my computer is using.	Section: Using IPCONFIG and WINIPCFG	187
How do I use PING to test my Internet connection?	Section: Using PING	189
How can I find out if my network adapter is working?	Section: I'm Not Sure My Network Adapter Is Working	363
How can I check my cabling?	Section: Troubleshooting Cabling	365
I connected my computer to the Uplink port on a switch or router and now I can't connect to the Internet.	Section: Troubleshooting Cabling	365
I'm having problems adding a computer to my wireless network.	Section: Troubleshooting Wireless Network Hardware	367
Can I use an 802.11a wireless network card with a Wi-Fi network?	Sidebar: Cautions and Warnings	371
I want to set up a computer as an Internet Connection Sharing (ICS) host, but I don't have room for another network card inside the computer.	Sidebar: Fast Track to Success	372
I turned on my computer before the ICS host was finished booting, and now I can't connect to the Internet.	Section: I'm Not Sure I Have a Valid IP Address	381
I can access the Internet, but I can't see other computers or shared resources on the network.	Section: I'm Not Sure My Network Settings Are Correct	379

Continues...

TROUBLESHOOTING

INTERNET AND NETWORKING PROBLEMS, *Continued*

PERIPHERAL AND PERIPHERAL CONNECTION PROBLEMS

Continues...

PERIPHERAL AND PERIPHERAL CONNECTION PROBLEMS, *Continued*

Symptom	Flowchart or Book Section	Page Number
I have an IEEE-1394 (FireWire, i.Link) port installed, but my system can't detect it.	Flowchart: Can't Detect Installed IEEE-1394 Port	53
My wireless input or pointing device doesn't work.	Flowchart: Wireless Input and Pointing Device Problems	50
I'm having a problem with a device connected to the IEEE-1394 port.	Flowchart: IEEE-1394 Device Troubleshooting	54
The Device Manager lists an I/O port or device with a problem.	Flowchart: I/O Port Is Detected but Not Working Properly	51
I'm having a problem with a device connected to my parallel port.	Flowchart: Parallel Port Troubleshooting	55
A drive or device attached to the SCSI interface isn't working.	Flowchart: SCSI Device Troubleshooting	57
I'm having a problem with a device connected to the USB port.	Flowchart: USB Device Troubleshooting	52
Where can I find drivers for Logitech, Microsoft, or IBM mice, trackballs, and keyboards?	Sidebar: On the Web	333
I just bought an adapter to connect my mouse to a different type of port. Why doesn't it work?	Section: Peripheral Adapters: When (and Why) They Don't Always Work	342
I just connected a bus-powered USB device to a USB hub, and it doesn't work.	Section: Using Device Manager to Troubleshoot USB Devices	338
Whenever I move my mouse around the desktop, it's dragging objects, even if I'm not holding down the left button.	Table: Refer to Table 6.4	347
I want to switch the mouse buttons around.	Table: Refer to Table 6.4	347
I'm having problems double-clicking objects.	Table: Refer to Table 6.4	347

Continues...

TROUBLESHOOTING

PERIPHERAL AND PERIPHERAL CONNECTION PROBLEMS, *Continued*

Symptom	Flowchart or Book Section	Page Number
I'm having a hard time seeing the mouse pointer.	Table: Refer to Table 6.4	347
The mouse pointer is too fast or too slow.	Table: Refer to Table 6.4	347
The scroll wheel on the mouse scrolls too slowly or too quickly.	Table: Refer to Table 6.4	347
I plug a mouse from another computer into the PS/2 port, but it doesn't work.	Section: Using the System BIOS to Solve Problems with PS/2 Pointing Devices	348
My USB keyboard works fine in Windows, but it doesn't work within the BIOS setup.	Section: Using the System BIOS to Solve Problems with USB Devices	349
I'm not sure my processor and case fans are running fast enough.	Section: Detecting Overheating and Incorrect Voltage Levels	412
I just installed a new processor, and now my computer won't start.	Section: My System Won't Start After I Installed a New Processor	431
The power supply is very warm to the touch.	Section: Troubleshooting an Overheated Power Supply	435
My computer restarts itself, even though I didn't do anything.	Section: Troubleshooting a Power Supply That Reboots the Computer	436
My computer works well in one room, but if I move it to another room, it crashes frequently.	Section: Checking Wall Outlets	446
I'm having a problem installing updated drivers for my hardware.	Section: Installing the Best Device Drivers—Look for the Microsoft Signature	152
I need to add more RAM (memory), but I don't have any empty memory sockets.	Section: Freeing Up Space for Additional Memory	402
I've opened the case, but I can't get to the memory sockets to perform an upgrade.	Table: Refer to Table 8.2	403

Continues…

PERIPHERAL AND PERIPHERAL CONNECTION PROBLEMS, *Continued*

Symptom	Flowchart or Book Section	Page Number
I installed new memory, but the system didn't detect it.	Table: Refer to Table 8.2 Section: Troubleshooting Defective Memory or Memory Sockets	403 407
I installed new memory, but the computer displayed a memory-size error when I restarted it.	Table: Refer to Table 8.2	403
My computer reports memory errors after I install new memory.	Table: Refer to Table 8.2 Section: Testing Installed Memory	403 408
I installed new memory, but the computer beeps instead of starting.	Section: Troubleshooting Memory with POST Beep Codes	409
I don't know how to test the memory installed in my computer.	Section: Testing Installed Memory	408
I need to add memory (RAM) but I don't know what type I should add.	Section: Determining What You Need	398
The brass spacers in my case don't line up with my new motherboard.	Section: I'm Having a Hard Time Fitting My New Motherboard into My Case	427
I just installed a new processor, and the system won't restart.	Section: My System Won't Start After I Installed a New Processor	431
I don't know how much power my USB hub has available for devices.	Section: Using Device Manager to Troubleshoot USB Devices	338
I'm having problems installing my new processor and heatsink.	Section: I'm Having a Hard Time Installing My New Processor	429
How can I tell if my new processor is running at the correct speed?	Section: My New Processor Isn't Running as Fast as It Should	432
How can I play sounds while I troubleshoot sound hardware?	Section: Sounds and Audio Devices	480
Where can I find the meanings of the error codes in Device Manager?	Table: Refer to Table A.2	482
What hardware, software, and firmware make up the different parts of the computer?	Table: Refer to Table B.2	511

TROUBLESHOOTING

PRINTER AND SCANNER PROBLEMS

Symptom	Flowchart or Book Section	Page Number
A printer on my network doesn't print.	Flowchart: Network Printer Doesn't Print	59
A printer attached to my computer doesn't print.	Flowchart: Local Printer Doesn't Print	58
My printer is producing poor-quality output.	Flowchart: Print Quality Problems	60
I'm having problems with my scanner.	Flowchart: Scanner Problems	61
My USB printer works great on my Windows XP computer, but doesn't work with Windows 98.	Section: USB Printing Issues	255
My printer won't display status messages when I use it with a switchbox.	Section: Switchbox Issues	256
I'm not sure what the best resolution is to use for scanning photos I want to print.	Section: Choosing Print-Worthy Images	261
When I print pages with a lot of graphics on my laser printer, they have to be ejected, and the page isn't completely printed.	Section: Out of Memory Error	266
Other users on the network can't see my printer.	Section: The Sharing Tab	271
My inkjet printer has gaps in its output.	Section: The Utilities Tab	274
My inkjet printer's vertical lines are out of alignment.	Section: The Utilities Tab	274
I'm not sure if Windows can communicate with my printer.	Table: Refer to Table 4.1	274
My document layout doesn't match the layout used by the printer.	Table: Refer to Table 4.1	274
The printer ejects pages in reverse order.	Table: Refer to Table 4.1	274

Continues...

TROUBLESHOOTING

PRINTER AND SCANNER PROBLEMS, *Continued*

Symptom	Flowchart or Book Section	Page Number
I want to put multiple pages on a single sheet of paper.	Table: Refer to Table 4.1	274
I am almost out of color ink but I need to print pages anyway.	Table: Refer to Table 4.1	274
I need to print my document on a printer I can't connect to over the network or locally.	Table: Refer to Table 4.1	274
I don't want to waste paper by printing documents that don't match the printer's configuration.	Table: Refer to Table 4.1	274
I cannot select all the features of my printer.	Table: Refer to Table 4.1	274
I want to put different paper/media sizes in the different paper trays of my printer.	Table: Refer to Table 4.1	274
I added additional memory to my laser or LED printer to fix out-of-memory problems, but I'm not sure Windows has detected the additional memory.	Table: Refer to Table 4.1	274
The printer is producing gibberish output.	Section: Troubleshooting Gibberish Output	277
The scanner is detected, but won't scan.	Section: Common Problems and Solutions for Scanners	354
My USB scanner isn't working correctly.	Section: Troubleshooting USB Scanners	355
My parallel-port scanner isn't working properly.	Section: Troubleshooting Parallel-Port Scanners	356
My SCSI scanner isn't working properly.	Section: Troubleshooting SCSI Scanners	356
My IEEE-1394a scanner isn't working properly.	Section: Troubleshooting IEEE-1394a Scanners	357

Continues...

TROUBLESHOOTING

PRINTER AND SCANNER PROBLEMS, *Continued*

Symptom	Flowchart or Book Section	Page Number
Windows can scan photos, but can't use the auto document feeder (ADF) or transparency adapter on my scanner.	Section: Common Problems and Solutions for Scanners	354
I can't get my network-ready scanner to scan from a remote computer.	Section: Common Problems and Solutions for Scanners	354
The scanner head won't move.	Section: Common Problems and Solutions for Scanners	354
One-button scanning doesn't work.	Section: Common Problems and Solutions for Scanners	354

STORAGE MEDIA AND DEVICE PROBLEMS

Symptom	Flowchart or Book Section	Page Number
I can't format or partition an IDE hard disk for use with any version of Windows.	Flowchart: Can't Prepare an IDE Hard Drive After Installing It	63
I can't copy files to an IDE hard drive.	Flowchart: Can't Change Contents of IDE Hard Drive	65
I can't delete or change files on an IDE drive.	Flowchart: Can't Change Contents of IDE Hard Drive	65
I can't format a floppy disk.	Flowchart: Can't Change Contents of a Floppy Disk	78
I can't erase files from a floppy disk.	Flowchart: Can't Change Contents of a Floppy Disk	78
I can't read a disk in the floppy drive.	Flowchart: Floppy Drive Problems	77
I can't save files to a floppy disk.	Flowchart: Can't Change Contents of a Floppy Disk	78
I can't boot from the ATA/IDE hard disk.	Flowchart: Hard Drive Doesn't Boot	64
I can't access a newly installed IDE/ATA hard drive.	Flowchart: IDE Hard Drive Installation Troubleshooting	62

Continues...

STORAGE MEDIA AND DEVICE PROBLEMS, *Continued*

Symptom	Flowchart or Book Section	Page Number
I can't use an optical or removable media drive connected to the IDE interface in my computer.	Flowchart: IDE Removable Media and Optical Drive Troubleshooting	75
I can't read optical media.	Flowchart: General Optical Drive Problems	66
I can't erase, format, or save files to a removable-media disk (LS-120/240 SuperDisk, Zip disk, Jaz, Orb, or others).	Flowchart: Removable Media Drive Problems	76
I'm having problems writing to CD-R or CD-RW media.	Flowchart: CD-R and CD-RW Drive and Media Troubleshooting	70
I can't read recordable (CD-R) media in the target drive.	Flowchart: Can't Read Recordable (CD-R) Media	71
I'm getting a buffer underrun error when I try to create a recordable CD using a drive or software that supports buffer underrun protection.	Flowchart: Buffer Underrun Problems on Drives with Underrun Protection	69
I'm getting a buffer underrun error when I try to create a recordable CD using a drive or software that doesn't support buffer underrun protection.	Flowchart: Buffer Underrun Problems on Drives without Underrun Protection	68
I can't copy (drag and drop) files to a CD-R or CD-RW disc.	Flowchart: Can't Copy or Drag and Drop Files to CD-R or CD-RW Media	73
I can't read CD-RW media in my target computer.	Flowchart: Rewritable (CD-RW) Media Problems	72
A drive or device attached to the SCSI isn't working.	Flowchart: SCSI Device Troubleshooting	57
I can't delete files from a CD-RW disc.	Flowchart: Can't Delete Files from a CD-RW or Rewritable DVD Disc	74
I can't read a particular recordable or rewritable DVD disc with my DVD drive.	Flowchart: DVD Drive Problems	67

Continues…

TROUBLESHOOTING

STORAGE MEDIA AND DEVICE PROBLEMS, *Continued*

Symptom	Flowchart or Book Section	Page Number
When I run error-checking or defrag with Windows 9x/Me, the process keeps restarting.	Section: Maintaining Windows with Drive and Anti-Virus Utilities	152
I've changed the hard disk BIOS setting from Auto to another setting, and now my computer won't start.	Section: Configuring a Hard Drive in BIOS	125
I'm not sure what software was used to prepare my hard disk.	Section: Special Procedures for Special Cases	127
I can't boot from the Windows CD-ROM.	Section: Troubleshooting Hard Disk or Optical Drive Bootup Problems	233
I installed Y-splitters to power additional drives, and now I'm having problems.	Section: Checking the Drive Connection to the Power Supply	196
I just installed a new ATA/IDE drive, and the screen is blank when I turn on the computer.	Section: Checking the Drive and Host Adapter Connection to the Data Cable	196
I've lost the documentation for my drive and need information about jumpers and other settings.	Sidebar: On the Web	202
I think my hard disk has failed.	Section: Determining When Your ATA/IDE Drive Has Failed	202
My IEEE-1394a or USB drive is detected when I plug it into the rear of the computer, but not when I plug it into a port on the front of the computer.	Sidebar: Cautions and Warnings	205
My USB drive has stopped working since I attached it to a longer USB cable.	Section: Troubleshooting Other Problems with USB Drives	207
My USB drive doesn't work if I attach it to a hub built into the keyboard.	Section: Troubleshooting Other Problems with USB Drives	207

Continues...

TROUBLESHOOTING

STORAGE MEDIA AND DEVICE PROBLEMS, *Continued*

Symptom	Flowchart or Book Section	Page Number
I just added a new SCSI drive to my system, and now I'm having problems with several SCSI devices.	Section: Troubleshooting Termination and Device ID Settings	209
My PC Card slots work, but a new PC Card drive I just plugged in isn't recognized.	Section: Troubleshooting a PC Card Drive	212
Windows XP recognizes my new hard disk, but Windows 98 can't read it.	Sidebar: Fast Track to Success	218
I need to install Windows 98 or Windows Me, but I don't have a bootable startup disk.	Sidebar: Fast Track to Success	226
When I run FDISK with Windows 98, it doesn't recognize the full capacity of my drive.	Section: Troubleshooting Problems with Recognizing Full Drive Capacity	229
I keep running FDISK but it can't partition the disk.	Section: Troubleshooting Disk Partitioning Problems	231
I keep running Disk Management but it can't partition the disk.	Section: Troubleshooting Disk Partitioning Problems	231
My new CD-mastering program doesn't recognize my writable drive.	Section: Troubleshooting CD-Mastering Drive Support Problems	239
I'm not sure which connectors to use for master and slave ATA/IDE drives.	Table: Refer to Table 3.2	201
I'm not sure how to jumper my ATA/IDE drives.	Table: Refer to Table 3.2	201

TROUBLESHOOTING

WINDOWS AND APPLICATION PROBLEMS

Symptom	Flowchart or Book Section	Page Number
Windows will start only in Safe Mode.	Flowchart: Windows Starts Only in Safe Mode	81
I'm getting an error message whenever I try to use a particular program.	Flowchart: A Program Displays an Error When I Use It	83
I can't start a program from its Start menu or Desktop shortcut.	Flowchart: I Can't Start a Program from a Shortcut	82
When I turn on my computer, it doesn't start up correctly.	Flowchart: The Computer Doesn't Start	79
When I turn on my computer, I see an error message.	Flowchart: The Computer Displays Error Messages at Startup	80
I want to create MP3 digital music files, but all I have is Windows Media Player.	Sidebar: On the Web	323
I'm not sure I can use Windows Media Player to view a DVD movie.	Section: Can't View a DVD Movie	324
Where can I get an update to DirectX?	Sidebar: On the Web	318
My computer starts only if I choose VGA mode or use VGA display drivers.	Section: Can't Start the Computer Using Normal Display Drivers	299
I want to find out what program or process is preventing Windows from starting properly.	Section: Understanding the Boot Log	131
I want to stop some programs from loading at startup.	Section: Using MSConfig	501
I'm having problems shutting down Windows.	Section: Shutdown Problems with Windows	134
Some of my programs won't run under Windows XP.	Section: Troubleshooting Programs That Won't Run Under Windows XP	138

Continues...

TROUBLESHOOTING

WINDOWS AND APPLICATION PROBLEMS, *Continued*

Symptom	Flowchart or Book Section	Page Number
I'm getting STOP errors on my system.	Section: Troubleshooting Stop Errors with Windows 2000/XP	142
	Section: Preventing and Reducing Occurrences of BSOD Errors in Windows	144
I'm getting fatal exception errors on my system.	Section: Troubleshooting Fatal Exception Errors with Windows 9x/Me	143
	Section: Preventing and Reducing Occurrences of BSOD Errors in Windows	144
I'm getting "blue screen of death" (BSOD) errors on my Windows XP/2000 computer.	Section: Troubleshooting Stop Errors in Windows XP	142
	Section: Preventing and Reducing Occurrences of BSOD Errors in Windows	144
I'm getting "blue screen of death" (BSOD) errors on my Windows 9x/Me computer.	Section: Troubleshooting Fatal Exception Errors with Windows 9x/Me	143
	Section: Preventing and Reducing Occurrences of BSOD Errors in Windows	144
I'm getting "Illegal Operations" errors on my computer.	Section: Troubleshooting Illegal Operations and Other Error Messages	145
I'm having problems running game programs.	Section: Troubleshooting Games	146
I'm not sure DirectX is working correctly.	Section: Using DirectX Diagnostics	497
I want to test my 3D sound and 3D video drivers.	Section: Using DirectX Diagnostics	497

Continues...

TROUBLESHOOTING

WINDOWS AND APPLICATION PROBLEMS, *Continued*

Symptom	Flowchart or Book Section	Page Number
I'm not sure what types of hardware my version of Windows supports.	Section: Windows Limitations	148
How can I make sure I have the latest fixes to Windows?	Section: Using Windows Update	150
My computer's slow and I'm wondering whether adding RAM (memory) would help.	Section: Troubleshooting Memory Bottlenecks	385
I've run out of space on the C:drive.	Section: Using Disk Cleanup	391
I need to move my paging (swap) file to another drive.	Section: Viewing and Adjusting Pagefile (Swapfile) Configuration	393
I'm having sound quality or performance problems when I play 3D games.	Section: Troubleshooting Problems with 3D Sound in Games	318
I can't play Windows Media Audio (WMA) files with Windows Media Player.	Section: Can't Play Back WMA Digital Files with Windows Media Player	322
Windows Media Player doesn't recognize my portable music hardware.	Section: Windows Media Player Can't Work with Some Devices or Types of Media	323
Windows Media Player can't play a new type of media file.	Section: Windows Media Player Can't Work with Some Devices or Types of Media	323
My advanced speaker system won't work with my DVD player software.	Section: Can't Use Advanced Speaker Systems with Your DVD Player	325
I don't know how to run the diagnostic software provided with my network adapter.	Section: I'm Not Sure My Network Adapter Is Working	363
How do I access the Microsoft Knowledge Base?	Section: Researching Your Program's Compatibility with Windows	454

Continues…

TROUBLESHOOTING

WINDOWS AND APPLICATION PROBLEMS, *Continued*

Symptom	Flowchart or Book Section	Page Number
I can't open some types of files in my favorite programs.	Section: I Can't Open a Particular Type of File	461
I can't see the file extensions in My Computer/Windows Explorer.	Sidebar: Fast Track to Success	475
I can't install programs or hardware in Windows XP.	Section: Add Hardware Section: Add or Remove Programs	469 470
Windows isn't working correctly since I installed some older software.	Section: Using File Signature Verification	496
A program or feature built into Windows isn't working correctly.	Section: Using System File Checker	496
I need to get help from a Windows XP user located at another computer.	Section: Remote Assistance in Windows XP	498
I need to help a Windows XP user located at another computer.	Section: Remote Assistance in Windows XP	498
I need to find out which startup program is causing problems.	Section: Using MSConfig	501
Windows 9x/Me is running very slowly or crashing when I have several programs open.	Section: Troubleshooting System Resource Shortages in Windows 9x/Me	503
Windows 9x/Me is running very slowly or crashing when I leave the system on for a long time.	Section: Troubleshooting System Resource Shortages in Windows 9x/Me	503

The Computer Starts, but the Screen Is Blank

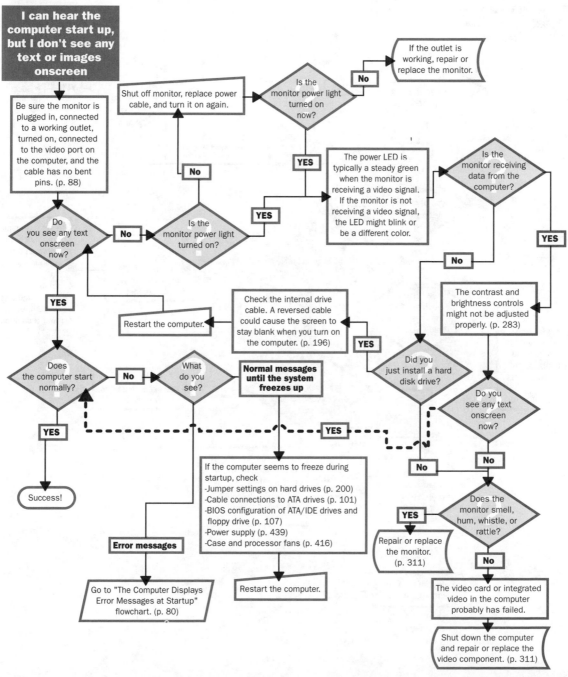

I can hear the computer start up, but I don't see any text or images onscreen

Be sure the monitor is plugged in, connected to a working outlet, turned on, connected to the video port on the computer, and the cable has no bent pins. (p. 88)

Shut off monitor, replace power cable, and turn it on again.

Is the monitor power light turned on now?

No → If the outlet is working, repair or replace the monitor.

YES

The power LED is typically a steady green when the monitor is receiving a video signal. If the monitor is not receiving a video signal, the LED might blink or be a different color.

Is the monitor receiving data from the computer?

Do you see any text onscreen now?

No → **Is the monitor power light turned on?**

YES

No

The contrast and brightness controls might not be adjusted properly. (p. 283)

YES

Restart the computer.

Check the internal drive cable. A reversed cable could cause the screen to stay blank when you turn on the computer. (p. 196)

YES

Did you just install a hard disk drive?

Do you see any text onscreen now?

YES

Does the computer start normally?

No → **What do you see?**

Normal messages until the system freezes up

YES

YES

Success!

If the computer seems to freeze during startup, check
- Jumper settings on hard drives (p. 200)
- Cable connections to ATA drives (p. 101)
- BIOS configuration of ATA/IDE drives and floppy drive (p. 107)
- Power supply (p. 439)
- Case and processor fans (p. 416)

No

No

YES → Repair or replace the monitor. (p. 311)

Does the monitor smell, hum, whistle, or rattle?

Error messages

Go to "The Computer Displays Error Messages at Startup" flowchart. (p. 80)

Restart the computer.

No

The video card or integrated video in the computer probably has failed.

Shut down the computer and repair or replace the video component. (p. 311)

Part of the Screen Image Is Missing

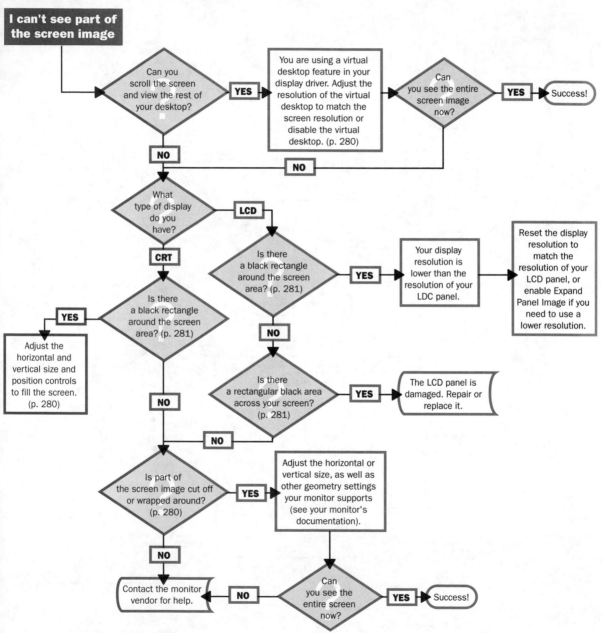

I can't see part of the screen image

Can you scroll the screen and view the rest of your desktop?

YES → You are using a virtual desktop feature in your display driver. Adjust the resolution of the virtual desktop to match the screen resolution or disable the virtual desktop. (p. 280)

Can you see the entire screen image now? **YES** → Success!

NO

What type of display do you have?

LCD → **Is there a black rectangle around the screen area? (p. 281)**

YES → Your display resolution is lower than the resolution of your LDC panel. → Reset the display resolution to match the resolution of your LCD panel, or enable Expand Panel Image if you need to use a lower resolution.

NO → **Is there a rectangular black area across your screen? (p. 281)** **YES** → The LCD panel is damaged. Repair or replace it.

CRT → **Is there a black rectangle around the screen area? (p. 281)**

YES → Adjust the horizontal and vertical size and position controls to fill the screen. (p. 280)

NO

NO → **Is part of the screen image cut off or wrapped around? (p. 280)**

YES → Adjust the horizontal or vertical size, as well as other geometry settings your monitor supports (see your monitor's documentation).

Can you see the entire screen now? **YES** → Success!

NO → Contact the monitor vendor for help.

Display Has Too Few Colors

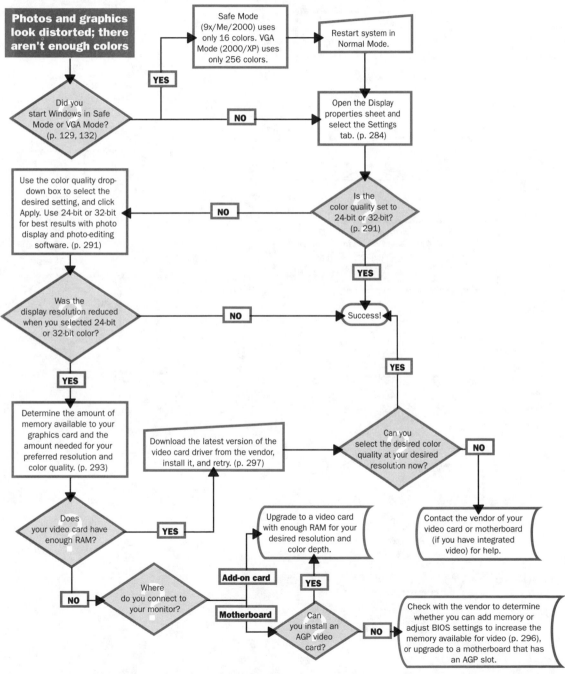

Photos and graphics look distorted; there aren't enough colors

Did you start Windows in Safe Mode or VGA Mode? (p. 129, 132)

YES → Safe Mode (9x/Me/2000) uses only 16 colors. VGA Mode (2000/XP) uses only 256 colors. → Restart system in Normal Mode.

NO → Open the Display properties sheet and select the Settings tab. (p. 284)

Is the color quality set to 24-bit or 32-bit? (p. 291)

NO → Use the color quality drop-down box to select the desired setting, and click Apply. Use 24-bit or 32-bit for best results with photo display and photo-editing software. (p. 291)

YES → Success!

Was the display resolution reduced when you selected 24-bit or 32-bit color?

NO → Success!

YES → Determine the amount of memory available to your graphics card and the amount needed for your preferred resolution and color quality. (p. 293)

Can you select the desired color quality at your desired resolution now?

YES → Download the latest version of the video card driver from the vendor, install it, and retry. (p. 297)

NO → Contact the vendor of your video card or motherboard (if you have integrated video) for help.

Does your video card have enough RAM?

YES → Upgrade to a video card with enough RAM for your desired resolution and color depth.

NO → Where do you connect to your monitor?

Add-on card → Upgrade to a video card with enough RAM for your desired resolution and color depth.

Motherboard → Can you install an AGP video card?

YES → Upgrade to a video card

NO → Check with the vendor to determine whether you can add memory or adjust BIOS settings to increase the memory available for video (p. 296), or upgrade to a motherboard that has an AGP slot.

Display Has Wavy Lines

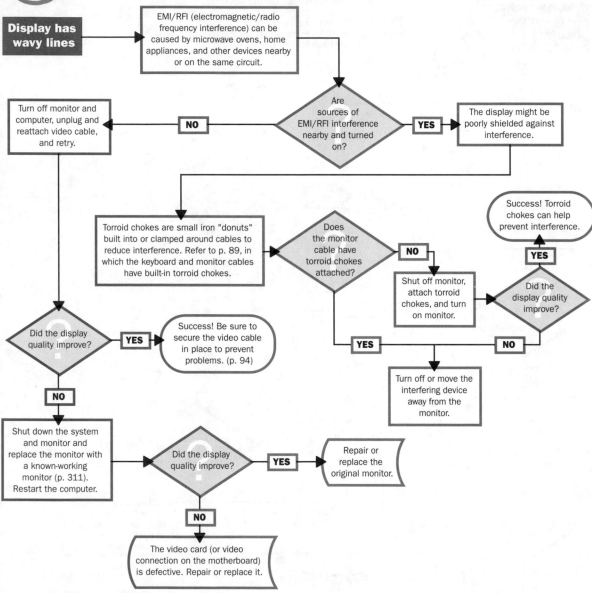

Display has wavy lines → EMI/RFI (electromagnetic/radio frequency interference) can be caused by microwave ovens, home appliances, and other devices nearby or on the same circuit.

Are sources of EMI/RFI interference nearby and turned on?

NO → Turn off monitor and computer, unplug and reattach video cable, and retry.

YES → The display might be poorly shielded against interference.

Torroid chokes are small iron "donuts" built into or clamped around cables to reduce interference. Refer to p. 89, in which the keyboard and monitor cables have built-in torroid chokes.

Does the monitor cable have torroid chokes attached?

NO → Shut off monitor, attach torroid chokes, and turn on monitor.

YES → Turn off or move the interfering device away from the monitor.

Did the display quality improve?

YES → Success! Torroid chokes can help prevent interference.

NO → Turn off or move the interfering device away from the monitor.

Did the display quality improve?

YES → Success! Be sure to secure the video cable in place to prevent problems. (p. 94)

NO → Shut down the system and monitor and replace the monitor with a known-working monitor (p. 311). Restart the computer.

Did the display quality improve?

YES → Repair or replace the original monitor.

NO → The video card (or video connection on the motherboard) is defective. Repair or replace it.

CRT Display Is Flickering

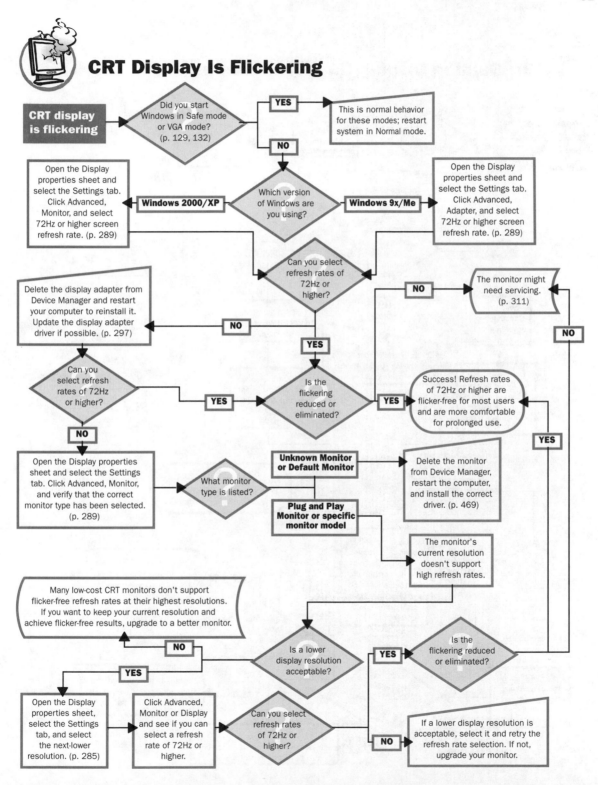

CRT display is flickering

Did you start Windows in Safe mode or VGA mode? (p. 129, 132)

YES → This is normal behavior for these modes; restart system in Normal mode.

NO ↓

Which version of Windows are you using?

Windows 2000/XP → Open the Display properties sheet and select the Settings tab. Click Advanced, Monitor, and select 72Hz or higher screen refresh rate. (p. 289)

Windows 9x/Me → Open the Display properties sheet and select the Settings tab. Click Advanced, Adapter, and select 72Hz or higher screen refresh rate. (p. 289)

Can you select refresh rates of 72Hz or higher?

NO → Delete the display adapter from Device Manager and restart your computer to reinstall it. Update the display adapter driver if possible. (p. 297)

NO → The monitor might need servicing. (p. 311)

YES ↓

Can you select refresh rates of 72Hz or higher?

YES → Is the flickering reduced or eliminated?

YES → Success! Refresh rates of 72Hz or higher are flicker-free for most users and are more comfortable for prolonged use.

NO → Open the Display properties sheet and select the Settings tab. Click Advanced, Monitor, and verify that the correct monitor type has been selected. (p. 289)

What monitor type is listed?

Unknown Monitor or Default Monitor → Delete the monitor from Device Manager, restart the computer, and install the correct driver. (p. 469)

Plug and Play Monitor or specific monitor model → The monitor's current resolution doesn't support high refresh rates.

Many low-cost CRT monitors don't support flicker-free refresh rates at their highest resolutions. If you want to keep your current resolution and achieve flicker-free results, upgrade to a better monitor.

Is a lower display resolution acceptable?

NO → (to "Many low-cost CRT monitors..." box)

YES ↓

Open the Display properties sheet, select the Settings tab, and select the next-lower resolution. (p. 285)

Click Advanced, Monitor or Display and see if you can select a refresh rate of 72Hz or higher.

Can you select refresh rates of 72Hz or higher?

YES → Is the flickering reduced or eliminated?

NO → If a lower display resolution is acceptable, select it and retry the refresh rate selection. If not, upgrade your monitor.

3D Gaming Display Quality Problems

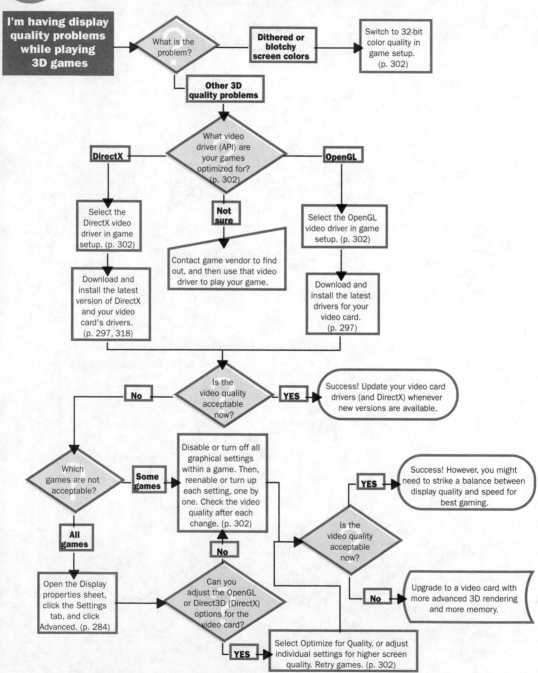

I'm having display quality problems while playing 3D games

What is the problem?

Dithered or blotchy screen colors → Switch to 32-bit color quality in game setup. (p. 302)

Other 3D quality problems

What video driver (API) are your games optimized for? (p. 302)

DirectX → Select the DirectX video driver in game setup. (p. 302) → Download and install the latest version of DirectX and your video card's drivers. (p. 297, 318)

Not sure → Contact game vendor to find out, and then use that video driver to play your game.

OpenGL → Select the OpenGL video driver in game setup. (p. 302) → Download and install the latest drivers for your video card. (p. 297)

Is the video quality acceptable now? — **No** / **YES** → Success! Update your video card drivers (and DirectX) whenever new versions are available.

Which games are not acceptable? — **Some games** → Disable or turn off all graphical settings within a game. Then, reenable or turn up each setting, one by one. Check the video quality after each change. (p. 302)

All games → Open the Display properties sheet, click the Settings tab, and click Advanced. (p. 284)

Is the video quality acceptable now? — **YES** → Success! However, you might need to strike a balance between display quality and speed for best gaming.

No → Can you adjust the OpenGL or Direct3D (DirectX) options for the video card?

No → Upgrade to a video card with more advanced 3D rendering and more memory.

YES → Select Optimize for Quality, or adjust individual settings for higher screen quality. Retry games. (p. 302)

3D Gaming Display Speed Problems

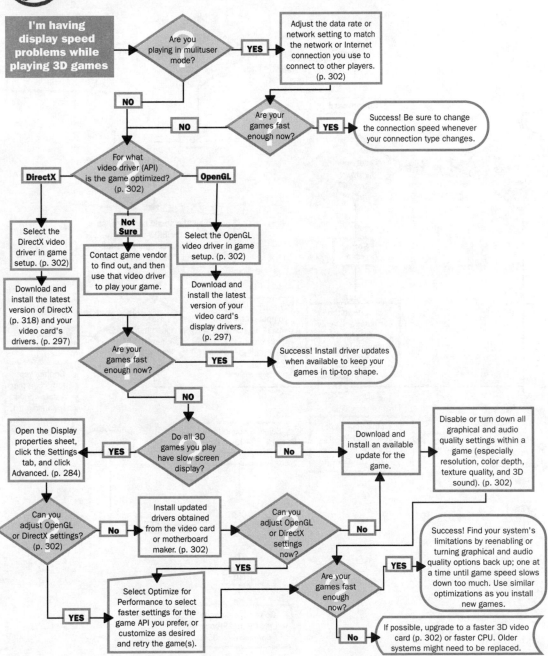

I'm having display speed problems while playing 3D games

Are you playing in mulituser mode?

YES → Adjust the data rate or network setting to match the network or Internet connection you use to connect to other players. (p. 302)

NO

NO → Are your games fast enough now? **YES** → Success! Be sure to change the connection speed whenever your connection type changes.

For what video driver (API) is the game optimized? (p. 302)

DirectX → Select the DirectX video driver in game setup. (p. 302) → Download and install the latest version of DirectX (p. 318) and your video card's drivers. (p. 297)

Not Sure → Contact game vendor to find out, and then use that video driver to play your game.

OpenGL → Select the OpenGL video driver in game setup. (p. 302) → Download and install the latest version of your video card's display drivers. (p. 297)

Are your games fast enough now? **YES** → Success! Install driver updates when available to keep your games in tip-top shape.

NO

Do all 3D games you play have slow screen display?

YES → Open the Display properties sheet, click the Settings tab, and click Advanced. (p. 284)

No → Download and install an available update for the game.

→ Disable or turn down all graphical and audio quality settings within a game (especially resolution, color depth, texture quality, and 3D sound). (p. 302)

Can you adjust OpenGL or DirectX settings? (p. 302)

No → Install updated drivers obtained from the video card or motherboard maker. (p. 302)

Can you adjust OpenGL or DirectX settings now?

No →

YES →

YES → Select Optimize for Performance to select faster settings for the game API you prefer, or customize as desired and retry the game(s).

Are your games fast enough now?

YES → Success! Find your system's limitations by reenabling or turning graphical and audio quality options back up; one at a time until game speed slows down too much. Use similar optimizations as you install new games.

No → If possible, upgrade to a faster 3D video card (p. 302) or faster CPU. Older systems might need to be replaced.

Audio Hardware Problems

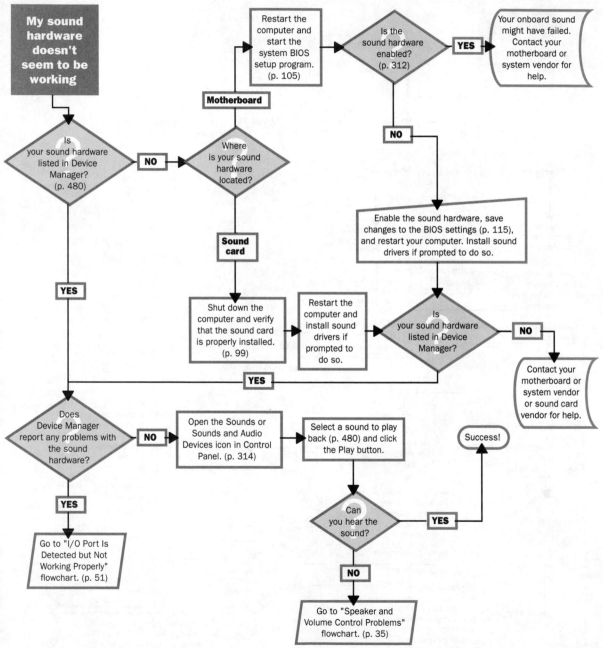

My sound hardware doesn't seem to be working

Restart the computer and start the system BIOS setup program. (p. 105)

Motherboard

Is the sound hardware enabled? (p. 312) — **YES** → Your onboard sound might have failed. Contact your motherboard or system vendor for help.

NO

Enable the sound hardware, save changes to the BIOS settings (p. 115), and restart your computer. Install sound drivers if prompted to do so.

Is your sound hardware listed in Device Manager? (p. 480) — **NO** → Where is your sound hardware located?

Sound card

YES

Shut down the computer and verify that the sound card is properly installed. (p. 99)

Restart the computer and install sound drivers if prompted to do so.

YES

Is your sound hardware listed in Device Manager? — **NO** → Contact your motherboard or system vendor or sound card vendor for help.

Does Device Manager report any problems with the sound hardware? — **NO** → Open the Sounds or Sounds and Audio Devices icon in Control Panel. (p. 314) → Select a sound to play back (p. 480) and click the Play button.

YES

Go to "I/O Port Is Detected but Not Working Properly" flowchart. (p. 51)

Success!

Can you hear the sound? — **YES** → Success!

NO

Go to "Speaker and Volume Control Problems" flowchart. (p. 35)

Speaker and Volume Control Problems

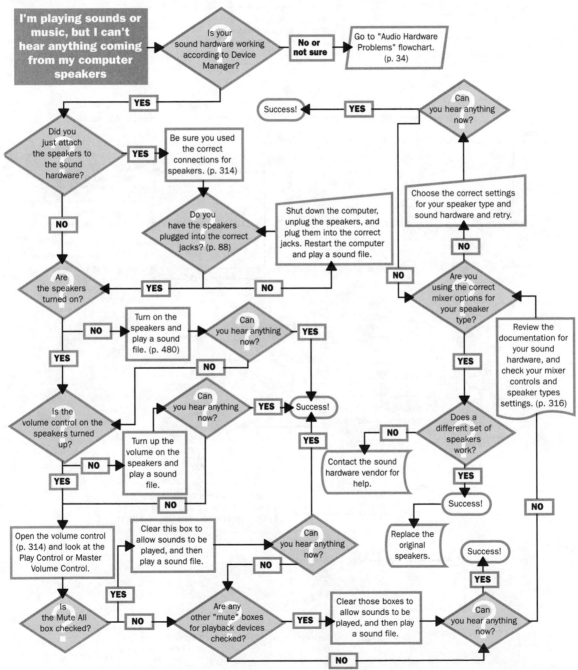

I'm playing sounds or music, but I can't hear anything coming from my computer speakers

Is your sound hardware working according to Device Manager?

No or not sure → Go to "Audio Hardware Problems" flowchart. (p. 34)

YES

Did you just attach the speakers to the sound hardware?

YES → Be sure you used the correct connections for speakers. (p. 314)

NO

Do you have the speakers plugged into the correct jacks? (p. 88)

Shut down the computer, unplug the speakers, and plug them into the correct jacks. Restart the computer and play a sound file.

Choose the correct settings for your speaker type and sound hardware and retry.

Can you hear anything now? **YES** → Success!

Are the speakers turned on?

YES ← **NO**

NO → Turn on the speakers and play a sound file. (p. 480)

Can you hear anything now? **YES**

NO

YES

Is the volume control on the speakers turned up?

YES → Can you hear anything now? **YES** → Success!

YES

NO → Turn up the volume on the speakers and play a sound file.

NO

Are you using the correct mixer options for your speaker type?

NO

YES

Review the documentation for your sound hardware, and check your mixer controls and speaker types settings. (p. 316)

Does a different set of speakers work?

NO → Contact the sound hardware vendor for help.

YES → Success!

Replace the original speakers.

Open the volume control (p. 314) and look at the Play Control or Master Volume Control.

Clear this box to allow sounds to be played, and then play a sound file.

Can you hear anything now?

NO

Is the Mute All box checked?

YES

NO → Are any other "mute" boxes for playback devices checked?

YES → Clear those boxes to allow sounds to be played, and then play a sound file.

NO

Can you hear anything now?

YES → Success!

NO

Can't Connect to the Internet
via a Dial-Up Connection

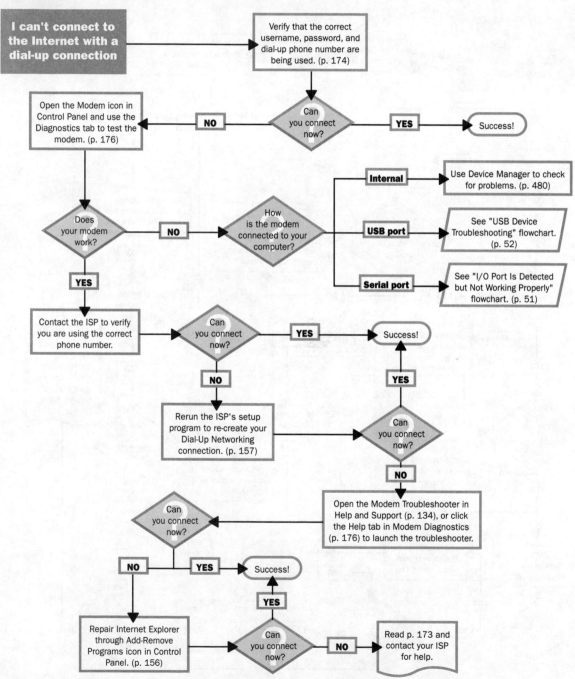

I can't connect to the Internet with a dial-up connection

Verify that the correct username, password, and dial-up phone number are being used. (p. 174)

Can you connect now?

NO → Open the Modem icon in Control Panel and use the Diagnostics tab to test the modem. (p. 176)

YES → Success!

Does your modem work?

NO → **How is the modem connected to your computer?**

Internal → Use Device Manager to check for problems. (p. 480)

USB port → See "USB Device Troubleshooting" flowchart. (p. 52)

Serial port → See "I/O Port Is Detected but Not Working Properly" flowchart. (p. 51)

YES → Contact the ISP to verify you are using the correct phone number.

Can you connect now?

YES → Success!

NO → Rerun the ISP's setup program to re-create your Dial-Up Networking connection. (p. 157)

Can you connect now?

YES → Success!

NO → Open the Modem Troubleshooter in Help and Support (p. 134), or click the Help tab in Modem Diagnostics (p. 176) to launch the troubleshooter.

Can you connect now?

NO → Repair Internet Explorer through Add-Remove Programs icon in Control Panel. (p. 156)

YES → Success!

Can you connect now?

YES → Success!

NO → Read p. 173 and contact your ISP for help.

Can't Connect to the Internet via a Broadband or PPPoE Connection

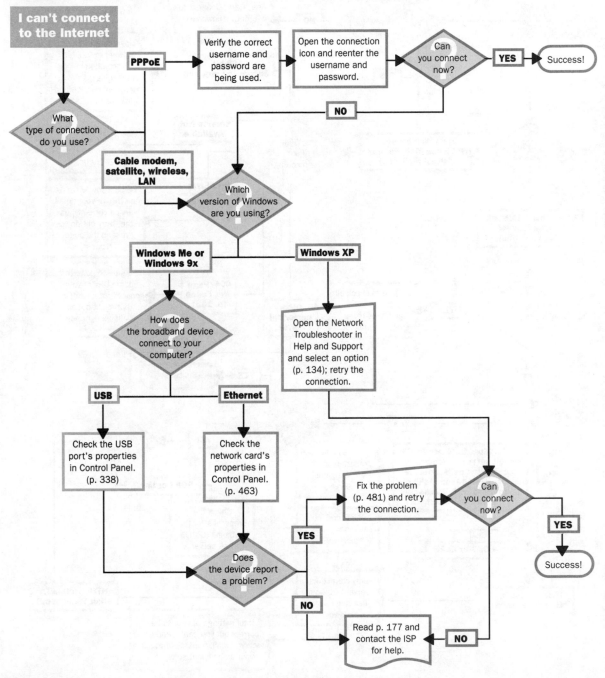

I can't connect to the Internet

What type of connection do you use?

PPPoE

Verify the correct username and password are being used.

Open the connection icon and reenter the username and password.

Can you connect now?

YES → Success!

NO

Cable modem, satellite, wireless, LAN

Which version of Windows are you using?

Windows Me or Windows 9x

Windows XP

How does the broadband device connect to your computer?

Open the Network Troubleshooter in Help and Support and select an option (p. 134); retry the connection.

USB

Ethernet

Check the USB port's properties in Control Panel. (p. 338)

Check the network card's properties in Control Panel. (p. 463)

Does the device report a problem?

YES

Fix the problem (p. 481) and retry the connection.

Can you connect now?

YES → Success!

NO

NO

Read p. 177 and contact the ISP for help.

Email Problems

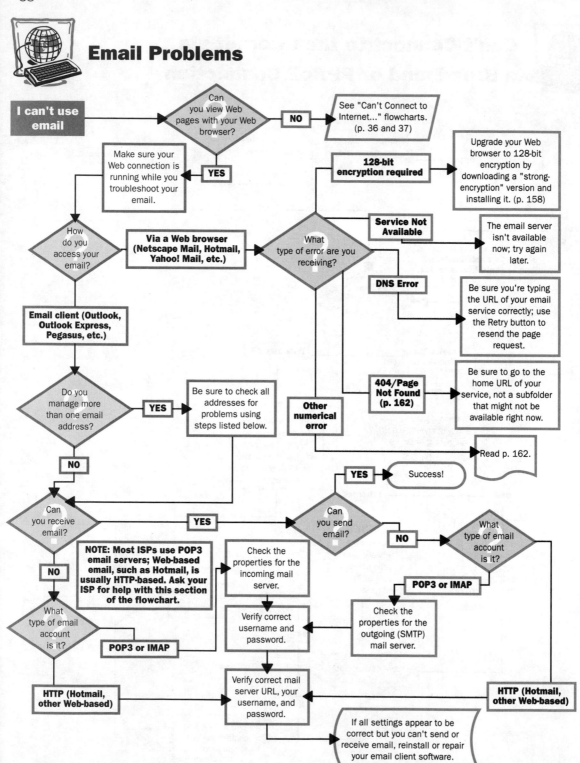

I can't use email → Can you view Web pages with your Web browser?

— NO → See "Can't Connect to Internet..." flowcharts. (p. 36 and 37)

— YES → Make sure your Web connection is running while you troubleshoot your email.

↓

How do you access your email?

— Via a Web browser (Netscape Mail, Hotmail, Yahoo! Mail, etc.) → What type of error are you receiving?

- **128-bit encryption required** → Upgrade your Web browser to 128-bit encryption by downloading a "strong-encryption" version and installing it. (p. 158)
- **Service Not Available** → The email server isn't available now; try again later.
- **DNS Error** → Be sure you're typing the URL of your email service correctly; use the Retry button to resend the page request.
- **404/Page Not Found (p. 162)** → Be sure to go to the home URL of your service, not a subfolder that might not be available right now.
- **Other numerical error** → Read p. 162.

— Email client (Outlook, Outlook Express, Pegasus, etc.)

↓

Do you manage more than one email address?

— YES → Be sure to check all addresses for problems using steps listed below.

— NO

↓

Can you receive email?

— YES → Can you send email?
  - YES → Success!
  - NO → What type of email account is it?
    - POP3 or IMAP → Check the properties for the outgoing (SMTP) mail server.
    - HTTP (Hotmail, other Web-based) → Verify correct mail server URL, your username, and password.

— NO → What type of email account is it?

NOTE: Most ISPs use POP3 email servers; Web-based email, such as Hotmail, is usually HTTP-based. Ask your ISP for help with this section of the flowchart.

- POP3 or IMAP → Check the properties for the incoming mail server. → Verify correct username and password.
- HTTP (Hotmail, other Web-based) → Verify correct mail server URL, your username, and password.

If all settings appear to be correct but you can't send or receive email, reinstall or repair your email client software.

Web Page Problems

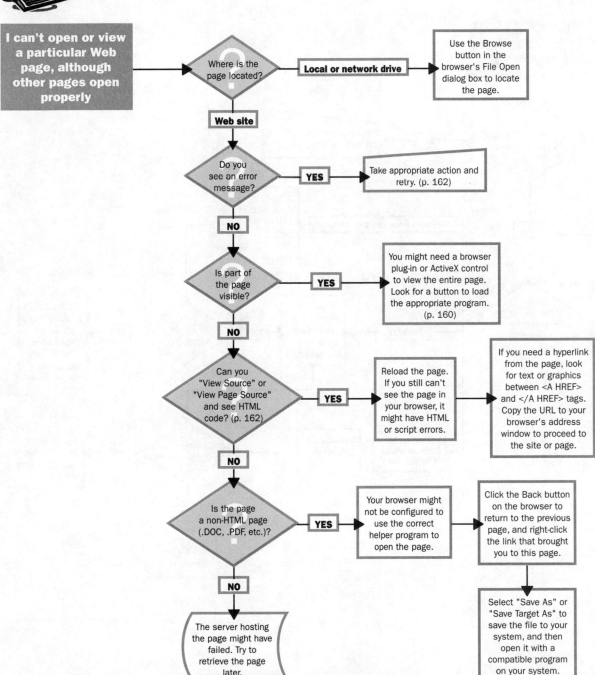

I can't open or view a particular Web page, although other pages open properly

Where is the page located?

Local or network drive → Use the Browse button in the browser's File Open dialog box to locate the page.

Web site

Do you see an error message?

YES → Take appropriate action and retry. (p. 162)

NO

Is part of the page visible?

YES → You might need a browser plug-in or ActiveX control to view the entire page. Look for a button to load the appropriate program. (p. 160)

NO

Can you "View Source" or "View Page Source" and see HTML code? (p. 162)

YES → Reload the page. If you still can't see the page in your browser, it might have HTML or script errors. → If you need a hyperlink from the page, look for text or graphics between <A HREF> and </A HREF> tags. Copy the URL to your browser's address window to proceed to the site or page.

NO

Is the page a non-HTML page (.DOC, .PDF, etc.)?

YES → Your browser might not be configured to use the correct helper program to open the page. → Click the Back button on the browser to return to the previous page, and right-click the link that brought you to this page. → Select "Save As" or "Save Target As" to save the file to your system, and then open it with a compatible program on your system.

NO

The server hosting the page might have failed. Try to retrieve the page later.

File Download Problems

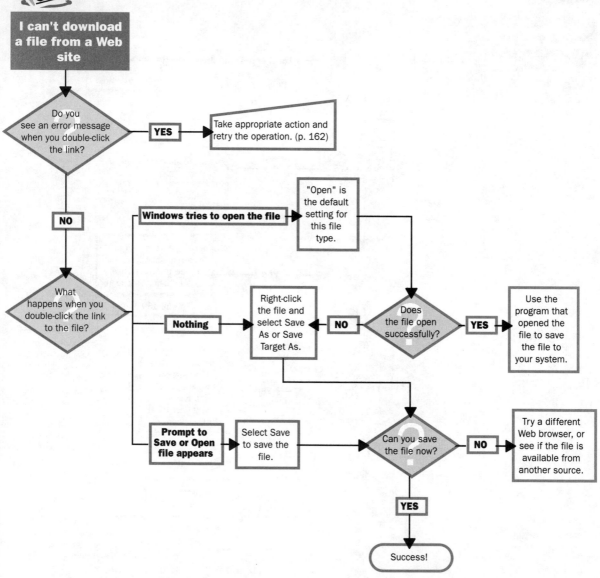

I can't download a file from a Web site

Do you see an error message when you double-click the link?

YES → Take appropriate action and retry the operation. (p. 162)

NO

Windows tries to open the file → "Open" is the default setting for this file type.

What happens when you double-click the link to the file?

Nothing → Right-click the file and select Save As or Save Target As.

Does the file open successfully?

NO → Right-click the file and select Save As or Save Target As.

YES → Use the program that opened the file to save the file to your system.

Prompt to Save or Open file appears → Select Save to save the file.

Can you save the file now?

NO → Try a different Web browser, or see if the file is available from another source.

YES

Success!

Can't Access Shared Files

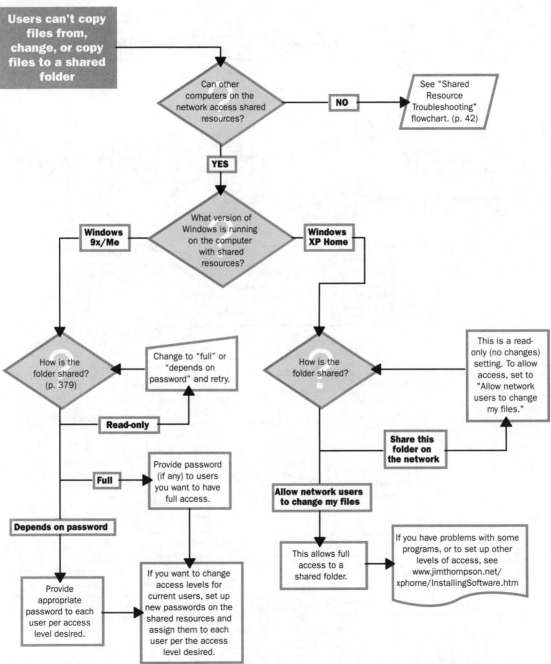

Users can't copy files from, change, or copy files to a shared folder

Can other computers on the network access shared resources?

NO → See "Shared Resource Troubleshooting" flowchart. (p. 42)

YES

What version of Windows is running on the computer with shared resources?

Windows 9x/Me

Windows XP Home

How is the folder shared? (p. 379)

Change to "full" or "depends on password" and retry.

Read-only

Full → Provide password (if any) to users you want to have full access.

Depends on password

Provide appropriate password to each user per access level desired.

If you want to change access levels for current users, set up new passwords on the shared resources and assign them to each user per the access level desired.

How is the folder shared?

This is a read-only (no changes) setting. To allow access, set to "Allow network users to change my files."

Share this folder on the network

Allow network users to change my files

This allows full access to a shared folder.

If you have problems with some programs, or to set up other levels of access, see www.jimthompson.net/xphome/InstallingSoftware.htm

42

Shared Resource Troubleshooting

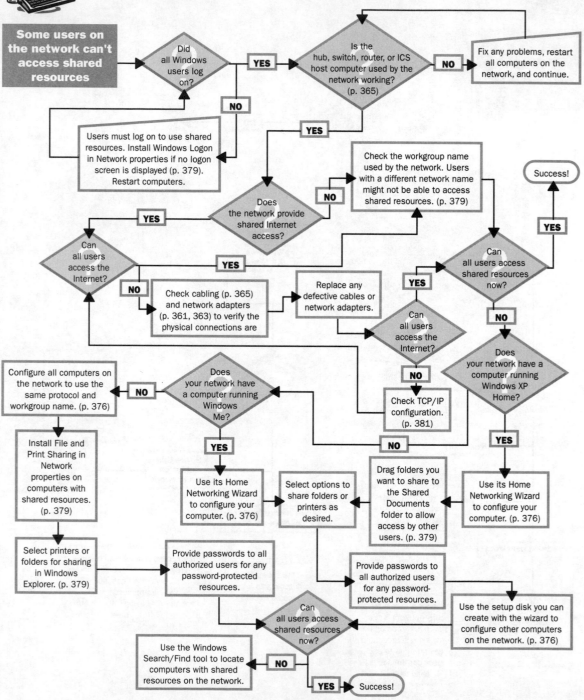

Some users on the network can't access shared resources

Did all Windows users log on?
— **NO** → Users must log on to use shared resources. Install Windows Logon in Network properties if no logon screen is displayed (p. 379). Restart computers.
— **YES** → Is the hub, switch, router, or ICS host computer used by the network working? (p. 365)
  — **NO** → Fix any problems, restart all computers on the network, and continue.
  — **YES** → Does the network provide shared Internet access?

Does the network provide shared Internet access?
— **NO** → Check the workgroup name used by the network. Users with a different network name might not be able to access shared resources. (p. 379)
— **YES** → Can all users access the Internet?

Can all users access the Internet?
— **YES** →
— **NO** → Check cabling (p. 365) and network adapters (p. 361, 363) to verify the physical connections are → Replace any defective cables or network adapters. → Can all users access the Internet?
  — **YES** → Check the workgroup name...
  — **NO** → Check TCP/IP configuration. (p. 381)

Can all users access shared resources now?
— **YES** → Success!
— **NO** → Does your network have a computer running Windows XP Home?
  — **YES** → Use its Home Networking Wizard to configure your computer. (p. 376) → Drag folders you want to share to the Shared Documents folder to allow access by other users. (p. 379) → Provide passwords to all authorized users for any password-protected resources. → Use the setup disk you can create with the wizard to configure other computers on the network. (p. 376)
  — **NO** → Does your network have a computer running Windows Me?
    — **YES** → Use its Home Networking Wizard to configure your computer. (p. 376) → Select options to share folders or printers as desired.
    — **NO** → Configure all computers on the network to use the same protocol and workgroup name. (p. 376) → Install File and Print Sharing in Network properties on computers with shared resources. (p. 379) → Select printers or folders for sharing in Windows Explorer. (p. 379) → Provide passwords to all authorized users for any password-protected resources.

Can all users access shared resources now?
— **NO** → Use the Windows Search/Find tool to locate computers with shared resources on the network.
— **YES** → Success!

My PS/2 Keyboard or Mouse Doesn't Work

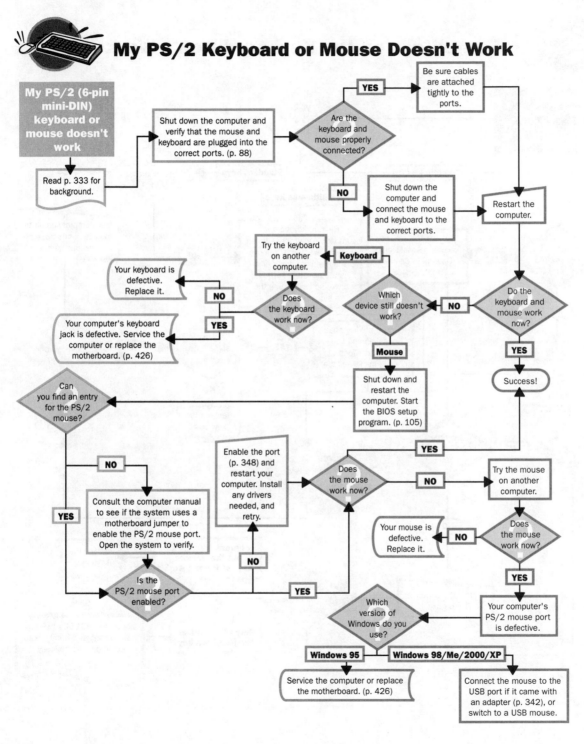

My PS/2 (6-pin mini-DIN) keyboard or mouse doesn't work

Read p. 333 for background.

Shut down the computer and verify that the mouse and keyboard are plugged into the correct ports. (p. 88)

Are the keyboard and mouse properly connected?

YES → Be sure cables are attached tightly to the ports.

NO → Shut down the computer and connect the mouse and keyboard to the correct ports.

Restart the computer.

Do the keyboard and mouse work now?

YES → Success!

NO → **Which device still doesn't work?**

Keyboard → Try the keyboard on another computer.

Does the keyboard work now?

NO → Your keyboard is defective. Replace it.

YES → Your computer's keyboard jack is defective. Service the computer or replace the motherboard. (p. 426)

Mouse → Shut down and restart the computer. Start the BIOS setup program. (p. 105)

Can you find an entry for the PS/2 mouse?

NO → Consult the computer manual to see if the system uses a motherboard jumper to enable the PS/2 mouse port. Open the system to verify.

YES → **Is the PS/2 mouse port enabled?**

NO → Enable the port (p. 348) and restart your computer. Install any drivers needed, and retry.

Does the mouse work now?

YES →

NO → Try the mouse on another computer.

Does the mouse work now?

NO → Your mouse is defective. Replace it.

YES → Your computer's PS/2 mouse port is defective.

Which version of Windows do you use?

Windows 95 → Service the computer or replace the motherboard. (p. 426)

Windows 98/Me/2000/XP → Connect the mouse to the USB port if it came with an adapter (p. 342), or switch to a USB mouse.

44

Some Keys on the Keyboard Don't Work

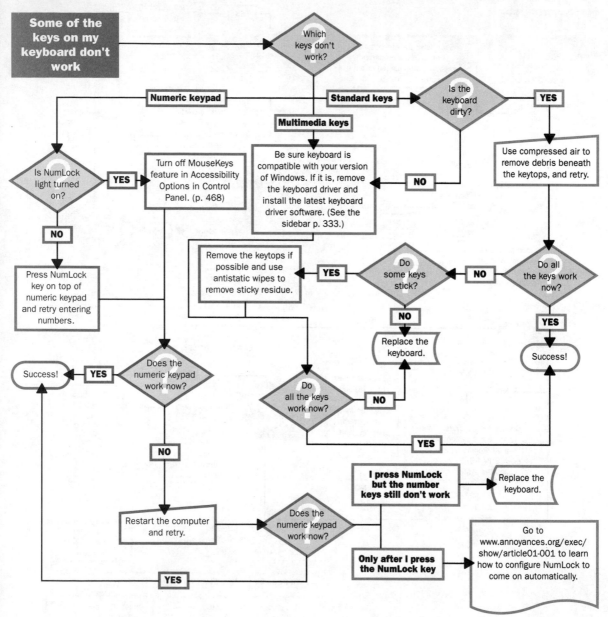

Some of the keys on my keyboard don't work

Which keys don't work?

Numeric keypad

Standard keys

Multimedia keys

Is the keyboard dirty?

YES

Use compressed air to remove debris beneath the keytops, and retry.

Is NumLock light turned on?

YES

Turn off MouseKeys feature in Accessibility Options in Control Panel. (p. 468)

Be sure keyboard is compatible with your version of Windows. If it is, remove the keyboard driver and install the latest keyboard driver software. (See the sidebar p. 333.)

NO

NO

Press NumLock key on top of numeric keypad and retry entering numbers.

Remove the keytops if possible and use antistatic wipes to remove sticky residue.

YES

Do some keys stick?

NO

Do all the keys work now?

Does the numeric keypad work now?

YES

Success!

NO

Replace the keyboard.

YES

Success!

Do all the keys work now?

NO

NO

YES

Restart the computer and retry.

Does the numeric keypad work now?

I press NumLock but the number keys still don't work

Replace the keyboard.

Only after I press the NumLock key

Go to www.annoyances.org/exec/show/article01-001 to learn how to configure NumLock to come on automatically.

YES

No Keys on the Keyboard Work

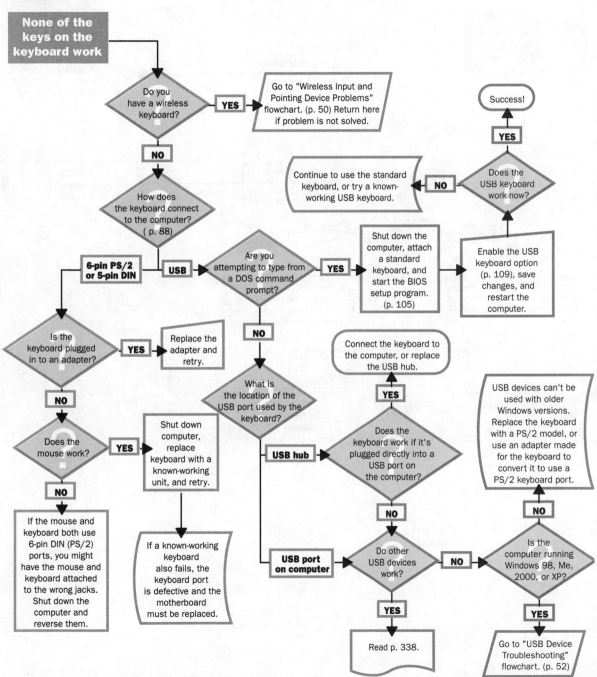

None of the keys on the keyboard work

Do you have a wireless keyboard?

YES → Go to "Wireless Input and Pointing Device Problems" flowchart. (p. 50) Return here if problem is not solved.

NO ↓

How does the keyboard connect to the computer? (p. 88)

6-pin PS/2 or 5-pin DIN | **USB**

Are you attempting to type from a DOS command prompt?

YES → Shut down the computer, attach a standard keyboard, and start the BIOS setup program. (p. 105)

→ Enable the USB keyboard option (p. 109), save changes, and restart the computer.

Does the USB keyboard work now?

YES → Success!

NO → Continue to use the standard keyboard, or try a known-working USB keyboard.

NO ↓

Is the keyboard plugged in to an adapter?

YES → Replace the adapter and retry.

NO ↓

What is the location of the USB port used by the keyboard?

Connect the keyboard to the computer, or replace the USB hub.

YES ↑

Does the keyboard work if it's plugged directly into a USB port on the computer?

USB devices can't be used with older Windows versions. Replace the keyboard with a PS/2 model, or use an adapter made for the keyboard to convert it to use a PS/2 keyboard port.

USB hub

Does the mouse work?

YES → Shut down computer, replace keyboard with a known-working unit, and retry.

NO ↓

If the mouse and keyboard both use 6-pin DIN (PS/2) ports, you might have the mouse and keyboard attached to the wrong jacks. Shut down the computer and reverse them.

If a known-working keyboard also fails, the keyboard port is defective and the motherboard must be replaced.

USB port on computer

Do other USB devices work?

NO → Is the computer running Windows 98, Me, 2000, or XP?

NO ↓

YES → Read p. 338.

YES → Go to "USB Device Troubleshooting" flowchart. (p. 52)

General Pointing Device Problems

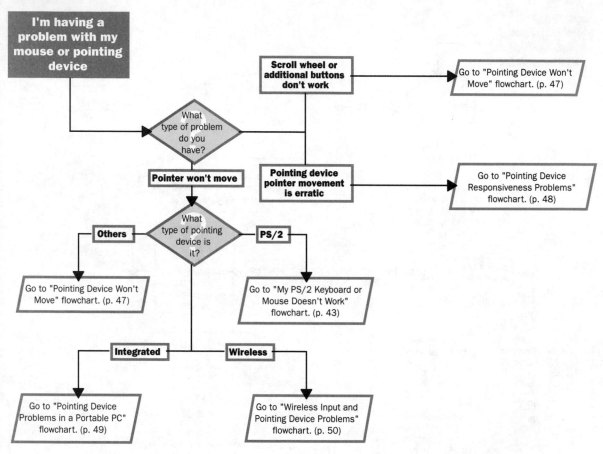

I'm having a problem with my mouse or pointing device

What type of problem do you have?

Scroll wheel or additional buttons don't work

Go to "Pointing Device Won't Move" flowchart. (p. 47)

Pointer won't move

Pointing device pointer movement is erratic

Go to "Pointing Device Responsiveness Problems" flowchart. (p. 48)

What type of pointing device is it?

Others

PS/2

Go to "Pointing Device Won't Move" flowchart. (p. 47)

Go to "My PS/2 Keyboard or Mouse Doesn't Work" flowchart. (p. 43)

Integrated

Wireless

Go to "Pointing Device Problems in a Portable PC" flowchart. (p. 49)

Go to "Wireless Input and Pointing Device Problems" flowchart. (p. 50)

Pointing Device Won't Move

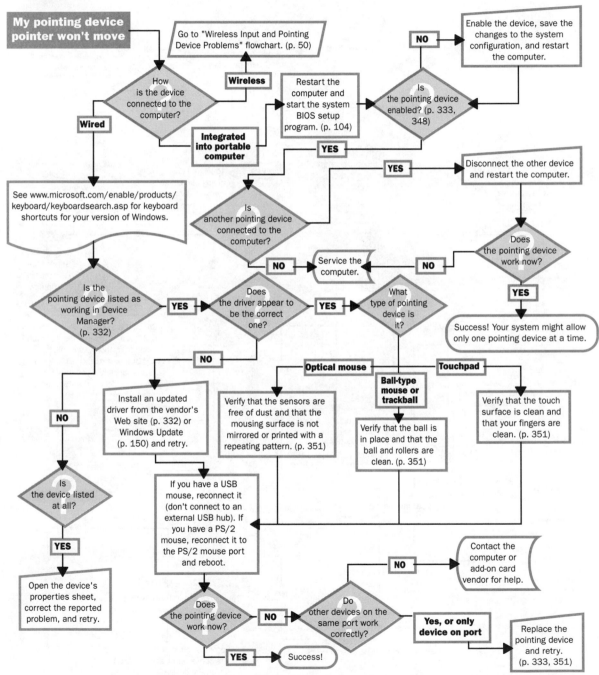

My pointing device pointer won't move

Go to "Wireless Input and Pointing Device Problems" flowchart. (p. 50)

How is the device connected to the computer?

Wireless

Wired

Integrated into portable computer

Restart the computer and start the system BIOS setup program. (p. 104)

Is the pointing device enabled? (p. 333, 348)

NO → Enable the device, save the changes to the system configuration, and restart the computer.

YES

YES → Disconnect the other device and restart the computer.

See www.microsoft.com/enable/products/keyboard/keyboardsearch.asp for keyboard shortcuts for your version of Windows.

Is another pointing device connected to the computer?

NO → Service the computer.

Does the pointing device work now?

NO → Service the computer.

YES → Success! Your system might allow only one pointing device at a time.

Is the pointing device listed as working in Device Manager? (p. 332)

YES → **Does the driver appear to be the correct one?**

YES → **What type of pointing device is it?**

NO

NO

Install an updated driver from the vendor's Web site (p. 332) or Windows Update (p. 150) and retry.

Optical mouse → Verify that the sensors are free of dust and that the mousing surface is not mirrored or printed with a repeating pattern. (p. 351)

Ball-type mouse or trackball → Verify that the ball is in place and that the ball and rollers are clean. (p. 351)

Touchpad → Verify that the touch surface is clean and that your fingers are clean. (p. 351)

Is the device listed at all?

YES → Open the device's properties sheet, correct the reported problem, and retry.

If you have a USB mouse, reconnect it (don't connect to an external USB hub). If you have a PS/2 mouse, reconnect it to the PS/2 mouse port and reboot.

Contact the computer or add-on card vendor for help.

Does the pointing device work now?

NO → **Do other devices on the same port work correctly?**

Yes, or only device on port → Replace the pointing device and retry. (p. 333, 351)

NO → Contact the computer or add-on card vendor for help.

YES → Success!

Pointing Device Responsiveness Problems

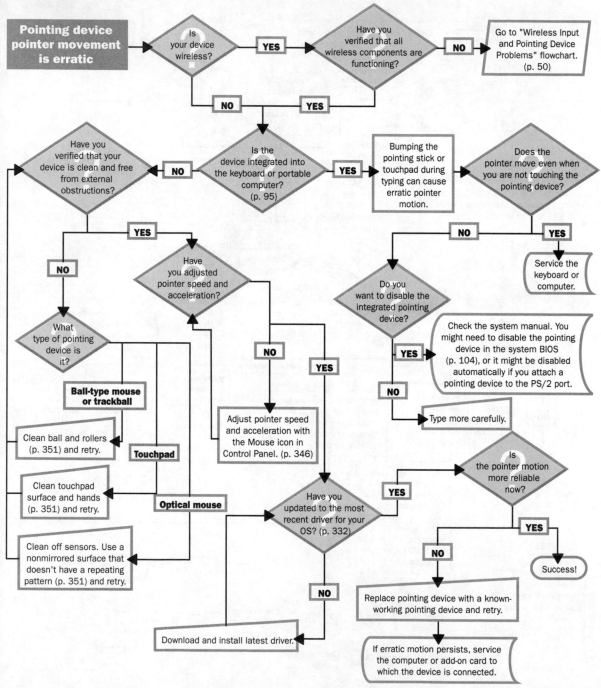

Pointing device pointer movement is erratic

Is your device wireless?

YES → Have you verified that all wireless components are functioning?

NO → Go to "Wireless Input and Pointing Device Problems" flowchart. (p. 50)

YES →

NO →

Have you verified that your device is clean and free from external obstructions?

NO ← Is the device integrated into the keyboard or portable computer? (p. 95)

YES → Bumping the pointing stick or touchpad during typing can cause erratic pointer motion.

Does the pointer move even when you are not touching the pointing device?

NO →

YES → Service the keyboard or computer.

YES → Have you adjusted pointer speed and acceleration?

NO →

Do you want to disable the integrated pointing device?

YES → Check the system manual. You might need to disable the pointing device in the system BIOS (p. 104), or it might be disabled automatically if you attach a pointing device to the PS/2 port.

NO → Type more carefully.

What type of pointing device is it?

Ball-type mouse or trackball

Clean ball and rollers (p. 351) and retry.

Touchpad

Clean touchpad surface and hands (p. 351) and retry.

Optical mouse

Clean off sensors. Use a nonmirrored surface that doesn't have a repeating pattern (p. 351) and retry.

NO → Adjust pointer speed and acceleration with the Mouse icon in Control Panel. (p. 346)

YES →

Have you updated to the most recent driver for your OS? (p. 332)

YES → Is the pointer motion more reliable now?

YES → **YES** → Success!

NO → Replace pointing device with a known-working pointing device and retry.

NO → Download and install latest driver.

If erratic motion persists, service the computer or add-on card to which the device is connected.

Pointing Device Problems in a Portable PC

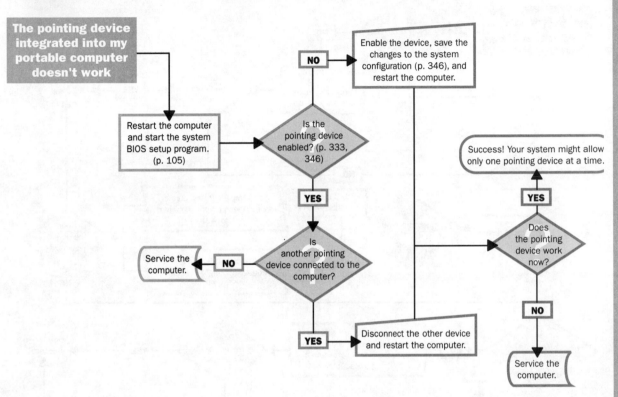

The pointing device integrated into my portable computer doesn't work

Restart the computer and start the system BIOS setup program. (p. 105)

Is the pointing device enabled? (p. 333, 346)

NO → Enable the device, save the changes to the system configuration (p. 346), and restart the computer.

YES ↓

Is another pointing device connected to the computer?

NO → Service the computer.

YES → Disconnect the other device and restart the computer.

Does the pointing device work now?

YES → Success! Your system might allow only one pointing device at a time.

NO → Service the computer.

Wireless Input and Pointing Device Problems

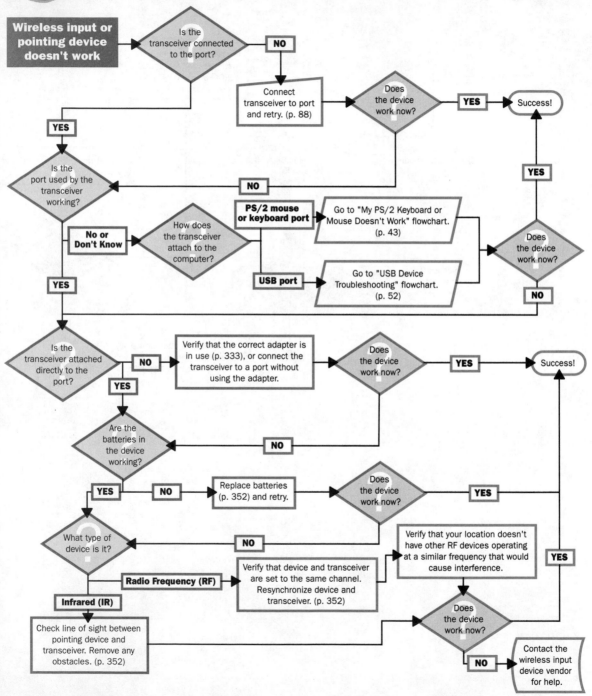

Wireless input or pointing device doesn't work

Is the transceiver connected to the port?

NO → Connect transceiver to port and retry. (p. 88) → Does the device work now? → **YES** → Success!

YES

Is the port used by the transceiver working?

NO

No or Don't Know → How does the transceiver attach to the computer?

PS/2 mouse or keyboard port → Go to "My PS/2 Keyboard or Mouse Doesn't Work" flowchart. (p. 43)

USB port → Go to "USB Device Troubleshooting" flowchart. (p. 52)

Does the device work now? → **YES** → Success!

NO

YES

Is the transceiver attached directly to the port?

NO → Verify that the correct adapter is in use (p. 333), or connect the transceiver to a port without using the adapter. → Does the device work now? → **YES** → Success!

YES

Are the batteries in the device working?

NO

YES   **NO** → Replace batteries (p. 352) and retry. → Does the device work now? → **YES**

What type of device is it?

NO

Radio Frequency (RF) → Verify that device and transceiver are set to the same channel. Resynchronize device and transceiver. (p. 352) → Verify that your location doesn't have other RF devices operating at a similar frequency that would cause interference. → Does the device work now? → **YES**

Infrared (IR) → Check line of sight between pointing device and transceiver. Remove any obstacles. (p. 352)

Does the device work now? → **NO** → Contact the wireless input device vendor for help.

I/O Port Is Detected but Not Working Properly

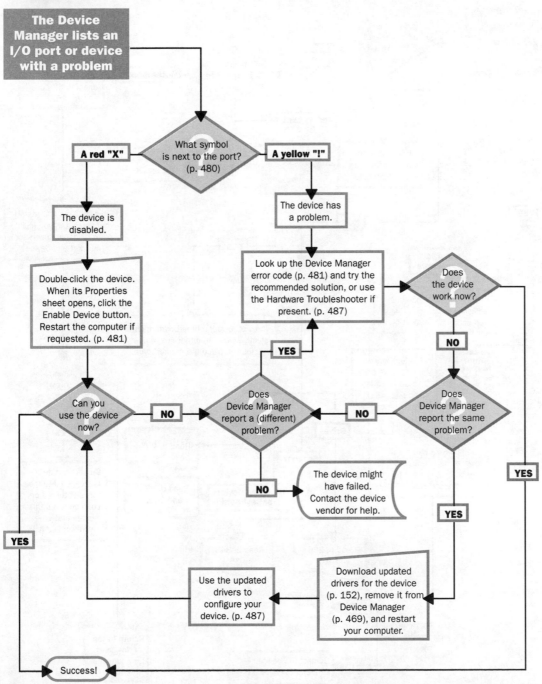

The Device Manager lists an I/O port or device with a problem

What symbol is next to the port? (p. 480)

A red "X"

The device is disabled.

Double-click the device. When its Properties sheet opens, click the Enable Device button. Restart the computer if requested. (p. 481)

A yellow "!"

The device has a problem.

Look up the Device Manager error code (p. 481) and try the recommended solution, or use the Hardware Troubleshooter if present. (p. 487)

Does the device work now?

NO

Can you use the device now?

NO

Does Device Manager report a (different) problem?

YES

NO

Does Device Manager report the same problem?

NO

The device might have failed. Contact the device vendor for help.

YES

YES

Download updated drivers for the device (p. 152), remove it from Device Manager (p. 469), and restart your computer.

Use the updated drivers to configure your device. (p. 487)

YES

Success!

USB Device Troubleshooting

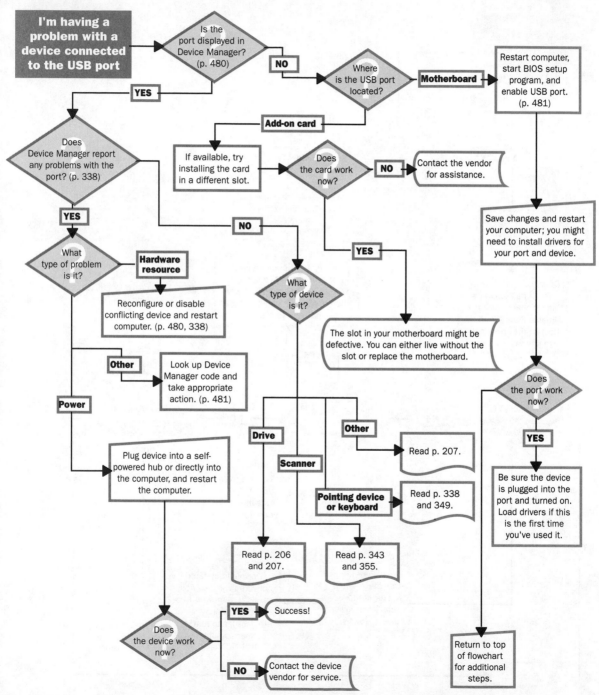

I'm having a problem with a device connected to the USB port

Is the port displayed in Device Manager? (p. 480)

NO

Where is the USB port located?

Motherboard

Restart computer, start BIOS setup program, and enable USB port. (p. 481)

YES

Add-on card

Does Device Manager report any problems with the port? (p. 338)

If available, try installing the card in a different slot.

Does the card work now?

NO

Contact the vendor for assistance.

Save changes and restart your computer; you might need to install drivers for your port and device.

YES

NO

What type of problem is it?

Hardware resource

Reconfigure or disable conflicting device and restart computer. (p. 480, 338)

YES

What type of device is it?

The slot in your motherboard might be defective. You can either live without the slot or replace the motherboard.

Other

Look up Device Manager code and take appropriate action. (p. 481)

Does the port work now?

Power

Drive

Other

Read p. 207.

YES

Scanner

Plug device into a self-powered hub or directly into the computer, and restart the computer.

Pointing device or keyboard

Read p. 338 and 349.

Be sure the device is plugged into the port and turned on. Load drivers if this is the first time you've used it.

Read p. 206 and 207.

Read p. 343 and 355.

YES → Success!

Does the device work now?

NO → Contact the device vendor for service.

Return to top of flowchart for additional steps.

Can't Detect Installed IEEE - 1394 Port

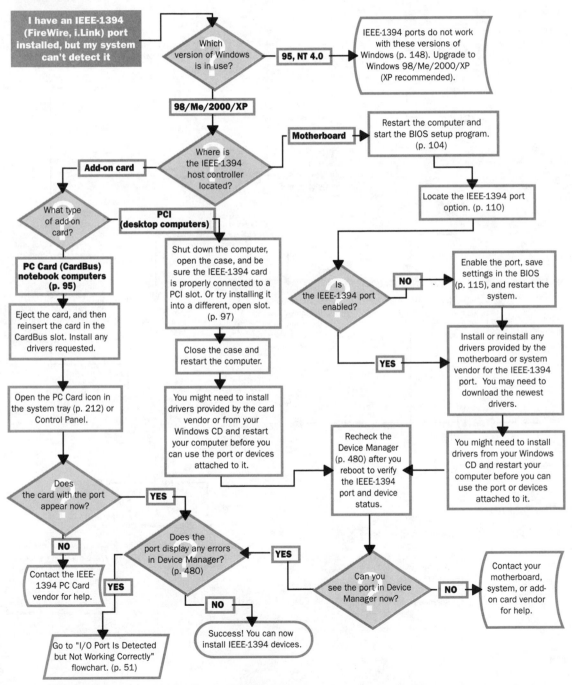

I have an IEEE-1394 (FireWire, i.Link) port installed, but my system can't detect it

Which version of Windows is in use?

95, NT 4.0 → IEEE-1394 ports do not work with these versions of Windows (p. 148). Upgrade to Windows 98/Me/2000/XP (XP recommended).

98/Me/2000/XP

Where is the IEEE-1394 host controller located?

Motherboard → Restart the computer and start the BIOS setup program. (p. 104)

↓ Locate the IEEE-1394 port option. (p. 110)

Add-on card

What type of add-on card?

PCI (desktop computers)

PC Card (CardBus) notebook computers (p. 95)

Eject the card, and then reinsert the card in the CardBus slot. Install any drivers requested.

↓

Open the PC Card icon in the system tray (p. 212) or Control Panel.

↓

Does the card with the port appear now?

YES →

NO ↓

Contact the IEEE-1394 PC Card vendor for help.

Shut down the computer, open the case, and be sure the IEEE-1394 card is properly connected to a PCI slot. Or try installing it into a different, open slot. (p. 97)

↓

Close the case and restart the computer.

↓

You might need to install drivers provided by the card vendor or from your Windows CD and restart your computer before you can use the port or devices attached to it.

Is the IEEE-1394 port enabled?

NO → Enable the port, save settings in the BIOS (p. 115), and restart the system.

YES → Install or reinstall any drivers provided by the motherboard or system vendor for the IEEE-1394 port. You may need to download the newest drivers.

↓

You might need to install drivers from your Windows CD and restart your computer before you can use the port or devices attached to it.

Recheck the Device Manager (p. 480) after you reboot to verify the IEEE-1394 port and device status.

Does the port display any errors in Device Manager? (p. 480)

YES →

YES ↓

NO ↓

Go to "I/O Port Is Detected but Not Working Correctly" flowchart. (p. 51)

Success! You can now install IEEE-1394 devices.

Can you see the port in Device Manager now?

NO → Contact your motherboard, system, or add-on card vendor for help.

IEEE-1394 Device Troubleshooting

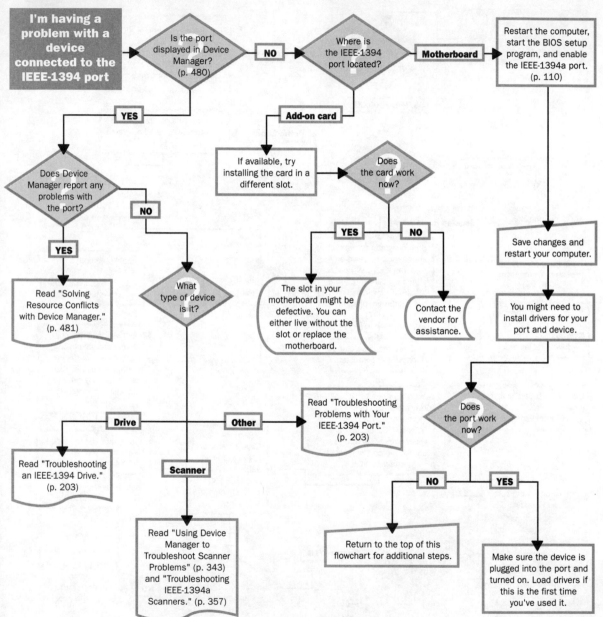

I'm having a problem with a device connected to the IEEE-1394 port

Is the port displayed in Device Manager? (p. 480)

NO

Where is the IEEE-1394 port located?

Motherboard

Restart the computer, start the BIOS setup program, and enable the IEEE-1394a port. (p. 110)

YES

Add-on card

If available, try installing the card in a different slot.

Does the card work now?

Does Device Manager report any problems with the port?

NO

YES

NO

Save changes and restart your computer.

YES

Read "Solving Resource Conflicts with Device Manager." (p. 481)

What type of device is it?

The slot in your motherboard might be defective. You can either live without the slot or replace the motherboard.

Contact the vendor for assistance.

You might need to install drivers for your port and device.

Drive

Other

Read "Troubleshooting Problems with Your IEEE-1394 Port." (p. 203)

Does the port work now?

Read "Troubleshooting an IEEE-1394 Drive." (p. 203)

Scanner

NO

YES

Read "Using Device Manager to Troubleshoot Scanner Problems" (p. 343) and "Troubleshooting IEEE-1394a Scanners." (p. 357)

Return to the top of this flowchart for additional steps.

Make sure the device is plugged into the port and turned on. Load drivers if this is the first time you've used it.

Parallel Port Troubleshooting

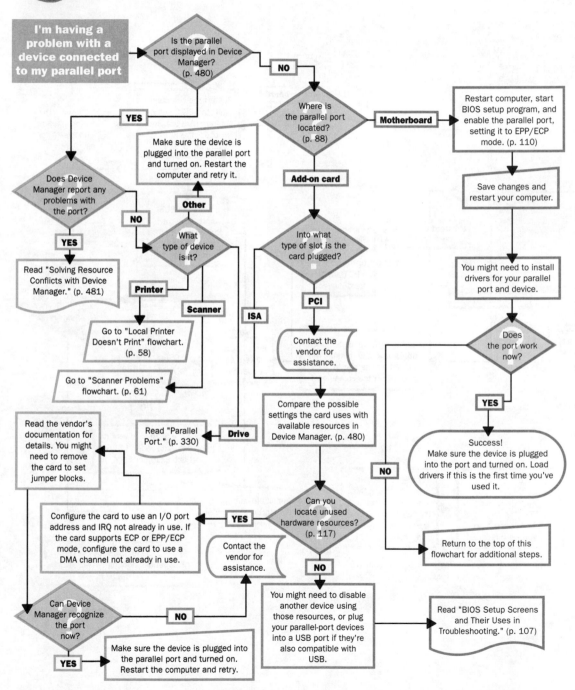

I'm having a problem with a device connected to my parallel port

Is the parallel port displayed in Device Manager? (p. 480)

NO →

YES ↓

Where is the parallel port located? (p. 88)

Motherboard → Restart computer, start BIOS setup program, and enable the parallel port, setting it to EPP/ECP mode. (p. 110)

Save changes and restart your computer.

You might need to install drivers for your parallel port and device.

Does the port work now?

YES ↓

Success! Make sure the device is plugged into the port and turned on. Load drivers if this is the first time you've used it.

NO → Return to the top of this flowchart for additional steps.

Add-on card ↓

Into what type of slot is the card plugged?

PCI ↓ Contact the vendor for assistance.

ISA ↓

Compare the possible settings the card uses with available resources in Device Manager. (p. 480)

Can you locate unused hardware resources? (p. 117)

YES → Configure the card to use an I/O port address and IRQ not already in use. If the card supports ECP or EPP/ECP mode, configure the card to use a DMA channel not already in use.

NO ↓

You might need to disable another device using those resources, or plug your parallel-port devices into a USB port if they're also compatible with USB.

→ Read "BIOS Setup Screens and Their Uses in Troubleshooting." (p. 107)

Read the vendor's documentation for details. You might need to remove the card to set jumper blocks.

Can Device Manager recognize the port now?

NO → Contact the vendor for assistance.

YES → Make sure the device is plugged into the parallel port and turned on. Restart the computer and retry.

Does Device Manager report any problems with the port?

YES ↓

Read "Solving Resource Conflicts with Device Manager." (p. 481)

NO →

What type of device is it?

Other → Make sure the device is plugged into the parallel port and turned on. Restart the computer and retry it.

Printer → Go to "Local Printer Doesn't Print" flowchart. (p. 58)

Scanner → Go to "Scanner Problems" flowchart. (p. 61)

Drive → Read "Parallel Port." (p. 330)

SCSI Port Troubleshooting

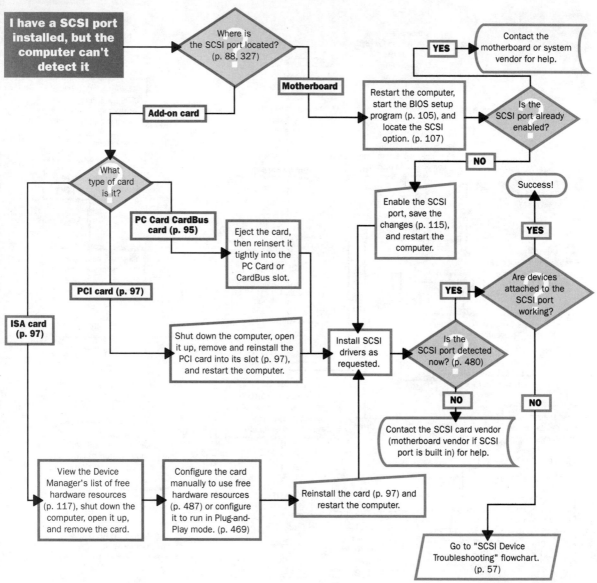

I have a SCSI port installed, but the computer can't detect it

Where is the SCSI port located? (p. 88, 327)

Motherboard

Add-on card

What type of card is it?

PC Card CardBus card (p. 95)

PCI card (p. 97)

ISA card (p. 97)

Eject the card, then reinsert it tightly into the PC Card or CardBus slot.

Shut down the computer, open it up, remove and reinstall the PCI card into its slot (p. 97), and restart the computer.

View the Device Manager's list of free hardware resources (p. 117), shut down the computer, open it up, and remove the card.

Configure the card manually to use free hardware resources (p. 487) or configure it to run in Plug-and-Play mode. (p. 469)

Reinstall the card (p. 97) and restart the computer.

Restart the computer, start the BIOS setup program (p. 105), and locate the SCSI option. (p. 107)

Is the SCSI port already enabled?

YES — Contact the motherboard or system vendor for help.

NO

Enable the SCSI port, save the changes (p. 115), and restart the computer.

Install SCSI drivers as requested.

Is the SCSI port detected now? (p. 480)

NO — Contact the SCSI card vendor (motherboard vendor if SCSI port is built in) for help.

YES

Are devices attached to the SCSI port working?

YES — Success!

NO

Go to "SCSI Device Troubleshooting" flowchart. (p. 57)

SCSI Device Troubleshooting

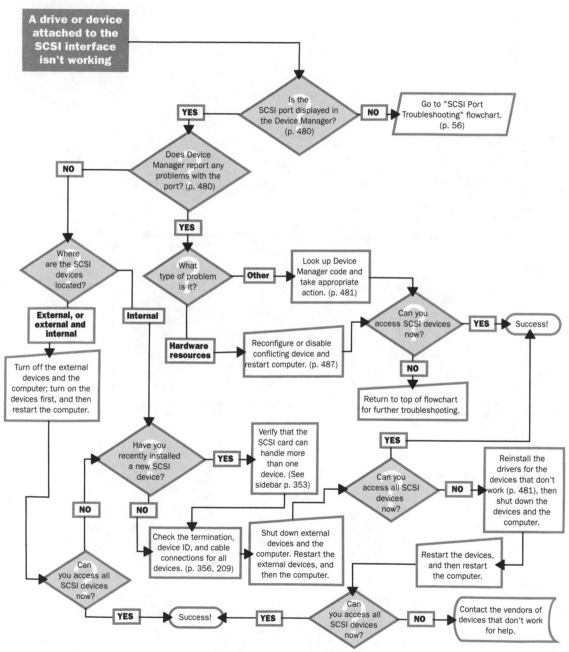

A drive or device attached to the SCSI interface isn't working

Is the SCSI port displayed in the Device Manager? (p. 480)

YES → **NO** → Go to "SCSI Port Troubleshooting" flowchart. (p. 56)

Does Device Manager report any problems with the port? (p. 480)

NO **YES**

Where are the SCSI devices located?

What type of problem is it?

Other → Look up Device Manager code and take appropriate action. (p. 481)

External, or external and internal

Internal

Hardware resources → Reconfigure or disable conflicting device and restart computer. (p. 487)

Turn off the external devices and the computer; turn on the devices first, and then restart the computer.

Can you access SCSI devices now?

YES → Success!

NO

Return to top of flowchart for further troubleshooting.

Have you recently installed a new SCSI device?

YES → Verify that the SCSI card can handle more than one device. (See sidebar p. 353)

NO **NO**

YES

Can you access all SCSI devices now?

NO → Reinstall the drivers for the devices that don't work (p. 481), then shut down the devices and the computer.

Check the termination, device ID, and cable connections for all devices. (p. 356, 209)

Shut down external devices and the computer. Restart the external devices, and then the computer.

Restart the devices, and then restart the computer.

Can you access all SCSI devices now?

YES → Success! ← **YES** ← Can you access all SCSI devices now?

NO → Contact the vendors of devices that don't work for help.

Local Printer Doesn't Print

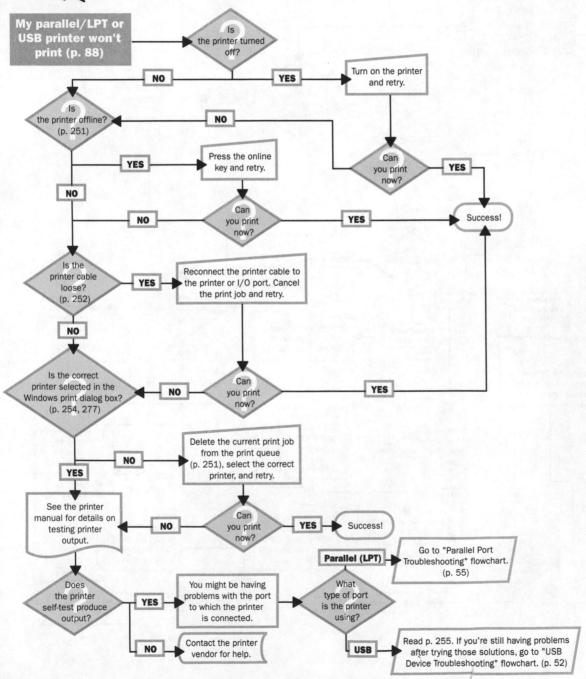

My parallel/LPT or USB printer won't print (p. 88)

Is the printer turned off?

NO

YES → Turn on the printer and retry.

Is the printer offline? (p. 251)

NO

YES → Press the online key and retry.

Can you print now?

YES → Success!

NO

Is the printer cable loose? (p. 252)

YES → Reconnect the printer cable to the printer or I/O port. Cancel the print job and retry.

Can you print now?

YES → Success!

NO

Is the correct printer selected in the Windows print dialog box? (p. 254, 277)

NO → Delete the current print job from the print queue (p. 251), select the correct printer, and retry.

Can you print now?

YES → Success!

YES

See the printer manual for details on testing printer output.

Does the printer self-test produce output?

YES → You might be having problems with the port to which the printer is connected.

NO → Contact the printer vendor for help.

What type of port is the printer using?

Parallel (LPT) → Go to "Parallel Port Troubleshooting" flowchart. (p. 55)

USB → Read p. 255. If you're still having problems after trying those solutions, go to "USB Device Troubleshooting" flowchart. (p. 52)

Network Printer Doesn't Print

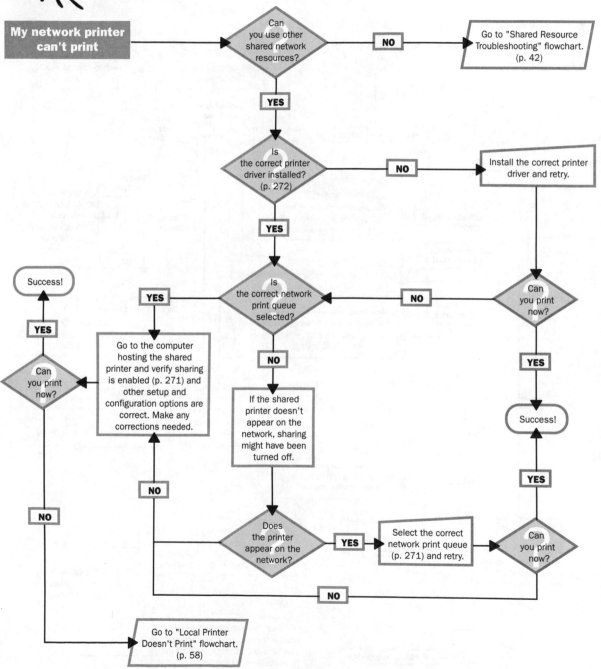

My network printer can't print

Can you use other shared network resources?

NO → Go to "Shared Resource Troubleshooting" flowchart. (p. 42)

YES

Is the correct printer driver installed? (p. 272)

NO → Install the correct printer driver and retry.

YES

Is the correct network print queue selected?

Can you print now?

NO

YES → Success!

Success!

YES

YES

Can you print now?

Go to the computer hosting the shared printer and verify sharing is enabled (p. 271) and other setup and configuration options are correct. Make any corrections needed.

NO

If the shared printer doesn't appear on the network, sharing might have been turned off.

NO

Does the printer appear on the network?

YES → Select the correct network print queue (p. 271) and retry.

Can you print now?

YES → Success!

NO

Go to "Local Printer Doesn't Print" flowchart. (p. 58)

Print Quality Problems

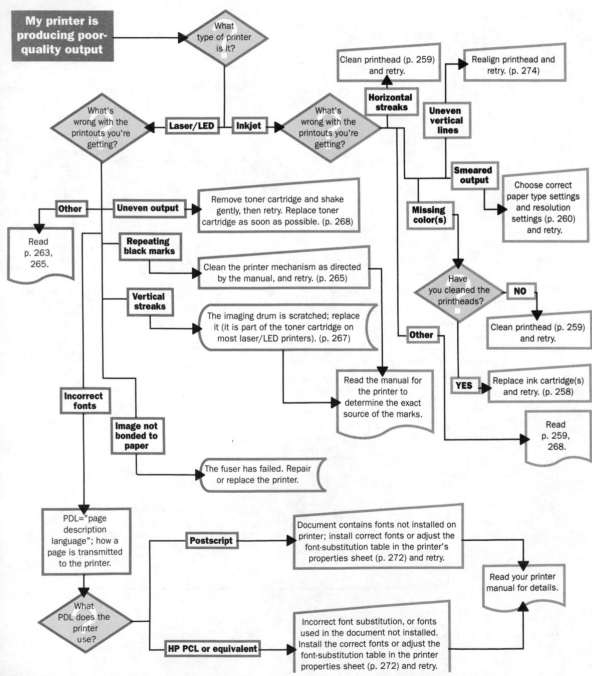

My printer is producing poor-quality output

What type of printer is it?

Laser/LED — Inkjet

What's wrong with the printouts you're getting?

What's wrong with the printouts you're getting?

Horizontal streaks → Clean printhead (p. 259) and retry. → Realign printhead and retry. (p. 274)

Uneven vertical lines

Smeared output → Choose correct paper type settings and resolution settings (p. 260) and retry.

Missing color(s)

Other

Have you cleaned the printheads?

NO → Clean printhead (p. 259) and retry.

YES → Replace ink cartridge(s) and retry. (p. 258)

Read p. 259, 268.

Read the manual for the printer to determine the exact source of the marks.

Other → Read p. 263, 265.

Uneven output → Remove toner cartridge and shake gently, then retry. Replace toner cartridge as soon as possible. (p. 268)

Repeating black marks → Clean the printer mechanism as directed by the manual, and retry. (p. 265)

Vertical streaks → The imaging drum is scratched; replace it (it is part of the toner cartridge on most laser/LED printers). (p. 267)

Incorrect fonts

Image not bonded to paper → The fuser has failed. Repair or replace the printer.

PDL="page description language"; how a page is transmitted to the printer.

What PDL does the printer use?

Postscript → Document contains fonts not installed on printer; install correct fonts or adjust the font-substitution table in the printer's properties sheet (p. 272) and retry.

Read your printer manual for details.

HP PCL or equivalent → Incorrect font substitution, or fonts used in the document not installed. Install the correct fonts or adjust the font-substitution table in the printer properties sheet (p. 272) and retry.

Scanner Problems

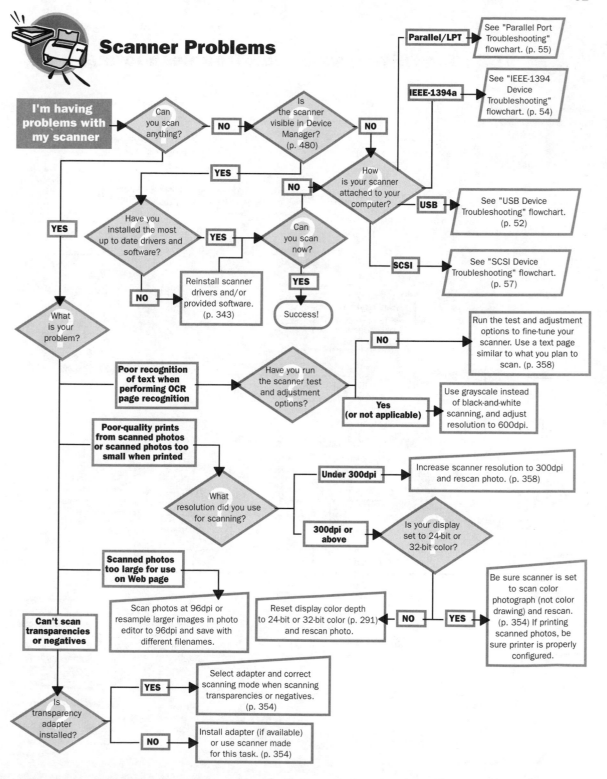

I'm having problems with my scanner

Can you scan anything? — NO → Is the scanner visible in Device Manager? (p. 480)

Is the scanner visible in Device Manager? (p. 480) — NO → How is your scanner attached to your computer?

How is your scanner attached to your computer?
- Parallel/LPT → See "Parallel Port Troubleshooting" flowchart. (p. 55)
- IEEE-1394a → See "IEEE-1394 Device Troubleshooting" flowchart. (p. 54)
- USB → See "USB Device Troubleshooting" flowchart. (p. 52)
- SCSI → See "SCSI Device Troubleshooting" flowchart. (p. 57)

Is the scanner visible in Device Manager? — YES → Have you installed the most up to date drivers and software?

Have you installed the most up to date drivers and software?
- YES → Can you scan now?
- NO → Reinstall scanner drivers and/or provided software. (p. 343)

Can you scan now?
- NO → How is your scanner attached to your computer?
- YES → Success!

Can you scan anything? — YES → What is your problem?

What is your problem?

Poor recognition of text when performing OCR page recognition → Have you run the scanner test and adjustment options?
- NO → Run the test and adjustment options to fine-tune your scanner. Use a text page similar to what you plan to scan. (p. 358)
- Yes (or not applicable) → Use grayscale instead of black-and-white scanning, and adjust resolution to 600dpi.

Poor-quality prints from scanned photos or scanned photos too small when printed → What resolution did you use for scanning?
- Under 300dpi → Increase scanner resolution to 300dpi and rescan photo. (p. 358)
- 300dpi or above → Is your display set to 24-bit or 32-bit color?

Is your display set to 24-bit or 32-bit color?
- NO → Reset display color depth to 24-bit or 32-bit color (p. 291) and rescan photo.
- YES → Be sure scanner is set to scan color photograph (not color drawing) and rescan. (p. 354) If printing scanned photos, be sure printer is properly configured.

Scanned photos too large for use on Web page → Scan photos at 96dpi or resample larger images in photo editor to 96dpi and save with different filenames.

Can't scan transparencies or negatives → Is transparency adapter installed?
- YES → Select adapter and correct scanning mode when scanning transparencies or negatives. (p. 354)
- NO → Install adapter (if available) or use scanner made for this task. (p. 354)

IDE Hard Drive Installation Troubleshooting

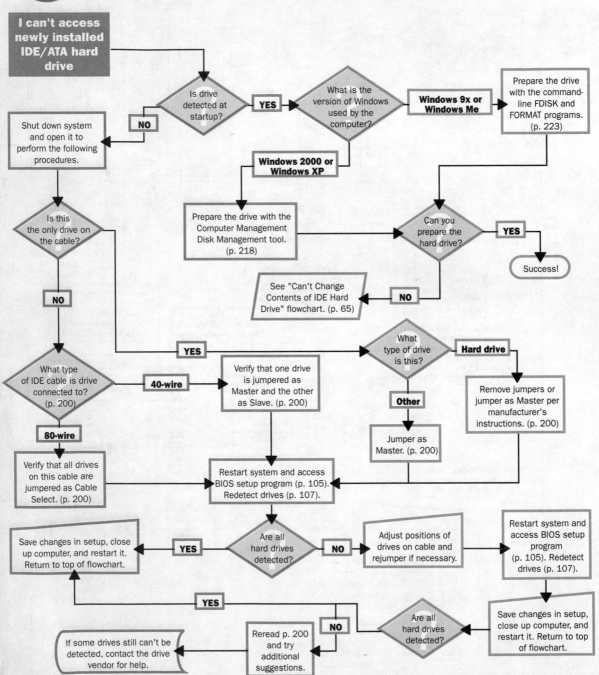

I can't access newly installed IDE/ATA hard drive

Is drive detected at startup? — **YES** → What is the version of Windows used by the computer?

→ **Windows 9x or Windows Me** → Prepare the drive with the command-line FDISK and FORMAT programs. (p. 223)

→ **Windows 2000 or Windows XP** → Prepare the drive with the Computer Management Disk Management tool. (p. 218)

NO → Shut down system and open it to perform the following procedures.

Can you prepare the hard drive? — **YES** → Success!

— **NO** → See "Can't Change Contents of IDE Hard Drive" flowchart. (p. 65)

Is this the only drive on the cable? — **NO** → What type of IDE cable is drive connected to? (p. 200)

— **YES** → What type of drive is this? — **Hard drive** → Remove jumpers or jumper as Master per manufacturer's instructions. (p. 200)

— **Other** → Jumper as Master. (p. 200)

What type of IDE cable is drive connected to? (p. 200) — **40-wire** → Verify that one drive is jumpered as Master and the other as Slave. (p. 200)

— **80-wire** → Verify that all drives on this cable are jumpered as Cable Select. (p. 200)

Restart system and access BIOS setup program (p. 105). Redetect drives (p. 107).

Are all hard drives detected? — **YES** → Save changes in setup, close up computer, and restart it. Return to top of flowchart.

— **NO** → Adjust positions of drives on cable and rejumper if necessary. → Restart system and access BIOS setup program (p. 105). Redetect drives (p. 107).

Save changes in setup, close up computer, and restart it. Return to top of flowchart.

Are all hard drives detected? — **YES** → (return to Save changes)

— **NO** → Reread p. 200 and try additional suggestions.

If some drives still can't be detected, contact the drive vendor for help.

Can't Prepare IDE/ATA Hard Drive After Installation

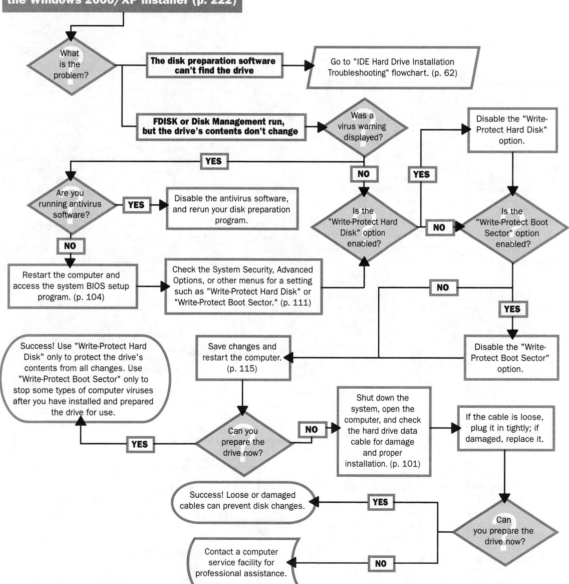

I can't prepare the hard disk for use with FDISK (Windows 9x/Me) (p. 223, 226), the Disk Management tool (Windows 2000/XP) (p. 218), or the Windows 2000/XP installer (p. 222)

What is the problem?

The disk preparation software can't find the drive → Go to "IDE Hard Drive Installation Troubleshooting" flowchart. (p. 62)

FDISK or Disk Management run, but the drive's contents don't change

Was a virus warning displayed?

Disable the "Write-Protect Hard Disk" option.

Are you running antivirus software?

YES → Disable the antivirus software, and rerun your disk preparation program.

NO

Is the "Write-Protect Hard Disk" option enabled?

Is the "Write-Protect Boot Sector" option enabled?

Restart the computer and access the system BIOS setup program. (p. 104)

Check the System Security, Advanced Options, or other menus for a setting such as "Write-Protect Hard Disk" or "Write-Protect Boot Sector." (p. 111)

Success! Use "Write-Protect Hard Disk" only to protect the drive's contents from all changes. Use "Write-Protect Boot Sector" only to stop some types of computer viruses after you have installed and prepared the drive for use.

Save changes and restart the computer. (p. 115)

Disable the "Write-Protect Boot Sector" option.

Can you prepare the drive now?

Shut down the system, open the computer, and check the hard drive data cable for damage and proper installation. (p. 101)

If the cable is loose, plug it in tightly; if damaged, replace it.

Success! Loose or damaged cables can prevent disk changes.

Can you prepare the drive now?

Contact a computer service facility for professional assistance.

Hard Drive Doesn't Boot

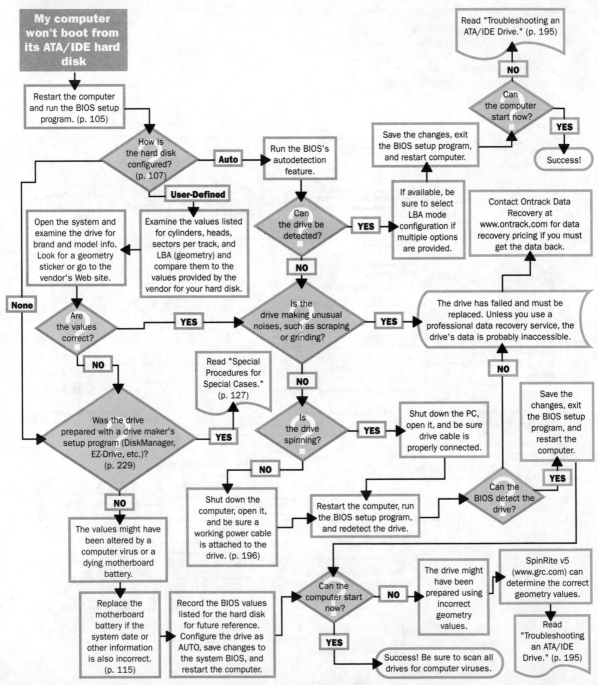

My computer won't boot from its ATA/IDE hard disk

Restart the computer and run the BIOS setup program. (p. 105)

How is the hard disk configured? (p. 107)

Auto → Run the BIOS's autodetection feature.

User-Defined → Examine the values listed for cylinders, heads, sectors per track, and LBA (geometry) and compare them to the values provided by the vendor for your hard disk.

None → Open the system and examine the drive for brand and model info. Look for a geometry sticker or go to the vendor's Web site.

Are the values correct?

YES → Is the drive making unusual noises, such as scraping or grinding?

NO → Was the drive prepared with a drive maker's setup program (DiskManager, EZ-Drive, etc.)? (p. 229)

YES → Read "Special Procedures for Special Cases." (p. 127)

NO → The values might have been altered by a computer virus or a dying motherboard battery.

Replace the motherboard battery if the system date or other information is also incorrect. (p. 115)

Record the BIOS values listed for the hard disk for future reference. Configure the drive as AUTO, save changes to the system BIOS, and restart the computer.

Can the drive be detected?

YES → If available, be sure to select LBA mode configuration if multiple options are provided.

NO → Is the drive making unusual noises, such as scraping or grinding?

YES → The drive has failed and must be replaced. Unless you use a professional data recovery service, the drive's data is probably inaccessible.

NO → Is the drive spinning?

YES → Shut down the PC, open it, and be sure drive cable is properly connected.

NO → Shut down the computer, open it, and be sure a working power cable is attached to the drive. (p. 196)

Restart the computer, run the BIOS setup program, and redetect the drive.

Save the changes, exit the BIOS setup program, and restart computer.

Can the computer start now?

NO → Read "Troubleshooting an ATA/IDE Drive." (p. 195)

YES → Success!

Contact Ontrack Data Recovery at www.ontrack.com for data recovery pricing if you must get the data back.

Can the BIOS detect the drive?

YES → Save the changes, exit the BIOS setup program, and restart the computer.

NO → The drive has failed and must be replaced. Unless you use a professional data recovery service, the drive's data is probably inaccessible.

Can the computer start now?

NO → The drive might have been prepared using incorrect geometry values.

SpinRite v5 (www.grc.com) can determine the correct geometry values.

Read "Troubleshooting an ATA/IDE Drive." (p. 195)

YES → Success! Be sure to scan all drives for computer viruses.

Can't Change Contents of IDE Hard Drive

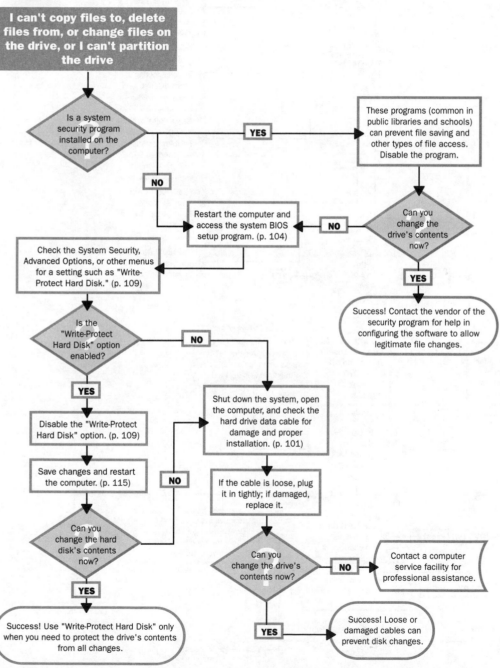

I can't copy files to, delete files from, or change files on the drive, or I can't partition the drive

Is a system security program installed on the computer?

YES → These programs (common in public libraries and schools) can prevent file saving and other types of file access. Disable the program.

NO

Can you change the drive's contents now?

NO → Restart the computer and access the system BIOS setup program. (p. 104)

YES → Success! Contact the vendor of the security program for help in configuring the software to allow legitimate file changes.

Check the System Security, Advanced Options, or other menus for a setting such as "Write-Protect Hard Disk." (p. 109)

Is the "Write-Protect Hard Disk" option enabled?

NO → Shut down the system, open the computer, and check the hard drive data cable for damage and proper installation. (p. 101)

YES

Disable the "Write-Protect Hard Disk" option. (p. 109)

Save changes and restart the computer. (p. 115)

If the cable is loose, plug it in tightly; if damaged, replace it.

Can you change the hard disk's contents now?

NO

YES → Success! Use "Write-Protect Hard Disk" only when you need to protect the drive's contents from all changes.

Can you change the drive's contents now?

NO → Contact a computer service facility for professional assistance.

YES → Success! Loose or damaged cables can prevent disk changes.

General Optical Drive Problems

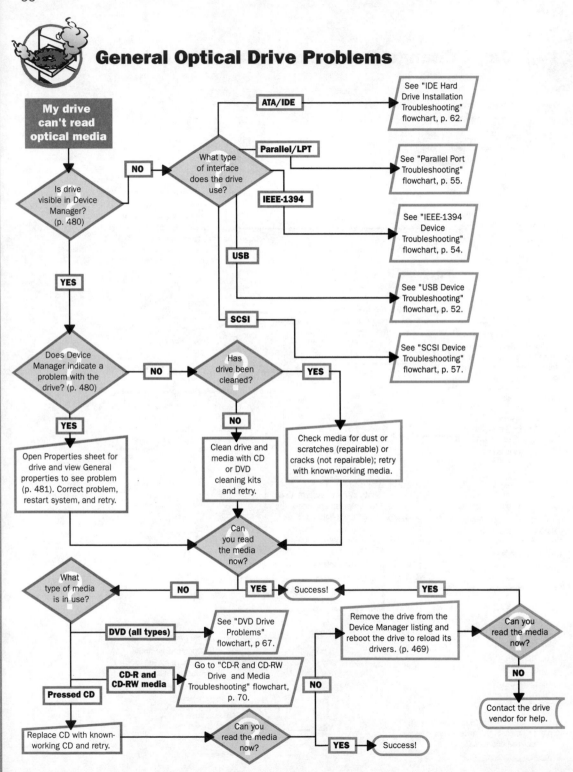

My drive can't read optical media

Is drive visible in Device Manager? (p. 480)

NO → **What type of interface does the drive use?**

- ATA/IDE → See "IDE Hard Drive Installation Troubleshooting" flowchart, p. 62.
- Parallel/LPT → See "Parallel Port Troubleshooting" flowchart, p. 55.
- IEEE-1394 → See "IEEE-1394 Device Troubleshooting" flowchart, p. 54.
- USB → See "USB Device Troubleshooting" flowchart, p. 52.
- SCSI → See "SCSI Device Troubleshooting" flowchart, p. 57.

YES →

Does Device Manager indicate a problem with the drive? (p. 480)

NO → **Has drive been cleaned?**

- YES → Check media for dust or scratches (repairable) or cracks (not repairable); retry with known-working media.
- NO → Clean drive and media with CD or DVD cleaning kits and retry.

YES → Open Properties sheet for drive and view General properties to see problem (p. 481). Correct problem, restart system, and retry.

Can you read the media now?

- YES → Success!
- NO → **What type of media is in use?**

What type of media is in use?
- DVD (all types) → See "DVD Drive Problems" flowchart, p 67.
- CD-R and CD-RW media → Go to "CD-R and CD-RW Drive and Media Troubleshooting" flowchart, p. 70.
- Pressed CD → Replace CD with known-working CD and retry.

Remove the drive from the Device Manager listing and reboot the drive to reload its drivers. (p. 469)

Can you read the media now?

- YES → Success!
- NO → Contact the drive vendor for help.

Replace CD with known-working CD and retry. → **Can you read the media now?**
- YES → Success!
- NO →

DVD Drive Problems

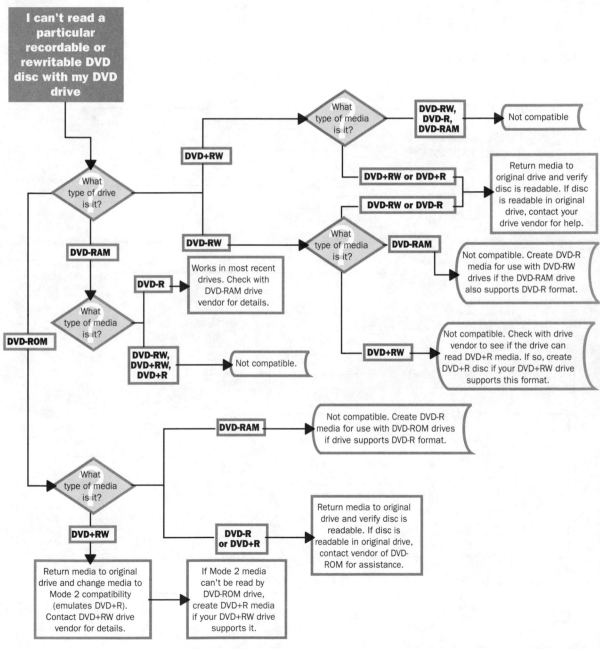

I can't read a particular recordable or rewritable DVD disc with my DVD drive

What type of drive is it?

→ **DVD+RW** → What type of media is it?

- **DVD-RW, DVD-R, DVD-RAM** → Not compatible
- **DVD+RW or DVD+R** → Return media to original drive and verify disc is readable. If disc is readable in original drive, contact your drive vendor for help.

→ **DVD-RW** → What type of media is it?

- **DVD-RW or DVD-R** → Return media to original drive and verify disc is readable. If disc is readable in original drive, contact your drive vendor for help.
- **DVD-RAM** → Not compatible. Create DVD-R media for use with DVD-RW drives if the DVD-RAM drive also supports DVD-R format.
- **DVD+RW** → Not compatible. Check with drive vendor to see if the drive can read DVD+R media. If so, create DVD+R disc if your DVD+RW drive supports this format.

→ **DVD-RAM** → What type of media is it?

- **DVD-R** → Works in most recent drives. Check with DVD-RAM drive vendor for details.
- **DVD-RW, DVD+RW, DVD+R** → Not compatible.

→ **DVD-ROM** → What type of media is it?

- **DVD-RAM** → Not compatible. Create DVD-R media for use with DVD-ROM drives if drive supports DVD-R format.
- **DVD-R or DVD+R** → Return media to original drive and verify disc is readable. If disc is readable in original drive, contact vendor of DVD-ROM for assistance.
- **DVD+RW** → Return media to original drive and change media to Mode 2 compatibility (emulates DVD+R). Contact DVD+RW drive vendor for details. → If Mode 2 media can't be read by DVD-ROM drive, create DVD+R media if your DVD+RW drive supports it.

Buffer Underrun Problems on Drives Without Underrun Protection

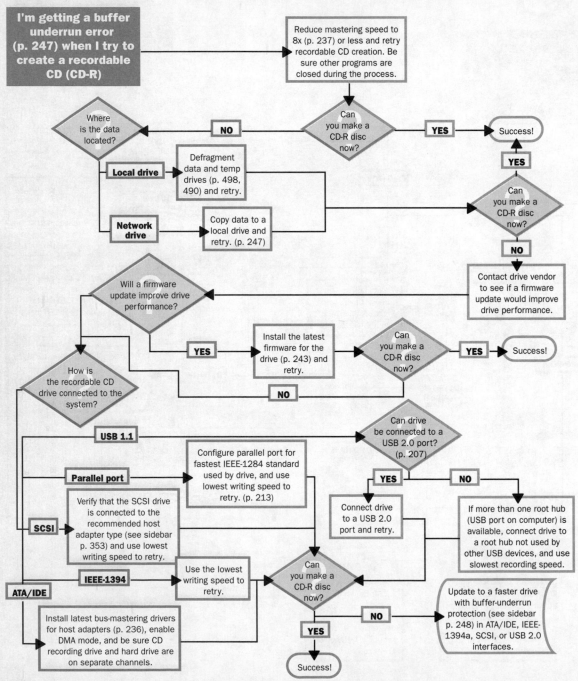

Buffer Underrun Problems on Drives with Underrun Protection

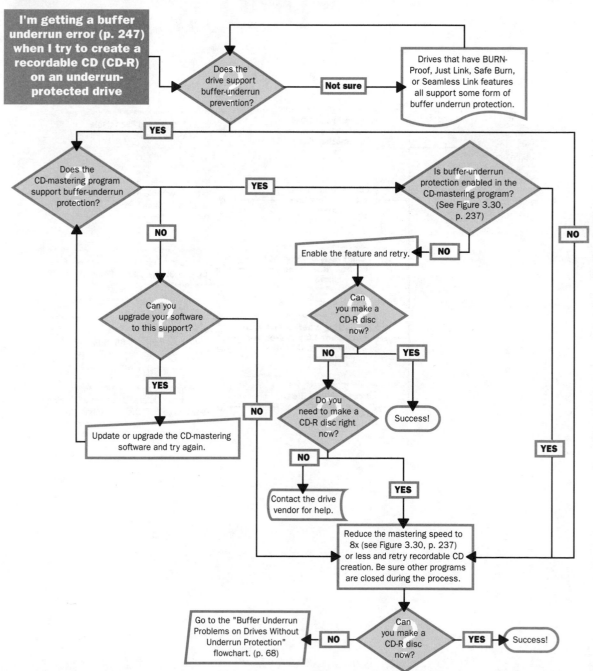

I'm getting a buffer underrun error (p. 247) when I try to create a recordable CD (CD-R) on an underrun-protected drive

Does the drive support buffer-underrun prevention?

Not sure → Drives that have BURN-Proof, Just Link, Safe Burn, or Seamless Link features all support some form of buffer underrun protection.

YES

Does the CD-mastering program support buffer-underrun protection?

YES → Is buffer-underrun protection enabled in the CD-mastering program? (See Figure 3.30, p. 237)

NO → Enable the feature and retry.

NO

Can you upgrade your software to this support?

YES → Update or upgrade the CD-mastering software and try again.

NO

Can you make a CD-R disc now?

NO → Do you need to make a CD-R disc right now?

YES → Success!

NO → Contact the drive vendor for help.

YES → Reduce the mastering speed to 8x (see Figure 3.30, p. 237) or less and retry recordable CD creation. Be sure other programs are closed during the process.

NO

YES

Can you make a CD-R disc now?

NO → Go to the "Buffer Underrun Problems on Drives Without Underrun Protection" flowchart. (p. 68)

YES → Success!

CD-R and CD-RW Drive and Media Troubleshooting

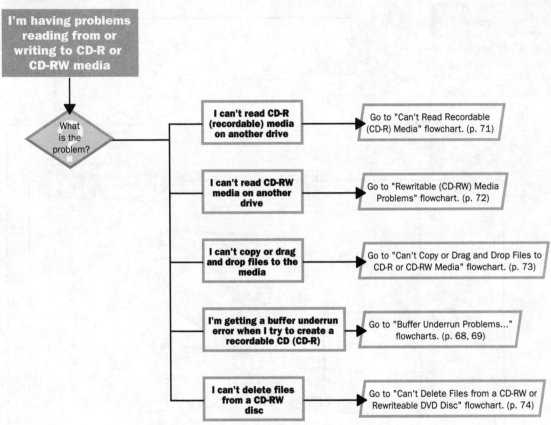

I'm having problems reading from or writing to CD-R or CD-RW media

What is the problem?

- **I can't read CD-R (recordable) media on another drive** → Go to "Can't Read Recordable (CD-R) Media" flowchart. (p. 71)

- **I can't read CD-RW media on another drive** → Go to "Rewritable (CD-RW) Media Problems" flowchart. (p. 72)

- **I can't copy or drag and drop files to the media** → Go to "Can't Copy or Drag and Drop Files to CD-R or CD-RW Media" flowchart. (p. 73)

- **I'm getting a buffer underrun error when I try to create a recordable CD (CD-R)** → Go to "Buffer Underrun Problems..." flowcharts. (p. 68, 69)

- **I can't delete files from a CD-RW disc** → Go to "Can't Delete Files from a CD-RW or Rewriteable DVD Disc" flowchart. (p. 74)

Can't Read Recordable (CD-R) Media

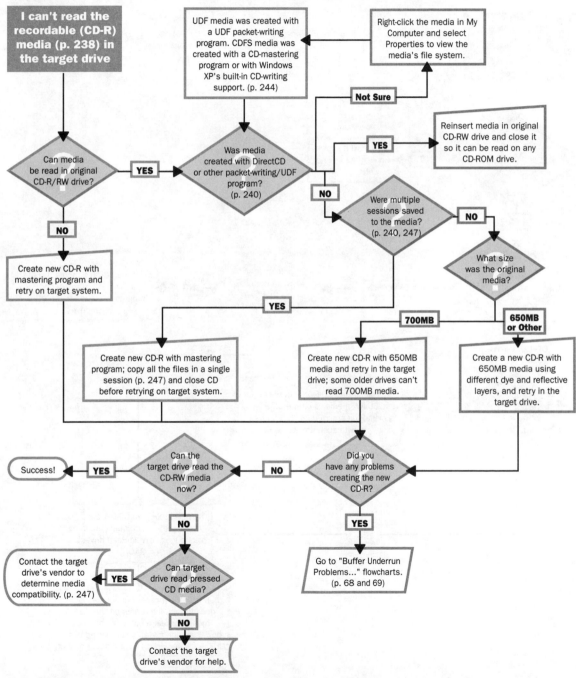

Rewriteable (CD-RW) Media Problems

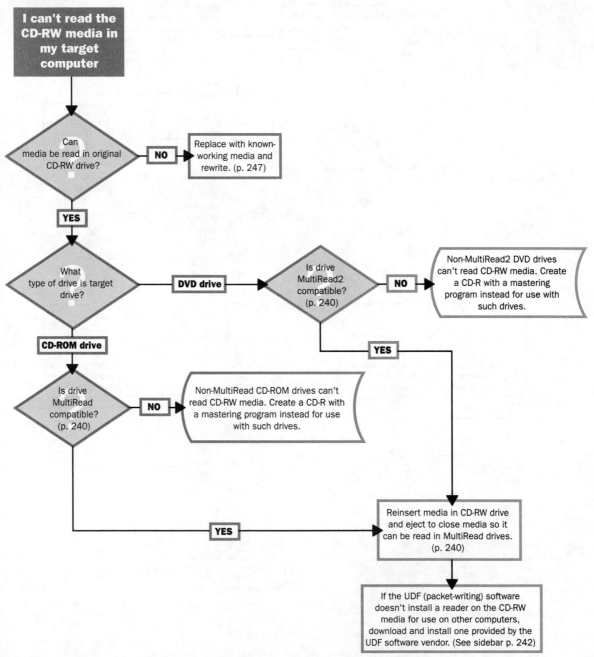

I can't read the CD-RW media in my target computer

Can media be read in original CD-RW drive?

NO → Replace with known-working media and rewrite. (p. 247)

YES

What type of drive is target drive?

DVD drive → Is drive MultiRead2 compatible? (p. 240)

NO → Non-MultiRead2 DVD drives can't read CD-RW media. Create a CD-R with a mastering program instead for use with such drives.

CD-ROM drive

Is drive MultiRead compatible? (p. 240)

NO → Non-MultiRead CD-ROM drives can't read CD-RW media. Create a CD-R with a mastering program instead for use with such drives.

YES

YES → Reinsert media in CD-RW drive and eject to close media so it can be read in MultiRead drives. (p. 240)

If the UDF (packet-writing) software doesn't install a reader on the CD-RW media for use on other computers, download and install one provided by the UDF software vendor. (See sidebar p. 242)

Can't Copy or Drag and Drop Files to CD-R or CD-RW Media

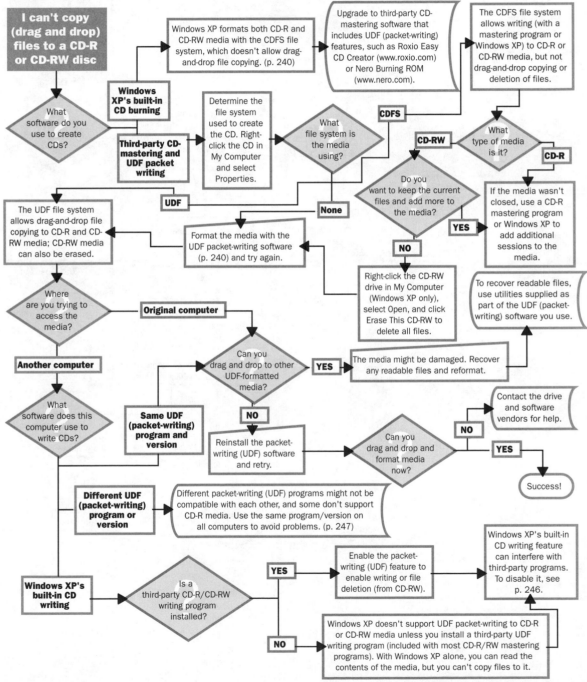

I can't copy (drag and drop) files to a CD-R or CD-RW disc

What software do you use to create CDs?

Windows XP's built-in CD burning

Third-party CD-mastering and UDF packet writing

Windows XP formats both CD-R and CD-RW media with the CDFS file system, which doesn't allow drag-and-drop file copying. (p. 240)

Upgrade to third-party CD-mastering software that includes UDF (packet-writing) features, such as Roxio Easy CD Creator (www.roxio.com) or Nero Burning ROM (www.nero.com).

The CDFS file system allows writing (with a mastering program or Windows XP) to CD-R or CD-RW media, but not drag-and-drop copying or deletion of files.

Determine the file system used to create the CD. Right-click the CD in My Computer and select Properties.

What file system is the media using?

CDFS

What type of media is it?

CD-RW

CD-R

UDF

None

Do you want to keep the current files and add more to the media?

YES

NO

If the media wasn't closed, use a CD-R mastering program or Windows XP to add additional sessions to the media.

The UDF file system allows drag-and-drop file copying to CD-R and CD-RW media; CD-RW media can also be erased.

Format the media with the UDF packet-writing software (p. 240) and try again.

Right-click the CD-RW drive in My Computer (Windows XP only), select Open, and click Erase This CD-RW to delete all files.

To recover readable files, use utilities supplied as part of the UDF (packet-writing) software you use.

Where are you trying to access the media?

Original computer

Another computer

Can you drag and drop to other UDF-formatted media?

YES

The media might be damaged. Recover any readable files and reformat.

NO

What software does this computer use to write CDs?

Same UDF (packet-writing) program and version

Reinstall the packet-writing (UDF) software and retry.

Can you drag and drop and format media now?

NO

Contact the drive and software vendors for help.

YES

Success!

Different UDF (packet-writing) program or version

Different packet-writing (UDF) programs might not be compatible with each other, and some don't support CD-R media. Use the same program/version on all computers to avoid problems. (p. 247)

Windows XP's built-in CD writing feature can interfere with third-party programs. To disable it, see p. 246.

Windows XP's built-in CD writing

Is a third-party CD-R/CD-RW writing program installed?

YES

Enable the packet-writing (UDF) feature to enable writing or file deletion (from CD-RW).

NO

Windows XP doesn't support UDF packet-writing to CD-R or CD-RW media unless you install a third-party UDF writing program (included with most CD-R/RW mastering programs). With Windows XP alone, you can read the contents of the media, but you can't copy files to it.

Can't Delete Files from a CD-RW or Rewriteable DVD Disc

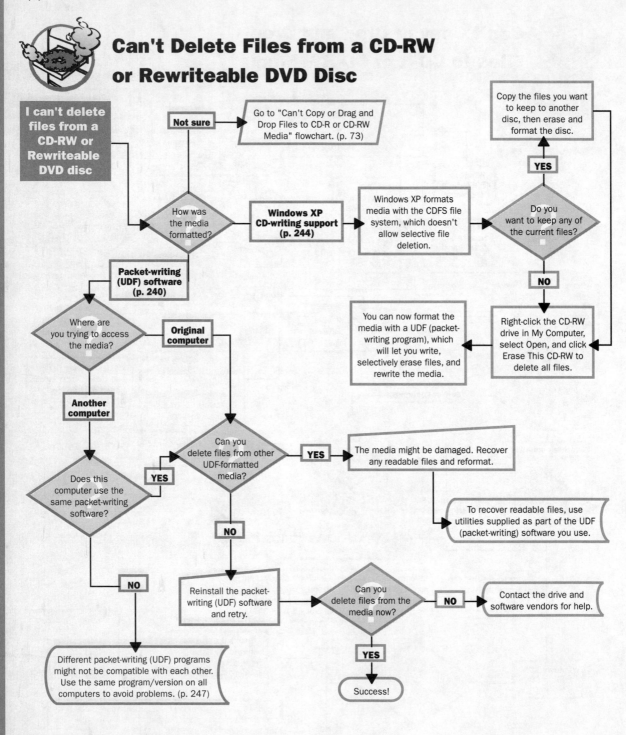

I can't delete files from a CD-RW or Rewriteable DVD disc

Not sure → Go to "Can't Copy or Drag and Drop Files to CD-R or CD-RW Media" flowchart. (p. 73)

How was the media formatted?

Windows XP CD-writing support (p. 244) → Windows XP formats media with the CDFS file system, which doesn't allow selective file deletion. → **Do you want to keep any of the current files?**

— **YES** → Copy the files you want to keep to another disc, then erase and format the disc.

— **NO** → Right-click the CD-RW drive in My Computer, select Open, and click Erase This CD-RW to delete all files. → You can now format the media with a UDF (packet-writing program), which will let you write, selectively erase files, and rewrite the media.

Packet-writing (UDF) software (p. 240)

Where are you trying to access the media?

— **Original computer** → **Can you delete files from other UDF-formatted media?**
  - **YES** → The media might be damaged. Recover any readable files and reformat. → To recover readable files, use utilities supplied as part of the UDF (packet-writing) software you use.
  - **NO** → Reinstall the packet-writing (UDF) software and retry. → **Can you delete files from the media now?**
    - **NO** → Contact the drive and software vendors for help.
    - **YES** → Success!

— **Another computer** → **Does this computer use the same packet-writing software?**
  - **YES** → Can you delete files from other UDF-formatted media?
  - **NO** → Different packet-writing (UDF) programs might not be compatible with each other. Use the same program/version on all computers to avoid problems. (p. 247)

IDE Removable Media and
Optical Drive Troubleshooting

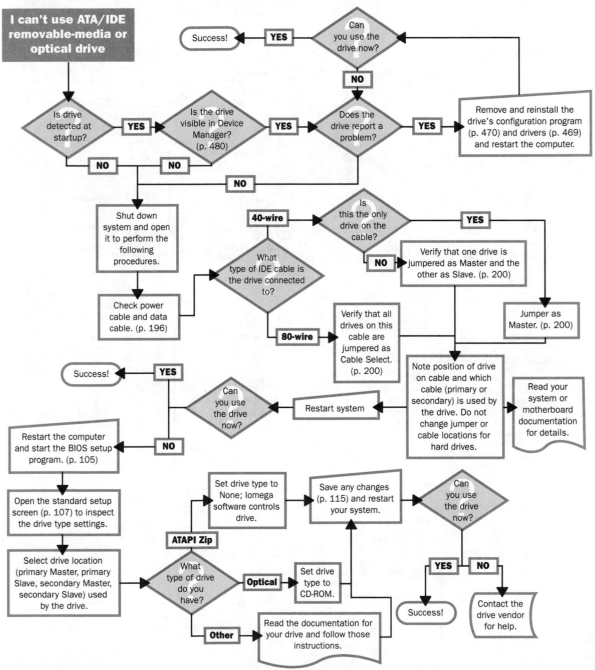

I can't use ATA/IDE removable-media or optical drive

Is drive detected at startup? — YES → **Is the drive visible in Device Manager? (p. 480)** — YES → **Does the drive report a problem?** — YES → **Remove and reinstall the drive's configuration program (p. 470) and drivers (p. 469) and restart the computer.**

Can you use the drive now? — YES → **Success!**

NO

Is drive detected at startup? NO ↓ NO

Is the drive visible in Device Manager? NO ↓

Does the drive report a problem? NO →

Shut down system and open it to perform the following procedures.

Check power cable and data cable. (p. 196)

What type of IDE cable is the drive connected to?
- 40-wire → **Is this the only drive on the cable?** — YES → **Jumper as Master. (p. 200)**
  - NO → **Verify that one drive is jumpered as Master and the other as Slave. (p. 200)**
- 80-wire → **Verify that all drives on this cable are jumpered as Cable Select. (p. 200)**

Note position of drive on cable and which cable (primary or secondary) is used by the drive. Do not change jumper or cable locations for hard drives. → **Read your system or motherboard documentation for details.**

Restart system → **Can you use the drive now?** — YES → **Success!**
- NO → **Restart the computer and start the BIOS setup program. (p. 105)**

Open the standard setup screen (p. 107) to inspect the drive type settings.

Select drive location (primary Master, primary Slave, secondary Master, secondary Slave) used by the drive.

What type of drive do you have?
- ATAPI Zip → **Set drive type to None; Iomega software controls drive.**
- Optical → **Set drive type to CD-ROM.**
- Other → **Read the documentation for your drive and follow those instructions.**

Save any changes (p. 115) and restart your system. → **Can you use the drive now?**
- YES → **Success!**
- NO → **Contact the drive vendor for help.**

76

Removable Media Drive Problems

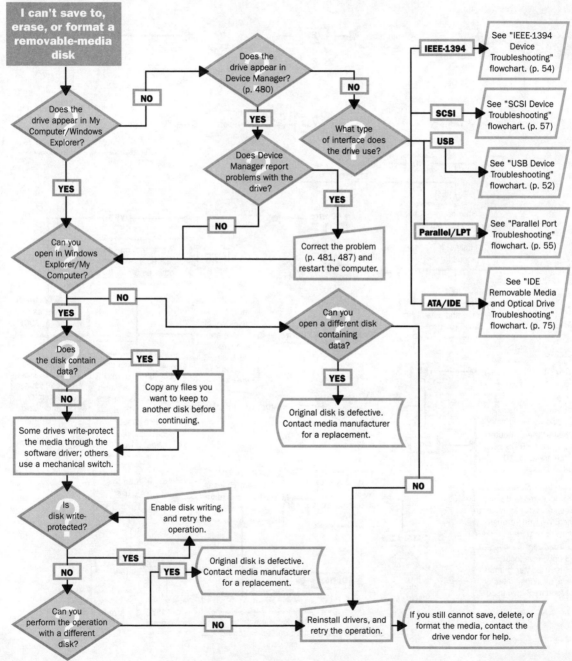

I can't save to, erase, or format a removable-media disk

Does the drive appear in My Computer/Windows Explorer?

NO → Does the drive appear in Device Manager? (p. 480)

NO → What type of interface does the drive use?

- **IEEE-1394** → See "IEEE-1394 Device Troubleshooting" flowchart. (p. 54)
- **SCSI** → See "SCSI Device Troubleshooting" flowchart. (p. 57)
- **USB** → See "USB Device Troubleshooting" flowchart. (p. 52)
- **Parallel/LPT** → See "Parallel Port Troubleshooting" flowchart. (p. 55)
- **ATA/IDE** → See "IDE Removable Media and Optical Drive Troubleshooting" flowchart. (p. 75)

YES → Does Device Manager report problems with the drive?

YES → Correct the problem (p. 481, 487) and restart the computer.

NO → Can you open in Windows Explorer/My Computer?

YES → Does the disk contain data?

YES → Copy any files you want to keep to another disk before continuing.

NO → Some drives write-protect the media through the software driver; others use a mechanical switch.

Is disk write-protected?

YES → Enable disk writing, and retry the operation.

NO → Can you perform the operation with a different disk?

YES → Original disk is defective. Contact media manufacturer for a replacement.

NO → Reinstall drivers, and retry the operation. → If you still cannot save, delete, or format the media, contact the drive vendor for help.

Can you open a different disk containing data?

YES → Original disk is defective. Contact media manufacturer for a replacement.

NO →

Floppy Drive Problems

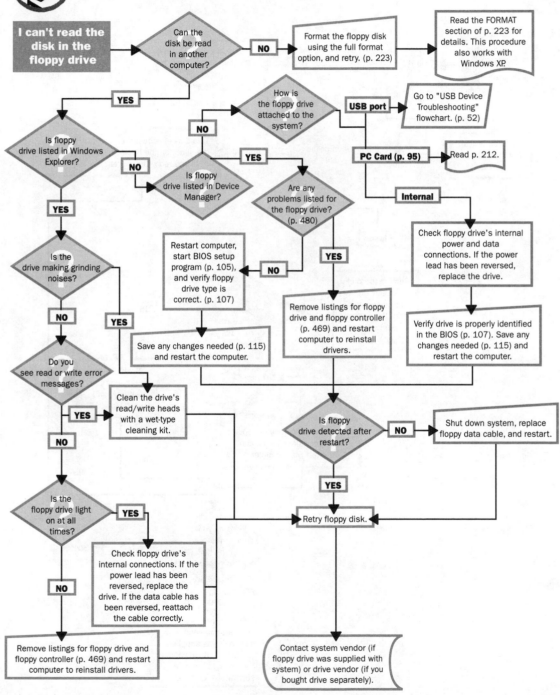

I can't read the disk in the floppy drive

Can the disk be read in another computer?

NO → Format the floppy disk using the full format option, and retry. (p. 223) → Read the FORMAT section of p. 223 for details. This procedure also works with Windows XP.

YES ↓

Is floppy drive listed in Windows Explorer?

How is the floppy drive attached to the system?

USB port → Go to "USB Device Troubleshooting" flowchart. (p. 52)

NO → Is floppy drive listed in Device Manager?

YES → Are any problems listed for the floppy drive? (p. 480)

PC Card (p. 95) → Read p. 212.

Internal → Check floppy drive's internal power and data connections. If the power lead has been reversed, replace the drive.

NO → Restart computer, start BIOS setup program (p. 105), and verify floppy drive type is correct. (p. 107)

NO → Remove listings for floppy drive and floppy controller (p. 469) and restart computer to reinstall drivers.

Verify drive is properly identified in the BIOS (p. 107). Save any changes needed (p. 115) and restart the computer.

YES ↓

Is the drive making grinding noises?

YES → Save any changes needed (p. 115) and restart the computer.

NO ↓

Do you see read or write error messages?

YES → Clean the drive's read/write heads with a wet-type cleaning kit.

NO ↓

Is floppy drive detected after restart?

NO → Shut down system, replace floppy data cable, and restart.

YES ↓

Retry floppy disk.

Is the floppy drive light on at all times?

YES → Check floppy drive's internal connections. If the power lead has been reversed, replace the drive. If the data cable has been reversed, reattach the cable correctly.

NO → Remove listings for floppy drive and floppy controller (p. 469) and restart computer to reinstall drivers.

Contact system vendor (if floppy drive was supplied with system) or drive vendor (if you bought drive separately).

Can't Change Contents of a Floppy Disk

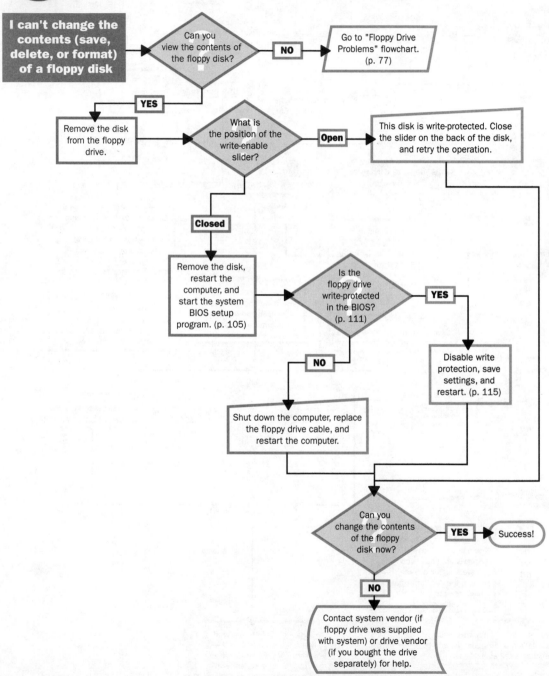

I can't change the contents (save, delete, or format) of a floppy disk

Can you view the contents of the floppy disk?

NO → Go to "Floppy Drive Problems" flowchart. (p. 77)

YES → Remove the disk from the floppy drive.

What is the position of the write-enable slider?

Open → This disk is write-protected. Close the slider on the back of the disk, and retry the operation.

Closed → Remove the disk, restart the computer, and start the system BIOS setup program. (p. 105)

Is the floppy drive write-protected in the BIOS? (p. 111)

YES → Disable write protection, save settings, and restart. (p. 115)

NO → Shut down the computer, replace the floppy drive cable, and restart the computer.

Can you change the contents of the floppy disk now?

YES → Success!

NO → Contact system vendor (if floppy drive was supplied with system) or drive vendor (if you bought the drive separately) for help.

The Computer Doesn't Start

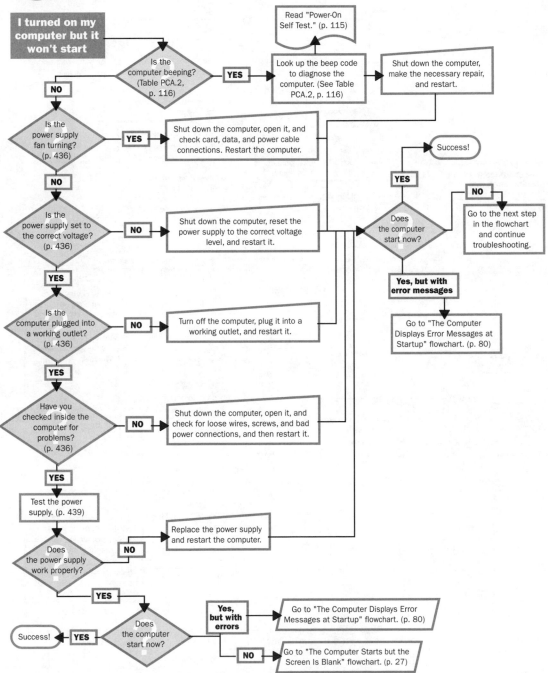

I turned on my computer but it won't start

Is the computer beeping? (Table PCA.2, p. 116)

NO / **YES**

Read "Power-On Self Test." (p. 115)

Look up the beep code to diagnose the computer. (See Table PCA.2, p. 116)

Shut down the computer, make the necessary repair, and restart.

Is the power supply fan turning? (p. 436)

NO / **YES**

Shut down the computer, open it, and check card, data, and power cable connections. Restart the computer.

Is the power supply set to the correct voltage? (p. 436)

YES / **NO**

Shut down the computer, reset the power supply to the correct voltage level, and restart it.

Is the computer plugged into a working outlet? (p. 436)

YES / **NO**

Turn off the computer, plug it into a working outlet, and restart it.

Have you checked inside the computer for problems? (p. 436)

YES / **NO**

Shut down the computer, open it, and check for loose wires, screws, and bad power connections, and then restart it.

Test the power supply. (p. 439)

Does the power supply work properly?

YES / **NO**

Replace the power supply and restart the computer.

Does the computer start now?

YES → Success!

NO → Go to the next step in the flowchart and continue troubleshooting.

Yes, but with error messages → Go to "The Computer Displays Error Messages at Startup" flowchart. (p. 80)

Does the computer start now?

YES → Success!

Yes, but with errors → Go to "The Computer Displays Error Messages at Startup" flowchart. (p. 80)

NO → Go to "The Computer Starts but the Screen Is Blank" flowchart. (p. 27)

The Computer Displays Error Messages at Startup

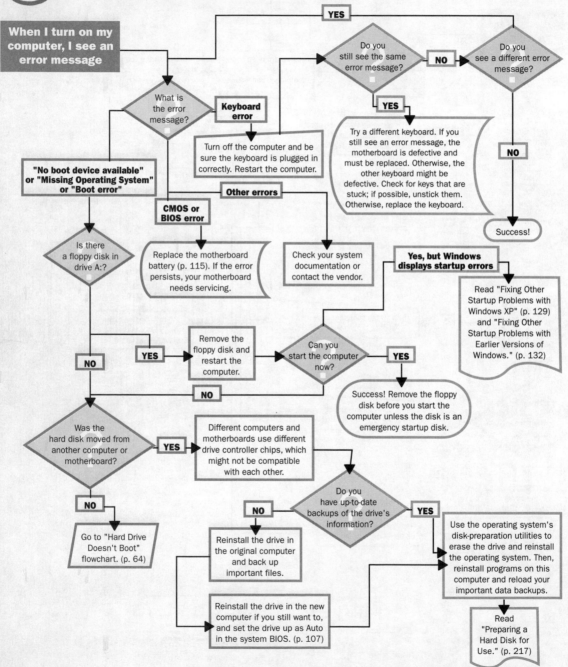

When I turn on my computer, I see an error message

What is the error message?

Keyboard error

Turn off the computer and be sure the keyboard is plugged in correctly. Restart the computer.

Do you still see the same error message?

YES

Try a different keyboard. If you still see an error message, the motherboard is defective and must be replaced. Otherwise, the other keyboard might be defective. Check for keys that are stuck; if possible, unstick them. Otherwise, replace the keyboard.

NO

Do you see a different error message?

NO

Success!

"No boot device available" or "Missing Operating System" or "Boot error"

CMOS or BIOS error

Other errors

Is there a floppy disk in drive A:?

Replace the motherboard battery (p. 115). If the error persists, your motherboard needs servicing.

Check your system documentation or contact the vendor.

Yes, but Windows displays startup errors

Read "Fixing Other Startup Problems with Windows XP" (p. 129) and "Fixing Other Startup Problems with Earlier Versions of Windows." (p. 132)

NO

YES

Remove the floppy disk and restart the computer.

Can you start the computer now?

YES

Success! Remove the floppy disk before you start the computer unless the disk is an emergency startup disk.

NO

Was the hard disk moved from another computer or motherboard?

YES

Different computers and motherboards use different drive controller chips, which might not be compatible with each other.

Do you have up-to-date backups of the drive's information?

NO

YES

Use the operating system's disk-preparation utilities to erase the drive and reinstall the operating system. Then, reinstall programs on this computer and reload your important data backups.

NO

Go to "Hard Drive Doesn't Boot" flowchart. (p. 64)

Reinstall the drive in the original computer and back up important files.

Reinstall the drive in the new computer if you still want to, and set the drive up as Auto in the system BIOS. (p. 107)

Read "Preparing a Hard Disk for Use." (p. 217)

Windows Starts Only in Safe Mode

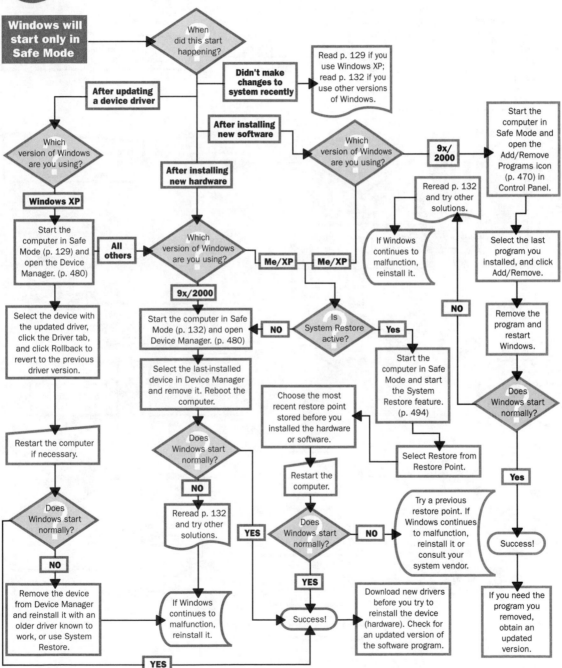

Windows will start only in Safe Mode

When did this start happening?

Didn't make changes to system recently → Read p. 129 if you use Windows XP; read p. 132 if you use other versions of Windows.

After updating a device driver

After installing new software → Which version of Windows are you using? → **9x/2000** → Start the computer in Safe Mode and open the Add/Remove Programs icon (p. 470) in Control Panel.

After installing new hardware

Which version of Windows are you using? → **Windows XP** → Start the computer in Safe Mode (p. 129) and open the Device Manager. (p. 480)

Which version of Windows are you using? — **All others** / **9x/2000** / **Me/XP** **Me/XP**

Reread p. 132 and try other solutions.

If Windows continues to malfunction, reinstall it.

Select the last program you installed, and click Add/Remove.

Select the device with the updated driver, click the Driver tab, and click Rollback to revert to the previous driver version.

Start the computer in Safe Mode (p. 132) and open Device Manager. (p. 480)

Is System Restore active? — **NO** / **Yes**

NO

Remove the program and restart Windows.

Select the last-installed device in Device Manager and remove it. Reboot the computer.

Start the computer in Safe Mode and start the System Restore feature. (p. 494)

Choose the most recent restore point stored before you installed the hardware or software.

Does Windows start normally?

Restart the computer if necessary.

Does Windows start normally? → **NO** → Reread p. 132 and try other solutions.

Restart the computer.

Yes

Does Windows start normally?

Select Restore from Restore Point.

Does Windows start normally? → **NO** → Remove the device from Device Manager and reinstall it with an older driver known to work, or use System Restore.

Try a previous restore point. If Windows continues to malfunction, reinstall it or consult your system vendor.

Success!

Does Windows start normally? — **YES** / **NO**

YES

YES

If Windows continues to malfunction, reinstall it.

Success!

Download new drivers before you try to reinstall the device (hardware). Check for an updated version of the software program.

If you need the program you removed, obtain an updated version.

YES

Can't Start a Program from a Shortcut

I can't start a program from its Start menu or Desktop shortcut

Did you boot in Safe Mode? (p. 129, 132)

YES → Some programs and devices aren't available in Safe Mode. Reboot normally and retry.

NO

Is the program located on a network drive?

YES → Can you access other network resources?

NO → Log off and log on to the system again so you can reconnect with network resources.

YES

NO

Right-click on the shortcut, select Properties, and view the path to the program or file.

Can you access the network now?

YES →

NO → Go to "Shared Resource Troubleshooting" flowchart. (p. 42)

Does the shortcut point to the correct file?

YES → Click Find Target (Windows will attempt to locate the file referenced in the shortcut).

NO → Shortcuts can be altered by installing or removing a drive or by other means. → Create a new shortcut to the file; see p. 503 for an example.

What is the result of Find Target?

Folder opens → Windows opens the folder containing the file and highlights the file. → Double-click the file to open it. → Can you open the file?

YES →

NO →

"Missing Shortcut" error → The file to which the shortcut points has been deleted or moved.

Do you see an error message?

YES → Go to "A Program Displays an Error When I Use It" flowchart. (p. 83)

NO → Reinstall the file referred to in the shortcut from a backup or by reinstalling the program.

A Program Displays an Error When I Use It

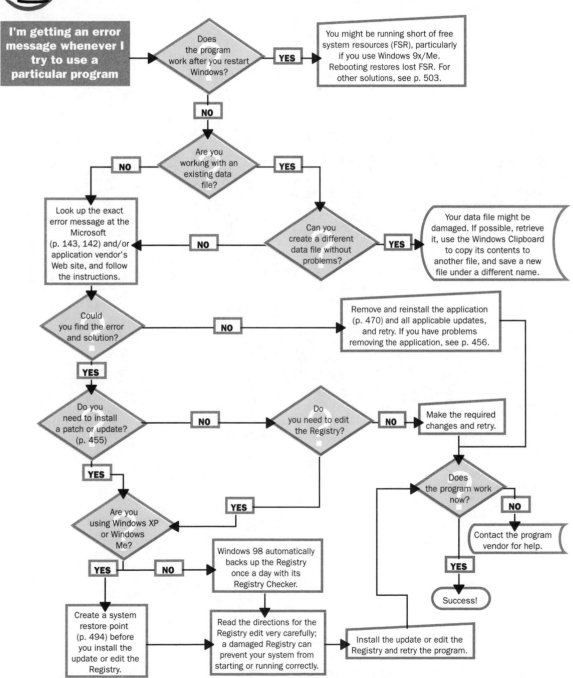

I'm getting an error message whenever I try to use a particular program

Does the program work after you restart Windows?

YES → You might be running short of free system resources (FSR), particularly if you use Windows 9x/Me. Rebooting restores lost FSR. For other solutions, see p. 503.

NO

Are you working with an existing data file?

NO →

YES →

Can you create a different data file without problems?

NO →

YES → Your data file might be damaged. If possible, retrieve it, use the Windows Clipboard to copy its contents to another file, and save a new file under a different name.

Look up the exact error message at the Microsoft (p. 143, 142) and/or application vendor's Web site, and follow the instructions.

Could you find the error and solution?

NO → Remove and reinstall the application (p. 470) and all applicable updates, and retry. If you have problems removing the application, see p. 456.

YES

Do you need to install a patch or update? (p. 455)

NO →

Do you need to edit the Registry?

NO → Make the required changes and retry.

YES

YES

Are you using Windows XP or Windows Me?

Does the program work now?

NO → Contact the program vendor for help.

YES

YES →

NO → Windows 98 automatically backs up the Registry once a day with its Registry Checker.

Create a system restore point (p. 494) before you install the update or edit the Registry.

Read the directions for the Registry edit very carefully; a damaged Registry can prevent your system from starting or running correctly.

Install the update or edit the Registry and retry the program.

Success!

PC Anatomy 101

Dissecting Your Computer

Before you can troubleshoot your computer, you need to understand what a computer is and how it's put together. A computer (or PC, for personal computer) is not a single unit, but is instead a collection of hardware subsystems including

- Video
- Storage
- Input devices
- Printers and other output devices
- Audio
- Networking
- Processor
- Memory
- Power

These subsystems, which include the device and its cables, are controlled by two types of software:

- A system BIOS (basic input-output system) chip on the mother-board—A BIOS chip is an example of "software on a chip" or firmware.

- The operating system and its device drivers (files that tell Windows how to use your PC's hardware). In this book, I concentrate on Microsoft Windows XP Home Edition and earlier versions such as Windows 9x and Windows Me. I occasionally reference Windows 2000, but as this is not a consumer operating system, it is not the focus of my troubleshooting efforts in this book.

Hardware and operating system software are both used by application programs such as Microsoft Office, Adobe Photoshop, Quicken, and many, many others to create, change, store, print, and transmit information.

With even the simplest devices and software depending upon so many other factors, troubleshooting your computer can be a challenge. But, if you don't know the details of what's inside a typical computer and how all this hardware and software relates, it's just about impossible.

This chapter introduces you to the major components you will find in typical computers, including those prone to being a *point of failure*. Think of it as an anatomy lesson, but without the formaldehyde or nasty smells.

What Is a Point of Failure?

In the following sections, I use the term *point of failure* to refer to a component or BIOS configuration which could cause problems for your system. This term isn't meant to suggest that computers are constantly on the verge of having a problem, but that some parts of the computer are more likely to cause problems than others.

The Outside Story of Typical Computers

While the "inside" story of computers is even more complicated than the outside, don't neglect taking a good look at the outside of your system when it's time to troubleshoot a computer problem.

The outside of the computer is where you'll find

- Cable connections for external peripherals such as cable modems, printers, monitors, and scanners
- Drive bays for removable-media and optical drives
- The power supply fan and voltage switch
- The power switch, reset button, and signal lights

All in all, the outside of the computer is a good place to start when your computer has stopped working, even if you're not sure that's where the problem lies.

The Front View of a Typical Desktop Computer

A typical "desktop" computer actually sits on the floor in most offices, and resembles Figure PCA.1.

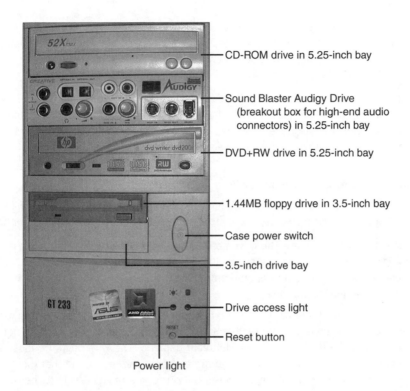

CD-ROM drive in 5.25-inch bay

Sound Blaster Audigy Drive
(breakout box for high-end audio
connectors) in 5.25-inch bay

DVD+RW drive in 5.25-inch bay

1.44MB floppy drive in 3.5-inch bay

Case power switch

3.5-inch drive bay

Drive access light

Reset button

Power light

Fast Track to Success

The term "desktop computer" is a bit misleading today, since few computers actually sit on the user's desk anymore (when I started working with computers in 1983, real "desktop" computers were virtually all there were). However, this term survives to describe computers that

- Use standard internal components such as motherboards, processors, memory, drives, sound cards, and video cards.
- Can be upgraded and rebuilt by the user without special tools.
- Use separate input devices (keyboard, mouse, or other pointing device).

Most (but not all) desktop computers are multi-piece units with a separate keyboard and monitor, although the iMac has inspired a few compact "all-in-one" PCs that incorporate a monitor.

The case shown in Figure PCA.1 is sometimes referred to as a *mid-tower* case. This computer has room for up to six internal drives (three in 5.25-inch bays and three in 3.5-inch bays; one of the 3.5-inch bays can't be seen in Figure PCA.1).

5.25-inch drive bays typically contain CD-ROM, CD-RW, DVD-ROM, and similar optical drives, as well as large removable-media drives such as the Castlewood Orb and Iomega Jaz. 3.5-inch drive bays usually house floppy drives, hard drives, and smaller removable-media drives such as Iomega Zip and SuperDisk LS-120/LS-240 drives.

As Figure PCA.1 also shows, you can add other types of devices to the 5.25-inch drive bays, such as the Sound Blaster Audigy Drive (a breakout box for this popular sound card), cooling fans, drive-selection switches, front-mounted connectors for IEEE-1394 and USB ports, and so on.

Note that the Sound Blaster Audigy Drive has connectors for some types of speakers and other multimedia devices. Unfortunately, front-mounted cable connections are still quite rare. Most devices still connect to the rear of the computer, which makes it more difficult to fix problems caused by loose cables.

Points of Failure on the Front of Your Computer

The front of your computer may provide valuable clues if you're having problems with your system. In case of problems, check the following common points of failure for help.

- Can't read CD media—The drive door on the CD-ROM or other optical drive might not be completely closed or the media might be inserted upside down; press the eject button to open the drive, remove any obstacles, reseat the media, and close the drive.

- Can't shut down the computer with the case power switch—The case power switch is connected to the motherboard on ATX and Micro-ATX systems, not directly to the power supply as with older designs. The wire might be loose or connected to the wrong pins on the motherboard. Keep in mind that most systems require you to hold in the power button for about four seconds before the system will shut down. If the computer crashes, you might need to shut down the computer by unplugging it or by turning off the surge suppressor to which the computer is connected.

- Can't see the drive access or power lights—As with the case power switch, these lights are also connected to the motherboard. These wires might also be loose or connected to the wrong pins on the motherboard.

- Can't use USB or digital camera (serial) ports on the front of the system— Some systems have these ports on the front of the computer as well as the rear. Front-mounted ports are connected with extension cables to the motherboard. If the cables inside the case are loose, the ports won't work. If the ports are disabled in the system BIOS, the ports won't work.

→ See "Inside a Typical PC," p. 97 for details.

As you can see from this section, in many situations, you will need to open the case to resolve a problem, even though the symptoms might first manifest themselves outside your computer.

The Rear View of Typical Desktop Computers

While the front view of a computer can help you determine whether there's room for another drive, the rear view is the most critical view if you're trying to locate a loose cable or a place to attach a new peripheral. Figure PCA.2 shows the rear of a typical desktop computer when common peripheral cables are attached, while Figure PCA.3 shows the rear of the same computer after the cables are removed.

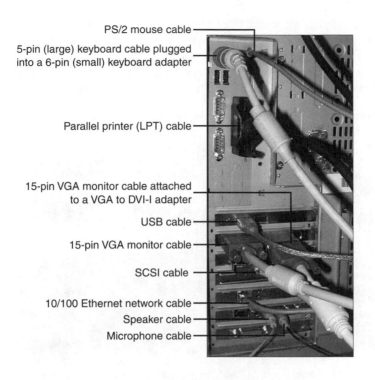

PS/2 mouse cable

5-pin (large) keyboard cable plugged
into a 6-pin (small) keyboard adapter

Parallel printer (LPT) cable

15-pin VGA monitor cable attached
to a VGA to DVI-I adapter

USB cable

15-pin VGA monitor cable

SCSI cable

10/100 Ethernet network cable

Speaker cable

Microphone cable

FIGURE PCA.2

The rear panel of a typical desktop computer with common external peripheral cables attached.

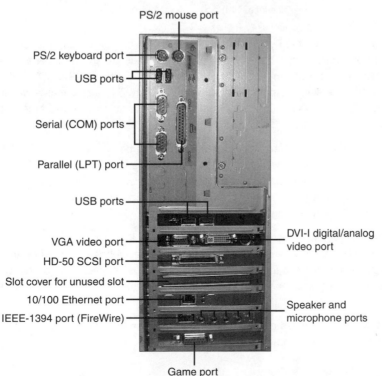

PS/2 mouse port

PS/2 keyboard port

USB ports

Serial (COM) ports

Parallel (LPT) port

USB ports

VGA video port

HD-50 SCSI port

Slot cover for unused slot

10/100 Ethernet port

IEEE-1394 port (FireWire)

DVI-I digital/analog
video port

Speaker and
microphone ports

Game port

FIGURE PCA.3

The rear panel of a typical desktop computer with built-in ports (top) and ports on add-in cards (bottom).

Figure PCA.2 and PCA.3 are typical of computers built in local computer shops (also called *box shops*) from standard parts. However, if you purchased your computer from a retail store, the rear panels shown in Figure PCA.4 might look more like your computer. Computers sold in retail stores often have built-in sound and VGA video ports, and some might also include built-in 10/100 Ethernet ports.

FIGURE PCA.4
The rear panel of a desktop computer with built-in VGA video and sound, and the standard peripheral cables.

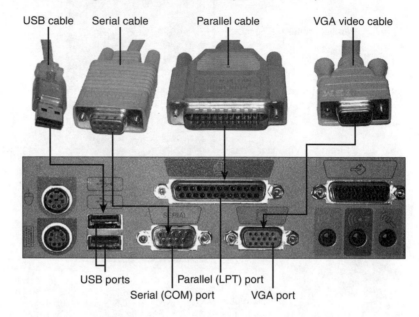

The computers pictured in Figures PCA.2—PCA.4 use motherboards that conform to an industry-standard form factor called ATX. The ATX design, and its more compact sibling Micro-ATX, is found in virtually all computers sold since 1997. ATX motherboards have six or seven expansion slots inside; Micro-ATX motherboards, which are used most frequently in low-cost retail-store computers, normally have three or four expansion slots.

Older types of computers use different types of motherboards which have built-in ports mounted under the expansion slots (LPX) or have built-in ports wired to connectors mounted in the expansion slots (Baby-AT). Because these systems are typically five years old or older (and are candidates for complete replacement), they are not discussed in this section.

Above the rear panel details shown in Figures PCA.2—PCA.4 is the power supply (see Figure PCA.5). Power supplies actually convert high-voltage AC power into the low-voltage DC power used inside the computer. Because conversions of this type create heat, the power supply has a fan to cool itself and also help overall system cooling.

While a few power supplies can switch between 115V and 230V services automatically, most use a sliding switch.

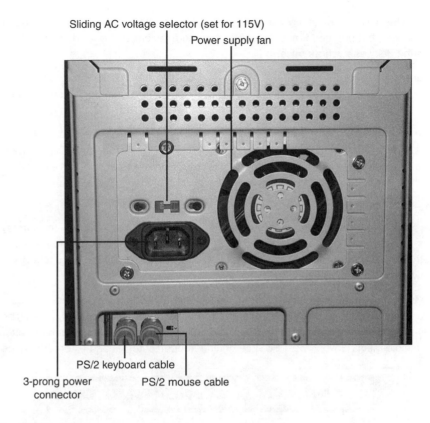

Sliding AC voltage selector (set for 115V)

Power supply fan

3-prong power connector

PS/2 keyboard cable

PS/2 mouse cable

FIGURE PCA.5
A typical power supply mounted in a computer.

The Parallel Port

The parallel port, shown in Figure PCA.4, is one of the oldest multipurpose interfaces found on a typical PC. The parallel port uses a DB-25F connector, and was originally designed for use with parallel printers. However, it has since been adapted for use with removable-storage drives of varying types (Zip, SuperDisk, CD-ROM, CD-RW), scanners, and for direct parallel (Direct Cable Connection or LapLink) file transfer. The parallel port is included as part of most ATX and Micro-ATX computers' rear panels as shown in Figure PCA.4, but it can also be built into an add-on card that can be installed into the PCI or ISA expansion slots on the motherboard. So-called legacy-free computers don't include built-in parallel ports.

If the parallel port is built into the motherboard, as in Figure PCA.4, it is considered an ISA device and its IRQ (normally IRQ 7) cannot be shared with other devices. For more details on the hardware resources used by the parallel port, see "Hardware Resources," p. 117.

The Serial Port

The serial port, shown in Figure PCA.4, was introduced along with the parallel port on the first PCs. The original serial ports used a DB-25M connector, but virtually all serial ports in recent years have used a DB-9M connector as seen in Figure PCA.4.

The serial port was originally intended for use with analog (dial-up) modems and serial printers, but has been most often used in more recent times for data transfer or pointing devices such as mice.

Whereas most recent computers have one or two serial ports built into the motherboard, legacy-free computers don't have any serial ports. Serial ports can also be added to the ISA or PCI expansion slots on the motherboard.

If the serial port is built into the motherboard, it cannot share its IRQ (normally IRQ 4 for COM1, and IRQ 3 for COM2) with other devices. For more details on the hardware resources used by the serial port, see "Hardware Resources," p. 117.

The SCSI Interface

The SCSI interface, which is not found in most home PCs, can have several forms, depending upon the type of SCSI card used by your computer (it's rare to have a motherboard with built-in SCSI). The most common types of SCSI connectors are shown in Figure PCA.6.

The HD-68 pin connector is used for high-performance Wide SCSI devices such as hard drives and tape backups. The other three interfaces are used for various types of Narrow SCSI devices, including CD-ROM, CD-R, and CD-RW drives; scanners; and removable-media drives. Most SCSI cards can support internal and external devices.

FIGURE PCA.6

Typical SCSI interfaces: HD-68 (top), HD-50 (second from top), DB25 (third from top), and Centronics 50 (bottom).

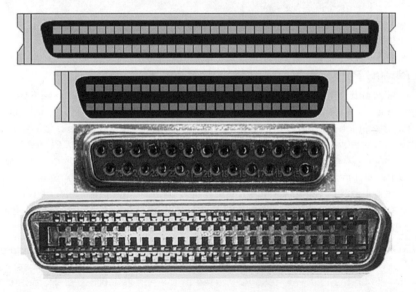

The 25-pin connector shown in Figure PCA.6 is found primarily on low-cost SCSI cards bundled with scanners or Zip drives. It uses the same DB-25F connector used by the parallel port, but is not interchangeable. To determine whether a 25-pin adapter on the rear of your system is a SCSI port, use these methods:

- A 25-pin SCSI connector will usually say SCSI on the card bracket at the rear of the computer.

- Open the Device Manager display of on-board hardware to see whether a SCSI device is listed; note that the Promise Ultra IDE controller built into some motherboards is listed under SCSI devices in Device Manager, but is used for IDE/ATA devices. A true SCSI card will list SCSI in the device description in Device Manager. For help using the Device Manager, refer to Appendix A, "Using Windows Diagnostics Tools."

Most SCSI cards plug into the PCI slot on the motherboard or the PC Card slot found in notebook computers. In these cases, the IRQ used by the card can be shared with other devices. However, older SCSI cards used the ISA slot; ISA IRQs cannot be shared with other devices. Narrow SCSI (25-pin or 50-pin interface) cards support up to 7 unique devices plus the host adapter, while Wide SCSI (68-pin) cards support up to 15 unique devices plus the host adapter. External SCSI devices have two ports, enabling you to create a daisy-chain of devices. Each device plugged into a SCSI card must have a unique device ID, and the end of the daisy-chain of devices must be terminated.

→ *For more details about SCSI daisy-chaining and device configuration, see "Troubleshooting SCSI Scanners," p. 356.*

The USB Interface

The USB interface (refer to Figure PCA.4) is currently replacing serial, parallel, and PS/2 mouse and keyboard ports; some systems feature only USB ports for external expansion. The original version of the USB port, USB 1.1, has speeds up to 12Mbps, while the newer USB 2.0 standard, also called Hi-speed USB, has speeds up to 480Mbps. Most recent computers built through mid-2002 include built-in USB 1.1 ports, but computers built from mid-2002 on might include both USB 1.1 and USB 2.0 ports. Both USB 1.1 and USB 2.0 ports can be added to systems through the use of a PCI or PC Card add-on card.

USB ports can be used for keyboards, mice and pointing devices, scanners, printers, removable-media drives, hard drives, optical drives, direct data transfer, modems, and networking. USB ports are thus the most versatile ports built into modern PCs.

USB devices can be daisy-chained, as can SCSI and IEEE-1394a devices, but there are several differences between how these technologies work, as shown in Table PCA.1.

TABLE PCA.1
SCSI, IEEE-1394a, and USB Compared

Interface	How Devices Are Daisy-Chained	Max. Number of Devices	How Devices Are Configured	MaximumSpeed
SCSI	Direct connection between devices	7 or 15 (depends on host adapter type)	Unique device ID; last device in daisy-chain must be terminated	10Mbps up to 320Mbps; speeds beyond 40Mbps are used primarily for hard drives
USB	Multi-port hubs	Up to 127	Plug-and-Play configuration in Windows	1.1: 12Mbps; 2.0: 480Mbps
IEEE-1394a	Hub, direct	Up to 63	Plug-and-Play configuration in Windows	400Mbps

The USB ports built into the computer are known as root hubs; most computers have at least two. External hubs, also called generic hubs, are connected to root hubs to allow multiple USB devices to share a single root hub. Different USB devices use different amounts of power. Bus-powered hubs (hubs which take power from the USB root hub) can provide no more than 100mA of power to each device, while self-powered hubs (connected to a separate power outlet) can provide the full 500mA of power required by some USB devices. Because USB root hubs, whether built into the motherboard or installed as an add-on card, are PCI devices, they can share IRQs with other PCI devices.

USB 1.1 devices can run at 1.5Mbps (keyboards, mice and pointing devices) or at speeds of 12Mbps (scanners, printers, and other devices). Because low-speed devices can slow down higher-speed USB 1.1 devices when plugged into the same USB 1.1 root hub, I recommend that you use separate generic hubs for low-speed and high-speed USB 1.1 devices. However, USB 2.0 is capable of managing both USB 1.1 and USB 2.0 devices at their top speeds.

→ For more information about troubleshooting USB devices, see "Using Device Manager to Troubleshoot USB Devices," p. 338.

The IEEE-1394a Interface

→ To see an illustration of the typical locations used for IEEE-1394 ports, see "Troubleshooting Other Problems with an IEEE-1394 Drive," p. 204.

The IEEE-1394a interface, commonly referred to as IEEE-1394, FireWire, or i.Link, is designed to be a high-speed replacement for SCSI, parallel, and other legacy port types. As Table PCA.1 indicates, IEEE-1394a is much faster than USB 1.1, but a bit slower than USB 2.0. The major difference between IEEE-1394a and USB, aside from speed, is that IEEE-1394a can be used to connect devices without using a computer, while USB 1.1 and USB 2.0 require that a computer be used to control the connection. For this reason, IEEE-1394a is very popular for use with DV camcorders and other multimedia devices. The speed of IEEE-1394a and its increasing popularity has also made it a popular choice for external hard drives. IEEE-1394a ports are occasionally built into a computer's motherboard, but are more often installed into PCI slots or CardBus PC Card slots.

Points of Failure on the Rear of Your Computer

The most likely point of failure on the rear of your computer is peripheral cabling. Fortunately, more and more devices use the lightweight USB cable shown in Figure PCA.4 instead of the bulky, heavy serial and parallel cables also shown in Figure PCA.4. Note that serial, parallel, and VGA cables all use thumbscrews; if you don't fasten the thumbscrews to the connector on the computer, your cables won't connect tightly and this could cause intermittent or complete failure of your peripherals.

Newer types of peripheral cables such as USB and IEEE-1394a are pushed into place and are very lightweight. No thumbscrews or other locking devices are needed. However, these cables can also be pulled out of the socket easily, precisely because they are lightweight and support a feature called hot-swapping. Hot-swap devices can be freely connected and disconnected while the PC's power is on.

When you attach cables to the ports at the rear of the computer, avoid tangling them together. Tangled cables could cause electrical interference with each other, leading to erratic performance of external devices such as your printer or monitor. Also, tangled cables put extra stress on ports, which could cause malfunctions or port failure.

The power supply shown in Figure PCA.5 is another likely point of failure. If the three-prong power cable is not plugged all the way into the computer, the system might not start up at all, or might shut down unexpectedly. If the voltage selector switch is not set correctly, the computer will not start at all, and if the power supply is set for 115V and is plugged into a 230V supply, the power supply and possibly other parts of the computer will be destroyed.

All Around a Notebook Computer

Notebook computers use the same types of peripherals, operating system, and application software as desktop computers use. However, notebook computers vary in several ways from desktop computers:

- Most notebook computers feature integrated ports which are not usually built in to desktop computers, including one or more PC Card (PCMCIA) slots, a 56Kbps modem, and a 10/100 Ethernet port.

- Some notebook computers support swappable drives, but less-expensive models require a trip to the service bench for a drive upgrade.

- More and more notebook computers use combo DVD-ROM/CD-RW drives to enable one optical drive to perform the work of two.

- Many notebook computers don't have an internal floppy drive, but rely on CD-RW or removable-media drives on USB connections to transfer or back up data.

- Notebook computers have integrated pointing devices built into their keyboards; most use a touchpad, but a few (primarily IBM and Toshiba models) have a pointing stick (which one is better is a matter of personal preference).

Figure PCA.7 shows you a composite view of a typical notebook computer, a Compaq Presario 700 series.

Points of Failure on a Notebook Computer

As with desktop computers, cabling can be a major point of failure on notebook computers. However, notebook computers also have a few unique points of failure. The PC Card (PCMCIA card) represents a significant potential point of failure for the following reasons:

- If a PC Card is not completely pushed into its slot, it will not function.

- If a PC Card is ejected without being stopped by using the PC Card system tray control, it could be damaged.

- Many PC Cards designed as 10/100 Ethernet network adapters or 56Kbps modems use dongles similar to the one pictured in Figure PCA.7. If the dongle is damaged, the card is useless until a replacement dongle is obtained.

- Some notebook computers that have the 32-bit CardBus version of the PC Card slot require the user to enable CardBus compatibility in the system BIOS, or else CardBus cards (used by USB 2.0, IEEE-1394a, and other high-bandwidth PC Card devices) will not work.

→ *For more information on troubleshooting PC Card and CardBus devices, see "Troubleshooting a PC Card Drive," p. 212.*

FIGURE PCA.7

Rear, left, and right views of the author's Compaq Presario 700-series notebook computer.

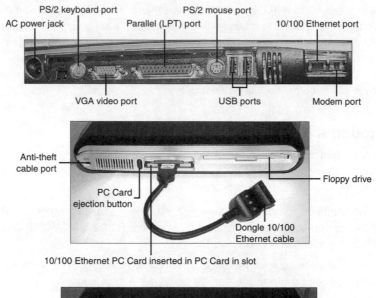

AC power jack
PS/2 keyboard port
Parallel (LPT) port
PS/2 mouse port
10/100 Ethernet port
VGA video port
USB ports
Modem port

Anti-theft cable port
PC Card ejection button
Floppy drive
Dongle 10/100 Ethernet cable
10/100 Ethernet PC Card inserted in PC Card in slot

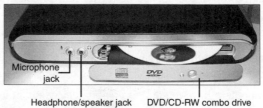

Microphone jack
Headphone/speaker jack
DVD/CD-RW combo drive

While a notebook computer's drives are much more rugged than those found in desktop computers, they are much more expensive to replace if damaged. While some mid-range and high-end notebook computers offer swappable drives, most lower-priced models do not. You can perform an upgrade to a hard disk without special tools on many models, but replacement of other types of drives on systems that don't support swappable drive bays can be expensive.

Although drives are expensive to replace on notebook computers, the biggest potential expense is the LCD screen. Most recent computers use active-matrix LCD panels in place of the dimmer (but less expensive to fix) passive-matrix panels that were once common.

Although LCD screen replacement is beyond the scope of this book, it represents a major threat to notebook computer users who travel frequently. I recommend purchasing an extended warranty which covers LCD replacement if you travel with your notebook computer frequently and depend upon it for your work.

Inside a Typical PC

As you have already learned, some problems which manifest themselves on the outside of the computer come from problems inside the computer. If you ever add memory, add an internal drive, upgrade your processor or motherboard, or add a card to your computer, you will need to work with the interior of the computer to complete these tasks.

The interior of a typical desktop computer is a crowded place, as Figure PCA.8 shows.

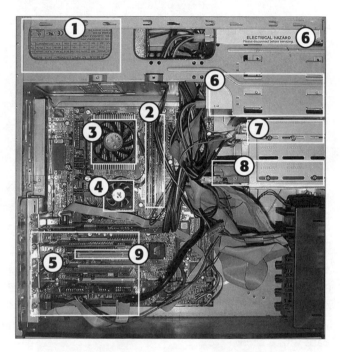

FIGURE PCA.8
The interior of a typical PC using an ATX motherboard.

1. Power supply
2. Memory modules
3. Processor with fan/heatsink
4. North Bridge chip with fan/heatsink
5. Add-on cards
6. Optical drives
7. Floppy drive
8. Hard drive
9. Empty PCI slot

Each device highlighted in Figure PCA.8, as well as the data, signal, and power cables that connect them to the motherboard and power supply, can cause significant system problems if they fail.

Expansion Slots

Typical desktop computers have three or more expansion slots, some of which might already be used for factory-installed devices such as video cards, network cards, or modems. Most computers have several PCI slots, and many also have a

single AGP slot for high-speed video. While AGP slots are faster than PCI slots, they are configured the same way in the system BIOS. See "PCI Configuration," p. 112 for details.

Most recent systems have no more than one ISA slot, and many no longer have ISA slots at all. ISA cards are much slower than PCI cards, and some can't be installed with Windows's normal Plug-and-Play automatic detection. You should avoid using ISA slots for upgrading your system if possible. Figure PCA.9 compares AGP, PCI, and ISA slots.

FIGURE PCA.9

ISA, PCI, and AGP slots compared.

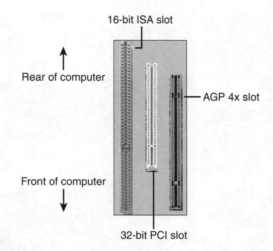

16-bit ISA slot

Rear of computer

AGP 4x slot

Front of computer

32-bit PCI slot

Regardless of the type of expansion slot your add-on card uses, you need to push the card connector all the way into the expansion slot when you install a card, as shown in Figure PCA.10.

After the card is properly inserted into the expansion slot, you need to fasten the card to the case with a screw.

Points of Failure Inside the Computer

Some of the problems you could encounter because of devices inside your computer include

- Overheating—Failure of the fans in the power supply or those attached to the processor, North Bridge chip, or video card can cause overheating and can lead to component damage. Each fan shown in Figure PCA.8 is connected to the motherboard to obtain power. Some case-mounted or older processor fans use a standard four-wire drive power connector instead (shown in Figure PCA.11).

- Loose add-on cards (see Figure PCA.10).

Card bracket not
flush with rear
edge of case

Bracket not
flush with rear
case wall

Connector not
pushed down into slot

FIGURE PCA.10
*A video card partly
inserted into the slot
(top) and fully inserted
into the slot (bottom).*

Card bracket
flush with rear
edge of case

Bracket flush with
rear case wall

Connector pushed
completely into slot

- Inability to start the computer—A loose processor or memory module can prevent the computer from starting (see Figures PCA.11 and PCA.12).
- Drive failures—If drives are not properly connected to power or data cables, or are not properly configured with jumper blocks, they will not work properly (see Figure PCA.13).

A socket-based processor before (left) and after (right) serious problems were corrected.

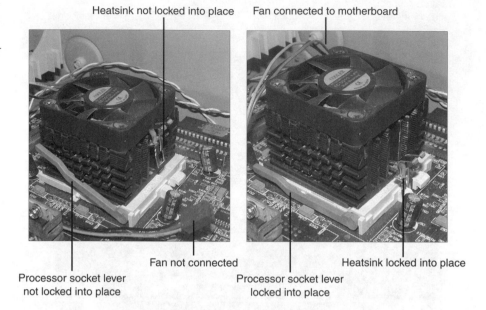

Heatsink not locked into place   Fan connected to motherboard

Fan not connected

Processor socket lever
not locked into place

Processor socket lever
locked into place

Heatsink locked into place

FIGURE PCA.12

A memory module before (top) and after (bottom) being locked into its socket.

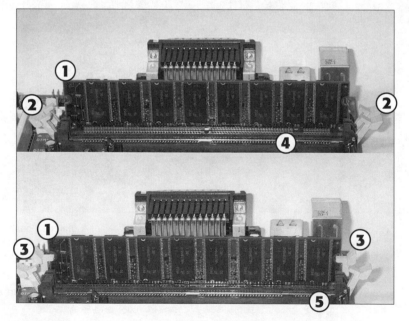

1. DIMM memory module
2. Module locks in open position
3. Module locks in closed position

4. Memory module edge connector before module fully inserted
5. Memory module edge connector after module fully inserted

The ATA/IDE Interface

Virtually every desktop computer built since the mid-1990s has featured two ATA/IDE interfaces on the motherboard. Each ATA/IDE interface can handle one or two drives, including hard drives, optical drives, and removable-media drives. Thus, you can install up to four ATA/IDE drives into a typical desktop computer.

The ATA/IDE interface uses a 40-pin connector (refer to Figure PCA.14), which connects to a 40-wire or 80-wire ATA/IDE cable. This cable has three connectors that go to the following locations:

- ATA/IDE interface on the motherboard
- Primary (master) drive
- Secondary (slave) drive

Forty-wire cables, which are now becoming outdated, support device bandwidth up to UltraDMA/33 (33MBps). Eighty-wire cables support all older devices plus the latest data bandwidth up to 133MBps (UltraDMA/133). See Figure PCA.13 to see examples of a drive that is properly connected and one that is not.

Each ATA/IDE interface uses an IRQ: IRQ 14 is used for the primary interface, and IRQ 15 is used for the secondary interface. These IRQs cannot be shared with other devices. For details, see "Hardware Resources," p. 117.

Cautions and Warnings

The original ATA/IDE drive cable, which contained 40 wires, allowed users to select primary (master) and secondary (slave) drives with *jumper blocks* on the rear or bottom of the drives. Some vendors, such as Western Digital, supported a no-jumper-block configuration for single hard drives. Most drives are labeled with the correct jumper settings as well as with the correct orientation for the power and data cables. If your drive lacks this information, look up the drive model on the vendor's Web site.

However, in most new systems today, drives are connected with an 80-wire ATA/IDE cable. This cable allows ATA/IDE drives such as hard drives, CD-RW drives, or DVD drives to be jumpered as *Cable Select*, giving control of master/slave settings to the cable. With these cables, the black connector at one end of the cable is used for master, the middle (gray) connector is used for slave, and the blue end of the cable connects to the system board or other ATA/IDE host adapter.

Cautions and Warnings

Most ATA/IDE drives and motherboard host adapters are designed to accept cables only when they are properly connected. The usual method is to match a *key* on one side of the cable plug (refer to Figure PCA.13) with a matching cutout on the cable connector. However, some low-cost cables don't feature keying, making it easy to install them incorrectly. If you use such a cable, note that the colored stripe indicating pin 1 on the cable is usually on the same side of the cable as the power supply connector. Check the motherboard (shown later in Figure PCA.14) for markings.

FIGURE PCA.13

A typical ATA/IDE CD-ROM drive before (top) and after (bottom) typical cabling and configuration problems have been corrected.

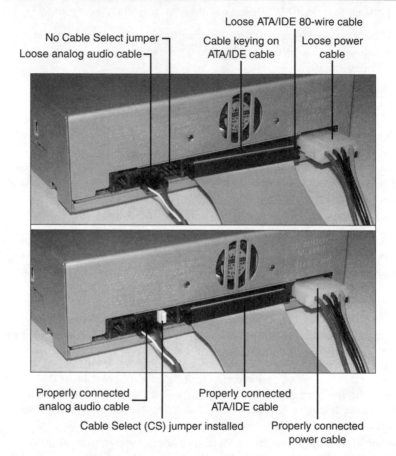

Even if you aren't installing a new drive, if you move existing ATA/IDE cables around inside your computer to gain access to memory, processor, or other components, you need to recheck the those cable connections, both to the drive and to the motherboard. It's very easy to accidentally pull these cables loose, which even if only partially detached, keeps your drives from functioning properly.

Figure PCA.14 shows a typical ATA/IDE motherboard connector.

- Multimedia failures—If the analog or digital audio cable running from the CD-ROM or other optical drive to the sound card is disconnected, you might not be able to hear CD music through your speakers. Some high-end sound cards also have connections to an external breakout box for additional speaker or I/O options. Be careful when you work inside your computer to avoid disconnecting these cables (see Figure PCA.15).

Blue motherboard ATA/IDE drive connector

Colored stripe indicating pin 1 on ATA/IDE cable

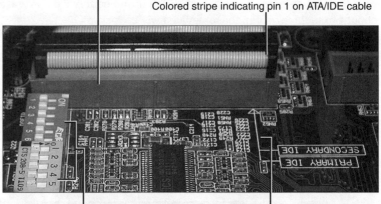

DIP switches for motherboard configuration

Motherboard marking for pin 1 on ATA/IDE connectors

FIGURE PCA.14

A typical ATA/IDE motherboard drive connector (top) and the DIP switches used on some motherboards for system configuration (left).

Cautions and Warnings

Some systems can transfer CD music through the standard ATA/IDE cable and don't require a separate patch cable. If you can play music CDs through your speakers and your system doesn't use analog or digital audio cables, don't worry about it.

Most CD-ROM and other types of optical drives include analog or digital audio cables, but if you need replacements, most computer stores also stock them.

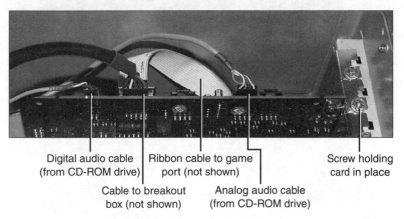

Digital audio cable (from CD-ROM drive)

Cable to breakout box (not shown)

Ribbon cable to game port (not shown)

Analog audio cable (from CD-ROM drive)

Screw holding card in place

FIGURE PCA.15

The top edge of a typical high-end sound card with multiple cable connections.

- Front panel failures—The tiny cables that connect the case power switch, reset switch, and status lights are easy to disconnect accidentally if you are working near the edges of the motherboard (see Figure PCA.16).

- Battery failure—The battery (see Figure PCA.16) maintains the system settings, which are configured by the system BIOS. The settings are stored in a part of the computer called the CMOS (more formally known as the non-volatile RAM/real-time clock—NVRAM/RTC). If the battery dies (average life is about two to three years), these settings will be lost.

- BIOS chip failure—The system BIOS chip (see Figure PCA.16) can be destroyed by electrostatic discharge (ESD) or lightning strikes. However, BIOS chips can also become outdated. While some systems use a socketed BIOS chip like the one shown in Figure PCA.16, others use a soldered chip. In both cases, software BIOS upgrades are usually available to provide additional BIOS features such as support for newer processors and hardware.

FIGURE PCA.16

The front-panel cables, BIOS chip, and battery on a typical motherboard.

System BIOS chip

Front-panel cables for system power button, status lights, and PC speaker

Battery

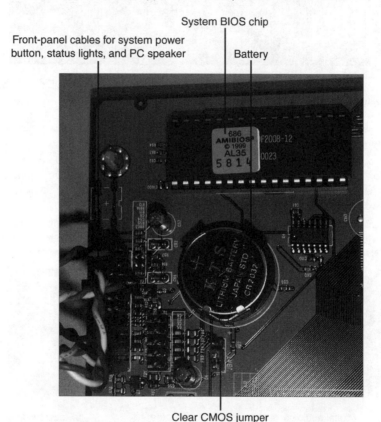

Clear CMOS jumper

BIOS Setup

The system BIOS chip shown in Figure PCA.16 is responsible for configuring many parts of your computer, including

- Floppy and hard drive configuration
- Memory size
- Drive boot sequence
- Built-in port configuration
- System security
- Power management

Essentially, the BIOS acts as a restaurant menu of possible choices, and the CMOS RAM (which might be a separate chip or be built into the South Bridge on some chipsets) stores the selections made from the menu of choices. When you received your computer from the factory, default selections were already stored in the BIOS, but as you add devices or customize your computer to perform certain operations, you might need to make additional choices. This section is intended to introduce the major BIOS setup options as an aid to troubleshooting your system.

On the Web

Contact your system or motherboard vendor's Web site for more information about particular configuration options you might see on your system, or check the manufacturer links, discussion groups, and all-around great coverage of BIOS-related issues available at Wim Bervoets's Wim's BIOS Web site

http://www.wimsbios.com

How the BIOS Displays Your PC's Components

While some computers display only a system manufacturer's logo at startup, forcing you to read the system manual to determine which key to press to start the BIOS setup program, others, particularly "white box" computers which use a collection of components from various vendors, or systems which use a replacement mother-board, can provide you with a lot of useful information at startup.

Figure PCA.17 shows a typical example of the BIOS chip's POST (power-on self-test) program's detecting onboard storage (the memory size is displayed briefly on many systems first). The display also shows which key to press to start the setup program.

FIGURE PCA.17

A typical startup screen displaying detected drives, chipset, and BIOS information.

1. BIOS vendor and release information
2. Motherboard vendor and model number
3. USB storage device(s)
4. Anti-virus feature enabled
5. Detected ATA/IDE drives
6. How to start the BIOS setup program
7. BIOS date and chipset information

Many systems that display information similar to that shown in Figure PCA.17 also display a condensed listing of onboard hardware before starting Windows (see Figure PCA.18). Because this information should not change on a day-to-day basis unless you change your system configuration (BIOS changes or hardware upgrades), displaying this information at startup is a valuable aid to troubleshooting a sick system.

FIGURE PCA.18

A typical system configuration screen displayed at system startup.

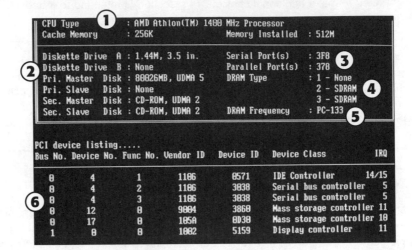

1. Processor type, speed, and memory size information
2. Drive information
3. I/O port addresses for serial & parallel ports
4. Memory slot usage
5. Memory speed
6. Onboard PCI devices

Fast Track to Success

Many computers sold at retail stores do not display the POST and configuration information screens shown in Figures PCA.17 and PCA.18 as configured from the factory. To display this information, start the computer's BIOS setup program and look for a BIOS option called Quiet Boot. Disable this option and save your changes. Some systems have an option called "Boot-Time Diagnostic Screen" instead; enable this option and save your changes. When your computer restarts, it should display hardware information.

Note that if your BIOS doesn't have an option such as Quiet Boot or Boot-Time Diagnostic Screen, you might not be able to view your hardware configuration at bootup.

One of the reasons it's so important to display this information when you start your computer (if your system permits it) is because you will know immediately whether there are any changes in your hardware configuration. If the configuration information displayed some day at startup differs from the normal information you see, it might mean that

- Someone has changed your BIOS configuration

- The computer has reverted to default settings for troubleshooting or other reasons
- The computer's battery is failing, causing stored setup information to be lost or corrupted
- The hardware inside your computer has failed, or been removed/replaced

To determine which of these has taken place, you need to press the key used by your computer to start the BIOS setup program. Common access keys used include

- F1 or F2 (various brands that use Phoenix BIOS)
- F10 (Compaq computers)
- Del (Award or AMI BIOS)

However, your computer or motherboard manual might list a different key or key combination to use for accessing the BIOS.

BIOS Setup Screens and Their Uses in Troubleshooting

Generally, system BIOS setup programs start in one of two ways:

- Some display a menu that allows you to go to any screen you desire.
- Others display a standard configuration screen along with a top-level menu for access to other screens.

BIOSes vary widely, but the screens used in the following sections are representative of the options available on typical recent systems; your system might have similar options, but place the settings on different screens than those shown here. You might find it useful to compare these screens to your computer's BIOS setup screens.

Cautions and Warnings

The setup screens shown in the following sections are typical of those found on "white-box" systems or replacement motherboards. However, if you use a major-brand desktop or notebook computer, don't be surprised if you have far fewer options. To reduce the chances of computer problems caused by incorrect configuration, some system and motherboard makers specify stripped-down BIOS setup programs.

Standard Setup

Most BIOSes have a main or standard setup screen similar to the one shown in Figure PCA.19. Generally, this screen is used to set date and time as well as drive configuration options. Many BIOSes also display the installed memory size on this screen.

Most systems' drives are usually configured as those shown in Figure PCA.19. The Auto setting for primary and secondary master and slave drives refers to drives connected to the ATA/IDE host adapters on the motherboard. Auto configuration enables the computer to detect the drive and use the correct settings at startup. While some users recommend that you configure the settings for hard drives to user-defined, which will list the exact settings for each hard drive, this can cause a major problem in case your BIOS settings are lost due to a virus, battery failure, or other causes. If you are not an experienced user, I highly recommend you let your computer do the work here.

FIGURE PCA.19

A typical main or standard BIOS setup screen.

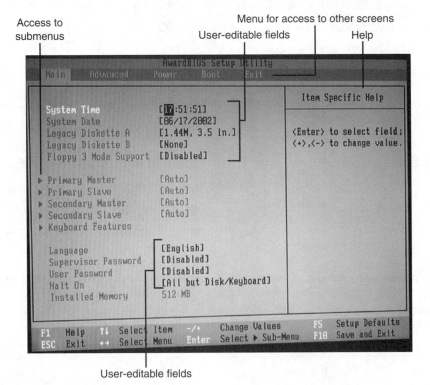

Cautions and Warnings

While hard drives, CD-ROM, and other ATA/IDE drives can be detected automatically by the system BIOS, floppy drives must be configured manually. When some systems revert to Setup Defaults (see the callouts for Figure PCA.19), they don't use the common 1.44MB, 3.5-inch floppy drive as the setup default. Believe it or not, some revert to 5.25-inch floppy drives, which haven't been in common use for more than a decade! Since Windows relies on the BIOS to properly identify drives so you can boot your system, an emergency startup disk won't work if your computer thinks its 3.5-inch drive is a 5.25-inch 1.2MB or 360KB model.

Be sure to check your floppy drive setting after you change a motherboard battery or use Setup Defaults to clear up a BIOS configuration problem.

Advanced Setup

Typical Advanced BIOS setup screens, such as the one shown in Figure PCA.20, can be used to adjust settings such as memory caching, USB, and PS/2 mouse configuration, and might also have settings such as boot order and anti-virus protection. Many recent systems also allow the user to adjust the CPU clock multiplier and memory speed settings as an alternative to struggling with DIP switches or jumpers on the motherboard. These functions are mainly used to overclock your PC's processor, a feat you should attempt only if you know what you're getting into.

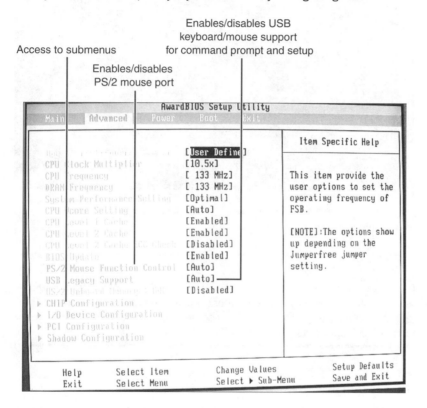

FIGURE PCA.20

A typical Advanced BIOS setup.

Chipset Setup

The Chipset setup screen (known as CHIP on some systems) typically is used to display or control memory and AGP video timing. Those settings should not be altered under normal circumstances (although some users like to experiment with faster settings than the defaults, faster settings can lead to instability).

Some computers also place the ATA/IDE host adapter settings on this screen (see Figure PCA.21). Both primary and secondary host adapters should be enabled unless the computer is using a faster ATA/IDE host adapter card in an expansion slot as a replacement for the onboard host adapters.

FIGURE PCA.21

A typical Chipset setup screen configured for default operations.

AGP video card settings

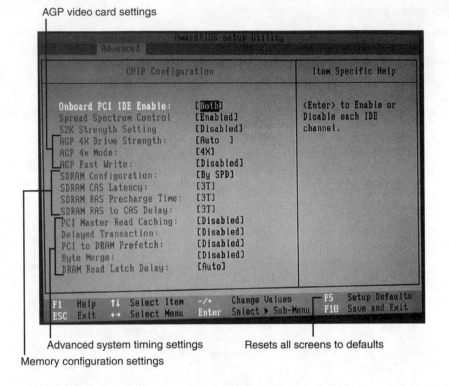

Advanced system timing settings   Resets all screens to defaults
Memory configuration settings

Fast Track to Success

If you start experimenting with this screen and foul up your system, use the Setup Defaults option available on most BIOSes to reset all screens to their defaults. Be sure to go through all the screens and make sure that drives and ports are configured as you desire.

I/O Device Setup

Depending on the system, you might need to check several BIOS setup screens to verify that your computer's onboard devices are all configured as you desire. The example shown in Figure PCA.22 configures serial, parallel, and onboard sound and modem settings only, while other ports (USB, PS/2 mouse, and IDE) are configured on different screens.

The parallel port setting in Figure PCA.22 (ECP+EPP) is recommended for use with virtually any parallel port printer or device because some devices prefer EPP mode and others prefer ECP mode. Note that you can disable parallel and serial ports if you no longer use parallel or serial devices.

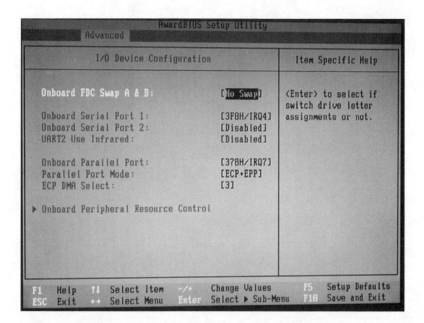

Fast Track to Success

Each serial and parallel port built into your system (most computers have two serial ports and one parallel port) gobbles up precious hardware resources, particularly IRQs. While PCI and AGP cards and onboard PCI devices such as USB ports can share IRQs, serial and parallel ports are ISA devices that can't share IRQs. The bottom line is that the rest of your peripherals will have more resources to use and share if you disable the ports you don't use.

Power Management

Power management features in the BIOS (see Figure PCA.23) can be used to save power and, on some systems, to protect your processor. While you might prefer to manage power through the Windows power management dialog, you can enable features such as CPU Fan Check at Power On or Fan Check Beeping through this dialog on some recent computers. Enabling these settings can help protect your processor from overheating.

Boot Setup

The boot configuration screen (part of the Advanced setup screen on some systems) is used to configure the order in which the computer looks for a bootable device, anti-virus BIOS configuration, the primary video card, and related settings (see Figure PCA.24).

➡ *To learn more about the recommended boot sequence for your version of Windows, see "Troubleshooting Hard Disk or Optical Drive Bootup Problems," p. 233.*

Helps protect processor if enabled

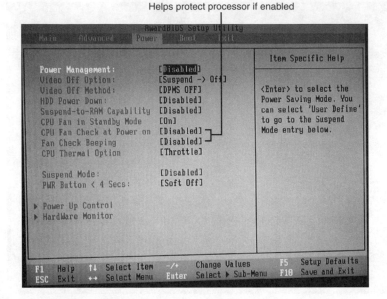

PCI Configuration

The PCI slot is the primary slot type used on most recent motherboards for add-in cards (the AGP slot for video cards is considered a PCI slot for configuration purposes).

While PCI devices can normally share IRQ resources, you might need to manually configure their hardware resource settings in a few cases, such as if Windows can't detect a PCI card you've installed. To do so, use the BIOS's PCI configuration screen, such as the example shown in Figure PCA.25. IRQs are discussed in much greater detail in "Hardware Resources," p. 117.

If Windows can't configure a PCI device inserted into a particular PCI slot, you might need to use the IRQ settings shown in Figure PCA.25. Note that slots 4 and 5 must use the same IRQ in this example; if cards in these slots can't work with each other, move one of the cards to another slot.

Fast Track to Success

Even if you aren't having any problems with the PCI (and AGP) cards already installed in your system, you might want to examine the Slot x IRQ options in your system BIOS to determine which IRQs your PCI cards can use. Originally, PCI cards could be configured to use only IRQs 9, 10, 11, and 12 (and 12 was often unavailable because it was used by the PS/2 mouse port). Newer systems (such as the one shown here) might also offer IRQs traditionally used by ISA devices such as serial (IRQs 3 and 4) and parallel (IRQ 7) ports. In such a case, disabling serial and parallel ports that you don't use makes it easier for Windows and your BIOS to find resource combinations that work correctly for all cards and motherboard-based devices, such as USB and integrated sound.

Enables Windows PnP control of installed devices

Configures order of boot devices

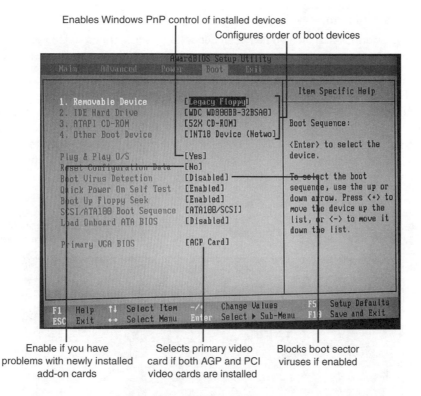

FIGURE PCA.24
A typical Boot Configuration screen.

Enable if you have
problems with newly installed
add-on cards

Selects primary video
card if both AGP and PCI
video cards are installed

Blocks boot sector
viruses if enabled

Configures IRQ usage per each PCI slot

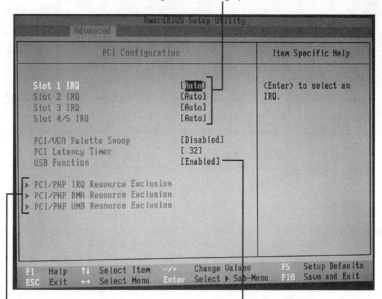

FIGURE PCA.25
*A typical PCI
Configuration screen.*

Use to prevent conflicts with ISA
devices that aren't PnP compatible

Enables/disables USB ports

Hardware Monitor

The Hardware Monitor screen has been added to newer systems to help you determine that your computer's temperature and voltage conditions are at safe levels for your computer (see Figure PCA.26).

Although it's useful to view these settings in the BIOS, temperature values are usually higher after the computer has been working for awhile (after you've booted to Windows and no longer have access to this screen). Generally, the major value of this screen is that its information can be detected by motherboard or system monitoring programs that run under Windows and enable you to be warned immediately if there are any heat or fan-related problems with your system.

Displays current motherboard and CPU temperatures

Displays CPU fan speed and speeds of other fans that are connected to the motherboard

FIGURE PCA.26

A typical Hardware Monitor screen.

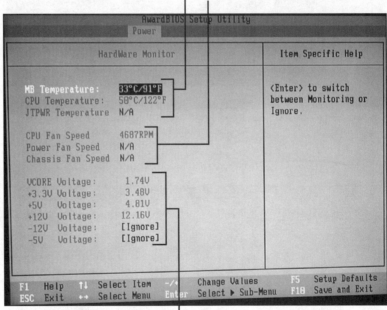

Displays current voltage levels (−12V and −5V are sometimes ignored because very few devices use these levels)

Cautions and Warnings

Figure PCA.26 doesn't list values for the power and chassis fans. That's because the fans inside this system aren't connected to the motherboard, and thus can't be monitored by the BIOS. If you buy chassis fans, make sure you buy the type that can connect to your motherboard so that you can get the full benefit of your computer's hardware monitor feature.

Saving Your Changes and Restarting the Computer

Most BIOSes offer two ways to exit:

- Exit Saving Changes
- Exit Discarding Changes

If you didn't intend to make any changes, choose the Exit Discarding Changes option. This might require you to return to the starting menu or to press the ESC key several times until you can select this option. Whether you save or discard changes, the computer reboots after you exit the BIOS setup program.

What to Do If Your Computer Can't Retain BIOS Setup Information

If your computer displays "Invalid BIOS information" messages whenever you start it up or the clock keeps reverting to the same date, you probably need to replace the battery on the motherboard. Most recent systems use a CR-2032 battery sold in the watch battery department of most stores. However, older systems might use any of a wide range of proprietary batteries, and a few use a combined NVRAM/RTC and battery chip made by Dallas Semiconductor or have a soldered-in-place battery. If your computer's battery is soldered in place, your motherboard probably has header pins for an external battery. Most full-line computer stores stock replacement batteries suitable for most models. Typical motherboard batteries last two to three years before you need to replace them.

On the Web

If your computer needs an unusual replacement battery, check the following sources:

Baber.com's extensive list is available at http://www.baber.com/baber/computer_clock_battery/generic.htm.

Batteries Plus has retail stores in many areas, and lists its computer battery replacements online at http://www.batteriesplus.com/Product/compclock.html.

After you replace the battery, you will need to restart your system and make any BIOS changes necessary to reflect your preferred configuration. Save the changes and exit the BIOS, and your system should restart normally.

Power-on Self Test

Every time your computer is turned on, the BIOS performs a Power-on Self Test, also known as the POST. If you see error messages displayed during startup or if the computer beeps during startup, the POST has located problems with your hardware configuration. Technicians can also display additional POST codes with a special add-on card called a POST card, which is installed into an empty PCI or ISA slot. However, the most common errors are reported through beep codes or onscreen error messages.

Onscreen error messages are usually fairly easy to understand, but POST beep codes vary by BIOS version. To determine what a particular beep code means, you need to know what BIOS brand and version your computer uses.

The major BIOS vendors include

- AMI (American Megatrends)
- Phoenix
- Award Software (owned by Phoenix)

The most common beep codes you're likely to encounter are listed in Table PCA.2.

TABLE PCA.2
Common System Errors and Their Beep Codes

Problem	Phoenix BIOS	Award BIOS	AMI BIOS	IBM BIOS
Memory	Beep sequences: 1-3-4-1 1-3-4-3 1-4-1-1	Beeping (other than 2 long, 1 short)	1, 3, or 11 beeps; 1 long, 3 short beeps	(None)
Video	(none)	2 long, 1 short beep	8 beeps; 1 long, 8 short beeps	1 long, 3 short beeps or 1 beep
Processor or motherboard	Beep sequence: 1-2-2-3	(none)	5 beeps or 9 beeps	1 long, 1 short beep

On the Web

For additional beep codes, see the following resources:

AMI BIOS—http://www.ami.com/support/doc/beep_codes.pdf

Phoenix BIOS—http://www.phoenix.com/resources/bios-postcode1.pdf

(These files require the free Adobe Acrobat Reader, available from Adobe at http://www.adobe.com.)

IBM BIOS—http://www.computerhope.com/beep.htm

Preventing ESD

ESD (electrostatic discharge) is a hidden danger to your data and your computer hardware, particularly when you open your computer to install new hardware or to troubleshoot a problem inside your system. ESD takes place when two items with different electrical potentials come close to each other or touch each other. ESD can happen even if you don't see a spark or feel a shock, but it takes very little ESD to damage or destroy computer parts. It takes about 800V of ESD for you to get a tingle or shock. It takes less than 100V (an amount you can't even feel) to ruin a CPU, memory module, or other computer part. Low-power construction makes these parts very vulnerable to ESD.

You can avoid ESD discharge when you're working inside your computer by following these tips:

- Use anti-static cleaning wipes to clean cases and monitors.
- Wear cotton or other natural fibers when you work on your PC; if you're working at home, ditch those synthetic-soled shoes and work in your stocking feet to avoid generating static electricity.
- Buy and use anti-ESD devices such as a wrist strap with an alligator clip and an anti-static mat. Connect the alligator clip to the computer *after* you disconnect it from power; this equalizes the electrical potential between you and the computer to prevent ESD.

  If you want to keep parts you remove from the computer safe as well as prevent ESD when you're inside the PC, look for a *field service kit*, which combines a grounding strap for your body with a grounded parts mat for components you are removing (or installing).
- Hold components by the case or card bracket, never by the circuit boards or data/power connectors.

On the Web

If you can't find ESD-protection devices locally, try these online sources:

e-Mat: http://www.anti-staticmat.com/

Radio Shack: http://www.radioshack.com/ (search for "anti-static")

Static Specialists: http://www.staticspecialists.com

Hardware Resources

There are four types of hardware resources used by both onboard and add-on card devices:

- IRQ
- I/O Port Address
- DMA Channel
- Memory Address

Each device needs its own set of hardware resources, or needs to be a device that can share IRQs (the only one of the four resources which can be shared). Resource conflicts between devices can prevent your system from starting, lock up your system, or can even cause data loss.

IRQs

IRQ is short for Interrupt Request. An IRQ is a signaling connection between a device and the processor (CPU). The device uses an IRQ line to "interrupt" the processor when the device needs attention from the processor. At least one IRQ is used by most major add-on cards (network, SCSI, sound, video, modem, and IEEE-1394); major built-in system components such as ATA/IDE host adapters, serial, parallel, and USB ports.

IRQs range from 0 to 15, as shown in Table PCA.3.

TABLE PCA.3
Typical IRQ Usage

IRQ	Standard Function	Bus Slot	Resource Type	Recommended Use
0	System timer	No	System	—
1	Keyboard controller	No	System	—
2	Second IRQ controller cascade to IRQ 9	No	System	—
8	Real-time clock	No	System	—
9	Available (might appear as IRQ 2)	Yes	PCI	Network Interface Card or VGA
10	Available	Yes	PCI	USB
11	Available	Yes	PCI	SCSI host adapter
12	Motherboard mouse port/available	Yes	ISA/PCI	Motherboard mouse port
13	Math coprocessor	No	System	—
14	Primary IDE	Yes	PCI	Primary IDE (hard disks)
15	Secondary IDE/ available	Yes	PCI	Secondary IDE (CD-ROM/tape)
3	Serial Port 2 (COM 2:)	Yes	ISA	COM 2:/internal modem
4	Serial Port 1 (COM 1:)	Yes	ISA	COM 1:
5	Sound/Parallel Port 2 (LPT2:)	Yes	ISA	Sound card
6	Floppy disk controller	Yes	System	Floppy controller
7	Parallel Port 1 (LPT1:)	Yes	ISA	LPT1:

Although Table PCA.3 shows you traditional IRQ usage, you should realize that your computer might list much different IRQ usage and still work correctly. Here's why:

- If your computer is a so-called legacy-free system without serial, parallel, or PS/2 mouse and keyboard ports, or if you have manually disabled them, IRQs 3, 4, 7, and 12 will also be treated as PCI IRQs. This means they can be used for PCI cards not listed on the chart, such as IEEE-1394a host adapters, SCSI host adapters, video capture cards, add-on multi-I/O (serial/parallel) adapters, and so forth.

- Beginning with late versions of Windows 95 and continuing on to today's Windows XP, PCI devices can share IRQs on most systems. While ISA devices such as built-in serial, parallel, and PS/2 mouse ports each need an exclusive IRQ, two or more PCI devices (as well as AGP video cards) can share IRQs as shown in Figure PCA.27.

I/O Port Addresses

I/O port addresses are used for the task of moving data to and from a device, and are used by every device in the computer, including motherboard devices, game ports, and other components that don't need IRQs. There are thousands of I/O port addresses available in today's computers, so resource conflicts are rare unless a user tries to assign two serial ports to the same address (refer ahead to Figure PCA.28).

As you look at I/O port address usage in your computer, you might see two different components that are working but are displaying the same I/O port address per the Windows Device Manager. In these cases, the devices listed use the same I/O port address as a way to communicate with each other. For example, the AMD-751 chipset processor to AGP controller and the TNT2 AGP video card in my computer use the same I/O port addresses to facilitate communication with each other (shown in Figure PCA.28).

DMA Channels

DMA stands for Direct Memory Access, a method of transferring data to and from memory at high speeds by avoiding the bottlenecks of management via the processor. While DMA transfers are very common today (high-speed ATA/IDE hard disks use a variation called Ultra DMA), only ISA devices such as the ECP or ECP+EPP parallel port and sound cards that emulate the Sound Blaster require specific DMA channels. Since there are more DMA channels than any user needs (0–7, with DMA 4 used as a cascade between the original DMA channels 0–3 and the newer DMA 5–7 range), DMA conflicts are rare. However, unlike IRQs, DMA channels can't be shared; data loss could result if two devices try to use the same DMA channel at the same time.

Memory Addresses

Like DMA channels, memory addresses are also abundant in computers. Add-on cards that have their own BIOS chips (some SCSI, some ATA/IDE, and some network cards as well as all VGA and 3D video cards), however, must use unique memory addresses that are found in the range between 640KB and 1MB. Since there's abundant memory address space and relatively low demand for memory addresses, conflicts are rare unless you manually configure a card to use an address already in use by another device.

Viewing Hardware Resources in Use

→ *For details, see "Using the Device Manager," p. 480 and "Using System Information," p. 491.*

You can view the current resource usage in your computer with the Windows Device Manager. To see the resource usage for a particular device, open the Device Manager, open the device's properties sheet and click Resources. You can also use the Windows System Information program to view resource usage.

If you need to install non-PnP devices, or if you are concerned about installing devices that have limited configuration options, you can also view all the resources currently in use. With Windows XP (and Windows 2000), start the Device Manager, select View, Resources by Type, and click the plus sign (+) next to each category. Figure PCA.27 shows the DMA channel, IRQ, and a portion of the memory resource usage in one of my computers, which runs Windows XP. Figure PCA.28 shows a portion of the I/O port address usage in the same computer. With Windows 9x/Me, double-click the computer icon at the top of the Device Manager listing to see resource usage.

FIGURE PCA.27

The Windows XP Device Manager configured to display IRQ, DMA, and Memory address usage.

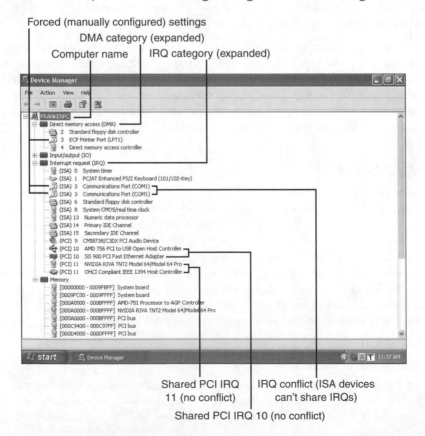
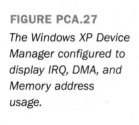

Note that in these two figures, forced (manually configured) settings are indicated with a white circle containing a blue i. Forced settings are seldom a good idea (Plug-and-Play configuration usually works much better, especially with Windows XP). Additionally, if two ISA devices have been forced to use the same hardware resource (such as the COM ports in Figure PCA.28), you have a hardware conflict that will prevent the devices from working.

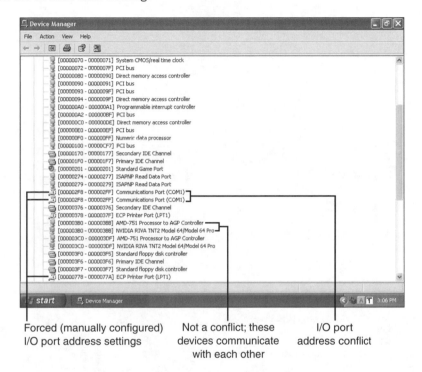

Forced (manually configured)   Not a conflict; these   I/O port
I/O port address settings   devices communicate   address conflict
                                  with each other

FIGURE PCA.28

The Windows XP Device Manager configured to display a portion of the I/O port address usage.

Using Your Computer's Anatomy for Troubleshooting

The overriding goal of this discussion of PC Anatomy has been to encourage you to learn about your computer before you have a problem. No matter how good the technical support your vendor might provide, most computers don't stay in as-delivered condition for long. New hardware, new software, and operating system changes all change the character of a computer over time. By using the methods covered in this chapter, you can determine how your computer works when it's healthy, which makes recovering from inevitable problems faster and easier.

Troubleshooting a Windows Installation

Startup Problems

If Windows doesn't start properly, you can't get anything done with your computer, because the Windows operating system manages your screen, your peripherals, your drives, your pointing devices—your entire computer life once the computer is turned on and completes its power-on self-test (POST) routine.

Causes for Windows startup problems vary, but the causes for most include

- Corrupted or missing boot files on your startup drive
- Incorrect hard disk configuration settings in the system BIOS
- Loading multiple programs that can't run at the same time because of software conflicts
- Damaged or missing Windows or application files that Windows requires access to upon startup
- Hardware resource conflicts

To troubleshoot a Windows installation that won't boot, it's important to understand what is supposed to happen when everything works. With that information firmly in hand, you can then try figure out where in the boot process everything screeched to a halt and use that knowledge to fix the problem.

Overview of the Computer Boot and Windows Startup Processes

Although it takes only a couple of minutes to go from power-on to seeing the familiar Windows desktop on your screen, many different tasks are performed in that time period to make this possible. When you turn on the computer, a chip on the motherboard called the system BIOS or ROM BIOS performs a power-on self-test (POST). This process ensures that the essential components of your system's hardware (processor, memory, graphics card, and so on) appear to be in working order. Problems detected during the POST might trigger beep codes, on-screen error messages, or might stop the boot process entirely. It all depends upon the problem and the BIOS version the computer uses. From there it goes on to load Windows, which performs its own set up of procedures.

The basic sequence of events looks like this:

1. The system BIOS checks for Plug and Play devices on the motherboard and expansion slots (such as network adapters, sound adapters, USB ports, video adapters, and so forth) and assigns hardware resources to each device that allow Windows to communicate that hardware.

2. The system BIOS searches for memory chips on video cards and add-on cards, and runs the programs located in those chips to enable those devices.

3. The system BIOS tests the system memory; on some computers, an error message will be generated if the amount of memory detected is different than the last-stored value.

4. The system BIOS searches for operating system boot files on the first bootable drive listed in the BIOS setup (most BIOSes can check up to three drives). This drive could be a floppy disk, a CD-ROM, or a hard disk drive (unless you need to install or repair Windows, your PC should boot from its hard drive).

Cautions and Warnings

All PCs provide a way to access and modify a set of configuration options for the BIOS (like which drives the PC should attempt to boot from). Usually you must press a specific key (or combination of keys) during the POST to access these options (what that code is varies from system to system, but should be visible on the POST screen).

Unless you are following instructions from this book, another experienced user, or if you *know* what you're getting into, it's best not to change any options found here. You could easily do more harm to your PC than good!

5. If the BIOS is unable to find boot files on the first drive listed, each additional bootable drive is checked until a valid bootable disk is found. If no disk can be found containing a valid boot record, the system displays a message such as "Non-System Disk or Disk Error" or "Disk Boot Failure."

6. If the BIOS locates a bootable drive, the instructions it contains are executed to start your operating system (Windows).

7. During the startup process, Windows loads *drivers* into memory for each device installed on the computer, runs programs that are found in the Windows Startup folder or have been set to run at startup by the Windows Registry, and displays a Windows logon screen (if Windows is so configured).

As you can see from this overview, any problems with either your system or Windows configuration can cause the startup process to fail.

Fixing Hard Disk Configuration Problems

If, following your PC's POST, instead of seeing the normal Windows splash screen when you start your computer, you see an error message such as "No operating system", "Searching for Boot Record from IDE-0", or others, there might be a problem with your hard drive. First, be sure you don't have a floppy disk inserted in your floppy drives (a floppy disk which lacks boot files could prevent your system from booting). From here it's time to take a look at your hard drive's master boot record.

The master boot record (MBR) is a section at the beginning of the drive's data storage area that defines the location of operating system files and how the drive is partitioned. It is possible that the MBR might have been erased or corrupted, or the drive might be configured incorrectly in the system BIOS so that it can't read the master boot record properly.

Most hard drives are installed using the Auto configuration option found in your PC's BIOS. When using this setting, the hard disk reports its configuration to the computer every time you start the system. Because this is rarely a flawed process, it's more likely that there's a problem with files found in your drive's boot sector than a problem with your drive's BIOS configuration. In the next two sections we take a look at both of these scenarios.

Configuring a Hard Drive in BIOS

Depending on the version of Windows you use, you could damage your Windows installation if you re-create a master boot record when the real problem is an incorrect BIOS configuration for your drive. To ensure this isn't the case, start your computer, and press the key or keys (usually DEL or F1) specified in your computer's instruction manual or displayed on-screen to start the system BIOS configuration program (see Figure 1.1). Note that many computers display a manufacturer's logo during the boot process, and might not tell you on-screen which key to press to activate the BIOS configuration program. Check your system or motherboard manual to determine the correct key to press in such cases.

While the interface varies from BIOS to BIOS, once you're into its main menu, you should see an option to access a Standard Setup screen. Use your keyboard to go to this screen and check how the hard disk is configured. If it is configured as User-Defined with LBA mode enabled or as Auto (see Figure 1.2), then the problem is most likely rooted in a damaged or missing master boot record. However, if LBA mode is disabled, you won't be able to boot from the drive since your computer won't be able to find the boot sectors to begin with.

Write down the current drive configuration settings, reset the configuration to Auto, save the changes, and restart the computer. If your computer still won't boot then the problem probably isn't with your hard disk drive's BIOS configuration.

FIGURE 1.1

A typical PC during startup.

BIOS vendor and version

Motherboard maker and model #   Detected ATA/IDE drives

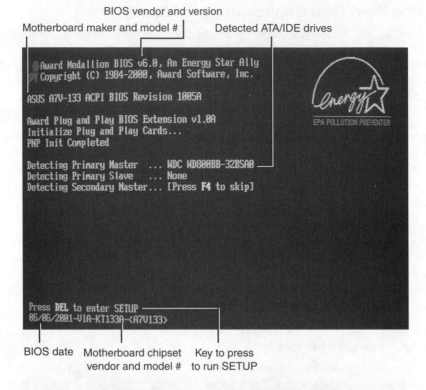

BIOS date   Motherboard chipset   Key to press
             vendor and model #   to run SETUP

FIGURE 1.2

If your drive is configured with incorrect options for cylinders, heads, sectors, or LBA mode, it won't be bootable. It's safer to use Auto mode when you install a new IDE/ATA hard drive.

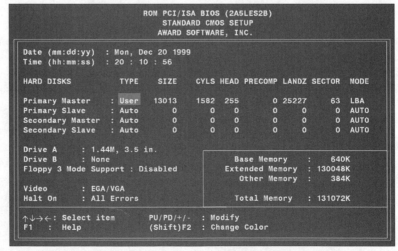

Repairing a Damaged Master Boot Record

If the master boot record (MBR) on your hard disk is damaged, the computer cannot read it to determine how your drive is partitioned or the location of your operating system boot files. The most typical cause for a damaged MBR is a boot-sector computer virus. Depending upon your version of Windows, you can use the Windows CD-ROM or an emergency startup disk to start your system and fix the problem.

Fast Track to Success

During the install process, Windows asks to create an Emergency Startup Disk (essentially a bootable floppy disk with a few key files and utilities). If you bought your system with Windows pre-installed, then hopefully the reseller provided you either with this disk or a "recovery" CD-ROM that could meet the same purpose.

If you use Windows 9x/Me and don't have an emergency startup disk, you should create one as soon as possible. Open the Control Panel, double-click the Add/Remove Programs icon and select the Startup Tab. From there just follow the on-screen instructions to create the disk. If you use Windows 2000 or XP, you can't create, nor do you need, this disk. Your Windows CD-ROM can be used to boot any necessary troubleshooting utilities.

In addition to a valid MBR, a bootable hard disk also needs to have the correct Windows bootable files installed on it. The error message displayed when a system can't boot will help you determine which problem the drive is having.

If the system displays a message such as "No Boot Sector on Fixed Disk" or "No Boot Device Available," the MBR has been corrupted. If the system displays a message such as "Non-System Disk or Disk Error" or "Invalid System Disk," the MBR is okay but the boot files are missing or corrupted.

Special Procedures for Special Cases

The procedures discussed in the following sections are designed to help you recover from a problem with a damaged MBR or missing boot files if your hard disk was prepared with the standard Windows utilities. However, if you used a program packaged with your hard disk (or downloaded from your hard disk vendor's Web site) to prepare your hard disk, you might not have a standard MBR.

Programs such as Maxtor's MaxBlast, Western Digital's Data Lifeguard Tools, Seagate's Disc Wizard, Ontrack Disk Manager, Phoenix/StorageSoft's EZ-Drive and DriveGuide, and others serve two purposes:

- They provide an easier-to-use replacement for FDISK/FORMAT or for the Windows 2000/XP Disk Management or Setup process
- Optionally, they can also provide a software-based BIOS replacement for BIOS chips which cannot handle the entire capacity of the drive

Using the repair procedures in the following section to fix an MBR problem on drives prepared with programs like this might overwrite the special MBR created by the hard disk setup program and prevent access to the drive.

If you used a vendor-supplied or third-party disk preparation program *and* if your computer displays a message such as "EZ-BIOS: Hold the CTRL key down for Status

Screen or to boot from floppy" or a message referring to "Dynamic Drive Overlay," your drive is being controlled by a special MBR created by the drive installation program.

To solve bootup problems with a drive that uses EZ-BIOS to control the drive, contact the drive vendor that supplied the setup applications, or the Phoenix/StorageSoft Web site at http://www.storagesoft.com/products/drive_utils/.

For bootup problems with a drive which uses Dynamic Drive Overlay to control the drive, contact the drive vendor or the Ontrack Web site at http://www.ontrack.com/diskmanager/.

Cautions and Warnings

Hard drive vendors have used both StorageSoft and Ontrack-produced versions of disk installation programs over the years, sometimes switching between one vendor and another. The surest way to tell whose product setup your drive uses is to watch the startup messages:

- A reference to "EZ-BIOS" indicates that a product created by Phoenix/StorageSoft was used to configure the drive and replace the system BIOS drive support.
- A reference to "Dynamic Drive Overlay" indicates that a product created by Ontrack was used to configure the drive and replace the system BIOS drive support.

Windows XP

If you use Windows XP, boot from the CD-ROM and select the Repair option displayed on the Welcome to Setup menu to fix your installation with the Recovery Console. When prompted, enter the number of the Windows installation you want to fix (normally 1: C:\WINDOWS). Then, enter the Administrator password to continue; if no Administrator password was set, press ENTER.

Enter the command FIXBOOT at the Recovery Console prompt that appears. This option installs new bootable files on your hard drive. Answer Y(es) when prompted to write a new boot sector. Enter the command FIXMBR to recreate the master boot record.

When complete, type EXIT and press the Enter key to restart the computer. Remove the CD-ROM so the computer can boot from the hard drive. These commands also work with Windows 2000.

If you use Windows XP, you may also want to consider ordering CPR for XP 3.0 from http://www.myezfix.com/ (about $30). This product provides fast rebuilding of unbootable Windows XP installations and also works with the Windows XP System Restore feature to handle problems encountered after Windows begins the boot process.

Fast Track to Success

You should configure the boot order in your system BIOS with the following settings to allow you to boot from a CD-ROM, floppy disk, or hard disk to make repairs easier:

- first boot device: CD-ROM
- second boot device: floppy
- third boot device: first hard disk (called hard disk 0 on some systems)

For details, see "Troubleshooting Booting Problems," p. 232.

Windows 95, Windows 98, and Windows Me

The basic process for fixing the master boot record and restoring boot files is similar in Windows 95, Windows 98, and Windows Me.

In all cases, you need to boot from the Windows Emergency Startup Disk. Then, with Windows Me, select #4 from the Startup menu; with Windows 98, select #2 from the startup menu (Windows 95 has no startup menu but boots straight to a command prompt). After you see the command prompt, type Scandisk /ALL and press ENTER to check all drives (this may take several minutes to complete; repair any errors found); type Sys C: and press ENTER to recopy new boot files to the hard disk. Remove the startup disk from drive A: and press Ctrl+Alt+Del to restart the computer.

If you don't have an Emergency Startup Disk or if your emergency disk has become corrupted (it can happen) you have a couple of options. If available, the simplest is to use another computer with your version of Windows (a PC at work, a friend's, and so on) to create a new emergency disk. If that's not an option, there are programs you can use that provide recovery utilities. Norton Utilities from Symantec, for example, provides a bootable CD-ROM, which you can use to recover from boot problems.

Fixing Other Startup Problems with Windows XP

If Windows XP starts but can't finish booting properly, or if it displays errors, you'll need to access the Windows Advanced Options menu. To do so, reboot your PC and press the F8 key repeatedly until the menu appears (this may take a couple tries to get the timing down). You can select different options from this menu to get your system back to work in a hurry. Table 1.1 provides a reference to which startup option is best to use depending upon your circumstances.

TABLE 1.1
Using the Windows XP Advanced Options Menu

Problem	XP Startup Option to Select	Notes
Windows won't start after you install new hardware or software	Last Known Good Configuration	Resets Windows to its last-known working configuration. You will need to reinstall hardware or software installed after that time.
Windows won't start after you upgrade a device driver	Safe Mode	After starting the computer in Safe Mode, open the Device Manager, select the device and use the Rollback feature to restore the previously used device driver. Restart your system. See "Using Device Manager," p. 480. This mode uses 800×600 resolution but retains the color settings normally used.
Windows won't start after you install a different video card or monitor	Enable VGA Mode	Most video cards should be installed when your system is running in VGA mode (256 colors, 640×480 resolution). Use Display Properties to select a working video mode before you restart. See "Can't Start the Computer Using Normal Display Drivers," p. 299 and "Display," p. 474.
Windows can't start normally, but you need access to the Internet to research the problem or download updates	Safe Mode with Networking	You can use Windows Update and the Internet, but some devices won't work in this mode. This mode also uses 800×600 resolution but retains the color settings normally used.
Windows doesn't finish starting normally, and you want to know what device driver or process is preventing it from working	Enable Boot Logging	This option starts the computer with all its normal drivers and settings while it also creates a file called ntbtlog.txt in the default Windows folder (usually C:\Windows or C:\WINNT). Restart the computer in Safe Mode and open this file with Notepad or Wordpad to determine the last driver file that loaded. You can update the driver or remove the hardware device using that driver to restore your system to working condition. See the next section for more on using the boot log.

TABLE 1.1 (continued)

Problem	XP Startup Option to Select	Notes
Windows is loading programs you don't need during its startup process	Boot computer in Normal Mode (or Safe Mode if the computer won't start in Normal Mode), click Start, Run, then type MSCONFIG	Use MSCONFIG to disable one or more startup programs, then re-start your computer. You can also use MSCONFIG to restore damaged files, or to start System Restore to reset your computer to an earlier condition. For details, see "Using MSCONFIG," p. 501, and "Using System Restore," p. 494.

Windows XP also provides a Startup/Shutdown Troubleshooter, available in the Help and Support Center, which can help you determine the reason for startup problems. To use this troubleshooter even if Windows won't start normally, boot your system in Safe Mode or Safe Mode with Networking.

If your computer cannot even boot to Safe Mode, yet the BIOS does properly identify your hard drive and locate Windows boot files on the master boot record files, then your problem is a bit more serious. If you're experienced with using the Windows XP Recovery Console (refer to Windows XP part of the section "Repairing a Damaged Master Boot Record"), you may be able to fix your system from there. Otherwise it's time to call tech support (most likely either your system vendor or Microsoft). It may help the tech support technician if you're able to access the boot log file described in the next section.

Understanding the Boot Log

The Windows XP bootlog file (ntbtlog.txt) is a plain-text file that lists the drivers that are loaded or not loaded during the boot process. Because Windows XP adds entries to the ntbtlog.txt file every time you start the system with boot logging enabled, follow this procedure to make it useful for troubleshooting:

1. Use the Advanced Options Menu (refer to the previous section) to create a bootlog as soon as you have successfully installed Windows XP.

2. Use the Search option to locate ntbtlog.txt and change the name of the file to bootlog.txt.

3. Whenever you install new hardware, delete the ntbtlog.txt and bootlog.txt files and create a new bootlog.txt file as in steps 1 and 2.

4. If Windows XP won't boot, create a new bootlog.

5. Restart Windows XP in Safe Mode and open bootlog.txt (your original bootlog) and the new ntbtlog.txt (which shows the current status of the computer). Compare the entries in each file, as shown in Figure 1.3 (if there is more than one section in ntbtlog.txt, scroll down to the section headed by the date and time of the last bootlog creation).

Cdaudio.sys driver loaded when system was working correctly

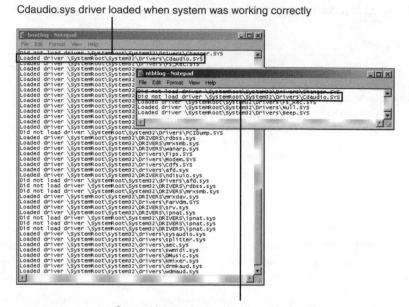

Same driver no longer loads; may be missing or corrupt

Similar to what is shown in this figure, what you should expect to see is a specific driver file (or set of driver files) that no longer loads properly. If you can identify the device the driver is attached to (audio card, video card, and so forth), then the best solution is to boot to Safe Mode and reinstall the driver. If you can access the Internet from Safe Mode with Networking (depends on your connection and the boot problem), you should check the device vendor's Web site for driver updates that you can download and install.

To reinstall drivers for a particular device, you can use the Device Manager (see "Using the Device Manager," p. 480) to reload the driver or to remove the device. Windows reinstalls the device with a fresh driver when it restarts.

Even if you can't identify what device to which the problem driver is attached, it can still be helpful information to provide a tech support operative.

Fixing Other Startup Problems with Earlier Versions of Windows

Other versions of Windows also provide you with troubleshooting startup options similar to those described previously for Windows XP, although the details vary with the version of Windows you use. Windows Me and 98 also feature a Startup/Shutdown Troubleshooter in their help systems. Table 1.2 shows you how to use the startup options available with Windows 2000, Windows Me, Windows 9x (98/95), or Windows 98 only. As with Windows XP, press the F8 key to display the startup menu.

TABLE 1.2

Using the Windows Startup Menus for Troubleshooting

Problem	Windows Version	Startup Option to Select	Notes
Windows won't start after you install new hardware or software	Me	Safe Mode	Boots computer with minimal devices installed; use System Restore (if available) to reset the computer to a previous working condition. If System Restore is disabled, refer to the Notes for a Windows 9x PC.
Windows won't start after you install new hardware or software	2000, 9x	Safe Mode	Boots computer with minimal devices installed. Use Device Manager to remove or reconfigure last-installed hardware, or Add/Remove Programs to remove last-installed software. Then, restart the computer. See "Using Device Manager," Appendix A, p. 480 for details.
Windows won't start after you install a different video card or monitor	2000	VGA Mode	Select PCI VGA adapter for the video driver in the Display Properties sheet, and restart the computer. Reinstall the drivers needed for the video card as prompted. See "Can't Start the Computer Using Normal Display Drivers," p. 299, and "Display," p. 474.
Windows won't start after you install a different video card or monitor	Me, 9x	Safe Mode	Select PCI VGA adapter for the video driver in the Display Properties sheet, and restart the computer. Reinstall the drivers needed for the video card as prompted. See "Can't Start the Computer Using Normal Display Drivers," p. 299, and "Display," p. 474.
Windows can't start normally, but you need access to the Internet to research the problem or download updates	Me, 9x, 2000	Safe Mode with Networking	You can use Windows Update and the Internet, but some devices won't work in this mode. This mode also uses 640×480 and 16-color display mode.

TABLE 1.2 (continued)

Problem	Windows Version	Startup Option to Select	Notes
Windows doesn't finish starting normally, and you want to know what device driver or process is preventing it from working	2000, 9x, Me	Enable Boot Logging	This option creates a file called ntbtlog.txt (Windows 2000) or bootlog.txt (Windows 9x/Me) in the default Windows folder (usually C:\Windows or C:\WinNT with Windows 2000) in the root directory of the boot drive (C:\ with Windows 9x/Me). Restart the computer in Safe Mode and open this file with Notepad or Wordpad to determine the last driver file that loaded. You can update the driver or remove the hardware device using that driver to restore your system to working condition.

On the Web

As long as you can get to the Internet (booting up your computer in Safe Mode with Networking will do it for you) with Windows 98, Me, 2000, or XP, you can get updated device drivers and Windows files straight from the source with Microsoft Windows Update. Start your Internet connection after you reboot, click Start, then Windows Update, and let Windows Update scan your system for the features you need.

If you're still running Windows 95, you can still download updates, but you'll need to do it manually. Go to http://www.microsoft.com/windows95/downloads/ for the current list of critical and security updates, service packs, and recommended updates. Generally, you will want to install the updates in chronological order; the newest are listed first in each category, so start at the bottom of the list and work your way up.

Shutdown Problems with Windows

Windows doesn't always shut down when you tell it to do so. Sometimes it hangs, or sometimes it reboots instead of shutting down. Windows XP, Me, and 98 all have a Startup/Shutdown Troubleshooter available that may be able to help you isolate the causes.

In Windows XP, open the Help and Support Center (in the Start menu) and use the Search field to find "List of Troubleshooters." In Windows Me, open Help (from the

Start menu), click Index, type Startup, and scroll down to the troubleshooter. In Windows 98, open Help, click the Contents tab, click Troubleshooting, and click Windows 98 Troubleshooters for a list of troubleshooters.

To use any of the troubleshooters, answer the question and click Next to go to the next step; the sequence of questions varies according to your answers. The troubleshooters might also direct you to use MSCONFIG, the Device Manager, or other Windows tools.

If you use Windows 95 or the Windows Troubleshooters aren't helping, try using the tips in Table 1.3 to find the problem and a solution.

TABLE 1.3
Troubleshooting Windows Shutdown Problems

Problem	Windows Version	Solution	Notes
Computer won't shut down after installing new hardware or software	XP, 2000, Me, 9x	First, download and install latest software patches or device drivers. If the computer still won't shut down, contact the hardware or software vendor for tech support or uninstall the hardware or software.	You can use System Restore in Windows Me or Windows XP to revert the computer to a point before you installed the hardware or software.
Computer restarts instead of shutting down	XP	Disable Automatic Restart in the System properties sheet.	Right-click on My Computer, select Properties, select Advanced, click the Settings button in the Startup and Recovery section, and clear the check mark next to Automatically Restart. Click OK.
Computer displays STOP message at shutdown	XP	Bad device drivers for one or more devices if STOP 0x9F, STOP 0x8E, or STOP 0x7B is displayed	Restart, press F8 during boot, and select the Last Known Good Configuration option, or use System Restore to go back to an older working configuration
Computer displays fatal exception errors or general protection faults at shutdown	9x, Me	Conflicts between hardware or device drivers and Windows	Look up specific error message at Microsoft's Knowledge Base (http://support.microsoft.com) and apply solution.

TABLE 1.3 (continued)

Problem	Windows Version	Solution	Notes
Computer won't shut down, but doesn't display an error message	XP, 2000, Me, 98	Programs installed at startup may not be working properly.	Click Start, Run and enter MSCONFIG. Then use the Startup tab to selectively disable startup events one at a time until the computer shuts down properly. Try to identify noncritical components first before disabling something more important like a virus scanner or registry backup utility. (MSCONFIG is not included with Windows 2000 or Windows 95)

On the Web

For additional advice on troubleshooting shutdown problems with any recent Windows version (98 through XP), I recommend James A. Eschelman's Windows Startup and Shutdown Center troubleshooters.

Find the Windows 9x/Me version at

http://www.aumha.org/a/shutdown.htm

The Windows XP version is available at

http://www.aumha.org/a/shtdwnxp.htm

Problems with Programs and Applications

Most problems that occur after Windows successfully boots involve the applications and programs you use on a day-to-day basis. Typical problems you might encounter include

- Programs which worked with earlier versions of Windows but don't work with Windows XP
- Programs that won't start from their desktop or Start button shortcuts
- Programs you can't open from Windows Explorer
- Programs which trigger a STOP error (Blue Screen of Death or BSOD)
- Programs which trigger fatal exception errors
- Programs which trigger illegal operation errors

This section helps you solve these problems. First, though, you should familiarize yourself with some of the tools Windows places at your disposal to monitor the health of your system.

Windows Tools to Keep You Out of Trouble

Windows XP features various tools to help you avoid problems with your system and your software. These tools won't necessarily help you fix a problem, but often they can help you identify the source of one.

If you press Ctrl-Alt-Del in Windows XP (or Windows 2000), you bring up the Windows Task Manager. This version of the utility is much more than a simple task list as it was in previous Windows versions. The Windows XP Task Manager displays running applications, detailed information about processes and the memory they use (see Figure 1.4), page file (swapfile) and CPU usage, network traffic, and users.

FIGURE 1.4
The Windows XP Task Manager displays all processes currently running on the system.

Because their Task Managers aren't nearly as useful, if you use Windows 9x or Windows Me, make sure that you've installed the following:

- Net Watcher to check network usage (helps you determine whether network traffic is flowing correctly)

- System Monitor to check CPU and page file usage (helps you determine whether your processor or system memory are under a heavy load)

- System Resource Meter to check free system resources (which can cause Illegal Operations errors when exhausted)

For more information about using the Windows XP Task Manager or the Windows 9x/Me System Monitor, see "Troubleshooting Memory Bottlenecks," p. 385. For more information about using the Windows 9x/Me System Resource Meter, see "Troubleshooting System Resource Shortages in Windows 9x/Me," p. 503.

If they aren't already, each of these programs can be installed from your Windows CD-ROM. Activate the Windows Control Panel and open the Add/Remove Programs utility. In the tab labeled Windows Setup, you can find check boxes that should allow you to install these programs.

You can also click Start, Run and enter the msinfo32 command to start the System Information utility. System Information (also available for Windows 2000, Windows Me, and Windows 98—with some differences) provides a fast method to determine the hardware, software, and Internet configuration of your system. The Tools menu found in the Windows XP version features:

- A Net Diagnostics tool for network troubleshooting
- One-click access to System Restore
- File Signature Verification to help you find incorrect versions of system files
- DirectX Diagnostic to help ensure stability in your games
- Dr Watson, which will intercept crashes and capture the details of the problem for analysis.

Use these tools to help you prevent problems before they start and find problems after they manifest themselves. For more information about using System Information and its associated tools, see "Using System Information," p. 491.

My Programs Won't Run

One of the most frequent problems you'll run into when using various applications in Windows is that the program simply will not run. Causes for this are various, but the key to identifying what that cause is lies in how you tried to launch the program.

Troubleshooting Programs That Won't Run Under Windows XP

Windows XP is the first consumer-level operating system to be based on Windows NT and Windows 2000, rather than Windows 95. This means that many programs which ran properly under older versions of Windows might not run properly under Windows XP unless you take advantage of its built-in Program Compatibility Wizard. To start the wizard, click Start, All Programs, Accessories, Program Compatibility Wizard.

Once the wizard is started, you can select from programs already installed on your computer, the current program in the CD-ROM drive, or you can browse to the program manually. After you select a program, you can select the version of Windows the program worked best under (see Figure 1.5).

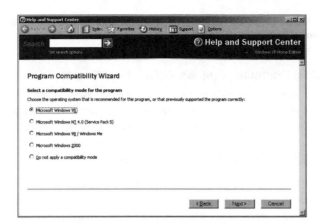

FIGURE 1.5

Using the Program Compatibility Wizard to run an older Windows program under Windows XP as Windows 95 would run it.

On the next screen, you can select one or more of the following options to aid compatibility:

- 256 colors; many older Windows programs can't run on 16-bit or higher color depths

- 640×480 screen resolution; many older Windows programs use a fixed screen size and can't run properly on a high-resolution screen

- Disable visual themes; many older Windows programs were created before visual themes were common

Click the box next to each option to select it if desired.

Fast Track to Success

If you are using the Program Compatibility Wizard to help you run an older game or educational program (circa 1996 or earlier) under Windows XP, you'll probably want to try all three of these options. Setting these options affects only the program you set them for. The rest of Windows will continue to look and function normally.

After you select any visual options you want to try, you can test the program, which will apply the visual options or compatibility mode selected, then start the program. After you close the program, Windows switches back to its normal screen settings if necessary, and you can decide whether to use these settings for your software, or try others. You can choose whether to inform Microsoft of your settings, and the settings you chose for the program are used automatically every time you run the program.

Keep in mind that the Program Compatibility Wizard won't work with all old Windows programs. However, Microsoft periodically offers Application Compatibility Updates through Windows Update which improve Windows XP's compatibility with older applications. If you can't get an older program to work with Windows XP now, it may be able to work in the future. To see which programs are affected by a particular Application Compatibility Update, click the Details button on the listing in Windows Update.

Troubleshooting Programs That Won't Run from Shortcuts

Windows stores shortcuts (.LNK files) to programs in a folder normally called \Windows\Start Menu\Programs on the default system drive (normally C:). The .LNK file points to the correct location for the actual program, so that if you open the .LNK file, it opens the actual program for you. If you open a shortcut but the program doesn't appear to start, check the following:

- Is there a "Missing Shortcut" error message?—This error means that the file the shortcut is pointing to has been deleted, moved, or renamed. If the shortcut points to a removable-media drive, make sure the program disk or CD is inserted into the correct drive and that the drive in question is functioning properly.

- The program you are trying to run may already be started, although it's not visible in the Windows Taskbar—Press Ctrl-Alt-Del to display the Task Manager and see if the program you are trying to run appears more than once. Select End Task for each reference to the program (you will need to press Ctrl-Alt-Del again to redisplay the Task List after you close a program), and try to run the program again after all references to the program have been closed. Some programs can't run properly if you try to start more than one instance at the same time.

Cautions and Warnings

After Windows displays a "Missing Shortcut" error, it will keep searching for a file with the same or similar name as the shortcut's original target. Once it finds a file it believes is close enough to the original shortcut's reference, it will offer to fix the shortcut. Unless you're sure the replacement file reference is the same file, don't let Windows link the shortcut to the file it shows you. Just delete the shortcut and remake a new one manually.

- The shortcut isn't broken, but the program won't run correctly (it may start, but quit immediately, or never start at all)—The Windows Registry entries for the program may be corrupted, and if the Registry can't find the program, it can't run. You may need to re-register the program's components with the Windows Registry. If the program has a re-registering utility, such as PFREG.EXE, supplied with some versions of the Corel WordPerfect Office suite, you can run it to re-register program components. Otherwise, reinstall the program from its installation disc(s). If you're unsure of whether or not your program can re-register itself, check its instruction manual or online help for more details.

Even though a shortcut not pointing to the right place is often the problem when you can't start an application, that's not the only possibility. To be sure that your program is installed properly and ensure that Windows knows where it is, your next step should be to try running the program from its application file as described in the next section.

Troubleshooting Programs That Won't Run from Windows Explorer

If you're having problems with a program's Start menu or desktop shortcut, or the program you want to launch doesn't have a shortcut, you can usually run it directly from the Windows Explorer (also called My Computer) file listing. The only trick is that you'll need to know the folder path to where the program is installed. Most applications install into a folder called Program Files, located on your C: hard disk drive. Once you've found the folder, you need to double-click the file icon for the application.

If you can't run the program directly from Window Explorer then it may be that it is already running, or needs to have its components reregistered into the Windows Registry. See the previous section, "Troubleshooting Programs That Won't Run from Shortcuts." Failing those two possibilities, you can check the following:

- Did you drag and drop the program from another folder or drive location?—If it's possible that you've somehow modified the name or location of the program's folders or files, the Windows Registry listing for the program will be out of date. Put the program back into the correct folder or drive location if possible, and try to run it again. If it cannot run or you don't recall how its files or folders may have been changed, uninstall it (if possible) and reinstall it in the desired location. For details, see "Add or Remove Programs," p. 470.

- Have you installed or uninstalled a program recently?—Many Windows programs used shared files which are stored in the \Windows\System folder. If incompatible versions of these files replace other versions during installation of new software, an existing program might stop working. Or, if shared files are deleted when you uninstall a program, other programs that might use the same files could also stop working. In that case you could try reinstalling the program to restore the missing files.

- Have you deleted any files recently?—Deleting files which are found in folders such as \Windows, \WinNT, or \Program Files or their subfolders can break programs if you delete program components instead of data or temporary files (data files should be stored in your personal document folder). Check the Recycle Bin and undelete any files which originated in \Windows or \Program Files or their subfolders and retry your program.

Cautions and Warnings

When you install a new program, pay attention during the installation process. If the installer asks if you want to replace an existing system file, use the option provided by some install programs to make a backup of the system file being replaced. When you uninstall a file, don't remove files stored in the \Windows\System or \Winnt\System folder if there's any possibility that other programs use the same file. Similarly, if you uninstall one part of a collection of applications from the same vendor, the uninstall program may offer to remove files from a shared folder used by that vendor's programs. Do so only if you're certain that no other program uses those same files.

What to Do Next

If none of the previous sections solve your problem then there's probably more than a simple program startup problem at work. You should ensure that your program is compatible with not only Windows (it's not unheard of for a retailer to stock, for example, Macintosh software in with the Windows software), but also your version of Windows (95, 98, Me, XP). You should also ensure that your PC meets or exceeds the program's minimum system requirements. In particular, verify that you have enough system RAM and hard disk space, adequate processor speed, and, especially in the case of games, an adequate graphics or audio card.

Blue Screen of Death Errors (BSODs)

If your program starts, but triggers a crash that locks up your computer and displays a technical error message with white text on a blue background, then you've encountered the dreaded Blue Screen of Death (BSOD). There are many possibilities for what can cause such an error. There might be a problem with a program's files, with its interaction with other software or hardware on your system, or your memory or other hardware. With so many possible causes, BSOD errors can be extremely difficult to troubleshoot. The next few sections take a look at what steps you can take to prevent or at least reduce these system killers.

Troubleshooting Stop Errors in Windows XP

In Windows XP (or Windows 2000), errors that result in a BSOD are called Stop Errors. When you see a stop error, be sure to record the numbers listed after the STOP message, such as STOP: 0x0000001E. You should also record the name of the error, such as: KMODE_EXCEPTION_NOT_HANDLED. You can then look up the error number and name on the Microsoft Knowledge Base (http://support.microsoft.com) to find Microsoft's suggested solutions. Or, you can contact Microsoft technical support and they may be able help you further.

On the Web

For a helpful guide to troubleshooting Stop errors in Windows XP, see

http://www.microsoft.com/windowsxp/pro/using/howto/gettingstarted/guide/troubleshoot.asp

Windows 2000 users will find a guide to Stop errors at

http://www.microsoft.com/windows2000/techinfo/reskit/en-us/default.asp?url=/windows2000/techinfo/reskit/en-us/prork/prhd_exe_qaco.asp

---

Troubleshooting Fatal Exception Errors with Windows 9x/Me

Because Windows 9x and Me use different technology than Windows 2000 and Windows XP (which are based on Windows NT), their version of the BSOD doesn't come in the form of a Stop error. Instead, their blue-screen errors are called Fatal Exception errors, and display messages similar to the following:

```
A fatal exception zz has occurred at [address] in [file or program name]
```

"zz" stands for codes ranging from 00 (divide fault) to 14 (page fault) with Pentium-class processors. Causes for fatal exceptions vary by many factors, including

- Outdated video or multimedia drivers
- Incorrect video acceleration settings
- Incompatible software
- Incorrect locations for driver files

Unlike a STOP/BSOD error, which shuts down the computer, a fatal exception error doesn't necessarily shut down the computer, although you should save any open work to a different filename, and, if possible, to a removable-media drive rather than your hard disk (in case system memory is corrupted).

To diagnose a fatal exception error, do the following:

1. Write down the error message, including the fatal exception code and the address.
2. Restart your computer in clean-boot mode (don't load any normal startup programs). With Windows 98 or Me, you can use MSCONFIG to disable startup events. With Windows 95, press the F8 key, and select step-by-step startup (choosing No for most items that come up while booting). In either case, you should load only the following files: Doublespace/drivespace driver, himem.sys, ifshlp.sys, dblbuff.sys, and the Windows GUI with all Windows drivers. For details, see "Using MSCONFIG," p. 501.
3. Run Scandisk to correct any disk errors.
4. Open your Web browser and go to http://search.microsoft.com and look up the error to find a solution. If a particular third-party driver or application appears to be the cause, also check with the vendor for a solution.
5. If you've not installed updated drivers for your PC's hardware in a while, download any updated files available from Microsoft or other sources and install them.
6. Make any other configuration changes suggested by Microsoft or by the third-party vendor.
7. Restart the computer normally.

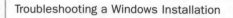

If the problem persists, your only recourse may be to reinstall Windows. While you should explore every other option first (your PC vendor's technical support, knowledgeable friends, and so on), if you do have to resort to starting over, be sure to back up as much data as you can. Don't forget often-forgotten items like your email inbox and address book, Internet Explorer Favorites, MP3 collections, and so forth.

If your system is pre-built you may have a "Restore CD" which resets your system to the "factory" condition in which you received it. However, if you need to reinstall Windows manually and you're not sure of what you're doing, don't go it alone! Get help from friends or family members with experience, or if you must, resort to paying for help from a support shop.

Cautions and Warnings

Unfortunately, most computers shipped with Windows don't come with a "real" version of Windows that works the way the retail versions do. Instead, they are supplied with a special Restore CD which is primarily intended to erase the hard disk, reinstall Windows, and set up the computer in its factory-shipped configuration. During the process, any data you have on the system is deleted, as well as any programs you've installed.

Before you use a System Restore CD, be sure you've backed up all your data. If your computer can't be booted, even in Safe Mode, and you have no backups, consider connecting your drive to another working computer and transferring the data to another drive.

Preventing and Reducing Occurrences of BSOD Errors in Windows

Whether using Windows 2000/XP or Windows 9x/Me, there are steps you can take to minimize or eliminate the occurrences of these errors. Follow these steps to help reduce the likelihood of repeated BSODs:

- If the BSOD occurred directly after you installed new hardware or software, uninstall the hardware or software and check for driver or program updates before you install it again. If it continues to occur, contact the technical support department for the product in question.

- BSODs that occur only after you've used the computer for awhile could be caused by excessive heat in your system causing corruption to the contents of your system's memory modules. If you have a system monitor program that displays internal case temperature, periodically check the temperature. If you see a temperature rise before the BSOD, install additional case fans and make sure your processor's fan is working properly. For details, see "VCore Settings and Overclocking," p. 413.

Cautions and Warnings

While AMD processors such as the Athlon and Duron are favored by many because of their low cost and high performance, they have a weakness: they can destroy themselves in a few seconds if their cooling fans stop working. If your system monitor program warns you that the fan has stopped, shut down your system immediately.

If you're comfortable poking around in your PC, go ahead: Open it up and verify the fan's condition visually. If necessary, replace it, either yourself (if you have the experience and know how) or contact your system vendor.

- While a lot of products claim to be compatible with each version of Windows, Microsoft has its own standards for Windows compatibility. Make sure your hardware is included on the Microsoft Hardware Compatibility Labs list of compatible hardware, which is available online at http://www.microsoft.com/hcl.

- As with hardware, Microsoft also likes to "digitally sign" (certify) device drivers for Windows. Be sure to use digitally signed drivers whenever possible; these drivers have been approved by Microsoft's Hardware Quality Labs.

- If the drivers you use with your hardware are meant for an older version of Windows than what you are using (typically, Windows 2000 drivers with Windows XP or Windows 98 drivers with Windows Me), attempt to replace these outdated drivers with the correct version as soon as possible. Note that the speed at which OS-specific drivers for your particular device and version of Windows appear is dependent on its manufacturer.

- You may find that removing the device and installing the correct driver when the device is redetected is more reliable than just updating the driver in Device Manager, since outdated files might still be retained if the drivers are updated instead of being removed and reinstalled.

- If you've overclocked your computer (adjusted its CPU, video, or memory speeds beyond the normal limits for your hardware), reset the component speeds and voltages to their default values. Your processor, memory, or one or more of your components may lose stability when overclocking your system.

Really, there are so many possible causes of BSODs that even taking the steps described here may not address your issue. Anything from a faulty or overtaxed power supply to system memory errors to a buggy application could be at the source of your problems. If the possibilities and solutions given here don't help, try to narrow down the behavior to times when a specific application or peripheral is in use. If all else fails, it's time to contact the technical support department for Microsoft, your system vendor, or the distributor of the software or peripheral you've identified as the root of your troubles.

Troubleshooting Illegal Operations and Other Error Messages

Conflicts between applications, driver problems, or running out of available memory can cause illegal operations errors, a blanket term for a variety of problems including invalid page faults, application errors, and others. Despite the unsettling name "illegal operation," these errors are not your fault. Unlike STOP or Fatal Exception errors, these errors don't cause a BSOD; rather they are displayed in a window on-screen.

To determine exactly what type of error and what program is involved in the error, click the Details button before you click OK (Figure 1.6). As soon as you click OK, the program mentioned in the error is closed down, but other programs you may have open should still work properly.

FIGURE 1.6

An illegal operation in Windows 98.

Type of illegal operation

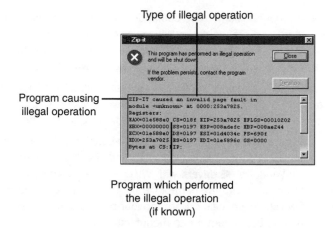

Program causing illegal operation

Program which performed the illegal operation (if known)

An illegal operation occurring in module "unknown" as in Figure 1.6 is usually the result of running too many programs at the same time with Windows 9x or Me, which causes the computer to run out of system resources. If a specific module is mentioned in the error message details, you can research the cause using the following method:

1. Record detailed error information before you close the program.
2. Run Scandisk to correct any disk errors.
3. Open your Web browser and go to http://search.microsoft.com and look up the error to find a solution. If a third-party program is listed, check with its vendor as well.
4. Make sure that you have the most up-to-date files available from whomever developed the offending program.
5. Make any other configuration changes suggested by Microsoft or by the third-party vendor.
6. Restart the computer if necessary.

Troubleshooting Games

While certainly the most fun and entertaining part of using a computer, games can be one of the biggest sources of troubles. Problems with Windows-based games come from a variety of sources, including

- Problems with the games themselves (bugs, lack of support for new hardware and operating systems)

- Outdated drivers for gaming hardware (sound cards, video, game controllers)
- Problems with DirectX (described later in this section)

Publishers frequently release games with both known and unknown problems. In order to help get things working properly for everyone, they frequently release a set of files, called a patch, to address known issues. To find out if a patch is available for your game, check the publisher's Web site (sometimes the game has an update link in its group in your Start menu). Do remember that not all publishers release patches for all games, and not all patches fix all problems (some even introduce new ones). If you find the game to be unplayable on your computer, take it back to the retailer from whom you purchased it.

You should also make sure you have installed the latest drivers for your gaming hardware (graphics card, audio card, and so on); if Windows Update doesn't have the files you need, go to the hardware vendor's Web site.

Finally, make sure your system meets the game's system requirements. Games can be some of the most demanding applications you'll find for a PC. If you've got an older system (2+ years) and are running fairly recent software, you shouldn't be surprised when your PC chokes on it. Also, if you are using Windows XP and the game was designed for older versions of Windows, use the Program Compatibility Wizard to run your game. For details, see "Troubleshooting Programs That Won't Run Under Windows XP," p. 138.

If these steps don't solve problems with your game, you might have a problem with DirectX. Most Windows-based games (as well as game-type educational software) depend upon the features of DirectX, an application programming interface (API) which provides a convenient way for software coders to access 3D video, 3D sound, game control, and other game features, regardless of the brand of video adapter, sound card, or controllers you use. If DirectX components are damaged or missing, you won't be able to play games that depend upon DirectX.

To keep DirectX in shape, follow these rules:

- Install the latest version of DirectX for your version of Windows; get it from Microsoft instead of using the outdated versions supplied with some games. Get DirectX from http://www.microsoft.com/windows/directx/default.asp.
- Run the DirectX Diagnostic tool (DXDIAG) available in the Tools menu of System Information to make sure your DirectX installation is working correctly. You can test, enable, or disable features such as DirectDraw, Direct3D, AGP Texture Acceleration, DirectSound, and DirectMusic with the Display (see Figure 1.7), Sound, and Music tabs. Use the More Help tab to troubleshoot the installation.

FIGURE 1.7

*Using the Display tab
of the Windows XP
DirectX diagnostic tool.*

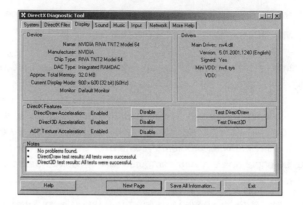

Windows Limitations

Some problems with Windows and certain combinations of hardware are due to limitations in some versions of Windows. In addition to the general rule that each new type of hardware requires updated drivers specific to the hardware and Windows version, there are two other significant types of limitations with some Windows versions:

- Limitations on supported types of hardware
- Limits on supported memory or hard disk size

Table 1.4 lists the major hardware limitations that exist on different Windows versions and their solutions.

TABLE 1.4
Hardware Support Limitations by Windows Version

Upgrade	95a	95B	98	Me	2000	XP	Notes
Hard disk over 32GB	No	No	Yes	Yes	Yes	Yes	Windows 98 may need ScanDisk patch on some systems with Phoenix BIOS. See MS Knowledge Base article Q243450 for details and fix.
							Windows 98 needs Fdisk patch on all systems. See MS Knowledge Base article Q263044 for details and fix.
IEEE-1394	No	No	Varies by device	Yes	Yes	Yes	Some devices support Windows 98SE only; some vendors don't support Windows 2000/XP.
USB 1.1	No	Varies	Yes	Yes	Yes	Yes	Some late releases of Windows 95B have incomplete USB support.

TABLE 1.3 (continued)

Upgrade	95a	95B	98	Me	2000	XP	Notes
USB 2.0	No	No	Varies by device	Yes	Yes	Yes	Some devices support Windows 98SE only.
AGP	No	No	Yes	Yes	Yes	Yes	Windows 98 users may need to install chipset-specific mini-port drivers with some mother-boards.
DVD	No	No	Yes	Yes	Yes	Yes	
RAM over 512MB	No	No	No	No	Yes	Yes	Windows 9x/Me's virtual memory manager cannot handle RAM over 512MB on systems with an AGP video adapter because of memory address conflicts.

Although Windows XP and other recent versions of Windows support IEEE-1394 and USB 1.1 and 2.0 devices in general, some vendors have developed Windows 9x or 9x/Me-only drivers and don't support Windows 2000 or Windows XP. Be sure to check with the vendor for the latest hardware drivers before you upgrade to a newer version of Windows.

Fast Track to Success

While you can see the major Windows version (Windows 98, Windows XP, and so on) whenever you open the Start button in Windows, you get much more accurate information about which revision of Windows you have by checking the System properties sheet. Right-click the My Computer icon and select Properties to see the exact release number for your version of Windows.

For example, the original version of Windows 98 lacks Internet Connection Sharing and doesn't work with some advanced hardware. The General tab of system properties lists original Windows 98 as Microsoft Windows 98, Version 4.10.1998. Windows 98, Second Edition, is listed as Microsoft Windows 98, Second Edition, Version 4.10.2222A.

Keeping Your Windows Installation Healthy

The best way to solve problems with Windows is to keep them from occurring in the first place. There are several ways you can use a little preventative maintenance to keep a Windows installation healthy:

- For Windows 98, Me, 2000, and XP, use Windows Update to install the latest Windows components.

- Keep an eye out for patches and updates to your applications.

- Install the latest digitally-signed hardware drivers for the components in your PC (video card, audio card, motherboard, and so forth).
- Perform system maintenance tasks such as error-checking disk drives and scanning for viruses.

Performing these four steps, which are detailed in the following sections, can help you postpone the all-too-common fifth way of ensuring reliable Windows usage:

- Installing a new version of Windows to a clean hard disk.

Using Windows Update

Before Windows 98 was released, keeping Windows up-to-date was a nightmare of downloading all types of patch files, installing them, and trying to remember which files had been installed and in what order. Starting with Windows 98, Microsoft provided a Windows Update feature on the Start menu. Click it to connect with Microsoft's Windows Update Web site (http://windowsupdate.microsoft.com), which detects your Windows and Internet Explorer version, inventories the software versions on your system, and provides a customized list of files your system needs, including

- Critical Updates and Service Packs (files which improve system security and stability)
- Picks of the Month (new versions of Internet Explorer, Media Player, or similar integrated tools)
- Recommended Updates (non-critical but useful fixes for hardware drivers, DirectX, networking, and other Windows features)
- Additional Windows Features (fonts, utilities, and other tools you can use for various Windows tasks; includes updated language-support files)
- Updated Device Drivers (Microsoft-approved drivers for your hardware)

Unlike the manual tracking process necessary with Windows 95 or Windows NT 4.0, Windows Update keeps track of the components you need and makes installation very simple. To make Windows Update work effectively for you, I recommend the following:

- Use Windows Update to check for updates at least once a week. If you hear of a flaw in Internet Explorer, Outlook Express, or the Media Player, check for updates immediately.
- Even update utilities need to be updated from time to time. Be sure to install updates to the Windows Update and Critical Updates tools when Microsoft informs you they need to be installed.
- Download Critical Updates and restart your computer before you install less-vital updates. If an update must be installed by itself, Windows Update prevents you from downloading and installing others at the same time.
- Keep in mind that Windows Update doesn't provide updates for applications, so be sure to visit your software vendors' Web sites for updates.

On the Web

Windows Update is actually a component of Internet Explorer, so a damaged IE installation may keep Windows Update from working. Other causes for Windows Update's failing to work are covered in the Microsoft Knowledge Base Article Q193385. Look up the step-by-step instructions for fixing a sick Windows Update at

http://support.microsoft.com

If you can't connect to this Web site because your browser is broken, open the Add/Remove Programs icon in Control Panel, select Internet Explorer from the list of programs, and click Add/Remove. You can uninstall or repair IE with this option.

Upgrading Applications

Although Windows XP uses a new side-by-side technology for managing dynamic link library files (.DLL files), files that form the building blocks of Windows applications, using outdated versions of programs can still cause problems for any version of Windows, especially Windows 9x and Windows Me. Because older applications in particular like to copy some of their .DLL files into the \Windows\System folder, you could have problems with an older application, or even Windows itself, if you insist on running programs designed for Windows 95 or Windows 98 with newer versions of Windows.

Follow these guidelines for painless updates:

- If you are installing an upgrade version, find out what proof of ownership is needed during installation. If the program's CD-ROM or floppy disk #1 is all that's needed to verify you owned the old version, consider removing the old version before you install the new version. Leftover DLL files and Registry entries are prime reasons for Windows and application crashes.

- If the new version of a program must locate the old version's installation on the hard disk, find out if it's acceptable to install the new version to a different folder. This will also avoid mixing up DLL files and Registry entries and make for a more reliable installation; you can remove the old version after you install the new version. You may also be able to remove the old version before you install the new version if you can use the old version's program CD to verify eligibility for the update. This option will save disk space and avoid any problems with data files being opened by the wrong version of the program.

- Before you install the updated version of an application, check the vendor's Web site for patches and service packs. If possible, download them before you install the main program so you can bring it up to the latest release quickly.

Installing the Best Device Drivers—Look for the Microsoft Signature

Starting with Windows Me, and continuing with Windows 2000 and the latest Windows release, Windows XP, Microsoft has emphasized the use of digitally-signed device drivers for hardware. In a perfect world, using Windows Update would assure you of a constant stream of these MS Hardware Quality Labs–approved, good-as-gold device drivers. In reality, Microsoft doesn't always have the latest drivers at its Web site.

You might need to get device drivers for urgent fixes, especially involving brand-new hardware, straight from the hardware vendor's Web site. In such cases, try to avoid beta (pre-release) or test versions of driver software. In general, the latest released versions of a driver are the best to use, but with some older motherboard or video card chipsets, an older driver might work better.

To avoid problems when you install updated drivers, follow these guidelines:

- Download the driver and uncompress it to a known folder location so you can look for Readme files or other information before you install it.

- Uninstall the old driver and use the browse feature of the Detect/Add Hardware wizard to locate the new driver files when the hardware is redetected. This is often more reliable than installing new drivers over old drivers, particularly with Windows XP if your old drivers were not digitally signed or were made for Windows 2000.

- If you install a new driver over an old driver in Windows XP and the hardware has problems, use the Rollback feature on the device's properties sheet to revert to the old driver.

- Windows Me, 2000, and XP are all configured by default to warn you if you try to install unsigned drivers. However, you can disregard this warning if you're confident in the source from which you're downloading the drivers.

Maintaining Windows with Drive and Anti-Virus Utilities

No version of Windows provides a complete system-maintenance solution. You must add a third-party antivirus program to every version of Windows for virus, email, and hostile script protection, run it frequently, and keep it updated. However, Windows does include tools for testing drives and keeping them well-organized.

To access these tools, right-click on a drive in My Computer or Windows Explorer and select Properties, then Tools.

All recent versions of Windows contain the following tools:

- Error-checking—Tests drives for errors and corrects them

- Defragging—Puts all sections of a file into contiguous sectors and puts all empty disk space into contiguous sectors

With Windows XP and Windows 2000's error-checking, you can't check the system drive (normally the C: hard drive) from the Windows desktop. When you select the system drive for testing, the test is scheduled to be performed the next time you start the computer. Thus, if you suspect a disk drive problem, you should select error-checking and restart right away so the system drive is tested immediately.

Windows 9x/Me can test any drive at any time. However, the system drive test may restart several times before it's completed if you have programs running, a screen saver active, or music playing (either from MP3/WMA files or from a music CD).

The Windows 2000 and Windows XP defragger provides a detailed analysis of the drive's condition before you start, while the Windows 9x/Me defragger provides a visual map of fragmentation with a less accurate rating of the drive's status. As with disk testing, running programs or even a screen saver while you run the Windows 9x/Me defragger can cause it to restart frequently before it finishes.

Fast Track to Success

To disable the background tasks that cause the Windows 9x/Me Defrag and Error-checking programs to restart repeatedly, start the computer in Safe Mode before you start either process. While the disk access is slower (because the system BIOS is used for drive control rather than 32-bit Windows device drivers), the net result is faster completion because these processes are no longer interrupted. If you use third-party tools such as Norton Utilities or System Works instead, though, this trick won't work (they rely on the 32-bit drivers which Safe Mode doesn't load). Instead, press Ctrl-Alt-Del to display the Task List and close background programs before you start the Norton Disk Doctor or SpeedDisk programs. In either case, be sure to disable the Windows screen saver with the Display properties sheet because it can also interrupt these processes.

As an alternative to using Windows's own disk maintenance programs, I recommend Norton System Works, which has better error-checking, powerful antivirus, and Registry repair programs. While System Works has a defragger called SpeedDisk, the Vopt program from Golden Bow Systems is much faster than either Norton's or Windows's own defrag programs and provides powerful analysis tools. For more information on System Works, see http://www.symantec.com. For more information on Vopt, see http://www.vopt.com.

Internet and Online Problems

CHAPTER 2

The Sources of Problems with Internet Connections

Problems with Internet connections tend to be fairly obvious. If your modem can't dial into your ISP, Web pages don't open, or you can't send and receive email, then you know something is wrong. Internet connection problems can be caused by many parts of your computer, including

- Missing or outdated software components such as browsers, plug-ins, and ActiveX controls
- Incorrect TCP/IP configuration settings
- Defective modem or network hardware
- Loose cables

Missing or outdated software might not keep you off the Internet, but can result in error messages or blank browser windows when you try to view some pages, particularly those with interactive or multimedia content.

However, if your TCP/IP configuration settings are incorrect or your hardware or cables are defective, you won't be seeing any of the Internet until you determine what's wrong and find a solution. Incorrect TCP/IP configuration settings can also prevent you from seeing any other users on a home or small-office network. Your first clue that your modem or network hardware is defective could be the signal lights most devices use to inform you when things are working (or not). Loose cables might be the most irritating problem of all, because they can result in a "connected today, off tomorrow" nightmare of erratic performance.

Because Internet access relies on Internet service provider (ISP) connections to the Internet, ISP problems can also cause you to lose Internet access. This chapter helps you figure out if the problem is with your side or your ISP's side of the connection.

Troubleshooting Missing or Outdated Software Components

Depending on the type of Internet access you have (dial-up or broadband) and the types of Web content you plan to access, you need to install a variety of Windows components and programs to fully enjoy the Internet.

Use the checklist in Table 2.1 to determine if your system has up-to-date components.

TABLE 2.1
Software Components Needed for Internet Access

Task	Software Needed	Where to Get It	Where to Get Updates
Dial-up (analog modem access)	Windows Dial-Up Net-working Windows 9x/Me (only)	Install from Windows CD-ROM	Windows Update [1]
Web browsing	Internet Explorer 5.x or above; Netscape 6.2x or above; older versions might not work correctly with many sites	Install from Windows CD-ROM (IE); Download (Netscape)	Windows Update (IE) http://home. netscape.com/ computing/download/ index.html (Netscape)
Reading Adobe Acrobat (.PDF) files	Adobe Acrobat Reader 4.x or above	Download from Adobe	http://www.adobe. com/products/ acrobat
Connecting to the Internet (all types)	Windows TCP/IP components	Install from Windows CD-ROM	Windows Update
Virtual Private Networking (VPN) [2]	Windows VPN components	Install from Windows CD-ROM	Windows Update
Email	Email client such as Microsoft Outlook Express or Netscape Mail (bundled with browsers) or others	Installed along with preferred browser	Windows Update (IE); http://home. netscape.com/ computing/download/ index.html (Netscape)
Viewing Flash animation (used for many Web site front ends)	Flash Player	Often preinstalled with browser	http://www. macromedia.com

[1] To access Windows Update, click the Windows Update icon on your Start menu, or set your Internet Explorer browser to http://windowsupdate.microsoft.com (for Windows 98, Me, 2000, XP).

[2] VPNs create a secure the connection between your remote computer and your office network.

Fast Track for Success

In some cases, even if your ISP provides you with a signup kit or a setup CD, you might need to install or reinstall some Windows components to configure your Internet connection or make it work better for you.

With any recent version of Windows, open the Add/Remove Programs icon in Control Panel to get started. Select Add/Remove Windows components, then select the Windows components you need from the list. Be sure to click the Details button, when available, to see the specific items in each category. (Most Internet-related options can be found in the Communications group.)

If you installed Windows yourself, insert the Windows CD when prompted. If Windows was pre-installed, a folder on your computer might have the Windows files you can install. If Windows asks you if you want to replace a newer component with an older file, either during the component installation process or at other times, answer No. You want the latest, freshest Windows components to keep Windows working properly.

Installing/Reinstalling ISP Setup Software

Most ISPs provide an installation kit on CD-ROM that installs at least the Dial-Up Networking (if needed), TCP/IP components, and Internet Explorer/ Outlook Express 5.x or above (some vendors might supply Netscape 6.2 or above instead of IE). You might need to provide the following information (assigned to you by your ISP) during the installation process:

→ *For more information on the TCP/IP protocol, see, "TCP/IP Configuration" p. 169.*

- Telephone number to use for Dial-Up Networking Access
- User name (for logging in to the Internet)
- Password
- Email name (usually the same as the user name)

Be sure to record this information in a safe place (**not** in a file stored on your PC, lest you lose it to a hard disk failure or nosy hacker) in case you need to reinstall your Internet access software.

If you damage your Internet software configuration through making changes to the Dial-Up Networking or Network Neighborhood/My Network Places (Network Neighborhood in Windows 9x/Me) properties sheets, rerun the installation software and provide the needed information to reconfigure your connection. You might need your Windows CD-ROM to complete the installation. Then, download and install updates as noted in Table 2.1.

Once you've installed the software your ISP has provided, you should run Windows Update to install security or other updates for Internet Explorer, Outlook Express, or TCP/IP software.

Use the Windows Update icon on your Start menu to access Windows Update (or enter http://windowsupdate.microsoft.com into your IE address window), which automatically detects the version of Windows and Internet Explorer installed on your system and selects the updates needed.

Stay Secure with Critical Updates

After you connect with Windows Update the first time, be sure to download and install the Critical Updates first. These help protect your system against various Internet threats. Many critical updates must be downloaded one at a time, and often require you to reboot your computer afterward. Then, select other updates listed according to your needs.

If you choose not to enable automatic Critical Updates, be sure to run Windows Update at least once a week, and whenever you find out about security issues that require new Critical Updates.

If your ISP doesn't provide a setup program, see either "TCP/IP Configuration", p. 169 to learn how a broadband Internet connection is configured, or "Dial-Up Networking Configuration," p. 164 if you use an analog (dial-up) modem.

Troubleshooting Problems with Secure Web Sites

If you can browse the Web, but can't connect to secure Web sites such as online stores, e-banking, or stock trading sites, you are probably using a browser with inadequate or incorrectly configured security settings. Most likely, your browser's security encryption schemes are inadequate, so we'll first take a look at that possibility.

Fast Track to Success

To determine whether a Web site is secure, look for these clues:

- A Web site URL that begins with https:// instead of http:// is a secured site (the "s" stands for secured).
- IE uses a padlock in the lower right side of the browser window to indicate a secure site.
- Netscape displays a key in the lower left side of the browser window to indicate a secure site.
- Opera displays a padlock symbol to the left of the URL address bar at all times: An open padlock means the site is not secure, while a closed padlock means the site is secure.
- You can browse most of a site normally, but find that specific pages won't load, like login pages, pages that request personal information or credit card numbers, and so on.

Security in online transactions is based upon the strength of the encryption used to scramble data in transit between your browser and the secured Web site. Encryption strength is commonly expressed in bits: The higher the bits, the greater the number of possible combinations of information which can be used to encrypt the data, and the greater the security.

On the Web

RSA Security, Inc., a major provider of Web site security technologies, has an easy-to-understand FAQ about basic Web site security that you should read if you'd like more information on the topic.

`http://www.rsasecurity.com/standards/ssl/basics.html`

Until January 2000, Web browsers with what is called 128-bit encryption could be distributed only to U.S. users. Many Web users in the U.S. and elsewhere installed browsers with less secure 40-bit or 56-bit encryption because a stronger-encryption version was not available for download or required extra steps to download. Now, all current browsers provide 128-bit encryption as standard for users in most world areas.

To check the encryption strength of your IE browser, click Help, About Internet Explorer. If the cipher (encryption) strength listed is 128-bit, as in Figure 2.1, your browser can connect with secure sites using this encryption strength (or less). If the browser lists 40-bit cipher strength, it should be updated. If you install IE 5.5 or above, you will get 128-bit encryption standard with most versions of Windows. Windows 2000 requires a separate High Encryption Pack.

Cipher (encryption) strength —

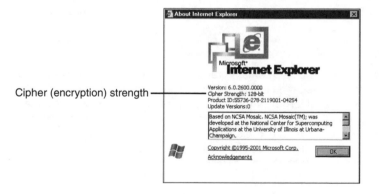

FIGURE 2.1
This version of IE has 128-bit encryption installed.

On the Web

If you prefer (or are required) to keep an earlier version of IE running on your Windows NT 4 or Windows 9x system, you can download the High Encryption Pack for IE 5.01, IE 5, and IE 4 from

`http://www.microsoft.com/windows/ie/downloads/recommended/128bit/default.asp`

Windows 2000 users need to download the High Encryption Pack, which can be found at

`http://www.microsoft.com/windows2000/downloads/recommended/encryption/`

To check the encryption strength of your Netscape browser, click Help, About Navigator or About Communicator. Scroll down to the section "Contains encryption software from RSA Data Security, Inc". Versions which support 128-bit encryption will display "This version supports U.S. Security". The browser will list "International Security" instead if it supports 40-bit encryption instead.

The latest version of Netscape, Netscape 7, features 128-bit encryption. Get it from http://home.netscape.com/computing/download/index.html.

If you prefer (or are required to use) Netscape 4.7x, you can still download it in a 128-bit "strong encryption" version from the same Web site.

If your browser uses 128-bit encryption, but you still cannot connect with secure sites, your browser's support for popular security standards may be disabled. You should check your Web browser's settings for security standards like SSL (Secure Socket Layers—the most common protocol used for secure Web sites) and TLS (a less-common security standard).

In Internet Explorer, click Tools, Internet Options, Advanced, and scroll down to Security. Make sure that Use SSL 2.0, Use SSL 3.0, and Use TLS 1.0 are all checked.

To check settings with Netscape 4.x, click Window, Security Info, Navigator, Advanced Security (SSL) Configuration. Make sure both Enable SSL (Secure Sockets Layer) v2 and Enable SSL (Secure Sockets Layer) v3 are checked. With Netscape 6, click Tasks, Privacy and Security, Security Manager, Advanced, Options. Make sure Enable SSL version 2, Enable SSL version 3, and Enable TLS are checked.

Cautions and Warnings

If you decide it's time to switch browsers, you don't need to lose your favorite sites. With IE, use the File, Import and Export menu to create an HTML file of your Favorites folder which you can transfer to another browser such as Netscape or Opera. If you want to move your bookmarks out of Netscape or another browser to IE, use the same menu. Follow the prompts and it's easy to use your favorites or bookmarks in other places.

Installing Site-Specific Software

While your Web browser is designed to display pages written in the Internet's Hypertext Markup Language (HTML) and some types of graphics, many Web sites have content or features which require you to install additional software to view the content or use the Web site's special features. If you don't have this additional software, the site either won't load or will be missing content or features.

Table 2.1 listed Adobe Acrobat and Macromedia Flash as two "must-have" additions to your browser installation, but you may encounter more. If you use the standard Microsoft Internet Explorer Web browser, sooner or later you will be asked if you want to install an ActiveX control or Java package to enable a particular Web site's content, as in Figure 2.2.

FIGURE 2.2
A typical Security Warning from the IE browser that prompts you to accept or reject the ActiveX or Java software that a Web site wants to install on your system.

Some Web sites will automatically offer you the control, as in Figure 2.2, so that you can access the site's special features, such as live music, animations, or movies. In other cases, the Web site will offer links you must click on to download the control.

When a security warning pops up, look carefully at the name of the program and its provider before you accept the program. Many advertising-sponsored Web sites have their own version of spam: they offer you unsolicited ActiveX controls, where the box offering the program pops up even though you didn't click on anything to request the download. Many of these programs are known as "spyware," since their primary function is to gather information about your Web-surfing habits. Typically, such programs offer to perform other services for you and you must look closely at the user agreement to discover that they are spying on you, using your computer's idle time to perform tasks for the software provider, and so forth. I recommend that if you didn't ask for an ActiveX control or the ActiveX control has nothing to do with the Web site's purpose, refuse it. In most cases saying no does not significantly (if at all) impair your ability to browse a Web site.

If you're worried about spyware, try downloading Ad-Aware, a freeware program which removes the contact feature from popular spyware programs such as Gator, Comet Cursor, Doubleclick, Webhancer, and others. This prevents them from reporting your browsing habits to their advertisers. Get it from http://www.webattack.com/get/adaware.shtml.

Fast Track to Success

As a result of litigation between Microsoft and Sun Microsystems (the creators of Java, a popular language for enhanced Web site features), Microsoft doesn't incorporate its Java VM (Java Virtual Machine) into most recent versions of Internet Explorer. If you go to a Web site which uses Java and the Java VM isn't installed on your computer, you will be prompted to install the Java VM from Microsoft. Since many Web site features won't work without Java, install it, although it could take several minutes (depending upon the speed of your connection).

If you have all the necessary software to view a Web site properly and you still experience problems, then the source of your troubles is elsewhere. The next section deals with those problems.

Troubleshooting Problems with Viewing Certain Web Sites

If a Web site displays a blank screen or the content looks distorted and you've already downloaded any necessary add-on software, then you need to determine if the problem is with your URL, the Web site, or with an out-of-date browser.

If you don't see the Web site you expected but you see a numeric error message instead, there's a problem with the Web site URL you entered or with the Web page itself, not your browser.

The most common numerical error is a 404—Not found error. This indicates the document you requested could not be found. If you typed in the URL yourself, check your spelling. If the URL was a link from another site, the link is out-of-date or mis-spelled. Some Web sites customize their 404 error message page to provide you with help in resolving the problem.

Other errors you might encounter include

- 401—Unauthorized—Your browser didn't supply the correct credentials for the Web page (such as a username and password); if you are an authorized user, you need to log in to the main Web site and then access the page. The 403 (Forbidden) error is similar.

- 500—Internal Error—The Web site server has a software error that prevents it from sending you the page.

- 502—Service Temporarily Overloaded—The Web site can't service your request because of too much traffic.

400-series errors indicate a problem with the URL address or with your credentials, while 500-series errors indicate a problem with the Web site server.

An error such as Host Unavailable or Unable to Locate Host could indicate a temporary problem with the Web site host, a lost Internet connection, or a mistyped URL. Check your spelling or try again later. If you can't browse to any sites, your connection is down.

On the Web

Of the numerous Web sites which list common numeric web browser/site errors, the Yahooligan Error Codes listing is one of the easiest to understand:
`http://www.yahooligans.com/docs/writeus/error.html`

A more complete list including non-numbered error messages is available at the Webopedia Web site

`http://www.webopedia.com/quick_ref/error.html`

If you can view some sites, but not others, and you don't see an error message, chances are your browser is outdated and can't interpret the contents of the Web site properly. Most Web sites today assume that you are using Internet Explorer 5.0 or above or Netscape 4.7x or higher. If you use older browsers, or if you use another vendor's browser, you might have problems viewing some sites.

Even if you prefer Netscape, Opera, or another third-party browser, don't forget to use IE if you can't view a particular site with some browsers. Since IE is the most popular Web browser now, many developers have gotten lazy and don't check their Web sites for usability with other browsers.

When you're having problems getting specific sites to open or display properly, there are some tricks that can help you get around the problem.

- Try a different browser—Both Microsoft and Netscape have added proprietary extensions to the official standards for Web pages. The most popular non-MS/Netscape browser to try is Opera 6.x, available in a free ad-supported version or a $39 no-ad version from http://www.opera.com.

- Highlight the text to reverse foreground and background colors—Many Web site designers have gone for "cool" instead of "readable." This can result in text that may be hard to read or even invisible depending on your browser's settings. Try using your mouse to highlight the text (or the areas where the text should be). This can make a lot of hard-to-read pages easy to read.

- Permanently force your browser to use your choice of colors rather than the designer's—See this Web page for details for various versions of both IE and Netscape:

    http://www.blind.org.uk/adjust_browser.html

- If you're desperate for the information that's available on a "blank" page and you understand HTML tags, use the View Source or Page Source option to display the contents of a "blank" page—Even if your browser is baffled by the HTML on a particular web page, you can click View, Source (IE) or View, Page Source (Netscape) to open a window which shows the actual HTML code used to create a page. If you're trying to find a link on the page, look for a URL inside the <a href> code, as in this example:

    <a href=http://www.mozilla.org/source.html>Source Code</a>

    Highlight the URL (which I have underlined in this example), copy it, and paste it into your browser to go to the Web site.

- Use the Text Size option in your browser to shrink oversized text or enlarge tiny text to make it easier to read—IE uses View, Text Size to display a list of choices. With Netscape, click Edit, Preferences, Appearance, Fonts and select the size desired.

Fast Track to Success

One of the best reasons to use the Internet is because it's the gateway to immense amounts of troubleshooting information. Instead of running your inkjet printer dry to print tutorials, FAQs, and articles, use your browser to capture the information you need to your hard disk.

If you want to save a picture or a file from a Web site where there's no specific "download it here" link, right-click on its picture or file reference and select Save

As or Save Target As from the menu. In some cases the link displayed is not the actual file but it displays another page where the actual link is displayed.

If you want to save the entire page as displayed in your browser with IE, click File, Save As, Web Archive, which creates a file ending with .MHT. This single file stores all the text and graphics, and you can view it in any recent browser and print it if you want to.

How Internet Connections Are Configured

Depending on the type of Internet connection you have and the version of Windows you use, your Internet connection is configured in different ways.

With Windows 2000 and Windows XP, all types of Internet and network connections are gathered together in My Network Places, while Windows 9x/Me uses Dial-Up Networking for analog modem connections and the Network icon in Control Panel for broadband and network connections.

Your ISP generally provides you with a setup disk or instructions on configuring your Internet connection. In the case of DSL, cable, or satellite service, your ISP may even do all the configuration tasks for you. If, however, you're having problems and need to check the configuration of your connection, you can do so. Open the appropriate location for your version of Windows (as described in the previous paragraph), right-click on the icon for your connection, and click the appropriate tabs to see the settings and change any incorrect settings.

Dial-Up Networking Configuration

If you need to manually configure a dial-up networking connection for an analog modem connection to the Internet or for connecting to a remote computer, here's the information you need for any connection:

- The telephone number, including area code for the ISP or remote computer
- Your username and password (if required)

By default, a dial-up connection assumes that you are connecting to an ISP's server. If you cannot connect, contact the ISP for additional settings which may be required. In rare cases, you might need to specify a particular Internet Protocol (IP) address provided by the ISP for your machine, but most dial-up Internet connections automatically assign you a new IP address whenever you connect. See Figure 2.3 for a typical example of dial-up networking with Windows XP. The following explains the different tabs:

- Options—click to change redial options and name and password prompts.
- Security—click to adjust how your identity is validated by the remote computer or to enable a custom login script.

- Networking—click to change the type of dial-up server you are calling or to change the type or properties of network software components needed for the connection.
- Advanced—click to share the connection with Internet Connection Sharing or to turn on the Windows XP Internet Firewall (which blocks unauthorized incoming traffic).

FIGURE 2.3
The properties sheet for a dial-up networking connection in Windows XP.

In most cases, you should never need to adjust the settings on these tabs, if your ISP provided a configuration program to set up your connection. However, if your ISP changes how it handles Internet connections, if you change locations, or if your ISP provided you with manual Internet connection instructions instead of a setup program, you might need to work with these tabs to create a new connection or correct problems with an existing connection.

The Dial-Up Networking General Tab

The General tab, shown in Figure 2.3, lets you view and configure the following settings:

- The modem used for the connection
- The telephone number
- Any dialing rules needed to make the connection
- Status icon display in the system tray

Generally, you should not need to change these options from the settings your ISP originally supplied, except in the following circumstances:

- You cannot make a reliable connection because of your modem's configuration—click Configure and adjust the settings as your ISP's help desk recommends (see Figure 2.4).

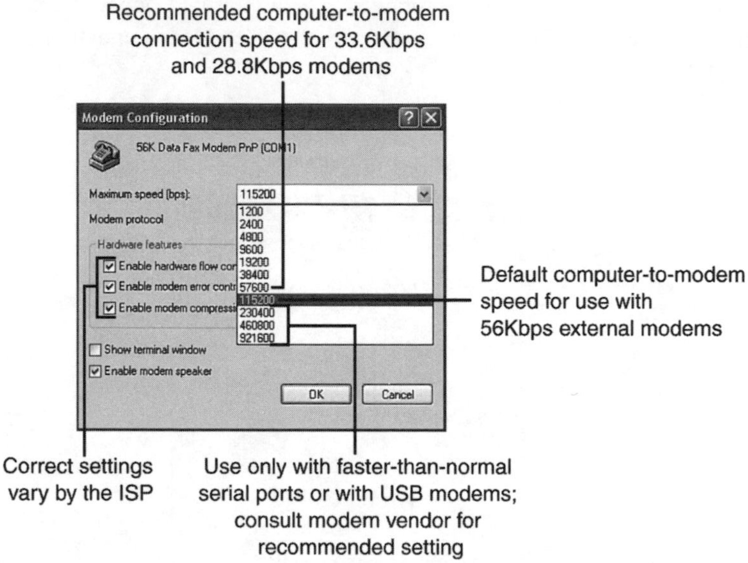

FIGURE 2.4

Adjusting the computer-to-modem connection speed and other modem settings in Windows XP.

Recommended computer-to-modem connection speed for 33.6Kbps and 28.8Kbps modems

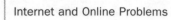

Default computer-to-modem speed for use with 56Kbps external modems

Correct settings vary by the ISP

Use only with faster-than-normal serial ports or with USB modems; consult modem vendor for recommended setting

- You cannot complete a connection because the ISP's dial-up telephone number has changed—With the explosion in new area codes and alternative telephone services, this might be the most common change you need to make. Enter the number and area code (if required) in the appropriate fields.

- You have moved your computer to a different location which requires you to enter additional codes to access an outside line or an area code—Click Use Dialing Rules, click the Dialing Rules button, and click New to add a location (recommended for temporary use at a hotel or office) or Edit to change the dialing rules for your default location. Figure 2.5 shows the General dialog, which is all that's required for local calls. If you will be calling from different area codes which require that the area code plus number need to be dialed to make the call, click Area Code Rules and specify how to handle calls using an area code. If you want to use a calling card, click Calling Card, select the calling card you use (or click New to create a new calling card setting) and enter the account and PIN number you use.

The Options Tab

Use the Options tab, shown in Figure 2.6, to configure redial options and whether to redial if the connection is dropped. These options can help you deal with overloaded dial-up services that are hard to connect to at peak periods. Other options let you specify different dial-up numbers, optional password prompts, and other dialing options.

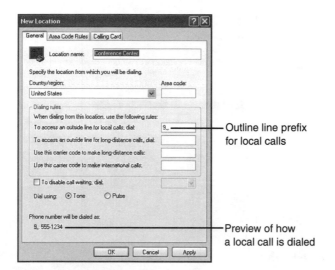

Outline line prefix
for local calls

Preview of how
a local call is dialed

FIGURE 2.5
Creating a new dialing rule for use when the modem is connected through a switchboard, which requires the user to request an outside line.

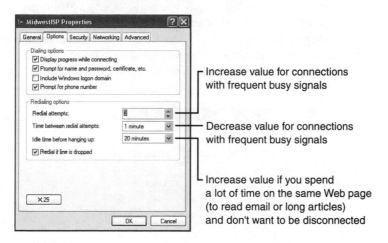

Increase value for connections
with frequent busy signals

Decrease value for connections
with frequent busy signals

Increase value if you spend
a lot of time on the same Web page
(to read email or long articles)
and don't want to be disconnected

FIGURE 2.6
Adjusting redialing options in Windows XP.

The Security Tab

Adjust the settings on this tab only if you need to change how you log on to the ISP's computer, or if your ISP requires you to display a terminal window for login or run a customized script provided by the ISP. If you have problems logging in to your ISP, contact your ISP to see if you need to make configuration changes with this dialog.

The Networking Tab

Use the Networking tab, shown in Figure 2.7, if your ISP requires you to adjust how the dialup server connection is made or if you need to modify the default settings for network software components. For example, if your ISP required you to specify a particular IP address for your computer, you would need to adjust the properties for Internet Protocol (TCP/IP) and add the IP address information that your ISP must provide for your account.

FIGURE 2.7

The Networking tab for Windows XP's Dial-Up Networking configuration.

The Advanced Tab

Use the Advanced tab, shown in Figure 2.8, to enable Windows XP's Internet Connection Firewall (which helps prevent unsolicited access to your computer from the Internet) or to configure your computer to share its Internet connection with Internet Connection Sharing (also available in Windows Me). Click the Settings button if you want to enable your computer to be an Internet server for various Internet services such as File Transfer Protocol, Telnet, and so forth.

FIGURE 2.8

Enabling Internet Connection Firewall with Windows XP's Advanced tab for Dial-Up Networking configuration.

➔ *For more about the hardware configuration needed for Internet Connection Sharing, see "Troubleshooting A Shared Internet Connection," p. 371.*

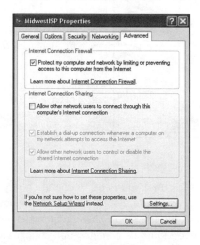

The Advanced tab is so named for a reason; you need to think hard about whether you need to use it. Use its features incorrectly and you could have big problems with your system. For example, don't enable the Internet Connection Firewall (ICF) on computers which share printers or folders with other computer users (it's recommended for use on the ICF host, but the host shouldn't share anything else with the rest of the network). ICF blocks the traffic to the shared resources, so that other computers can't use them, even those on the same network. Instead of trying to configure Internet Connection Sharing (ICS) manually, I recommend you use the

Network Setup Wizard link seen in Figure 2.8. You don't need to use the Settings button unless you are configuring a Web server.

TCP/IP Configuration

TCP/IP, the Transport Control Protocol/Internet Protocol (often referred to in Windows as simply Internet Protocol), can be called the language of the Internet. It doesn't matter what type of computer you have; any computer or device on the Internet needs to use TCP/IP to share information with the rest of the world's largest network.

Unfortunately, the flip side of the power of TCP/IP is that it can be very hard to configure. Every computer or device on the Internet needs an IP address; a public address which is unique to that computer or device. However, most Internet users don't connect directly to the Internet, but connect to an intermediate device or service (like your ISP) that provides an IP address as needed. By default, Windows installs TCP/IP to receive an IP address from a special computer or device, called a Dynamic Host Control Protocol (DHCP) server. This is a feature of most ISPs as well as broadband modems, routers, and Internet sharing programs. A DHCP server automatically assigns an IP address when your computer makes the connection to the Internet.

However, if your ISP doesn't provide a setup CD for TCP/IP configuration, or if you need to make changes to your configuration because you are using Internet sharing products such as a router, you might need to manually configure your computer's TCP/IP settings. This might include entering your computer's IP address, the IP addresses of the DNS servers the computer relies on to convert URLs into IP addresses, the IP address of the gateway to the Internet, and so forth. If you need to change these settings, open the properties sheet for the connection in Windows XP or Windows 2000, or open the Network icon in Control Panel in Windows 9x/Me. Click on the TCP/IP setting and select Properties.

→ *To learn how to view these settings in an easier-to-read list, see "Using IPCONFIG and WINIPCFG," p. 187.*

Using a Fixed IP Address with a Dial-Up or PPPoE Broadband Connection in Windows XP/2000

While not as common as it used to be, some ISPs assign you a fixed IP address (that is, an IP address unique to your computer). If Windows is configured to obtain this address automatically or if it's using the wrong one, you won't have Internet access. To change the TCP/IP settings for a dial-up connection in Windows XP or Windows 2000, follow these instructions:

1. Open the My Network Places folder and click View Network Connections.
2. Right-click the connection you need to change and select Properties.
3. Click Networking, Internet Protocol (TCP/IP), and Properties (see Figure 2.9).
4. Click Use the following IP address and enter the IP address provided by the ISP for your computer.

5. Click Use the following DNS server addresses and enter the IP addresses for the DNS servers used by the ISP.

6. If you need to make additional changes required by the ISP such as WINS server IP addresses or additional DNS servers, click Advanced.

7. Click OK when finished.

FIGURE 2.9
Configuring a Windows XP dial-up connection for the default server-assigned IP address (left) and for a fixed IP address (right).

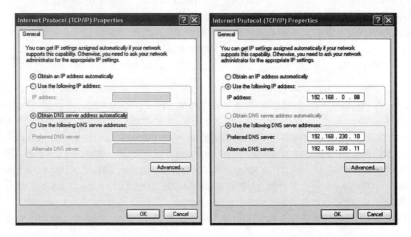

If your broadband Internet connection requires you to log in and provide a user name and password, the provider is using PPPoE (Point-to-Point Protocol over Ethernet) for your account. DSL broadband accounts are the primary users of PPPoE, but other types of broadband might use it as well. Use the same procedure listed here to configure PPPoE broadband accounts with a fixed IP address.

Using a Fixed IP Address with a Dial-Up Connection in Windows 9x/Me

In Windows 9x/Me, dial-up networking connections are stored in a folder called Dial-Up Networking. This folder can be accessed through the Windows Explorer; you can also click Start, Settings, Accessories, Communications, Dial-Up Networking. To change the TCP/IP settings for a dial-up connection using Windows 9x/Me, follow these instructions:

1. Open the Dial-Up Networking folder.

2. Right-click the connection you need to change and select Properties.

3. Click Server Types, TCP/IP Settings.

4. Click Specify an IP address and enter the IP address provided by the ISP for your computer.

5. Click Specify name server addresses and enter the addresses for the DNS servers your ISP uses (see Figure 2.10). If your ISP uses WINS servers, enter those values in the spaces provided.

6. If your ISP doesn't use IP header compression, clear the checkmark next to this option.

7. Click OK when finished.

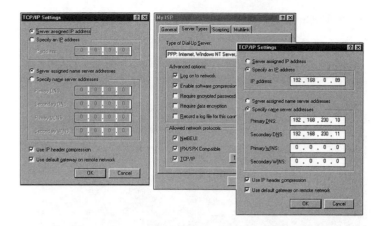

FIGURE 2.10
Configuring Dial-Up Networking in Windows 9x for the default server-assigned IP address (left) and for a fixed IP address (right).

Using a Fixed IP Address with a LAN, Cable Modem, or Fixed Wireless Connection in Windows XP/2000

By default, Windows configures all types of Internet connections to use server-assigned IP addresses. In most cases, this is the correct setting because broadband Internet devices and routers (which are used to share a single Internet connection among multiple users) are normally configured to use DHCP to automatically provide IP addresses to the devices connected to them. However, in some cases, an Internet connection using a LAN or connected directly to a cable modem or other broadband device might need to use a fixed IP address.

To configure a LAN or broadband Internet connection with a fixed IP address in Windows XP/2000

1. Open the My Network Places folder and click View Network Connections.

2. Right-click the connection you need to change and select Properties.

3. Click Networking, click Internet Protocol (TCP/IP), and click Properties.

4. Click Use the following IP address and enter the IP address your ISP has provided for your computer.

5. Click Use the following DNS server addresses and enter the IP addresses for the DNS servers that your ISP uses.

6. Click Advanced and click Add under the Gateway section; enter the IP address of the default gateway.

7. Click OK when finished.

Using a Fixed IP Address with a Cable Modem, Fixed Wireless, or Internet Connection in Windows 9x/Me

To configure a LAN or broadband Internet connection with a fixed IP address in Windows 9x/Me

1. Open the Control Panel.

2. Open the Network icon.

3. Click the TCP/IP entry for your network card and select Properties.

4. Click Specify an IP address and enter the correct IP address and subnet mask (see Figure 2.11).

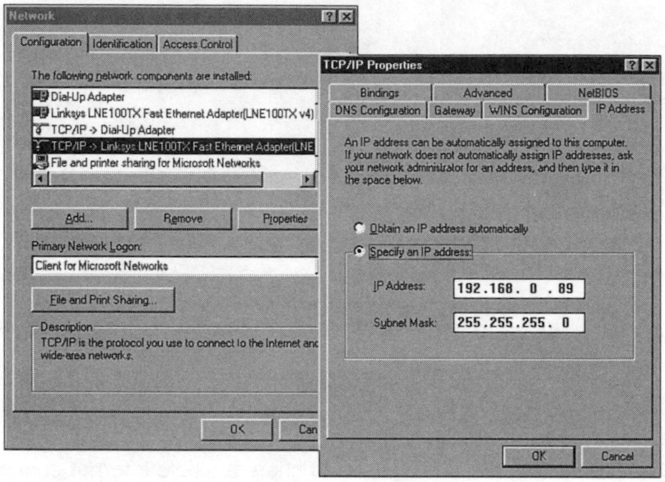

FIGURE 2.11

Configuring a network card in Windows 9x with a fixed IP address.

5. Click Gateway and enter the gateway's IP address; click Add (see Figure 2.12).

6. Click DNS, Enable DNS, and enter the correct host and domain names.

7. Enter the IP address for the first DNS server and click Add; repeat with the address for the second DNS server (see Figure 2.13).

8. Click OK and restart the computer.

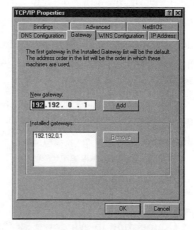

FIGURE 2.12

Specifying a gateway for an Internet connection with a fixed IP address in Windows 9x.

FIGURE 2.13

Specifying the DNS configuration for an Internet connection with a fixed IP address in Windows 9x.

Troubleshooting a Dial-Up (Analog Modem) Connection

An analog modem connection can fail for any of the following reasons:

- Incorrect telephone number
- Incorrect username or password
- Loose or damaged RJ-11 telephone cable
- No dial tone
- Modem failure
- Driver corruption or incorrect driver installed
- Windows software component corruption
- Busy signal or server problems at the ISP

Modem Has No Dial Tone

If your modem can't dial into an ISP's server or other remote computer's telephone number, you can't complete your connection. Modems, like phones, can't dial if there is no dial tone. Check the following if you get a "no dial tone" error message:

- Loose or damaged RJ-11 telephone cable—Make sure the cable is attached correctly to both the wall jack and the modem. Try replacing the cable with one known to work. If it does, you have a damaged cable that you must replace.

- Telephone cable is plugged into the wrong jack on the modem—Most modems have two jacks, one for the phone line and one for sharing the line with a telephone. Use the jack marked "line" for the cable to the wall jack, and the jack marked "phone" for an extension phone. Some modems can use either jack for either task.

- A phone on the same circuit is off the hook—Pick up your phone and listen for a dial tone. If you can't hear a dial tone, make sure all extension phones are properly hung up and try the connection again.

- Your phone service is dead—If all phones are hung up but you still can't connect or make a voice call with your phone, your phone service is dead. Contact the phone company for repair assistance.

- Your modem is damaged or destroyed—If you can't connect after a lightning strike or a power outage, your modem may have been damaged or destroyed. To see if it's still working, see "Using Analog Modem Diagnostics," p. 176.

PC Can Dial but Does Not Connect

If you can dial the remote computer but can't complete the connection, check the following:

- You may be dialing the wrong number—Open the modem properties sheet and increase the speaker volume to maximum. Try the connection again and listen for the tones played by the remote device when it answers. If you hear a series of hisses, that's a modem at the other end. However, if you hear a repeated warble, that's a fax machine, not a modem—and that's a wrong number. If you hear a live human being or an answering machine, that's also a wrong number.

- The remote computer might not be accepting your password or username (normally, an error message tells you if this is the case)—Re-enter the correct username and password on the connection screen (see Figure 2.14) and retry your connection.

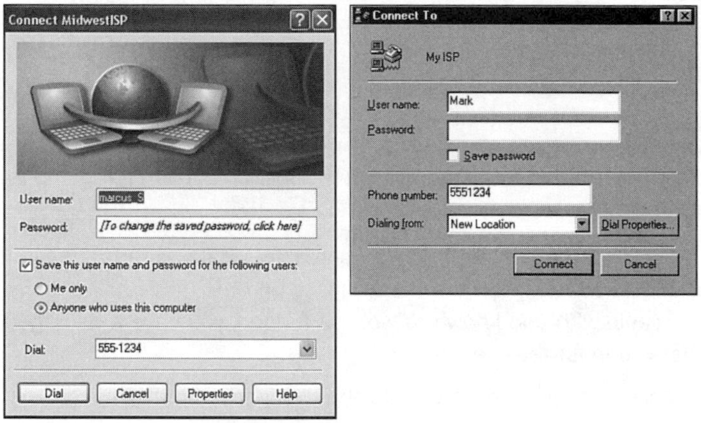

FIGURE 2.14

The dial-up connection dialog in Windows XP (left) and Windows 9x (right). Re-enter the username and password if the remote computer doesn't recognize them.

- The software configuration may be damaged—Rerun the installation program provided by the ISP, or call the ISP for assistance and manually check the configuration as instructed by their help desk.

- The ISP's telephone number might be busy—If repeated attempts to connect result in a busy signal each time, contact the ISP by telephone to determine if there are alternate numbers you can call to connect. Adjust the redial options (see "The Options Tab," p. 166) to redial more frequently to make your connection.

- You might have problems with your TCP/IP configuration—Call your ISP's tech support desk and ask them to walk you through the TCP/IP configuration for the service to make sure your system is properly configured.

If your computer locks up when you try to make the connection, your modem (or the port the modem is connected to) has a hardware conflict (probably an IRQ conflict) with another device. Restart your computer and open Device Manager to check for IRQ conflicts between modem and another device (usually a COM port);

you can also use the Conflicts/Sharing section of the Windows System Information utility to check for conflicts. Change the modem to another IRQ or disable the COM port if you don't use it; you might need to restart your computer and access the system BIOS setup program to change or disable the COM port on the computer. See "Using Device Manager," p. 480; "Using System Information," p. 491; and "I/O Device Setup," p. 110.

Port Already Open

If you see a "port already open" error message when you try to make the connection, another program is trying to use the modem. Try these solutions:

- Be sure you are not trying to send a fax with your modem at the same time. Complete the fax transmission and retry the connection.

- If you formerly used AOL, but no longer use it, make sure you remove it from your system with the Add/Remove Programs icon in Control Panel. You might also need to remove AOL adapters from the Windows 9x/Me Network properties sheet. Remove and reinstall the Dial-Up Networking Adapter in Windows 9x/Me if necessary.

  To remove AOL from your system

  1. Open the Add/Remove Programs icon in Control Panel.

  2. Select each program which mentions AOL or America Online (except AOL Instant Messenger) and click remove. If you use AOL Instant Messenger, you don't need to remove it, since it works with any Internet connection.

  3. Open the Network icon in Control Panel and remove items such as AOL Adapter, Client for America Online, or other AOL/America Online references.

  4. Restart your computer and retry your normal dial-up connection.

- If you still can't connect with your normal dial-up networking (DUN) connection, you should remove and reinstall DUN if you use Windows 9x/Me.

  To remove and reinstall Dial-Up Networking for Windows 9x/Me

  1. Open Control Panel.

  2. Open Add/Remove Programs.

  3. Click Windows Setup.

  4. Click Communications to select the category, then click Details.

  5. Clear the check box next to Dial-Up Networking.

  6. Click OK twice and restart your computer to remove your current installation of DUN.

  7. After the computer restarts, repeat steps 1–4, and click the box next to Dial-Up Networking to select it.

  8. Click OK twice. Provide your Windows CD if required to reinstall DUN. Restart your computer when prompted.

- Disable the Quicken Download Manager (Qagent) if you use Windows 2000 or Windows XP—This utility is part of Quicken 2000, and is used to download financial information into Quicken even when Quicken is not in use. To prevent Qagent from running in the background

    1. Start Quicken.

    2. Click Edit, Options, Internet Options.

    3. Click Connection on the Customize Quicken 2000 Download window.

    4. Select Don't Use Background Downloading Option.

    5. Click OK.

    6. Close Quicken.

    7. Restart your computer to use this new configuration.

    This problem might also be resolved if you upgrade to newer versions of Quicken. If you want to re-enable Qagent because you've switched to a broadband Internet service, see http://www.intuit.com/support/quicken/2000/win/1935.html for instructions.

If your modem won't respond when you try to open a connection, test it with Windows's modem diagnostics. The next section, "Using Analog Modem Diagnostics," discusses these diagnostic tools in more detail.

Using Analog Modem Diagnostics

Windows contains a built-in modem diagnostics feature which you can use to determine if your modem is working, even if you cannot dial out to make an Internet connection.

To run the modem diagnostics with Windows XP:

1. Open the Phone and Modem Options icon in the Control Panel.

2. Click the Modems tab.

3. Select your modem and click Properties.

4. Click Query Modem.

If you're using Windows 9x/Me, open the Modems icon in Control Panel to perform modem testing; use the Diagnostics tab and select the modem you want to test.

Upon running the test, you should see various AT commands (AT commands are used by dial-up networking and other software to control the modem) and the modem's response in the Command/Response window as in Figure 2.15.

You can also open the Device Manager, select the modem from the list of hardware devices, and access its properties sheet to perform this test.

If the modem fails to respond, an error message will be displayed suggesting that you need to turn on the modem (if external) or check for hardware conflicts (if internal).

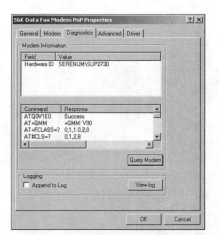

FIGURE 2.15
A successful modem test; the modem responds to the commands listed.

If an internal modem has no hardware conflicts with other devices or an external modem is connected to a working port and is turned on but doesn't respond during the modem diagnostics test, it is probably defective. You will probably have to replace it, but first try contacting the modem vendor's tech support center for help.

Troubleshooting a Broadband Internet Connection

Because broadband Internet connections such as cable modems, fixed wireless, DSL, and satellite use either 10/100 Ethernet or USB connections to your computer, connection failures are caused by different problems than those afflicting analog modem Internet connections. Regardless of the type of broadband connection, these problems include

- Loose or damaged cables—Check the connections between the computer, the modem, and the external signal source; tighten loose cables and replace damaged cables. See Figure 2.16.

- Disabled or defective USB or 10/100 Ethernet ports—Connect a USB cable to a different USB port; use the Device Manager to determine if the ports are configured correctly (see "Using Device Manager," p. 480 for details); use any diagnostics software provided with the network adapter to test it.

- Conflicts between USB or 10/100 Ethernet ports and other hardware devices—See "Using Device Manager," p. 480, for details.

- Incorrect TCP/IP configuration—See "Using TCP/IP Diagnostics to Toubleshoot Your Connection," p. 186 for details.

- Router failure (a router lets you share a broadband Internet connection among multiple computers)—See "Troubleshooting a Router," p.183 for details.

In addition to these problems common to all types of broadband Internet connections, each type of broadband connection can have unique problems.

Loose Category 5 cable;
not plugged into
socket completely

FIGURE 2.16
*Loose (top) and
properly-connected
(bottom) Category 5
Ethernet cables con-
nected to a typical
10/100 Ethernet card.*

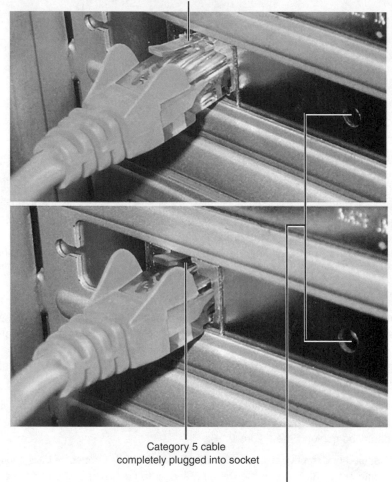

Category 5 cable
completely plugged into socket

Signal lights indicate a
connection only for the
properly connected cable

Troubleshooting a Cable Modem Connection

Cable modems, which use the same connection into your location as cable TV, are
the most popular form of broadband Internet. Here are solutions to problems
unique to cable modems:

- If you have cable TV and cable Internet, and you cannot see any cable TV
  channels or receive cable Internet service, contact the cable provider to
  report a service outage.

- If cable TV is working, but cable Internet service is not working, check the cable connections to your PC and cable modem (refer to Figures 2.16 and 2.17). Loose cables should be tightened; damaged cables should be replaced.

- If your cable Internet service is a one-way service, which uses a dial-up (analog) modem to send page requests and email, problems with your analog modem can prevent you from making an Internet connection. To diagnose dial-up modem problems, see "Troubleshooting a Dial-Up (Analog Modem) Connection," p. 173 for details.

- If the connections between the cable modem and the computer appear to be correct, check the signal lights on the cable modem to see if they indicate problems. See "Using Signal Lights to Troubleshoot Your Connection," p. 182 for details.

- If the cable modem doesn't report any problems, your computer's TCP/IP address may not be valid. To diagnose problems with your computer's TCP/IP configuration by using programs such as PING, IPCONFIG (Windows 2000/XP), and WINIPCFG (Windows 9x/Me), see "Using TCP/IP Diagnostics to Troubleshoot Your Connection," p. 186.

Loose coaxial cable; note large amount of screw thread visible

Coaxial cable correctly screwed into place

FIGURE 2.17
Loose (left) and properly-connected (right) coaxial cables on a typical cable modem.

Troubleshooting a DSL Connection

Digital Subscriber Line (DSL) connections also share a common connection into your location: your telephone line. However, unlike cable modem service, which is usually provided over an upgraded cable TV network which also provides digital cable TV, DSL connections share your telephone line. Because DSL is carried over the telephone line (which wasn't originally designed to handle high-frequency, high-speed DSL traffic), telephone-related problems can cause havoc with your DSL connection.

- If you lose voice telephone service because of a problem with the telephone wiring outside your home, you've also lost DSL service, since both services are carried over the same lines. However, other types of DSL problems don't necessarily affect your phone lines.

- If your telephone service is working, but your DSL connection is not working at all, check the connections between the DSL modem, your computer, and the telephone wall jack.

- A slow DSL connection, or one that doesn't work at all, may be caused by interference from telephones, answering machines, or fax machines. If you installed DSL yourself (self-install), you should have connected small devices called microfilters (see Figure 2.18) between each of these devices and the telephone wall jack to block interference. To determine if your microfilters are defective, disconnect all telephone-type devices from the telephone jacks and try your DSL connection again. If your connection starts working, or runs much faster than before, replace the microfilters. You can buy them at Radio Shack or other electronics stores.

FIGURE 2.18
A typical DSL microfilter. Photo courtesy of 2Wire.

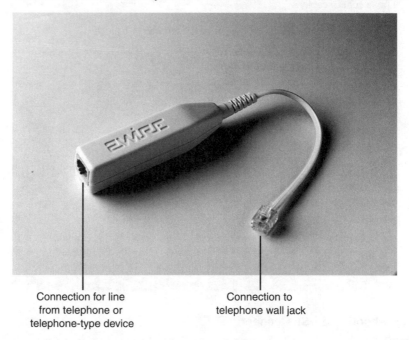

Connection for line
from telephone or
telephone-type device

Connection to
telephone wall jack

- Check the signal lights on the DSL modem to see if they indicate problems with your connection. See "Using Signal Lights to Troubleshoot Your Connection," p. 182 for details.

- If the DSL modem doesn't report any problems, your computer's TCP/IP address may not be valid. To diagnose problems with your computer's TCP/IP configuration by using programs such as PING, IPCONFIG (Windows 2000/XP), and WINIPCFG (Windows 9x/Me), see "Using TCP/IP Diagnostics to Troubleshoot Your Connection," p. 186.

Troubleshooting a Satellite Connection

Satellite-based connections such as DirecWay (formerly DirecPC) and StarBand can be knocked off the air by antenna misalignment, cabling problems, and satellite modem problems.

- If you are unable to connect to the Internet after a storm, earthquake, or other event which may have caused the antenna to be misaligned, check the signal strength if your software installation includes this feature. If your signal strength is low or zero, or if you have no signal-strength feature, contact the satellite Internet provider for assistance unless you have the older DirecPC/DirecWay one-way satellite connections. Note that heavy rain or snow can also cause slow connections or interruptions, but this type of disruption should stop when the rain or snowstorm is over.

- If you see physical damage to the satellite dish with any type of satellite Internet service, contact the vendor for repair assistance.

- If you have one-way DirecPC/DirecWay service, you can realign the antenna yourself using the software provided with the service. However, you should attempt this only if you installed the antenna yourself or are handy with tools. It's easiest to adjust the antenna if two people are involved; one to move the antenna and the other to check the signal strength displayed on the computer screen and transmit the results to the user.

- One-way DirecPC/DirecWay service will be interrupted if your dial-up modem (used for sending page requests and email) stops working. To diagnose dial-up modem problems, see "Troubleshooting a Dial-Up (Analog Modem) Connection," p. 173 for details.

- If the satellite modem doesn't report any problems and the signal strength appears to be within acceptable limits, your computer's TCP/IP address may not be valid. To diagnose problems with your computer's TCP/IP configuration by using programs such as PING, IPCONFIG (Windows 2000/XP), and WINIPCFG (Windows 9x/Me), see "Using TCP/IP Diagnostics to Troubleshoot Your Connection," p. 186.

Troubleshooting a Fixed Wireless Connection

Fixed wireless Internet connections have some of the characteristics of a satellite-based and a cable modem-based service. Like a satellite-based system, fixed-wireless systems use a directional antenna to connect to the ISP. Like both satellite-based and cable modem services, some fixed wireless services depend

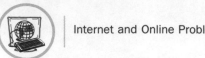

upon a dial-up (analog) modem to send page requests and email. And, some fixed wireless ISPs provide Internet service along with wireless cable TV service.

- If you are unable to connect to the Internet after a storm, earthquake, or other event which may have caused the antenna to be misaligned, contact the Internet provider for assistance. You may need to have a new site survey performed to realign the antenna.

- If you see physical damage to the antenna, contact the vendor for repair assistance.

- If you lose wireless cable TV service, don't be surprised if your Internet connection also stops working. A problem at the ISP could knock both services off the air. Report the connection problem to the ISP.

- If your wireless Internet service is a one-way service, which uses a dial-up (analog) modem to send page requests and email, problems with your analog modem can prevent you from making an Internet connection. To diagnose dial-up modem problems, see "Troubleshooting a Dial-Up (Analog Modem) Connection," p. 173 for details.

- Check the signal lights on the wireless broadband modem or router to see if they indicate problems with your connection. See the following section for details.

- If the wireless broadband modem or router doesn't report any problems, your computer's TCP/IP address may not be valid. To diagnose problems with your computer's TCP/IP configuration by using programs such as PING, IPCONFIG (Windows 2000/XP), and WINIPCFG (Windows 9x/Me), see "Using TCP/IP Diagnostics to Troubleshoot Your Connection," p. 186.

Using Signal Lights to Troubleshoot Your Connection

Most broadband Internet modems, particularly those used for DSL, cable modem, and fixed wireless connections, are external devices. The signal lights on the unit can be used to help you diagnose problems with your Internet connection (see Figure 2.19).

The following tips are general guidelines; to determine exactly what the signal lights are called and what they indicate on your broadband modem, consult your broadband modem's instruction manual.

- If the broadband modem is not receiving power, check the power cable and the connection to the wall outlet or surge protector.

- If the signal light for the connection to the computer indicates a problem with the modem's connection to the computer, check the USB or RJ-45 cable connection between the device and the computer. If the cable is attached correctly, check the USB or Ethernet port on the computer and make sure it's working correctly. See "Using Device Manager," p. 480 for details.

- If the signal light for the connection to the broadband network indicates a problem, reset the broadband modem. When the modem resets it must reacquire the cable signal. This should only take a minute or two, but may take longer. If the modem still indicates a problem after about 30 minutes or so, contact the ISP; the ISP may have a problem.

- If the self-test light on the modem indicates a problem, reset the modem. If resetting the modem doesn't solve the problem, contact the ISP (if you leased the modem from them) or the modem vendor (if you purchased the modem outright).

- If the ready light on the modem indicates a problem, reset the modem. If the ready light still indicates a problem, check the cables and contact the ISP for help.

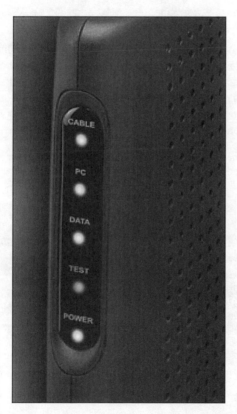

FIGURE 2.19
The signal lights on the front of a typical broadband modem (Toshiba's PCX2500, a cable modem).

Troubleshooting a Router

Routers resemble a networking hub or switch, which are devices that allow multiple PCs to share data or peripherals. However, routers also have a special WAN or Internet port which connects them to broadband modems, providing a hardware method for sharing a single Internet connection among computers on a network. (Some routers only connect to one computer, but most can connect to four or more.) Like the modems themselves, routers can suffer from a number of problems that could interrupt your Internet service.

- If your ISP changes the type of IP address you have (the most common switch is from a static IP address which never changes to a dynamic IP address), you need to reprogram your router to use dynamic IP addressing, or your connection will fail. See Figure 2.20.

- Some ISPs dislike home networks, and might shut off service to your computer if they determine that you are using a router to share your Internet connection—To avoid this problem, use the MAC Address cloning feature in your router's setup to have the router report the same MAC address used by the network adapter originally connected to the cable modem to the ISP. To learn how to view your network adapter's MAC address, see "Using IPCONFIG and WINIPCFG," p. 187.

- Your router or gateway has lost its connection to the broadband modem—Reset the router or gateway and retry your connection. If you still can't connect, contact the ISP and verify the settings for your account. Make sure your router configuration is using the correct settings for fixed or server-assigned IP (fixed IP addresses also require settings for gateway and DNS servers) and any other configuration options used by your ISP.

FIGURE 2.20

The setup screen for a typical router (the Linksys BEFSR41); this screen controls the LAN (network) and WAN (Internet connection) IP addresses.

Configures the LAN (local network address) used for the router

Select if the router receives its IP address automatically from the ISP

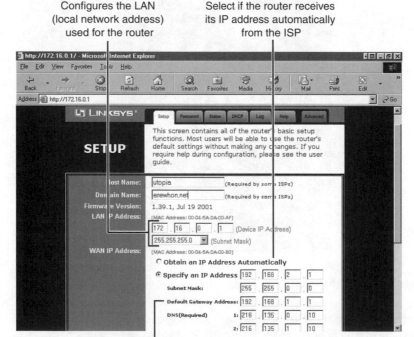

Select and complete per the ISP's instructions if your ISP has assigned your computer a fixed IP address

- If the signal lights on the router don't indicate a connection with some computers which are turned on, check for loose or damaged network cables.

- No computers on the network can connect to each other or to the Internet if the router loses power—Check the power connections in the event of a power failure on the circuit that the router is connected to.

- Most networks use a feature called Dynamic Host Configuration Protocol (DHCP) to provide Internet Protocol (IP) addresses to the computers on the network. If you change sharing methods, such as switching from using Windows Internet Connection Sharing (ICS) to a router, or if your router wasn't powered on when you started your computer, you won't have a valid IP address. To solve this problem by using programs such as IPCONFIG (Windows 2000/XP) and WINIPCFG (Windows 9x/Me), see "Using IPCONFIG and WINIPCFG," p. 187. You might need to power down the computers connected to the router or to the computer with the shared Internet connection and restart them to get a working IP address.

- If you add computers to your network, you might need to reconfigure your router to provide additional IP addresses (see Figure 2.21).

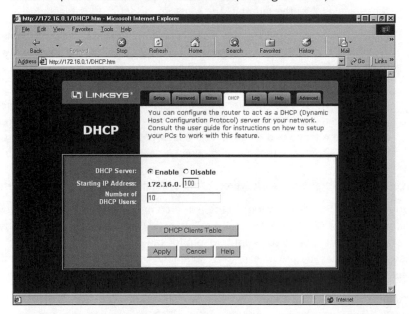

FIGURE 2.21
Configuring a typical router (the Linksys BEFSR41) to use DHCP to provide IP addresses for up to 10 computers. The router has a built-in Web server which lets you use your Web browser to configure it or view settings.

- If one computer on the network can't access the Internet, but others can, check the cabling between that computer and the router. Most routers incorporate what is called an *uplink port*, which enables the router to be daisy-chained to another hub or switch to allow more computers to share data or Internet access across a network. If you plug a computer into the uplink port (which has its connections reversed from a normal network cable) instead of into a normal port, it won't be able to "see" the Internet or the rest of the network. And, if you use the uplink port, the adjacent port is disabled (see Figure 2.22).

FIGURE 2.22
The ports on a typical 4-port router with integrated switch.

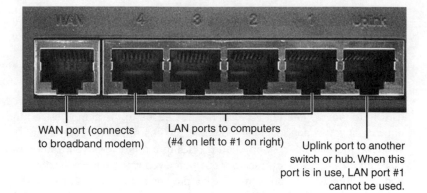

WAN port (connects to broadband modem)

LAN ports to computers (#4 on left to #1 on right)

Uplink port to another switch or hub. When this port is in use, LAN port #1 cannot be used.

Using TCP/IP Diagnostics to Troubleshoot Your Connection

Microsoft provides several TCP/IP diagnostics programs as part of the TCP/IP protocol, the "language" of the Internet. The most important of these include

- PING—This program sends data to a specified IP address or server name. The target IP then returns data to your computer, which helps you to determine if you have a live connection and how fast it is. You can also use Ping to make sure your computer has TCP/IP installed.

- WINIPCFG (Windows 9x/Me) or IPCONFIG (Windows 2000/XP)—These programs display the IP address and other details about your computer, and can be used to release and renew IP addresses provided by a DHCP server (often built in to a router or broadband modem).

The commands listed here are covered in more detail in the upcoming sections.

To run PING and IPCONFIG, you need to open a command-prompt window. With Windows 2000 or Windows XP, click Start, Run, type CMD, and click OK. Then, type the command and options you want to use after the command prompt (>), and press ENTER. After you are finished with command-line programs, type EXIT and press ENTER to return to the Windows desktop.

To run PING with Windows 9x or Windows Me, click Start, Run, type COMMAND, and click OK. Then, type the command and options you want to use after the command prompt (>), and press ENTER. After you are finished with command-line programs, type EXIT and press ENTER to return to the Windows desktop.

To run WINIPCFG (Windows 9x/Me), click Start, Run, type WINIPCFG, and click OK. Close the window when you're finished with the program.

Using IPCONFIG and WINIPCFG

If you're not a whiz at networking, digging around in the Networks icon in Control Panel probably isn't your idea of a good time. Fortunately, running IPCONFIG (Windows XP/2000) or WINIPCFG (Windows 9x/Me) provides a fast way to see TCP/IP configuration information about your computer.

Windows XP and Windows 2000 users run IPCONFIG from the command line. If you use Windows 9x or Windows Me, you also use Start, Run to launch WINIPCFG, but you don't need to open a command prompt window first. Just type WINIPCFG and click OK to start it.

Type IPCONFIG and press Enter to display the name of the DNS server (the server which matches IP addresses to server names), the computer's IP address and subnet mask, and the default gateway (which connects your computer to the Internet). If you need more detailed information, type IPCONFIG /ALL and press ENTER as in Figure 2.23.

DHCP enabled; if yes, computer
gets its IP address from the
DHCP server; if no, the IP address
is manually configured

Physical (MAC) address

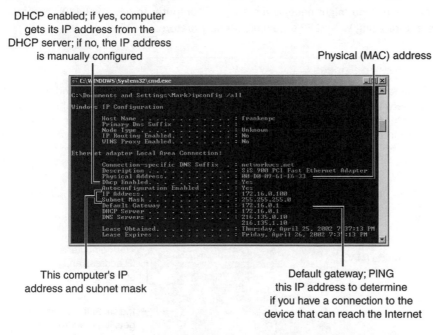

This computer's IP
address and subnet mask

Default gateway; PING
this IP address to determine
if you have a connection to the
device that can reach the Internet

FIGURE 2.23
IPCONFIG/ALL displays your MAC address (physical address) along with your computer's IP address, whether you use DHCP to get an IP address, and other information that tech support people might need to know about your system.

If you see invalid IP addresses such as 0.0.0.0 and your computer uses dynamic IP addressing, type IPCONFIG /RELEASE and press Enter to release current IP addresses. Then type IPCONFIG /RENEW and press Enter to get new IP address information for your system. If you still see 0.0.0.0 as the IP address, you need to

- Make sure you have a working connection to the device which gives you your IP address (a router, a computer running a sharing program such as Internet Connection Sharing [ICS], or a broadband modem). If you use a separate switch and router, make sure both are turned on and that the switch is properly connected to the router and to all the computers.

- Make sure the router, computer with shared Internet access, or modem is turned on. If you connect through a computer running ICS or a third-party sharing program, see if you can access the Internet from that computer. If not, you need to get that computer working first before others can use its connection.

- Restart the router, computer with shared Internet access, or the broadband modem. Wait for a computer which shares Internet access with others to complete booting.

- Restart your computer and see if you can connect to the Internet.

If you use Windows 9x/Me, WINIPCFG's basic display shows the adapter's MAC address, IP address, subnet mask, and default gateway. Click More Info to see additional details similar to those shown by IPCONFIG (see Figure 2.24). If you can't connect to your router or cable modem because the IP address information is out-of-date or invalid (169.x.x.x or 0.0.0.0), click Release All to release the current IP address; click Renew All to get a new IP address. With some Windows installations, you might need to restart your computer to get a valid IP address instead of using WINIPCFG's Release/Renew feature.

Fast Track to Success

By default, WINIPCFG displays the PPP adapter (a logical adapter used for dial-up networking); click the down arrow next to it and select your actual network adapter to see the information you need to solve problems with your broadband Internet connection.

FIGURE 2.24

WINIPCFG displays your MAC address (physical address) along with your computer's IP address, whether you use DHCP to get an IP address, and other information that tech support people might need to know about your system.

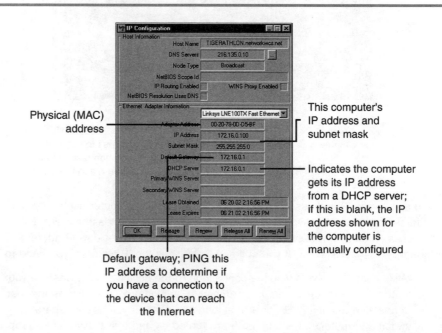

Physical (MAC) address

This computer's IP address and subnet mask

Indicates the computer gets its IP address from a DHCP server; if this is blank, the IP address shown for the computer is manually configured

Default gateway; PING this IP address to determine if you have a connection to the device that can reach the Internet

Using PING

PING must be used from a command prompt, as described in the previous section. It can be used to determine

- Whether you have TCP/IP installed on your system
- Whether you have a connection to a specified IP address or server name
- The speed of your connection to a specified IP address or server name

To view the options you can use for PING, type PING /? and press ENTER. Normally, you will use a command such as PING *hostname* (replace *hostname* with the IP address or server name). If PING can reach the specified *hostname*, it determines the *hostname*'s IP address (a process called resolving), sends data to the *hostname*, and displays the round trip time (also called site latency), the host's IP address, and the time to live (TTL) value for that site (in milliseconds). Figure 2.25 shows a typical PING command and output.

FIGURE 2.25
Using PING to test the connection to a popular Internet news site. Note the average round-trip time (also called the ping rate or latency of the Web site).

Checking Your TCP/IP Configuration with PING

To make sure that you have TCP/IP installed on your system, type PING 127.0.0.1 (this IP address is called the local loopback address) and press ENTER. If you don't have TCP/IP installed, you will get an "unknown host" error message instead of output similar to that shown in Figure 2.9. Reinstall the TCP/IP protocol through the Network icon in Control Panel.

Checking Your Connection to Your Broadband Modem or Router or ICS Host with PING

To determine the IP address of your broadband modem or router or the computer which shares its Internet connection with the network, use IPCONFIG or WINIPCFG, depending upon your version of Windows. The value shown for the default gateway is the address to use in your PING command. For example, if the default gateway is listed as 192.168.0.1, use PING 192.168.0.1.

If you get a timeout error instead of a display similar to that shown in Figure 2.9, you might have a cabling problem or the router or modem might not be working. Restart your computer and try your connection again. If it fails, then check the broadband modem or router to see if the device is working correctly. If your computer uses another computer's Internet connection, restart the computer with the shared connection and make sure it's completely booted and is running the sharing software before you try your Internet connection again.

If you can PING the IP address of your broadband modem, router or computer with the shared Internet connection, but you cannot PING remote IP addresses or Web sites, there is a problem with your Internet connection beyond your network. Restart the broadband modem, router, or computer with the shared connection and try the Internet connection again. If the connection still doesn't work, see "Using Signal Lights to Troubleshoot Your Connection," p. 182, this chapter to troubleshoot your broadband modem or "Troubleshooting a Router," p. 183 to solve router problems.

If Ping displays "Unknown Host" when you ping another computer or IP address, make sure you specified the correct host name and check your TCP/IP settings to verify that you can reach a DNS server.

Fast Track to Success

Because PING can be used to measure the round-trip speed between your computer and any other computer that responds to PING (a few computers block PING for security reasons), you can use PING to check your connection speed to a game server (PING *gameservername* or PING *Ipaddress of game-server*). The lower the ping rate, the faster your connection.

Internet connections can be very complex, particularly if your ISP has provided you with a fixed IP address or if you use a network to provide shared Internet access. Using tools such as IPCONFIG and WINIPCFG to determine your network configuration when it's working properly will make troubleshooting a broken system a lot easier to perform.

Troubleshooting Storage Devices

CHAPTER 3

Overview of Drive Installation and Preparation Tasks

When you install a new storage device into your computer, you can't just use it until you "prepare" it for use. A storage device in this case could be anything from a hard disk drive, to a ZIP Drive, to a CD-RW or DVD drive. The process varies based on the specific type of device, but the first step always involves the physical installation and cabling of the drive. For an internal device, this means you must open your PC and mount it in an available drive bay. Whereas an external device is usually a simple matter of connecting a cable or two and ensuring the device has power.

When the physical installation is complete, the next step is to ensure that your PC and Windows can properly identify it. If your computer can't "see" the device, you can't use it. In the case of a hard, floppy, or optical drive, this means you must ensure that your PC's BIOS can properly identify it. Some removable media devices, such as a ZIP drive, might require only a driver installation in Windows to make it usable.

After the drive is configured, it's time to make sure the same is true of the media it uses. How complicated this process is depends greatly on the type of media for which your device is designed. A hard disk requires much more preparation than a CD-ROM drive, which outside of inserting a disc, requires no media preparation at all. Generally, the process involves some combination of

- Inserting any necessary media (like a recordable CD in a CD-RW drive; not applicable for hard drives)

- Partitioning the drive (hard disk only)
- Formatting the drive's media (this process varies depending on the media type)

Partitioning, Formatting, and File Systems, Oh My!

Partitioning is the process of identifying which portions of a physical hard disk you want to use. You can partition a hard disk as a single drive letter or as two or more drive letters. You can also partition some large (1GB and larger) removable-media drives, but optical drives and small removable-media drives don't require partitioning.

Formatting is the process of dividing up the disk surface into sectors; both hard disks and removable-media disks of any size need to be formatted. The standard Windows format command is used with hard disks and standard floppy disks, while Zip, Superdisk, and other types of removable and optical media are usually formatted with a proprietary program provided by the drive vendor. Rewriteable optical media that will be used for drag-and-drop file copying with programs such as Roxio DirectCD must also be formatted before it can be used. Formatting is not necessary for optical media that will be used with a CD mastering program such as Easy CD Creator or Nero Burning ROM.

During the format process, the file system is created on the media. The file system determines how efficiently a drive stores information, how large a drive letter can be, and whether special Windows 2000 and Windows XP features such as encryption, enhanced file security, and real-time data compression can be used on the drive.

With Windows 9x/Me, the partitioning and formatting process used separate programs (FDISK and FORMAT), but Windows 2000 and Windows XP use a single Disk Management tool to perform these tasks.

➜ *For more information about the ATA/IDE interface, see "The ATA/IDE Interface," p. 101.*

➜ *For more information about USB, see "The USB Interface," p. 93.*

➜ *For more information about SCSI, see The SCSI Interface," p. 92.*

➜ *For more information about IEEE-1394, see "The IEEE-1394a Interface," p. 94.*

➜ *For more information about the parallel port, see "The Parallel Port," p. 91.*

Depending on your level of experience, all this might seem a little basic. However, as simple as the process might seem, there's a whole lot that can go wrong. Cables can be installed incorrectly, the system BIOS might not recognize the drive, the drive's media could be incorrectly formatted or even defective. It's a landscape full of pitfalls! This section helps you solve many of the problems you may encounter as you prepare a new (or even existing) drive for use.

Troubleshooting Drive Detection Problems

Your computer can't prepare a new hard disk or use removable-media or optical disks until it recognizes the drive. Symptoms of a drive not being recognized can vary with the type of drive interface (ATA/IDE, USB, IEEE-1394, SCSI, parallel port).

The following are some typical symptoms:

- Internal drives aren't displayed at startup on systems that display configuration information
- SCSI BIOS on SCSI host adapter cards used with hard disks can't locate drive
- ATA/IDE BIOS on ATA/IDE host adapter cards used with fast, large hard disks can't locate drive
- Hard disk isn't displayed in drive preparation utilities like Computer Management (Windows XP/2000) or FDISK (Windows 9x/Me)
- Proprietary disk-preparation or disk setup programs supplied with IEEE-1394, parallel port or USB drives can't locate drive

Table 3.1 provides a quick-reference to the most common reasons drives aren't recognized by the system. See detailed solutions in the sections following the table.

TABLE 3.1
Quick-Reference to Drive Detection Problems

Type of Drive	How Drive Connects to System	Why Drive Isn't Detected	Solution
IDE/ATA	Any	System power supply might not be connected to drive	Shut down system, attach power connectors to drive and restart
		Data cable is not connected at all or not connected properly	Reconnect cable to drive and ATA/IDE interface
		Drive is configured as "no drive present"	Configure system BIOS to detect all drives at startup
	40-pin, 40-wire* cable	Incorrect master/slave jumpering	If two drives are connected via the same cable, both drives must be correctly jumpered as master or slave
	40-pin, 80-wire* cable	Incorrect drive jumpering	All drives on cable should be jumpered as cable select
IEEE-1394	All cable types	Port disabled	Verify port is working by using Device Manager

TABLE 3.1 (continued)

Type of Drive	How Drive Connects to System	Why Drive Isn't Detected	Solution
		Drive not powered on	Check power going to drive
		No drivers for your version of Windows	Download and install correct drivers for device/Windows version in use
		Windows version not compatible with IEEE-1394 devices	Upgrade to a supported Windows version or use a different type of drive
USB	All cable types	Port disabled	Verify port is working by using Device Manager
		Drive not powered on	Check power going to drive
		No drivers for your version of Windows	Download and install correct drivers for device/Windows version in use
		Windows version not compatible with USB devices	Upgrade to a supported Windows version or use a different type of drive
SCSI	All cable types	Incorrect termination	Last device in SCSI daisy-chain must be terminated; other devices should not be terminated
		Duplicate device ID numbers	Each device attached to a particular SCSI host adapter must have a unique device ID
		Drive not powered on	Check power going to drive

TABLE 3.1 (continued)

Type of Drive	How Drive Connects to System	Why Drive Isn't Detected	Solution
		Mismatch between SCSI version support in host adapter and drive	Determine what level of SCSI support your host adapter provides, and buy SCSI drives that match
PC Card (PCMCIA)	All cable types	PC Card not completely inserted	Eject and reinsert PC Card
		PC Card handlers not installed in operating system	Run Add New Hardware wizard
Parallel port	All cable types	Incorrect parallel port mode	Check drive documentation for correct mode; most require EPP or ECP mode
		Parallel port doesn't have an IRQ assignment, or shares an IRQ with other ISA devices	Check port status with Device Manager; ISA parallel ports can't share IRQs with other devices
		Drive not powered on	Check power going to drive

*Count the number of ridges in a drive cable to determine the number of wires (if necessary).

Troubleshooting an ATA/IDE Drive

An IDE/ATA drive cannot be detected by the system if any of the following are true:

- **The drive is not connected to power or the power cable is loose**—During installation of the drive, be sure to firmly connect the drive to a power cable coming from the power supply. If you use a Y-splitter or power cable extender, be sure the splitter or extender is in good condition and is firmly connected to the power cable and to the drive.

- **The drive is not properly connected to the ATA/IDE interface on the motherboard or add-on card**—Some low-cost cables are not keyed, making it possible for the cable to be installed upside down at either the host adapter or drive end.

- The drive is configured as "Not present" or "none" in the system BIOS—The drive should be configured using the Auto setting to enable the drive to report its configuration to the system.

- The drive is not jumpered correctly—The older 40-wire cables require that one drive be jumpered as master and the other as slave; some brands of drives don't use jumpers if only one drive is on the cable. 80-wire cables use cable select jumpers for both drives, using the position of the drive on the cable to determine which drive is the primary (master) and which the secondary (slave) drive.

In the following sections, you will learn how to check an existing drive installation for problems; if you are installing a brand-new ATA/IDE drive, you can follow the same steps to make sure you are performing the installation correctly.

Checking the Drive Connection to the Power Supply

Most ATA/IDE drives use a four-pin Molex power connector, while a few removable-media drives use a small four-pin power connector instead. In either situation, the drive must be connected to a matching lead from the power supply.

If the power supply doesn't have a free connector available, you can disconnect a power cable from another device and attach a Y-splitter to the end of the cable to enable two devices to be powered from a single cable (see Figure 3.1).

It takes a bit of force to make a solid connection with the Molex connectors seen in Figure 3.1; make sure the drive is attached solidly to the power cable.

Cautions and Warnings

If your computer has a power supply under 300 watts, think twice about using a lot of splitters to power additional drives and case fans. To avoid problems, don't use a split cable to power a processor fan, and don't use a split cable to power two optical drives (the laser and motor mechanism in an optical drive such as a CD-RW or DVD requires much more power than a hard drive does). It's acceptable to split power between a hard drive and an optical drive or a drive and a case fan, but it's better to upgrade to a larger power supply that provides more power connectors for drives and fans.

Checking the Drive and Host Adapter Connection to the Data Cable

The connection between the ATA/IDE host adapter and the drive is made with a 40-pin cable. If the cable is not connected correctly to either the host adapter or the drive, the drive will not be detected and cannot be used.

The contrasting-colored markings on the cable indicate pin 1; line up this side of the cable with pin 1 on the drive and the host adapter. In almost all cases, the location of pin 1 is next to the power connector (see Figure 3.2). Most drives also indicate the location of pin 1 on the bottom or rear of the drive.

Master/slave/cable
select jumper on drive

ATA/IDE data
cable connector
on drive

Extra power
connector provided
by splitter

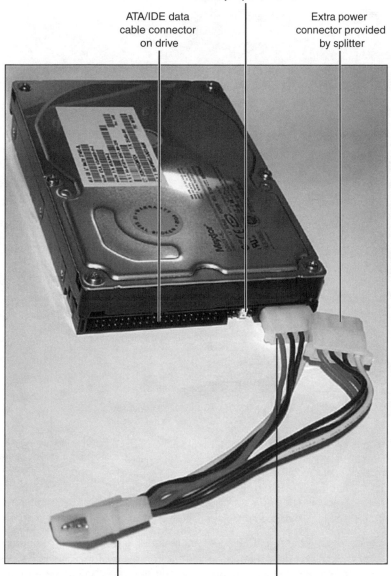

FIGURE 3.1
*A typical ATA/IDE
hard drive attached to
a Y-splitter power cable
before installation into
a system.*

Connection to power
supply (using a Y-splitter cable)

Power connector to hard drive

FIGURE 3.2

Data cable connections to a typical ATA/IDE drive. Pin 1 should be next to the power connector.

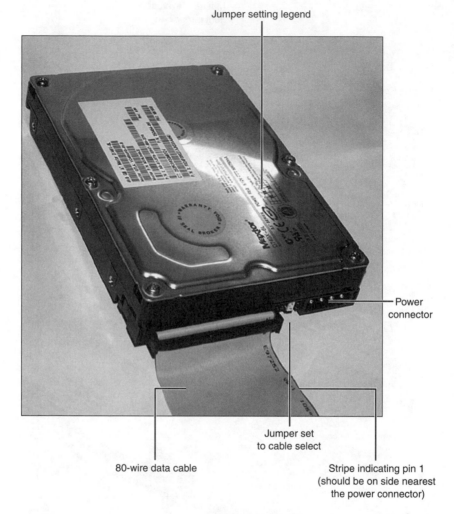

Jumper setting legend

Power connector

Jumper set to cable select

80-wire data cable

Stripe indicating pin 1 (should be on side nearest the power connector)

Note that some cables don't have a plugged hole or a raised protrusion to prevent the cable from being inserted incorrectly (see Figure 3.3).

On some systems, if the ATA/IDE cable is connected in reverse, the computer will not display anything on the screen after you turn on the system. This is because some computers can't continue the power-on self test (POST) until a connected ATA/IDE hard drive responds to a spin up command. Because the drive can't receive the command from a reversed cable, the computer can't proceed in the POST process and can't display any messages.

Figure 3.4 shows how an ATA/IDE cable should be attached to the host adapter. Note the markings for pin 1 on the motherboard and how the keyed cable prevents incorrect installation.

Cable key

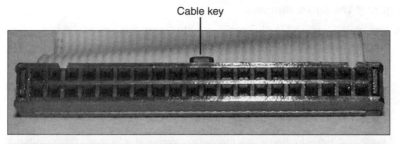

FIGURE 3.3
Keyed (top) and unkeyed (bottom) ATA/IDE data cables.

No cable key

Stripe indicating pin 1
orientation on cable

Keyed cable inserted into
host adapter socket

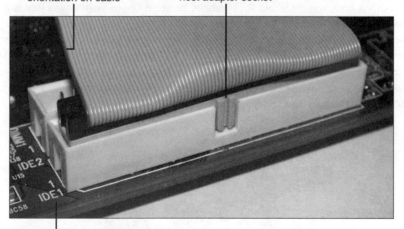

FIGURE 3.4
An 80-wire ATA/IDE cable properly attached to the host adapter on the motherboard.

Host adapter number and pin 1
markings on motherboard

Cautions and Warnings

Some motherboards don't surround the ATA/IDE or floppy cable connections on the motherboard with a plastic skirt as shown in Figure 3.4. It's very easy on such motherboards to incorrectly connect the cable to just one row of pins or to miss some pins entirely; these also prevent the drive from being detected. Avoid problems with all types of ribbon cables by using a flashlight and a magnifier to help you see the cable and the connector during installation.

Configuring the Drive Jumpers

Depending on the type of ATA/IDE cable used to connect drives to the host adapter, the jumpers or the position of the drives on the data cable are used to determine which drive is primary and which is secondary.

Jumpers are pins on the rear (or, occasionally the underside) of a drive that are closed with jumper blocks to set the drive's configuration. ATA/IDE drives have three basic configurations, which can be selected with jumper blocks (see Figure 3.5):

- Master—A drive jumpered as master becomes the primary drive on the cable; if you have your hard disk and optical drive on the same cable, the hard drive should be jumpered as master, and the cable should be plugged into IDE connector number 1 on the motherboard.

- Slave—A drive jumpered as slave becomes the secondary drive on the cable.

- Cable select—The position of the drive on the cable determines which drive is master and which is slave; requires an 80-wire Ultra ATA cable.

Figure 3.5 shows the most common jumper location and the various jumpering options supported on a typical hard disk.

Some drives have additional configuration options that are designed to handle BIOS limitations on some systems. For example, Western Digital hard drives that are not recognized at full capacity on systems with older BIOS chips can be configured with two jumper blocks; installing the second jumper block reduces the drive capacity that's reported to the system BIOS, enabling the drive to be handled by the system BIOS. But, to use the full capacity of the drive, the user must install the drive with Western Digital's EZ-Install or Data Lifeguard Tools, which load a special driver to override the BIOS's disk capacity limitations.

FIGURE 3.5

The jumper pins and jumpering options available for Western Digital hard disks.

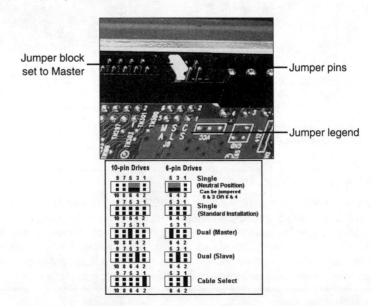

Table 3.2 lists the jumper options for both 40-wire and 80-wire cables. I recommend using an 80-wire cable, even if you don't use drives that are designed for the faster speeds it accommodates, because the additional wires provide cleaner, better signaling to all types of ATA/IDE drives.

TABLE 3.2
Correct Jumpering for a New ATA Drive Installation

Cable Type	Drive Installed As	How to Jumper	Which Cable Connector to Use	Jumper Original Drive As
80-wire	Slave	Cable Select	Gray connector (middle of cable)	Cable Select
	Only drive on cable	Cable Select	Black connector (end of cable)	N/A
	Master	Cable Select	Black connector (end of cable)	Cable Select
40-wire	Slave	Slave	Either	Master
	Only drive on cable	Master or single drive (check drive manufacturer recommendation)	Either	N/A
	Master	Master	Either	Slave

Before You Change It, Write It Down!

If you need to change the jumpering or cable position of an existing drive when you install a new drive, write down the original settings. Note that any drive plugged into an ATA/IDE cable, even if it's an optical or removable-media drive, follows the rules in Table 3.2.

If you install two different brands of drives on the same ATA/IDE cable, in some cases, one or both drives might not be recognized, even if you jumper and connect them correctly to the data cable. This is because of manufacturer-specific differences in their implementation of the ATA/IDE standards.

To avoid this type of problem, I recommend you install the same brand of drive originally used in your system. To see the brand and model of the current drive in your system, open the Device Manager in Windows and open the disk drives category.

However, if you've already purchased a hard drive that won't coexist on the same cable with your current drive, here are some solutions you can try:

- Swap the drive positions on the cable—Use master and slave jumper positions rather than the default cable select jumper positions for an 80-wire cable to preserve the current drive letter sequence.

- Move the new drive to the secondary IDE cable—If you already have an optical or removable-media drive connected to the cable, it's acceptable to install the new drive as a slave. This eliminates any possibility of drive conflicts, since each hard drive is on a separate cable.

- Install an ATA host adapter into an empty PCI expansion slot on your computer and connect your new drive to it—Using the ATA-100 or ATA-133 host adapters packaged with some drives and available separately from various sources will also enable you to bypass BIOS limitations you might have with an older system, and could help your system run faster.

On the Web

To learn more about the drives in your system, including performance, jumper settings, and setup utilities, check the manufacturer's Web sites. Major desktop drive makers include

- Seagate—For Seagate and Conner Peripherals drives, see http://www.seagate.com
- IBM—For IBM drives, see http://www.ibm.com
- Maxtor—For Maxtor and Quantum drives, see http://www.maxtor.com
- Western Digital—For Western Digital drives, see http://www.wdc.com

Determining When Your ATA/IDE Drive Has Failed

Although today's ATA/IDE hard drives are extremely reliable, it's still possible the drive itself has failed. Look for these indications of drive failure:

- Drive will not power up—To check this, shut down the computer, place your hand on the top of the drive case and turn on the computer. If you can't feel any vibration through the case (or you can't hear the drive turning) and the drive is connected to a working power supply, it's probably dead.

- Drive makes excessive noise when the system is turned on—If the drive sounds like it has a marble loose inside, makes scraping or coffee-grinder noises as soon as you turn it on, it's sustained physical damage and is probably dead.

- Computer won't turn on when the drive is attached to the power supply—If your computer appears to be dead when you start it with the drive attached, but powers up normally when you disconnect the power supply from the drive, the drive has a short-circuit and is probably dead.

If ATA/IDE optical and removable-media drives don't display any power lights at any time and won't spin up when you insert media, check their power, data cable, and jumper configuration as described previously.

If the drive's configuration checks out okay, and another drive works when connected to the same cable, the original drive is certainly damaged or dead and should be replaced.

Troubleshooting an IEEE-1394 Drive

IEEE-1394 drives are the newest way to add a high-performance hard drive to your system. They offer Plug-and-Play installation, hot-swap capabilities, and capacities rivaling desktop drives. However, if any of the following are true, your drive won't be detected by your system and can't be used:

- Disabled IEEE-1394 port on your computer
- Resource conflict between IEEE-1394 port and another device
- Drive is not powered on
- Your computer uses a version of Windows that doesn't support IEEE-1394 devices
- You haven't installed the correct drivers for your version of Windows and your drive

Before you connect an IEEE-1394 drive to your system, make sure the port is enabled and supported by your version of Windows. To do this, open the Device Manager and verify that the port is listed and that it is not reporting any problems.

To check your version of Windows for IEEE-1394 compatibility, see "Windows Limitations," Chapter 1. Also, make sure you have drivers for your drive and version of Windows. You might need to download drivers for your version of Windows from the manufacturer, particularly if you use Windows XP.

→ *For details, see "Using the Device Manager," p. 480 for details.*

Troubleshooting Problems with Your IEEE-1394 Port

If the IEEE-1394 port is not displayed in Device Manager then you must enable the port.

If the port is built in to your system, restart the computer, access the BIOS setup program, and enable the port (see Figure 3.6). Save changes and exit the system.

Make sure port is enabled

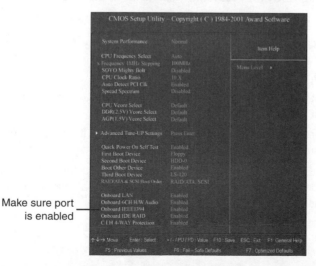

FIGURE 3.6
Enabling the IEEE-1394 port with the computer's BIOS setup program.

If the port is on an add-on card, use the Add Hardware wizard to detect the port and install drivers.

➜ *For more details about using the system BIOS setup program, see "BIOS Setup," p. 104.*

If the port is present but reports problems then you must correct these problems before you can expect the port or your drive to function normally. Some of the problems you might encounter could include

- Incorrect driver loaded for the port's chipset

- Hardware resource conflict with another port

➜ *For more details about using the Add Hardware wizard, see "Add Hardware," p. 469.*

- Corrupt driver loaded

- Device is disabled

These problems can be detected and resolved with the Windows Device Manager (see Figure 3.7).

FIGURE 3.7
A disabled IEEE-1394 port as displayed by the Windows XP Device Manager.

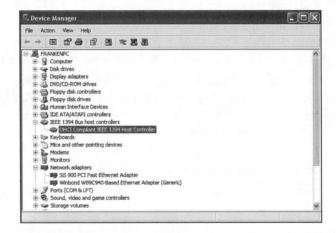

➜ *For details, see "Using Device Manager," p. 480.*

Troubleshooting Other Problems with an IEEE-1394 Drive

If the port is working but the drive is not detected when you attach it to the system

- If the drive's instructions require you to install driver or configuration software before you attach the drive, disconnect the drive from the system, install the software, and reconnect the drive.

- Unplug the device cable from the IEEE-1394 port on the computer and reattach it.

- Make sure the drive is connected to AC power (if it isn't powered by the port) and turned on.

- If the IEEE-1394 ports on the computer are connected to the motherboard by a header cable (see Figure 3.8), make sure the cable is properly and securely attached to the motherboard.

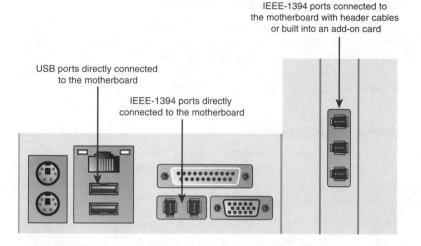

IEEE-1394 ports connected to
the motherboard with header cables
or built into an add-on card

USB ports directly connected
to the motherboard

IEEE-1394 ports directly
connected to the motherboard

FIGURE 3.8
*Two typical locations
for built-in IEEE-1394
and USB ports on the
rear of a computer.*

Cautions and Warnings

The rear of the computer isn't the only place you might have IEEE-1394 or USB ports. Many home-market computers now feature these ports on the front of the computer as well as the rear. Front-mounted ports always use header cables that plug into the motherboard. If you need to unplug cables from the motherboard to perform memory or other internal upgrades, make sure you plug the cables back in the same way they were originally connected.

- Make sure that the IEEE-1394 cable is attached securely to the drive.

- If, after you've reconnected the power and IEEE-1394 cables, Windows does not automatically detect the device, run the Add Hardware wizard. Open the Control Panel through the Start menu, click Add Hardware (called Add New Hardware on some Windows versions), and follow the prompts to detect and install your new drive.

- Replace the IEEE-1394 cable if the drive still can't be detected, and retry.

Cautions and Warnings

If you attach devices to an IEEE-1394 CardBus (32-bit PC Card) adapter in a notebook computer, make sure the devices are self-powered or attach an AC adapter to the IEEE-1394 card. The PC Card slot can't provide enough power to support bus-powered IEEE-1394 devices. If your IEEE-1394 PC Card wasn't shipped with an AC adapter, contact the vendor for details about compatible units.

Determining Your IEEE-1394 Drive Has Failed

If you've checked your software and hardware configuration as described above but your drive still won't function, it might be damaged or dead. This is particularly likely if the drive won't spin up or makes a lot of noise while running. However, if you have other IEEE-1394 devices connected to your computer and none of them are working, the host adapter is probably defective; contact the vendor for help.

Troubleshooting a USB Drive

The USB interface is a flexible interface used for many devices, including portable hard drives. USB hard drives offer Plug-and-Play installation, hot-swap capabilities, and capacities rivaling desktop drives. However, if any of the following are true, your system won't detect your drive:

- USB ports on your computer are disabled; a device connected to a disabled port cannot be detected until the port is enabled.
- The USB data cable is too long or is defective.
- A resource conflict exists between the USB port and another device.
- Drive is not powered on.
- Your computer uses a version of Windows that doesn't support USB devices.
- You haven't installed the correct drivers for your version of Windows and your drive.
- Your drive requires more power than the USB port can provide.

Troubleshooting USB Port Configuration

Before you connect a USB drive to your system, make sure the port is enabled and supported in your version of Windows. To do this, open the Device Manager and verify that the port is listed and that it is not reporting any problems. Also, make sure you have drivers for your drive and version of Windows. You might need to download drivers for your version of Windows from the manufacturer, particularly if you use Windows XP with the newer USB 2.0 ports and devices. Depending upon the drive, you might need to install its drivers first before you connect the drive to the system; check the drive's documentation to find out.

If the USB port is not displayed in Device Manager then you must enable it. If the USB port is built in to your system (as on most recent computers), restart the computer, access the BIOS setup program, and enable the port. Save changes and exit the system. If the port is on an add-on card, use the Add New Hardware wizard to detect the port and install drivers.

Troubleshooting Other Problems with USB Drives

If the USB port is working but the drive is not detected when you attach it to the system or doesn't work after being detected

- Unplug the cable from the USB port on the computer and reattach it; check the cable for damage.

- Make sure the drive is connected to AC power (if it isn't powered by the port) and turned on (if it has a power switch).

- Make sure that the power and USB cables are attached securely to the drive.

- Make sure the USB cable is attached securely to the computer.

- Unplug the drive from the USB port and reinstall the drive installation software provided by the vendor.

- If the drive is supposed to be detected by the system and prompt you for drivers, run the Add New Hardware wizard after connecting the drive to the system and powering it up if it isn't detected automatically.

- Open the properties sheet for the USB hub the drive is connected to and check the available power for that hub.

➜ See "Using Device Manager to Troubleshoot USB Devices," p. 338 for details.

All recent versions of Windows (Windows 98, Me, 2000, XP) support USB 1.1 ports; USB 2.0 is supported in all of these Windows versions except for Windows 98 First Edition.

➜ To determine which version of Windows you use, see "Windows Limitations," p. 148.

However, as with any device, you need to make sure you have drivers for your drive and version of Windows. You might need to download drivers for your version of Windows from the manufacturer, particularly if you use Windows XP.

If the USB port is not displayed in Device Manager then you must enable the port. If the port is built in to your system, restart the computer, access the BIOS setup program, and enable the port. Save changes and exit the system.

➜ For more details about using the system BIOS setup program to troubleshoot USB devices, see "Using the System BIOS to Solve Problems with USB Devices," p. 348.

If the port is on an add-on card but the card wasn't detected when the computer was started, use the Add Hardware wizard to detect the port and install drivers.

If the port is present but reports problems, you must correct them before you can expect the port or your drive to function normally. Some of the problems you might encounter could include

➜ For more details about using the Add Hardware wizard, see "Add Hardware," p. 469.

- Incorrect driver loaded for the port's chipset

- Hardware resource conflict with another port

- Corrupt driver loaded

- Device is disabled

➜ For details, see "Using Device Manager," p. 480.

These problems can be detected and resolved with the Windows Device Manager.

If the USB port is working but the drive is not detected when you attach it to the system

- Unplug the device cable from the USB port on the computer and reattach it.

- Replace a damaged or suspect USB cable with a known-working cable of the same length (or shorter) and retry.

- Make sure the drive is connected to AC power (if it isn't powered by the port) and turned on.

- USB ports located on the rear of the computer are connected directly to the motherboard (refer to Figure 3.8), but USB ports on the front of the computer might be connected to the motherboard with a header cable. If the USB ports on the computer are connected to the motherboard by a header cable, make sure the cable is properly and securely attached to the motherboard.

- Make sure that the cable is attached securely to the drive.

→ *For more details about using the Add Hardware wizard, see "Add Hardware," p. 469.*

- If, after you've reconnected the power and data cables, Windows does not automatically detect the device, reinstall the installation software provided with the drive or use the Add Hardware wizard (check the drive documentation for which installation process is recommended). To use Add Hardware, open the Control Panel through the Start menu, click Add Hardware (called Add New Hardware on some Windows versions) and follow the prompts to detect and install your new drive.

- If the drive is connected to a bus-powered generic USB hub (such as those built into keyboards and monitors) and the drive itself is bus-powered, connect the drive directly to the USB root hubs (ports) on the front or rear of the system if possible; root hubs provide the USB maximum of 500mA per port. If this is not convenient, connect the drive to a self-powered USB hub (which also provide 500mA per port) and connect the hub to the computer. Bus-powered hubs provide no more than 100mA of power per port, while bus-powered removable-media drives could require almost 500mA of power to run (see Figure 3.9).

Determining the USB Drive Is Defective

If you've checked your software and hardware configuration as described above, but your drive still won't function, it may be damaged or dead. This is particularly likely if the drive won't spin up or makes a lot of noise while running, but other devices attached to the USB port are working correctly.

However, if no devices attached to the USB port are working, the motherboard or host adapter containing the USB port is probably defective; contact the vendor for help.

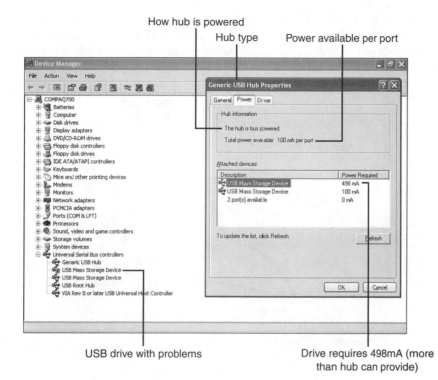

How hub is powered

Hub type   Power available per port

USB drive with problems

Drive requires 498mA (more than hub can provide)

FIGURE 3.9
The USB Mass Storage Device (drive) isn't working because it draws more power than a bus-powered hub can provide.

Troubleshooting a SCSI Drive

Although SCSI drives were actually developed before ATA/IDE drives, they're not nearly as popular as other types of drives in desktop computers. However, SCSI drives and other types of devices are popular choices for high-performance video and graphics editing workstations and for servers. SCSI drives can't be recognized by the system if any of the following are true:

- Incorrect termination of the ends of a SCSI daisy-chain
- Duplicate device ID numbers in a daisy-chain
- Drive not powered on
- SCSI interface not enabled
- SCSI interface has resource conflicts with another device
- Incorrect cable used to connect the drive

Troubleshooting Termination and Device ID Settings

If you have added a drive to a system with other SCSI devices on-board, you might need to adjust termination settings for the existing and new drives/devices. The ends of any SCSI daisy-chain must be terminated to allow the host adapter to properly detect and control all devices. See Figure 3.10 for typical configurations. If you connect the new drive to the end of the daisy-chain, you need to disable termination on the device that was formerly at the end of the daisy-chain and enable termination on the new drive.

FIGURE 3.10
A properly configured SCSI device daisy-chain.

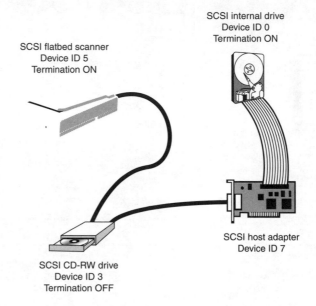

SCSI internal drive
Device ID 0
Termination ON

SCSI flatbed scanner
Device ID 5
Termination ON

SCSI host adapter
Device ID 7

SCSI CD-RW drive
Device ID 3
Termination OFF

You also might have a duplicate device ID. Some SCSI host adapter vendors, such as Adaptec, offer a SCSI diagnostics program that can list the device IDs already in use. Each device must have a unique device ID.

Internal SCSI drives use jumper blocks to set both termination and device ID values. External drives and devices might use a dial, slider, or pushbutton to set termination and device ID (see Figure 3.11). High-speed external SCSI devices often use an external terminator that plugs into the unused SCSI port.

If the new drive has been connected to a SCSI port that has no other devices attached to it

- The port might be disabled or have a conflict. Open the Device Manager to check the port's status. If the port is disabled, enable it. Correct any problems indicated by Device Manager. See "Using Device Manager," p. 480.

- You must terminate the new device.

- Verify that an external drive is turned on after you connect it to the system; the drive must be turned on before the computer is turned on to enable it to be detected.

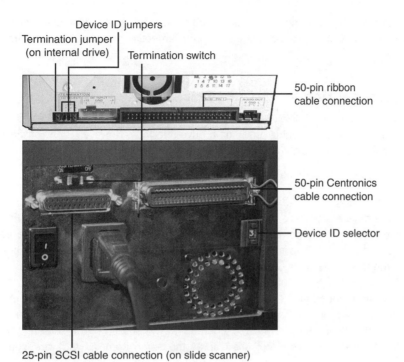

Device ID jumpers

Termination jumper
(on internal drive)   Termination switch

50-pin ribbon
cable connection

50-pin Centronics
cable connection

Device ID selector

25-pin SCSI cable connection (on slide scanner)

FIGURE 3.11
A typical SCSI internal drive (top) and external scanner (bottom) demonstrating the types of SCSI cable connections, device ID and termination options on different SCSI devices.

If the drive is connected to an external port

- You must use the correct type of cable. Some SCSI devices use cables with the same DB25M connector used for parallel-port switchboxes and Direct Parallel/Cable Connection (LapLink/Interlink) cables, but the cables are not the same. Use a cable made especially for SCSI.

- Make sure the last device in the daisy-chain is terminated. If you attach the SCSI drive after other existing devices, turn off the termination on the last device present before the new drive is added, connect the new drive, and enable termination on the new drive.

- Make sure the new drive and all other SCSI devices are powered up before you start the computer.

After the hard drive is installed and the SCSI host adapter has detected it, you must use a utility supplied with the SCSI host adapter vendor to perform a low-level format on the drive before you can prepare it for use with Windows.

Determining That the SCSI Drive Is Defective

If other SCSI devices on the same daisy-chain are working correctly, and you've checked all the settings (device ID, termination, power, cables) discussed above, your drive is probably defective. Contact the vendor for repair or replacement.

However, if no device works when connected to your SCSI card, regardless of configuration, the SCSI host adapter card is probably defective and should be repaired or replaced.

Troubleshooting a PC Card Drive

PC Cards (also called PCMCIA cards) provide a wide variety of I/O services to portable computers, including providing a drive interface. However, if any of the following are true, your PC Card-interfaced drives won't work properly:

- PC Card is not completely inserted
- PC Card handlers are not installed in the operating system
- The drive attached to the PC Card is not connected to a power source (if it requires external power) or turned on—While most PC Card devices are powered by the PC Card slot, some devices that can be connected to multiple interface types have on/off switches.

If a PC Card is not completely inserted into the PC Card slot, you need to eject it and slide it in all the way. When it is installed, you should see a PC Card icon appear in the Windows system tray, by default, at the bottom of the screen (next to the clock). Windows XP refers to this icon as the Safely Remove Hardware icon.

If you have fully inserted a PC Card into the PC Card slot, and it is not recognized, there are three possible reasons:

- Windows cannot locate drivers for the PC Card
- The PC Card configuration software used by Windows is not loaded
- The PC Card configuration software used by Windows might have a problem

→ See "Using the Device Manager," p. 480 for details on troubleshooting hardware devices.

→ See "Hardware Resources," p. 117 for details on how IRQs, I/O port addresses, and memory addresses are used by hardware.

Open the Device Manager and verify that the PC Card or CardBus (PCMCIA) controller is available and working properly. If the controller is visible, but doesn't report any problems, look for the icon for the device you installed. If it was recognized as a PC Card or CardBus device, it will be listed in the PCMCIA category in Device Manager. If you don't see the device listed in the PCMCIA category, it might be listed in the Other Devices category (see Figure 3.12). Open the device's properties sheet to verify that the device is installed in the PCMCIA slot. Follow the troubleshooting instructions listed; normally, you will need to install the correct driver for the device to enable Windows to recognize it.

If the controller is not visible, run Add New Hardware and install or troubleshoot it. A PC Card or CardBus controller is a very resource-hungry beast, using an IRQ, several memory ranges, and several I/O port address ranges. However, it should work correctly unless its drivers have been corrupted or another device is using one or more of the same memory or I/O port address ranges. If the controller is displayed, but has problems, use the status listed in the controller's properties sheet to determine the problem and solve it.

Device is connected to the CardBus slot

Problem with device

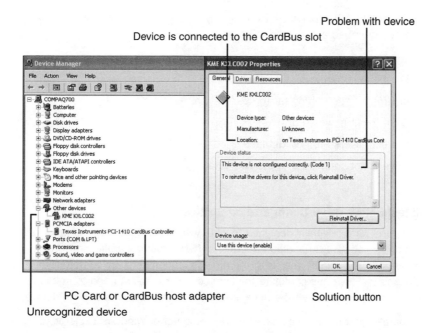

PC Card or CardBus host adapter

Solution button

Unrecognized device

FIGURE 3.12
An unrecognized device installed in a PCMCIA (PC Card or CardBus) slot.

→ *For more information on using the Solution button shown in Figure 3.12, see "Solving Resource Conflicts with Device Manager," p. 481.*

If the drive attached to the PC Card is not connected to a power source (if it has one) or turned on, the card might be recognized, but the drive will not work. Turn the drive on. If the drive won't power up, check the power connection to the drive.

Determining That the PC Card Drive Is Defective

A PC Card drive is a more complex device than other drives because the drive itself may be working but the PC Card interface might not work correctly. If the PC Card drive can be connected to another type of interface and the drive works correctly, the PC Card interface is probably defective and should be replaced. If the PC Card slot in the computer works with other types of PC Card devices (modems, network adapters, I/O ports, and so forth), but won't work with your PC Card drive, the drive (or its device drivers) is clearly at fault.

If you have loaded the correct drivers for your PC Card drive on a system with a working PC Card slot and the drive can't be detected after trying all the steps listed above, contact the vendor for help. The drive might be defective and need to be serviced or replaced.

Troubleshooting a Parallel Port Drive

Before the advent of USB and IEEE-1394 ports, parallel ports were commonly used for external drive interfacing with both desktop and notebook computers; they are still useful for situations in which you want to share a drive among systems that lack USB or IEEE-1394 ports. However, if any of the following are true, you won't be able to detect or use a parallel-port drive:

- You haven't run the configuration software supplied with the drive
- Parallel port hardware resources conflict with another device
- Incorrect mode setting for the parallel port
- Drive is not powered on
- Correct drivers are not installed
- Drive is not connected to the computer

Troubleshooting Drive Configuration Software

Parallel ports were originally designed to work with parallel printers; all other uses require driver software. In addition to driver software, some parallel-port drives (such as the Iomega Zip) require the user to run configuration software to detect the parallel port and the drive and configure the connection. You might need to install this software before you connect the drive; see the drive's documentation for details.

If your parallel port drive is not visible in My Computer or Windows Explorer, you should rerun the configuration software program, even if you've run it before. If the configuration program can't locate the drive, check the other items listed below to locate the source of your problem.

Troubleshooting Hardware Conflicts with Parallel Ports

→ See "Using the Device Manager," p. 480, for details.

If you find that your parallel port was already configured properly, or if changing it to the proper setting hasn't alleviated the problem, then it's time to look elsewhere for the cause. To see if there are hardware conflicts or driver problems with the parallel port, open the Device Manager.

Parallel ports built into the motherboard are usually configured as ISA devices, which means they cannot share IRQ settings with other devices. Parallel ports on ISA cards are also ISA devices. Parallel ports on PCI cards are PnP devices that can share IRQ settings with other cards.

Troubleshooting Parallel Port Mode Settings

→ For details, see "Using the Device Manager," p. 480, for details.

→ For more details about accessing and using the system BIOS setup program, see "BIOS Setup," p. 104.

While Windows can print to many parallel port printers regardless of the port settings, most parallel port drives require that the port be configured as an EPP or ECP port and not have any hardware resource conflicts with other devices.

To check or change the parallel port mode and hardware resource settings currently in use for a built-in parallel port

1. Restart the computer.
2. Start the system BIOS setup program.
3. Display the menu that contains the parallel (LPT) port settings (see Figure 3.13).

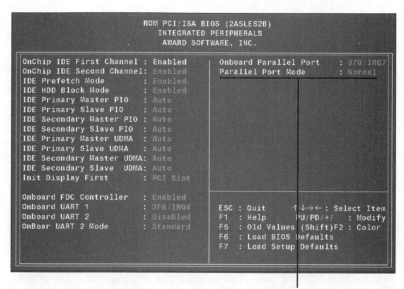

Parallel port setting

FIGURE 3.13
A typical computer's BIOS configuration screen for built-in parallel ports; the NORMAL setting shown here doesn't support bi-directional devices such as drives and should be changed to bi-directional, EPP, or ECP as recommended by the drive vendor.

4. Compare the current parallel port setting to the setting recommended for the drive. If the current parallel port setting is not configured properly for the drive, change it to a suitable setting. This setting most likely should be EPP or ECP, but check your drive's manual to be sure.

5. If you need to change hardware resource settings such as IRQ, DMA, or I/O port address to avoid conflicts with another device (as displayed by Device Manager), select non-conflicting settings.

6. Save any changes you made to the BIOS configuration, and restart the computer.

Troubleshooting Add-On Parallel Port Configuration Issues

If you have installed an add-on parallel port card (see Figure 3.14), you need to configure the card using its own setup features. If the card uses an ISA expansion slot, it might use jumper blocks or a software setup program to configure card settings such as parallel port mode or hardware resource settings. PCI parallel port cards are configured with Windows's Plug and Play technology.

➔ *See "PCI Configuration," p. 112 for more about the differences between PCI and ISA slots and resource usage.*

If you are using an add-on parallel port card, see the card's documentation for details on how to configure it.

Cautions and Warnings

Don't panic if the Windows Device Manager shows your second parallel port cheerily sharing IRQ settings with other devices. A PCI parallel port is designed to do this. However, an ISA parallel port card is just as limited as the built-in parallel ports on most systems; it needs its own IRQ to work correctly.

Troubleshooting Storage Devices

FIGURE 3.14

A typical computer with a built-in parallel port and an add-on parallel port card.

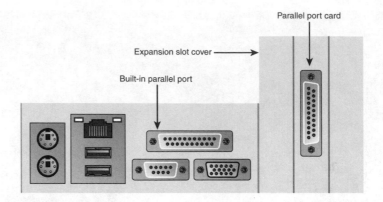

Troubleshooting Parallel Port Cabling and Power Issues

Because many different types of cabling with different pinouts are used for parallel-port devices, make sure you use the cable provided by the vendor for your parallel-port drive. If the cable is not long enough, you might need to extend the cable with a straight-through cable, such as the type sold for computer to parallel switchbox connections. Don't use a cable made for file transfers, as it crosses some wires and omits other wires needed for parallel devices. If the cable has cracks or cuts in the jacket, the signal wires inside might be damaged; order a replacement from the drive vendor.

If you have your computer's parallel port configured as an EPP, ECP, or EPP/ECP port, make sure any extension cable you use corresponds to the IEEE-1284 parallel port standard. Cables that aren't IEEE-1284 compliant might not work because some pins in the cable connector which are needed for fast IEEE-1284 modes aren't used in non-compliant cables.

Be sure you use the power adapter provided with the drive; buy a replacement from the drive vendor instead of looking for a generic replacement. Most power adapters made for drives have non-standard voltage and amperage ratings, and third-party generic replacements won't work and might damage the drive.

Use the thumbscrews on the parallel cable to securely attach the cable to the parallel ports on the drive and the computer. Since the parallel cable is very heavy, pushing the cable into place could cause a poor connection.

As with other external drives, parallel-port drives must be turned on before they can be recognized and used. If the drive's software was installed and the drive was turned on and connected to a properly configured parallel port without any resource conflicts, but the drive can't be recognized, you might need to update the drive's device drivers. Check with the vendor's Web site for updates and details.

Troubleshooting Parallel Port Daisy-Chaining Issues

Because parallel ports were not originally designed to connect to devices other than printers, daisy-chaining a drive and another device other than a printer to a parallel port might not work (normally, a drive plus a printer works with little difficulty).

If you have the drive plugged into another device that is plugged into the parallel port, make sure the other device and the drive are turned on before you turn on the computer. If the drive still won't work, shut down the computer and all devices and plug your drive directly into the parallel port. If the drive works when it's plugged directly into the parallel port, but not when it's connected to the other device, you might not be able to use the two devices on the same port. Try adjusting the mode (EPP, ECP, EPP/ECP) and connect the other device to the drive to see if reversing the order of devices in the daisy-chain will work correctly.

Determining That a Parallel Port Drive Is Defective

If you have checked parallel-port settings and hardware resources, verified proper connection of cables and power, and adjusted the connection order of the drive and any other parallel-port, and the drive doesn't work, but a printer or other parallel-port devices are working, the drive is probably defective.

However, if no devices (solely or in a daisy-chain) will work with the parallel port, the port itself is defective. Contact your vendor for service.

Preparing a Hard Disk for Use

Preparing a hard disk for use in your PC is the process by which you set up the drive so that it can hold your data (everything from Windows to programs and documents files). Usually you'll only need to go through this process when installing a new drive. Occasionally, however, you might decide it's time to give your PC a fresh start, by erasing everything on your drives, re-preparing them, and installing fresh copies of your software. (If you ever decide to do this, be very sure that you've backed up any essential data to another storage medium.)

In most PCs, the system BIOS handles configuration duties for ATA/IDE hard drives (the standard type of hard drive found in most systems). The more expensive (and slightly more advanced) SCSI hard drives are configured by the SCSI BIOS, which is usually found on special SCSI controller cards designed for connecting these devices.

Preparing either of these types of hard disks requires the use of your operating system's disk preparation utilities (Disk Management in Windows XP or Windows 2000; FDISK and FORMAT in Windows 9x/Me). These programs process the disk according to what the system or SCSI BIOS report. If the system BIOS is not configured properly, an ATA/IDE drive will not be recognized at its full capacity. An outdated SCSI BIOS can also prevent SCSI hard drives from being recognized at their full capacity.

Most systems are set to auto-detect the capacity of ATA/IDE hard disks when you install them and turn on the computer; this type of hard disk is the most common type. You can determine if your version of Windows can view the entire capacity of the drive during the disk preparation process.

SCSI drives are detected by the SCSI BIOS built into SCSI host adapters built for hard drives (low-end SCSI host adapters made for scanners and optical drives don't have a BIOS and can't be used for bootable drives). After the SCSI BIOS detects the drive, the drive must be prepared with a host-adapter-specific low-level formatter program before they can be prepared by Windows; see the manual for your SCSI host adapter for details.

Preparing an Additional Hard Disk with Windows XP/2000

The process of installing a hard disk varies according to whether the drive is being added to your computer or is being installed as a replacement. The process described in this section assumes that you are adding an additional hard disk to your existing computer.

Before you start this process

1. Make sure your computer recognizes the hard disk.

2. Decide whether you want to treat the new drive as a single drive letter, or subdivide it into two or more logical drives (having a single drive letter is easier to configure).

3. Decide which file system you want to use for your new drive (usually FAT32 or NTFS).

Fast Track to Success

If all you use is Windows XP, you should use the NTFS (New Technology File System) option to format your disk. NTFS lets you use advanced features such as encryption (which can be used to "hide" files on your system from other users) and compression (which uses less disk space). However, if you installed Windows XP to work in a dual-boot configuration with Windows 98 or Windows Me (you select the Windows version you want to work with when you boot), you might prefer to choose FAT32 for your new drive. Both NTFS and FAT32 can work with large drives, but FAT32 drives can be read by Windows 98 and Windows Me.

What if you want to share your files over a network? Use NTFS, no matter what version of Windows other users have. The network software will take care of recognizing the drive's contents, and NTFS lets you apply better security to each shared folder.

To prepare an additional hard drive for use with Windows XP/2000

1. Open the Start menu, right-click on My Computer and select Manage.

2. Click the Storage icon in the left-hand window of the Computer Management screen.

3. Double-click Disk Management (local) in the right-hand window. The new drive will appear as Unallocated in the display window if the drive is brand-new (see Figure 3.15). If the drive has already been partitioned, the display will indicate what type of a partition is on the drive. You can right-click on the additional drive's partition to remove it, but this will delete its contents. You should use My Computer to view the drive's contents first and copy any files you want to keep to another drive before you continue.

The drive's listed capacity should be similar to the capacity listed on the drive's faceplate or box. If not, see "Troubleshooting Problems with Recognizing Full Drive Capacity," p. 229.

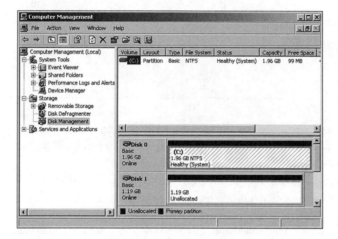

FIGURE 3.15
A 1.2GB drive (Disk 1) before partitioning and formatting (which assigns drive letters to the drive) as displayed by the Windows XP Disk Management tool.

4. Right-click the Unallocated drive and select New Partition to start the New Partition Wizard.

5. Click Next after reading the introduction to the wizard.

6. Select Extended partition and click Next to create an extended partition (which will be divided into one or more logical, non-bootable drive letters).

Cautions and Warnings

If you want to boot from a drive you add to your system as well as from your normal drive, you will need to install a boot manager program such as Boot Magic (provided as part of PowerQuest's Partition Magic) or V-com's System Commander (also part of Partition Commander) and prepare the drive as directed by the vendor. See the documentation for the boot manager program you prefer for details.

Learn more about Partition Magic and Boot Magic at http://www.powerquest.com.

Learn more about Partition Commander and System Commander at http://www.v-com.com.

7. If you want to use the entire hard disk for one or more logical drives, click Next. To leave some empty space on the drive to format under a different file system or for use by another operating system, adjust the partition size and click Next (see Figure 3.16).

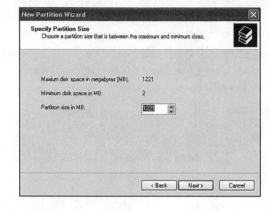

8. The wizard displays the settings you have selected; click Finish to perform the listed operations and convert the drive to an extended partition containing free space.

9. Right-click the free space and select New Logical Drive to set up drive letter(s) to use the free space inside the extended partition (Figure 3.17). Click Next.

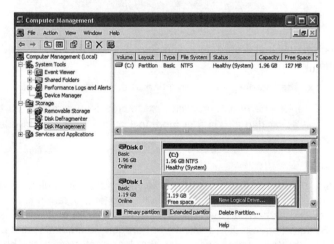

10. Click Next to create a logical drive.

11. Specify the size of the logical drive if you want to create more than one logical drive; if you click Next without specifying a size, the entire free space will be converted into a single drive letter.

12. By default, Windows assigns the next available drive letter; click Next to accept it, or use the pull-down menu to choose a different drive letter and

then click Next. Other options listed (mount in empty NTFS folder or Do not assign a drive letter) are for advanced users.

13. Select a format option (see Figure 3.18); I recommend you use the defaults (NTFS and default allocation unit size) unless you need to access the drive by booting the computer with Windows 98 or Me, in which case, use FAT32. Change New Volume to a descriptive name you prefer. Select Enable file and folder compression if you want the option to try it later. Click Next.

Change to FAT32 only if Windows 98/Me will be used to boot the system and access this drive.

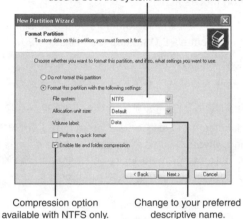

FIGURE 3.18
Selecting format options for the new logical drive.

Compression option available with NTFS only.

Change to your preferred descriptive name.

14. The wizard displays the settings you have selected (see Figure 3.19); click Finish to perform the listed operations and convert the free space into a drive letter or click Back to make changes. The format operation takes a few minutes to complete.

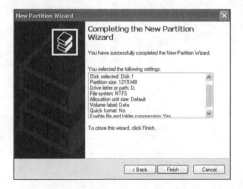

FIGURE 3.19
The New Partition Wizard displays the settings selected for preparing the new drive.

15. When the format process is completed, the drive is identified with a drive letter and its status should be displayed as Healthy (contact the drive vendor if the drive is not identified as Healthy). Click File, Exit to close Computer Management. You can use the newly prepared drive immediately.

Preparing a Bootable Hard Disk with Windows XP

You can prepare a drive with a primary partition (primary partitions are bootable) with the Disk Management tool described in the previous section. Simply select Primary partition when prompted and follow the general outline given above. Generally, you will select this option if you are planning to install a boot manager program and another operating system on your computer.

➔ *To learn more about accessing your BIOS and changing its settings, see "BIOS Setup," p. 104.*

➔ *The drive's listed capacity should be similar to the capacity listed on the drive's faceplate or box. If not, see "Trouble-shooting Problems with Recognizing Full Drive Capacity," p. 229.*

However, if you want to prepare a new hard drive on a brand-new system (one that doesn't have Windows XP already installed), you can perform this task as part of the Windows installation process.

1. Verify that your CD-ROM drive is listed before your hard disk in the boot sequence of your computer's BIOS setup (see Figure 3.20).

2. Insert the Windows XP CD-ROM into your CD-ROM drive.

3. Start your computer.

4. The Windows XP installation program starts after the CD boots the computer.

5. When prompted, select the type of file system (NTFS or FAT32) you want for the hard disk and whether you want to use the hard disk as a single drive letter or subdivided into two or more logical drives. Windows XP will prepare each drive letter you specify during its setup process.

FIGURE 3.20
This computer needs to have the CD-ROM moved before the hard disk in the boot sequence to enable the computer to boot from the Windows XP CD-ROM.

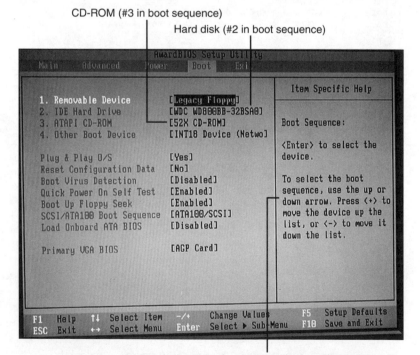

CD-ROM (#3 in boot sequence)

Hard disk (#2 in boot sequence)

Instructions for changing the boot sequence

On the Web

Read Microsoft Knowledge Base article "HOW TO: Partition and Format a Hard Disk in Windows XP" (#Q313348) to learn more about the process of preparing a hard disk with Disk Management or with the Windows XP setup program. Set your browser to http://support.microsoft.com and enter Q313348 in the search box.

Preparing an Additional Hard Disk with Windows 9x/Me

The process for installing a hard disk with Windows 9x/Me is similar whether you are adding a hard disk to a working system or preparing a hard disk for a new installation of Windows 9x/Me. Unlike the wizard-driven Disk Management interface used by Windows XP (and Windows 2000), Windows 9x/Me use separate programs for disk partitioning (FDISK) and disk formatting. Disk partitioning must be started from the command prompt, but you can use Windows Explorer/My Computer to format the hard disk after it's been partitioned with FDISK. In this section, you will learn how to prepare a hard disk you are adding to an existing system already running Windows.

In Windows 9x/Me

1. Click Start, Run.

2. Type FDISK and click OK.

3. Press Y (yes) and ENTER to accept large hard disk support on the first screen you see after starting FDISK; this option enables you to use all of the space on a hard disk as a single drive letter with Windows by using the FAT32 file system; you can also create multiple drive letters if you like. If you press N (no) and ENTER, your maximum size per drive letter is just 2GB.

4. FDISK displays the startup menu (see Figure 3.21). To select a menu option, type the number of the option and press ENTER.

Current drive number

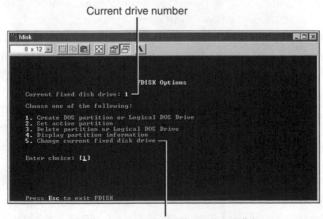

Omitted on systems with one hard disk

FIGURE 3.21
The FDISK main menu on a system with two or more hard disks installed; FDISK omits menu item #5 if the system has only one hard disk.

5. By default, FDISK works with hard disk #1. To switch to the newly-installed drive (drive #2 or higher), type 5 (Change current fixed disk drive) and press ENTER. The capacity of the newly-installed drive will be displayed without any drive letter as free space (Figure 3.22). The drive's listed capacity should be similar to the capacity listed on the drive's faceplate or box. If not, see "Troubleshooting Problems with Recognizing Full Drive Capacity," p. 229. Type the number of the newly-installed drive and press ENTER to select the drive and return to the FDISK main menu.

Cautions and Warnings

If you are adding an additional hard disk to your computer, it's critical that you switch to the new disk drive with FDISK before you run commands. FDISK destroys any information already on the drive.

Use the #4 option (Display partition information) from the main FDISK menu after you select a drive number to see if the current drive contains any disk partitions. If it does, there might be data on the drive. Copy any files you want to keep before you re-partition the disk with FDISK.

FIGURE 3.22
An unpartitioned drive as seen by FDISK.

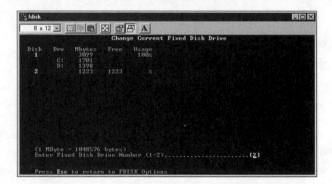

6. To create a partition on the drive, type 1 (Create DOS partition) from the FDISK main menu and press ENTER.

7. To create a new partition whose drive letters will follow the current hard drive letters on your system, type 2 (Create Extended DOS partition) in the Create DOS Partition or Logical DOS Drive Menu (see Figure 3.23) and press ENTER.

8. Unless you want to leave room for another operating system in the future, press ENTER to accept the default (entire drive as an extended partition). The extended partition size will be displayed on screen. Press ESC to continue.

   The drive's listed capacity should be similar to the capacity listed on the drive's faceplate or box. If not, see "Troubleshooting Problems with Recognizing Full Drive Capacity," p. 229.

9. Specify the size of the logical drive if you want to create more than one logical drive (see Figure 3.24); if you press ENTER without specifying a size, the entire free space will be converted into a single drive letter.

Used most often when you are
preparing a drive in a brand-new system
for a Windows 9x/Me installation.

Use to add a drive to an existing
system and keep the current drive.

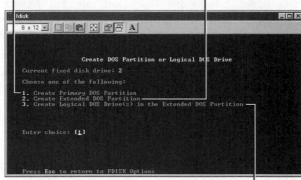

FIGURE 3.23
*The Create DOS
Partition Menu in
FDISK.*

Starts automatically after you
create an extended partition.

Change to indicate desired
size of logical drive.

Total size of extended partition.

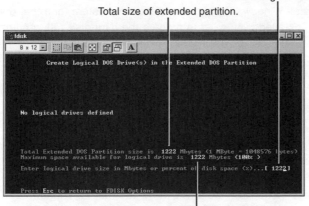

FIGURE 3.24
*Specifying the size of
the logical drive in
FDISK.*

Amount remaining for logical drives.

10. The logical drive letter and size will be displayed If you didn't use all the
    extended partition for the logical drive, you will be prompted to repeat step 8.
    Press ESC to continue.

11. After you have allocated all the space in the extended partition to logical dri-
    ves, you will return to the FDISK main menu. Press ESC to exit the menu;
    press ESC again after you read the reminder to shut down Windows and
    reboot before you format the drive letter(s) you created in FDISK.

12. Shut down Windows and restart.

13. After Windows restarts, open the Windows Explorer. Your newly-created drive
    letter(s) will be displayed. Click on each one and Windows will display a Disk is
    not Formatted dialog. Click Yes to format the drive; enter a label (a descriptive

name for the drive), click Full (format type), and click Start. Click OK to format the disk and click Close after the format process is over. Go to step 14.

14. If Windows doesn't display the "Disk is Not Formatted" prompt, right-click on the drive you want to format and select Properties. The drive's file system should be displayed as RAW with 0 bytes of used space and 0 bytes of free space. Click OK.

   Right-click on the drive again and select FORMAT. Make sure you are NOT formatting a drive that contains data (unless you either no longer need that data or it you have backed it up to another medium). The FORMAT option lists the capacity of the drive. Enter a label (a descriptive name for the drive), click Full (format type), and click Start. Click OK to format the disk and click Close after the format process is over.

At this point, your drive should be ready to go. As a final check, right-click on the newly formatted drive's Windows icon, select Properties, select Tools, and select Error-checking to check the drive for errors before you use the drive.

Preparing a Bootable Hard Disk with Windows 9x/Me

If you need to install Windows 9x/Me on a brand-new system (one that doesn't have Windows already installed), you need to prepare the hard disk with a primary (bootable) partition that can be used for the Windows installation.

You will need to create a Windows Emergency Startup Disk from your Windows CD to perform this task.

Fast Track to Success

The Windows 98 CD-ROM contains a program called FAT32EBD.EXE that can be used to create a startup disk; you can run this from another computer that uses Windows to create a startup disk if you don't have one handy.

Read Microsoft Knowledge Base article "How to Create a Windows 98 Startup Disk that Supports FAT32" (Q187632) for details.

Set your browser to http://support.microsoft.com and enter Q187632 in the search box.

If you're now using Windows Me, you can still use a Windows 98 startup disk to partition and format your hard disk before installing Windows Me.

To set up your new hard disk as a single bootable drive

1. Boot the computer with the Windows emergency startup disk.

2. Type FDISK at the command prompt and press ENTER.

3. Press Y to enable Large Disk Support when prompted. If you select N (no), FDISK will prepare only the first 2GB of your disk.

4. Select #1, Create DOS Partition or Logical DOS Drive from the main FDISK menu (refer to Figure 3.21).

5. From the Create DOS Partition or Logical DOS Drive menu (refer to Figure 3.23), press Enter to select #1, Create a Primary DOS partition.

6. Press Enter again to select the entire usable capacity of the drive as a single primary partition and make it active.

7. After you press Enter again to accept these changes, you're prompted to shut down the system and reboot it.

   This creates a single primary partition on the hard disk that must be formatted by the Format program using the system option before it can be used to boot the system.

8. After your computer reboots, start the system with CD-ROM support.

9. Type FORMAT C:/S at the command prompt and press ENTER.

10. Follow the prompts to format your hard disk and transfer system files.

11. After the format process is over, you can install Windows from your CD-ROM drive.

To use FDISK to set up the only hard drive on a system as two or more drive letters with a bootable partition, follow this procedure:

1. Boot the computer with the Windows emergency startup disk.

2. Type FDISK at the command prompt and press ENTER.

3. Choose Enable Large Disk Support when prompted to allow partitions larger than 2GB in size.

4. Select #1, Create DOS Partition or Logical DOS Drive from the main menu.

5. From the Create DOS Partition or Logical DOS Drive menu, press Enter to select #1, Create a Primary DOS Partition.

6. Type N (no) when asked if you want to use the entire capacity of the drive.

7. Enter the amount of space you want to use for the primary partition in either MB or percentages (for example, to use 2GB, enter 2048; to use 50% of the drive, enter 50%) and press Enter (see Figure 3.25).

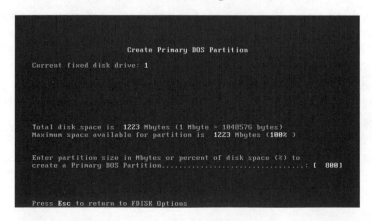

FIGURE 3.25
The primary partition on this 1.2GB drive is being set as 800MB by FDISK.

The drive's listed capacity should be similar to the capacity listed on the drive's faceplate or box. If not, see "Troubleshooting Problems with Recognizing Full Drive Capacity," p. 229.

8. Press Esc to return to the main FDISK menu.

9. Because you created a primary partition using only a portion of the disk space, a warning appears to remind you that the primary partition is not yet active; it must be marked active to be bootable.

10. To mark the primary partition as active, type 2 (Set Active Partition) from the FDISK main menu and press Enter to display the Set Active Partition menu.

11. Type the number of the partition you want to make active (normally 1), and press Enter. The status line will display an A for active partition, as in Figure 3.26. Press Esc to return to the main FDISK menu.

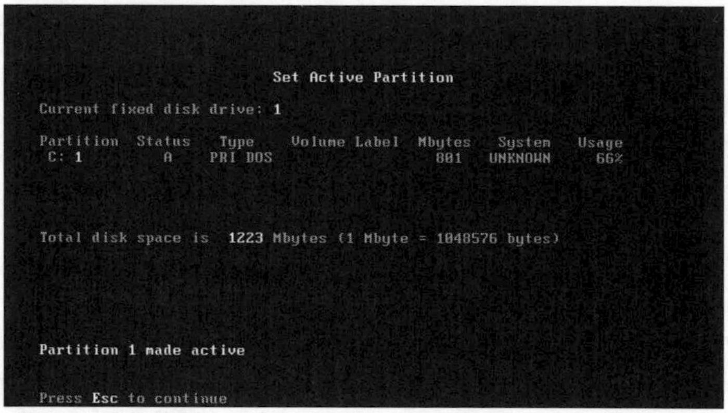

FIGURE 3.26
The 800MB primary partition after FDISK sets it as Active. To be bootable, this partition must also be formatted with the /S (system) option.

```
                              Set Active Partition

Current fixed disk drive: 1

Partition  Status    Type    Volume Label   Mbytes   System    Usage
   C: 1       A     PRI DOS                    801    UNKNOWN    66%



Total disk space is  1223 Mbytes (1 Mbyte = 1048576 bytes)




Partition 1 made active


Press Esc to continue
```

12. To prepare the rest of the drive for use by Windows 98, select #1, Create DOS Partition or Logical DOS Drive from the FDISK main menu.

13. From the Create DOS Partition menu, select #2, Create an Extended Partition.

14. Press Enter to accept the default (the remaining capacity of the drive); the logical drives will be stored in the extended partition.

15. Create one more or logical drives when prompted, specifying the size you want for each letter. The drive letter for each logical drive is listed; note the letters because you will need to format each logical drive after you finish using FDISK and reboot.

16. When the entire capacity of the drive is used, the FDISK display will resemble Figure 3.27. Press Y to view the logical drives stored in the extended partition.

17. After you press Enter again to accept these changes, you're prompted to shut down the system and reboot it.

18. After your computer reboots, start the system with CD-ROM support.

19. Type FORMAT C:/S at the command prompt and press ENTER.

20. Follow the prompts to format your hard disk and transfer system files; specify a descriptive name for the drive when prompted such as WINDOWS.

The Volume Label remains blank until the drive is formatted; both Format and Label can apply a volume label, or the user can choose not to use a volume label.

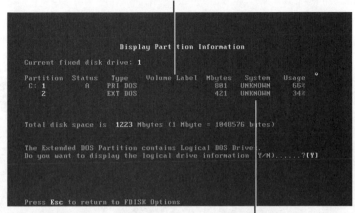

FIGURE 3.27
This drive contains both a primary and an extended partition; logical drives in the extended partition make this entire drive available to Windows 98.

The system is listed as unknown on an unformatted drive.

21. Type FORMAT D: at the command prompt and press ENTER to format the D: drive; follow the prompts to complete the procedure. Specify a descriptive name for the drive when prompted such as DATA. Repeat as needed for any additional drive letters you created with FDISK.

22. After the format process is over, you can install Windows from your CD-ROM drive.

Troubleshooting Problems with Recognizing Full Drive Capacity

If Disk Management or FDISK doesn't report the full capacity of the drive during the preparation process, check the following:

- Windows 95 can recognize only 32GB of disk space, regardless of the actual capacity of your drive or your system BIOS. If you want to use a larger drive with Windows 95, you must prepare it with the special disk-setup tools provided by the drive vendor instead of with FDISK and FORMAT, or upgrade to a newer version of Windows.

- If you are using Windows 98 or Windows 98SE with a hard disk greater than 64MB, you need updated versions of the FDISK program; the original versions of FDISK displays only the capacity of the drive above 64MB. For example, an 80GB drive would be displayed as only about 16GB (80-64=16). Use the search engine at www.microsoft.com for article number Q263044, which contains links to the updated FDISK files. Unfortunately, these problems aren't limited to FDISK. FORMAT for Windows 98/Me won't display the correct size either; see article number Q263045 at the same Microsoft site to download updated files. If updates to FDISK and FORMAT still don't display the correct size for the drive, keep reading.

- Make sure you are using Auto-configure in the system BIOS setup for the hard disk (see Figure 3.28); this enables LBA (logical block addressing) mode, which allows the entire capacity of the drive to be available in Windows.

FIGURE 3.28

A typical system BIOS hard disk setup screen with both User-Defined and Auto-Configured drives listed.

```
                       ROM PCI/ISA BIOS (2A5LES2B)
                          STANDARD CMOS SETUP
                          AWARD SOFTWARE, INC.

    Date (mm:dd:yy)  : Mon, Dec 20 1999
    Time (hh:mm:ss)  : 20 : 10 : 56

    HARD DISKS         TYPE    SIZE    CYLS HEAD PRECOMP LANDZ SECTOR  MODE

    Primary Master   : User   13013   1582  255      0  25227     63  LBA
    Primary Slave    : Auto       0      0    0      0      0      0  AUTO
    Secondary Master : Auto       0      0    0      0      0      0  AUTO
    Secondary Slave  : Auto       0      0    0      0      0      0  AUTO

    Drive A    : 1.44M, 3.5 in.
    Drive B    : None
    Floppy 3 Mode Support : Disabled        ┌──────────────────────────────┐
                                            │ Base Memory     :      640K  │
    Video      : EGA/VGA                    │ Extended Memory : 130048K    │
    Halt On    : All Errors                 │ Other Memory    :      384K  │
                                            │                              │
                                            │ Total Memory    : 131072K    │
                                            └──────────────────────────────┘

    ↑↓→←: Select item        PU/PD/+/-  : Modify
    F1  : Help               (Shift)F2  : Change Color
```

- If the drive is Auto-configured but is recognized as only about 8GB by Disk Management or FDISK regardless of its actual size, the system BIOS doesn't support a feature called extended disk drive (EDD—also known as INT13h extensions), which enable drives up to 137GB to be supported by the BIOS.

- If the system locks up after installing the new drive, or is recognized as only 2.1GB or 4.2GB regardless of its actual size, the system BIOS is not compatible with the full capacity of the drive.

To enable the computer to work with the entire capacity of the drive, use one of the following options, listed in order from the best to worst option:

- Upgrade the system BIOS if an upgrade is available to handle the larger hard disk; download and install the BIOS upgrade from the system or motherboard maker's Web site and retry the drive installation.

- Install an ATA BIOS support card; these cards have on-board BIOS chips that override the limitations of your system BIOS and enable your computer to use the larger drive. Your computer must have an open PCI or ISA slot on its motherboard to use this option (see "Expansion Slots," p. 97).

- If you use Windows 9x/Me, check to see if the drive's manufacturer provides a utility program that also includes a BIOS override software option. If they do have one, you may need to install that to allow your PC to recognize your drive's full capacity. Examples of these types of programs include Disc Wizard, EZ-BIOS, or Disk Manager. As a general rule, I don't recommend going this route. It prevents you from using standard boot sector repair programs if your drive becomes unbootable, limiting your recovery options in an emergency. On the other hand, these programs don't cost any money; they either should be included on a utility disk packaged with the drive or are made available for downloaded from the drive manufacturer's Web site.

BIOS Upgrade Cards to the Rescue

If your computer can't handle your ATA/IDE hard disk at full capacity and a BIOS upgrade isn't available or doesn't solve the problem, your best option is to install a BIOS override card. Some drives, such as certain Maxtor 120GB and 160GB drives, include a high-speed PCI interface card that enables the drives to be used at full capacity; the card is also available separately. Get more information about the Maxtor ATA/133 PCI Adapter Card from http://www.maxtor.com.

Other cards from different vendors include

- MicroFirmware's ATA Pro Flash (uses an ISA slot); http://www.firmware.com
- ESupport's LBA Pro (uses an ISA slot); http://www.esupport.com
- Promise Technology's Ultra100 TX2 and Ultra133 TX2 (uses a PCI slot); http://www.promise.com
- SIIG's UltraATA 133 PCI (uses a PCI slot); http://www.siig.com

The PCI cards also have on-board ATA/IDE controllers, enabling you to connect up to four additional drives to your system.

If you are installing a SCSI hard disk, the BIOS on the SCSI host adapter, rather than the system BIOS, is used to report the capacity of the drive to the operating system. If the full capacity of your SCSI hard disk is not detected by your host adapter's BIOS setup program, contact the SCSI host adapter manufacturer for a BIOS upgrade.

Troubleshooting Disk Partitioning Problems

If you run FDISK or the Disk Management disk preparation wizard and find that you are unable to partition your drive, or that the drive you partitioned has reverted to an unpartitioned state after you restart your system, you might have the write-protect hard disk feature enabled in your system BIOS.

Many systems have this feature, which is designed to prevent boot sector viruses from attacking your computer. However, this feature also prevents the boot sector from being changed during the disk preparation process. To disable this feature

1. Restart the computer.
2. Press the key(s) that start the BIOS setup program when prompted.

3. Check the BIOS Features or Advanced BIOS setup menus for an option such as "Write-Protect Boot Sector" or "Anti-Virus Boot Sector." Disable this option.

4. Save the changes and exit to restart your computer.

5. Retry disk preparation.

On the Web

The Trend ChipAway anti-virus feature used by some motherboards does not need to be disabled to enable you to prepare a new hard disk. Your motherboard might display Trend ChipAway if it's active during system startup, or you would see this option in your system BIOS setup. To learn about the difference between ChipAway and conventional write-protect or anti-virus hard disk BIOS options, see the Trend Micro ChipAway Web site:

http://www.antivirus.com/products/chipaway/

If your BIOS doesn't have write-protect or anti-virus boot sector protection enabled but you can't prepare the hard disk, check the following:

- Disable anti-virus software during the hard disk preparation process; some programs of this type can interfere with disk preparation.

- Shut down the computer, open the case, and inspect the data cable running between the drive and the host adapter. Remove and reattach the data cable where it connects to the drive and host adapter; a loose data cable can prevent successful disk preparation.

- Replace any data cables that are damaged (cut, scuffed, excessively creased).

Troubleshooting Booting Problems

After you've prepared a drive as a bootable drive, your computer can use it to start your system. However, the drive and your computer must be properly configured to enable this to take place.

Before you can use any type of hard, floppy, removable-media, or optical disk as a bootable drive (a drive that can start your system), the following must be true about the disk:

- The drive must be selected as a bootable device in the system BIOS (see Figure 3.29).

- The drive must be properly prepared to be bootable. A hard disk must be prepared with a primary partition, be formatted, and have system files transferred to it. Other types of media must be formatted and have system files transferred to the media.

- The drive must be properly identified in the system BIOS.

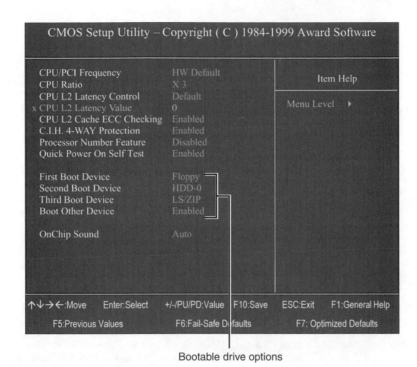

FIGURE 3.29
A typical advanced BIOS setup screen featuring a bootable drive selection option.

Bootable drive options

Troubleshooting Hard Disk or Optical Drive Bootup Problems

If you cannot start your system from a hard disk you were previously able to boot from, or you can't boot your system from a bootable Windows CD-ROM, check the following:

- A floppy disk in Drive A:—A non-bootable floppy can't be used to start a system and also stops the entire system boot process if the floppy drive is listed before the CD-ROM and hard disk in the BIOS boot sequence. Remove the disk and try to restart the system.

- The BIOS setup for the drive—Most drives use Auto as the setup type. If your drive is configured as User-Defined, check with the drive vendor's Web site to see if the values listed are correct for the drive. If they are not, reset the drive to Auto or enter the correct values, save the changes, and restart your system.

- The boot order—Your hard disk should be listed somewhere in the boot order. In Windows 2000 or XP, I recommend that order be: CD-ROM, 1st hard disk, and then any other bootable device you may have. In Windows 9x or Me (which use a floppy disk as an emergency startup disk), I recommend: floppy disk, CD-ROM drive, and then your 1st hard disk.

- Whether the drive has an active partition. A hard disk must be prepared as a primary partition and must be set as active before it can be used to start (boot) the system. Although FDISK for Windows 9x/Me isn't designed to be used with Windows 2000 or Windows XP, it can be used with any of these Windows versions to remark a primary partition as active:

1. Start the computer with a Windows 9x/Me emergency startup disk. You can borrow one from a friend or make one from a Windows 98 CD-ROM.

2. Type FDISK and press ENTER from the system prompt.

3. Press Y to accept large hard disk support.

4. Press Y to treat NTFS partitions as Large (displayed only if your hard disk was set up as NTFS initially).

5. If no partition is set active, FDISK will display a warning. Type 2 from the FDISK main menu and press ENTER, then enter the number of the partition you want to make active (normally #1). If you see more than one partition listed, select the partition listed as NTFS or FAT32.

6. Exit FDISK.

7. Remove the startup disk and restart the computer.

On the Web

If your computer can't boot from a CD-ROM drive, you might want to create a boot floppy disk that enables you to start Windows XP or Windows 2000 in an emergency. Go to http://search.microsoft.com and search for the following articles:

- Q305595 for the procedure for creating a Windows XP boot floppy disk
- Q119467 for the procedure for creating a Windows 2000 boot floppy disk

---

→ *See "Overview of Startup Problems," p. 123 for other types of startup problems and solutions.*

If you are having problems booting your system and your drives and boot sequence are configured correctly, you might be having Windows-related startup problems.

Preparing Other Drives to Act as Bootable Devices

Having a bootable storage device other than your hard disk drive in case your hard drive fails for some unforeseen reason can be critical in recovering from a PC disaster. In cases where you cannot boot your PC from its hard disk, you could be helpless if you don't have some other means to boot up. While having bootable media for a floppy, CD-ROM, or other device won't fix the source problem, it can allow you to keep troubleshooting tools and utilities accessible in case of emergency. If you want to boot from other types of drives

- The drive type you want to use must be listed as a bootable device in your system BIOS.
- You must make sure the drive appears in the boot order before the hard disk.
- You must prepare the media to act as a bootable device.

Most recent computers can use optical drives (CD-ROM, CD-RW, DVD-ROM), floppy drives, and SCSI drives as bootable devices. Some can also use removable media drives such as LS-120/LS-240 SuperDisk drives and Zip drives as bootable devices. On most systems, all but SCSI drives must be connected to the ATA/IDE interface; drives other than hard disks that use this interface are often referred to as ATAPI drives. Some systems can also boot from drives connected to the USB port.

Windows 2000 and Windows XP can be started from the hard disk, high-capacity removable media that is prepared as a fixed disk, or from the Windows 2000 or Windows XP upgrade or OEM CD. See the previous section for information on how to make a bootable floppy disk.

If you want to prepare a CD-R, CD-RW, or recordable/rewriteable DVD disc as a startup disc with Windows, see the instructions for your CD mastering program. If you are a Windows 9x/Me user, keep in mind that you still need to create a bootable floppy in order to provide a source for boot files.

You can create a bootable floppy disk you can use to start your computer in case of emergencies with Windows 9x or Windows Me through the Add/Remove Programs icon in Control Panel.

1. Open Add/Remove Programs
2. Click Windows Startup Disk
3. Follow the prompts to create a startup disk

The Windows 98 and Windows Me emergency disks contain drivers compatible with most CD-ROM or similar optical drives so it can be used to reinstall Windows from the CD-ROM. If you still use Windows 95, the Windows 95 emergency disk doesn't contain CD-ROM device drivers. You can add them yourself or borrow a Windows 98 emergency disk from another user to start your computer with CD-ROM support.

Fast Track to Success

If you want more powerful diagnostics tools (including anti-virus) that you can run from a bootable disk than what the Windows emergency boot disk provides, consider picking up Norton System Works 2003 for your Windows 98, Me, 2000, or XP computer, particularly if your XP/2000 drives are formatted as FAT32 drives. Get more information at the Symantec Web site

http://www.symantec.com

If you're still using Windows 95, you need to use Norton System Works 2001. It's no longer sold at most retail stores, but various Internet closeout outlets might still have copies for sale. Use a search engine such as Google and you're likely to track down several sources.

The Professional (Pro) versions add support for drive imaging and faxing, but if you don't need those features, the standard versions work very well.

Solving UDMA Mode Problems with ATA/IDE Drives

Originally, all ATA/IDE drives used an access method called PIO (programmable input/output). Today, ATA/IDE hard drives (and some types of ATAPI drives) support faster access modes known as UDMA (also called Ultra DMA or Ultra ATA), which range from 33MHz to 66MHZ, 100MHz, and the latest 133MHz speed. If you notice the following problems, your system probably doesn't have UDMA configured correctly:

- Very slow hard disk and optical drive performance
- Inability to use disk-mastering software with your CD-RW or writeable DVD drive

To achieve a particular UDMA speed, all of the following must be present:

- The correct cable must be used. While UDMA/33 drives can use the older 40-wire IDE cable, UDMA/66 and faster drives must use the 80-wire UDMA cable.
- The drive must be configured for the fastest UDMA speed supported by both the drive and the host adapter.
- The host adapter (motherboard or slot-based) must have its Windows device drivers installed for maximum performance. View the ATA/IDE host adapters in Device Manager to determine if you need to install device drivers; if the host adapter listing in Device Manager indicate that the correct drivers are not installed, download them from the motherboard or system builder's Web site and install them. See "Using Device Manager," p. 480 for details.
- The correct UDMA speed must be selected in the system BIOS setup for the drive if User-defined, rather than AUTO, is used to configure the drive.

Because drives with fast UDMA modes are frequently used on motherboards that support slower UDMA modes, most drives are shipped with their faster UDMA modes disabled. Use the utility disk supplied with the drive, or download a utility from the drive maker's Web site, to view and change the UDMA support for your drive.

Solving Problems with Writeable CD and DVD Media

One of the most popular add-ons for computers (and an increasingly popular standard feature) is a writeable CD or DVD drive. Some of the problems you might encounter with such drives include

- Inability to write to the media
- Inability to read written media on another system
- Buffer underruns

The following sections will help you solve these problems.

Figure 3.30 displays the Record CD Setup and Project screens used by Roxio Easy CD Creator 5.x, a popular CD mastering program. This figure will be referred to frequently in the following sections.

Select to avoid buffer underruns or slow creation if your files are on removable media or network drives

Enable to avoid creating a useless "coaster" due to a buffer underrun (requires a writeable drive with this feature)

Select the write speed that matches your media

Drive selection menu

Number of CD copies to make

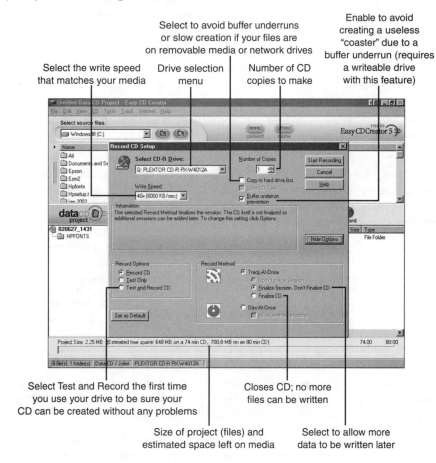

FIGURE 3.30
The Record CD Setup dialog in Roxio Easy CD Creator 5.

Select Test and Record the first time you use your drive to be sure your CD can be created without any problems

Closes CD; no more files can be written

Size of project (files) and estimated space left on media

Select to allow more data to be written later

Solving Can't Write to Media Problems

If your drive can't write to writeable media, check the following issues:

- You are trying to use the wrong type of media for your drive
- Your CD-mastering program doesn't support the drive
- You are trying to use media that has been closed (write-protected)
- You aren't running packet-writing (drag-and-drop) software
- You haven't formatted your media for packet-writing (drag-and-drop) file copying
- Your drive is damaged
- Windows XP doesn't support your writeable drive

Troubleshooting Incorrect Media and Media Usage Problems

There are more types of writeable media at your local electronics and computer store than ever before, which means that the chances are increasing that you could buy the wrong type of media for your drive or for the task you want to perform.

If you have a CD-RW drive, you can use

- CD-R media
- CD-RW media

Both types of media are single-sided; you can write on the printed surface with soft-tip markers.

CD-R media is designed to be used with CD mastering programs; you can write to it and add files to non-closed media, but you can't delete files from it. Some packet-writing programs can also use it for drag-and-drop file copying. CD-R media has a colored recording surface that might appear gold, silver, light green, or light blue depending upon the reflective surface and dye layer.

CD-RW media is designed to be used with packet-writing programs. Like conventional removable-media drives (floppy, Zip, SuperDisk, and others), you can erase CD-RW media and use it again. CD-RW media's recordable surface looks like a mirror.

Both CD-R and CD-RW media are speed-rated. If you use slower CD-R media with a faster drive, you can reduce the write speed of the drive (refer to Figure 3.30) or you can try to write at top speed and try the completed media on other drives to see if it's readable. CD-RW media, on the other hand, comes in only two speeds, but you can't cheat when you use it. High-speed CD-RW media (10x) can be used only in CD-RW drives with 10x or faster rewrite speeds. If you want to transfer data stored on CD-RW media from a 10x drive to a drive with the slower 2x or 4x rewrite speed, you must use standard speed (2x/4x) CD-RW media in your fast drive.

A number of manufacturers now make various types of writeable DVD drives. There are actually five types of writeable DVD media, and since most drives can use only one or two types, it's essential that you buy the correct type.

- DVD-RAM—A rewriteable/erasable media similar to CD-RW, but can be single or double-sided. DVD-RAM is usually kept in a closed disc caddy to protect its surfaces.
- DVD-R—A writeable/non-erasable media similar to CD-R; some DVD-RAM and all DVD-RW drives can use DVD-R media.
- DVD-RW—A single-sided rewriteable/erasable media similar to CD-RW. DVD-RW drives can also write to DVD-R media.
- DVD+RW—A rewriteable/erasable media. Also similar to CD-RW, but not interchangeable with DVD-RW or DVD-RAM.
- DVD+R—A writeable/non-erasable media. Also similar to CD-R, but not interchangeable with DVD-R. Most second generation DVD+RW drives also support this media, though early models (despite claims to the contrary) do not.

DVD media is not speed-rated as of mid-2002, but as faster drives reach the market, you might begin to see media rated for different drive speeds (the drives, however, are rated).

Most DVD+RW and DVD-RW drives, along with a few DVD-RAM drives, can also use CD-RW and CD-R media.

All rewriteable media (CD-RW, DVD-RAM, DVD-RW, and DVD+RW) must be formatted before it can be used for drag-and-drop file copying. Depending upon the media type, this process can take as much as a half-hour or longer.

While CD-mastering programs can also use rewriteable media, you should not use such media with these programs, as the media might not be erasable after being mastered. Use CD-R, DVD-R, or DVD+R media for CD or DVD-mastering tasks.

Troubleshooting CD-Mastering Drive Support Problems

Originally, the only way to write to CD-R media was with a mastering program such as Roxio Easy CD Creator (originally developed by Adaptec) or Nero Burning ROM. These and similar programs typically feature a Windows Explorer-style interface that you use to create a list of files and folders you want to write to a CD.

Unfortunately, if your particular brand and model of writeable drive isn't supported by the mastering program you want to use, you can't use the program to write to your media.

Here are some indications your mastering program doesn't work with your drive

- The program doesn't detect your drive at all
- The program doesn't list your drive as a target drive for writing files
- The program detects your drive, but displays an error message when you try to write files to the drive.

To solve problems like these, try the following:

- Download the latest CD recorder support files from the vendor's Web site—Most vendors provide a database of supported recorders and software versions you can query. If your recorder appears on the list of supported recorders, but the version of software listed is more recent than the one you use, download an the recommended update. Keep checking the software vendor's Web site for further updates if your recorder isn't listed yet.

- Upgrade to the latest version of your preferred software—If you use a no-longer current version of CD mastering software and your recorder isn't listed as supported, see if the latest version will support it, and purchase the upgrade if a free update isn't available.

- Use the recording software provided with the drive instead of a third-party product—While many writeable drives come with bare-bones software that might lack the features of a commercial product, the program packaged with the drive will work.

- Change to a different brand of software—While Roxio Easy CD Creator's basic version has been very popular with major drive vendors, some users prefer the more advanced features of Ahead Nero Burning ROM, and Nero sometimes supports new drives before Roxio adds support.

Troubleshooting Problems with Closed Media

All but the earliest CD-ROM drives are designed to read media that can be added to (multiple session) or media that has been closed (write-protected).

If your CD mastering program displays an error message indicating that you need to insert media which has enough room for the files you want to write, and the media has more than enough space, the media was closed when it was created, and no more files can be placed on the media. You can determine how much space is used on a writeable CD with Windows Explorer/My Computer. Right-click on the drive and select Properties to see the amount of space used. 74-minute media can hold about 650MB, while 80-minute media can hold about 700MB of information. The properties sheet might also say the media has 0 bytes free, but this is misleading. Most mastering programs also list the amount of space used by the files you want to transfer to CD.

If you want to write files to the media more than once, be sure to select the option that doesn't close (finalize) the CD when you create the CD (refer to Figure 3.30). Some programs choose this option for you by default, while others might close (finalize) the CD unless you choose otherwise.

Troubleshooting Drag-and-Drop (Packet Writing) Problems

CD mastering is an excellent way to copy a large number of files to a CD all at once, but it's not designed to allow files to be dragged from their original location and dropped (copied) to a CD. Hence, most CD mastering programs come with separate packet-writing programs to allow drag-and-drop file copying. For example, Easy CD Creator comes with DirectCD, and Nero Burning ROM comes with InCD (or you can download a copy if your version of Nero didn't include it). Packet-writing software writes files that correspond to a standard called Universal Disk Format (UDF).

Floppy disks, Zip disks, SuperDisk (LS-120/LS-240), and other types of magnetic removable-media storage are preformatted; you can copy files to them as soon as you insert them into the drive. However, optical media must be formatted before you can use it for drag-and-drop copying.

The packet-writing software supplied with your drive (or as part of a CD-creation program you bought at the store) is used to perform this task (see Figure 3.31). After you start the program, insert your media and click the Format button.

You should provide a label (descriptive name) for your media to make it easy to distinguish between different CD-RW discs (the label is displayed in Windows Explorer/My Computer). Use compression to save space.

Opens Format dialog box

Selects writeable
CD drive to use

Enables compression to
store more on the media

Optional label for media

Starts the format
with selected options

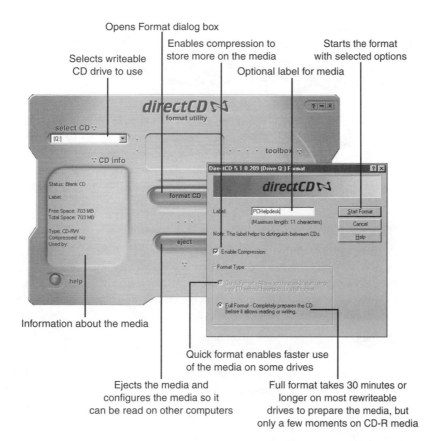

FIGURE 3.31
*The Roxio DirectCD
formatting program
preparing a blank
CD-RW disc for use.*

Information about the media

Quick format enables faster use
of the media on some drives

Ejects the media and
configures the media so it
can be read on other computers

Full format takes 30 minutes or
longer on most rewriteable
drives to prepare the media, but
only a few moments on CD-R media

If you're unable to start the formatting process, check the following:

- If you have another writeable drive installed, close any resident software used by the other drive (check the system tray).

- Use the correct type of media for your recorder and packet-writing program— Drives that rewrite at 10x or faster can use 10x or 4x media, but drives that rewrite at only 4x can't use faster media. If your packet-writing program doesn't support CD-R media, you must use rewriteable media.

At the end of the formatting process, be sure to properly eject the media. Use the Eject option provided by your packet-writing software to make sure the media is properly set for use in other systems (see Figure 3.32).

FIGURE 3.32
*The Roxio DirectCD pro-
gram after ejecting for-
matted CD-RW media. The
media must be read with
a CD-RW or a CD-ROM
drive with UDF Reader.*

If the drive reports an error during the formatting process, try another CD-RW disc and retry the process. If the problem repeats itself, contact the drive vendor for help.

When you insert the media into your drive for copying files, make sure the packet-writing program recognizes the media before you try to use it.

When you want to remove the media, use the Eject command built into your packet-writing software to close the media so it can be read. Unlike closing the media on a CD-R mastering program, closing CD-RW media doesn't prevent re-use of the media by the packet-writing program. By default, the media is closed so it can be read on any CD-ROM equipped with compatible UDF (Universal Disk Format) reading software (some programs, such as DirectCD, copy the reader to the media for you) and by other CD-RW drives.

If you are unable to read a CD-RW disc on another drive, check the following:

- The drive must be MultiRead or MultiRead2 compliant—Almost all CD-ROM drives that are 24x or faster are MultiRead compliant, and most recent DVD drives are MultiRead2 compliant (MultiRead/MultiRead2 drives use different types of lasers to read rewriteable media because it has lower reflectivity than ordinary pressed or CD-R media).

- Return the media to the original computer and use the packet-writing program's Eject feature to properly close the media.

- Install a UDF reader program compatible with the media—If the media didn't include such a reader, download one from the CD mastering program's vendor.

On the Web

If you want to read media created with Roxio DirectCD on systems that don't have this program, you need the latest UDF Reader. Go to the Roxio Web site (http://www.roxio.com), click on Downloads, and look for the UDF Volume Reader (works with Windows 95 through XP).

Ahead Software offers EasyWrite Reader for users who want to read InCD-created media. Go to http://www.nero.com, click InCD, and then click Downloads.

For other UDF reader solutions, contact the vendor of your drive or packet-writing software.

Some packet-writing programs support CD-R media as well as CD-RW media. CD-R media is less expensive and more durable than CD-RW media, but you need to make sure you select the most suitable option for closing it; you might be prompted for a closing method, or need to select one in the packet-writing program's options menu. If you choose Close to UDF Reader, the target computer needs to use a UDF Reader program to recognize the information on the CD. I recommend you select the Close to Read on Any Computer option so that most CD-ROM and other optical drives can read the files on the CD without using special software.

Troubleshooting Problems with the Writeable Drive Hardware

If your writeable drive has any of the following symptoms, it might be defective and in need of service:

- You must remove and insert media a couple of times before the packet-writing or mastering program will recognize it
- Your drive is no longer recognized as a writeable drive by your mastering or packet-writing program
- Your drive isn't displayed in My Computer or Windows Explorer
- Your drive ejects and retracts its media tray when you didn't press the Eject button or use the Eject option in your software

Before you contact your vendor for help, try the following:

- Review the troubleshooting sections earlier in this chapter for the drive interface your writeable CD uses—Most internal drives are ATA/IDE, while external drives usually connect to the USB or IEEE-1394 ports.
- Check the settings for the drive in Device Manager—Check the vendor's documentation for the correct DMA setting (enable or disable). If the drive's settings tab indicates the drive is not using DMA and the drive manufacturer recommends it, enable it. If DMA is already enabled, disable it (the drive will create CDs more slowly).
- Install the latest bus-mastering drivers available for your motherboard's chipset—Check your system or motherboard vendor's Web site for details and files to download.
- Check the data cable and make sure it's tightly connected to both the drive and the host adapter—Replace a defective cable.
- Use an 80-wire UDMA cable instead of a 40-wire cable on an ATA/IDE drive—You might need to change the jumpering from master/slave to cable select.
- Download the latest drivers for your writeable drive and the latest software updates for your CD-mastering and packet-writing programs.
- Check with the drive vendor for a list of recommended media—Substandard media, particularly CD-R media, can cause major problems with reliable writing.

→ See "Configuring the Drive Jumpers," p. 200.

Who Made Your Media?

You can download the freeware CD-R Identifier program from http://www.gum.de/it/download/english.htm.

You can use it to determine important information about any CD-R media you have, including the actual manufacturer (which is often *not* the name on the package) and the type of dye it uses (some colors work better with some recorders than others).

→ *For details on using Device Manager, see "Using the Device Manager," p. 480.*

- Check your drive vendor's Web site for a firmware upgrade—A firmware upgrade changes the instructions inside the drive similar to the way a system BIOS upgrade changes the instructions built into your computer's BIOS chip. Install the firmware upgrade if you don't have the latest one. The Settings tab on the drive's properties sheet in Device Manager indicates the firmware release installed.

Troubleshooting Problems with Windows XP and Writeable Drives

Windows XP supports writeable drives…badly. Instead of providing CD-mastering and packet-writing software, Windows XP uses a very slow and inefficient way of copying files to a CD-R or CD-RW disc. The process works this way:

1. Select the files you want to transfer to the writeable drive in My Computer.
2. Select Copy the Selected Items and select the writeable drive as the destination. The files are copied to a temporary folder.
3. Click the CD icon in the system tray to view the files waiting to be copied to the CD (see Figure 3.33).
4. Click Write these items to CD to start the CD Writing Wizard.

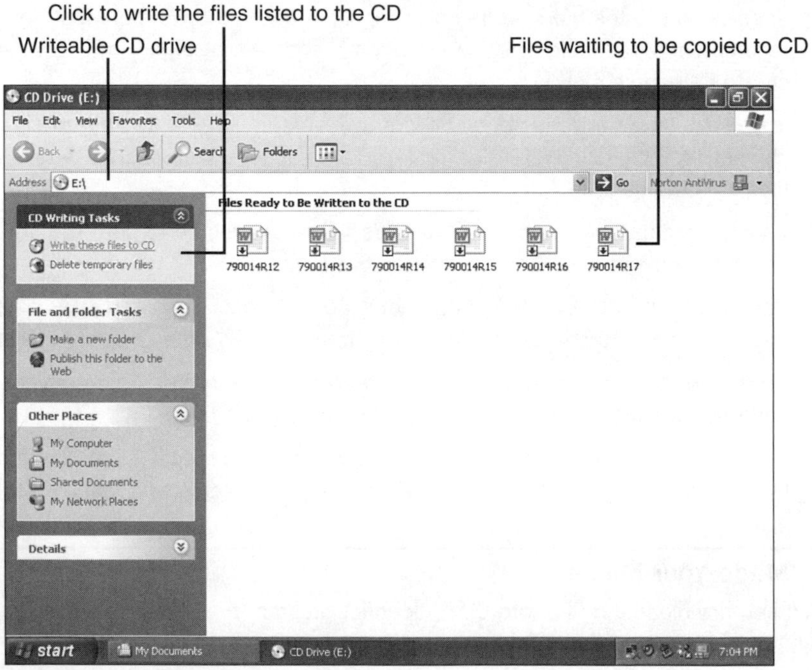

Click to write the files listed to the CD
Writeable CD drive
Files waiting to be copied to CD

FIGURE 3.33
The Windows XP CD writing program prepares to write files to the CD.

5. By default, the CD Writing Wizard uses the current date for the name of the CD it creates; change it if desired. You can also select Close the wizard after the files have been written; do this if you want to create only one copy. Click Next to continue.

6. Windows XP creates a CD image and writes the files to the CD. The process is fairly quick if you select only a few files, but is very slow if you want to fill a CD with your files. You can add more files to the CD at a later time if you want.

7. Click Finish to exit the wizard.

To see how much space is left on the CD, right-click on it in My Computer. One advantage of Windows XP over earlier versions of Windows is that it can display used and free space on a writeable drive; earlier versions treat both CD-ROM and writeable drives as having 0 bytes free.

Some of the problems you might have with Windows XP's writeable CD support include

- Doesn't recognize some CD-RW drives

- Writes non-erasable files to CD-RW media

- Prevents your packet-writing software from writing to CD-RW media

- Automatically prompts you to write files to the media when you insert a blank writeable CD

Troubleshooting Drives That Windows XP Doesn't Recognize

By default, Windows XP is designed to work with most CD-RW drives on the market (including DVD drives that support CD-RW media). Windows XP features a built-in driver called the Advanced SCSI Programming Interface (ASPI) layer. The Generic layer supplied with Windows XP supports most drives, but if your drive is not supported by the standard Windows ASPI driver, Windows XP will treat it as a CD-ROM or DVD-ROM drive.

If Windows XP doesn't recognize your drive as a writeable drive, try the following:

- Go to Windows Update (http://windowsupdate.microsoft.com) or to http://support.microsoft.com and download the update to the Windows XP CD writing feature discussed in document Q320174—This fix also helps solve other CD writing problems.

- Download and install the Adaptec Windows ASPI Package (you don't need an Adaptec or any other SCSI host adapter to use it); it frequently solves the problem. Go to the Adaptec Web site:

  http://www.adaptec.com

  Click Support, Downloads, SCSI Software to locate the link for the program.

Erasing CD-RW Media Created with the Windows XP CD Writing Feature

The Windows XP CD writing feature creates CDFS (CD File System) CDs that can't be erased by other programs. If you use CD-RW media with the Windows XP writing feature and want to use it with a UDF program, you need to use the Erase This CD button on the CD Writing Tasks menu. You can then format the media as needed.

Adjusting and Disabling the Windows XP CD Writing Feature

It's very likely that you will replace Windows XP's built-in CD-writing software with a third-party product that offers true CD mastering and packet-writing capabilities. However, even after you install the program you prefer, XP's built-in CD writing features could interfere with your third-party software. Even if you are content with XP's CD-writing feature, you might want to fine-tune it.

To adjust how the Windows XP CD-writing feature works, or to disable it, right-click on the drive in My Computer, select Properties, and click the Recording tab (see Figure 3.34).

FIGURE 3.34
The Recording tab for a writeable CD drive in Windows XP.

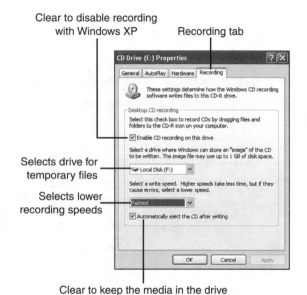

Clear to disable recording with Windows XP

Recording tab

Selects drive for temporary files

Selects lower recording speeds

Clear to keep the media in the drive

If you want to use third-party software to record CDs, clear the checkbox next to "Enable CD recording." This prevents Windows XP from trying to run its own wizard when you insert a blank CD and stops Windows XP from interfering with your packet-writing software.

If you can't read the media you wrote with Windows XP with any drive, including the drive that created it, your drive might have experienced a buffer underrun. A buffer underrun takes place when a recordable drive runs out of data to transfer to the media. Because CDs must be recorded in a continuous spiral of data from the center to the edge, a disc with a buffer underrun is unreadable; such a disc is called a "coaster" by some users. You can select a slower record speed than Fastest if you have problems reading the CDs you create.

If your default drive for temporary files is short of space, it could slow down the CD creation process and might cause a buffer underrun (resulting in a useless coaster). Use My Computer to determine which hard disk has the most empty space if you have more than one hard disk drive letter, and use the pull-down menu to select that drive as the location for temporary files.

If you prefer to remove a disc you write from the drive, enable the eject feature, but if you prefer to view it with My Computer to make sure it's readable, clear the Automatically eject option.

Fast Track to Success

If your computer doesn't display the Recording tab for your writeable drive, it could mean that

- Windows XP doesn't recognize your drive as a recordable drive; follow the tips given in the section "Troubleshooting Drives That Windows XP Doesn't Recognize," p. 245.
- Your third-party CD mastering or packet-writing software has disabled this tab for you to prevent problems.

Troubleshooting Recorded Media You Can't Read on Another System

Even if you create CDs primarily as backups of your own data or music, you should be concerned about whether other systems can read the media you create. This is definitely a concern if you regularly create media for use by others. If other users can't read the CDs you create, check the following:

- Make sure you are using a type of media the target system can use—The safest type of media to use is a high-quality CD-R used with a CD mastering program. Unless you choose the "close to read on any computer" option in your packet-writing software, packet-written CD-R media relies on UDF reader software to be readable on CD-ROM drives. CD-RW must be read in another CD-RW drive or by CD-ROM drives with a compatible UDF reader program installed. CD-RWs also don't work in most older portable stereo systems and non-MultiRead CD-ROM drives. CD-R is inexpensive and works virtually everywhere.

- Record all the data you want to put on the CD in a single session and close the CD—Some very early CD-ROM drives can read only single-session discs, and by creating a single-session disc you avoid compatibility problems.

- If you need the read/write/erase capability of CD-RW media, make sure you eject it correctly; don't shut off the computer until the media is ejected. The ejection process closes the media so it can be read on other systems.

- Try the media on your own system—If the drive that created the media can read it, but others cannot, you can try reducing the recording speed, closing the CD, or try a different type of CD media with a different combination of dye and reflective layers. However, if even the original drive can't read the media, you might have a defective drive or a buffer underrun.

Troubleshooting Buffer Underruns

Ever since the first recordable CD drive was introduced, users have created untold numbers of useless coasters because of buffer underruns. A buffer underrun takes place when the writeable CD drive transfers data to the disc faster than the computer can provide it to the drive. Because the flow of data is interrupted, the recording stops and the media is useless.

Depending on the CD recording/mastering software you use, you might get immediate notification of a buffer underrun, or discover it only after you can't read the disc you created in any drive.

All current writeable CD drives include some type of buffer-underrun prevention technologies such as BURN-Proof, SmartBurn, and others. These technologies work by suspending the CD creation process whenever the buffer memory in the CD runs out of information, and continue the process when more data is available. Upgrading from a drive that lacks this feature to a drive that supports this feature is the easiest way to avoid buffer underruns and enjoy much faster disc creation times.

Here are some other ways to avoid creating a coaster with your drive:

- If your drive supports buffer-underrun prevention, make sure your CD mastering software also supports this feature and make sure you leave it enabled (refer to Figure 3.30). Generally, the CD mastering programs supplied with drives with buffer-underrun prevention include this feature, as do the latest versions of retail CD mastering programs.

- If your preferred CD-mastering program doesn't offer a buffer-underrun prevention feature, upgrade to a version that does if your drive also has this feature.

- If your drive or CD-mastering program doesn't support buffer-underrun protection, use the fastest mastering speed that is reliable. I don't recommend recording speeds above 8x when buffer underrun-prevention isn't available.

- If your CD-mastering software offers a Test option (refer to Figure 3.30), use it to simulate CD recording at various speeds—If the program reports an error at a specific recording speed, reduce the speed and try the test again.

- Copy your data files to a fast, unfragmented hard disk—If your files are scattered across multiple drives, are located on another optical drive, or are on a different computer on a network or a serial or parallel direct connection, the likelihood of a buffer underrun is very high. Copy the files you want to transfer to CD into a single folder and defragment the drive containing that folder.

- Leave your computer alone while the CD mastering task is running—Don't play Solitaire, read email, or surf the Web; any activity on the system other than CD mastering can cause a buffer underrun. You should also disable screen savers, prevent anti-virus programs from scanning the system, and turn off all other unnecessary programs.

On the Web

Buffer-underrun prevention features are now universal, and many vendors sell drives for around $100 or less that are faster and more reliable than their predecessors. Check the latest reviews at *PC World* (http://www.pcworld.com) and *PC Magazine* (http://www.pcmag.com) to find a new writeable CD drive.

Printer Types, Technologies, and Common Problems

Most printers used at home and in the office fall into one of three major categories:

- Inkjet
- Laser/LED
- Impact

Inkjet printers use one or more ink cartridges and a print head which sprays tiny drops of ink onto the paper to make the image. Laser and LED printers use a laser beam or LED array to transfer an electrically-charged image of the page stored in the printer's memory onto a rotating drum, which attracts toner that is transferred to the paper to make the printout; a fusing mechanism bonds toner to the paper to complete the process. Impact printers have multi-wire print heads that use a ribbon to transfer images onto the paper, and are used primarily in warehouse or point-of-sale applications today.

Just as printers fall into separate categories, so do printer interfaces. These include

- Parallel (LPT) ports
- USB ports

If your computer is connected to a network, you might also have access to shared printers over the network.

Each printer type and each interface type provides different possibilities for printing problems. Regardless of whether your printer is a laser, inkjet, and so on, the major problems your printer might have can be broken down into three major categories:

- Complete inability to print
- Problems with print quality
- Gibberish output

When a printer can't print at all, the usual causes can include

- Disabled or incorrectly configured I/O ports
- Loose, damaged, or incorrect cabling
- Paper jams
- Running out of ink or toner
- Incorrect network configuration
- Incorrect printer configuration
- Internal damage to the printer

Problems with print quality can usually be traced to

- Dirty printer components
- Incorrect or damaged printer driver software
- Incorrect matching of print options to media type in use
- Running out of printer memory (with laser/LED printers)
- Failure to make use of the options available in the printer properties sheets
- Trying to print an image or document of too low a quality for satisfactory reproduction

Problems with gibberish output can usually be traced to

- Using the wrong printer driver with a printer (such as an HP LaserJet printer driver with an Epson inkjet printer)
- Damage to the printer port or printer cable

Generally, if a printer can't print at all, the cause is often not unique to a type of printer. On the other hand, problems with the quality of a printed image can vary widely and are often entirely dependent on the type of printer you use.

Printer Does Not Print

Regardless of the type of printer you have (Laser/LED, inkjet, or impact), all printers can suffer from common problems which can cause them to fail to print.

Because Windows normally sends print jobs to a print queue (a temporary file which holds the print job until the printer is ready for it), you might not see an error message right away when the printer can't print. You can view the contents of the print queue by opening the printer icon in Windows System Tray (see Figure 4.1). However, if a printer problem is so severe that the document doesn't print, Windows should eventually display an error message on its own (without you having to check up on it).

Click Help, Troubleshooter in Windows XP to activate the Printer Troubleshooter Print queue window

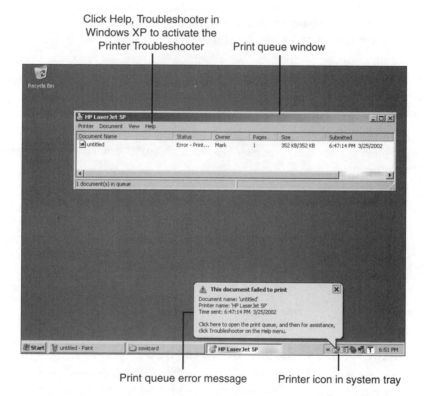

Print queue error message Printer icon in system tray

FIGURE 4.1
Windows XP's print queue (top) will try to sent a print job to a local printer for several minutes, but if it cannot do so, it will eventually display an error message (bottom).

If you're completely lost at sea about why you can't print, you can use the printer troubleshooter in Windows 98, Me, 2000 and XP. Even if you use Windows 95, however, the detailed solutions provided in the following sections should be all you need to identify the source of your problem.

Printer Is Offline

A printer has two basic conditions in relation to the computer it's connected to: Online (ready to receive data) and Offline (can't receive data). Every printer, regardless of type, should have a button that can toggle this state off and on (refer to your printer documentation for specifics). When you turn on a printer, assuming there's not any immediate problem, its default condition is online (some printers, like laser printers, need time to warm up when first powered on). You should take the printer offline if you need to

- Change toner or ink cartridges
- Add paper
- Eject a partially-printed sheet of paper
- Fix a paper jam or other problem

In many of these cases, a printer can take itself offline if it is capable of automatically detecting any of the listed conditions. A printer also automatically goes offline if the printer cable is loose or if it runs out of paper.

If the printer is offline because it's out of paper, turned off, or for some other reason, you can't print. See "Troubleshooting an Inkjet Printer with Its Status Lights," p. 258 or "Laser Printer Status Lights and Messages," p. 263 to determine whether your printer is online.

If there is nothing wrong with the printer when you set it to online mode, it should begin printing immediately (or after a short warm up). If it still cannot print, check the following:

- Cable connections
- Port problems
- Paper supply and paper jams
- Ink and toner levels
- Power connections

See the following sections for details.

Printer Cable Is Loose or Detached

Printers are normally connected to the computer through either the parallel (LPT) port or the USB port. Parallel port cables and connectors are heavy, and should be screwed securely into place at the computer end and clipped into place at the printer end (see Figure 4.2). If you need to tighten or reconnect a parallel cable, shut down the computer and printer to avoid damaging the ports.

Unlike their parallel equivalents, USB cables and connectors are very lightweight and are easily pushed into place without the need for screws or clips. USB cables are also hot-swappable, so you can attach them while the computer and printer are turned on without having to worry about doing damage to the ports (see Figure 4.3).

Parallel port (called DB25F)

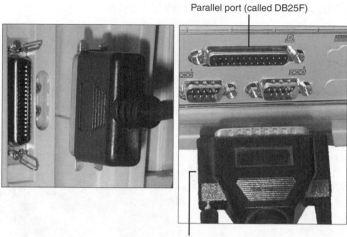

Parallel connector (called DB25M)

FIGURE 4.2
Attaching the parallel (LPT) cable to the printer (left) and computer (right).

USB Type B cable connector

USB Type B port (on printer)

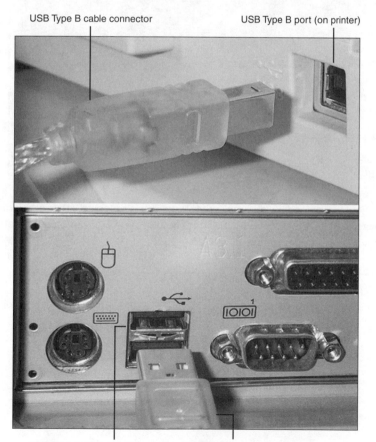

USB Type A ports (on computer)   USB Type A cable connector

FIGURE 4.3
Attaching the USB cable to the printer (top) and computer (bottom).

Wrong Printer Is Selected in Windows

If you have more than one printer, Windows automatically uses whichever one is set as the default printer. This is the printer that is used if you select the Print icon from the top-level toolbar in Web browsers or other applications. If you want to use a different printer connected to your computer, you need to use the File, Print options on the application's menu bar. This will open a Print dialog box that allows you to select any available printer for this job. Usually you must select the desired printer from a drop-down menu or an icon-based list as in Figure 4.4.

FIGURE 4.4
Selecting a different printer than the default in Windows XP.

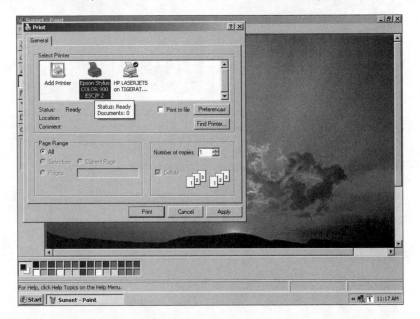

If the selected printer still does not print, there must be some other problem at work. Use the "Local Printer Doesn't Print" flowchart on p. 58 or scan the other sections in this chapter to find a solution.

Fast Track to Success

You can change the default printer in Windows from within the Printers folder.

1. Open the Printers folder. In Windows XP, click Start, Control Panel, Printers and Other Hardware, View Installed Printers. In other Windows versions, click Start, Settings, Printers.

2. Right-click on the printer you want to make the default printer and select Set as Default from the shortcut menu that appears.

Port Problems

A printer cannot print if the port it's connected to isn't working properly, isn't configured properly, or isn't present. You can use the Windows Device Manager to view the current configuration of the ports your printer uses, and to correct any conflicts.

➜ See "Using Device Manager," p. 480 for details.

While you can install an add-on card that has USB or parallel (LPT) ports built in to it, most relatively recent computers have these ports built in. These ports are enabled, disabled, and configured through the system BIOS.

➜ See "Using Device Manager to Troubleshoot USB Devices," p. 338 for details about USB port configuration.

USB Printing Issues

Windows XP has built-in drivers for most USB devices, including printers. However, you may need to install printer-specific USB support before you can use a USB printer with Windows 2000, Windows 98, or Windows Me. Windows 95 is essentially incompatible with USB devices, although some late OEM releases of Windows 95 came with a USB support patch installed which works with a few USB devices.

Parallel Port Modes

Parallel (LPT) ports can be configured to operate in several modes. What mode you should use depends both on the connectors at the PC and printer ends and the cable used to make the connection. If it looks like your port's configuration is causing your inability to print, you may need to select a different mode. Possible parallel printer port modes include

- Standard—This mode (also called compatible mode) is designed for output only, and sends data very slowly; it is the default setting on many computers, but should be changed to one of the other modes to support modern printers or other parallel-port devices.

- Bi-directional—This mode (also called PS/2 mode) can send and receive data at the same rate, and requires a bi-directional cable. It is not as fast as EPP or ECP, but will allow you to receive information such as ink or toner levels from your printer.

- EPP—Enhanced Parallel Port—This mode is much faster than either bi-directional or compatible, and supports printers and storage devices you might want to attach to your parallel port.

- ECP—Enhanced Capabilities Port—This mode is designed for use with printers and scanners.

- ECP/EPP—Combines features of EPP and ECP; an excellent choice if you are trying to connect devices which prefer different modes on the same port.

EPP and ECP are parts of the IEEE-1284 parallel port specification, which also requires that an IEEE-1284-compliant parallel cable (also compatible with earlier modes) be used with the port.

If you can print, but you cannot receive ink levels or other information back from your printer, or can't use the port for devices other than a printer, you probably have the wrong parallel-port mode set in the BIOS. To change the parallel port setting:

1. Shut down all running programs

2. Click Start, Shut Down, and Restart

➜ *For more informa-
tion on accessing your
PC's BIOS, refer to
"Configuring a Hard
Drive in BIOS," p. 125.*

3. When the computer restarts, press the key(s) used to access your computer's BIOS setup program.

4. Navigate to the screen where parallel port configuration is performed. The title of this screen (and the controls used to navigate there) will vary based on the BIOS used in your PC. Generally there is an option or tab that refers to Port Configuration.

5. Select the port setting recommended for your printer and any other hardware attached to the parallel port; if you're not sure what to use, use EPP/ECP if available. If this option is already set to EPP/ECP, it could be that your printer or cable does not support the interface. Try using just the Standard print mode. If, when you reboot, you can now print normally (albeit slow), it may be time to replace your printer cable (virtually all current printers support EPP/ECP mode).

6. Save the changes and restart the computer.

Switchbox Issues

Switchboxes allow multiple computers to share a printer, or multiple printers to share a single parallel port. If you use a switchbox to allow two or more printers to share a single parallel port and you fail to switch to the correct printer before printing, you could send a print job intended for one printer to another printer. Since different brands and models of printers use different printer languages, garbage output will usually result.

If you use a switchbox with IEEE-1284 parallel ports (EPP, ECP, and EPP/ECP), you need to make sure that the switchbox and the special cable which connects the switchbox to the computer are also IEEE-1284 compliant. Otherwise, slower printing will result and you won't be able to receive status messages from the printer.

The solutions to other types of printer problems vary with the type of printer you have.

Anatomy of an Inkjet Printer

Inkjet printers are far-and-away the most common type of printer found in homes and home offices. Many businesses also find that the quiet printing and ability to print great color pages make inkjet printers very popular at the office as well.

While most printing problems with inkjet printers are caused by cartridge or print-head problems, mechanical problems with the drive mechanism or paper feed can also lead to print failures.

Figure 4.5 shows the major features of a typical inkjet printer when the cover is opened.

Printhead support rod and belt drive   Black (K) ink cartridge
Paper clamp   Paper feed tray   Three-color (CMY) ink cartridge

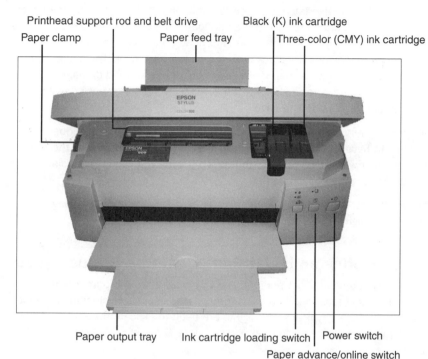

Paper output tray   Ink cartridge loading switch | Power switch
Paper advance/online switch

FIGURE 4.5
A typical inkjet printer with a rear-mounted paper feed.

While early inkjet printers used a black ink cartridge only, later models added color (sometimes by requiring you to interchange the black and color cartridges). Today, all inkjet printers support at least four colors, and some use separate ink cartridges for each color:

- Black (K)
- Cyan
- Magenta (M)
- Yellow (Y)

Some photo printers also feature light (photo) cyan and light magenta cartridges for a total of six colors.

When the print command is sent to an inkjet printer, a ribbon cable (not visible in Figure 4.5) carries print signals from the computer to the printheads, which spray droplets of ink onto the surface of the paper to form the image.

If the printhead control cable is damaged, you won't be able to print, but this is a very rare problem. However, it's not unheard of. Recently, a colleague of mine made a house call to check out a printer whose LEDs were blinking erratically and wouldn't print. He opened the cover to find that the client's pet ferret had gnawed on the flex ribbon cable attached to the print head.

In terms of physical damage to the printer, there are a couple of other, more common, scenarios to check. Damage could occur to the drive train that moves the print head back and forth. Also latches (on certain models) designed to hold the ink cartridges in place can often break. If you don't "park" the print head correctly before you try to remove the ink cartridges, the print head could actuate and not be able to move because the latches are blocked by the printer enclosure. This could crack the latches or damage the drive train if allowed to continue. To avoid damage to these moving parts, also be sure to shut down the printer with its own power switch before you remove any paper jams.

If your printer has sustained physical damage similar to what is described here, you'll need to have a professional repair it. Depending on the cost of the repair, it may be cheaper with some printers to replace it with a new one (especially if the damaged printer is out of date).

Most non-physical inkjet printing problems can be diagnosed through using the printer's status lights or its properties sheets.

Troubleshooting an Inkjet Printer with Its Status Lights

The power light on most inkjet printers glows steadily when the printer is resting. When the printer is receiving data or performing a task such as cleaning its printheads, it blinks. Other typical status lights are used to indicate the status of the ink cartridges and paper tray. In many cases, these lights stay off unless there's a problem.

Figure 4.6 shows the status lights on a typical inkjet printer, the Epson Stylus Color 900.

FIGURE 4.6
Status lights and controls on a typical color inkjet printer.

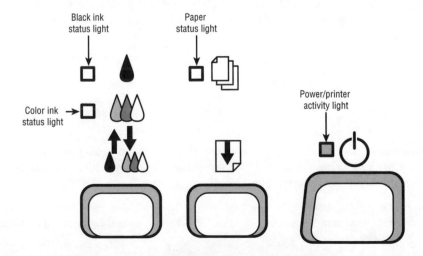

In this example, if the paper status light blinks, there is a paper feed problem; add paper or remove a paper jam. Press the button beneath the status light to eject paper or to put the printer into online mode after installing paper. If the black ink status light or color ink status light blinks, press the button beneath the ink status lights to move the ink cartridges to the installation position and install a new ink cartridge. If the printer uses a separate cartridge for each ink color, there is likely an ink-status monitoring tool installed with your printer driver. Use this on-screen status indicator, which is often displayed during printing, to determine which color(s) needs to be replaced.

Troubleshooting Inkjet Printer Problems

Some of the typical problems you might encounter with inkjet printers include

- Dirty printer components
- Incorrect print quality/media selections
- Paper jams
- Failure to make use of the options available in the printer properties sheets
- Trying to print an image or document of too low a quality for satisfactory reproduction
- Running out of ink

Cleaning an Inkjet Printer

The signs of a dirty inkjet printer include

- Random ink smudges on the front and rear of printed pages
- Breaks and gaps in printed output

To clean an inkjet printer, start by purchasing a set of inkjet cleaning sheets from your office supply dealer and using one or two in your printer. These sheets normally come with a spray cleaner, which is applied to one side of the sheet before it is run through the printer. This removes most of the ink residue from rollers and print heads.

If you have an HP or Canon inkjet printer, you can remove the print heads from the printer (HP's print heads are part of the ink cartridge, while Canon's ink cartridges and print heads can be changed separately or as a unit). After removing the print heads, you can wipe them off with a standalone inkjet cartridge cleaning kit before inserting them back into your printer. Epson print heads are built in to the printer, and you should not remove the ink cartridges until they are exhausted.

Finally, you can use a damp cloth to wipe off the rollers visible below the print head while you work the paper-feed button to move the rollers. To avoid ink smears, be sure to shut down the printer with its own power switch instead of with a surge

→ See "The Utilities Tab," p. 274 for details.

protector. By using the printer's own power switch, it will self-cap its ink cartridges to prevent them from drying out or leaking ink onto the rollers.

If breaks and gaps in printed output remain after you clean the printer, you need to use the printer's built-in head-cleaning routine to clean the print heads. With most printers, you can activate this routine and test the effectiveness of cleaning through the Utilities menu of the printer's properties sheet. The test feature makes a printout using each color separately, so you can determine which ink cartridge is causing the problem.

Some printers also allow you to run the same routine by pressing buttons on the printer itself. If the print quality doesn't improve after you run the print head cleaning utility three or four times, you should replace the ink cartridge that is producing poor-quality printing.

Fast Track to Success

Before you spend 10 or 15 minutes printing a high-resolution photo-quality enlargement onto glossy photo paper, take a few moments to clean the print heads and test the output. Many inkjet printers will develop minor clogs if they're left on for protracted periods of time, and cleaning the print heads will help prevent a spoiled print.

Incorrect Print Quality/Media Selections

By default, the typical inkjet printer is configured to print to plain paper at a relatively low print resolution of 300 to 360 dpi (dots per inch). If you want to print at higher resolutions or use photo quality paper, transparencies, or other types of special media, the paper-type and output selections you make in the printer properties sheet are critical to the quality of your output (see Figure 4.7).

FIGURE 4.7
The media choices available for a typical inkjet printer as shown in the Windows XP print dialog.

Inkjet printers vary the amount of ink used and how the print head moves to create the printout based upon the media choice you make and the print quality you select. If you mismatch the media option in the print dialog with the actual media used for the printout, you might soak your printout with excessive ink or cause gaps in the printed output.

If you want to print to plain paper at higher resolutions than the default settings allow, you may need to select Custom print options.

Avoid using paper that has a rough surface or loose fibers. This can cause ink wicking. Loose fibers might stick to the print head and cause problems with all your printouts. High-quality paper made for inkjets is a bit more expensive than copy paper, but the results are worth the extra cost.

Preventing and Fixing Paper Jams

You can prevent paper jams with your inkjet printer by

- Proper installation of paper into the paper tray—Be sure to adjust the paper guides correctly and make sure the stack is even before you insert it into the printer. Don't use more than the maximum number of sheets in the feeder.

- Adjusting the head gap for thick media—If you print on envelopes, labels, or transparencies, be sure to adjust the head gap wider than normal to avoid smudges and possible paper jams. Adjust the head gap back to normal after you switch back to normal paper. (See your printer's documentation for instructions on how to adjust your printer's head gap.)

If you need to remove a paper jam, turn off the printer with its own power switch, open the printer, and carefully remove all jammed sheets of paper and any residue.

Choosing Print-Worthy Images

Often people incorrectly confuse the source of a print quality problem as something wrong with the printer. While it's true that many issues involving print quality have to do with things like clean print heads or using the right paper stock, it's easy to forget that the source image or document counts too. Your printer can't produce a Van Gogh from a kindergartner's stick figure.

For example, if you've ever saved a photo from a Web site and tried to print it out at a larger size, you've probably been disappointed with the results. There's a simple reason: Web site pictures are designed to be as small as possible to load quickly and take up minimal space on-screen. They don't have enough pixels to be reproduced properly by a printer if you try to enlarge the image, even at the printer's low-quality setting.

The low-quality setting on a typical inkjet printer is 300 to 360 dpi (dots per inch), while the resolution of your monitor is about 96 dpi. As a result, a three-inch tall image on-screen only has enough dots to make a decent quality printout that's about one inch tall (96 is about 1/3 of 300).

Similarly, if you're scanning photos you want to print out later, be sure to scan at resolutions of at least 150 to 200 dpi if you want to print a snapshot (4×6-inch) or larger printout. If you want to enlarge a section of your original, scan at 300 dpi. However, if you're using a 35mm slide or negative scanner, you will need to use 1,800 to 2,700 dpi or higher scans because of the small size of the original slide or negative

Cautions and Warnings

The resolutions suggested here might seem too low for printers which boast of resolutions such as 2,880×720 dpi or 2,400×1,200 dpi, but these settings work very nicely. The reason is that printers use their very high output dpi to perform color mixing and halftoning of the image. If you tried to create a 4×6-inch scanned image that was 1,200 dpi, you'd chew up hundreds of megabytes of disk space, your printer would take much longer to print the page, and the quality would not be any better.

Tracking Ink Consumption

Usually when an inkjet printer's output quality starts to go South, it's because ink levels are getting low (this becomes obvious when printing a color image where the coloring is suddenly all out of whack).

Many recent inkjet printers are designed to report ink levels back to the user through a dialog box which is displayed during the print job. A report on these levels might also be available through the Utilities tab on the printer's properties sheet. To receive ink level information from the printer, your printer must support the feature and have its proper drivers installed in Windows. The printer must be turned on and you must

- Use a bi-directional printer interface such as EPP, ECP, EPP/ECP (parallel port), or USB
- Use an IEEE-1284–compliant parallel cable (if you use the parallel port)

Figure 4.8 shows a typical display of ink levels as reported by the Epson Stylus Color 900 printer in my office.

In cases where a printer combines all of its color inks into one cartridge, if any one of the three colored inks runs out, the entire ink cartridge must be replaced. The waste inherent in this type of design is why many of the newest printers, such as the Epson Stylus C80 I use at home, feature a separate ink cartridge for each color.

While it may seem more expensive to buy multiple ink cartridges for each color, you will find that you use a specific color or two much more often than the others. In this case, it's a lot cheaper (and less wasteful) to have to replace just one or two colors rather than all of them.

Color ink levels   Black ink levels

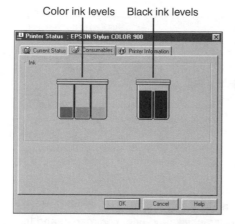

FIGURE 4.8
The consumables (ink levels) display from this Epson printer indicates that the printer has plenty of black ink, but has only about 1/3 of its colored inks remaining.

Fast Track to Success

Before you spend 10 or 15 minutes printing a high-resolution photo-quality enlargement onto glossy photo paper, take a few moments to check the ink levels in your printer. If you run out of ink partway through the printout, the effort (and the ink) is wasted.

To avoid using up your colored inks on non-critical printouts (such as Web pages), I recommend that you select Black ink in the print dialog as shown earlier in Figure 4.7. The printer will use grayscale shading to reproduce colors with black ink so you will still see the graphics on the printed result. This will cause you to go through your black ink cartridge more quickly, but black ink cartridges are usually cheaper to replace.

Anatomy of a Laser/LED Printer

Unlike inkjet printers, in which most moving parts are readily visible to the naked eye (refer to Figure 4.5), a laser or LED printer's mechanism is concealed within the printer cover. In fact, much of the imaging process is performed within the printer's toner cartridge. Figure 4.9 diagrams a typical laser printer's internal components.

An LED printer is identical to a laser printer, except that a fixed array of light-emitting diodes (LEDs) is used in place of a moving laser beam to place the image on the rotating drum inside the toner cartridge. Because most models of laser printers use a toner cartridge which contains the imaging drum, replacing the toner cartridge is a fast way to fix many types of printing problems with laser or LED printers.

Laser Printer Status Lights and Messages

Laser and LED printers work differently than inkjet printers. As soon as an inkjet printer receives data, it starts printing in a line-by-line fashion. Problems are visible right away because the printout starts right away, right in front of your eyes.

FIGURE 4.9

The components of a typical laser printer based on the Canon/ HP laser engine. Some laser printers use toner which is separate from the imaging drum, but most models use a design similar to the one shown in this figure.

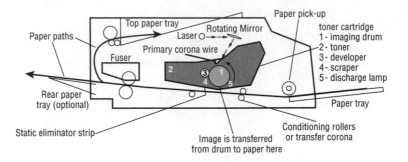

By contrast, laser and LED printers are page printers; they must receive an entire page's worth of text, graphics, and print commands and transfer them to the imaging drum, which transfers them to the paper before the paper emerges from the printer. Because of their more complex operation, more things can go wrong; correct interpretation of the printer's signal lights or status messages is extremely important.

Because every printer brand is different, and most printers now use signal lights instead of an alphanumeric message display to indicate problems, our discussion of laser printer problems is a general guide; for the specific meaning of a given light pattern or message, see your printer's manual or check the printer vendor's Web site for technical documents.

Generally, most laser/LED printers have a light on their control panel which glows steadily to indicate the printer is online (ready to receive a print job). This same light blinks when the printer is receiving a print job.

Most printers have two or more other lights that will shine or blink in various patterns to indicate problems such as

- Out of memory (the contents of the page are larger than the printer's available memory)
- Paper jam
- Paper out
- Toner cartridge problems

While a few printers might use an alphanumeric display panel to provide the error message, you will normally need to look up the light pattern for your printer to determine the problem and its solution.

The bottom line is: Learn the difference between normal and abnormal light displays on your printer.

Common Laser/LED Problems and Solutions

Typical problems with laser and LED printers include

- Dirty printer components
- Running out of printer memory
- Failure to make use of the options available in the printer properties sheets
- Trying to print an image or document of too low a quality for satisfactory reproduction
- Running out of paper

Use the following sections to solve the most common problems you are likely to encounter with your laser printer.

Cleaning a Laser or LED Printer

Because of the different sizes used by the rollers which are part of a laser or LED printer's paper path, you can often determine the exact cause of repeating or continuous extraneous markings on your printer's output by examining the distance between repeated markings on the output.

For example, with the HP LaserJet 1100 and 1200 series printers, a repetitive print defect which occurs every 1.25 inches indicates that the developing cylinder (part of the toner cartridge) is dirty or defective, while a defect every 1.8 inches indicates a dirty or defective transfer roller. The exact values for your laser printer are normally provided in the documentation for the printer, or can be viewed online at the printer manufacturer's Web site. Follow instructions for removing the toner cartridge to expose the rollers that need to be cleaned, and then wipe the rollers off with a soft cloth. If the damaged or dirty rollers are within the toner cartridge, you might need to replace the toner cartridge. A continuous vertical black streak along all pages of the printout usually indicates a damaged toner cartridge that must be replaced.

Cautions and Warnings

There are several potential hazards inside a laser or LED printer, including

- The imaging laser (laser printers only)
- High-voltage electricity (both types)
- Hot fusing assembly (both types)

If you need to clean the printer or remove a paper jam, you should turn off and unplug the printer. If you need to clean the fuser rollers, let the printer cool down for a few minutes before you clean this part of the printer.

If you clean your printer and replace the toner cartridge but still find extraneous marks and smudges on your printouts, the printer might have internal damage which requires professional service.

Out of Memory Error

Even the lowest-cost laser printers should be able to print a page of text, or a page with small graphics. However, if you try to print a page composed mostly of graphics or that has several different fonts, you may run out of laser printer memory, causing an out-of-memory error. Since the printer could not finish printing the page, the page will remain in the printer until you eject it.

- *Error Recovery*—To recover from this error, eject the current page (see your printer's manual); note that the page will not be completely printed but will appear to be cut off at the point where the page contents exceeded the laser printer's memory.

➜ See "Under-standing Your Printer's Properties Sheets," p. 268 for details.

- *Workaround*—The easiest way to print the page is to decrease the graphics resolution of the printer in the printer's properties sheet. For example, reducing a 1,200 dpi (dots per inch) laser printer's graphics resolution to 600 dpi reduces the amount of required printer memory by a factor of 4. While graphics won't be as finely detailed, text quality is unaffected.

- *Solution*—Install more memory in the laser printer. The amount of RAM required to print a page varies with the printer's resolution, the size of the graphics, the number of fonts on the page, the size of the page (letter or legal size paper) and the printer's ability to compress graphic data. For a 600 dpi laser printer, your memory upgrade should add at least twice the amount of memory originally installed in the printer. For example, if your printer has 2MB of onboard memory, you should add at least 4MB (total 6MB of RAM). If you are upgrading a 1200 dpi laser printer, add at least four times the amount of memory originally found in the printer. This will enable you to print complex pages at their highest resolution, enable you to print two or more pages on a single sheet of paper, and may also speed up printing because the printer doesn't need to spend as much time compressing data.

Depending on the printer, you might be able to add a standard SIMM or DIMM module similar to those used by PCs, or you might need to add a proprietary memory module or card. Proprietary memory modules or cards must usually be purchased from the printer manufacturer or from an authorized reseller. Always expect to have to pay a little more when purchasing proprietary components.

Paper Jam

Paper jams can be caused by incorrect paper loading, wrinkled or damaged paper, or damp paper.

- *Error recovery*—Shut down the printer and open the printer to locate the paper jam. You might need to remove the toner cartridge on some models to find the paper jam. Remove the misfed sheet(s) and be sure to remove any torn paper or loose labels. Resend the print job after you turn on the printer.

If the paper jam is located near the end of the paper path, beware of the hot fusing assembly when you remove the paper jam.

- *Solution*—Be sure to load the paper tray properly and insert it completely into the printer. Use only laser-compatible labels; copier labels aren't designed to handle the heat of laser printing and can come off inside the printer, possibly causing damage. If you can switch to a straight-through paper path (usually an optional rear paper tray) for labels and similar heavy stock, do so to minimize the chances of a paper jam (refer to Figure 4.7). Avoid using paper that is damaged, stuck together, warped, or wrinkled. Don't use media that is thicker or heavier than the printer is rated to accept.

Paper Out

Running out of paper is a normal part of printing, but you can minimize the interruption to your printing task by filling the paper tray before you start printing a long document.

- *Error recovery and solution*—Open the paper tray and properly install new paper. Some printers will print normally as soon as you close the paper tray, while others require you to press the online/paper feed button to continue printing after you insert paper.

- *Workaround*—If the paper tray is defective or if it isn't completely inserted into the printer, you might continue to get a paper-out signal even after you fill the paper tray and re-insert it. In these cases, use the manual paper tray option (if available), use a replacement paper tray, or service the printer if the paper tray isn't a removable item.

Cautions and Warnings

It's long been true that most inkjet printers aren't worth servicing once the warranty period is up; changes in technology and performance along with the throwaway nature of their design make replacement the rule. Laser printers have also dropped in price and improved in resolution and performance, so be sure to determine the servicing cost before authorizing a repair on an out-of-warranty laser printer. You may find that a new laser printer's a better way to spend your money.

I recommend the 50% rule: If a repair costs at least 50% of the cost of a comparable new printer, scrap the old printer and put the money toward a new model.

Toner Cartridge Problems

A damaged toner cartridge will put extraneous marks or smudges on every page it prints, and an empty toner cartridge can't print anything. Sooner or later, you will need to replace the toner cartridge for one reason or the other.

Error recovery and solution—Shut down the printer and remove the toner cartridge (refer to your manual for specifics). Verify that the toner cartridge is properly inserted and contains toner. Watch for print quality problems when the first print jobs emerge after you reinstall an existing toner cartridge or install a new one. If the new toner cartridge doesn't improve print quality, recheck the printer for other problems; you may need to have it serviced.

Fading or Uneven Text

Error recovery and workaround—You're probably running out of toner. Remove the toner cartridge and shake it gently side-to-side to redistribute the remaining toner more evenly. Print only necessary documents and check print quality until you can install a new toner cartridge.

Solution and prevention—Install a new toner cartridge immediately. To maximize toner cartridge print life, use the EconoMode (toner saving) mode if available when you print draft copies.

Understanding Your Printer's Properties Sheets

The Windows properties sheets for your printer enable you to control your printer's print quality, extend the life of consumables such as toner, perform print head cleaning and other maintenance tasks, and solve various printer performance and output problems.

While specific printers vary in the details of their properties sheets, most laser and LED printers offer similar options. Similarly, most inkjet printers are similar to each other in their properties sheets. Use the examples in this section as a general guide, and see the documentation for your printer for the specific features of your printer.

Accessing the Properties Sheets for Your Printer

To display the installed printers on your system in Windows, click Start, Control Panel. In Windows XP, click Printers and other Hardware, View installed printers or fax printers. In Windows 9x/Me, simply double-click the Printers icon.

If you have more than one printer installed, the default printer (the printer automatically selected unless you choose another one) is indicated with a checkmark. To view the properties sheet for the printer, right-click on the printer's icon and select Properties from the menu (see Figure 4.10).

FIGURE 4.10
Preparing to view the printer properties sheet for the default printer in Windows XP.

Virtually all printers of any type supported by Windows XP have the following properties sheets:

- General
- Sharing
- Ports
- Device Options

Each of these properties sheets is described in the following sections. Earlier versions of Windows feature similar options for their printers, although the placement of options on each tab will vary.

The General Tab

General displays the printer name, location, comments, features, and test print option (see Figure 4.11).

Clicking the Printing Preferences button opens a new window with three tabs. Use the Layout tab to select page orientation, number of pages per printed page, and page order. Click the Paper/Quality tab, shown in Figure 4.12, to adjust paper type and tray usage, and, with inkjet printers, to select print quality and media type settings.

The Advanced button, available from one or more of the tabs in the Printing preferences properties sheets, typically controls graphics resolution, output options, and printer features (see Figure 4.13).

FIGURE 4.11

The General tab provides a quick overview of the printer's features and provides access to the most common adjustments through the Printing Preferences button.

FIGURE 4.12

The Paper/Quality tab for the Printing preferences for a typical inkjet printer.

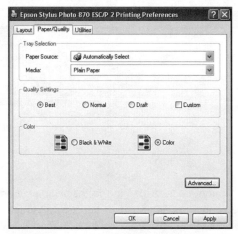

FIGURE 4.13

The Windows XP Advanced Options dialog for a typical laser printer (left) and inkjet printer (right); to change current settings, click on the underlined text next to each option.

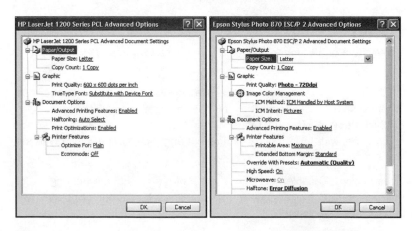

The Sharing Tab

If your computer is on a network, use this tab to enable or disable printer sharing (see Figure 4.14). If you enable printer sharing, specify a descriptive share name; this can be any name that will help you tell this printer from others, such as "Joe's Inkjet."

Use the Additional Drivers button to install printer drivers for other Windows versions, so they can be downloaded by other computers on the network if needed. For example, if your network has Windows 9x and Windows Me computers which want to share the printer on your Windows XP computer, use this option to make sure that the correct drivers for those Windows versions will be available on your computer. When Windows 9x or Me computers connect to your computer to use your printer for the first time, they can download and install the drivers from your computer instead of needing to install the driver from their Windows CD or from an Internet download.

FIGURE 4.14
The Sharing dialog for a typical printer in Windows XP.

The Ports Tab

Use this tab to select the port (local or network) to be used for this printer (see Figure 4.15). If your printer is Plug and Play, the correct port should be selected automatically for you. Assuming your printer connects through a paralell port, this should be LTP1.

FIGURE 4.15
Scroll down past LPT and COM ports to select a network print queue or USB port.

The Advanced Tab

Use this tab to adjust printer priority, spooling options, separator page options, printer availability, and the data type sent to the printer (Print Processor button) (see Figure 4.16). By increasing printer priority (default is 1, maximum is 99), documents with higher priority are printed before documents with lower priority. To prevent printer use during certain hours (such as overnight), select Available from and adjust the start and end times. You can also elect to keep printed documents in the print spool (the list of documents to be printed) for reprinting later, prevent mismatched documents (documents with incorrect settings such as paper orientation or size) from printing with Hold Mismatched Document, and bypass the print spool entirely if you can't print using print spooling. Changing the data type is not recommended unless the printer vendor specifically recommends it.

FIGURE 4.16
The Advanced properties sheet controls every aspect of how documents travel to your printer.

The Device Settings Tab

While most printer properties sheets are similar from printer to printer, regardless of the printer type, the Device Settings properties sheet will vary a great deal because it controls printer-specific features. Figure 4.17 displays the Device Settings for a typical laser printer, while Figure 4.18 displays the device settings for a typical inkjet printer.

Color Management Tab

A color printer (whether inkjet, laser, or LED) is also likely to have a Color Management tab, which enables you to specify a color profile. The color profile is used to help you match the colors you see on-screen to the tone and shading of the colors you see in the final printout (see Figure 4.19).

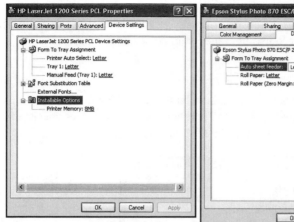

FIGURE 4.17
The Device Settings properties sheet for a typical laser printer lets you specify the default paper type for each tray, control font substitutions, and see (or change) the printer's memory size.

FIGURE 4.18
The Device Settings menu for a typical inkjet printer lets you specify paper sizes for each type of paper feed supported by the printer.

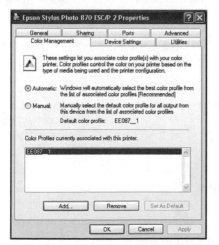

FIGURE 4.19
Color profiles used with the Color Management tab are supplied by the printer vendor.

Generally, the automatic color profile selection provides the best results. However, if you download or create a different color profile, you should click Manual and select the color profile you want to use from the list of color profiles displayed.

The Utilities Tab

Most inkjet printers' properties sheets also feature a Utilities tab; use it to check the condition of the printhead, clean the printhead when needed, or check/adjust the vertical alignment of the printhead (see Figure 4.20).

FIGURE 4.20

Use the Utilities menu to keep your inkjet printer in top working condition.

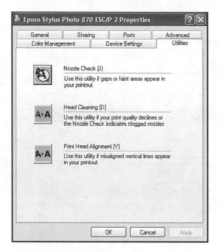

Using Printer Properties to Troubleshoot Your Printer

By using the properties sheets for your printer, you can solve many print problems, including layout, the order in which pages are printed, print quality, and others.

Use Table 4.1 to help you use your printer's properties sheets to solve printing problems. Most of these sheets have appeared in figures in the previous sections.

TABLE 4.1

Troubleshooting Your Printer with Properties Sheet Options

Problem	Properties Sheet	Solution
You're not sure whether Windows can communicate with printer	General	Use the test print button; if the test print doesn't work, applications can't print either. Use Flowchart, "Local Printer Doesn't Print," p. 58 to isolate the problem.
Printed document orientation doesn't match document layout	Layout	Select correct paper orientation for document layout and reprint.

TABLE 4.1 (continued)

Problem	Properties Sheet	Solution
Paper ejects from printer in reverse order.	Layout	Select Page Order Back to Front so that document will emerge from printer in correct page order.
You want to put multiple pages on a single sheet of paper	Layout	Select the desired Pages per Sheet; for example, to print four pages on a single sheet, select 4.
You are almost out of color ink	Paper/Quality	Select Black & White to map all colors to grayscale and print with black ink only. Note that some printers will not print if any of the color ink cartridges have run out, even if you select black ink.
You are using special media with your inkjet printer	Paper/Quality	Select the correct media type to optimize printing.
You want to customize the normal print settings with your inkjet printer	Paper/Quality and Advanced	Select Custom on the Paper/Quality menu and then click Advanced; adjust print quality and other settings as desired.
You need to print your document on a printer you can't connect to over the network or locally	Ports	Install the printer driver for the printer you want to print to, select Print to File, and specify a drive and filename when you print. A print file will be created in the specified location. Copy the file to a floppy disk or other media and take the file to the computer connected to the printer. Copy the file to the printer port the printer is connected to: COPY MYPRINT.PRN LPT1. Note: This will not work with a USB printer. However, you can use a freeware program called PrintFile to perform this task with USB or other printers. Download it from http://www.lerup.com/printfile/

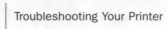

TABLE 4.1 (continued)

Problem	Properties Sheet	Solution
You don't want to waste paper by printing documents that don't match the printer's configuration	Advanced	Enable the Hold Mismatched Documents option.
You are printing a large document and may need additional copies later	Advanced	Enable the Keep Printed Documents option and print the document; to reprint the document, open the printer icon and select the document for reprinting.
You cannot select all the features of your printer	Advanced	Use the New Driver button to install a new driver for your printer, or use Windows Update.
You want to put different paper/ media sizes in the different paper trays of your printer	Device Settings	Select the paper tray or location where you want to use specially sized paper or envelopes, and select the size.
You have added additional memory to your laser/LED printer and want to be sure it's being used	Device Settings	View the Printer Memory size and adjust it if necessary to reflect the memory upgrade. You should compare its before-upgrade and after-upgrade value to determine whether you need to make any adjustments.
There are lines and gaps in the output from your inkjet printer.	Utilities	Use the Head Cleaning option (if available) to clean the printhead; then, use the Nozzle Check option or run a test print to verify proper operation. Repeat Head Cleaning if needed. If your printer lacks a Head Cleaning option on the Utilities menu, check the manual for the procedure for cleaning the heads. If cleaning the heads doesn't solve the problem, your ink cartridge is almost out of ink and should be replaced.

Troubleshooting Gibberish Output

While it may appear to be a "quality" problem with your printer, if the result of a print job looks like gibberish, the source of your problem is entirely different from those discussed so far. Gibberish output from a printer is usually caused by

- Using the wrong driver for the printer
- A loose or damaged printer cable
- Damage to the printer or the printer port

To determine whether the correct driver is being used with Windows XP

1. Right-click on the printer icon and select Properties.
2. Click the Advanced tab and view the driver listed.
3. If the driver listed is incorrect, click New Driver to start the Add Printer Driver Wizard. Select the correct brand and model from the lists displayed. If you have downloaded the correct driver, click Have Disk and browse to the folder containing the correct driver.
4. If the driver listed is correct, check the cable and port. If a switchbox is used, make sure the switchbox is set correctly.
5. To make sure the driver is working correctly, reinstall it and retry the print job. If the printer still outputs gibberish, go to the next test.

To determine if a defective or loose parallel (LPT) cable is causing gibberish output

1. Shut down the computer and the printer.
2. Remove the cable and examine the cable jacket for nicks, cuts, and exposed wires. Examine the cable connector for bent or broken pins.
3. If the cable appears to be okay, reconnect it to the computer and the printer. Be sure to secure the cable at both ends.
4. Turn on the printer, then the computer, and retry the print job.

If the printer still produces gibberish, or if the cable appears damaged, shut down the printer and computer, replace the cable with a known-working cable, and repeat step 4. If the output is still gibberish, the printer may need servicing.

To determine if the port or the printer is defective

1. Connect a different printer to the port using the same cable.
2. Install the correct printer driver and retry the print job.

If a different printer prints correctly, the original printer is defective. If every printer prints gibberish, the parallel port on the computer is defective.

There aren't many good options for getting around this problem. If your printer supports an interface other than parallel (many support both parallel and USB), try using the other interface. You could also install an add-in board with a parallel port that can take the place of the port built in to your computer. If your printer is dated and you were planning to replace it anyway, you could purchase a new printer that has support for a different (functioning) port on your PC. Finally, you could also replace the motherboard, though this could necessitate that you upgrade other various components of your PC as well (like the CPU and memory type).

Troubleshooting Display, Audio, and Multimedia Problems

CHAPTER 5

Troubleshooting Monitor and Display Adapter Problems

Next to the keyboard and pointing device, the display subsystem (the monitor and display adapter/video card) may be the most important part of your computer's user interface. The display subsystem essentially gives you a visual representation of what's happening inside your computer, so keeping it working properly is very important.

Monitor problems typically fall into the following categories:

- Physical problems such as desktop sizing, image distortion, missing portions of the desktop, overly dim or bright text and images, and dull text and images
- Windows configuration problems such as monitor flicker, icon and text sizing issues, text color issues, and driver problems

Display adapter problems typically fall into the following categories:

- Physical problems such as BIOS configuration for single and multiple display adapters and inability to install multiple display adapters
- Windows configuration problems such as distorted colors, inability to select the desired color depth and resolution, driver problems, inability to start the computer, frequent lockups, and slow 3D game performance

The following sections will help you keep your monitor and video card working properly.

There's a Problem with the Size or Position of the Windows Desktop

Because the Windows desktop is so familiar, viewing it carefully is an easy way to tell if you have problems with the size or positioning adjustments of your display, such as

- One of the edges of the desktop is cut off.
- There's a black border all around the desktop.
- The edges of the desktop are curved in or out.

Use the following sections to solve these display annoyances.

One of the Edges of the Windows Desktop Is Cut Off

If one of the edges of your Windows desktop isn't visible (see Figure 5.1), the most likely solution is one of the following:

- You might need to adjust the screen position with controls on the monitor.
- You might have a virtual desktop enabled. A virtual desktop uses the screen as a movable window around a larger desktop.

FIGURE 5.1

An LCD display that needs to have its vertical screen position adjusted.

Blank area at top of screen

Windows toolbar is partially cut off

To adjust the vertical or horizontal position, look at the front of your monitor. Most monitors have controls on the front or under the front edge of the monitor for adjusting vertical and horizontal position, size, and other settings. If you need help using these controls, you must consult your monitor's documentation.

To determine whether you are using a virtual desktop, watch your Windows desktop as you move your pointing device into each corner of the screen. If the visible screen area moves or shifts as you move your pointing device, particularly when you move it near one edge of the visible display, your display driver has a virtual desktop feature enabled. To configure or disable this feature, see the documentation for your video card.

There Are Black Lines or Rectangles Across the Desktop with an LCD Display

If you use an LCD monitor and you see thick black horizontal lines or rectangles across the desktop, the LCD is damaged and should be replaced. The black areas are areas where the transistors that activate the display have failed.

There's a Black Border All Around the Desktop

If you see a thin black border all around the desktop with a CRT monitor, this is normal; you can increase the actual screen size by using the horizontal and vertical size and position controls mentioned in the previous section.

Fast Track to Success

If you want to adjust the size of the visible display on your CRT the fast way, look for a zoom control in the onscreen control functions. This adjusts both vertical and horizontal size at the same time. If you zoom the screen larger and start to cut off one edge of the screen as seen later in Figure 5.7, adjust horizontal or vertical position as needed.

However, if you see a wide black border on an LCD display panel, particularly the type built in to a notebook computer, the problem might be that you are not using the native resolution of the panel. LCD panels, unlike CRT monitors, are designed to work at a single resolution (often called the native resolution). Some panels automatically handle scaling to lower resolutions, although the results might be much worse than with a CRT, but others must use only a portion of the screen for a lower resolution (see Figure 5.2).

To adjust how your LCD panel handles lower resolutions than normal, click the Settings tab on the display adapter's properties sheet and click Advanced. Look through the properties sheets to find a setting such as Scale Image to Panel Size or Expand Panel Image (see Figure 5.3). If this option is enabled, setting the resolution lower than normal will cause the display to stretch the image to fill the LCD panel; depending upon the display adapter and panel, the results might be acceptable or might be terrible. If you find the results are not acceptable, but you need to use a lower resolution to enable your system to connect to a lower-resolution display projector or monitor, disable this option.

1024×768 display area not used by lower-resolution setting

FIGURE 5.2

How a typical 1024×768 LCD notebook display panel will look when configured to use 800×600 resolution if scaling is not used.

800×600 display setting fills only a portion of the display

FIGURE 5.3

Enabling the Expand Panel Image option on this Compaq notebook computer fills the 1024×768 display with an 800×600 image. The actual onscreen display was not as clear as this screen shot.

On the Web

If you'd like an easier way to adjust font and icon size in the Windows desktop, check out Portrait Display, Inc.'s new LiquidView program. Learn more about it at http://us2.portrait.com/products/lv.htm

The Edges of the Windows Desktop Are Curved

Because CRT monitors can be adjusted to a wide range of screen sizes, the edges of the Windows Desktop (or any other screen display) may become curved, particularly if you increase the size of the desktop to fill the screen. The most common problems include

- Barrel distortion—The edges of the screen display are curved outward
- Pincushion distortion—The edges of the screen display are curved inward
- Wave distortion—The edges of the screen display curve back and forth

To compensate for these display-quality problems, use the geometry controls available on most monitors to straighten the edges of the screen.

Cautions and Warnings

If you change resolutions or refresh rates, you might need to adjust the geometry settings the first time you select a new resolution or refresh rate. However, most monitors will save these settings for you and automatically reuse them when needed.

The Text and Icons Onscreen Are Hard to Read

If you're having problems reading the text or seeing the icons onscreen, these problems can have several causes, including

- Incorrect contrast or brightness settings on the monitor
- Screen resolution set too high or too low
- The color scheme used by Windows
- The refresh rate used by your monitor

The Text Is Too Dim or Too Bright

If you notice that the text is too bright or too dim, or that there's not enough difference between bright and dark colors, you should adjust the brightness and contrast controls on your monitor, and, if possible, adjust the monitor gamma in Windows.

To adjust the brightness and contrast controls on your monitor

1. Open a command-prompt window: Click Start, Run, and type CMD (Windows XP or Windows 2000) or Command (Windows 9x/Me) and press Enter.

2. If you can still see the Windows desktop behind the window, press Ctrl+Enter to switch to the command-prompt window to full-screen mode.

3. Adjust the brightness display until the text display is at medium brightness.

4. Adjust the contrast display until the background is a solid black.

5. Type Exit and press the Enter key to return to the Windows desktop.

This optimizes the monitor display for command-prompt applications, but the appearance of the Windows desktop might still be too dark or too light. You can further optimize your monitor display if you have a gamma option included in your display adapter's Advanced properties sheet; look for an option such as Color or Gamma. Gamma controls are also installed by some graphics and photo-editing programs. Gamma controls enable the user to adjust brightness and contrast for all Windows-based programs, and are especially important if you want to see matching results from displayed and printed images. If you have a gamma control, see the instructions for your display adapter driver or graphics software for details of how to use it. The gamma control also might be found in Control Panel.

To access the Advanced display properties sheet

1. Right-click on the Windows desktop (not on an icon).

2. Select Properties.

3. Click the Settings tab.

4. Click Advanced.

On the Web

For more information about controlling gamma, see the monitor/printer calibration and gamma Web site at http://www.normankoren.com/makingfineprints1A.html.

The Text and Icons Are Too Large or Too Small

By default, Windows uses fixed-size icons; the higher the resolution (the number of dots in each direction horizontally and vertically) onscreen, the smaller the icons. Windows also uses fixed-size fonts instead of scalable fonts for its standard windows and menus. Generally, very large icons and text might indicate that the display resolution is set lower than the best size for your monitor.

Other signs that your resolution is set too low include

- You need to scroll horizontally to read the contents of many Web sites.

- You need to scroll vertically to see all your program shortcuts when you click All Programs (Windows XP) or Programs (other Windows versions), even though you only have a few programs installed.

Fast Track to Success

If the desktop icons and text are large, but you don't need to scroll horizontally or vertically to view Web sites or to see program shortcuts, you might be using the Use Large Icons option.

While it's more likely that your display resolution is set too low—resulting in annoyances like very large icons—if you're experiencing the opposite problem, that text and icons are too small to read comfortably, or if the screen has an annoying flicker, your display resolution might be set too high.

→ *See also "The CRT Monitor Flickers," p. 289.*

To see the current display resolution and color settings your computer uses, right-click on the Windows desktop and select Properties. Click the Settings tab to display this information (see Figure 5.4).

Display type   Display adapter type

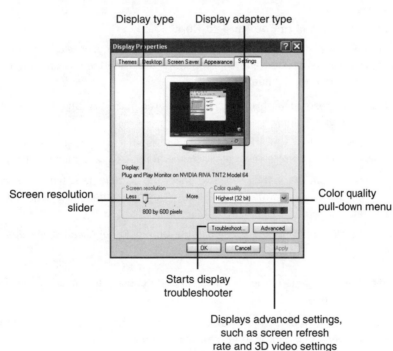

FIGURE 5.4
The display settings properties sheet in Windows XP.

Screen resolution slider

Color quality pull-down menu

Starts display troubleshooter

Displays advanced settings, such as screen refresh rate and 3D video settings

Compare your computer's current screen resolution setting to the suggestions in Table 5.1. If you are using a different setting than the one recommended for your monitor and you are not comfortable with the screen display, select the recommended resolution with the Screen Resolution slider and click Apply to preview the results. If you are satisfied, click OK to accept the new setting. If you are not satisfied, the monitor will revert to the old setting in a few seconds.

TABLE 5.1
Suggested Screen Resolution Settings by Monitor Size and Type

Screen Resolution	Resolution Name	CRT Monitor Size	LCD Monitor Size
640×480	VGA	14-inch or less	12-inch or less
800×600	Super VGA	15-inch	13-inch
1024×768	XGA	17-inch	15-inch
1280×1024	UltraXGA	19-inch	17-inch
1600×1200	(None)	21-inch	19-inch

Windows XP requires 800×600 (SuperVGA) resolution or higher.

The Text Is Too Small or Too Hard to Read

If you find that larger monitors, with their correspondingly smaller text and icon sizes for the Windows desktop and applications, are making the screen harder for you to read, you have four options:

- Reduce the resolution of your display, which will make text and icons larger (see previous section).

- Spend time fiddling with the Display Properties sheet's Appearance tab, which allows you to customize your color scheme, font sizes, and much more.

- Use the custom DPI setting available under the Settings tab; click Advanced, General, and select Normal, Large size, or Custom settings to enlarge all desktop objects.

- Select a high-contrast display through the Control Panel Accessibility Options icon.

→ To learn more about using the Appearance tab, see "Fonts and Icons Overlap on the Windows Desktop," p. 287.

The high-contrast option is particularly well-suited to users with limited vision. To try a high-contrast display

1. Click Start, Control Panel (Windows XP) or Start, Settings, Control Panel (other Windows versions) and open Accessibility Options.

2. Click the Display tab from the Accessibility Options dialog box that appears.

3. Enable the Use High Contrast check box.

4. Click the Settings button. To select a high-contrast or other Windows color scheme as your standard color scheme, click the down-arrow next to your current high-contrast scheme, and choose from those listed (in non-XP versions of Windows, first select the Custom radio button). True high-contrast schemes include High Contrast #1, High Contrast #2, High Contrast Black, and High Contrast White. All of these are available with regular, large, or extra large icons and text. Click OK, Apply, and then OK to activate the high-contrast color scheme.

5. If you want to be able to switch back and forth between your high-contrast and normal Windows color schemes, click the box next to Use Shortcut, and then select the high-contrast color scheme you want (see Figure 5.5). Click OK, Apply, and then OK. The screen switches to the high-contrast scheme you selected, but when you press the shortcut combination (Alt+Left Shift+PrintScreen), the screen reverts to the normal Windows color scheme.

FIGURE 5.5

Enabling switching between standard and the specified high-contrast color scheme in Windows XP.

6. To change back to the high-contrast color scheme after you switch to the normal color scheme, press the shortcut keys again.

Figure 5.6 shows how a typical Windows XP desktop will look after being switched into High Contrast Black (Extra Large).

If you decide to disable a high-contrast color scheme, follow this procedure:

1. Click Start, Control Panel (Windows XP) or Start, Settings, Control Panel (other Windows versions) and open Accessibility Options.

2. Click the Display tab from the Accessibility Options dialog box that appears.

3. Clear the Use High Contrast check box.

4. Click the Settings button and select the same color scheme you are using as your high-contrast color scheme. Click OK, Apply, and then OK to activate the changes.

Fonts and Icons Overlap on the Windows Desktop

If you decide to use a high contrast or other color scheme that uses large or extra large fonts, as in Figure 5.6, you will have overlapping icons on the Windows desktop.

FIGURE 5.6

The Windows XP High Contrast Black (Extra Large) color scheme.

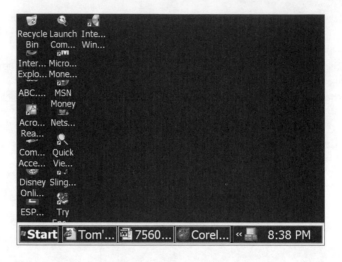

There are two ways to solve this problem:

- Adjust the setting for icon spacing in the Appearance tab of the Display Properties sheet.
- Manually drag icons into position.

To adjust the setting for icon spacing:

1. Open the Display Properties sheet and click the Appearance tab; with Windows XP, click Advanced.

2. Click the pull-down menu and select Icon Spacing (Horizontal).

3. Select a number that's about twice the default setting if you are using a large color scheme, or about 2.3 times the default setting if you are using an extra-large setting. For example, if the normal setting is 43, use 86 for a large color scheme or 100 for an extra-large color scheme. Click OK.

4. Click the pull-down menu and select Icon Spacing (Vertical).

5. Select a number that's about 70% larger than the default setting for either large or extra-large color schemes. For example, if the default is 43, use 70. Click OK.

6. Click Apply and OK to finish the process.

The problem with resetting the horizontal and vertical icon spacing is that if you decide to change back to a different color scheme with a different font size, your desktop will still be configured for the old spacing, which will then be too wide. If you decide to change the icon spacing, you should record the original values so you can change them back to their original values if you decide to switch back to your previous display.

Instead, I recommend that you follow this procedure to cure overlapping text and icons:

1. Switch to the high-contrast setting you prefer using the steps described in the previous section.

2. Right-click on the desktop and select Arrange Icons (by).

3. Deselect Auto Arrange (so that no check mark appears next to it in the menu) and click on the desktop to close the menu.

4. Drag the desktop icons around as desired until you can read the descriptions and see the icons.

To keep your desktop arrangement as you desired, don't use "Auto Arrange." Note that the desktop icons will be in the same locations if you switch back to your normal desktop, even though the icons and their text labels will be smaller.

Fast Track to Success

Windows XP doesn't clutter your desktop as much as earlier versions of Windows, but if you prefer desktop icons with XP or any other versions of Windows, consider making a folder on your desktop for the shortcuts you use most often. Although it will take an extra double-click to open a desktop folder, it's still faster than navigating through the Start menu to locate your programs.

To relocate desktop shortcuts (icons with the curved arrow) to a folder on the desktop, follow this procedure:

1. Right-click on an empty area of the desktop and select New, Folder.

2. Name the folder "Shortcuts".

3. Drag your desktop shortcuts into the folder.

Don't drag the Recycle Bin or other desktop icons that are not shortcuts (My Computer, Network Neighborhood, and so on) into the folder.

The CRT Monitor Flickers

The most common reason why CRT monitors flicker is that the vertical refresh rate is set too low. The vertical refresh rate indicates how quickly the screen is redrawn. By default, most Windows display drivers use low refresh rates (60Hz is typical). While 60Hz doesn't produce much flicker on traditional 640×480 VGA monitors, higher-resolution monitors running at 800×600, 1024×768, and above will flicker annoyingly if the refresh rate isn't increased. Your ability to adjust the refresh rate is dependent on the capabilities of your display adapter, your CRT monitor, and whether Windows can properly identify them.

Cautions and Warnings

Screen flicker can be just as annoying as the flickering light emitted by a defective fluorescent tube. But, screen flicker can be much worse for you. It can cause headaches and eyestrain, making a long day at the computer even longer. And, display flicker (which is also a problem with TV sets) has been known to trigger epileptic seizures in some computer users and TV viewers.

If you never want to worry about flicker again, switch to LCD display panels if you can afford them. But for economy and versatility, CRTs are still the monitor to beat.

If you are annoyed by screen flicker, open the Display Properties sheet, click Settings, and click Advanced. Depending upon the version of Windows you use, you will find the vertical refresh rate controls on either the Adapter tab (Windows 9x/Me) or the Monitor tab (Windows 2000/XP); see Figure 5.7. To reduce or eliminate flicker, choose a refresh rate of 72Hz or higher.

FIGURE 5.7

Adjusting the vertical refresh rate in Windows 9x/Me.

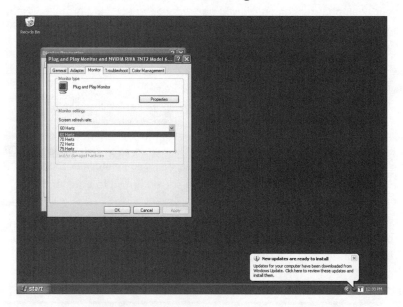

Cautions and Warnings

It's important to realize that Windows will *not* show you refresh rates that are too high for your monitor unless you clear the check box called Hide Modes That the Monitor Cannot Display in Windows XP. I don't recommend this, because you can damage your monitor if you try to force it to run refresh rates beyond its capabilities.

With Windows XP only, you can select resolution, color quality, and refresh rate with one mouse click from the Adapter tab. Click List All Modes to see all the available modes that will work with your display (see Figure 5.8).

FIGURE 5.8
Selecting resolution, color quality, and refresh rate with Windows XP's List All Modes option.

For Windows to accurately determine your refresh rates, it must properly identify your monitor and your display card. If your monitor uses a custom driver, the name and model number will be displayed on the Monitor tab of the Advanced Display Properties sheet. However, most monitors are Plug and Play, reporting their valid range of settings to Windows automatically. If the monitor is displayed as "Unknown" or "Default Monitor," though, you won't be able to safely set high refresh rates until you solve the problem with the display adapter. After the display adapter is properly configured with the correct driver, Windows can usually identify your monitor. If Windows cannot identify your monitor, contact the monitor vendor for a customized driver file or for technical support.

➔ *If Windows cannot properly identify your display card, see "Reinstalling or Updating Your Display Adapter Driver," p. 297.*

Colors Are Distorted

If you watch movie trailers, play 3D games, or work with digital camera pictures or scanned photos on your computer, your display needs to be configured to display a full range of colors. Figure 5.9 compares the display color choices available in Windows XP (left) and Windows 9x/Me (right).

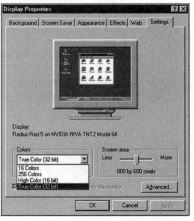

FIGURE 5.9
The Windows XP Color Quality settings (left) compared to the Windows 9x/Me Color Quality settings (right). Windows XP is optimized for high-color settings, while Windows 9x/Me can support older video cards that might have limited color settings.

Table 5.2 provides more detail about the color settings available in different versions of Windows.

TABLE 5.2
Windows Color Quality Settings

Windows XP Quality Setting	Windows 9x/Me Quality Setting	Number of Colors	Also Known As	Notes
Highest	True Color	16.8 million colors	32-bit or 24-bit color	32-bit setting is used by 3D display adapters; 24-bit setting is used by older display adapters that lack 3D modes
Medium	High Color	65,536 colors	16-bit color	Lowest quality setting typically available in Windows XP
Low	256 Colors	Same	8-bit color	Use Windows XP Compatibility Wizard to run programs in this mode (see "Troubleshooting Programs That Won't Run Under Windows XP," p. 138) or start computer in VGA mode
N/A	16 Colors	Same	4-bit color	Not available in Windows XP

Figure 5.10 compares a photograph scanned in 32-bit color (left) with the same picture scanned in 8-bit color (right).

If your display is set to 256-color or 16-bit mode, the images you scan or edit on your computer will be saved in that color mode, which, as Figure 5.10 shows, can reduce or eliminate fine details.

→ See "3D Games Run Too Slowly," p. 302.

Generally speaking, you should use the highest quality (32-bit or 24-bit) color setting whenever possible, since this provides the best appearance for scanned photos, digital pictures, and streaming video. Some 3D games run faster when medium (16-bit) color quality is used, but you can often select this mode within the game.

With most recent display adapters and on-board video, you should be able to set your display to 1024×768 resolution and use 32-bit or 24-bit color. This combination of resolution and color depth makes the best use of the popular 17-inch CRT or 15-inch LCD displays, and provides virtually unlimited colors.

FIGURE 5.10

A photo saved in 32-bit mode (left) compared to one saved in 256-color (8-bit) mode (right). Note the blotchy appearance of the 256-color mode photo.

The Display Color Quality Setting Is Reduced when You Select a Higher Resolution

You might discover, especially if you use an older computer, a computer with built-in video (instead of a separate display adapter), or a notebook computer, that you might not be able to select True Color (32-bit or 24-bit color) at some resolutions. This can be caused by any of the following:

- If the computer's display adapter (video card) doesn't have enough on-board memory to handle the color quality and resolution combination you selected. This doesn't apply to systems with integrated video adapters.

- If the computer has a built-in display adapter, you need to adjust the system BIOS settings to provide more onboard memory for display usage.

- You are not using the correct driver for the display adapter.

- The display driver is outdated or corrupt.

- Windows cannot correctly identify the display adapter.

How can you determine which of these villains is the real cause of your problem? First, you should determine the amount of display memory on your video card.

With Windows XP or Windows 2000, right-click the desktop and choose Properties to open the Display Properties sheet, click Settings, and click Advanced. The Adapter Information section displays the chipset, onboard memory, and other information (see Figure 5.11).

With Windows 9x/Me, right-click the desktop and choose Properties to open the Display Properties sheet. Look for a Details tab, which might contain this information (if it's there, select it). If there is no Details tab, you need to run the DirectX Diagnostic program or use a third-party reporting program such as SiSoftware Sandra to see the amount of memory on the display card.

→ *To learn more about using the DirectX Diagnostic program, see "Using DirectX Diagnostics," p. 497.*

FIGURE 5.11

Use Windows XP's Adapter Properties sheet to determine the amount of memory available to the adapter. Windows 2000 uses a similar Properties sheet.

Memory on display adapter

On the Web

SiSoftware Sandra is one of the most powerful system reporting programs ever created. Download the standard version (free for personal use) and learn about the professional version from the Sandra Information Page

http://www.sisoftware.demon.co.uk/sandra/

To use DirectX Diagnostics to determine the video card memory size, do the following:

1. Click Start, Run.

2. Type DXDIAG.

3. Click OK.

4. Click the Display tab. The video card's memory will be displayed in the Device section of the screen that appears (see Figure 5.12).

Note that the amount of memory DirectX Diagnostics lists for the display adapter might not be completely accurate. The memory size shown in Figure 5.12 was estimated at 31.5MB, while the actual size of the memory is 32MB. Regardless, the estimate is close enough in most cases to determine whether you have enough display memory to achieve a particular combination of colors and resolution. Table 5.3 shows how much display memory is required for various resolutions and color depths on 3D-capable display adapters. The values given in Table 5.3 for memory needed are the common memory sizes available on video cards; the exact values will be somewhat less than those shown.

Memory on display adapter

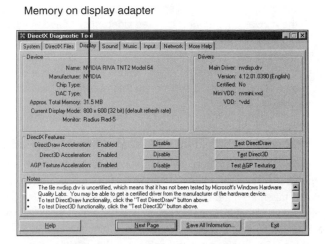

FIGURE 5.12
Use Windows's DirectX Diagnostic program to determine the memory available to the display adapter.

TABLE 5.3
Display Memory Required for Common Resolutions

Resolution	Color Depth	Video Card Memory Requirement (3D Operation)
640×480	32-bit	8MB
	24-bit	4MB
	16-bit	2MB
800×600	32-bit	8MB
	24-bit	8MB
	16-bit	4MB
1024×768	32-bit	16MB
	24-bit	16MB
	16-bit	8MB
1280×1024	32-bit	32MB
	24-bit	16MB
	16-bit	16MB
1600×1200	32-bit	32MB
	24-bit	32MB
	16-bit	16MB

If the amount of memory detected by the Windows XP Adapter Properties sheet, by DirectX Diagnostics, or by third-party programs such as SiSoftware Sandra indicates that you should be able to select a particular color quality setting, and you cannot, you

→ *For details, see "Reinstalling or Updating Your Display Adapter Driver," p. 297.*

should check the specifications for your display adapter (or integrated video) at the vendor's Web site. If the display adapter or integrated video specifications indicate that you should be able to select the color quality and resolution you want, visit the video adapter vendor's Web site and update the video driver. If you still cannot select the color quality setting and resolution you want, contact the display adapter vendor for help (or the motherboard or system vendor if the video is integrated); you might have a defective adapter or motherboard.

Increasing Available Display Memory on Systems with Integrated Video

In many notebook and desktop computers, video functions are built into the motherboard, rather than added through a separate adapter card. In these systems, the video memory is actually taken from the available system memory. If this is true of your system, you might need to adjust how the computer shares main memory with the display adapter to be able to configure the system to a particular combination of color quality and screen resolution. Depending upon the computer, this might require that you

- Install additional memory on the motherboard
- Adjust a setting in the system BIOS

The amount of system memory used in early integrated video systems varies according to the version of Windows used and the amount of RAM installed. In Table 5.4, you can see the relationship between video and system memory in systems using the Intel 810- and 815-series motherboard chipsets.

TABLE 5.4
Intel 810- and 815-Series Chipsets Display Memory Sizing

Total System Memory →	32MB	64MB	128MB or more
Windows Version	**Memory Used for Display**		
Windows 98/Me	6MB	10MB	10MB
Windows NT 4.0	(can't run)	9MB	9MB
Windows 2000/XP	(can't run)	9MB	10MB

More recently, motherboard chipsets with integrated video, such as the Intel 845G and 845GL, support much larger amounts of display memory:

- For systems with 128MB of RAM, these chipsets provide 32MB of RAM for the video display.
- For systems with more than 128MB of RAM, these chipsets provide 48MB of RAM for the video display.

Systems based on these chipsets don't always provide complete or accurate display memory size information using the Adapter Properties sheet or DirectX Display tab; use the information provided here instead.

Fast Track to Success

If your computer doesn't report the chipset at startup, you can run SiSoftware Sandra or other reporting programs to determine this information. If you downloaded and installed SiSoftware Sandra

1. Open the program through the Start menu.

2. Double-click the System Summary icon.

3. Scroll down to the Mainboard and BIOS section.

4. Read the information listed for System Chipset.

Desktop and notebook computers that use other chipsets with integrated video might require you to adjust a setting in the system BIOS to increase the amount of RAM available to the display adapter function. For example, the ASUS A1 series notebooks offer a BIOS setting called Video RAM Size on the Main BIOS Setup screen that allows the built-in display adapter to use anywhere from 2MB up to 64MB of RAM; its default is 16MB.

To determine whether your computer with built-in display adapter offers a similar function, see your system's instruction manual for details.

Reinstalling or Updating Your Display Adapter Driver

One of the best fixes for problems with the display adapter in Windows is to remove the display adapter from the Device Manager and restart the computer. This forces Windows to redetect the display adapter and reinstall the driver. This solves problems caused by damaged Registry entries for the display adapter. To perform this task

→ See "Using the Device Manager," p. 480 for general instructions on accessing and using the Device Manager.

1. Open the Device Manager.

2. Click the plus (+) sign next to the Display Adapters category.

3. Click the display adapter and click the Remove button (Windows 9x/Me), or click the display adapter and press the Del key (Windows 2000/XP).

4. Click OK to remove the display adapter.

5. Shut down the computer and turn off the power if the computer doesn't power down automatically.

6. Wait about 30 seconds and restart the computer; the display adapter will be redetected and the driver reinstalled when you restart the computer.

In some cases, you might also need to update the display adapter to a newer version. Follow these steps:

1. Run Windows Update to see if Windows Update has a new display adapter driver; if it does, it can install it for you automatically.

2. If Windows Update doesn't have an updated driver, go to the display adapter vendor's Web site (for an add-on card) or the computer vendor's Web site (for built-in video) and download the latest driver.

3. The Web site should provide you with specific directions for driver installation; if the driver doesn't install itself automatically during this process, note the location to which you downloaded it.

4. Follow the vendor's instructions for installing the new video driver with your version of Windows.

System Starts in 640×480 Mode

If the computer starts in the low-res 640×480 mode, even though you were previously using a higher resolution and you did not start the computer in VGA mode or Safe Mode, you might be experiencing one of the following problems:

- Your AGP display adapter is not assigned an IRQ in the system BIOS.
- Windows cannot identify your display adapter.
- Your display drivers might be corrupted.

If Windows cannot identify your display adapter or if your display driver is corrupt, you might not be able to select any other setting than 640×480 resolution and 16 colors.

To determine whether your display adapter is working correctly

1. Open the Device Manager and view the display adapter properties.

2. If the display adapter is shown with a yellow circle containing an exclamation point (!) in the Device Manager list of installed devices, look at the General tab of its properties sheet to determine the problem (see Figure 5.13).

FIGURE 5.13

How the Device Manager indicates a "can't start" problem with a display adapter.

Problem device shown in Device Manager

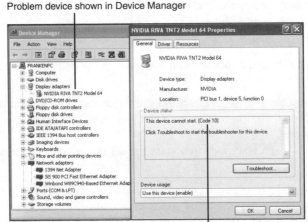

Explanation of error in device properties sheet

3. If the problem is listed as This Device Cannot Start (Code 10), shut down the computer and restart it.

4. Start the system BIOS setup program and navigate through the Advanced or Chipset menus until you find an option labeled Assign IRQ to VGA. If this option is disabled, enable this option and save the changes to the BIOS setup.

   This change enables Windows to accurately detect and configure your video card.

5. Restart the computer and open the Device Manager after the computer restarts. The display adapter should not report any problems.

If your display adapter is listed as Standard VGA or PCI-compatible VGA Adapter in Device Manager, Windows cannot identify it. You need to download new drivers from the vendor and direct Windows to use the new driver for the display adapter.

Can't Start the Computer Using Normal Display Drivers

If you can't start the computer in normal mode, but you can start it in Safe mode (Windows 9x/Me) or in VGA mode (Windows XP/2000), the problem might be the display drivers. All video chipsets used in Windows-based computers for the last several years use various methods to speed the transfer of video/graphics information to the display. By default, Windows enables all the video acceleration features available for your display adapter. However, if the display drivers aren't working correctly, full video acceleration could cause lockups or display problems or even prevent your computer from starting.

To determine whether your display drivers are preventing Windows from starting normally, follow this procedure:

1. Start the computer in VGA mode or Safe mode.

2. If the computer starts normally, disable all video acceleration. Right-click the desktop and select Properties. On the window that appears, select the Settings tab and click the Advanced button. Select the Troubleshoot tab (Windows XP) or Performance tab (other versions) and adjust the slider all the way to the left. This should disable all video acceleration. Windows XP users should also clear the Enable Write Combining check box (see Figure 5.14). Close all Display Properties windows.

3. If the computer restarts normally, download updated display adapter drivers and install them.

4. If you cannot restart Windows after adjusting the acceleration settings, restart Windows XP/2000 in VGA mode, download updated display adapter drivers, and install them. If Windows 9x/Me won't start normally after adjusting the acceleration settings, set up your display adapter as a VGA-compatible PCI adapter, restart the computer, download new display adapter drivers, and

→ If the Device Manager lists a different error code for the display adapter, or if the system BIOS doesn't have an option for enabling the IRQ for the VGA card, see "Solving Resource Conflicts with Device Manager," p. 481 for details.

→ For details about accessing the BIOS, see "BIOS Setup," p. 104.

→ To install a new video driver, see "Reinstalling or Updating Your Display Adapter Driver," p. 297.

→ For other reasons why Windows won't start, and to learn how to start Windows in Safe or VGA modes, see "Fixing Other Startup Problems with Windows XP," p. 129 and "Fixing Other Startup Problems with Earlier Versions of Windows," p. 132.

→ To switch to the standard VGA-compatible PCI adapter, follow the directions given for "Reinstalling or Updating Your Display Adapter Driver," p. 297, but specify this adapter type from the list of standard display adapters.

install them. If Windows still cannot correctly detect and configure your display adapter, it may be defective; contact the vendor for help.

FIGURE 5.14

Adjusting the acceleration settings to troubleshoot the display adapter in Windows XP.

Default (full) acceleration setting

Disables all video acceleration

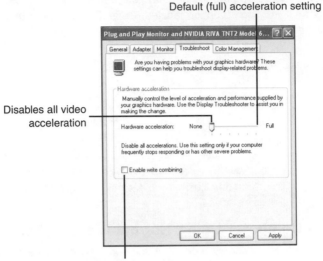

Disables the Enable Write Combining option when cleared

Computer Locks Up Frequently or Has Display-Quality Problems

If your computer starts correctly, but has frequent lockups or screen corruption when you move your mouse, your display, mouse, or DirectX drivers are probably defective and should be upgraded. However, as a workaround, you can reduce the video acceleration using a procedure similar to the one described in the previous section and illustrated in Figure 5.14. Use Table 5.5 to determine the best setting to use for the display problem you're having with Windows XP. With other Windows versions, use Table 5.6.

TABLE 5.5
Using Graphics Acceleration Settings to Troubleshoot Windows XP

Acceleration Setting	Left	One Click from Left	Two Clicks from Left	Two Clicks from Right	One Click from Right	Right
Effect of Setting	No acceleration	Disables all but basic acceleration	Disables DirectX, DirectDraw, Direct 3D acceleration (mainly used by 3D games)	Disables cursor and drawing accelerations	Disables mouse and pointer acceleration	Enables full acceleration
Long-Term Solution	Update display, DirectX, and mouse drivers	Update display, DirectX, and mouse drivers	Update DirectX drivers	Update display drivers	Update mouse drivers	N/A

Table note: Disable write combining, a method for speeding up screen display, whenever you select any setting other than full acceleration to improve stability. Re-enable write combining after you install updated drivers and retry.

TABLE 5.6
Using Graphics Acceleration Settings to Troubleshoot Other Windows Versions

Mouse Pointer Location	Left	One Click from Left	One Click from Right	Right
Effect of Setting	Disables all acceleration	Basic acceleration	Disables mouse pointer acceleration only	Full acceleration
Long-Term Solution	Update display and mouse drivers	Update display and mouse drivers	Update mouse drivers	N/A

If you're not certain of which setting is the best for your situation, use this procedure:

1. Start the computer.

2. Open the Troubleshooting or Performance dialog as described in the previous section.

3. Slide the acceleration pointer one notch to the left from its current position.

4. Click Apply, OK, and OK again to close the Display Properties dialog.

Use your normal software and perform typical tasks.

If the computer now performs acceptably, continue to use this setting until you can obtain and install updated drivers. If the computer continues to have problems, repeat steps 2–4 and move the pointer one step to the left each time until the problems go away or until you can install updated drivers as specified in Tables 5.5 or 5.6.

3D Games Run Too Slowly

If your 3D games run too slowly, the causes can vary according to the nature of the game and the hardware in your PC. If you are playing a single player game or with another human player on a single PC, then the solutions in this section should speed up your game. However, if you are playing a multiplayer game with other players using PCs located on your network or over the Internet, you may also need to adjust the network or Internet options in your game.

The best ways to speed up your visual display also cost money, such as

- Replacing your older video card with a video card using the latest chipsets made by nVidia or ATI

- Replacing integrated video with an AGP video card with the latest nVidia or ATI chipsets (if your computer has an AGP slot)

To speed up the visual display of 3D games with your current hardware, you can

- Reduce the color depth (number of colors) used in the game from 32-bit to 16-bit; displaying fewer colors can greatly improve performance.

- Reduce visual quality settings by disabling options such as anti-aliasing and anisotropic texture filtering; these settings create smoother and more realistic onscreen objects, but older display adapters become much slower when these options are enabled.

- Specify a 16-bit Z-buffer (the memory used to store 3D scene detail) instead of a 24-bit Z-buffer. Reducing the size of the Z-buffer reduces the amount of data the video card has to manipulate.

Some games allow you to adjust display quality settings within the game setup (see Figure 5.15); if not, you can adjust the 3D effects properties sheets provided as part of a 3D display adapter's properties sheets (see Figure 5.16).

It's important to understand that if you adjust video options from within a game, the interface and options you can choose vary from game to game. You should check its documentation for more information. Additionally, display quality adjustments made from within a game do not affect settings outside it.

Fast Track to Success

If you don't see any 3D configuration tabs for your 3D display adapter as shown in Figure 5.16, you are probably running the bare-bones Windows drivers provided on the Windows CD-ROM or through Windows Update. You should visit your display adapter vendor's Web site for card-specific or motherboard video-specific drivers.

While you might be able to use generic nVidia or ATI display drivers for third-party video cards built with those chipsets, you may be better off with drivers optimized for your particular hardware. The same is true for video drivers for motherboards with integrated video.

Some display adapter vendors provide preconfigured high-performance and high display-quality settings for OpenGL and Direct3D configuration, enabling you to quickly switch modes or make custom configuration changes. If you're not familiar with all the options available on your display adapter's 3D configuration options, consult the help function provided in the driver; click the ? (question mark) button in the upper-right corner of the properties sheet and click on the term or menu item you need help with.

FIGURE 5.15

Quake III is a popular 3D game that allows you to adjust resolution, 3D lighting, texture detail, and other effects within the game itself.

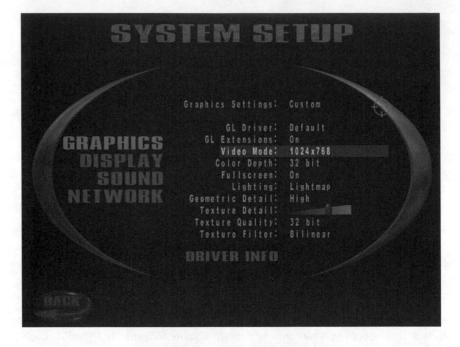

Use the Direct3D tab to adjust
3D effects for games that require DirectX

FIGURE 5.16

The OpenGL 3D Properties sheet for display adapters based on the popular nVidia TNT2 graphics chipset. Some games use OpenGL 3D graphics, while others use DirectX 3D graphics.

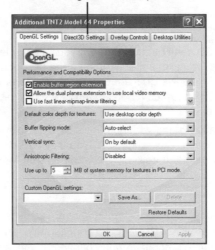

On the Web

The following Web sites provide reviews, white papers, and other resources that you can use to bolster your knowledge of 3D graphics:

- Tom's Hardware—http://www.tomshardware.com, a Web site that reviews the latest 3D hardware (and all other major computer subsystems) with incredibly detailed technical information and benchmarks.

- Anandtech—http://www.anandtech.com, another outstanding review and technology Web site for 3D hardware and other computer components.
- nVidia—http://www.nvidia.com, the leading maker of 3D graphics chipsets such as TNT2, GeForce series, and the nForce motherboard chipsets with integrated 3D graphics. Products using nVidia chips are sold by many vendors around the world.
- ATI—http://www.ati.com, a strong rival of nVidia, ATI is now selling 3D and motherboard chipsets to many other vendors as well as producing a broad line of graphics cards under the ATI label. 3D chipsets include the Radeon family, the Rage 128 family, and the Radeon IGP motherboard chipset with integrated 3D graphics.

Most of the time, altering the settings described in this section is a matter of choosing between better graphics and better performance. If your game stutters badly as it tries to draw the screen or suffers from other problems, try lowering the resolution and/or color depth from within the game's configuration options. Additionally, if your system contains hardware technology that is two or more years old, you may find that it simply cannot keep up with newer game titles (no matter what speed versus quality trade-offs you attempt to make).

Troubleshooting Multiple Displays

Windows 98 introduced support for multiple displays to the Windows/ PC world; it's also present in Windows Me, Windows 2000, and Windows XP. There are two ways to add a second monitor to your system:

- Install a second video card.
- Install a dual-display video card (if you don't already have one).

The simpler way by far is to move to a dual-display video card. Video cards using high-performance and mid-range 3D accelerator chips from both ATI and nVidia offer a wide range of prices and features. However, you can also recycle an older video card with recent ATI, nVidia, and other chipsets by installing it as your second video card.

Use the following sections to learn how to enable multiple-monitor support and solve common problems you might encounter.

Enabling Multiple-Monitor Support

The process of enabling multiple-monitor support varies with the type of display adapter you're using. If you have a dual-display adapter, including notebook computers with an LCD display and an external VGA port that run Windows XP, the process works like this:

1. Verify the system works correctly with the current (primary) monitor (this is the built-in LCD display on a notebook computer).

2. Turn off the system and all monitors.

3. Attach the secondary monitor to the other video port on the display adapter, or to the external video port on a notebook computer running Windows XP.

4. Turn on both monitors, and then the computer. During the boot process, you should see the same information on both monitors. If you don't see anything on the secondary display, check the data cable between the secondary monitor and the data port on the display adapter.

5. When the computer boots to the Windows desktop, open the Display Properties sheet and click the Settings tab.

6. You should see two icons displayed; your original monitor is displayed as monitor #1, while the new secondary monitor is displayed as monitor #2. To make monitor #2 active, click on the icon for monitor #2 and click the box next to Extend my Windows desktop onto this monitor (see Figure 5.17). Click Apply. Your Windows desktop background should appear on the second monitor (but no icons unless you drag them there).

7. Adjust the resolution and color quality for monitor #2 with the sliders shown in Figure 5.17.

Fast Track to Success

If you're not sure which monitor is which, click Identify, which places a huge number across each monitor for a few seconds.

FIGURE 5.17

Enabling multiple monitors in Windows XP; other Windows versions use a virtually identical interface.

Each monitor can use a different refresh rate, color depth, and resolution setting (except for Windows 2000). To adjust the settings for each monitor, click it in the Display Properties dialog box, then move through the properties sheets as discussed earlier in this chapter.

Cautions and Warnings

While Windows 2000 does offer multiple-monitor support, you will *not* be able to freely adjust refresh rates and resolutions with this version of Windows as you can with Windows 98, Me, and XP. In Windows 2000, both monitors must use the same resolution and refresh rate. This can make it very difficult to use a CRT and LCD monitor on the same system, since CRT monitors need high refresh rates to avoid flicker, and LCD panels use lower refresh rates (and don't have problems with flicker at any refresh rates). To avoid problems with Windows 2000

- Use two LCD panels or two CRTs; avoid mixing and matching.
- Make sure both panels or CRTs use similar ranges of refresh rates and resolutions.
- Avoid mixing and matching larger and smaller monitors.

If you're a big multiple-monitor fan, you'll find these limitations very frustrating—and a good reason to move to Windows XP.

If you're adding a second display adapter to an existing system, the start of the procedure is a bit different and more can go wrong:

1. Shut down the computer and the existing (primary) monitor.

2. Open the computer and locate an empty card slot for the secondary display adapter. You can add a PCI display adapter to systems that have PCI or AGP video.

3. Insert the new video card and connect the secondary monitor to the card.

4. Close the computer, turn on the monitors, and start the computer.

5. During the startup process, you should see information on both monitors.

6. Install drivers for the display adapter and monitor as prompted. Use the latest display adapter drivers provided by the vendor, not the one from the Windows CD, for best results.

7. When the computer boots to the Windows desktop, open the Display Properties sheet and click the Settings tab.

8. You should see two icons displayed; continue as described earlier in this section to configure your new display adapter and monitor.

If you are using compatible display adapters, the process of using two (or more) display adapters should go as smoothly as with a multiple-display card. However, if you have problems, see the following sections.

I Can't Get the Second Display to Work

If you're adding a separate video card to support an additional display and you're having problems, make sure that you

- Check the compatibility of both video cards with each other and with your motherboard or computer. While Microsoft has some information on multiple-display support available on its Web site and on the Windows CD, the chipsets mentioned are not current. I find the best source for researching video chipset and motherboard issues is the Realtime Soft UltraMon Web site (UltraMon is a terrific low-cost add-on to Windows that enhances multiple-monitor configuration and setup). The Web site has an enormous database of user-reported configurations; look up the video cards and motherboard/system you have to see if someone's already tried your combination and to learn what happened.

On the Web

The Realtime Soft UltraMon Web site is located at

http://www.realtimesoft.com/multimon/

Another useful multiple-monitor resource is available in the Technical Articles section of Arash Ramin's Web site:

http://www.digitalroom.net

You can search the microsoft.public.win98.display.multi_monitor newsgroup with Google (http://groups.google.com/) for more user comments and discussions.

- Make sure you have an available slot for the second video card. If you want to have dual-display support on a desktop computer with built-in video, you will need to install a multiple-display card or two separate single-display cards, because built-in video needs to be disabled whenever you install add-on display adapters. If you don't have room for a second video card, replace your existing card with a multiple-display video card.

Cautions and Warnings

While some computers with built-in video automatically disable the onboard video adapter when you install another video card, some require you to adjust a setting in the system BIOS or adjust a jumper block on the motherboard to disable onboard video. Consult your computer or motherboard documentation for details.

→ For details about accessing the BIOS, see "BIOS Setup," p. 104.

- If Windows can't recognize the secondary display adapter, try adjusting the priority of the display cards in your system. Most recent system BIOSes with AGP slots have a BIOS setting that lets you select either AGP or PCI as the primary display. You might need to configure the slower PCI display card as the primary display adapter to enable dual-display support if your system already has an AGP display adapter installed. Because the secondary display adapter can't be used for advanced 3D gaming or accelerated video, you want to avoid this situation if possible. Study the online resources provided earlier to determine which combinations of AGP and PCI display adapters will enable you to continue to use the faster AGP video card as the primary adapter and have dual-display support.

- Install updated drivers for both video cards. The video drivers provided by Microsoft often don't support multiple displays or other advanced features. Go to the card manufacturer's Web site and download the latest drivers they offer for your card and your version of Windows.

- Make sure the primary display works correctly before you install the second video card.

- To verify that the secondary display adapter works if Windows can't detect it, remove the primary display adapter and use the secondary adapter as the only video card in the system. If it works by itself, but not with the original primary adapter in the system, you might not be able to use that particular combination of cards in your system. Try the other fixes listed, try a different card as the secondary display adapter, or upgrade to a dual-display card.

→ *For details, see "Reinstalling or Updating Your Display Adapter Driver," p. 297.*

The Second Display Won't Run 3D Graphics

This is a normal limitation of multiple-display setups. The faster video card should be used with the primary display. If you are unable to use two separate display cards with the faster AGP card as the primary display, I recommend that you replace your existing AGP card with a dual-display card using an nVidia or ATI 3D graphics chip; see the nVidia or ATI Web sites for details about their latest offerings.

The Second Display Shows What's on the First Display

This is normal if you've attached a secondary monitor to a multiple-monitor display adapter. To enable the secondary monitor to display different programs than the primary adapter, open the Display Properties sheet, click Settings, and click the icon for the secondary monitor (refer to Figure 5.17). Answer Yes to the dialog box that asks if you want to enable the monitor, and then click Apply. Adjust the color depth, resolution, and refresh rate as desired.

If you don't see multiple displays listed on the Settings tab, you need to upgrade your display drivers to the enhanced versions available from the display card or chipset vendor; the display drivers supplied with Windows might not support multiple displays.

If you're already using up-to-date enhanced display adapter drivers, check the configuration of add-on software. Many vendors provide special software that enables multiple displays to be used as one large desktop, mirrored displays (both displays show the same information), and other features. Disable the mirror feature to enable each display to show different information.

The Secondary Display Doesn't Show Any Programs

To display programs on the secondary display, click the Restore button in the upper-right corner of your program's display to shrink the program into a window. Then, you can drag the window to the secondary display. Click the Restore button again to maximize the program window on the secondary display.

The Secondary Display Is Using the Same Driver As the Primary Display

Windows can't always determine what type of monitor you're using for a secondary display. To select the correct driver in Windows XP

1. Open the Display Properties sheet and click the Settings tab.

2. Select the secondary monitor.

3. Click Advanced.

4. Click Monitor.

5. Click Properties, and then Driver.

6. Click Update Driver.

7. Click Install from a List or Specific Location, and then Next.

8. If you have downloaded the correct driver or have a driver on CD or floppy disk, keep the default (search for the best driver) and specify the locations to search. If you want to choose the driver from a list, click Don't Search.

9. If you select Search, Windows will locate the correct driver and install it for you. If you select Don't Search and want to see a list of drivers, clear the Show Compatible Hardware checkbox and scroll through the vendor list to select a vendor, and then through the model list to select the model. Click Next, and then Finish.

To select the correct driver in Windows 9x/Me

1. Open the Display Properties sheet and click the Settings tab.

2. Select the secondary monitor.

3. Click Advanced.

4. Click Monitor.

5. Click Change, and then Next.

6. Click Display a List of All the Drivers.

7. To install from a downloaded driver file, floppy disk, or CD, click Have Disk and navigate to the driver. Follow the prompts to install the driver.

8. To select from all drivers, click Show All Hardware and scroll through the vendor list to select a vendor, and then through the model list to select the model. Click Next, and then Finish.

Troubleshooting Damaged or Defective Displays or Display Adapters

Damaged or defective displays might have the following symptoms:

- Rectangular blank areas or pixels that are stuck on or off (LCD panels)
- Discolored or extremely dim CRT monitor displays
- Periodic colored flickers
- Buzzing or humming
- Display can't power on

If resetting the display with its onscreen controls, degaussing a CRT display with the degaussing button available on some models, or tightening the data cable doesn't resolve these problems, you might have a defective monitor. If you can, borrow a replacement monitor from another computer, shut down the computer and monitor, attach a different monitor to the computer, and try the operation again. If the problem is solved by using a different monitor, service the original monitor. If the problem persists, replace the display adapter.

Keep in mind that if Windows doesn't recognize the new monitor correctly, you will need to install drivers for the monitor. Check the monitor's documentation to determine whether the monitor should be configured as a Plug and Play monitor or if it uses special drivers.

Fast Track to Success

Be sure to check the data cable running between the monitor and the display adapter for damage. When you remove it, check the connector for bent or broken pins. If you find bent pins, straighten them if possible and retry the monitor. If you can't fix the cable but you can remove it, try a replacement cable for a low-cost fix that won't require a trip to the repair shop. Unfortunately, most low-cost and mid-range monitors use fixed cables.

Troubleshooting Sound Problems

Sound hardware has become very important to all types of computer users. Whether you're a hardcore gamer, a fan of Internet radio, or like to watch DVD movies on your computer, you need to fix sound problems quickly. Use the following sections to make sure your sound works the way you need it to work.

Can't Record or Play Back Sounds

Sound recording and sound playback depend upon several factors, including

- Correct connection of speakers and microphones
- Correct installation of the sound card and its drivers
- Correct use of sound mixer controls
- Installation of the proper audio codecs

The following sections deal with these issues.

Troubleshooting Problems with Sound Card Installation and Drivers

Generally, sound card installations are simple *if*

- The computer doesn't have built-in sound.
- No other sound card has been installed in the computer previously.

However, if you have installed a new sound card in a computer that has built-in sound or you are upgrading from an older sound card, the old hardware could cause you problems. Check the following:

- Disable on-board sound hardware before you install a new sound card—Most systems with on-board sound control that feature through the system BIOS setup program (see Figure 5.18).

FIGURE 5.18

On-board audio settings on a typical system; these must be disabled to avoid conflicts with a sound card.

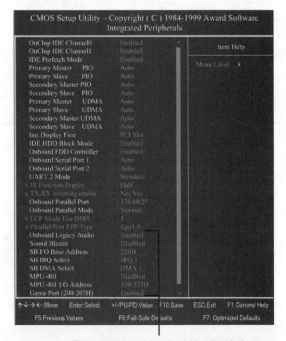

These audio settings should be disabled.

- Remove listings for old sound hardware from Device Manager before you install the new sound card—The Sound, Video, and Game Controllers category in Device Manager (see Figure 5.19) lists sound card and on-board sound hardware. Sound card (audio) hardware and drivers should no longer be loaded after you disable on-board sound. If you see the drivers listed, remove them. Similarly, if you are upgrading to a new sound card, remove the sound card from Device Manager before you install the new card.

➔ *For tips on using Device Manager, see "Using Device Manager," p. 480.*

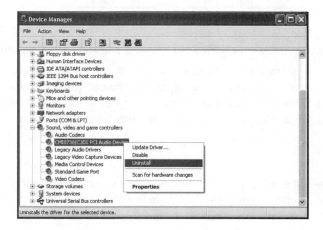

FIGURE 5.19

Preparing to remove existing sound hardware from the Windows XP Device Manager.

Cautions and Warnings

At one time you could assume that all the devices listed in the Sound, Video and Game Controllers section of the Windows Device Manager were part of the sound card. However, if you have a Webcam or a TV tuner, you might also find video capture tools for those devices in this category. When you delete your old sound hardware from Device Manager, I recommend you delete only the sound card or chipset driver itself; drivers associated with the sound card will also be deleted in the process. If you still use gameport devices and your motherboard has a gameport, but your new sound card doesn't, keep the gameport enabled in the system BIOS settings shown in Figure 5.17, and don't delete the gameport from the Device Manager.

- Download the latest drivers for your sound card before you start the installation process—This is especially important with Windows XP, since many vendors were slow about developing Windows XP drivers. Regardless of the Windows version you use, you might find that the drivers packaged with your sound card are inadequate or buggy.

- Load the software included with your sound card in the correct order— Depending upon the sound card you are installing, you might need to install the driver software before you install the sound card or let the sound card prompt you for drivers when Windows detects it. Generally, software for sound recording, digital audio conversion, and so forth should be installed only after the sound card is installed and tested.

Fast Track to Success

If you're moving up from built-in sound or an entry-level sound card to a better model, you can save yourself a lot of grief if you label both internal and external cables before you remove them. If you don't have specialized data-cable labels, address labels will do for temporary use. Since different types of cables use the same connectors, you can save yourself a lot of frustration if you mark what each cable does before you unplug it.

Troubleshooting Problems with Speaker and Microphone Connections

Generally, if your sound card is working and you attach speakers to your sound card, you should hear Windows play its startup sound as soon as the Windows desktop appears. Unfortunately, standard sound cards and built-in sound features use identical mini-jacks for speakers, microphones, and other input-output connections.

To make sure you connect the correct devices to the correct jacks, check the following:

- Use the color-coding provided on many recent sound cards, microphones, and speakers to attach the correct cables to the correct ports. The standard color used for speaker cords and jacks is lime green; microphone and line-in jacks use a light blue connector.

- Check the markings on the rear of the sound card or computer if the color coding systems don't match (some vendors don't follow industry standards) or aren't present.

If the cables are connected correctly, check the volume and mixer controls.

Troubleshooting the Sound Volume Controls

While basic sound cards are limited to the traditional mini-jacks, more and more sound cards offer optical and digital connections to 5.1 speaker systems, home theater systems, DVD drives, and other exotica. Whether you use a simple two-speaker hookup or have your system patched into your home theater system, you must configure your sound card's mixer controls to correctly identify which speakers you plan to use. Similarly, if you are recording sound, the mixer controls are also used to determine the source for recorded sound (microphone, line in, and so on).

To access the sound volume control, check the Windows system tray. In most cases, you will find a speaker icon. Click it to open the volume control (see Figure 5.20). If you don't see the volume control in the Windows system tray, open the Control Panel. In Windows XP, select Sounds, Speech and Audio Devices, and then Sounds and Audio Devices. In other Windows versions, double-click the Sounds (or Sounds and Multimedia) icon. In either case, enable the Place Volume Icon in the Taskbar check box and click OK.

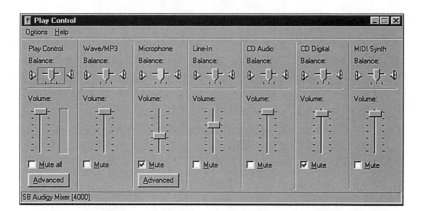

FIGURE 5.20
The volume control for the Creative Labs Sound Blaster Audigy Platinum.

If your sound card's default volume control has settings for devices and music types you will never use, you can configure the volume control to display only the controls you need. Click Options, Properties, Playback and clear the check marks from devices you don't use for playing sounds (see Figure 5.21). Click Options, Properties, Record and do the same for devices you don't use for recording.

If you can work with some types of sounds but not others, the volume control for the type of audio source probably has its volume turned down too far or the volume control is muted. For example, in Figure 5.20, you won't be able to record sounds through the microphone until you clear the check mark from the Mute setting. If you don't see a volume control for the sound source you are using, it is probably disabled. Open the Options menu, select Properties, and re-enable the volume control for that sound source.

FIGURE 5.21
Customizing the play-back volume control for the Creative Labs Sound Blaster Audigy Platinum.

Table 5.7 lists audio types and their uses. If you are having problems with sound recording or playback, use this table to determine which volume control to adjust.

TABLE 5.7

Audio Types and Volume Control Settings

Audio Type	Volume Control	Notes
All audio types	Play control	This overrides all other settings if set to a low volume or Mute.
Digital music	Wave/MP3	(WAV, MP3, WMA)
MIDI tracks	MIDI	
Music CDs	CD Audio or CD Digital	If you use the standard four-wire cable between the CD-ROM drive and the sound card, use CD-Audio. CD-Digital uses a two-wire cable that won't work with older CD-ROM drives.
Auxiliary	TV tuner card or additional CD-ROM drive	Uses the same four-wire cable as CD Audio.
Line-In	Any external sound source, particularly stereo systems, tape players, and so on	Might be the same as the microphone jack on some sound cards.
TAD-In	Works with internal modems that had a telephone answering device feature	
Microphone	Headset, boom, and handheld microphones	It is muted by default to prevent accidental recording.

Correct adjustment of the volume control is only half the battle. If you want to use more than two speakers, digital speakers, or other non-standard sound sources or outputs, you need to properly configure the sound mixing controls provided with the sound card.

Can't Hear Sound from Additional Speakers

Generally, if all you have is the traditional pair of stereo speakers that attach through a minijack, you don't need to do anything other than adjust the volume control to have acceptable sound playback. However, most users want more and better speakers, or might be using headphones instead of speakers. If you use analog speakers or headphones, you need to adjust the Sounds and Audio Devices properties in Windows. If you want to use advanced audio features or if you use digital speakers, you also need to adjust settings in the proprietary mixer program provided by the sound card vendor (in this case, consult your audio card's documentation).

If you can't hear anything from the additional speakers you've added to your system, or you've changed your speaker type (even if you have the same number of speakers), you need to adjust your audio configuration to reflect your new speaker setup.

1. Open the Control Panel. In Windows XP, select Sounds, Speech and Audio Devices, and then Sounds and Audio Devices. In Windows Me, double-click the Sounds and Multimedia icon and select the Audio tab. In Windows 9x, open the Multimedia icon.

2. Click the Advanced button in the Speakers section (Windows XP) or the Sound Playback section (other versions). An Advanced Audio Properties sheet appears; the Speakers tab is displayed by default.

3. Click the pull-down Speaker setup menu and select the type of speaker setup you use (see Figure 5.22); the speaker configuration you select is displayed onscreen.

4. After you select the correct speaker configuration, click OK when you're finished.

FIGURE 5.22
Selecting the speaker type in Windows XP.

If you've selected the correct speaker types, but you can't hear any sounds, check the volume control. If the volume control is set correctly, you might need to adjust the mixer controls to enable digital speakers. Consult the instructions for your sound card for details.

You might also have problems with the speaker cables, or with the speakers themselves. For example, you might have connected the additional speakers to the wrong jack, or you might need to adjust the built-in volume control on the speakers themselves before you can fine-tune the volume with Windows's own volume control. If you don't hear any sound from additional speakers after checking mixer controls, cable connections, and built-in volume controls, you might have defective speakers.

Troubleshooting Problems with 3D Sound in Games

3D sound makes games sound as realistic as 3D video makes them look. If you're not experiencing directional sound (even if you have just two speakers) or are having other sound quality problems, check the following:

➔ *For details, see "Can't Hear Sound from Additional Speakers," p. 316.*

- The speaker configuration—Even if you have just two speakers, speakers built into the monitor or headphones need a different configuration than the typical tabletop speakers you might have received with your system.

- The environmental audio settings for your sound card—If you have a Creative Labs Sound Blaster series card, for example, you should enable the EAX (environmental audio effects) feature through the EAX control panel (part of the Creative Audio HQ program included with the card).

- Make sure you have installed the latest DirectX drivers—Most games that use 3D sound use DirectX drivers.

On the Web

You can download the latest version of DirectX from the Microsoft DirectX Web site:

http://www.microsoft.com/windows/directx/default.asp

- Audio acceleration features—The default setting for audio acceleration is full, but you might need to try reduced acceleration for certain games if the default setting produces poor-quality sound.

To adjust the audio acceleration setting

1. Open the Control Panel. Then, in Windows XP, select Sounds, Speech and Audio Devices, and then Sounds and Audio Devices. In Windows Me, double-click the Sounds and Multimedia icon and select the Audio tab. In Windows 9x, open the Multimedia icon.

2. Click the Advanced button in the Speakers section (Windows XP) or the Sound Playback section (other versions); an Advanced Audio Properties sheet appears.

3. Click the Performance tab and adjust the Hardware acceleration slider one notch to the left from the default Full position (see Figure 5.23).

4. Try your game. If audio performance improves, use that acceleration setting for that game. If audio performance is still poor, repeat steps 1–3 and try each lower setting with your game.

5. Update the audio drivers as soon as possible and retry full audio acceleration after updating them.

Hardware acceleration slider

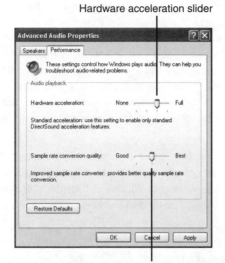

FIGURE 5.23

Adjusting the Hardware acceleration and sample rate conversion quality settings in Windows XP.

Sample rate conversion quality slider

A second option for improving game quality is also located on the Performance tab; if you need to adjust acceleration settings downward, also try adjusting sample rate conversion quality (how well and how quickly digital samples are converted to audio). Depending upon the speed of your sound card and your system, the default for your system might be set to Good. If it is, slide the control one notch towards the middle; this improves audio conversion quality, but requires a bit more processing power from your computer.

Fast Track to Success

Check with your game vendor for updates and patches for your game before you fiddle around with the acceleration and sample rate conversion sliders. You should also install the latest software drivers and DirectX version and retry your game. Also, be sure to check your games' own menus for sound playback options. Use these controls as a workaround if you can't improve sound quality any other way.

The following Web site has a terrific grab-bag of assorted workarounds, fixes, drivers, and patch sources for many recent systems and games with sound problems. Even if you don't have the particular sound card or program listed, it's a valuable resource for options to check on your system.

http://www.qsl.net/ad7db/tech/sound.txt

Troubleshooting Playback Problems with Music CDs

Playing music CDs on your computer is an enjoyable way to entertain yourself, but it depends upon proper cable connections and volume controls. If you can't hear anything while a music CD is playing, check the following:

- Volume control on your music player software and the Windows volume control—Whether you use Windows Media Player or some other playback software, its volume control must be coordinated with the Windows master volume control. Generally, you should set the Windows volume control as high as possible so you can use the application's volume control to reduce the volume (be careful not to damage your speakers by setting the volume too high). If you have your application's volume control turned up full blast but the Windows volume control is set to low levels or is muted, you won't hear your music.

- Power and volume controls used by external speakers—If the external speakers aren't turned on or have their built-in volume control turned down, you can't control the speakers with Windows. Turn them on and adjust their volume controls, and then fine-tune the volume with the Windows volume control.

- Patch cables between your CD-ROM or other optical drive and your sound card—If digital audio downloads such as MP3 and WMA files and WAV files in games sound great but you can't hear a thing when you play your CDs, this cable is probably not plugged in properly. Note that recent (7.x and above) versions of Windows Media Player can play music CDs without a patch cable on some systems, although other CD playback programs still require a patch cable.

There are two ways to connect your optical drive to a sound card:

- Older CD-ROM drives and low-cost sound cards use a four-wire analog cable.

- Newer CD-ROM, CD-RW, and DVD drives can use either the four-wire cable or a two-wire digital CD cable that connects to the CD SPDIF port on the sound card.

  Whenever possible, use the digital cable to provide better sound than with the analog cable. Figure 5.24 shows how these interfaces look on typical optical drives and sound cards.

- Sound mixer controls—By default, music CD playback programs assume that you are using the CD Audio (analog) cable; if your drive and sound card can use the CD SPDIF cable for superior digital sound, you must change the mixer settings to use CD Digital sound. See your sound card's instruction manual or help file for details.

- Dirt on the CD or in the drive—If the CD won't play at all or skips, its surface may be dirty. Use a wet-type radial CD cleaner to clean the CD surface, and also use a cleaning CD to clean the lens of the CD-ROM drive. If you have a DVD drive, try to use a DVD-specific cleaning CD for better results.

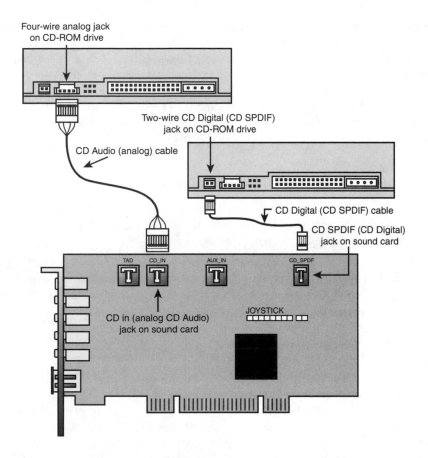

FIGURE 5.24

A typical four-wire analog connection (top) and the newer two-wire SPDIF connection (middle) between optical drives and sound cards.

Troubleshooting Multimedia Problems

Problems with multimedia devices such as media players and DVD
players can be caused by problems with sound, CD-ROM and DVD hardware, and display adapter hardware. You should make sure that basic sound and display features work correctly before you try to view streaming video, convert CDs into digital music tracks, or view a DVD on your computer. This section will help you solve problems that are not caused by basic problems with your audio or display hardware.

Troubleshooting Windows Media Player (WMP)

Windows Media Player is the default media player used in Windows
9x/Me/2000/XP. Use this section to keep WMP working properly.

Can't Access the Internet with Windows Media Player

Windows Media Player, particularly in version 7.x and above, functions as Internet Explorer's default media player as well as providing playback for locally stored audio and video media. When you start Windows Media Player (WMP) and click the Media

Guide button, WMP attempts to connect to the WindowsMedia.com Web site, which displays links to current movie, music, and news clips and features and displays them in the WMP window. This connection works automatically when you have an always-on connection to the Internet. However, if you use a dial-up, PPPoE, or other connection that requires you to log on, you must start that connection before Media Guide will work. If your Web browser is set to connect to the Internet automatically when you open it, Media Guide should also be able to connect to its Web site automatically.

If you don't see the contents of the WindowsMedia.com Web site when you click on Media Guide, check the following:

- Are you already connected to the Internet? If not, start your connection first.

- If you've already started your connection, make sure you can view Web pages with your browser. If your browser can't view Web pages, Media Guide (which acts as a specialized Web browser) won't work either.

- Are you on a corporate network? WMP needs special configuration settings to work behind a firewall or with a proxy server. Click Tools, Options, Network to open the Network dialog, and contact your network administrator for the specific settings you need for your network.

➜ *To troubleshoot your Internet connection, see Chapter 2, "Internet and Online Problems."*

Can't Play Back WMA Digital Files with Windows Media Player

Unlike MP3 player programs, which generally don't have any provision for controlling access to digital recordings (and have thus spawned a huge, unregulated market in MP3 file swapping), WMP is designed to manage use of digital recordings. By default, Windows Media Player automatically acquires licenses for CDs you copy with Windows Media Player. The details of these licenses might vary, but in practice, many licenses that WMP obtains automatically from the music CD publisher can limit you to playing back Windows Media Audio (WMA) files on your original computer only, or on portable devices that are attached to your computer. Unlike MP3 files, which you can move freely from computer to computer, WMA files that are created with the default settings can't be moved freely. You can even lose the ability to play back WMA files you created yourself if you don't properly maintain Windows licenses.

To prevent problems with playback of WMA files you create yourself, follow these precautions:

- Disable the default rights management/contact protection settings when you copy CDs from your own collection. Click, Tools, Options, Copy Music, and clear the Protect Content (Windows XP) or Use Enable Personal Rights Management (other Windows versions) check box. If you disable these options, your WMA files can be moved to any computer or portable device you use.

- If you have already copied CDs using WMP's default settings with Windows Media Player 7.x (Windows 9x/Me/2000), you should download and use the Personal License Update Wizard from http://www.microsoft.com/windows/windowsmedia/wm7/drm/pluwiz.asp.

This wizard enables you to play protected files on up to 10 computers or devices.

- Back up your personal licenses with Tools, License Management, Backup Now. You can transfer licenses for any type of digital media (CD copies, Internet downloads, and so on) to another computer through Back Up and Restore (Tools, License Management, Restore Now).

- Be sure to back up your licenses to a floppy disk before you perform a CPU upgrade or a motherboard/CPU upgrade. Digital rights management tracks the location of your licensed digital media based on your CPU type. Follow the instructions provided by Microsoft at http://support.microsoft.com/default.aspx?scid=kb;EN-US;Q301082.

- Consider using MP3 encoding instead of WMA encoding. Standard MP3 encoding doesn't use licensing, and thus can't cause you problems if you move a CD of your favorite "greatest hits" from your home PC to your office PC. I don't believe in piracy or swapping songs with friends, but in my opinion the digital license management features in Windows Media Player are a problem just waiting to trip up the honest, unwary user. You can add third-party MP3 encoders to Windows Media Player, or just use your favorite MP3 encoders as separate applications.

On the Web

The Crazy 4 MP3s.com Web site has an excellent collection of basic techniques for converting all types of music (tape, LP, and CD) into digital form:

http://www.crazy4mp3s.com/q&a.shtml

Two of the best MP3 creators and players include

- MUSICMATCH Jukebox 7.x—http://www.musicmatch.com
- Nullsoft Winamp—http://www.winamp.com

If you decide to re-create CD music tracks in MP3 format, be sure to start with the original music CD; converting from one compressed digital format to another (such as from WMA to MP3) will only reduce the quality of the resulting files.

Windows Media Player Can't Work with Some Devices or Types of Media

As new portable media players and media types are released, Windows Media Player might need to be updated. If you cannot work with a particular media player or type of media

1. Open WMP.
2. Open the Help menu and select Check for Player Updates.
3. If updates are available, WMP will display information on what the updates include. Click Next to download and install the updates.

Fast Track to Success

By default, WMP checks for updates monthly. To change the frequency of this update, open the Tools menu and select Options. On this screen you can choose between daily, weekly, and monthly updates. In any case, make sure that the Download codecs (compression/decompression programs) check box is selected.

You might also need to install driver support for the portable audio player; contact the audio player vendor's Web site for the latest driver files and updates.

Can't View a DVD Movie

If you want to watch a DVD movie on your computer screen, there's more to the process than just sliding your favorite comedy or epic into the DVD drive. You must use a DVD player program to convert the movie into computer-readable form. Most DVD drives, including those built in to notebook computers and many high-end display adapters come with a movie player program. If you didn't install the program, dig out the discs you received with your DVD drive, notebook computer with built-in DVD drive, or display adapter and, if available, install the provided player program.

Note that WMP can be used as a DVD movie player only if you install a DVD movie player application on your system; it doesn't include the DVD decoding software needed to see the movie.

To determine whether you have a DVD decoder compatible with Windows Media Player already installed

1. Insert your DVD movie into the DVD drive.
2. Start WMP.
3. Click Play.
4. If the menu lists Audio CD or DVD, you have a compatible DVD decoder installed and WMP can be used to view your movie; if the menu lists only Audio CD, you need to install a DVD decoder before you can use WMP to view your movie.

If you didn't receive a software DVD player with your DVD drive or video card, two of the leading products are WinDVD and PowerDVD.

On the Web

InterVideo, Inc is the producer of WinDVD and WinDVD Plus. Get more information or order the latest versions from their Web site:

http://www.intervideo.com

CyberLink Corp is the producer of PowerDVD. Get more information or order the latest versions from their Web site:

http://www.gocyberlink.com

Both vendors offer free trial versions you can download.

Can't Use Advanced Speaker Systems with Your DVD Player

To get the full benefit of watching DVD movies on your computer, there's nothing like connecting your system to a 5.1 or other advanced speaker system. However, standard DVD movie players (particularly those that are bundled with hardware) might not include support for advanced speaker configurations and sound systems. If you aren't getting the full benefit of your speaker system when you watch a DVD movie on your PC, check the following:

- Have you connected your speakers correctly? Check your speaker connections against the wiring diagrams provided with your sound card.

Cautions and Warnings

To accommodate the greater number of connections needed for advanced speaker systems, many high-end sound cards use external breakout boxes for the extra connections. For example, some models of the Sound Blaster Audigy series from Creative Labs feature the Audigy Drive, which fits into a CD-ROM–sized drive bay and offers extra speaker connections, easy-to-reach volume controls, and other benefits. If you connect your speakers to a breakout box like the Audigy drive, make sure the breakout box is properly connected to your sound card. If it requires a power connector, make sure it's receiving power as well. Without data and power connections, it's just a paperweight.

- Is your sound card mixer correctly configured for your speaker system? Some 4.1 and 5.1 speaker systems are analog, while others are digital. If you select the wrong setting in your mixer, your speakers won't work.

Fast Track to Success

If your sound card has a test option, use it to verify that all your speakers are working correctly and that your mixer controls are set correctly. If your speakers work with the test setup, the problem lies with your DVD movie player software.

- Have you configured your DVD player program to use your speaker configuration? Until you configure the player program to use your speaker system, it won't work correctly while you're watching movies. If your player program doesn't have an option for your speaker system, contact the vendor to determine whether an upgrade has the speaker support you need. You can usually upgrade a bundled player at a reduced price.

Troubleshooting Input Devices

CHAPTER 6

Common Input Devices

Your computer just sits on its desk or in your lap until you tell it what to do. And, until you can talk to a computer a la *Star Trek*, your hands do the "talking" through devices such as keyboards and pointing devices such as mice, trackballs, or touch pads. If you prefer a notebook computer to a full-size model, your notebook computer's keyboard typically includes an integrated trackball, touchpad, or mouse stick (such as the IBM TrackPoint II, III, or Toshiba AccuPoint). Finally, you might use a scanner to input photographic prints or other documents for image storage or text recognition.

Obviously, a problem with almost any of these input devices, your mouse or keyboard in particular, is going to leave your computer high and dry until you find a solution—and that's what this chapter is all about.

Input devices connect to your computer through many different types of ports, including

- Serial (COM)
- Parallel (LPT)
- PS/2
- USB

All these ports are commonly built in to computers today, as shown in Figure 6.1; these ports can be used for keyboards, pointing devices, scanners and more.

- SCSI
- IEEE-1394a

FIGURE 6.1

Input device ports on the rear of a typical computer.

6-pin mini-DIN (PS/2) mouse port   LPT (parallel) port

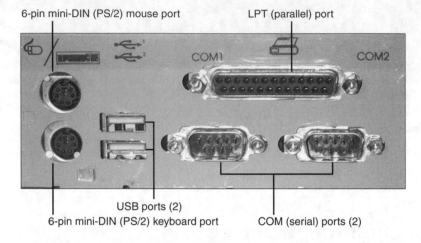

USB ports (2)

6-pin mini-DIN (PS/2) keyboard port   COM (serial) ports (2)

There are two other types of ports that usually require the installation of an add-in card for your PC to use them (though more recent PC motherboards may also have them built-in as well). See Figure 6.2.

FIGURE 6.2

SCSI (left) and IEEE-1394a (right) host adapters installed in a typical PC.

HD-50 SCSI port

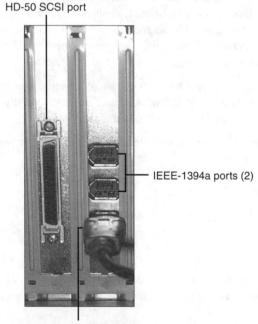

IEEE-1394a ports (2)

Cable attached to IEEE-1394a port

Ports used by input devices can be divided up into two categories:

- Legacy ports
- High-speed ports

The differences between these ports and the input devices which use them are discussed in the following sections.

Legacy Ports (Serial, Parallel, PS/2)

Legacy ports, as the name implies, are ports which today's computers have inherited from the PCs of 15 and 20 years ago. While serial, parallel, and PS/2 ports are different in many ways, they have several features in common:

- None of these ports are compatible with hot-swapped peripherals; you must shut down the computer before you can attach or remove devices attached to these ports.
- These ports were originally designed to handle a narrow range of devices, although ingenuity has enabled some (such as the parallel port) to be more flexible than originally intended.
- These ports are much slower than more recent high-speed ports such as SCSI, USB, and IEEE-1394a.

Legacy ports are typically used for keyboards, pointing devices, and scanners, but are used less often today than previously. In fact, recent so-called "legacy-free" systems don't have these ports at all, forcing you to use peripherals that support only recent connector types like USB and IEEE-1394.

Serial Port

Originally, mice and similar pointing devices were connected to the serial port, which was originally provided for modems and other serial communications devices. However, Windows XP no longer supports serial pointing devices. Serial ports are still used by specialized devices such as label printers, LapLink file transfer, and PDA synchronization cradles, but the latest versions of these products are now using the USB port instead. Similarly, most mouse products now use either a PS/2 or USB port.

PS/2 Mouse and Keyboard Ports

The major legacy ports used by both pointing devices and keyboards are the PS/2 mouse and keyboard ports.

While the PS/2 mouse and keyboard ports have the same physical connector, they cannot be interchanged. PS/2 ports, unlike serial and parallel ports, can't be used for any other purpose than pointing devices or keyboards. If you use a pointing device connected to the USB port, you can disable the PS/2 port and free up the hardware resources (such as IRQ 12), which it uses, for other components you may have installed.

→ *For more information about hardware resources, see "Hardware Resources" in p. 117.*

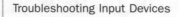

Parallel Port

The parallel (LPT) port, originally used for printing, has also been a favorite interface for low-cost scanners. Parallel-port scanners, as well as parallel-port drives, have two connectors:

- One port leads to the parallel port on the computer
- The other port enables the device to daisy-chain to a printer

➔ *For more informa-tion about parallel-port modes, see "Parallel Port Modes," p. 225.*

In order to accommodate the need to receive data (with a scanner or drive) as well as send data (to a drive or printer), parallel ports have become bi-directional devices, using various modes known as PS/2, EPP, ECP, or EPP/ECP.

A problem with the operation or configuration of a legacy port will affect any input or other device connected to it.

High-speed Ports (SCSI, USB, and IEEE-1394a)

High-speed ports such as SCSI, USB, and IEEE-1394a (which is also called FireWire by Apple and i.Link by Sony) are used for mid-range and high-performance scanners. USB and IEEE-1394a also work with other types of input devices.

SCSI

SCSI has been a popular choice for high-performance flatbed and slide scanners. SCSI is also used for

- high-performance PostScript laser printers
- various types of optical and removable-media drives
- tape backups

Because SCSI is expensive, difficult to configure, and does not support hot-swapping, it is being replaced for many tasks by USB and IEEE-1394a ports and devices.

USB 1.1 and 2.0

The original version of USB, USB 1.1, is a bit slower than a high-speed EPP or ECP parallel port, running at about 12Mbps. USB 1.1 is the most flexible port found on today's PCs, since it can accommodate any of the following types of devices:

- Input devices such as keyboards, pointing devices, scanners
- Removable-media, optical, hard disk and tape drives
- Printers
- File transfer cables
- Network adapters
- Analog modems
- PDA synchronization cradles
- Flash memory card readers

Most computers have two or more USB ports, which are built in to the motherboard. Additional USB ports can be added through USB cards, or through the use of USB hubs, which enable multiple USB devices to share a single port.

USB 2.0, which runs at up to 480Mbps, is built in to the latest computers, and can be retrofitted to older computers through the use of add-in cards. USB 2.0 supports all USB 1.1 devices, enables multiple USB 1.1 devices to work better on the same port, and is fast enough for true high-speed data access.

Both types of USB support hot-swapping, making it easy to add or remove USB devices as needed without having to reboot your computer for it to recognize a newly connected device.

IEEE-1394a

IEEE-1394a is becoming the replacement for SCSI in the eyes of many users. It's faster than low-cost SCSI cards, it supports hot-swapping, it's easy to install and use, and some computers even have IEEE-1394a ports built in. Otherwise, look for add-on cards (including some high-end sound cards or combo IEEE-1394a/USB cards) to add this interface to your computer.

In addition to supporting high-end scanners, IEEE-1394a also works with

- DV camcorders
- Portable hard drives
- Large capacity removable-media drives
- Networking

➔ *For more information about these ports, see "PC Anatomy 101."*

Fixing Problems with Input Devices

When an input device stops working, your ability to use your computer may be crippled or even eliminated. Because input devices are the principal way to interact with the computer and create new information, finding fast, accurate solutions to input device problems is critical.

There are three major sources of trouble with input devices:

- The port the device is plugged into
- The device itself
- The device driver in Windows

The Problem and Solution flowcharts in Part 2 are designed to help you determine which of these is the cause of your input device woes. In this section, you'll learn the details of each solution.

Diagnosing Port and Driver Problems with Device Manager

→ See "Using Device Manager," p. 480.

In many cases, the Windows Device Manager provides you a fast, reliable way to figure out if the problem with a device is caused by problems with the port it's attached to or with the port's or device's own device driver.

To access the Device Manager quickly, right-click on My Computer (either on the Windows Desktop or, in Windows XP, after clicking Start), and select Properties. Then, if you're using Windows XP or 2000, click the Hardware tab, then the Device Manager button. With Windows 9x or Me, click Device Manager. Figure 6.3 shows the Windows XP Device Manager displaying normal, disabled, and problem devices.

FIGURE 6.3

The Windows XP Device Manager.

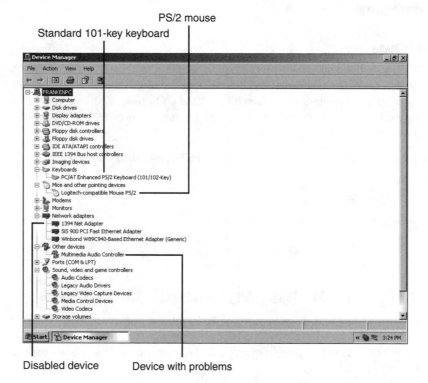

PS/2 mouse

Standard 101-key keyboard

Disabled device   Device with problems

If you're using Device Manager to figure out a problem with your input device, you need to know two pieces of information: what port it's using (for example, if you use USB input devices, you need to expand the Universal Serial Bus category), and how it's listed in Device Manager. You also need to understand the symbols that can sometimes appear on a device listed in Device Manager:

- An exclamation point (!) in a yellow circle

  This indicates a problem with the port, device, or driver. Right-click the device or port and choose Properties to get the details.

- A red X indicates that the port or device has been disabled.

  You might be able to use the properties sheet to re-enable the port or device. But, if the port or device is controlled by the system BIOS, you might need to reboot the computer and use the BIOS setup program to re-enable the port.

→ *For details about accessing the BIOS, see "BIOS Setup," p. 104.*

- A blue "I" in a gray circle indicates a Plug-and-Play device that has been configured manually (in Windows 9x/Me only). Windows normally handles all configuration issues associated with Plug-and-Play devices. The appearance of this icon means that for whatever reason, Windows is not in control of the Plug-and-Play settings for the device or port. It doesn't necessarily mean there is a problem.

An input device cannot work if you attach it to a port that

- is disabled
- is not recognized in the Device Manager
- has a conflict with another port
- has a defective driver

Even if the port is working properly, the device won't work if you don't have a driver for it, it is defective or didn't load, or if the device has a problem that the Device Manger cannot diagnose.

On the Web

Grab the latest device drivers for your Microsoft mouse, trackball, or keyboard from Microsoft's Hardware Web site at http://www.Microsoft.com/hardware.

Prefer Logitech? Drivers for Logitech mice, trackballs, and keyboards are yours for the asking at http://www.logitech.com/cf/support/downloads.cfm.

Search for IBM keyboard and mouse drivers at http://www-1.ibm.com/support/all_download_drivers.html.

Using Device Manager to Troubleshoot a PS/2 Mouse or Keyboard

Table 6.1 provides a quick reference to how problems with your PS/2 mouse or keyboard are reflected in Device Manager, and how to resolve them. The solutions described in Table 6.1 are covered in greater detail following the table.

TABLE 6.1

The PS/2 Ports and the Device Manager

Device Manager Display	Device Status	Problem	Solution
Mouse or keyboard displayed with (!) symbol	Attached to port	Problem with mouse, keyboard, or driver	Open properties sheet and follow instructions for resolving problem. See Table A.2, "Device Manager Codes," p. 482.
Mouse or keyboard displayed with Red X	Attached to port	Mouse or keyboard disabled by Device Manager	Open properties sheet for mouse or keyboard; enable mouse or keyboard. See flowchart "Pointing Device Won't Move," p. 47.
Mouse or keyboard displayed normally but doesn't work	Attached to port	Mouse not compatible with PS/2 port or wrong driver loaded; keyboard or keyboard adapter defective	Check or replace adapter. If you're using an adapter with a mouse not meant for use with a PS/2 port, it won't work. If the mouse is a PS/2 mouse, reload the driver. If you're using a 5-pin DIN keyboard with a PS/2 adapter, replace the adapter.
No mouse displayed	Mouse attached to port	PS/2 mouse port disabled	Enable port in BIOS or with motherboard jumper (see system/ MB manual for details).
		Mouse is defective	Replace mouse after verifying PS/2 mouse port is enabled.
No mouse or keyboard displayed	Mouse or keyboard not attached to port (or not plugged in properly)	Windows can't detect mouse or port	Shut down system and attach mouse or keyboard to correct PS/2 port, then restart system.

The PS/2 mouse port (also called the 6-pin mini-DIN port) is designed for use with a PS/2 mouse. Other types of mice which include a PS/2 mouse port adapter can also be used with this port. Similarly, the PS/2 keyboard port, which has an identical physical connector but is not interchangeable with the mouse port, is designed for use with a PS/2 keyboard, or with an older 5-pin DIN keyboard equipped with a PS/2 adapter. Figure 6.4 shows examples of these adapters.

5-pin DIN keyboard cable   Serial mouse cable

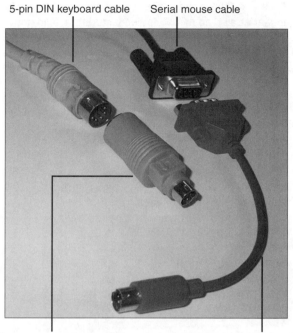

FIGURE 6.4

PS/2 keyboard and mouse port adapters.

PS/2 keyboard port adapter   PS/2 mouse port adapter

Unlike some other types of input devices, which list the port separately from the device, the Windows Device Manager lists the PS/2 mouse as a mouse and the PS/2 keyboard as a keyboard (as seen in Figure 6.3), but doesn't list the ports separately. If you have more than one mouse installed, such as a USB and a PS/2 mouse, you can tell which one is the PS/2 mouse because the Device Manager entry for the PS/2 mouse normally lists PS/2 as part of the description.

The PS/2 mouse is also emulated by the integrated pointing devices built in to notebook computers (usually in the form of a touchpad or stick built in to the keyboard assembly). If you use a USB mouse instead of a PS/2 mouse, you might prefer to disable the integrated pointing device so that you don't move the mouse pointer accidentally. You can disable the PS/2 mouse port or integrated pointing device in one of two ways:

- through the system BIOS
- through the Windows Device Manager

To disable the PS/2 mouse or integrated pointing device with the Device Manager, open the properties sheet for the mouse or pointing device and select Do not use this device (disable), as shown in Figure 6.5.

If you disable the PS/2 mouse with the Device Manager, it will be displayed with a red X as shown earlier, in Figure 6.3. However, if your PS/2 mouse port is not enabled or if you plug the mouse into the wrong PS/2 port, it will not appear in Device Manager at all. In fact, the Mice and Other Pointing Devices or Mouse category in Device Manager will not appear at all if no mouse is connected to a valid port. Similarly, if the PS/2 keyboard is attached to the mouse port by mistake, or is not plugged into the system at all, it will not appear in Device Manager, and the Keyboard category will not be listed (unless another keyboard is connected via the USB port).

FIGURE 6.5

Disabling a PS/2 mouse or integrated pointing device with the Windows XP Device Manager.

Fast Track to Success

Regardless of the computer, if you have two PS/2 ports stacked on top of each other on the rear of the computer as in Figure 6.1, the bottom PS/2 port is for the keyboard, and the top one is for the mouse. While some computers and input devices are color-coded to help you plug the correct device into each one, the physical connectors for the keyboard and mouse are identical. While you won't hurt the ports or the devices if you mix up the ports, the keyboard and pointing device won't work if they're plugged into the wrong ports.

If you attach a mouse to the PS/2 mouse port or a keyboard to the PS/2 keyboard port but they aren't displayed in Device Manager, they might not be connected tightly to the ports. Also, if the port is disabled in the system BIOS, the PS/2 mouse port will not be displayed, even if the mouse is properly attached. If you need to enable the port, see "Using the System BIOS to Solve Problems with PS/2 Pointing Devices," later in this chapter.

Fast Track to Success

Remember, that although the connectors are the same, the two PS/2 ports on the back of your PC aren't compatible with each other. Unlike USB where it doesn't matter, one PS/2 port is for a mouse, and the other is for the keyboard. If you mismatch which device is plugged into which port, neither will work. Look for a keyboard or mouse logo near each port to identify which port is which. If you don't see these logos, then just plug your keyboard into the "top" port.

However, a defective mouse or keyboard attached to the correct PS/2 port will not be visible either. To determine if the port or the device is at fault, perform this test:

1. Shut down Windows; if the mouse doesn't work, press Ctrl+Esc or the Windows key to open the Start button menu. You can use arrow keys to select Turn Off Computer; press the Enter key when you have highlighted Turn Off Computer.

2. If the PS/2 mouse isn't working, make sure the PS/2 mouse port is enabled in the system BIOS. See "Using the System BIOS to Solve Problems with PS/2 and USB Devices," later in this chapter.

3. If the port is enabled, try plugging a known-working keyboard or mouse into the correct PS/2 port; you can borrow one from another working computer at home or at the office (different brands are interchangeable). If you don't have a spare, buy a cheap mouse or keyboard for testing purposes (you'll spend all of ten or fifteen dollars each to get them).

4. Restart the computer. If the original mouse or keyboard was defective, you should be able to use the replacement and see it displayed in the Device Manager. If the port is defective, the replacement won't work either.

5. Replace the defective component; if the PS/2 port on the motherboard is bad, you need to replace the motherboard. Alternatively, you could replace your keyboard or mouse with a USB version that eliminates the need for a functional PS/2 port.

Fast Track to Success

Because Device Manager really looks only at the connection to a device and not the device itself, it's limited in its ability to solve problems with input devices. When it comes time to troubleshoot, it pays to have spare input devices you can use for swapping. This ensures that the problem is the device itself (and not the port it's connected to).

Worried about the expense? Don't be. For very little cash, you purchase a bare-bones mouse or cheap-jack keyboard to use as a pinch-hitter when things go wrong. By swapping a known-working device for one whose condition is unknown, you can get to the bottom of problems in a hurry.

In the case of USB devices, even this is unnecessary. You can use any USB device (even a scanner, Webcam, or drive) to confirm that a USB port or hub is working properly *provided you have the drivers needed for the device and the version of Windows you're using*. Remember, if nothing works when you plug it into a particular port, the port is either disabled or defective. But, if the replacement works, the original device is the source of the problem. Try downloading updated drivers compatible with your version of Windows. If the device still won't work, it's defective and should be repaired or replaced (most devices are much cheaper to replace than repair).

Using Device Manager to Troubleshoot USB Devices

Table 6.2 provides a quick reference to help you use the Device Manager to fix problems with your USB input devices. The solutions described in Table 6.2 are covered in greater detail following the table.

TABLE 6.2
USB Input Devices and the Device Manager

Device Manager Display	Input Device Status	Problem	Solution
Red X	Attached	Device is disabled	Enable device with its properties sheet's General tab. If you can't enable the device, remove the listing from Device Manager and restart the computer. It should be detected and reinstalled.
Yellow !	Attached	Device has a problem (various codes)	View device condition with its properties sheet's General tab; use codes or Troubleshooter to find solution. See Table A.2, "Device Manager Codes," p. 482.
Yellow !	Attached	Device Cannot Start (Code 10)	Check Power tab on properties sheet for hub used to connect input device; if not enough power is present, move input device to a hub with adequate power or supply AC power to the generic hub.
Device not visible in Device Manager; USB Controllers category present in Device Manager	Attached	Device may not be connected to working USB port or hub	If USB controllers category shows problems with controllers or hubs, correct them to enable USB devices to work. Try connecting the device directly to a USB port on your computer; if the device starts working, the hub or port previously used is defective.
Device not visible in Device Manager; USB Controller category not present in Device Manager	Attached	USB controllers are not enabled or are not compatible with this version of Windows	Remember that Windows 95 is either incompatible with or unstable in supporting USB (depending on version). If you are using a compatible version of Windows, restart the computer and enable the USB ports in the system BIOS.

TABLE 6.2 (continued)

Device Manager Display	Input Device Status	Problem	Solution
Visible in Device Manager but properties sheet doesn't indicate location	Attached	Some advanced features (such as programmable buttons on the keyboard) don't work	Install driver and application software for input device. If some buttons/features still don't work, download and install updated drivers. If the features still don't work, contact the vendor for a replacement device.
Keyboard visible in Device Manager	Attached	Web buttons don't activate desired features	Download updated keyboard setup program, run the setup program, and specify desired action for each button.

As you can see from Table 6.2, USB pointing devices and keyboards present a completely different troubleshooting task than PS/2 mice and pointing devices do. The Universal Serial Bus (USB) category in Device Manager is used for host controllers, root hubs (ports built into your computer), and external hubs (see Figure 6.6). However, USB devices are listed under the normal categories. For example, USB mice and pointing devices are listed under Mice and Other Pointing Devices or Mouse (varies with version of Windows used), and USB keyboards are listed under Keyboard. USB scanners are listed under Imaging Devices.

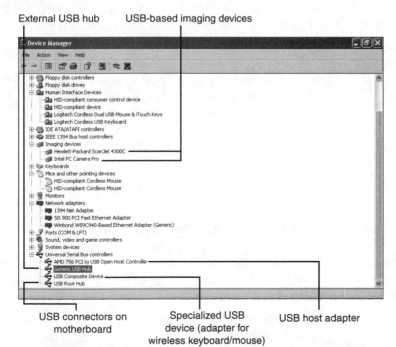

FIGURE 6.6
Typical Windows XP Device Manager listings for USB ports, devices, and hubs.

USB keyboards and pointing devices are referred to as *Human Interface Devices (HID)*, and each HID-compliant device has at least two listings in Device Manager, as in Figure 6.7. One listing is for the device, and the other listings are for the HID functions of that device.

FIGURE 6.7

A wireless USB mouse and USB keyboard as listed in the Windows XP Device Manager. There are several listings for both because the keyboard includes a mouse scroll wheel, Internet control keys, and multimedia control keys.

Listings for a USB wireless keyboard

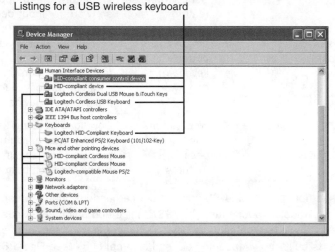

Listings for a USB wireless mouse and keyboard's mouse features

HID-compliant devices can be plugged into a computer at the same time as older PS/2 or serial input devices, allowing either to be used. Also, HID allows an input device to support additional buttons or features, such as the multimedia or Web browser-control buttons common on many new keyboards.

Fortunately, the Windows Device Manager provides many tools to help you diagnose problems with USB input devices. For example, the properties sheets for USB root (internal) and generic (external) hubs feature a Power tab in addition to the normal General and Driver tabs. Self-powered USB devices consume different levels of power, while bus-powered devices use the maximum 500mA provided by each USB port (see Figure 6.8).

There are two different types of USB hubs:

- Self-powered
- Bus-powered

Self-powered hubs are plugged into an AC outlet. The multi-port USB hubs you can buy as standalone accessories are almost always self-powered. Bus-powered hubs are often incorporated into other devices such as a keyboard or monitor; they are powered from the USB port they're attached to. Bus-powered hubs must subdivide the 500mA provided by a USB port built in to the computer among the ports built in to the hub.

Hub power source

Maximum available power per port

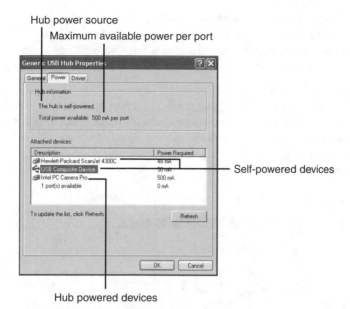

Self-powered devices

Hub powered devices

FIGURE 6.8

The Power properties sheet for a generic USB (external) hub which has several devices connected to it. Note the lower power levels used by self-powered devices.

If a self-powered hub is disconnected from its AC power source (which turns the hub into a bus-powered hub), some power-hungry devices won't work. If you plug too many bus-powered devices (devices which draw their power from the USB port) into a USB port or hub, particularly a bus-powered hub, they might stop working, as shown in Figure 6.9.

Hub is getting its power from the PC

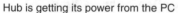

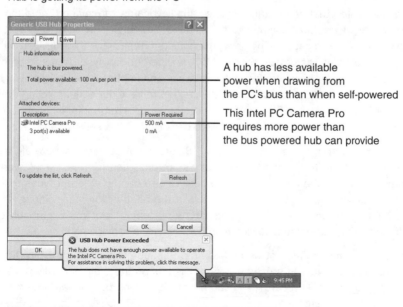

A hub has less available power when drawing from the PC's bus than when self-powered

This Intel PC Camera Pro requires more power than the bus powered hub can provide

Windows XP's warning that the hub requires more power

FIGURE 6.9

The Power properties sheet for a bus-powered generic USB (external) hub which has a device requiring more power than is available connected to it. Note the warning on the taskbar.

When you view the properties sheet for an HID device, check the Location information on the General tab (see Figure 6.10). If the Location information is not present, the device's specialized drivers and support software have not yet been loaded. Until the drivers and support software are loaded, some features of the device may not work.

While drivers are normally loaded as part of a device's initial setup, you might be tempted to just plug in the HID mouse or keyboard and start using it, since its basic functions don't require drivers. However, you should read the documentation for your device to determine when you install the drivers. You might need to install the drivers before you attach the device to your computer; see the documentation included with your device for details.

Name of the HID-compliant device

FIGURE 6.10

The General tab for an HID-compliant device indicates the correct location (device name) only after you install its drivers and support software.

Peripheral Adapters: When (and Why) They Don't Always Work

By now you realize that peripherals like mice and keyboards can support more than one connection type. Most commonly, they'll connect to either a PS/2 or USB port. To simplify store stock, most pointing device manufacturers package their devices with an adapter that enables the device to work with two different port types, rather than have separate products for each interface. The most common option today is to package a USB device with a PS/2 port adapter. In the case of mice, older serial pointing devices were often packaged with a PS/2 mouse port adapter as seen earlier in Figure 6.4. Conversely, some PS/2 pointing devices were packaged with a serial adapter.

Although retail stores sell serial-to-PS/2 or PS/2-to-serial adapters separately, trying to use an adapter with a pointing device that's not designed for it just won't work. The firmware inside the mouse has to be designed to handle different types of connectors for an adapter to work. What if you lose the adapter for your pointing device? You *might* be able to use a third-party replacement, but you're probably better off contacting the pointing device manufacturer for a replacement.

The situation is much different with keyboards. Because the old, large 5-pin DIN connector used by older PCs uses the same signals as the 6-pin mini-DIN PS/2 connector used by newer keyboards, you can adapt either type of keyboard to either type of system—no problem.

If that's not complicated enough for you, then keep in mind that adapters that allow you to attach a USB mouse or keyboard to a PS/2 port are proprietary. Both keyboards and mice designed for USB ports won't work with adapters unless the manufacturer designs that capability into the device—and if they do, they supply the adapter. Using one manufacturer's USB-to-PS/2 adapter with another's device won't work.

The bottom line is that if the pointing or input device was an OEM unit bundled with a computer, it's not designed to work with other interfaces. If you buy it at retail *and* an adapter is included, it will work with that adapter. Otherwise, you're probably out of luck.

Using Device Manager to Troubleshoot Wireless Mice and Keyboards

Wireless mice and keyboards present a special challenge when they aren't working properly for three reasons:

- Problems with their transceivers (which plug into the same connectors as normal input devices) can cause the devices to fail
- Problems with the devices' transmission and reception of signals from the transceivers can also cause device failure
- Problems with battery life will cause temporary device failure when the batteries are exhausted

Most wireless input devices from major vendors such as Microsoft and Logitech use radio signals, but a few low-cost devices from second-tier vendors use infrared (IR) signals instead.

One major weakness of the Windows Device Manager is that it detects problems with the transceiver, not the device connected to the transceiver. For example, if the batteries in your wireless mouse or keyboard fail, the Device Manager will still report that the device works correctly. You can use the Device Manager to detect problems with how the transceiver is connected to your system. For transceivers which connect to the PS/2 port, see "Using Device Manager to Troubleshoot a PS/2 Mouse" and Table 6.1. For transceivers which connect to the USB port, see "Using Device Manager to Troubleshoot USB Mice and Keyboards" and Table 6.2.

To troubleshoot wireless-specific problems, see "Troubleshooting Wireless Input Devices," later in this chapter.

Using Device Manager to Troubleshoot Scanner Problems

As with other types of input devices, scanners might have problems caused by two factors:

- Problems with the port
- Problems with the scanner itself

Most scanners today connect through the USB port (see "Using Device Manager to Troubleshoot USB Devices" for details). However, scanners might also connect to your computer through these other port types:

- LPT (Parallel); see "Troubleshooting Printers" for details
- SCSI
- IEEE-1394a

For a scanner to work correctly, the port the scanner is attached to must work properly and the scanner's device drivers must also be installed correctly. However, with some versions of Windows, you might find that your scanner works properly even though it appears in Device Manager as an "Other Device," without drivers.

Fast Track to Success

If your scanner is working correctly within an application with Windows 9x, even though Device Manager is reporting problems with it, you're not crazy—and neither is your scanner. Most scanners come with installation software that uses a driver technology called TWAIN (which stands for nothing in particular, by the way). TWAIN installs drivers that work with popular photo-editing and graphics programs such as Adobe Photoshop, Corel Draw, and even humbler apps such as Microsoft Paint. When you use the Acquire command from one of these applications and then specify your scanner, TWAIN opens the scanning program that was installed with your scanner, allowing you to digitize your favorite photos, love letters, or tax forms.

Windows Me, Windows 2000, and Windows XP use a new technology called WIA (Windows Image Acquisition) and use their own built-in imaging tools to run scanners that they recognize. But, in a pinch, you can usually install TWAIN drivers made for your scanner and Windows versions and they'll work, even if the Device Manager is clueless about your scanner.

Table 6.3 shows you how to use Device Manager to run down problems with your parallel-port, SCSI, or IEEE-1394–based scanner.

TABLE 6.3
Device Manager and Non-USB Scanners

Problem	Port Type	Device Manager Port Status	Solution
Scanner displayed in Device Manager but can't scan images	Parallel (LPT)	!—Properties sheet reveals a resource conflict	Use Resources tab to resolve conflict or connect scanner to USB port.
Scanner displayed in Device Manager but can't scan images	SCSI, IEEE-1394a	!—Properties sheet reveals a resource conflict	Use Resources tab to resolve conflict or remove and reinstall card. See "Using Device Manager," p. 480.

TABLE 6.3 (continued)

Problem	Port Type	Device Manager Port Status	Solution
Scanner displayed in Device Manager but can't scan images	All	!—Properties sheet indicates other problems	See Table A.2 p. 482.
Scanner not visible in Device Manager	All	Device-specific problems prevent the scanner from being detected	See "Common Problems and Solutions for Scanners," p. 354.
Scanner not visible in Device Manager	SCSI	May have same device ID as another device or improper termination of SCSI daisy-chain	Correct problems with device ID or termination. See "Troubleshooting a SCSI Drive," p. 209.

A resource conflict means that two devices want to use the same IRQ, DMA channel, I/O port address range, or memory address. Since SCSI and IEEE-1394a ports are not commonly built in to PCs and must be added through installing a card, a resource conflict could take place when the card is installed. While the Plug and Play installation feature of Windows makes resource conflicts less of an issue today than a few years ago, they can still take place. You can resolve resource conflicts by

→ *For more information about hardware resources and conflicts, see "Hardware Resources" p. 117.*

- Removing the card from Device Manager and installing the card in another PCI slot
- Changing the PCI/PnP settings in the system BIOS setup

Troubleshooting Input Device Problems Not Solvable with Device Manager

While the Windows Device Manager provides powerful tools for solving many problems with input devices, it is limited by several factors. It can't solve problems caused by

- Ports which have never been recognized by Windows
- Ports which have been disabled in the system BIOS
- Devices whose hardware isn't configured properly
- Wireless devices which cannot send or receive signals, although the transceiver is detected and configured by Windows
- Hardware failure

In this section, you'll learn how to solve these problems.

Troubleshooting Pointing Device Problems with Control Panel

The Windows Control Panel contains a Mouse properties sheet (which also works with touchpads, trackballs, and other mouse substitutes). Use it to improve the performance, compatibility, appearance, and movement of your pointing device.

Table 6.4 shows you how to use the Mouse properties sheet for Windows XP to solve common pointing device problems. Other versions of Windows offer similar features, although some advanced options might not be present. All properties sheet tabs are shown in Figure 6.11.

FIGURE 6.11
The Mouse properties sheets in Device Manager for a Windows XP system.

TABLE 6.4
Using the Pointing Device Properties Sheet

Problem	Properties Sheet Tab to Use	Solution
I need to set up mouse for left-handed user	Buttons	Select Switch primary and secondary buttons box
Double-click doesn't work consistently	Buttons	Use Double-click speed slider and test box to adjust speed
Items are dragged around the screen after I click on them, even if I don't hold down the primary mouse button	Buttons	Clear the ClickLock option box; if the ClickLock option isn't selected, the primary mouse button is probably broken and the mouse should be replaced
Need different (larger, animated, high-contrast) mouse pointers	Pointers	Select desired mouse scheme from menu; install mouse software provided by mouse vendor to provide additional schemes
Pointer moves too fast or too slow	Pointer Options	Adjust Motion slider to desired speed
Pointer hard to move over short distances or hard to stop	Pointer Options	Enable Enhance Pointer Precision option
I'm tired of moving pointer to dialog box to click OK	Pointer Options	Enable Snap to option
Pointer disappears when moved quickly (especially on LCD displays)	Pointer Options	Enable Pointer Trails option and select desired length of trail
Pointer covers up typed text	Pointer Options	Enable Hide Pointer While Typing option
Pointer is hard to find on a cluttered screen	Pointer Options	Enable Show Location When I press CTRL key option
Scroll wheel motion too fast or too slow	Wheel	Select number of lines to scroll with each click of the wheel, or select one screen at a time
Not sure which pointing devices are active	Hardware	Displays current device(s) and provides shortcuts to Troubleshooter and Properties
Mouse pointer disappears or only appears on parts of the screen	Pointer Options	Enable Show Location When I press CTRL key option. You might also want to minimize and maximize the active application to force Windows to rewrite the screen

Using the System BIOS to Solve Problems with PS/2 Pointing Devices

If your PS/2 mouse won't work when you attach it to the PS/2 port, boot your computer and ensure that you don't have any other devices using IRQ 12 (see "Using Device Manager," p. 480); if no other devices are using IRQ 12, then the port might not be enabled.

→ *For more information about the system BIOS, see "BIOS Setup," p. 104.*

Most computers with a PS/2 mouse port control the port through a setting in the system BIOS, although some older systems may use a jumper block on the motherboard to enable or disable the port. To view the current setting, shut down your computer, restart it, and press the key(s) which start the system BIOS setup program; if the correct key(s) are not displayed on-screen, check your computer or motherboard reference manual for the correct key(s) to press. Depending upon the system, you might need to look in the Advanced Menu (as in Figure 6.12), the Integrated Ports menu, or other places.

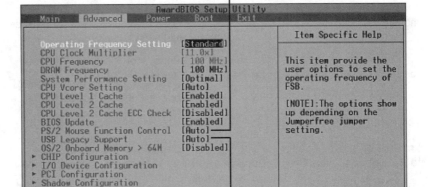

PS/2 mouse control

USB Legacy (keyboard/mouse) control

FIGURE 6.12

A typical Advanced (Award BIOS) setup screen which controls the PS/2 mouse and USB Legacy (keyboard/ mouse) functions. The Auto setting enables the devices when they are attached.

Depending on the system, there are two or three options available for configuring ports in the BIOS:

- Enabled—This setting enables the port and uses IRQ 12 for the mouse, even if no mouse is present.

- Disabled—This setting turns off the port and frees up IRQ 12 for other devices.

- Auto—This setting, seen in Figure 6.12, enables the mouse only if it is present. If it is not present, IRQ 12 can be used for other devices.

If the mouse pointer won't move when you use a PS/2 pointing device, check the following:

- Determine if the PS/2 Mouse BIOS option is configured to Enabled or Auto (either of which will enable a PS/2 pointing device to work). If the setting is set to Disabled, enable it, and restart the computer. Retry the mouse.

- If the PS/2 Mouse was already configured as Enabled or Auto, but the mouse pointer won't move, open the mouse and make sure the rollers and ball are clean and working. If they are dirty, clean them and retry. If they appear to be okay, replace the pointing device with a known-working PS/2 mouse and retry. If a replacement mouse works, the original pointing device is defective and should be replaced. If the replacement doesn't work, the PS/2 mouse port is defective.

- If you determine that your PS/2 mouse port is defective and you don't want to replace your motherboard, use a USB mouse instead (if you have Windows 98 or newer) or a serial mouse (if you are still using Windows 95).

- If the mouse is connected to the PS/2 port by an adapter, the adapter could be defective, or the mouse might not be compatible with an adapter. Use a mouse without an adapter for testing the PS/2 port.

Using the System BIOS to Solve Problems with USB Devices

System BIOS settings can affect USB input devices in two ways:

- If the USB ports are disabled, no USB devices, including input devices, will work.

- If the USB Legacy Mode (also called USB DOS mode) is not enabled, USB mouse and keyboard will work when the Windows desktop is displayed. However, the keyboard and mouse might not work within the system BIOS setup program or at a command-prompt mode such as the Windows XP Recovery Console, the Windows 9x/Me Command prompt, or MS-DOS mode operations. USB devices are also disabled in Safe Mode on some older versions of Windows, although USB keyboards and pointing devices will work in Safe Mode on Windows XP.

Figure 6.13 shows a typical BIOS setup screen which contains the USB BIOS setup options. Note that some early systems with USB ports don't have the USB Legacy or USB DOS mode functions shown in Figure 6.13. Compare Figure 6.13 to Figure 6.12, which shows a different BIOS in which USB Legacy and PS/2 mouse controls are on the same screen, but the USB controller option is on a different screen.

Use the following tips to help troubleshoot your USB pointing and keyboard devices. Note that you might need to use a keyboard connected to the PS/2 keyboard jack to access your system BIOS to enable USB controllers or USB Legacy keyboard support on some systems.

- If the Device Manager doesn't list the Universal Serial Bus controllers category, then no USB devices will work. You need to enable the USB controller option in the BIOS and restart the computer. Install drivers for USB devices as required.

- If the Device Manager doesn't list the Universal Serial Bus controllers category, but the USB controller option is enabled in the System BIOS and you are using Windows 98, Me, 2000, or XP, your USB controller is not supported by Windows. Contact the system or motherboard vendor for a BIOS upgrade and install it. If the controllers are still not recognized by Windows, disable USB controller setting in BIOS and install a USB 1.1 or USB 2.0 card if you want to use USB devices. I recommend a USB 2.0 card because it supports faster USB 2.0 peripherals and works better with multiple USB 1.1 or USB 2.0 devices.

- If your USB keyboard or pointing device works within Windows, but not at a command prompt or within the BIOS setup program (a few BIOS setup programs are graphical and support a pointing device), you need to enable USB Legacy mode within the BIOS, as shown in Figures 6.11 and 6.12. In the short term, you can attach a PS/2 keyboard to the system to access the BIOS if you can't activate the BIOS setup program with your USB keyboard. If this mode is already enabled, contact your system or motherboard vendor for a BIOS update. On some systems, USB Legacy Keyboard and USB Legacy Mouse are separate options; enable either or both as desired.

FIGURE 6.13

A typical Advanced (AMI BIOS) setup screen which controls the USB functions.

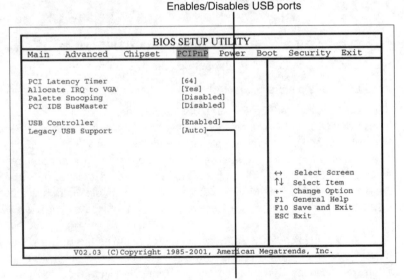

BIOS SETUP UTILITY

Enables/Disables USB ports

Enables/Disables use of USB keyboards and mouse outside Windows

Why It Pays to Keep an Old PS/2 Keyboard Around

Unless your computer is a so-called "legacy-free" model that has eliminated the venerable PS/2 keyboard and mouse connectors, it can be very useful to keep a PS/2 keyboard around even after you've switched over to a USB keyboard.

For example, as this section demonstrates, you may need to enter your system BIOS setup program to enable USB Legacy mode if you need to use your keyboard for the Windows XP Recovery Console or for other tasks outside the

Windows GUI. If you don't have a PS/2 keyboard, you might not be able to enable the USB Legacy feature you need to use your USB keyboard at all times. Even if you've turned on the feature once, a battery failure or virus attack could require you to dive back into the BIOS again—but without a PS/2 keyboard, you're out of luck. On some systems running Windows XP, a USB keyboard can't display the troubleshooting startup menu which is activated by pressing the F8 key, but a PS/2 keyboard will.

So, keep that old PS/2 keyboard around—or choose a USB keyboard which comes with a PS/2 adapter. You never know when you'll need it.

Using Other Methods to Diagnose Problems with Input Devices

As you have seen, the Windows Device Manager can fix many problems with input devices, but a defective input device might still be reported as "OK" by the Device Manager or might be connected to a fully BIOS enabled and functioning port. If the BIOS settings are correct for your device and the Device Manager reports it as having no problems, but it still doesn't work, the device itself may be to blame. How can you tell? Use physical inspection of the device, cleaning the device, unplugging and reattaching the device, and swapping the device with another to make sure the device itself is to blame.

- Physical inspection—Take a good look at the device. If the device's cabling is cracked, frayed, or has loose wires, replace the device. If one or more of the pins in the connector are bent or broken, replace the device. If the mouse's ball is missing, find the ball and reinstall it, or replace the mouse. If the mouse has broken or missing rollers, replace the mouse. Test the batteries on a wireless device; if they're weak or dead, replace them. If you're using one of the popular optical mice, make sure its LED is working, and make sure that the mousing surface isn't reflective and doesn't have a repeating pattern (both of which can confuse the motion sensor in the mouse).

- Cleaning—Gunk and dirt on mouse or trackball rollers can cause erratic pointer movements, or in extreme cases, no pointer movement at all. Use a mouse cleaning kit or carefully clean the rollers with alcohol-dipped swabs. Keyboards with sticky keys should be vacuumed out or blown out with compressed air. The cover glass on a scanner should be cleaned before each use, and as often as needed during use. Be sure to use a soft pre-moistened cloth to clean the cover glass. A dry cloth or towel could scratch the cover glass, making image quality worse.

- Unplugging and reattaching the device cable—In many cases, this simple process fixes the problem. If the device connects to a PS/2 port, you will need to shut down the computer first, but if the device plugs into the USB port, you can unplug it and reattach it while the power's on, thanks to the hot-swap nature of USB connections.

- Parts swapping—Swap a suspicious keyboard, mouse, or pointing device with another (preferably one that's known to be working) and see if the new device works OK. If it does, replace the old device. If no device works on the port, the port itself is defective, regardless of what the Windows Device Manager says about it or how it is configured in the BIOS.

Cautions and Warnings

If you've decided it's time to swap a balky keyboard or mouse for one that works to figure out why you can't type or use your mouse anymore, don't forget to shut down and turn off your system if you're swapping PS/2 devices. Unlike newer USB devices which can be hot-swapped, PS/2 keyboards, mice, and pointing devices can only be recognized if they're attached while the system is turned off. And, make sure you attach the cable correctly. Push the keyboard, mouse, or pointing device cable in at an angle, and you could break the solder joints which carry signals between the connector and the motherboard. The only cure for *that* problem is a new motherboard!

If known-working devices don't work, you can replace on-board USB ports with a USB card, but defective PS/2 ports mean that you're in the market for either new USB peripherals or a new motherboard.

Troubleshooting Problems with Wireless Input Devices

Even if the transceiver used by a wireless input device is working properly, the device itself might fail to work for one of the following reasons:

- Inability to exchange radio signals with the input device
- Loss of line-of-sight with an infrared (IR) input device
- Power failure due to dead batteries or dirty/corroded battery terminals

If you are using a radio-controlled input device, the input device and the transceiver both need to use the same radio frequency. Depending upon the input device, you might need to select a frequency manually by pushing a button or rotating a dial, or the device might select a frequency for you. You can reset the frequency used by removing the batteries from the input device and reinstalling them.

IR-based input devices need to establish a clear line-of-sight between the transceiver and the input device. This is relatively simple to do with an input device which is placed on the desktop, but can be a lot harder if you use a wireless keyboard or keyboard/mouse combo on your lap.

Typical wireless devices have a battery life of three to six months. Look for a battery-test light on the device to determine if the batteries are working, or remove them and use a separate battery tester. While most recent wireless input devices use standard battery sizes such as AA or AAA, some older models might use less-common sizes. You should make sure you keep a spare set of batteries around to avoid running out of battery power at an inconvenient time.

Some radio-frequency (RF) wireless keyboards have a control and troubleshooting properties sheet such as the one shown in Figure 6.14. Use this to check the RF channel in use, the battery life, check connections, or for other tasks.

iTouch keys setup

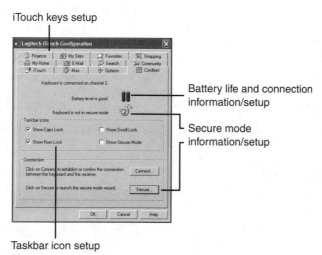

Battery life and connection information/setup

Secure mode information/setup

Taskbar icon setup

FIGURE 6.14
The Wireless tab on Logitech's iTouch wireless keyboard is used to troubleshoot the connection and configure the connection type. Use the other tabs shown to configure the keyboard's special iTouch buttons.

Troubleshooting Scanner Problems Not Related to Port Issues

Scanners are almost always external devices (though some internal slide scanners do exist), and are frequently connected in series (daisy-chained) to other devices. If your scanner isn't connected properly to other devices, isn't turned on, or isn't configured properly, Windows can't detect it, and you can't use it.

The next section covers common problems and solutions for all types of scanners, while subsequent sections cover problems and solutions for USB, parallel, SCSI, and IEEE-1394a scanners respectively, followed by scan quality issues.

Cautions and Warnings

Quite a few of today's scanners have multiple interfaces, either as a standard feature or through an optional adapter card. What should you choose?

- USB—Choose USB for basic flatbed scanning of 300 to 600 dpi with recent Windows versions (98, Me, 2000, XP), and when you want to move your scanner anywhere at a moment's notice. However, if you want to scan transparencies, USB 1.1 flatbed scanners are too slow and limited to do a good job. Take a look at USB 2.0 scanners if you want faster performance (but remember you'll also need a USB 2.0 card).

- IEEE-1394a—Looking at 1,600 dpi and higher scanning resolutions? USB 1.1 will slow you down, and SCSI can't hot-swap. For speed and hot-swap flexibility, go with IEEE-1394a if your version of Windows will support it. If your scanner supports transparency scanning, this interface is more than fast enough to make high-resolution scans worthwhile. Just keep in mind that most systems don't have an IEEE-1394a port until you add one.

- Parallel—Use this venerable interface only if USB isn't feasible. It can be painful trying to use a scanner along with another parallel device on the same LPT port.

- SCSI—Tougher to configure than other interface types, SCSI scanners are compatible with older Windows versions as well as with Windows XP. Keep in mind that many vendors of SCSI scanners ship them with very bare-bones SCSI cards not designed to work with multiple devices, although the scanners will also work with other SCSI cards which will support daisy-chaining.

Common Problems and Solutions for Scanners

If the scanner is not detected or can't scan, but the port the scanner is connected to is okay, then

→ See "Using Device Manager to Troubleshoot USB Devices," p. 338 for details about USB power usage.

- Turn on the scanner and reboot the system (if the scanner is SCSI or parallel) so the scanner will be recognized. If the scanner doesn't have a power switch, make sure the scanner is plugged into a working AC power source. Many USB scanners are powered by the hub, so make sure that the scanner is receiving adequate power from the USB hub.

- Make sure the scanner data cable is properly attached to the port on the computer and to the scanner. For USB and IEEE-1394a scanners, you can unplug and reconnect the data cable without shutting down the scanner or system. For other interface types (parallel and SCSI), shut down the system, unplug and reattach the scanner, and restart the system.

- Download and reinstall the latest TWAIN drivers and software for the scanner; use Windows Update to check for updates, then the scanner vendor's own Web site. The software or drivers currently installed may be corrupt.

- Check the meaning of any signal lights flashing on the scanner. The lights could be reporting an error; if so, correct the error and retry the scan.

- The scanning head may be locked, particularly if you hear the scanning head trying to move. Unlock the head and try again. Note that moving the scanner with an unlocked scanning head is not recommended, nor is trying to use the scanner while the head is locked; both can damage the scanner.

If you can't use special features such as one-button scanning, copying, network scanning, or an automatic document feeder (ADF) or transparency adapter provided with the scanner

- Install (or reinstall) the one-button scanning software, if you press the scan button but the scanner won't scan.

- Configure the scanning software to select the correct program or activity to run when you press the email, copying, or other special buttons.

- Make sure the transparency adapter or ADF is properly installed and that you have selected the correct scanning mode in the scanning software (low-cost flatbed scanners don't come with transparency adapters and can be used only for scanning prints and documents). Note that Windows's built-in Windows Imaging Architecture (WIA) scanning feature (the Camera and Scanner Wizard) in Windows Me and Windows XP might not support transparency adapters or ADFs. In that case, use the software provided with the scanner. Software provided with the scanner works through the Acquire command within a graphics editing application rather than through the Windows Explorer as with WIA devices.

- To use a network-compatible scanner from a different computer, you must activate the scan server software on the computer connected to the scanner, and the scan client software on any other computer on network which will be used for scanning. You may need to rerun the client software after each image is scanned with some programs.

Troubleshooting USB Scanners

The most common interface used in new scanners today is USB. This section helps you get your USB scanner back into operation in a hurry.

If your scanner is not detected or can't scan and the USB port is okay, check the following:

- The length of your USB cable. Standard USB cables should be no more than six feet long; if you need a longer run between your computer and your scanner, attach the scanner to a generic (external) USB self-powered hub. With the hub in between your scanner and the PC, you effectively double the length of your cabling (by using two six foot cables).

- The power required by your USB scanner, particularly if the scanner is bus-powered.

→ See "Using Device Manager to Troubleshoot USB Devices," p. 338 for details about USB power usage.

- Make sure your version of Windows supports your scanner and that you have installed the correct drivers. As with any USB device, you must use a USB-compatible version of Windows (98, Me, 2000, XP; 95's USB support was incomplete and buggy when present). Use the parallel or SCSI interface (if the scanner provides this option) if you need to run the scanner on a computer running Windows 95.

- Find out if the scanner works only with pre-installed versions of Windows if you have upgraded from a previous version of Windows. Check the documentation for your scanner to see if this applies. If you upgraded your system to its current version of Windows, check for driver updates. If none are available, contact the vendor to see if the scanner will work if you perform a clean install of Windows to an empty hard disk before installing the scanner.

- Disconnect and reconnect the scanner data cable.

- Check the power cable if the scanner uses AC power.

- Open the Windows Device Manager and click Refresh or Scan for Hardware Changes to redetect connected devices.

Troubleshooting Parallel-Port Scanners

Until the advent of USB scanners, parallel-port scanners were the most common type of low-cost flatbed scanners. Use the tips in this section to get your scanner back into action.

If your scanner is not detected or can't scan and the LPT port it's using is okay, check the following:

→ For more information about the system BIOS, see "BIOS Setup," p. 104.

- The LPT port configuration. Check scanner manual for correct LPT port mode setting (bi-directional, EPP, ECP, EPP/ECP). Restart computer, start the system BIOS setup program, and change LPT port configuration if necessary. Save changes and restart system.

- The cable type. Use the cable supplied with the scanner. If this cable isn't long enough, use an IEEE-1284–compatible straight-through extension cable between the scanner and the port. These cables can be purchased at most outlets where computers and computer hardware are sold.

- Other peripherals daisy-chained to the port. The scanner should connect to the computer, followed by the printer. Most scanners don't daisy-chain properly with removable-media drives (Zip, CD-ROM, CD-RW, and so on). Install a second parallel port if necessary for parallel port drives, or use USB devices to free up the parallel port for use with the scanner.

- The software drivers. Some users have found that using the software drivers for a different parallel-port model from the same vendor work better than the allegedly "correct" drivers do, particularly with Windows XP. If you are using Windows XP, make sure you are using XP-compatible drivers if possible; Windows 2000 drivers might work, but aren't recommended unless you can't get Windows XP-specific drivers.

Troubleshooting SCSI Scanners

While SCSI devices are becoming less common today, many high-performance flatbed and slide scanners still use this interface. Use this section to get back into action.

If your scanner is not detected or can't scan and the SCSI port is okay, check the following:

- Check the device ID#. Each SCSI device on a daisy-chain must have a unique device ID#. Change the scanner's device ID# to an ID# not in use by other SCSI devices and reboot system. See Figure 6.15.

- Make sure that the last device in the daisy-chain is terminated. The last device in a SCSI daisy-chain (even if there is only one device) must be terminated with a switch or a terminating connector. If both internal and external SCSI drives/devices are attached to a single card, both ends must be terminated. Enable or reattach the terminator and restart the system. See Figure 6.15.

- Make sure that all other devices in the daisy-chain are turned on. Turn on all external devices before you turn on the computer.

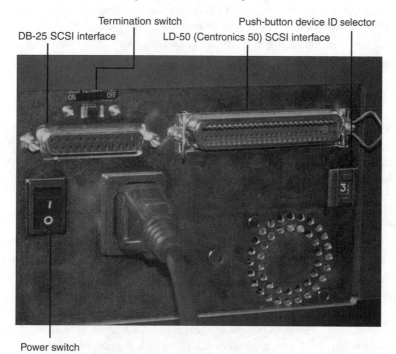

Termination switch   Push-button device ID selector

DB-25 SCSI interface   LD-50 (Centronics 50) SCSI interface

Power switch

FIGURE 6.15
SCSI interfaces and configuration controls on the rear of a typical SCSI transparency/ negative scanner.

Troubleshooting IEEE-1394a Scanners

Serious photography fans are switching from SCSI to IEEE-1394a scanners for high-powered digital imaging. Use this section to keep your scanner working reliably.

If your scanner is not detected or can't scan and the IEEE-1394a port is okay, check the following:

- The power switch. Turn on the scanner and reboot system if the scanner isn't detected by Windows.

- The scanner may have gone into a power-saving mode. Turn off the scanner and turn it on again. Contact the host adapter and scanner vendor(s) for updated driver software.

- Your scanner might not be supported by your version of Windows. Some IEEE-1394a scanners are supported by Windows 2000 only; if you use the scanner with other Windows versions, check for driver updates or reconfigure the scanner to work with its USB or SCSI interface.

- Your scanner might not work if you upgraded to your current version of Windows instead of using a pre-installed version. If you upgraded your system to its current version of Windows, check for driver updates that will allow it to work with an upgraded system. If none are available, contact the vendor to see if the scanner will work if you perform a clean install of Windows to an empty hard disk before installing the scanner.

- The IEEE-1394a add-on interface board on the scanner might not be connected properly. Disconnect the scanner from the computer, shut down the scanner, and remove the interface board. Reinsert it carefully and restart the scanner. Reconnect the scanner to the computer and retry scanning.

- The data cable may be too long. The maximum length for an IEEE-1394 cable is 4.5 meters (about 14.8 feet); use a high-speed hub or repeater if you need to place your scanner further than 4.5 meters away from your computer.

If the scanner runs slowly when connected to other IEEE-1394a devices, reconfigure the IEEE-1394a daisy-chain to attach low-speed devices such as 200MBps hubs or repeaters at the far end of the daisy-chain, after scanners, DV camcorders, and other high-speed devices.

Troubleshooting Scan Quality Problems

Even if a scanner has a working connection to your system, you can still have scan quality problems. Use this section to diagnose and solve typical scanning quality problems you might encounter.

If photos look good on screen, but the quality of the printed output is poor (jagged edges, unsharp), the photo was scanned at too low a resolution. Scan prints at 200 dpi or higher. Scan 35mm negatives and slides at 1350 dpi or higher. Use higher resolutions if you want to enlarge a portion of a print, slide, or negative.

If color photos have distorted colors when scanned, you probably selected the wrong image type during the scan process. Scan color photographs with a setting such as photographs, millions of colors, or similar settings. Don't use the color drawing or thousands of color settings offered with some scanner. For negative/slide scanners, select the correct film type. If your scanner has a color-adjustment setting, use it if your colors are distorted and you are already using the correct millions of colors/photographs scan setting.

If the scanned image doesn't show all the detail in the original photo, you have used the wrong exposure setting during the scan process. Rescan the image if possible, using correct exposure settings. If the original photo can't be rescanned, adjust the level, brightness, and contrast with a photo editing program.

If the scanned image has a moiré (cross-hatched) pattern, the original image was a halftone print. Rescan the image with the scanner's de-screening option if available. If the scanner lacks this feature, descreen the image in the photo-editing program (see your program's help file or documentation for details).

Troubleshooting Your Network

Troubleshooting Network Hardware

If your network adapter, cables, or other hardware don't work, you can't connect to other computers, and if you depend upon your network to reach the Internet, you won't have Internet access either. Use this section to help you troubleshoot problems with network hardware.

Network hardware can be divided into the following categories:

- Network adapters—A network adapter enables a computer to connect to other computers. Some computers have built-in network adapters, but most computers require you to add a network adapter in order to join a network. Network adapters used for wireless networks have fixed or detachable antennas, while network adapters used for wired networks have jacks for network cable (see Figure 7.1).

- Network switches or hubs—10/100 and other wired Ethernet networks transfer data between computers through these multi-port devices. Hubs subdivide the total data transfer rate, or bandwidth, among connected devices (that is, all PCs on the network share the same bandwidth). Switches provide full-speed connections to each device (that is, they can transmit to all connected PCs at peak bandwidth at the same time).

- Routers and gateways—A router enables computers on a local network to access another network, such as the Internet. Access points are used by wireless networks to pass data between stations; they can also include routers for access to the Internet. Routers and access points can also incorporate switches.

- Network cables—Wired networks use cable to connect each computer to the rest of the network. 10/100 Ethernet networks use Category 5 cables, which use an RJ-45 connector. HomePNA networks use telephone cables to piggyback on your existing telephone network.

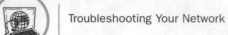

FIGURE 7.1

Typical 10/100 Ethernet network adapters. Photos courtesy of Linksys.

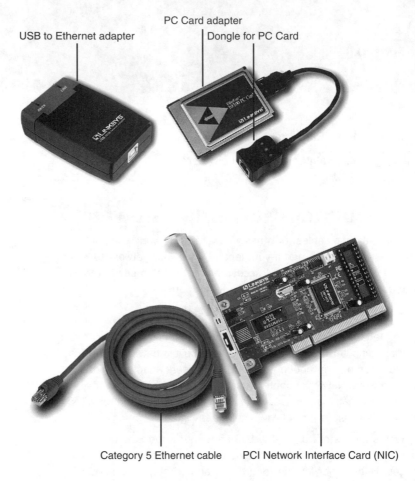

USB to Ethernet adapter

PC Card adapter

Dongle for PC Card

Category 5 Ethernet cable   PCI Network Interface Card (NIC)

When a problem occurs in any of these devices, it has the potential to bring down the entire network. Problems with network adapters can be caused by

- Loose or incorrectly installed network adapters
- Hardware conflicts between network adapters and other devices
- Incompatibilities between network adapters and routers or access devices
- Incorrect configuration of wireless network hardware

Problems with network cables can be caused by

- Incorrectly wired network cables
- Loose or damaged network cables
- Connecting network cables to the wrong port on a router, switch, or hub

Problems communicating between computers on a network can be caused by

- Incorrect configuration of wireless network access points
- Incorrect cabling
- Incorrect configuration of network software
- Switch or hub failure

In this chapter I examine each of these possibilities and how to correct them.

Troubleshooting Network Adapter Installations

The types of problems you can have with a network adapter vary depending on where it's installed and how it connects with other computers. Keep in mind that your computer might already have a 10/100 Ethernet network adapter built into the rear of the computer (a frequent feature on the latest desktop and notebook computers). Some notebook computers might also have a Wi-Fi Wireless Ethernet network adapter included; consult your computer documentation for details.

→ *To determine whether your desktop or notebook computer has built-in 10/100 Ethernet networking, compare the ports on the rear of your computer to those pictured in "PC Anatomy 101," Figure PCA.3, p. 89 and Figure PCA.7, p. 96.*

Adding a Network Adapter

If you need to add a network adapter, you can connect it to any of the following locations:

- USB port
- PCI expansion slot
- PC Card/CardBus expansion slot

I recommend using the USB port if you are adding a network port primarily to access a shared Internet connection. However, if you want to connect to shared folders or printers on other computers on your network, the other types of connections are faster than USB 1.1 (the most common type of USB port).

When you connect your network adapter to a USB port, it will work as long as the USB port is already working and can supply sufficient power for the adapter.

If you use PCI or PC Card/CardBus expansion slots, however, Windows and the system BIOS must detect the card and locate non-conflicting hardware resources to enable the network card to work properly. Windows and the system BIOS can do this only if the cards are properly installed.

If a card plugged into a PCI slot is not inserted completely into the expansion slot and fastened tightly into place (see Figure 7.2), the card will not work. Similarly, if you don't slide a PC Card or CardBus card all the way into the slot on a notebook computer, the card will not work.

→ *For details about troubleshooting USB ports, see "Using Device Manager to Troubleshoot USB Devices," p. 338, and "Using the System BIOS to Solve Problems with USB Devices," p. 348.*

Fast Track to Success

To determine whether a PC Card or CardBus card is correctly connected to the slot, check the Windows system tray for an icon called Safely Remove Hardware (Windows XP) or PC Card (other versions). Double-click the icon to display a dialog box. If your network card is displayed, it's been detected and installed.

FIGURE 7.2

Fastening a 10/100 Ethernet PCI card into place.

Fast Track to Success

CardBus cards use a 32-bit internal design, instead of the original PC Card's 16-bit design; thus, CardBus cards and slots can transmit or receive twice the data per operation and support much faster devices than normal PC Card cards and slots can. CardBus slots can use normal PC Card devices, but not vice versa.

CardBus cards are recommended for 10/100 Ethernet and other high-speed tasks, but they do cost a little more than normal PC Card devices.

After Windows has detected your network adapter (either upon rebooting your PC, inserting the PC Card, or attaching the USB adapter), follow these steps to complete the process:

1. After Windows identifies your network adapter, it usually asks you to provide network drivers from the adapter's CD-ROM or floppy disk. These drivers are usually more up-to-date than those provided with Windows. However, for the most up-to-date drivers, visit the vendor's Web site.

2. Provide your Windows CD-ROM if requested to complete the installation; Windows installs a default set of network protocols that vary by version whenever a network adapter is installed.

Cautions and Warnings

During the installation of the network card's drivers and Windows's own network software, the Windows installer may pause and indicate it can't find a particular file. This usually takes place when the installer is switching back and forth between installing the network adapter's own files and Windows network files. Use the Browse button to redirect the installer to the correct drive and folder to finish the process.

If Windows is unable to locate unique hardware resources for your network adapter, or you don't provide the correct drivers, the network adapter will not function. To determine whether your network card is installed properly or has a problem, open the Device Manager.

→ See "Using Device Manager," p. 480 for details.

I'm Not Sure My Network Adapter Is Working

To determine whether your network adapter is working after you install it, you can use the following procedures:

- Check the Windows Device Manager listing for the network adapter to see if Windows has recognized it and doesn't report any problems.

- Check for signal lights on the rear of a 10/100 Ethernet or HomePNA network adapter after you attach a network cable to the card; attach the other end of the cable to a powered hub, switch, or router (Ethernet) or to the telephone jack (HomePNA); and turn on the computer.

- Run diagnostic software provided by the network adapter vendor.

→ For more about using the Windows Device Manager, see "Using Device Manager," p. 480.

10/100 Ethernet and HomePNA network adapters have signal lights indicating proper operation. Normally, a signal light glows when the network adapter has a working connection to the rest of the network. Some network adapters have other signal lights to indicate network speed or other information.

If your network adapter's connection signal light doesn't glow after you have connected the network adapter to its cable, connected the other end of the cable to the network, and turned on the computer, see "Troubleshooting Cabling," p. 365.

You should also make sure the network adapter is working correctly. The best way to find out is to use the Windows Device Manager to see whether Windows can initialize the network adapter. You might also want to test the network adapter with its own diagnostics if you're having problems (these diagnostics typically come with the network adapter; consult your documentation for their use).

Diagnostic software for your network adapter might be located on the network adapter driver floppy disk, or can be downloaded from the vendor. It must be run by booting with a Windows 9x or Windows Me boot disk, even if you use Windows 2000 or Windows XP. If you use Windows 9x, you can start your system in Safe Mode Command Prompt and then run the diagnostics program. You can use the Emergency Startup Disk created during the installation of Windows 9x or Windows Me as a boot disk.

Cautions and Warnings

If you try to run the network adapter diagnostic program from within a Windows command-prompt window, the program might lock up partway through or not be able to find the network adapter at all because the diagnostics program must have exclusive access to the adapter's hardware.

→ *For details about changing the boot order, see "Boot Setup," p. 111, and "Troubleshooting Hard Disk or Optical Drive Bootup Problems," p. 233.*

To run network adapter diagnostics from a floppy disk

1. Insert a Windows 9x boot disk into drive A:; use this even if you normally run Windows 2000 or XP on your computer.

2. Start your computer.

3. If the computer doesn't boot from the floppy disk, you need to change the boot sequence so that the floppy drive is listed first.

4. During the boot process, select Boot Without CD-ROM Support if you are prompted for a startup option.

5. When the system completes booting (the screen will display an A:\> prompt), wait for the light on the floppy drive to go out, press the eject button to release the floppy disk from drive A:, and insert the floppy disk containing the diagnostics files.

6. Follow the instructions provided with the network adapter card for running diagnostics (the instructions might be found on a Readme.txt file on the disk). For example, the driver disk supplied with Linksys NICs contains a \DIAG folder that contains DIAG.EXE. To run a program in a folder, change to the folder (CD DIAG) and enter the name of the program (DIAG). Figure 7.3 shows the output from the Linksys diagnostics program.

FIGURE 7.3

The Linksys diagnostics program, DIAG.EXE, testing a properly working network card. To check network cabling, run the program on two different computers and enable the Network Function Test to send data between computers.

```
Linksys LNE100TX Fast Ethernet Adapter (LNE100TX v4) Diagnostic Program
Ver 1.14   01-06-2000   (C) Linksys Group

                                      ┌── Node ID: [ 00 20 78 0D D5 BF ] ──┐
#0LNE100TX   IRQ:255Port:8000          Tx Count    :           0   Packets
                                       Rx Count    :           0   Packets
Configuration Test    : PASS
I/O Test              : PASS           CRC Error   :           0
ID Test               : PASS           ALG Error   :           0
Internal Loopback Test: PASS           COLLISION   :           0
Link Status Test      : PASS
Interrupt Test        : PASS
Network Function Test : OFF
                                       Tx Perf.    :           0   Mbps
                                       Rx Perf.    :           0   Mbps
                                       Performance :           0   Mbps
F10 -> Change Turbo Mode
Turbo Mode : ENABLE
                                       Time        :           0   Seconds
F3  -> [ACPI Test]                     -->Burst 01 packets at most each time
                                       ( PgUp, PgDn to change burst number)

      Press <F1> to Reset Counters, <F2> to Toggle ON/OFF, <ESC> to Exit
```

If tests such as internal loopback, I/O, or Interrupt fail, the card is defective and should be replaced. Some diagnostics programs will display a FAIL message for network function or other tests that involve sending and receiving data; disregard this error message unless you are running the diagnostics program on another computer and have configured both to send and receive data.

After you complete the tests, exit the program, remove the floppy disk from drive A:, and restart the computer.

Troubleshooting Hubs, Switches, and Routers

If your network adapter passes its diagnostics tests but you can't get an IP address or the network signal lights don't indicate a connection, you might be having a problem with your switch, hub, or routing device (router, gateway, access point).

Both wired and wireless switches, hubs, and routing devices all have signal lights indicating power and connection status. If the power light is off, no computers will be able to connect through the device. Check the AC adapter connection to the power source and to the device (most of these devices don't have an on-off switch).

If power is flowing to the unit, check the diagnostics light; if it indicates a problem, reset the unit. You might need to unplug it for a minute or two and plug it back into AC power, or you might need to press a reset button. If you reset the unit, you might need to reconfigure it.

Cautions and Warnings

Many of the power cord plugs for hubs, switches, routers, cables modems, and so on have similar connectors that appear interchangeable. They aren't. Be careful that you always plug the correct plug into the correct device.

Plugging a 12v cable modem power connector into a 5v router/switch power connector, for example, will kill the router.

If the unit is a wireless unit, move a client computer within a few feet of the unit. Turn on the client and see if the wireless device can connect with the client. If it can, you might be experiencing signal loss at greater distances. Try adjusting the antenna position. If that doesn't help or the antenna is fixed, reduce the signaling rate of the wireless device to help make the connection more reliable.

If most clients can connect through the unit, but one cannot, you might be using the wrong port. On many of these devices, there is an uplink port designed to allow the unit to connect to another device. In such cases, you cannot use both this port and the adjacent LAN port for a client PC at the same time. Move the cable to an empty port, or connect another switch through the uplink port if you're out of empty ports.

If the switch, hub, or routing device appears to be working correctly, but nobody can connect to the Internet, check the configuration of the routing device. See "Troubleshooting Your Router, Gateway, or Access Point," p. 368. If the configuration appears to be correct, check the cabling between the routing device and the broadband Internet modem.

Troubleshooting Cabling

10/100 Ethernet networks depend upon hubs or switches and a type of twisted-pair cabling called Category 5 UTP (Unshielded Twisted Pair) to transfer data between computers. HomePNA networks use the same RJ-11 telephone cable used by telephones, modems, and fax machines.

A functioning hub has a signal light called Link or Link/Activity for each cable connection (switches and routers with built-in switches will have additional signal lights) as shown in Figure 7.4. The Link signal light glows when a working network cable is plugged into the hub and the computer at the other end of the cable is running. If the signal light doesn't appear, make sure the hub or switch and the computer at the other end of the cable are turned on.

FIGURE 7.4

The front of a typical router with a built-in switch. Photo courtesy of Linksys.

Link/activity lights
for the network ports

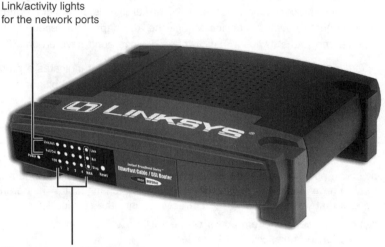

The numbers 1-4 identify each
of the switch's network ports

If the link signal light still doesn't light up, check the following:

➔ *See Figure 2.17, p. 179, for examples of correctly and incorrectly installed Category 5 (RJ-45) network cables. RJ-11 telephone cables used by HomePNA networks connect in the same way.*

- Is the cable tightly connected to the network adapter? Both RJ-45 cables (used by 10/100 Ethernet) and RJ-11 cables (used by HomePNA) are designed to lock tightly into place. If the cable is loose, the network connection won't work and the signal light won't come on.

- Are you using the correct type of cable on a 10/100 Ethernet network? The only time a "crossover" Category 5 cable should be used is to connect two computers together without using a hub or switch, or to connect a hub or switch to another hub or switch when an uplink port is not available. Use straight-through Category 5 cabling between hubs, switches, or routers with built-in switches and network adapters.

Fast Track to Success

A normal (straight-through) Category 5 or 5e network cable used with 10/100 Ethernet connections has the wire pairs in the same order at both ends; you can see them through the transparent plastic connector. A crossover cable will have different wire pair matchups at each end.

- Is the cable connected to the Uplink port, or to the port next to the Uplink port on the hub, switch, or router? If the Uplink port is used to connect the hub or switch to another hub or switch, the port next to the Uplink port can't be used for a network connection. The Uplink port itself is used only to connect to another hub or switch, never for connections to a computer.

- Is the cable damaged? If any part of the cable is cracked or broken, including the plastic connector at the ends of the cable or the cable jacket, replace the cable. A cable whose locking clip is broken can still be pushed into a jack and work, but the cable may work loose over time and create an unreliable connection.

- Is the cable connected to a dongle? If you use a PC Card network adapter that uses a dongle (a small patch cable that runs between the PC Card and the regular network cable), you might not have properly attached it to the PC Card. If the dongle isn't tightly connected, you won't see a connected signal from the signal lights on the dongle or on the routing device, switch, or hub.

- Have you tried another port on the hub, switch, or router? If one connection on a hub or switch isn't working, connect the cable from the computer to another port to see if the hub or switch is working properly.

→ See Figure 2.23, p. 187 for an example of a router/switch combination with an uplink port.

A defective cable can cause both network adapters and hubs/switches to appear to be malfunctioning. If you suspect a defective cable, try another cable between the hub or switch and a computer. If the hub or switch is turned on, the network adapter appears to be working properly, and a replacement cable works, then the original cable was defective. However, if every cable you attach between the hub or switch and the network adapter doesn't activate the signal lights (and the computer can't access the Internet), the hub or switch could be defective. Replace it and retry your network connection.

Troubleshooting Wireless Network Hardware

Wireless networks such as Wi-Fi (also called IEEE 802.11b), other IEEE 802.11-class networks, and HomeRF replace cabling with radio waves. Wi-Fi and HomePNA can be used in a peer-to-peer mode that allows computers to connect directly with each other. However, if you want to use your network to share broadband Internet access, you will need to connect a compatible router, base station, or gateway to your broadband modem (the exact name of the device varies by the network type and brand name).

Whether you connect to other computers in your local network only (also called an ad hoc network with Wi-Fi) or use the network to connect with the Internet (also called an infrastructure network with Wi-Fi), each computer on the network and the Internet access device (if any) must be configured to use the same network settings. The process can be difficult, so it's important to follow the vendor's instructions carefully.

If some computers on a Wi-Fi (IEEE 802.11b) or other wireless network can't connect with each other or with the Internet, check the following:

- The access point and computer have different SSIDs (IEEE 802.11) or different security codes (HomeRF)—The SSID or security code is a unique name for

→ If your hub or switch is part of a router (a device that enables network users to connect to the Internet), see "Troubleshooting a Router," p. 183. For an illustration of incorrect and correct cable connections, see Figure 2.17, p. 179.

the wireless network that prevents access from unauthorized users. The default value for the SSID or security code should be changed to the same value for each device on the network.

- The settings for WEP (Wireless Equivalent Privacy) aren't configured correctly (IEEE 802.11)—Wireless networks can be accessed by anyone with compatible hardware if you don't enable WEP encryption. For this reason, you should enable WEP features on your network. The access point and gateway to the Internet and every computer must use the same WEP settings to protect your network from snooping and to enable every computer on the network to work correctly. See your Wi-Fi or other IEEE 802.11-series access point/gateway manual for details.

- Your wireless network hardware doesn't support the same levels of WEP encryption—Encryption strengths (expressed as 40-bit, 56-bit, or 128-bit: larger is better) used by the WEP features of Wi-Fi and other IEEE 802.11-series networks can vary among brands of equipment. When you enable WEP, you need to select an encryption strength supported by all the equipment on the network.

- Incorrect installation of PC Card hardware into PCI cards used on desktop computers—Some vendors of wireless network cards sell PCI cards for desktop computers that act as a docking station for the PC Card network adapter used by notebook computers. If you don't completely insert the PC Card into the slot on the desktop computer's adapter card, you can't connect with the network.

- Incorrect positioning of the gateway, base station, or router—If the gateway, base station, or router can't be accessed by all the stations because of range issues or interference, those stations can't connect to the Internet or with each other. Follow the recommendations for device positioning very carefully. With IEEE 802.11-series networks, consider configuring the network adapters to run at lower speeds to increase range, or add another access point to relay signals from the more distant computers to the Internet gateway.

Troubleshooting Your Router, Gateway, or Access Point

If you are using a router, gateway, or access point to provide a hardware firewall or share an Internet connection with the network instead of using Windows Internet Connection Sharing (ICS), you need to configure it before you can configure the stations on the network.

→ See "Using IPCONFIG and WINIPCFG," p. 187.

Because the router, gateway, or access point replaces the original single-computer connection to the broadband Internet modem, it must use the same settings as you originally used for the computer that was attached directly to the broadband Internet modem. Use the Windows Run command (click Start, Run) and enter the IPCONFIG or WINIPCFG commands (using the computer currently connected to the broadband Internet connection) to display your current settings.

Most routers are already configured to automatically obtain an IP address from the broadband modem. You will need to configure the router to provide Internet Protocol (IP) addresses for all the computers on your network. Otherwise, some or all of your computers might not be able to access the Internet.

Your routing device will need additional configuration settings if any of the following are true about your connection:

- If your Internet connection uses a static (fixed) IP address provided by your broadband ISP, you will need to manually enter the computer's IP address and the IP addresses for DNS servers and your ISP's gateway into the routing device's configuration. (Consult your ISP for IP and DNS information, and your router's documentation for how to configure your router.)

- If you must log in to your broadband service using a user name and password then your service probably uses an option called PPPoE. You will need to select PPPoE in your router configuration and specify your username and password.

- If you have an ISP that requires you to provide the hardware address (called a MAC address) of your network card when your system was first configured. A MAC address is a unique number assigned to every network component manufactured. Most routing devices offer an option called "MAC address cloning" that enables the routing device to display the MAC address you specify (the one from your original network card) rather than its actual MAC address when it connects to the ISP's network. This option effectively hides your router from your ISP, making it look like your PC is connected directly to their network. (Since many ISPs will not support users with routers, this can be a very valuable feature.)

You have two options in determining whether these special settings apply to your configuration: Ask your ISP or examine your network configuration yourself.

To examine your network configuration in Windows XP/2000

1. Click Start, Control Panel, Network and Internet Connections, Network Connections.

2. If your connection is listed under LAN or High-Speed Internet, it doesn't use PPPoE. If your connection is listed under Broadband and includes PPPoE in its description, you will need to configure the router to use PPPoE in its Login configuration, and enter the username and password you normally use to connect to the Internet.

3. To determine the IP address configuration of your connection, right-click the connection icon and select Properties. In the window that appears, click Internet Protocol (TCP/IP), and then the Properties button.

If your connection uses a server-assigned IP address (that is, your ISP provides your IP address when you connect), the Obtain an IP Address Automatically and Obtain DNS Server Address Automatically options should be selected on the General tab. If, instead, you see specific addresses specified on the General tab for the computer's IP address and DNS servers, record the addresses for use with your router. Click the Advanced button. Record the default gateway's IP address and other IP address and server name information provided so you can enter this information into the router's configuration screen.

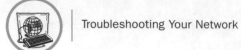

If you're using Windows 9x/Me

1. Right-click the Network Neighborhood or My Network Places icons on the Windows desktop and select Properties.

2. Scroll down through the configuration window, which lists the network components that are installed. If you see PPP over Ethernet protocol or PPPoE, your Internet connection uses PPPoE; you will need to set up your routing device to use PPPoE and provide it with your username and password.

3. Click the TCP/IP listing for the network adapter that is connected to your broadband modem and click Properties.

If your connection uses a server-assigned IP address, Obtain an IP Address Automatically and Obtain DNS Server Address Automatically will be selected on the IP Address tab. If you see specific IP addresses specified on the IP Address tab for the computer's IP address and DNS servers, record the addresses for use with the routing device configuration and click Gateway. Record the default gateway's IP address. Click DNS Configuration and note the DNS server and name server IP address information provided.

→ For details, see "Using IPCONFIG and WINIPCFG," p. 187.
Even if your ISP doesn't indicate that they track this information, you should still record and clone the MAC address of your network adapter. To display the MAC address for your network adapter, use IPCONFIG with Windows XP or Windows 2000, or WINIPCFG with Windows 9x/Me.

Fast Track to Success

The easiest way to make sure you're recording the correct information you need to configure your routing device is to open the instruction manual included with the router, gateway, or access point; turn to the pages that discuss the configuration process; follow the instructions listed previously; and use the humble Post-It note from 3M to attach the correct values to the pages. You might even want to number each Post-It note to correspond with the figure numbers on the page.

If your instruction manual is electronic, print out the pages and use the Post-It note trick. It's better than writing on the pages themselves because you might discover you've made a mistake the first time you configure the device.

Follow the instructions provided with the routing device to configure it. Most use a Web-based configuration utility that requires you to connect a computer to the routing device and log in to it through a Web browser such as Internet Explorer; the instruction manual for your routing device will provide the correct IP address to access the routing device's setup program. Even if you're using a wireless routing device, you might find it easier to connect a computer via an Ethernet cable when it's time to configure it (if you have a choice).

In addition to configuring the connection between the routing device and your broadband Internet modem (often referred to as the WAN connection), you also need to configure the routing device to serve as a DHCP server so it can provide IP address information to the computers on the network. Once you have completed the configuration of the router, connect your computers to the routing device and configure your network software. See "Troubleshooting Network Software Configuration," p. 376.

If you use a wireless network, you need to follow additional steps before you can configure the computers on the network. You should configure the access point to use WEP encryption and select an encryption level compatible with both your access point and your network adapters. If you don't configure your wireless network to be secure, anyone with compatible wireless gear who's within range of your network could sneak onto your network and use your Internet connection for free. See "Troubleshooting Wireless Network Hardware," p. 367 for more information.

Cautions and Warnings

A hallmark of 10/100 Ethernet is compatibility between different brands of hardware. I've mixed and matched two, three, or even four brands and models of NICs, routers, hubs, and switches (not to mention using both premade and bulk network cables) on a single network without any problems.

However, Wi-Fi (the popular name for IEEE-802.11b wireless networks), isn't completely standardized, despite the multi-vendor testing that the Wi-Fi trade organization performs. Because different vendors use different methods for configuring their access points and might add additional proprietary features to their hardware, you're better off if you get your access points/routers and NICs from the same vendor.

And, don't be confused by the many new IEEE 802.11-series wireless networks. Despite the similarities in name, IEEE 802.11a, 802.11b, and 802.11g aren't compatible with each other unless you use special multi-mode network hardware.

Troubleshooting a Shared Internet Connection

Originally, computer networks at home or in small offices were intended to enable resources to be shared and email to be sent between computers. However, the popularity of the Internet and the development of low-cost ways to share a broadband or LAN-based Internet connection has led many users to create networks that are mainly intended to share an Internet connection.

There are two ways you can configure your network for Internet sharing:

- Configure a computer on the network to provide Internet access to all computers on the network. The computer uses a network adapter to connect to the other computers on the network. The connection to the Internet could be made with a dial-up modem, another network adapter, or a USB port (the latter two options are used with broadband connections such as DSL, USB, or satellite or wireless connections).

- Connect all computers on the network to a router or gateway that provides Internet access equally to all PCs on the network. A 10/100 Ethernet network can use a combined router/switch, enabling all computers on the network to connect directly to the router. Other routers only have one Ethernet port, which must be connected to a separate hub or switch in order to allow all networked PCs access to the Internet. Wireless and other types of networks might call the router a gateway, home base, or Internet access device, but it works in the same way.

The first method is the one supported by Microsoft Internet Connection Sharing (ICS), which was originally introduced with Windows 98 Second Edition and is also included with Windows Me, Windows 2000, and Windows XP. Third-party sharing programs such as WinProxy, Sygate Home Network, and WinGate also use this method.

Fast Track to Success

Whether you want to attach a broadband Internet modem to your computer or need to add a second network port for sharing your connection, don't overlook USB. While USB 1.1 isn't as fast as an internal 10/100 Ethernet card, it's more than fast enough to connect a broadband Internet modem to your computer. In fact, you might not even need a USB-to-Ethernet adapter with some broadband modems; they're already USB ready right out of the box.

The second method was originally too expensive for home or small-office use, but the widespread popularity of home networking and broadband Internet has made router or gateway-based sharing a less-expensive and much more desirable option.

Figure 7.5 diagrams two typical 10/100 Ethernet networks that have been configured to provide shared Internet access.

ICS Host

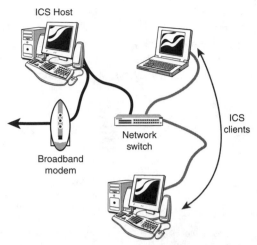

Broadband
modem

Network
switch

ICS
clients

Network sharing Internet access through Windows

FIGURE 7.5

Two 10/100 Ethernet networks configured for Internet sharing; one uses Windows Internet Connection Sharing (ICS) with two network adapters to share the connection, while the other uses a router with a built-in switch.

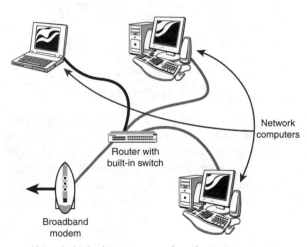

Network
computers

Router with
built-in switch

Broadband
modem

Network sharing Internet access through a router

Figure 7.6 diagrams a wireless network that has been configured to provide shared Internet access.

The problems and solutions encountered when you troubleshoot networks used for shared Internet connections vary according to how sharing is performed:

- If ICS or another computer-based sharing method is used, it's possible for the computer with the Internet connection (the host) to connect to the Internet but for other computers on the network to lack an Internet connection. This typically happens if the host computer is not correctly configured to share its Internet access or if other computers on the network are not configured to look to the host for Internet access.

→ *For more information on troubleshooting your current Internet connection before sharing it with other computers, see "Troubleshooting a Broadband Internet Connection," p. 177, or "Troubleshooting a Dial-Up (Analog Modem) Connection," p. 173, depending upon the Internet connection type you use.*

- If a router or gateway is used, it's possible for some computers to have Internet access while others don't, or for all computers to lack Internet access. If only some computers are configured correctly, others will not be able to connect to the Internet. If the router or gateway fails, or if no computers are connected correctly, no computers on the network will have an Internet connection.

FIGURE 7.6

A typical wireless network that uses a wireless gateway/access point to provide shared Internet access. The access point can also include a switch for supporting 10/100 Ethernet clients.

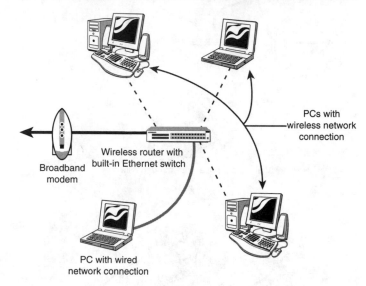

PCs with wireless network connection

Broadband modem

Wireless router with built-in Ethernet switch

PC with wired network connection

Troubleshooting ICS

ICS has been one of the most popular and low-cost ways developed to share an Internet connection, but behind the scenes it can be very complex to install and troubleshoot, particularly if the ICS host (the computer sharing its Internet connection with others) is running Windows 98SE. Because ICS is more difficult to use with Windows 98SE than with Windows Me or Windows XP, I recommend upgrading a Windows 98SE computer to Windows XP Home Edition before installing ICS.

On the Web

The Practically Networked Web site offers a series of excellent tutorials on the installation and configuration of Internet Connection Sharing. Visit the site before you install ICS at http://www.practicallynetworked.com/sharing/.

My book, *The Absolute Beginner's Guide to Cable Internet Connections* (Que), also provides detailed step-by-step tutorials and checklists for ICS installation as well as detailed network diagrams. Learn more at http://www.quepublishing.com.

Some of the common problems you can have with any version of ICS include

- Installing ICS on more than one computer—ICS is needed only on the ICS host computer. The computers that share the ICS connection use normal TCP/IP (Internet protocol) software, and don't even need to be running Windows!

- Forgetting which network adapter is used for the connection to a broadband modem, and which is used for ICS—This can be particularly problematic if you use Windows 98SE's version of ICS. With this version, you need to select which network adapter is used for the Internet, and which for sharing with the network. The Home Networking Wizard used by later versions of Windows usually determines this information for you.

  If you need to use two network adapters (essential for sharing most broadband modems), open the Device Manager before you install the second network adapter to see the brand and model of network adapter you are currently using (if you use a separate network card for the broadband modem). I recommend you buy a different brand and model of network adapter for your network to prevent confusion during ICS setup.

  Alternatively, determine the MAC address for both devices. (The networking device's MAC address is always unique, like a fingerprint.)

- Not installing all the ICS software components needed—You might need to insert the Windows CD during ICS initial setup to load the additional software components that ICS uses. If this installation attempts to install older copies of files you already have, you'll receive a warning. Tell Windows to keep the newer files, but don't skip any files during installation. If Windows can't find a particular file on your CD, make sure your Windows CD-ROM is properly inserted, has a clean surface, and is being referred to by the correct drive letter. If the drive letter for the CD-ROM or other optical drive has changed since you installed Windows, use the Browse button to change where Windows looks for the CD.

- Not connecting the broadband modem and network connections to the correct network adapters—If you have disconnected networking cables and later reconnected them, it can be surprisingly easy to miss a cable or not connect them properly. Because the ICS host uses the Internet connection and network connection in different ways, mixing them up will keep the host and the entire network off the Internet.

Fast Track to Success

To prevent mixups on your ICS host computer, I recommend you attach a label to the cable running from the broadband modem to the ICS host; call this cable "Internet." Label the cable running from the ICS host to the switch or hub as "Network." Label the network adapters on the computer the same way, and you'll never need to worry about which cable (and network adapter) does which job.

- Forgetting to turn on the ICS host when using a network computer to access the Internet—If your ICS host PC isn't turned on, no computer on the network has Internet access. It's also not enough to just turn it on. You must also allow it to boot up completely before trying to access the Internet from any computer on the network. Once the ICS host is running and can access the Internet, then other computers can start up and access the Internet as well.

- Not running the Home Networking Wizard on computers using Windows Me, 2000, or XP—While you can configure the ICS host and its clients manually, the Home Networking Wizard built into these Windows versions makes configuring ICS almost foolproof.

→ *See the relevant section of Chapter 2 for details about troubleshooting your Internet connection.*

- Not making sure the ICS host can access the Internet before installing ICS—If the ICS host can't access the Internet, don't install ICS or try to access the Internet from other computers (until the host computer is working).

- Not configuring ICS client computers correctly if the Home Networking Wizard is not available. See "I'm Not Sure My Network Settings Are Correct," later in this chapter, for details.

Troubleshooting Network Software Configuration

Each computer that shares Internet access, either with ICS or through a router or gateway, needs the following software installed:

- TCP/IP—The protocol required for all computers on the Internet; this is normally installed automatically during the installation of a network adapter.

- Client for Microsoft Networks—Permits logon to a Microsoft network to share resources.

- File and Printer Sharing for Microsoft Networks—Required only for systems that need to share drives, folders, printers, or other resources.

The following settings are needed for each ICS client:

- Server-assigned (dynamic) IP addressing—The ICS host, router, or gateway assigns the IP address to each computer

- A workgroup name (the same name must be used by all computers on the network)

- A unique computer name for each computer on the network

→ *For more information about TCP/IP and DHCP, see "TCP/IP Configuration," p. 169.*

The easiest way to add these components to most Windows networks is to use the Home Networking Wizard included with Windows Me and Windows XP.

Even though the latest Windows versions make configuring your network simpler than before, you still need the following information to configure your network with any version of Windows:

- Are you adding a Windows XP computer to an existing network that wasn't used for Internet access? If you use your network strictly to share folders and printers, you might not be using the TCP/IP protocol used by networks and the Internet. Some small networks use an older network protocol called NetBEUI. Windows XP doesn't support this protocol officially, but does provide it on the retail version of the Windows XP CD-ROM in the ValueADD folder.

On the Web

See the Microsoft Knowledge Base article #Q301041 to learn how to install NetBEUI if you need it. You need NetBEUI *only* for networks that don't access the Internet.

Go to http://support.microsoft.com and use the search option.

- How are you sharing an Internet connection? If you decide to use ICS or another computer-based sharing program such as WinGate or WinProxy, you need to configure the computer with the shared Internet connection in a different way from the rest of the network; with products other than ICS, you might need to install special software on the other computers in the network to enable them to use the shared connection. If you use a router or gateway, all computers on the network are configured in the same way, using the same software.

- How will computers get an IP address? Generally, you should use the default of server-assigned IP addresses for the easiest configuration. Providing a fixed IP address to each computer on the network can lead to problems. For example, if you assign two computers the same IP address, neither computer will have Internet or network access.

- What name will you use for the workgroup? Every computer on the network must use the same workgroup name, or shared resources such as folders, drives, and printers won't be available to some users. Some ISPs require you to use a particular workgroup name, while others don't care.

- Which name will you assign to each computer? While the workgroup name is common to all computers, each computer needs a unique computer name. If more than one computer has the same name, those computers won't be able to access shared resources.

- What resources do you want to share? You might want to share document folders or printers on some computers, but not others. Most versions of the Home Networking Wizard enable you to share the My Documents (Windows 9x/Me) or Shared Documents (Windows XP) folders with others, but you can skip this step on some computers if you don't want those folders shared. You can manually select other folders or printers for sharing later with Windows Explorer or the Printers folder.

While several steps are involved in this process, you can complete the configuration task very simply by using the Windows Home Networking Wizard with Windows XP or Windows Me. If your network has computers running Windows 95, 98, or 98SE as well as computers running Windows Me or XP, you can still use the Windows XP or Windows Me Home Networking wizards to configure systems with older versions of Windows by creating a Home Network Setup floppy disk on the XP or Me systems.

To start the Home Networking Wizard with Windows Me, click Start, Programs, Accessories, Communications, Home Networking Wizard.

To start the Home Networking Wizard with Windows XP, click Start, All Programs, Accessories, Communications, Network Setup Wizard.

If you are configuring the computer as an ICS host, make sure you specify that this computer has a direct connection to the Internet and that you want to share the connection with others. If you are configuring the computer as a client (connecting through an ICS host, a router, or a gateway), make sure you specify that the computer will access the Internet through another computer (a router or gateway is considered a computer by the wizard). In either case, you can select to share a document folder and a printer with other users on the network. You must specify a workgroup name (the same for all computers) and specify a unique computer name for each computer.

At the end of the process, you can create a Home Networking Wizard floppy disk that you can use to configure other Windows computers on the network, including Windows 9x computers.

The Home Networking Wizard floppy disk you can create with Windows Me or XP contains a program called NETSETUP.EXE. Run NETSETUP.EXE to configure other Windows computers on the network; select The Computer Connects to the Internet Through Another Computer and specify whether you want to share a document folder or a printer.

If you don't have Windows Me or Windows XP on your network (so you can't use their wizards to set up your Windows 9x systems), make sure each computer has TCP/IP installed, has a server-assigned IP address, and uses the same workgroup name. Each computer needs its own computer name, and you can choose whether or not to share resources on a computer-by-computer basis. Use the Networks icon in the Control Panel to view or change these settings.

If your network is not a wired Ethernet network, you might need to run special setup software provided by the network vendor in addition to, or instead of, using the Home Networking Wizard. See your network hardware's instruction manual for details.

After you have configured the network software on the host and each client computer and rebooted the host, followed by the client computers, each one should be able to access the Internet and shared resources on the network.

If your network isn't working after you have installed it, use the following sections to discover what's wrong and learn how to fix it.

I Can't Access Other Computers on the Network

If you can't see other computers on the network, one of the following could be the reason:

- The network hardware has failed
- You didn't log on to the network at startup
- You don't have a working connection to the network

Connecting to a shared Internet connection requires that your computer has the TCP/IP protocol installed and has a valid IP address. If you can connect to the Internet, your network hardware is working correctly. If not, this is the first place to check. See "Troubleshooting Network Hardware," p. 359, earlier in this chapter if you can't connect to the Internet.

Windows XP automatically logs you on to the network when it starts up. However, with Windows 9x and Me, if you click Cancel when the logon screen appears, you can't access any network resources.

To determine whether failing to log on is the reason why you can't access network resources with Windows 9x/Me, click Start, Shutdown, Log Off. When the username and password dialog appear, enter your username and password (press Enter in the password field if you don't use a password), and Windows will log you on to the system.

If you still can't access network resources, check the other options listed in the following sections.

I'm Not Sure My Network Settings Are Correct

The following problems might indicate a problem with your network software configuration:

- You can see other computers on the network but you can't see any shared folders or printers.
- You can access the Internet, but you can't see other computers.
- You can't access the Internet or see other computers.

To solve the first problem (can't see shared folders or printers), make sure that the computers which have folders that should be shared are running File and Printer Sharing and have specified folders to share. You can rerun the Home Networking Wizard on these computers or manually configure each computer's network settings to install File and Printer Sharing. The wizard will also permit you to share the My Documents folder on computers running versions of Windows other than Windows XP, and to select shared printers. For Windows XP, the Shared Documents folder is shared by default.

You can also manually set up folder and printer shares. Open My Computer or Windows Explorer, right-click a folder you'd like to share, select Sharing from the menu, and specify a share name (a descriptive name for the shared resource that is visible to other users on the network). To share a printer, open the Printers folder, right-click a printer, select Sharing, and specify a share name. Passwords are optional but recommended for security. If you share a printer on a Windows XP or Windows 2000 computer on a network that has other versions of Windows running on it, click the Additional Drivers button to install drivers that can be used by other versions of Windows (see Figure 7.7). The drivers will be downloaded to the other computers when they browse to the shared printer on the network.

FIGURE 7.7
Using the Additional Drivers option in Windows XP to provide drivers for other Windows versions.

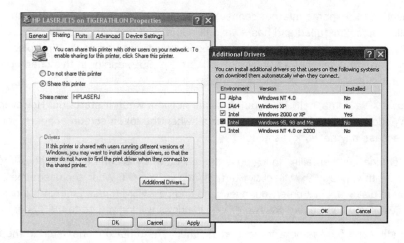

If you can access the Internet but not other computers on the network, your work-group name doesn't match the workgroup name of the other computers on the net-work. You can rerun the Home Networking Wizard and enter a common workgroup name, or change the name manually.

To change the workgroup name in Windows XP

1. Open the Start menu, right-click My Computer, and select Properties.

2. Click the Computer Name tab on the System properties sheet.

3. Click Change.

4. Enter the correct workgroup name and click OK (see Figure 7.8).

5. Reboot the computer.

In Windows 9x or Me

1. Right-click My Network Places or Network Neighborhood icons on the Windows desktop, and select Properties.

2. Click Identification.

3. Enter the correct workgroup name and click OK.

4. Reboot the computer.

FIGURE 7.8
Changing the work-group name in Windows XP.

Cautions and Warnings

Another reason you might not be able to connect with the home network is because you've moved a notebook computer from an office network to your home network. If your office network uses server-assigned IP addresses and you use 10/100 Ethernet, you should be able to get on the Internet at home just by connecting your computer to a network cable and powering it up. However, if you use a wireless network or you use a static IP address at the office, you could be in for a messy reconfiguring job when you want to bring your notebook computer home.

Check out Globesoft's Multinetwork Manager, a low-cost solution for managing multiple network configurations on your computer. Learn more about it and download a trial version at http://www.globesoft.com/mnm_home.html.

If you can't access the network or see other computers, the solution is usually pretty simple if you connect to the Internet through a routing device (router, gateway, or access point): Rerun the Home Networking Wizard, or make sure you have configured your network as discussed in "Troubleshooting Network Software Configuration," p. 376.

If you use Internet Connection Sharing, make sure the computer with the shared Internet connection (also called the ICS host) can connect with the Internet. If it can't connect, nobody can. Restart it, then rerun its Home Networking wizard if it still can't connect; if you use the Windows 98 or Windows Me version of ICS, you might want to remove and reinstall it. If the ICS host can connect to the Internet, but other users can't, or if no users can connect to the Internet on an ICS or router-based network, check the following sections.

I'm Not Sure I Have a Valid IP Address

Whether you connect through a routing device or through an ICS host, your computer should have received a valid IP address from the server included inside the routing device or from the ICS host. Use IPCONFIG or WINIPCFG to check your IP address.

→ *For details on updating all types of drivers, see "Using the Device Manager," p. 480.*

If you use ICS or a third-party sharing program, the computer with the shared Internet connection must be turned on and completely booted before it can provide a valid IP address to other computers on the network. If not, all computers should be shut down, the host computer should be started and finish booting, and then the client computers should be started. If this process is followed and the client PCs still can't get a valid IP address (they have an IP address of 0.0.0.0. or an address starting with 169.), you could have problems with your network adapter, cabling, or switch.

If your computers are connected to the Internet through a router, any computer can be used to access the Internet independently of the others, since the router provides a valid IP address to each user. If one or more computers don't have a valid IP address (IP address shows up as 0.0.0.0 or 169.x.x.x), check the router. If the router is turned off, has its power supply cable disconnected, or isn't connected to the network cables running to your computers (or to a separate network switch or hub used by the computers on the network), it can't provide valid IP addresses to the computers on the network. Recheck the cable connections, turn the router off and on again, shut down and restart the computers on the network, and retry connecting to the Internet.

Updating Network Hardware Drivers

If you discover problems with your network hardware, a driver or firmware update might be necessary to solve the problem. Follow these guidelines to ensure success in your update:

- Switches and hubs made for home-office and small-office use (brands such as Linksys, D-Link, Netgear) don't use firmware and can't be updated. If they fail, replace them.
- Some network adapters have upgradable firmware and some don't, but all of them use drivers, which can be updated.
- If Windows Update doesn't have an updated driver for a network adapter, go to the vendor's Web site.

If your normal broadband Internet connection isn't working because of router or network adapter problems, here are some alternatives that can help you get the driver or firmware updates you need:

- Connect a working PC directly to the broadband Internet modem. If the routing device has a problem, bypass it until you can get a replacement. To avoid problems with ISPs who identify your connection by its MAC address, see "Troubleshooting a Router," p. 183.
- Use the USB connection instead of the 10/100 Ethernet connection on the broadband Internet modem if the Ethernet card needs a new driver. While the Ethernet connection is a bit faster in practice, USB will work well enough, especially if you plug it directly into your computer and not into a hub that's already handling other USB devices.

- Use your computer's dial-up (analog) modem to connect to the Internet and get updates. Some broadband ISPs offer a limited amount of dial-up service as a backup in case of failures, or you can use a free service offer (AOL, anyone?). If you decide to use AOL, MSN, or some other Internet service that uses proprietary software, just remember that you will need to uninstall it and reinstall your normal Internet connection software after you are finished. If you have problems after you remove AOL or similar programs, run System Restore with Windows XP or Me and select a system restore point before the date you installed the proprietary online software.

- Buy prepaid Internet access from companies such as Slingshot (http://www.slingshot.com).

- Follow the instructions for updating the firmware on a routing device very carefully. If you don't update the firmware correctly, you will ruin the device's BIOS chip and a trip to the repair shop will be required. Make sure you write down the current settings used by the routing device before you update its firmware.

→ *For details, see "Using IPCONFIG and WINIPCFG," p. 187.*

Fast Track to Success

If your network's routing device uses a Web-based interface for configuration, you can use your Web browser's Print option to record its settings before you update its firmware.

Troubleshooting Memory Problems

Troubleshooting Memory Bottlenecks

Regardless of the speed of your computer's processor, adding more RAM memory provides faster performance in almost every case. How can you tell if your computer needs more memory? Check out these symptoms:

- You see the Windows "I'm busy" hourglass appear frequently when you have multiple program windows open

- The hard disk activity light is blinking furiously as you work

- Switching between programs takes measurable time instead of being instantaneous

If your computer has the preceding symptoms, try the following methods to find out whether or not you are facing performance bottlenecks caused by a lack of RAM:

- Determine the amount of memory you currently have installed on your system

- Determine how many programs you run at the same time (on average)

- Check the performance of your system

To determine the amount of installed RAM on your Windows computer, right-click My Computer and select Properties, or open the System icon in the Control Panel. You will see a display similar to the one in Figure 8.1.

Compare the amount of available memory in your system to the figures in Table 8.1 to determine if adding memory could speed up your system.

FIGURE 8.1
The General tab of the System properties sheet indicates the version of Windows in use and the amount of installed RAM memory available to Windows.

Windows version

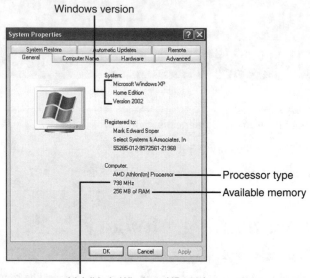

Processor type

Available memory

Current processor speed (visible in Windows XP only); might vary slightly from the processor's rated speed

TABLE 8.1

Recommended Memory Sizes for Applications You Use

Number of Programs You Have Open at One Time (on Average)	Types of Programs	Recommended Minimum RAM
1 to 2	Word processing and email, card and board games, Web browsing	128MB
1	3D games	512MB
2	Office suites, Web browsing	192MB
3	Office suites, games, Web browsing	256MB
3 or more	Office suites, photo and graphics editors, Web browsing	384MB
3 or more	Office suites, photo and graphics editors, CAD, multimedia, Web browsing	512MB

TABLE 8.1 (continued)

3 or more	3D CAD or modeling software, Web browsing	2GB (motherboard might limit maximum memory size)

As you can see from Table 8.1, it makes sense to upgrade your system to 512MB of RAM, particularly if you work with multimedia or digital imaging or play 3D games. Keep in mind that if your computer runs out of actual RAM, it will use its *virtual* memory, which is stored in a file called the *paging file* (also called the *swapfile*). The paging file is an area of free space on your hard disk that the computer treats like additional RAM. Unfortunately, the difference between accessing data from system RAM and your hard drive is like the difference between making photocopies in your office or driving across town to a Kinko's. It's a very slow substitute.

Fast Track to Success

If you use a low-cost computer with video integrated into the motherboard, or a notebook computer, you might have seen an unusual memory size such as 63MB (instead of 64MB) or 240MB (instead of 256MB) when you viewed your system properties (refer to Figure 8.1). This is because Windows cannot "see" memory which is set aside for use by your integrated video. Video integrated into the motherboard typically uses anywhere from 1MB to as much as 32MB of RAM, depending upon the computer and your version of Windows.

When you add memory, I recommend you keep this factor in mind. If you are planning to upgrade to 256MB of RAM and your system uses 16MB or more of main memory for video, add an extra 64MB to 128MB to the amount you were planning to add to make sure you have plenty of RAM after video takes its cut.

The figures in Table 8.1 are estimates based on typical usage. To determine more precisely if you need to add RAM, you can use the Task Manager in Windows XP and Windows 2000 to display real-time statistics for memory usage.

1. Press the CTRL-ALT-DEL keys to display Task Manager.
2. Click the Performance tab (see Figure 8.2).
3. Open the programs you plan to run at the same time.
4. Open typical data files within these programs.

Note the figures for Commit Charge (Total) and Physical Memory (Total) in Figure 8.2. If Commit Charge (Total), which refers to the amount of memory in use, is frequently or consistently larger than Physical Memory (Total) with typical combinations of programs and data in use, you should upgrade your RAM to meet or exceed the amount of RAM indicated in Commit Charge (Total). When Commit Charge (Total) is larger than Physical Memory (Total), the virtual memory paging file is used to make up the difference, and your system slows down because disk drives are far slower than RAM memory.

FIGURE 8.2

The Performance tab in Windows XP. This computer has 256MB of RAM installed, which is more than sufficient to handle the Commit Charge size of 141MB required by the programs currently in use.

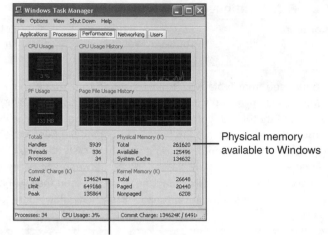

Physical memory available to Windows

Memory currently used by Windows

If you use Windows 98 or Windows Me, use a tool called System Monitor instead to determine if your memory size is adequate. System Monitor is an optional program accessed by clicking Start, Programs, Accessories, System Tools, System Monitor. If it is not already installed on your system, open the Add/Remove Programs icon in Control Panel, click the Windows Setup tab, and then click System Tools, Details to see the program listing. Click System Monitor to checkmark it, and click OK to install it. Provide your Windows CD-ROM if requested to complete the installation.

To measure memory use with System Monitor, click Edit, Add Item and select the following items from the Memory Manager category:

- Page faults (program requests data which is not stored in physical memory, and must fetch the information from virtual memory)

- Swapfile size (by default, Windows adjusts the size of your swapfile to keep pace with your system's need for virtual memory)

Figure 8.3 shows System Monitor in use displaying page faults. Note that the number of page faults per second is generally low, even though this computer has several programs open at the same time.

If the Page Faults per second value is consistently above 1K with a typical combination of programs and data, you should add memory to your system, up to 512MB total. (Windows 9x/Me have problems with more than 512MB of RAM when AGP video cards are used.)

Page faults per second

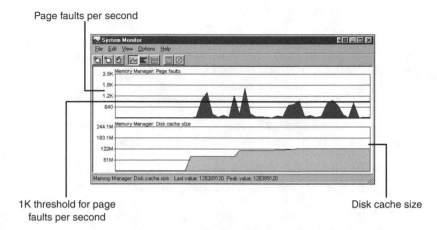

FIGURE 8.3
The System Monitor utility in Windows 98 configured to display page faults (per second) and disk cache size. The amount of RAM installed is sufficient for the programs and data in use, as shown by the generally low level of page faults.

1K threshold for page
faults per second

Disk cache size

Improving Virtual Memory Performance

Even if you add more memory, working with large data files or running many programs at once will still force your system to make occasional use of its paging file. The real goal is to minimize its use, as eliminating the need for virtual memory isn't realistic at this time. So, if you have to use it, you should make sure your PC is using it effectively. Because a lack of memory is a major bottleneck, improving how your virtual memory works is a necessity.

You can improve how quickly virtual memory works in these ways:

- Defragment the drive containing the paging file frequently
- Move the paging file to a separate hard drive which your commonly used programs and data don't use much; this drive letter should contain least 1GB or more free space before you move the paging file to it

Normally, Windows uses a variable-sized paging file to save disk space. However, when Windows adjusts the size of this file, the system can slow down, particularly if the drive containing the paging file is badly fragmented (has many files whose sectors are scattered around the drive) and has less than 1GB of free space.

Defragmenting Your Drive

Defragmenting your hard disk realigns the sectors in each file with each other and puts the empty space on the hard disk together. The result is that the hard disk can locate all the parts of a file faster, improving performance for virtual memory and for other disk activity such as saving and opening files.

Cautions and Warnings

The Windows Defragment program can't move some types of files, so it's normal to see a few files still in a fragmented state after the program is finished. However, most data files and program files will be defragmented, resulting in a performance boost for your system.

All versions of Windows from Windows 95 through Windows XP (except for Windows NT 4.0) include a built-in defragmentation program. To start it

1. Open My Computer or Windows Explorer.

2. Right-click on your hard disk and select Properties.

3. Click Tools.

4. Click Defragment Now.

If you use Windows XP/2000, you can select a drive and click Analyze to determine the fragmentation status of the drive in Windows before you run Defragment.

Windows will suggest that you defragment the drive if it determines that the drive contains many file fragments. For details, click View Report and scroll through the Volume information and Most fragmented files windows. Some files might be stored in hundreds of fragments (see Figure 8.4).

FIGURE 8.4

Displaying the fragmentation analysis on a Windows XP system with two hard drives.

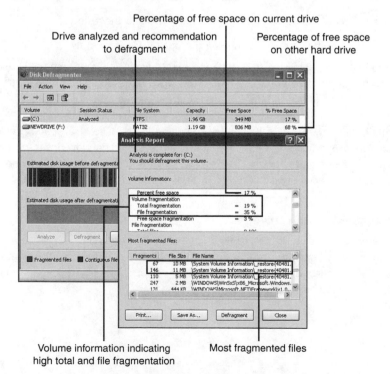

Click Defragment to begin the process if you have more than 15% free space on the drive as in Figure 8.4. Depending upon the size of the drive, the speed of the drive, and the amount of fragmentation on the drive, the operation could take anywhere from a few minutes to several hours.

Note that if Windows XP finds less than 15% free space on the drive, it might not be able to run properly and displays an on-screen warning. Free up space and try again if your system has less than 15% free on the drive you want to defragment.

The Windows 9x/Me Defragment program checks the drive for errors before it starts; if it finds errors on your drive, you will need to run ScanDisk or another disk-repair tool to correct them. While the Windows 9x/Me Defragment program doesn't recommend a particular percentage of free disk space, keeping at least 15% of your hard disk free is a good idea with these versions of Defragment as well.

Fast Track to Success

If you need to free up some disk space to allow defragment to work properly with any recent version of Windows, try this:

➜ *See "Using Disk Cleanup," p. 391.*

- Run Disk Cleanup to delete temporary files (including temporary Internet files), files in the Recycle Bin, and compress old files.

➜ *See "Viewing and Adjusting Pagefile (swapfile) Configuration," p. 393.*

- Disable the paging file on the current drive and place the paging file on another drive.

I recommend you run Disk Cleanup first, restart Defragment, and adjust the pagefile configuration if you're still below the recommended amount of disk space free.

While the Windows 95 Defragment program displays an analysis of the disk fragmentation and a recommendation of whether or not to defragment the drive, it is often incorrect; Windows 98 and Me don't offer an analysis, although you can scroll through the disk map displayed after Defragment starts and compare the disk condition to the legend to see if the drive is badly fragmented.

Because all versions of Windows create temporary files for printing and other program functions and resizes its swapfile as needed, I recommend that you defragment your drive about twice a month or more often if you notice a definite slowdown in system performance.

➜ *For more information about using the Windows 9x/Me Defragmentation program, see "Maintaining Windows with Drive and Anti-Virus Utilities," p. 152.*

Using Disk Cleanup

Because defragmentation uses empty space on your drive as a temporary location for files before it places them in their correct sequence, having enough empty space on your drive is critical to the correct operation of Defragment.

Starting with Windows 98, you can use the Disk Cleanup tool to free up disk space. Disk Cleanup can remove downloaded Internet temporary files, other types of Internet files, and compress old files you want to keep (Windows XP/2000 using NTFS only). To start Disk Cleanup

1. Click Start, (All) Programs, Accessories, System Tools, and Disk Cleanup.

2. Select the drive you want to clean up and Disk Cleanup scans the drive for files to process.

3. Disk Cleanup displays the file types it can process. Select each type of files you want to process and Disk Cleanup displays the disk space you can gain (see Figure 8.5).

4. Click OK to process the files; files in the Compress Old Files category will be compressed to save space and can still be used afterward, but files in all other selected categories will be discarded.

5. Disk Cleanup closes automatically after processing the selected file categories.

Displays dialog box for uninstalling unused Windows components, unused programs, and to display other options to free up disk space

FIGURE 8.5

Selecting file types for deletion or compression by Disk Cleanup in Windows XP.

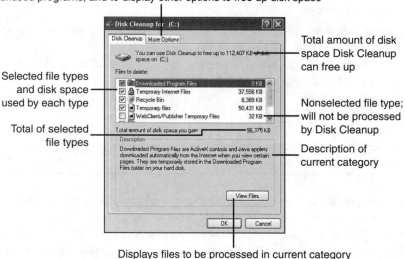

Selected file types and disk space used by each type

Total of selected file types

Total amount of disk space Disk Cleanup can free up

Nonselected file type; will not be processed by Disk Cleanup

Description of current category

Displays files to be processed in current category

Fast Track to Success

Windows defines an "old" file as one which hasn't been accessed for a specified time period. Click the Options button displayed when you select Compress Old Files to select the amount of days Windows waits before compressing a file.

Click the More Options tab to free up more space by uninstalling Windows components or third-party programs you don't use. Windows XP and Me users can also discard older System Restore checkpoints. Windows 98 and Me users who aren't using the more-efficient FAT32 file system can convert the selected drive to FAT32. Select the option you want to use and follow the wizard's prompts to perform the selected action.

Viewing and Adjusting Pagefile (Swapfile) Configuration

If your default Windows drive (normally C:) has less than 15% of free space left on it and you have other hard disk drive letters, consider changing the location of your paging file to another drive with more space, particularly if you've already used Disk Cleanup to free up space and you still haven't been able to free up at least 15% of your hard disk drive. Moving your paging file to a drive with more space makes it easier to defragment your default Windows drive and can provide faster system performance.

To see how much of your hard disk is available, you can run Defragment in Windows XP/2000 (refer to Figure 8.4), or with any recent Windows version

1. Open My Computer or Windows Explorer.

2. Right-click your hard disk and select Properties. A pie chart displays the free and used space (see Figure 8.6).

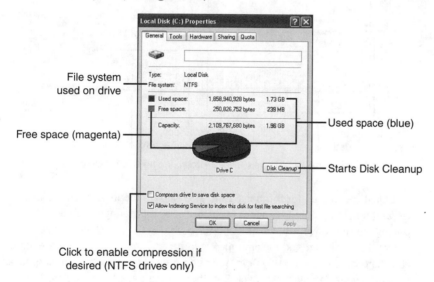

File system used on drive

Free space (magenta)

Used space (blue)

Starts Disk Cleanup

Click to enable compression if desired (NTFS drives only)

FIGURE 8.6
Displaying free and used space on a hard disk with Windows XP.

The drive shown in Figure 8.6 has about 11% of its total capacity free; not enough to run Defragment effectively. By default, Windows puts the paging file on the Windows system drive (normally C:, as in this case). To free up enough space to run defragment, you could disable the paging file temporarily (not recommended), remove some unused Windows components or programs, or configure this system to place its paging file on another drive.

To view or adjust the size or location of the paging file in Windows XP or Windows 2000

1. Right-click My Computer and select Properties.

2. Click Advanced.

3. In the Performance section, click Settings.

4. Click the Advanced tab, then Change (Virtual Memory). Windows displays the recommended and current size for the paging file, and displays how much space is available on the drive used for the paging file (see Figure 8.7). To see the amount of space which could be used on another drive, click the drive.

FIGURE 8.7

Viewing the paging file size and location in Windows XP after configuring each hard disk drive letter with a system managed paging file.

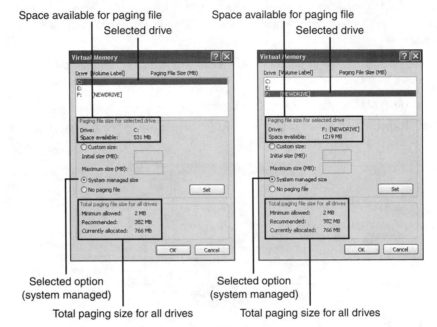

Space available for paging file
Selected drive

Space available for paging file
Selected drive

Selected option
(system managed)

Selected option
(system managed)

Total paging size for all drives

Total paging size for all drives

5. To adjust the values for the paging file size and its location, click the drive letter and select System Managed size (Windows will manage the swapfile), No paging file (the drive will not be used for a paging file), or Custom size (you select the minimum and maximum). I recommend that you configure each of your hard drives to use a System managed paging file to avoid running out of space on your default drive. Click Set, then OK to save the changes.

You can place paging files on more than one drive or place the entire paging file on a different drive than the default if you are short of space on the default drive.

Because Windows must reboot if you make changes to the page file, it requests that you restart the computer (you should heed this request).

Cautions and Warnings

Windows XP, unlike older Windows versions, can store all or part of its paging file on removable-media drives. This is a potentially-dangerous feature, because if you remove the disk containing part of the paging file, you could crash the system. If Windows XP displays multiple drive letters you can use for the paging file as in Figure 8.7, make sure you choose only hard disk drive letters for your paging file locations. You can determine what type of drive each drive letter refers to by opening My Computer and viewing the list of drives.

To change the swapfile size or location in Windows 9x/Me, open your System Properties sheet (right-click My Computer and choose Properties). Then click the Performance tab in the System properties sheet. Click the Virtual Memory button and adjust the settings as desired. Unlike Windows XP/2000, Windows 9x/Me support only one swapfile location and requires you to select a size for the swapfile if you move it from the default drive (C:). Reboot after making any changes.

Cautions and Warnings

You should periodically check your drives for errors with the error-checking feature on the Windows Tools menu for your drives. It's especially important to perform this test before you adjust the size or location of your pagefile or swapfile. For more information, see "Maintaining Windows with Drive and Anti-Virus Utilities," p. 152.

Upgrading System Memory

If you decide that you need to add memory to your system, you should check the manual packaged with your computer or motherboard to determine what type of memory you can use. Depending upon the system type, your desktop computer normally uses one of the following memory types:

- DDR SDRAM DIMM modules (see Figure 8.8)
- SDRAM DIMM modules (see Figure 8.8)
- RDRAM RIMM modules (see Figure 8.9)

Systems that use 72-pin SIMM modules (see Figure 8.10) are too old to justify upgrading.

A notebook computer might use

- SDRAM SO-DIMM or DDR SO-DIMM (see Figure 8.11)
- Proprietary memory (memory that is designed specifically for your brand and model of notebook)

Each type of memory uses a different type of socket.

FIGURE 8.8

A DDR SDRAM DIMM module (top) compared to a regular SDRAM DIMM module (bottom). Photos courtesy Micron Technology.

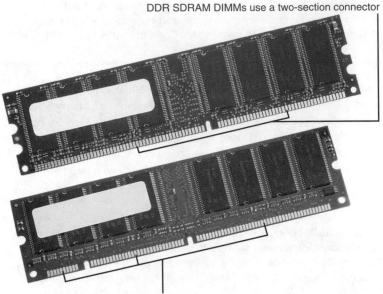

DDR SDRAM DIMMs use a two-section connector

SDRAM DIMMs use a three-section connector

FIGURE 8.9

An angled view of an RDRAM RIMM module. Photo courtesy Kingston Technology.

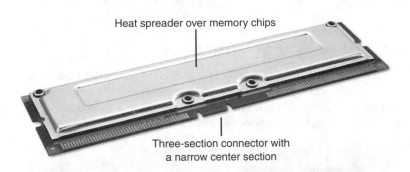

Heat spreader over memory chips

Three-section connector with a narrow center section

FIGURE 8.10

An SDRAM DIMM memory module (top) compared to a SIMM memory module (bottom). SIMMs are generally found in computers which are more than five years old and are too old to be cost-effective to upgrade.

32MB

FIGURE 8.11

Two types of SO-DIMM (Small Outline DIMM) memory modules used with notebook computers; the SDRAM SO-DIMM (top) is being replaced on the newest systems by the DDR SDRAM SO-DIMM (bottom). Photos courtesy Micron Technology.

It's important to realize that your computer is designed to handle specific types, speeds, and sizes of memory modules. If you install a memory module that's the wrong speed, you could have system lockups. If you install a memory module that's an unrecognized size, the computer might not recognize it, or might incorrectly identify it.

While your system or motherboard manual will tell you what sizes and types of RAM you can install, it can't tell you what's already installed. There are several ways to determine what memory is already installed in your system:

- To see the overall memory size, view the General tab of the system properties sheet in Windows (refer to Figure 8.1).

- Some computers display the specific memory size and speed of each module when the computer is started (see Figure 8.12).

- You can run a system analysis program such as SiSoftware Sandra to identify the memory modules in your system by brand, speed, and size (see Figure 8.13, later in this chapter).

Fast Track to Success

It can be tricky to determine the size of each module if your system doesn't display this information at startup and if you don't use a system analysis program. However, the following rules of thumb can help you determine this information:

- The most common sizes of memory modules include 32MB, 64MB, 128MB, 256MB, and 512MB.

- If the computer has one memory module installed, the total amount of memory is the same as the size of the memory module installed.

- If the computer has two memory modules installed *and* the total size of memory equals one of the common sizes listed above, each module is one-half that size. For example, in Figure 8.8, the total memory size is 512MB on a system with two modules. Divide 512MB by two, and each module is 256MB.

- If the computer has two memory modules installed *and* the total size of memory does *not* equal the common sizes listed above, the modules are different sizes. For example, a computer which reports a total memory size of 192MB has a 64MB memory module and a 128MB memory module.

- If the computer has three memory modules installed, you will need to inspect each module physically or with software to determine its size, since the possible combinations are virtually unlimited.

FIGURE 8.12
This computer has three memory sockets, of which two are in use, providing a total of 512MB of RAM. The memory runs at PC-133 frequency.

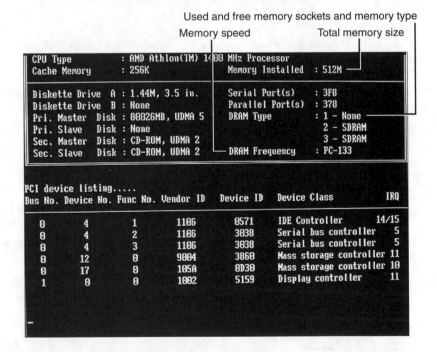

Determining What You Need

To determine what memory you can add to your system, you need to know the following:

- How many memory sockets are open
- What size(s) of memory modules are already installed
- What type and sizes of memory modules you can install in your system

You need to know how many memory sockets are open to determine whether you can add memory to your system or whether you must remove low-capacity memory to make room for larger memory modules. You need to know the sizes of the memory modules to determine which module(s) you should remove to make room for larger modules if you don't have any memory sockets remaining. You need to know what type and sizes of memory modules your system uses to be sure of buying the right memory for your system.

In addition to looking for information displayed at startup about your computer's memory size, speed, and memory socket usage, you should also consult your computer's documentation to see the type, size(s) and speed of modules you can use. If your computer uses SDRAM modules such as PC-100 or PC-133 or DDR SDRAM modules such as PC1600 or PC2100, you can generally add these one at a time. However, virtually all systems that use RDRAM RIMM modules such as PC600 or PC800 require that you add them in matched pairs.

If you know the motherboard or system brand and model (it might be displayed on the system properties sheet shown in Figure 8.1, at startup, or on a sticker on the side or rear of your computer), you can use interactive buying guides available from various memory vendors to choose the right memory for your system. Most "white-box" systems built from generic motherboard use standard memory modules, but many name-brand systems require proprietary modules which might be more expensive.

On the Web

Here are some of the major memory vendor Web sites which offer interactive memory selection guides

- Crucial.com—http://www.crucial.com; also lists memory for major motherboard vendors/models
- Kingston—http://www.kingston.com; also lists memory for major motherboard vendors/models
- PNY—http://www.pny.com
- Viking Components—http://www.vikingcomponents.com

You can use system analysis programs such as SiSoftware Sandra or Belarc Advisor to help you determine more information about your system's memory and motherboard, which is very helpful if your system doesn't report these details when you start it and you can't locate the information in your documentation.

On the Web

SiSoftware Sandra is available from SiSoftware online at http://www.sisoftware.co.uk/sandra.

The standard version of Sandra is free; the professional version, with added features, is about $30.

If you want a simpler display of memory and system information, try the free Belarc Advisor from Crucial Technology's Web site (Crucial.com sells Micron memory) at http://www.crucial.com/support/belarc_download.asp.

To determine motherboard and memory information on your system with SiSoftware Sandra, start Sandra and open the Mainboard Information icon. Scroll down to the System Memory Controller field and note the memory socket types and current usage (see Figure 8.13).

FIGURE 8.13
SiSoftware Sandra indicates this system has two of its three memory sockets in use; the third can be used to upgrade the system.

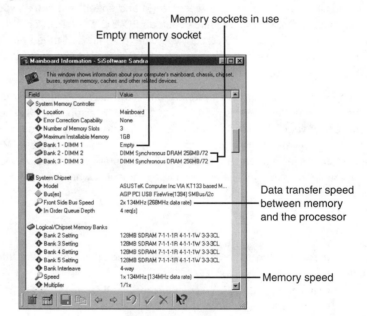

When you download and run Belarc Advisor, it opens a Web browser window to display its text-based report of your computer's contents, including motherboard brand and model, memory type, and memory size. You can click the Buy More button to go to Crucial's Web site, select your motherboard, and choose your memory.

Generally, you don't need to remove existing memory from your computer unless you have no more open memory sockets or if you want to see the labeling some manufacturers place on the memory modules for size and speed.

You should install the same speed of memory modules already found in your system. For example, if your system uses PC2100 DDR modules, don't install PC1600 DDR modules. Although they'll plug into the socket, your computer could have problems because the memory is slower than what's already installed.

Dumbing Down Fast Memory

Most retail memory outlets have stopped selling PC-66 and PC-100 speeds of SDRAM DIMM memory modules, since PC-133 is used in virtually all systems which still use SDRAM modules. Fortunately, in most cases you can pop a PC-133 module into a system which uses slower memory and it will work okay. Note that systems which use specially designed proprietary memory modules instead of standard DIMMs won't be able to accept standard PC-133 memory.

Installing System Memory

After you've determined that you need a memory upgrade and have purchased memory of the speed and type designed for your system, it's time to get it installed. Follow this procedure for installing new memory:

1. Shut down Windows and the computer.

2. Unplug the power cord to the computer.

3. Touch metal parts on the computer to equalize electrical potential before you open the case.

4. Open the case. The procedure for opening a PC case varies from PC to PC. You may have to remove two to four screws on the back. On other cases, you may have to remove the front bezel (face plate) and then one or two screws on the front of your case. Most current cases allow you to remove just one side panel or the other. In this case you need only remove the right side relative to the front of the PC.

5. Touch metal parts on the computer to equalize electrical potential before you open the package containing the memory module.

6. Locate the memory sockets. If you cannot see the memory sockets (see Figure 8.14), you might need to remove the motherboard from your system before you can upgrade the memory.

7. Install the memory module into the correct slot. Line up the connectors on the DIMM or RIMM with the connectors on the socket. Push the memory module straight down into the socket until the locking levers flip into position (see Figure 8.15).

8. If you removed the motherboard to install the memory, secure the motherboard back into the case.

9. Plug the power cord back into the computer.

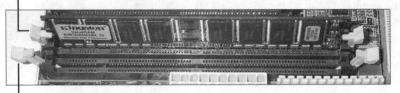

Memory module locked into place

Empty socket with open locking tabs

FIGURE 8.14
Typical SDRAM DIMM memory sockets; the one in the rear already contains a module, while the front socket is empty. Memory sockets for DDR SDRAM and RIMM modules also use swiveling locking tabs.

Locking clips not engaged

Locking clips engaged; module locked in place

FIGURE 8.15
A DIMM module partly installed (top) and fully installed (bottom); the memory module must be pushed firmly into place before the locking tabs will engage.

→ *If the system doesn't boot or reports a memory error, see "Troubleshooting Memory Upgrade Problems," p. 403.*

10. Restart the computer and watch for startup messages or open the System properties sheet after Windows boots to verify that the new memory has been detected.

11. Shut down running programs, Windows, and the computer.

12. Close the case and secure it.

Freeing Up Space for Additional Memory

If your computer has one or more empty memory sockets as seen earlier in Figures 8.12 and 8.13, you can install the additional memory you need in the empty socket. However, if your motherboard's memory sockets are already full, you will need to remove one or both modules to make room to add memory. In such a case, consider installing just one large memory module rather than two smaller modules: for example, a single 256MB module rather than two 128MB modules. This strategy allows you to add additional memory in the future.

If your total memory is a non-standard size such as 96MB (64MB+32MB), 192MB (128MB+64MB), or others, look at the labeling on the module to determine which module is smaller if you want to remove only one of your existing modules. If the markings are hard to read, keep in mind that the memory module with memory chips on both sides is usually the larger one, and the smaller one usually has chips on only one side.

Cautions and Warnings

While most systems let you remove or install one memory module at a time, there are some exceptions. Systems which use RDRAM RIMM modules must have every memory socket occupied by either an actual RIMM module or a continuity module (which resembles a RIMM module without memory chips). Systems which use the Intel 850-series chipsets use matched pairs of identical RIMM modules; if you need to add or remove memory on these systems, you must do it in pairs.

Programs such as SiSoftware Sandra and Belarc Advisor will inform you of the motherboard chipset on your system, enabling you to look up the vendor to get more information about memory usage and other features.

Troubleshooting Memory Upgrade Problems

Memory upgrades are normally very easy to perform, but you can run into problems, particularly if you haven't upgraded a system before. Table 8.2 provides a quick-reference to the problems you might encounter, and their solutions. More details for each solution are provided in the following sections.

TABLE 8.2

Memory Upgrade Problems and Solutions

Symptom	Cause	Solution	Tips
Memory sockets are not accessible after the case is opened	Components inside the case, such as the power supply or drives, are blocking access to memory	Remove the motherboard from the case if possible, or temporarily remove the component that's blocking access to the memory.	Take a look at your system documentation before you plan to perform the memory upgrade to determine if you need to remove the motherboard (it's necessary on some

TABLE 8.2 (continued)

Symptom	Cause	Solution	Tips
			of the smaller retail-store systems). If you're not comfortable performing this job, ask a friend for help, or pay the store's service department to perform the memory installation.
New memory not detected after it was installed	The new memory is not fully inserted into the socket	Be sure the memory is locked into place (see Figure 8.15).	The memory socket is keyed to accept the memory the correct way only; if the memory won't go into the socket, you might be inserting it backward.
	The memory is not inserted into the correct socket	Install the memory into the socket next to the currently used socket(s)	Check your system manual to determine if the order in which you populate memory sockets can cause problems.
	The new memory is the wrong size or type	Install the correct size and type of memory.	Use the interactive memory configurator and software tools discussed earlier to make sure you order the correct memory for your system.
	The new memory is defective	Test the new memory in a socket you've already used successfully with your	Be sure to keep your fingers away from the contacts on the bottom of the module during installation to

TABLE 8.2 (continued)

Symptom	Cause	Solution	Tips
		older memory modules.	avoid static damage to the module.
	The memory socket is defective	Test the socket by installing existing memory that works when used in a different socket.	If the memory socket is defective, you should replace the motherboard or use larger memory in the other sockets.
Computer displays a memory-sizing error after you install new memory	The BIOS information about memory is out of date	Restart the computer, enter the BIOS setup program, and save changes.	Most systems automatically test the memory at startup without displaying sizing errors.
Computer reports memory errors after you install new memory	The new memory may be defective	Remove and reinstall the new memory and retry. If the computer still reports memory errors, replace the memory.	Many systems lock up if memory is defective, but lockups can also happen for other reasons. Ask the vendor to test the memory for you, or try a memory test program.

The most likely cause for new memory not being detected after installation is that the memory is not properly installed. Refer to Figure 8.15 and note that you must not only insert the memory into its socket, but also ensure it is firmly pushed into place, so that the locking clips can engage. Until the locking clips engage, proper contact between the motherboard and the memory module will not take place and the new memory will not work.

SDRAM and DDR SDRAM DIMMs and RDRAM RIMMs must be inserted straight down into the memory sockets, and are keyed so that they can only be inserted one way. If you cannot push the memory into place, you might not have the module lined up correctly with the guides incorporated into the locking clips, you might be trying to install the memory facing the wrong direction, or you might be trying to install the wrong type of memory into the socket. Refer back to Figures 8.9, 8.10, and 8.11; each type of memory has a notch on the bottom of the memory connector to prevent improper installation.

If you have an older system, it may use a type of memory based on what are called 72-pin SIMM modules. Most likely, any upgrade you make to this system will involve replacing the motherboard (and the memory type with it). However, if you do find yourself just upgrading the memory, note that it must be inserted at an angle and snapped into place (rather than pushed straight in); see Figure 8.16. The keying on these modules doesn't prevent them from being inserted incorrectly, but will prevent you from snapping them into place.

FIGURE 8.16
Locking a 72-pin SIMM module into place.

Swing top of module upright to lock into place

Module inserted into socket

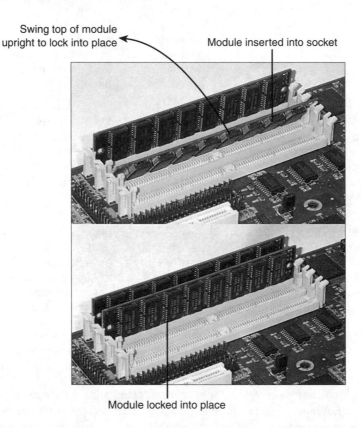

Module locked into place

Because motherboards and systems are designed to use only specific types, sizes, and speeds of memory, installing incorrect memory sizes and speeds, even if the module physically attaches to the system, can also prevent the system from detecting and using the new memory. For example, if you install a 512MB memory module into a system which is designed to work with 64MB, 128MB, or 256MB memory modules only, it won't work.

Troubleshooting Defective Memory or Memory Sockets

To determine whether a defective memory module or a defective memory socket is preventing your computer from detecting the newly installed memory, first open the case using the steps described for installing a memory module. To determine whether a memory module or socket is defective if you have two or more modules installed

1. Verify that the newly installed memory is the correct type, speed, and size; check the markings on the package with the system or motherboard manufacturer's requirements.

2. Remove the newly installed memory module.

3. Restart the computer and note the size of memory reported; it should be the size of the remaining module(s). Shut down the computer.

4. Remove one of the existing memory module(s).

5. Insert the newly installed memory module into the socket used by the existing memory module you removed in step 4.

6. Restart the computer; the memory size displayed should be the size of the new memory module plus the size of any other module still in the system. If the memory size displayed doesn't reflect the size of the new memory module, the module might be defective or might be the wrong size or speed for the motherboard. Return it to the vendor for replacement.

7. If the memory size displayed does reflect the size of the new memory module, shut down the computer and reinsert the existing memory module into the empty socket. Restart the computer. If the memory size displayed doesn't reflect the size of the additional memory module (which you already know is working from step 3), the memory socket is defective and the motherboard should be replaced.

For example, assume that your motherboard has three memory sockets, one with a 64MB module, one with a 128MB module, and the third is empty, for a total of 192MB. If you add another 128MB module, the memory should add up to 320MB if the memory module and the socket are okay.

If you remove the 128MB module which was installed before upgrading memory and install the new 128MB module in its place, you should still have 192MB of memory if the new module is working correctly. If you have only 64MB of RAM, the module is defective.

If the new 128MB module works correctly in slot 2, but is not recognized when you install it in slot 3, the slot itself is defective. You must either replace the motherboard or avoid using that slot for memory.

Troubleshooting Installed Memory

Troubleshooting memory problems after it's been installed in a system for awhile can be more difficult than discovering a module that's failed directly out of the package. Early PC systems displayed memory parity errors when the contents of memory were corrupted, but this type of memory went out of fashion in the mid-1990s. Today, many servers and some high-performance workstations use memory and motherboard chipsets which can detect and correct memory errors using a technology called ECC, but this feature is extremely rare on typical home, home-office, and corporate computers.

➡ *To learn more about detecting problems with your system's power supply, see "Determining You Have a Power Supply Problem," p. 434.*

When a system locks up during operation, the problem could be memory-related, but it could also be attributable to problems with other hardware or with Windows. The contents of memory can be corrupted by excessive heat or by problems with the system power supply.

You can test installed memory with a memory-testing program; your computer also tests memory during its power-on self-test (POST) process.

➡ *To learn more about reducing heat buildup inside your system, see "Troubleshooting Cooling Problems," p. 416.*

Testing Installed Memory

While today's memory modules are generally very reliable, it's still possible to have occasional memory errors after your memory is installed and working. To track down memory problems which might manifest themselves only after your computer's been running for awhile, you can use memory testing programs to provide a much more thorough test than what your computer's Power-on Self Test (POST) performs when you turn on your computer.

Most memory-testing programs require you to boot your computer with a DOS or Windows 9x/Me floppy disk; if you use Windows XP select the option Create an MS-DOS Startup Disk when you format the floppy disk in My Computer.

While memory testing programs are limited by the features of your motherboard and aren't as thorough as the dedicated memory testers used by some computer service shops, they can still help you determine if you have marginal memory modules which need to be replaced. Memory testing programs work by writing various patterns into memory and reading back the patterns; if the pattern of data written into memory don't match what the program reads back, the memory module is probably defective. For the most thorough test, set memory testing programs to run their most thorough testing processes over a several hour period; this is sometimes referred to as "burning in the system."

On the Web

SIMMTester.com offers its free DocMemory testing program on its Web site at http://www.simmtester.com/PAGE/products/doc/docinfo.asp

#1-PC Diagnostics Company has a free limited-feature version of its system and memory diagnostics software, #1 TuffTEST-Lite, available for download; more powerful versions are available for about $10 and $30 each

http://www.tufftest.com

Qualitas RAMexam is available for about $24 download; a free demo which checks only the first 640KB of RAM is also available

http://www.qualitas.com

Troubleshooting Memory with POST Beep Codes

If your system beeps when you turn it on and doesn't finish the normal power-on process, your system BIOS is reporting a significant hardware error.

Memory is one of the parts of the computer which your BIOS checks during its Power-on Self-Test (POST) process. BIOS beep codes are designed to report memory problems when you start the computer. Beep codes vary by BIOS brand and version; you can use the methods described earlier in this chapter to determine the BIOS vendor your system or motherboard uses.

If your computer has an AMI BIOS, the following beep codes are used to report memory problems

- One beep—Memory refresh failure
- Two beeps—Memory parity failure
- Three beeps—Memory failure in base (first 64KB) memory
- Continuous beeps—Memory failure (could also indicate video memory failure)

The Award BIOS uses one long beep or a continuous beep to indicate memory failure.

The Phoenix BIOS version 4.0 Release 6 also has several beep codes used to indicate memory failures, including

- One beep, followed by three beeps, four beeps, one beep
- One beep, followed by three beeps, four beeps, three beeps
- One beep, followed by four beeps, one beep, one beep

If your computer is beeping at you at power-on but the beep pattern doesn't match any of these, your computer might use a different BIOS or the problem might be with some other part of your computer. Contact your system or motherboard vendor for help.

→ *For more information about how the BIOS reports errors, see "Power-on Self Test," p. 115.*

Troubleshooting Processors and Motherboards

CHAPTER 9

How Processors Can Fail

While generally reliable, processors can and do fail. Causes can vary, but if you're dealing with a damaged or dead CPU, the only recourse is to replace it. The major reasons for processor failure include

- Overheating
- Power surges
- Heatsink failure
- Heatsink detached from processor
- Incorrect heatsink installation
- Wrong heatsink for processor
- Incorrect insertion into the motherboard

The first four causes can affect any user, even if you never open your system to install a new processor. The last three are concerns for users who replace their older processor with a new processor or for users who build their own systems from components.

Cautions and Warnings

In most cases, moving from an older processor such as an Intel Pentium II, Pentium III, Celeron, AMD K6, or Duron to a newer processor such as an Intel Pentium 4 or AMD Athlon XP also requires a motherboard and memory upgrade to get the greatest benefits from the new processor. In such cases, it's safer to install the new processor and memory on the motherboard before you install it in the case. If you don't install these components until after the motherboard is mounted in the case, you risk damaging the motherboard because of excessive flexing caused by the force needed to clip a heavy heatsink to the processor and lock it into place, and the force needed to push memory modules into the locked position.

Even if your existing motherboard can handle a faster processor, you're better off to remove the motherboard from the case before you remove the old processor and heatsink. Installing a new CPU/heatsink requires the application of thermal grease or paste to ensure proper transfer of heat away from the CPU. This precise process makes it essential that you are able to work without the restrictions of a case while you perform the installation.

The details of such an installation are beyond the scope of this book. For those looking for advanced technical information about CPUs and motherboards, pick up a copy of *Upgrading and Repairing PCs, 14th Edition*, by Scott Mueller (Que, 2002).

For a more basic, visual guide on performing PC upgrades, including the CPU and motherboard, check out *How to Expand and Upgrade PCs, 3rd Edition*, by Preston Gralla (Que, 2002).

Detecting Overheating and Incorrect Voltage Levels

The best way to prevent destroying your processor is to use the features provided by recent systems to help you monitor your PC's condition.

Most recent PCs and motherboards incorporate a series of hardware monitors that measure system temperature, voltage levels, and fan operation. Some computers display this information in the BIOS setup program, while others make this information available to you only if you install and run a hardware monitoring program. Some vendors include such a monitoring program with their systems or motherboards, while you might need to use a third-party program to view this information with other programs.

Figure 9.1 shows a typical hardware monitoring program supplied with my Athlon-based motherboard.

Detailed screens for each item monitored display the current values and the threshold value. To change the threshold value (the value that triggers an alarm), the user opens the Settings dialog.

On the Web

Some motherboard and system makers might offer a hardware monitor program for your system, although they didn't package it with the motherboard or computer. Contact your motherboard or system vendor for details.

Other third-party hardware monitors include

- Hmonitor—Download it from http://www.hmonitor.com.
- Motherboard Monitor—Download it from http://mbm.livewiredev.com.

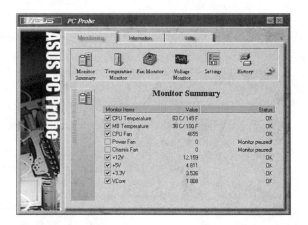

FIGURE 9.1
The Asus PC Probe hardware monitoring program supplied with the author's mother-board. The Power Fan and Chassis Fan are not selected for monitoring because they aren't connected to the motherboard.

Hardware monitoring programs alert you when voltage levels, fan speeds, or temperature levels exceed threshold limits; a few can be configured to shut down your system if limits are exceeded for a protracted period of time.

You should pay attention to fan or temperature warnings you receive from your hardware monitor, particularly if you use a hot-running processor such as the AMD Athlon or AMD Duron. Unlike recent-model Intel processors that have automatic slowdown or shutdown features built into the processor if they overheat, Athlon and Duron processors will keep running even if the fan built into the heatsink fails. A few seconds of overheating will destroy these processors unless a motherboard specially designed to shut down the computer in case of overheating is used.

On the Web

The great Tom's Hardware Web site crash-tested AMD and Intel CPUs to determine their resistance to overheating in the following article:

http://www.tomshardware.com/cpu/01q3/010917/index.html

A follow-up article discussing AMD's response to the problem, a motherboard-based fix you should demand on your next Athlon motherboard, is available at

http://www4.tomshardware.com/column/01q4/011029/index.html

Finally, the DVD packaged with the 14th edition of *Upgrading and Repairing PCs* also features footage showing what happens to an Intel Pentium 4 and AMD Athlon XP processor when run without the protection of a fan and heatsink.

VCore Settings and Overclocking

The VCore (core voltage setting) displayed in Figure 9.1 indicates the voltage used by the processor core. This is set automatically by the following processors:

- Intel Celeron
- Intel Pentium II
- Intel Pentium III
- Intel Pentium 4
- AMD Athlon (all series)
- AMD Duron (all series)

Because these processors automatically set the correct voltage, how is it possible to damage the processor by using incorrect voltages?

Even though the processor has a default setting for voltages, the motherboard is actually what controls how much power it gets. Some users attempt to *overclock* their processors. That is, configure them to run faster than their rated speed. Doing this often requires small voltage increases to provide the CPU with more power, but can also damage the processor. Overclocking is a popular hobby with many computer users, particularly gamers, but it can be dangerous to your processor and your system. In some cases, certain unscrupulous vendors will "remark" an overclocked CPU and sell it as if it were originally rated to run at the higher speed. This is, of course, highly illegal.

Because overclocking increases heat, extra cooling beyond the normal case fans and the stock heatsink fan is necessary. To achieve higher speeds with stability, you might need to increase the default VCore voltage (usually set in the BIOS or by setting jumpers on the motherboard), but if the voltage is set too high without adequate cooling, you can fry your processor as surely as if you didn't use a powered heatsink at all.

If you want to overclock, follow these guidelines to stay out of trouble:

- Buy an OEM version of the processor you want to use (OEM processors are sold in bulk to vendors primarily for sales to computer makers, but are also sold by component vendors) and buy the best third-party heatsink fan you can afford that will fit on your motherboard. An OEM processor has a very short manufacturer's warranty (often just 30 days), but some sellers will provide a year or longer warranty for processors sold with a heatsink or assembled with a heatsink fan on a motherboard sold by the same vendor.

  It's essential that you choose a heatsink fan that matches the speed of your processor as well as your processor model. Figure 9.2 compares a heatsink fan designed for Athlon and Pentium III/Celeron processors running at up to 1.5GHz with a heatsink designed for faster Athlons. The larger heatsink has a bigger fan and uses a more-efficient copper core to dissipate heat along with a copper contact surface, while the smaller heatsink uses less-efficient all-aluminum construction.

Cautions and Warnings

AMD's latest Thoroughbred-core Athlon processors have an even smaller surface area for dissipating heat than previous models. AMD requires that these processors use a copper, rather than aluminum, surface for the heat transfer surface (the part of the heatsink that touches the processor core) as shown in the larger heatsink in Figure 9.2.

If you cheap out and use an all-aluminum heatsink and fry your processor, AMD won't replace it (regardless of warranty).

- You shouldn't combine a retail boxed processor with a third-party heatsink unless you don't care about warranty coverage; removing the stock heatsink from a retail boxed processor voids the warranty.

FIGURE 9.2

Top and bottom view of a typical all-aluminum heatsink fan (left) compared to a copper/aluminum heatsink fan (right). The all-aluminum version is suitable for processors up to 1.5GHz, while the copper/aluminum model can support processors beyond 2GHz. Equipment courtesy of Computers Plus.

- Add extra case fans to the front and rear of the case. Front-mounted fans should be installed to blow cool air into the unit, while rear-mounted fans should be installed to blow hot air out of the unit.

- You should adjust the clock frequencies and voltages very cautiously. While some systems use jumper blocks on the motherboard to vary these settings from the factory specification, most overclocker-friendly motherboards use BIOS configuration screens to set these values.

- Add a fan to the North Bridge chip on the motherboard if it doesn't have a fan or a passive heatsink. See "Preventing Overheating Damage to the Motherboard," p. 420 for details.

On the Web

The Overclockers.com Web site (http://www.overclockers.com) is a true one-stop shop for overclocking and system cooling tips, products, guides, and reviews. Find out what works and what needs work.

You can find a more detailed explanation of overclocking at

http://www.basichardware.com/overclocking.html

...and how to overclock your system at

http://www.basichardware.com/how_to_overclock.html

Note that Intel-made motherboards don't provide any means to overclock either the clock multiplier or the FSB speed. Most third-party boards do, but check the specifications for the board and look for those that have BIOS-controller overclocking features for greater safety and control.

Troubleshooting Cooling Problems

If your hardware monitor warns you of excessively high processor or motherboard temperatures but the fan monitor doesn't indicate failures, check the following:

- Be sure the air intakes and fans on the front, sides, and rear of the computer are free of dust and grime. Use a computer vacuum cleaner or an anti-static spray cleaner such as Endust for Electronics to clean them.

Cautions and Warnings

If you use a spray cleaner to remove dust and gunk, be sure to spray your cleaning cloth and then wipe the component with the cloth. Spraying computer equipment directly, even if the equipment is turned off, can ruin it if the components are still damp when the power is turned back on.

- Replace heatsink or case fans that are noisy or don't spin fast enough with high-quality fans that use ball-bearing mechanisms. Sleeve-bearing fans are less expensive but will fail when their lubricant dries out.

- Clean the air intakes going into the power supply with a soft dry cloth or computer vacuum cleaner. You should unplug the power supply before you wipe it off or attempt to clean its internal or external fans.

- Add active heatsinks (heatsink and fan) to the North Bridge chip on high-performance (1GHz or faster) systems.

- Check fans already present on video cards or motherboard chipsets for proper operation and replace them if they are noisy or don't spin fast enough.

- Add additional fans to the front and rear of the case.

→ For more details about replacing the power supply, see "Replacing Your Power Supply," p. 443.

If the hardware monitor indicates that one or more fans have failed (very low or no RPMs for more than 10 seconds), shut down the system *immediately* and replace the fan that failed. If the fan on the power supply stops turning, shut down the system *immediately* and replace the power supply with a higher-rated unit. It is essential that you replace any failed fan before running your PC. Opening the case and pointing a home cooling fan at it is not an adequate solution (and significantly hampers air flow through the PC's case).

Troubleshooting Voltage Problems

→ For details on power supply testing, see "Determining You Have a Power Supply Problem," p. 434.

If the hardware monitor indicates problems with your motherboard voltages, your best course of action is to test the power supply with a digital multimeter. If the power supply provides out-of-range readings on one or more voltage lines, replace the power supply.

How Motherboards Can Fail

Motherboard failures are exceptionally serious to your system because a damaged motherboard can damage every component connected to it, including your processor, memory, add-on cards, and even external devices connected to motherboard-based ports.

Motherboards can fail for the following reasons:

- Electrostatic discharge (ESD).
- Power spikes, surges, or other power problems.
- Physical damage (tool marks or impact damage) during installation.
- Excessive flexing during processor or memory upgrades or board installation. Understand that I do emphasize the word *excessive* in this statement. Motherboards are designed with a small degree of give in mind.
- Damage to components near the processor socket during processor installation.
- Loose components inside the system causing impact damage when the system is moved.
- Overheating of the North Bridge chip.
- Shorting out of components after installation.

Although some of these topics are a greater concern to you if you install internal system upgrades yourself or have someone else install them for you, some of these can affect any system, even if you never open the computer.

Preventing Electrostatic Discharge Damage to Your Motherboard

If you are planning to perform a motherboard upgrade yourself, be sure to guard against electrostatic discharge (ESD). Touch the inside of the case before you remove the old motherboard, keep the new motherboard inside its anti-static packaging until it's time to install it, and hold the new motherboard by its edges. Keep your fingers away from the solder traces on the underside and the chips on the topside of the board, since these can conduct electricity and can carry ESD to ESD-sensitive components on the motherboard.

→ *For more details, see "Preventing ESD," p. 116.*

Although motherboards are less likely to be damaged by ESD after they are installed, you should still avoid touching chips on the motherboard surface when you install memory, processor, or add-on card upgrades unless you are properly grounded to the system.

Preventing Powerline Damage to Your Motherboard

The first line of defense against power spike or surge damage to your motherboard is a true surge suppressor that has a UL-1449 approval, has a let-through voltage rating of no more than 330V, and provides features such as signal lights to indicate that protection is active and to warn you of wiring faults.

➔ *For more details, see "Powerline Protection," p. 446.*

If your area suffers frequent blackout or brownout conditions, you should also consider connecting your computer to a battery backup unit. Most battery backup units have surge-suppression features built-in. Typical models can provide power for up to 15 minutes of computer operation.

By keeping high-quality power flowing into your system, you help prevent motherboard and component damage.

Preventing Motherboard Damage During Installation

During motherboard installation, you need to push the motherboard into place so that you can line up the holes in the motherboard with the standoffs attached to the case. The process of attaching the motherboard to the case can lead to physical damage to the motherboard that's not covered by the manufacturer's warranty if you're not careful.

You can prevent motherboard damage by using the following tips:

- Use hex-head screws and a hex driver to install your motherboard instead of a Phillips-head screwdriver. Hex drivers are less likely to slip, which can scratch the wire traces on the surface of the motherboard (see Figure 9.3).

- If your case has a removable motherboard tray, take the tray out of the system before you attach the motherboard to the tray.

➔ *For additional tips on proper motherboard installation, see "I'm Having a Hard Time Fitting My New Motherboard into My Case," p. 427.*

- Before you insert the new motherboard into the case, make sure the brass standoffs in the case line up with the screw holes (holes with metal rims) in your motherboard. If they don't, or if a brass standoff would line up with a hole that doesn't have a metal rim (see Figure 9.3), move the brass standoff (refer to Figure 9.9) to a different location.

Screw hole (metal rim);
use with brass standoffs

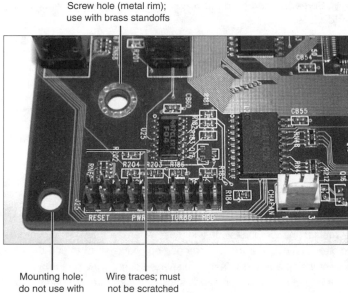

FIGURE 9.3
A typical motherboard has two types of holes; use only metal-rimmed holes to fasten the motherboard into place.

Mounting hole;   Wire traces; must
do not use with   not be scratched
brass standoffs   or otherwise damaged

Preventing Damage to Your Motherboard During Memory and Add-on Card Installations

Your motherboard is not very thick, but within its layers are power, data, and signaling lines that carry vital information to every component built into or connected to your computer. If you put too much downward pressure on the motherboard when you install your memory or add-on cards, you can crack the wire traces on the surface or inside your motherboard and ruin it.

To avoid damaging your motherboard during component installation, try these tips:

- If you are performing a motherboard installation, add the memory to the motherboard before you install it inside your system—If the memory sockets are not visible when you open the case, you might need to remove the motherboard to perform a memory upgrade at a later date.

- When you install memory or add-on cards, make sure you line up the memory with the socket or the add-on card connector with the expansion slot before you push it into place. If you put downward pressure on the wrong part of the expansion slot or memory socket, you could damage it and cause it to short out. You might also damage nearby components when you attempt to slide the card into place if you don't have the card lined up correctly.

→ *For more details about memory module installation, see "Installing System Memory," p. 401.*

Cautions and Warnings

If you are installing an AGP video card, be particularly careful that you don't damage nearby components such as the memory socket locking levers or the voltage regulator used to send the correct voltage to the processor (refer to

Figure 9.4). Some motherboards have very little clearance between the AGP slot and other devices.

Also, some AGP slots are designed for AGP Pro cards (which use a longer connector than normal AGP cards) as well as normal AGP cards; if you accidentally connect a normal AGP card into the AGP Pro *section* of the connector, you'll fry your card. Many of these slots have a protective cover over the AGP Pro section of the slot; remove this cover only if you install an AGP Pro card.

After the processor is installed into its socket, you will need to attach a heatsink fan to the processor. To learn how to avoid damage during this process, see "Protecting Your Motherboard and Processor from Installation Damage," p. 430.

Preventing Damage from Loose Components Inside the Case

If you hear a rattle, bang, or ding inside your case when you move your computer, put it down immediately, pull out your toolkit and open up your system to find the cause. Any loose component inside a system, from a misplaced screw lying on the surface of the motherboard to a dislodged heatsink, can cause short circuits or impact damage to your system.

To minimize the chances of system damage due to loose components, use the following tips:

- Be sure you retrieve any loose screws or other parts you might drop inside a system whenever the case is open. Since the motherboard "floats" above the case on standoffs, it's easy for loose screws to get under the motherboard, touch some of the solder points, and cause the system to short out.

- Secure loose cables inside the case with cable ties. Don't overtighten the cable tie, or you might damage your cables, but take up enough slack to prevent cables from blocking airflow to fans.

- Be sure the memory modules, processor, and heatsink are locked into place whenever you open the system. A loose heatsink, in particular, is heavy enough to cause damage if it comes loose from the processor and could cause processor damage if it's not securely in place. See "I'm Having a Hard Time Installing My New Processor," p. 429 for details.

Preventing Overheating Damage to the Motherboard

Most motherboards have two surface-mounted, non-removable chips that handle data transfers between the processor and other components:

- The North Bridge chip, also called the Memory Controller Hub or System Controller, is the chip responsible for handling high-speed traffic such as processor to memory or processor to video. Because of the speeds at which this chip operates, it can become very warm.

- The South Bridge chip, also called the I/O Controller Hub or Peripheral Bus Controller, is the chip responsible for handling lower-speed traffic passed from the North Bridge to the hard disk, network and modem interfaces, USB ports, and similar devices.

The North Bridge chip is larger than the South Bridge chip and is usually located near the processor socket. On many recent systems and motherboards, the North Bridge chip is covered with a heatsink. Some systems use a passive-cooling heatsink that uses metal fins to dissipate heat away from the chip, while other systems use a heatsink and fan (an active heatsink); see Figure 9.4.

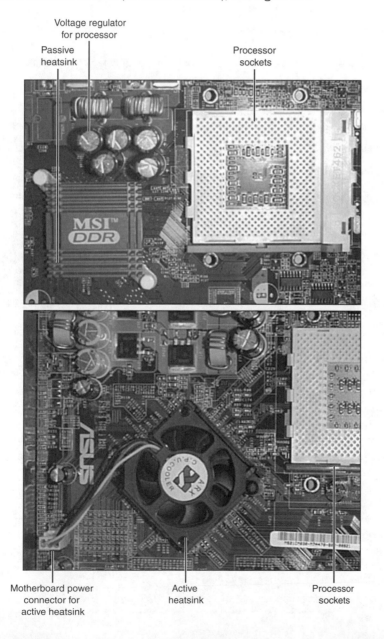

Voltage regulator
for processor

Passive
heatsink

Processor
sockets

Motherboard power
connector for
active heatsink

Active
heatsink

Processor
sockets

FIGURE 9.4

Typical factory-installed passive (top) and active (bottom) North Bridge heatsinks. Note the close proximity of the North Bridge chips to the processors.

If your motherboard or system uses a heatsink fan that draws its power from the motherboard (as in Figure 9.3), it might be monitored by the PC Health feature built in to many recent systems. Use the monitoring software provided with your system to verify that the fan is working properly.

If your North Bridge chip doesn't have a heatsink, I recommend you add one, particularly if your processor is faster than 1GHz or if you're planning to overclock your system. You have two options for mounting the heatsink:

- Plastic pegs that attach to holes on either side of the North Bridge chip
- Thermal tape that attaches the heatsink to the top of the North Bridge chip

Figure 9.5 shows a typical aftermarket kit containing both types of North Bridge heatsinks.

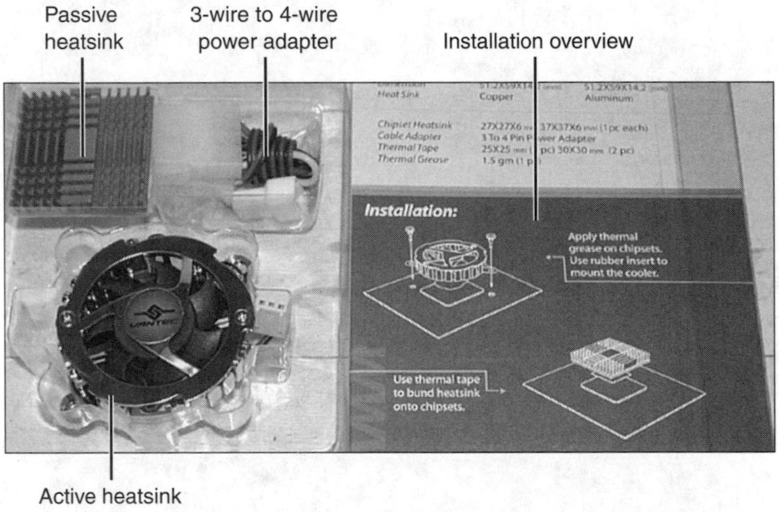

FIGURE 9.5

A typical North Bridge chipset heatsink kit. This kit features both passive and active heatsinks, but only the active heatsink can be attached with mounting pins; the passive heatsink uses thermal tape.

Passive heatsink   3-wire to 4-wire power adapter   Installation overview

Active heatsink

If your heatsink is equipped with mounting pegs, use them if the motherboard has mounting holes near the North Bridge chip. Be sure to apply the recommended amount of thermal paste between the heatsink and the North Bridge chip. Although some North Bridge heatsinks are supplied with double-stick adhesive thermal tape as in Figure 9.5, I don't recommend this mounting method if mounting holes are available on the motherboard and heatsink. If the thermal tape adhesive dries out, the heatsink could fall off the North Bridge chip and possibly cause this chip to overheat and fail. Since the North Bridge chip can't be removed from the system, you must replace the motherboard if its North Bridge chip fails.

On the Web

Zalman Tech Co, Ltd, a popular maker of heatsink and other cooling solutions, has produced a very informative animated tutorial covering how to install a North Bridge heatsink. Find it at

http://www.zalman.co.kr/english/product/nb32j.htm

If you prefer an active heatsink, for additional safety, connect the power lead on the heatsink to a monitored power connector on the motherboard so you can be notified of any problems with fan performance. Use the 3-pin to 4-pin (drive power connector) adapter to power the fan directly through your PC's power supply only if you can't plug the heatsink power lead into the motherboard.

→ For more information about system monitoring, see "Detecting Overheating and Incorrect Voltage Levels," p. 412.

Diagnosing Other Motherboard Problems

Because motherboards have so many on-board components, many problems with various devices can be traced back to motherboard problems:

- If you can't get your computer to recognize any type of add-on card inserted into a particular slot, the slot connector could be bad. Try inserting the card into another open slot.

- If your computer turns on but won't start the POST (Power-on Self-Test), you might have a loose socketed BIOS chip or a damaged flash BIOS. A socketed BIOS can become loose through chip creep (chips working loose from their sockets as a result of the motherboard heating up during use and cooling off when turned off), while a flash BIOS could be damaged by a computer virus, a power surge, or by an unsuccessful attempt to upgrade the BIOS.

  A socketed BIOS chip can be pushed into place, but a damaged flash BIOS needs to be reprogrammed or replaced. Contact your system or motherboard vendor for assistance.

→ A BIOS failure is one of the less likely reasons for a system to fail to start. See "Troubleshooting Booting Problems," Chapter 3, p. 232; "Startup Problems," p. 123; and "Troubleshooting a Computer That Won't Turn On," p. 436.

- If you smell an unusual odor inside your computer, a resistor, capacitor, or other component may have shorted out or burned up. Resistors look like small light-colored Christmas lights on two-wire connectors, and can be found on motherboards and add-on cards. Capacitors look like miniature soft drink cans and are part of the motherboard's voltage regulator (refer to Figure 9.4). If a resistor or a capacitor fails (look for discoloration on the component), test the power supply to make sure it is working correctly (replace it if it has failed or is out of specification), and then replace the device containing the defective component.

→ For details about power supply testing, see "Troubleshooting System Lockups," p. 439.

Troubleshooting Motherboard and Processor Upgrades

Motherboard and processor upgrades are the ultimate upgrade for your computer; no other upgrade can breathe new life into your computer like these upgrades can. Use this section to prevent and fix common problems you might encounter during this process.

Understanding Processor Sockets and Slots

Intel and AMD have used several different naming systems for processor sockets and slots over the years. The now-obsolete Intel Pentium and AMD K6-series processors used Sockets 5 and 7. The early models of the Intel Celeron, all Intel Pentium II, and early Intel Pentium III processors used a slot-based mounting system called Slot 1. Initial versions of AMD's Athlon CPU used a similar connector called Slot A. Later, Intel and AMD abandoned the slot mounting method and returned to socket-based processors.

Intel has three types of sockets that it uses for recent and current processors, and these socket types are named after the number of pins in the sockets:

- Socket 370 is used for socket-based Pentium III and most Celeron processors based on a Pentium III core.

- Socket 423 is used for the original Pentium 4 processors.

- More recent and current Athlons, the Athlon XP, and all AMD Durons use AMD's own Socket A, also called Socket 462. For details, see the AMD processor Web site at http://www.amd.com/us-en/Processors/.

You can see all three of these sockets and an example of the processor that matches them in Figure 9.6. Note that, as indicated in the figure, when installing these processors, pin 1 on the processor must match up with pin 1 on the socket.

FIGURE 9.6

Socket 370 with the Intel Celeron, Socket 423 with the Intel Pentium 4, and Socket A (Socket 462) with the AMD Athlon.

Pin 1 on Socket 370 and Celeron processor Pin 1 on Socket 423 and Pentium 4 processor Pin 1 on Socket A (Socket 462) and Athlon processor

Pin 1 on Socket 370 and Celeron processor Pin 1 on Socket 423 and Pentium 4 processor Pin 1 on Socket A (Socket 462) and Athlon processor

- Socket 478 is used for Intel Pentium 4 and Celeron processors released in the fourth quarter of 2001 (see Figure 9.7). Socket 478 itself is smaller than Socket 423, but many systems feature a large heatsink support outside the processor socket itself. For details, see the Intel Developer's Web site at http://developer.intel.com/design/processor/.

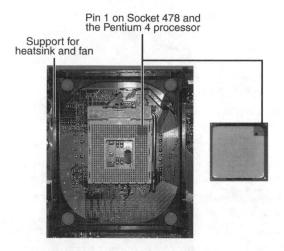

Support for
heatsink and fan

Pin 1 on Socket 478 and
the Pentium 4 processor

FIGURE 9.7
*Socket 478 with the
Intel Pentium 4. This
motherboard features
a built-in support for
the Pentium 4's large
and heavy heatsink fan
(not shown).*

I'm Not Sure What Type of Processor I Can Use in My Motherboard

Motherboards are designed to use certain types of processors running at certain speed ranges only. Some of the reasons a particular processor might not work in your motherboard include

- Wrong form factor—If you have a Slot A motherboard (the original AMD Athlon) or a Socket 7 motherboard (used by the Intel Pentium, MMX Pentium, and AMD K6 series), your motherboard cannot work with current processors, all of which use different sockets. Intel's Slot 1 is no longer current, but some Slot 1 to Socket 370 adapters allow older Socket 370 processors to work in a Slot 1 motherboard. The original Intel Pentium 4 used a 423-pin socket, while most current Pentium 4 versions use a 478-pin socket. AMD's current Athlon and all AMD Duron processors use a 462-pin socket called Socket A. You're better off in all cases to upgrade your motherboard as well.

- Wrong pinout—Some of the early Socket 370 motherboards were designed for the economy Intel Celeron processor only, not the Socket 370 Pentium III processor. The Pentium III has a few pins with different uses than the Celeron.

- Wrong voltage—While current processors can automatically adjust the voltage of the motherboard as needed, this feature depends upon the motherboard being designed to handle the voltage range used by the processor. Many older motherboards lack the correct voltages to handle newer processors. Some motherboards can handle the voltage requirements of newer processors if you upgrade the BIOS.

- BIOS limitations—Faster processors might require BIOS features and options not present on an older system. However, BIOS upgrades (which are usually available from the system or motherboard vendor) can sometimes allow an older system to handle a newer processor.

Visit your computer or motherboard vendor's Web site to see the most up-to-date information on the processors your computer or motherboard can use to avoid ordering a faster processor that won't work in your system.

Fast Track to Success

Here are two ways to find out what motherboard you have if your manual doesn't provide this information:

- Watch the system startup screen for brand-name and model information.
- Run third-party software such as SiSoftware Sandra or the eSupport.com BIOS Agent.

Because many current systems don't display system information at startup, I recommend using SiSoftware Sandra or BIOS Agent.

Get SiSoftware Sandra from http://www.sisoftware.demon.co.uk/sandra/.

Get the BIOS Agent from http://www.esupport.com/biosagent/index.cfm.

I'm Not Sure My New Motherboard Will Fit into My Case

Five types of case/motherboard designs have been used for desktop PCs since the late 1980s:

- ATX
- Micro-ATX
- NLX
- Baby-AT
- LPX

Notebook computers don't use standard motherboards, and have more limited upgrade options than desktop computers do.

ATX (and ATX variants) is the only current standard for PCs, and has been since the mid to late 1990s. If you have an ATX system, you can install virtually any motherboard you like into the case, assuming your power supply is capable of handling the requirements of your new processor.

→ *For details on power supply sizing, see "Right-Sizing a New Power Supply," p. 445.*

A Micro-ATX motherboard, the form factor used in many retail stores for low-cost, smaller PCs, can also be upgraded, although the choices available aren't nearly as wide as they are for full-size ATX systems (unless you replace the case with one designed for full ATX). You can, however, use a Micro-ATX board in an ATX case.

The Baby-AT motherboard design, which was once very upgradable, is now outdated. If you have a system with one of these boards, you're probably better off purchasing or building a system from scratch.

Figure 9.8 compares these motherboard designs to each other. Compare these drawings (which have been simplified to show only major components) to the motherboard in your current system to determine which motherboard type you can use for upgrades.

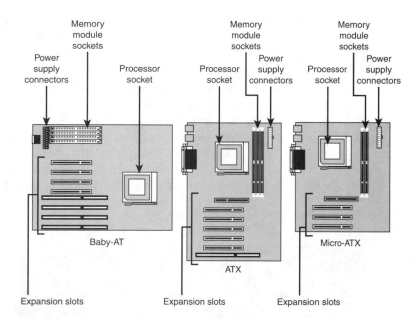

FIGURE 9.8
Baby-AT (left), ATX (center), and Micro-ATX (right) motherboards.

NLX systems are seldom sold to home-office or small-office users, but are popular in some corporate environments because their motherboards can be changed very rapidly.

The last option, the LPX, isn't a true standard at all but is used to describe systems that plug a riser card containing expansion slots into the "real" motherboard (NLX systems slide the motherboard into the riser card and are standardized). Some LPX systems have a T-shaped riser card, while others have a straight riser card that places the expansion slots parallel to the motherboard. Many low-cost systems have been sold with LPX motherboards, but systems with these boards are much less upgradable. Micro-ATX has largely replaced LPX in recent systems.

I'm Having a Hard Time Fitting My New Motherboard into My Case

After you determine what type of motherboard you can use for upgrades and install your processor and memory on the new motherboard, you need to remove the old motherboard so that you can install the new motherboard.:

To avoid problems with this process, follow these suggestions:

- Compare the current locations for screws in your current motherboard with screwholes in your new motherboard. If your old motherboard has screwholes in locations where your new motherboard doesn't, you should move the brass spacers visible after you unscrew and remove the old motherboard to a mounting hole that corresponds to a screwhole in your new motherboard.

- If you are installing a Pentium 4 motherboard into a case that originally used a non–Pentium 4 motherboard, you may have problems. Because of the

→ *You might also need to add a special ATX 12V power adapter to your power supply (if it's at least 350 watts) or buy a new power supply to properly operate a Pentium 4 motherboard. See "Replacing Your Power Supply," p. 443 for details.*

Pentium 4's unique design, you either need to use a motherboard equipped with a special support device for the processor, or you must replace your case with a Pentium 4–specific case. The Pentium 4 heatsink is so heavy that it's designed to be supported by the case, not the motherboard.

- When you slide the new motherboard into the case, you need to slide the I/O shield in first. The I/O shield is the metal shield at the rear of the system that has the cutouts and markings for the USB, sound card, parallel, serial, and other ports on your motherboard (see Figure 9.9). It has small metal fingers that press against the ports on your motherboard, so you need to use some force to push the board into place. After you push the motherboard into place against the I/O shield, attach one or two of the screws to hold the motherboard in place.

FIGURE 9.9
The I/O shield on a typical ATX motherboard as seen from the inside of the case. The holes to the right of the brass standoff can be used for additional standoffs if the motherboard needs them.

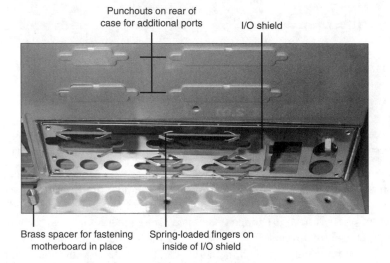

Punchouts on rear of case for additional ports   I/O shield

Brass spacer for fastening motherboard in place   Spring-loaded fingers on inside of I/O shield

My System Beeps Abnormally After I Restart It with the New Motherboard in Place

The system BIOS uses beep codes to report problems with your system, such as processor, memory, or other types of problems. The beep codes vary by BIOS brand and version.

Some of the most common reasons for a computer to beep after you upgrade the motherboard include

- The processor isn't plugged in correctly.
- The memory isn't installed or isn't locked into place.
- The video card isn't installed or isn't connected properly to the AGP or PCI slot.

If you know the BIOS type and count the beeps, you can determine the exact problem with your system.

Before you check any of these items or other problems that could be indicated by beep codes, be sure you shut down the computer and unplug it.

I'm Having a Hard Time Installing My New Processor

Whether you are installing a new processor into an existing motherboard or you are upgrading both components, getting your new processor properly installed is essential to your computer's proper operation.

Some of the most common problems you might encounter include

- Difficulty in locking the heatsink in place—Most processors use a heatsink that attaches to both sides of the processor socket (see Figure 9.10). If the heatsink is installed incorrectly or the wrong heatsink is used, the processor is ruined. If you buy an OEM processor and separate heatsink, make sure you verify that the heatsink you buy is designed for your CPU type and speed (retail boxed processors come with a matching heatsink, although third-party heatsinks often provide superior cooling).

Processor locking
lever in closed position

Heatsink clip
attached to top
of socket

Swivel lock
before being
snapped into place

Swivel lock after
being snapped
into place

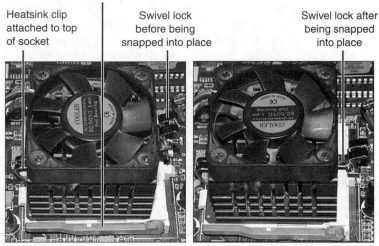

FIGURE 9.10
A typical processor heatsink being locked into place on the processor socket.

On the Web

AMD provides the "Socket A AMD Processor and Heatsink Installation Guide," a very detailed instruction manual for installing their processors with typical heatsinks on their Web site at

http://www.amd.com/us-en/assets/content_type/white_papers_and_tech_docs/23986.pdf

Intel's "Thermal Management for Systems based on Boxed Pentium 4 Processors" technical paper includes detailed instructions on installing the processor's heatsink. See it at

http://support.intel.com/support/processors/pentium4/thermal.htm

If you have an older Socket 423 Pentium 4 or Celeron processor, read this instead:

http://support.intel.com/support/processors/pentium4/intnotes.htm

- Not using a monitored fan connection for the processor's heatsink fan—Look at the motherboard documentation carefully to determine which connection is designed to power the CPU fan and monitor its performance. Some motherboards might have two or three fan connections near the processor socket.

- Failing to use proper thermal interface material between the processor and the bottom of the heatsink—Boxed processors that include a heatsink normally use thermal tape, while the third-party heatsinks made for OEM processors might not always include thermal tape or the more efficient thermal paste. If you install an OEM processor and third-party heatsink, be sure to find out if thermal paste is included. If you need to order it, the most efficient thermal paste is a product called Arctic Silver, which is, as the name suggests, a liquid silver thermal paste. Most companies that stock third-party heatsinks also sell Arctic Silver (note the spelling; a very poor counterfeit product called Artic Silver is sold by some stores).

  You *must* use either thermal tape or thermal paste between the heatsink and the processor, or the heatsink is useless. If you replace your heatsink, make sure you remove the old thermal tape or thermal paste residue from the surface of your processor and apply new thermal material before you install the new heatsink. If you reuse an existing heatsink with a new processor, make sure you verify that the old heatsink will work with the new processor and clean its surface before you install it on the new processor.

On the Web

Thermal paste or thermal tape should be placed only on the heat-transfer surface of the processor; AMD processors have a small rectangular core, while Intel processors have a larger-square heat-spreader plate.

For a detailed tutorial on the entire thermal paste application and surface cleaning process, see the Arctic Silver Web site:

http://www.arcticsilver.com/arctic_silver_instructions.htm

- Incorrect alignment of pin 1 on the processor with pin 1 on the socket—Refer to Figures 9.5 and 9.6. The AMD and Intel Web sites provided earlier in this chapter can also help you with this issue.

Protecting Your Motherboard and Processor from Installation Damage

It's all too easy to let your screwdriver slip during heatsink or motherboard installation. However, a scratched motherboard might stop working because some of the wire traces that carry power and signals are on the surface of the motherboard. To minimize the risk, try these tips:

- Use a hexagonal driver rather than a screwdriver to secure the hex screws used to hold most motherboards in place. Phillips-head screwdrivers can slip fairly easily, but hex drivers rarely do.

- Instead of pushing the heatsink mounting clip into place with a flat-bladed screwdriver as recommended by both AMD and Intel, you might try using a hex driver if you have one that is about the same diameter as the clip's locking lever. As with fastening the motherboard into place, there's less chance of a slip with the hex driver for this task as well. Be sure to practice using the hex driver or screwdriver to position the lever before you attach the heatsink to the processor to determine which tool you prefer.

- Before you order a high-performance third-party heatsink for a particular processor, find out if there's enough clearance between the components on the motherboard and the heatsink. The voltage regulator is located very close to the processor socket on some motherboards (refer to Figure 9.4), and if you damage its capacitors or other components with an oversized heatsink, say goodbye to your motherboard. Consult reviews of the motherboard at sources such as Tom's Hardware (http://www.tomshardware.com) or Anandtech (http://www.anandtech.com) to see which heatsinks have been tried with the board.

On the Web

Because AMD processors don't use a metal heat spreader over the CPU core (the small rectangular area in the middle of the processor) the way that Intel Pentium 4 processors do, they can be easily damaged by improper heatsink installation.

You can buy low-cost shims from various vendors to protect the processor from damage. The 3Dxtreme Web site has a review of a very good one at http://www.3dxtreme.org/xpshim.shtml.

You can order CPU shims for both AMD and Intel Socket 370 processors (older Celeron and most Pentium IIIs) from HighSpeed PC, LLC, at http://highspeedpc.com.

My System Won't Start After I Installed a New Processor

If your system won't start after you installed a new processor, check the following:

- **Make sure you're using the correct fan connector for the type of processor heatsink fan you have**—One vendor has a "Guardian" feature built in to their motherboard (it's enabled with a jumper) that, when enabled, prevents the system from starting if you don't have your processor fan plugged into the processor fan connector. Before he discovered this setting, my son Jeremy spent six frustrating weeks trying to figure out why the vendor could make his motherboard work and he couldn't. Disable this feature if you don't use a compatible processor fan; for example, if you attach the fan to a drive power connector instead of the motherboard.

- **Double-check the processor connection to the motherboard**—You usually can't lock the heatsink on a socketed processor unless it's properly inserted into the processor socket and the socket locking lever is closed, but a slot-mounted processor might appear to be in place, although not be locked into position.

- Close the lever on the processor socket—The system can't do anything until the processor is properly secured.

- The wire from the case switch isn't properly attached to the motherboard— Unlike older systems, ATX and Micro-ATX systems are turned on and off via the motherboard.

My New Processor Isn't Running as Fast as It Should

If you install a fast processor and find out through speed measurements with SiSoftware Sandra or by watching bootup messages that it's not running at top speed, here are some possible solutions:

- Your system has reverted back to a fail-safe setting—Some motherboards use a low clock multiplier and slow FSB setting if the system didn't boot properly on the previous attempt. So, if you shut off the system just a few seconds after you turned on the power, the system might have reverted to this state. Reset the correct values and try it again.

- You used the wrong clock multiplier and memory speed settings if your motherboard doesn't automatically set these for you—Consult your processor and system documentation to determine the correct settings for your memory speed and processor speed/type. If the reported clock speed is wildly faster or slower than what it's supposed to be, you have probably entered the wrong values.

- You might have a remarked processor—Component counterfeiting, including the marking of low-speed processors as faster processors, has been an epidemic in recent years. If you buy OEM processors (which are shipped to computer vendors in large trays rather than factory-sealed boxes), be sure you buy from a reputable vendor.

Cautions and Warnings

Because there are subtle differences in the appearance of different versions and speeds of processors, you might find it useful to visit a site such as Tom's Hardware (http://www.tomshardware.com) and print out a picture of the processor you plan to buy. If the actual processor doesn't match the photo, you might be getting scammed. The technical information available at the AMD and Intel Web sites can also help you avoid getting ripped off.

Before you buy a processor at a computer show (a frequent target for counterfeit goods), check out the vendor with other attendees or by calling the Better Business Bureau.

Troubleshooting Power Supplies

Why Power Supplies Fail

If there is an overlooked component in a PC, it has to be the power supply. Perhaps because it doesn't appear to affect a system's performance or features, it's not something most users put much thought into. Consequently, it's the first component most PC vendors attempt to skimp on. Not surprisingly, a lot of the problems PC users experience that get blamed on memory, Windows, and so on can all be traced to a faulty or poor-quality power supply.

A defective power supply prevents your computer from running reliably, can cause bus-powered USB and IEEE-1394 devices to be unreliable, and can even cause the computer to reboot spontaneously or fail to boot at all. In this chapter, you learn how to determine if you have a defective power supply, how to protect your power supply, and how to replace your power supply with the right model for your needs.

Despite the name, power supplies don't produce power; instead, power supplies convert potentially deadly high-voltage AC wall current into safe low-voltage DC power. A by-product of the transforming process is heat; hence, power supplies contain a built-in fan that pulls air through the power supply to dissipate heat. This also helps to cool the system.

Some of the major causes for power supply failure include

- Excessive wattage demand by the system—If your power supply doesn't have a high enough wattage rating (larger is better) to handle the power needs of your computer and the components plugged into it, the power supply will wear out prematurely. (Remember, any time you add to the components in your PC, you increase the load on your power supply.) Bus-powered IEEE-1394 and USB devices can cause a marginal power supply to become completely unreliable because the computer provides power to these devices.

→ *For details about cleaning your computer, see "Trouble-shooting Cooling Problems," p. 416.*

- Overheating—Overheating can be caused by dirty power supply air intakes or by excessive power demands. Both can cause the power supply to fail.

- AC power quality problems—Although power supplies can handle moderate surges (up to 600 volts AC) by themselves, much larger surges can take place as a result of lightning strikes or other power disturbances. In addition to power surges and spikes, excessive electrical "noise" (interference from other devices on a circuit) or frequent periods of lower-than-normal voltage can also lead to power supply failure.

- Poor airflow—Most power supplies cool your system by acting like vacuum cleaners, pulling air through the system to the power supply's air intakes and out the rear of the system. Dirty air intakes on the case or the power supply or a lack of free space behind the system can block airflow and lead to over-heating and eventual power supply failure.

- Higher-than-normal input voltage—There are two major voltage standards supported by personal computers: the 115-volt/60-cycle standard used in North America and the 230-volt/50-cycle standard used in most of the rest of the world. While most notebook computer power supplies automatically adjust to incoming voltage, most desktop computer power supplies must be manually set, using a switch on the back of the power supply, to use the correct voltage level.

In the following sections you will learn how to determine which of these is causing problems for your power supply and find out how to solve or prevent these problems.

Determining You Have a Power Supply Problem

The principal symptoms of a power supply problem include

- The rear of the power supply is too hot to touch while the computer is running.

- Your computer reboots spontaneously, running the memory test again during the reboot.

- You cannot turn on the computer.

- The computer locks up or generates Windows errors (like the blue screen of death) at random intervals.

These symptoms might not indicate the power supply is damaged, but they do indicate serious problems that must be dealt with before you can work with your computer.

Troubleshooting an Overheated Power Supply

An overheating power supply will eventually fail if you don't prevent the conditions that lead to overheating. Check the following:

- Make sure the air intakes on the computer case, the air intakes into the power supply, the power supply fan, and the exhaust are clean and free of obstructions.

- Make sure the power supply fan is turning at full speed; if the power supply has a fan facing inside the system, make sure it is turning as well. If the power supply fan has failed, replace the power supply.

- Fold or cable-tie drive ribbon cables inside the case to prevent them from blocking airflow. You can also replace flat cables with pre-rounded cables available from many vendors (these cables, however, do not conform to industry standards, so weigh the benefits and the risks).

- Check the wattage rating of the power supply and compare it to the wattage requirements of your computer's onboard and connected equipment. To see the wattage rating of your current power supply, open your system and look for a printed label on the unit (you might need to remove the power supply from your computer to see this information).

Figure 10.1 shows a typical power supply label.

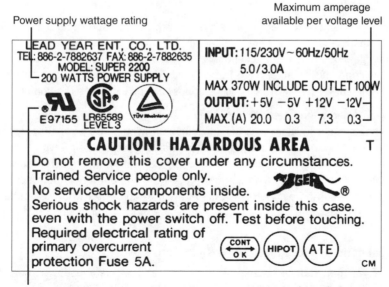

FIGURE 10.1
The label from a typical 200 watt power supply.

As Figure 10.1 suggests, you should never buy a power supply that has not been approved by safety ratings authorities such as CSA (Canada), UL (USA—the backward UR is the UL marking for components), or TÜV (Germany). If you have components that require a high amperage level on some voltage lines, knowing the amount of amperage available on each of the four voltage lines (+5V, –5V, +12V, and –12V) is useful to help you determine if your power supply is adequate.

However, as Figure 10.1 also warns you, do not open the power supply cover under any circumstances. Even when the computer is turned off and unplugged, the wire coils inside the power supply retain potentially lethal levels of electricity. When a power supply fails, don't even think about repairing it; throw it away.

If the power supply continues to overheat even after you have improved airflow to and through the unit, you should replace it with a unit with a higher wattage rating.

On the Web

PC Power and Cooling's interactive power supply selector can help you find out if the current size of power supply you have is adequate or if you need a larger unit (they also sell great power supplies). Try it out for yourself at

http://www.pcpowercooling.com/products/power_supplies/selector/index.htm

Troubleshooting a Power Supply That Reboots the Computer

Another sign of an overloaded power supply is if the power supply reboots itself. One of the pins on the power supply connector is known as the Power Good line; when voltage drops below or exceeds the range established for Power Good (nominally +5V with an acceptable range from +3V to +6V), the computer is sent a reset signal by the power supply. In essence, the power supply reboots the computer.

While a rare spontaneous reboot is nothing to worry about (glitches happen!), frequent reboots might indicate your computer has an overloaded power supply that needs to be replaced with a unit with a higher wattage rating. Before you assume the power supply is at fault, though, try plugging the system into a different wall outlet. Wiring faults in power outlets can also cause the computer to reboot spontaneously. However, if the computer reboots on its own no matter what wall outlet you use, it's safe to assume that the power supply needs to be replaced.

Troubleshooting a Computer That Won't Turn On

If you can't turn on your computer, there are several possible causes you need to eliminate before you determine the power supply is at fault:

- The computer might not be plugged in.
- The surge suppressor the computer is plugged into might be turned off.
- The power switch on the rear of the power supply might be turned off (not all power supplies have this switch).

- The wiring from the case's on-off switch might not be properly connected to the correct jumpers on the motherboard.

- The power connectors to the motherboard might not be properly connected to the motherboard. For adequate power, some motherboards require you to connect one of two additional connectors, called ATXAux or ATX12V, as well as the primary connector.

- You might have the wrong input voltage selected on the rear of the power supply.

- You might have an internal short that shuts down the power supply as soon as you start the system.

- The motherboard has a "Guardian" function that prevents you from starting the computer unless a working processor fan is plugged into a particular jack.

→ See "My System Won't Start After I Installed a New Processor," p. 431.

The first couple of possibilities might seem too obvious to list, but lots of people have concluded their computers, vacuum cleaners, typewriters, and so on were dead because they weren't connected to a working power source. Check the simple stuff first. Remember that even if the device is plugged in, that doesn't necessarily mean the power jack is getting juice. Try testing the outlet by plugging in some other electric device that you know works (or plugging your PC into a different outlet that you know functions).

You're probably using a surge suppressor between your computer and the wall outlet, so don't ignore the possibility that the surge suppressor is turned off or has failed. If the computer runs when you plug it into a wall outlet, but won't work when you plug it into a surge suppressor that's turned on, look for a reset button on the surge suppressor and press it. If the surge suppressor doesn't have a reset button, or it still doesn't work after you try it, the suppressor is dead and needs to be replaced.

→ For more about troubleshooting philosophy and methods, see "The Troubleshooting Process," p. 507.

The third possibility (the power switch on the rear of the power supply is turned off) might not apply to you. Many ATX power supplies don't have an external on-off switch, since the motherboard is responsible for controlling the power. However, some power supply vendors prefer to add this switch as an extra safety precaution; this switch enables you to shut off your system even if the connection to the motherboard fails.

You should suspect a problem with the wiring of your case switch if you have been working inside your system to perform upgrades or system maintenance. It's possible you accidentally disconnected the wire from the case switch to the motherboard. Before you reconnect this wire or unplug and replug it, unplug the computer from power.

The sliding switch on the rear of most desktop power supplies is used to select 115- or 230-volt input voltage levels. It's a harmless (but annoying) prank to set the switch to 230 volts if you are using the computer in North America. The keyboard light might flash before the computer shuts down completely because the input voltage setting is too high. However, don't try the reverse trick in a country that uses 230 volts; setting the input voltage to 115 volts and starting the computer will destroy the power supply and might also destroy the motherboard and other components!

Internal shorts can be caused by

- Loose screws inside the computer case
- Defective components in the power supply
- Bare wires on the power supply wires or splitter/extensions (which extend or split one four-pin drive connector to service two devices)
- Damaged components plugged into the power supply, such as drives or fans

Check for these problems and try turning on your computer again. If the computer won't start after you installed an internal upgrade, such as a drive or fan, disconnect that device from power and restart your system. If your system starts, the newly installed upgrade is either defective and should be replaced, or was installed incorrectly. Poorly constructed Y-splitters (used to divide one drive connector to support two drives or fans) can also cause shorts; don't use them unless you have no other way to power drives or fans and you know your power supply can handle the extra load. One hidden benefit of upgrading to a large-wattage power supply is the greater number of drive connectors built into the new power supply.

Because a defective motherboard or other components can cause your power supply to appear to be defective, it's a really good idea to test the power supply in isolation from the motherboard, fans, and drives. Several power supply vendors, including Antec and PC Power and Cooling, sell self-contained power supply testers; I found the one pictured in Figure 10.2 (sold by Antec) at a local "white box" computer and component store.

Signal LED indicates power
supply is working when lit

Connect lead to motherboard
to this connector

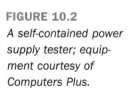
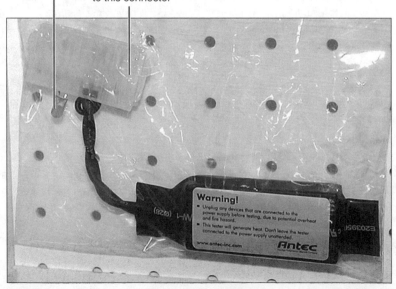

FIGURE 10.2
A self-contained power supply tester; equipment courtesy of Computers Plus.

Using the tester is simple:

1. Unplug the computer from AC power.

2. Open the computer case.

3. Disconnect the power supply from the motherboard, drives, and fans.

4. Plug the computer into AC power.

5. Connect the motherboard power connector from the power supply to the tester.

6. If the green LED on the tester lights up, the power supply is working.

If the power supply is dead, replace it. If the power supply is working, it might not be providing correct power levels. The tests in the next section will help you determine whether your power supply is providing correct power levels and a valid Power Good signal to the motherboard.

On the Web

In the opinion of many users, the very best power supplies, testing, and cooling accessories around are sold by PC Power and Cooling:

http://www.pcpowerandcooling.com

Antec is another high-quality vendor that is also famous for its cases:

http://www.antec-inc.com

If you have eliminated all these possibilities and the computer still won't start up, you probably need a new power supply.

Troubleshooting System Lockups

System lockups can be caused by many factors:

- Defective or overheated memory modules

- Hardware resource conflicts, particularly IRQ conflicts

- Incorrect voltage levels on the motherboard

Generally, defective memory modules trigger a beep code when the computer is turned on, and overheated memory modules will have problems only after the system has been running for a long time. You can detect hardware resource conflicts with the Windows Device Manager or with System Information.

➜ See "Using Device Manager," p. 480 for details.

Voltage problems can also cause reliability problems such as lockups, although it takes more effort to track them down. To check the voltage levels coming out of the power supply, you need the following:

- A multimeter that can be set to DC voltage

- A pinout of the power supply connectors so you know which ones to test

Cautions and Warnings

Starting in September 1998 and continuing through 2000, Dell Computers began to use motherboards and power supplies with a proprietary pinout. Although the physical connectors mimic the ATX standard, the wiring and voltage levels are completely different. If you connect a standard power supply to a Dell computer, or install a standard motherboard in a Dell computer, call the fire department or at least have a fire extinguisher handy. At the very least, you'll smoke either the motherboard or power supply, and it is possible one of these components will catch fire as soon as you turn on the power!

Hardware superstar Scott Mueller (author of the classic *Upgrading and Repairing PCs* series) has placed a detailed report about this problem on his Web site. The article includes the pinouts you need if you want to test a Dell motherboard.

Read it at

http://www.upgradingandrepairingpcs.com/articles/upgrade3_01_01.asp

If you need to replace the power supply in your Dell computer but don't want to replace the motherboard at the same time, some vendors sell Dell-specific power supplies.

To test voltage levels on your motherboard

1. Open the computer case and locate the power connector.
2. Turn on your multimeter and set it for DC power.
3. Turn on the computer.
4. Check Power Good, +5V, –5V, +12V, and –12V voltage levels; insert the red lead into the top of the power connector to touch the metal connector inside, and touch the black lead to a ground such as the case frame or power supply case (see Figures 10.3 and 10.4).
5. Check the readings against those shown in Table 10.1 (shown later). If you see a rating that falls outside the range listed, the power supply is defective and should be replaced.

DC voltage readout

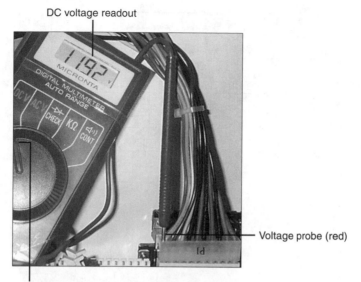

Voltage probe (red)

Digital multimeter set to DC voltage

FIGURE 10.3
Testing a +12V line on a standard ATX mother-board. The actual voltage (+11.92V) is well within specifications.

FIGURE 10.4
Testing the Power Good line on a Baby-AT motherboard. The actual voltage (+5.06V) is well within specifications.

Figure 10.5 shows the pinouts for a standard 20-pin power supply used with ATX, Micro-ATX, and similar systems. Figure 10.6 shows the pinouts for the older 10-pin LPX power supply used with Baby-AT and LPX systems. Table 10.1 lists the acceptable voltage ranges for the power connectors on the motherboard.

FIGURE 10.5

The pinout for an ATX standard (non-Dell) power supply connector. The shape of the individual pins keys the connector so it can be inserted only one way.

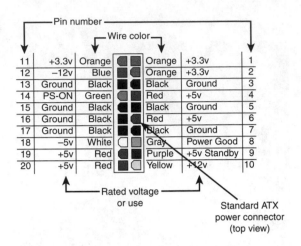

FIGURE 10.6

The pinout for the LPX power supply connectors used on Baby-AT and LPX motherboards. Because there are two connectors, it's possible to connect them to the motherboard in a variety of incorrect configurations.

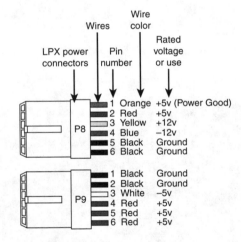

Cautions and Warnings

If you still have a computer with an LPX power supply, you need to watch out for the following issues:

- Make sure you attach the P8 and P9 power supply connectors to the motherboard so that the black wires are together as shown in Figure 10.6. If you connect the wires so that they are offset on the motherboard connector or are reversed, you can destroy the motherboard when you start the computer.

- Don't touch the wires running from the power supply to the switch, whether the computer is turned on or not. The power supply switch on LPX systems uses the same potentially-lethal AC voltage levels present in wall current (115V AC in North America, 230V AC in Europe and Asia).

Fortunately, most systems that use LPX power supplies are obsolete; your odds of seeing a system with an LPX power supply are quite low unless your computer is more than four or five years old.

Table 10.1 lists the acceptable voltage ranges for all types of power supplies, including Power Good. If your power supply doesn't provide power within these limits, replace it.

TABLE 10.1

Acceptable Voltage Ranges

Rated Voltage	Minimum	Maximum
+5V	+4.8V	+5.2V
–5V	–4.5V	–5.4V
+12V	+11.5V	+12.6V
–12V	–10.8V	–12.9V
Power Good	+2.4V	+6.0V

Fast Track to Success

Even if you don't have a multimeter, you can still check your system's power output if your BIOS supports hardware monitoring and you have a BIOS screen or software that displays the voltage readout. See "Detecting Overheating and Incorrect Voltage Levels," p. 412 for details.

Replacing Your Power Supply

The process of replacing your power supply involves

1. Determining the correct form factor, wattage rating, and special features you need in a new power supply.

2. Disconnecting drives and fans from the old power supply.

3. Removing the old power supply from your system.

4. Installing the new power supply in your system.

5. Reconnecting drives and fans to your new power supply.

6. Restarting the computer and verifying proper operation with a multimeter or the PC.

Cautions and Warnings

If your power supply caused a lot of system crashes before you replaced it, you might need to reinstall some of your applications and possibly even your operating system after you install a new power supply. A bad power supply can cause files to be corrupted if the power supply fails or restarts the computer during disk access.

So, if you see program or Windows errors after you install a new power supply *and* you have the expertise, reinstall the program or Windows; the error messages might be indicating that your old power supply corrupted some files during its death throes.

Use these tips to make the upgrade process easier:

- If you are replacing your power supply because you are upgrading to a new motherboard, make sure the power supply you choose will support the motherboard and processor you plan to buy. For example, many ATX-form factor Intel Pentium III motherboards require a six-pin auxiliary power connector (ATXAux; see Figure 10.7) as well as the normal 20-pin ATX connector for proper operation. Motherboards for the Intel Pentium 4 require that the power supply features an ATX12V connector (see Figure 10.7), and some might also use the six-pin auxiliary power connector.

FIGURE 10.7
The ATX12V power connector (left) and the ATXAux power connector (right) from a typical high-performance power supply.

On the Web

While AMD formerly tested specific power supplies for compliance, the widespread popularity of AMD Athlon and Duron processors means that most high-quality power supplies will work properly with these processors. Instead, AMD has developed a series of recommended features to look for when you buy your next power supply (or case/power supply combination). To get the official AMD recommendations, go to http://www.amd.com and click Search.

Enter "Power Supplies" (with quotes) as the search text.

- Take a careful look at your current power supply before you order a new one. The interactive buying guide available at the PC Power and Cooling Web site provides sketches that will help you determine which form factor you need for your system. Compare the sketches to your actual power supply.

- When you disconnect your drives from the old power supply, wriggle the connectors before you pull them apart to loosen the connection.

- If you are using Y-splitters or extenders, remove them and examine them carefully to see if they're in good enough condition to reuse. Reinstall them only if the new power supply doesn't have enough leads or if they can't reach the power connectors on your drives. If your power supply is under 300 watts, note that using too many Y-splitters could overload your power supply.

- Don't mix up the case and power supply screws when you open the case and remove the power supply. Some vendors use different screw types.

- If you need to remove components from your system to gain access to the power supply, carefully remove them and place them on anti-static material to avoid damage from ESD.

  → *For details about preventing ESD, see "Preventing ESD," p. 116.*

- When you insert the new power supply, make sure the mounting holes line up correctly with the corresponding holes in the rear of the case.

- Use the drive cables to connect to your drives before you reinstall extenders or Y-splitters. Since extenders and Y-splitters can cause shorts, you're better off without them if you don't need them.

- If a case fan needs to use a drive connector for power, use a power connector that's not being shared with another device if possible, or choose a connector that is not used much, such as the power connector to the floppy drive.

Right-Sizing a New Power Supply

When you replace your existing power supply of less than 300 watts, you should always opt for a model with a higher wattage rating than your existing power supply, even if an interactive buying guide suggests that your current wattage rating is sufficient. A larger (in watts) power supply doesn't require any more electricity than your existing power supply, but provides a greater safety margin (the difference between the actual power required and the power supply's maximum output) and more power for additional devices you might install later.

For example, if you are switching from serial and parallel devices (these are self-powered) to USB or IEEE-1394 devices that are bus-powered (powered by your computer), such as keyboards, mice, scanners, webcams, or drives, you need a power supply with a larger wattage rating. Adding internal upgrades such as additional memory, hard drives, or optical drives also add to the demand on your power supply.

A good rule of thumb for full-size ATX computers is to replace an existing power supply with one that is at least 100 watts more powerful than your current model if your current power supply is under 300 watts. For example, if you're replacing a 200-watt power supply, get one that is at least 300 watts. If you can afford it, I recommend going all the way to a high-quality 400-watt power supply. These units provide plenty of power for any processor/hardware combination.

If you're replacing a power supply in a retail store computer that uses a Micro-ATX motherboard (these systems use SFX power supplies), your options are more limited. The largest SFX power supply on the market is 180 watts, compared to the standard 145-watt model. Although Micro-ATX systems have more limited expansion capabilities compared to full-size ATX systems, the 180-watt models are recommended as replacements to provide additional power and a wide safety margin.

Powerline Protection

Most computer users connect their computer, monitor, and external devices such as printers and scanners to a multiple-outlet device called a surge suppressor or surge protector. Even if you use a high-quality surge suppressor (many sold at retail stores aren't very good), this is just the beginning of the steps you should take to ensure that your computer is receiving high-quality, reliable power.

A complete powerline-protection strategy should include

- Checking wall outlets for proper wiring.
- Using surge suppressors with filtering, wiring-fault warning, and high levels of protection against surges and spikes for all AC-connected equipment.
- Isolating electrically noisy devices such as laser printers from computers or other devices by using surge suppressors with separate filter banks or separate surge suppressors for the printer and other devices.
- Using a battery backup system for your computer and monitor if your area is subject to frequent electrical blackouts (complete loss of power) or brownouts (voltage sags below 100V AC).

Checking Wall Outlets

The polarized and grounded design used by wall outlets today is intended to provide high-quality power to your computer and peripherals and other devices in your home or office. However, all too often, incorrect wiring is present, regardless of whether the wiring was performed by professional or do-it-yourself electricians. If you don't determine that the wiring is correct, you could damage your computer or, at least, decrease its reliability by plugging it into an improperly-wired outlet.

Fortunately, it's not difficult or expensive to test your electrical outlets for problems such as incorrect grounding or reversed hot/neutral polarity. You can purchase an outlet tester similar to the one shown in Figure 10.8 from many electronics and home-improvement stores. The signal lights on the tester indicate if the outlet is wired properly, or, if it's wired incorrectly, what type of wiring fault is present. Testers include a chart (often attached to the unit as in Figure 10.8) indicating the meaning of the signal lights.

Cautions and Warnings

Many mid-range and high-end surge suppressors feature a single signal light to indicate if your wiring has a fault or is correct. While this is a useful feature to warn you of an incorrectly wired outlet, such units don't provide enough information to help you fix the problem. If your surge suppressor indicates that you have a wiring problem, get a tester similar to the one in Figure 10.8 and find out the exact problem.

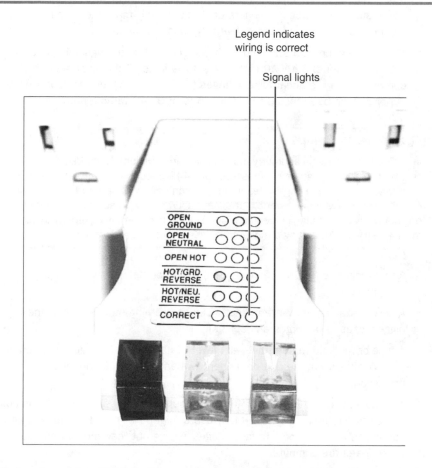

FIGURE 10.8
A typical receptacle/outlet tester in use; the signal lights indicate the outlet is correctly wired.

Choosing the Right Surge Suppressor for Your Equipment

There are two types of power problems that a properly-designed surge suppressor can handle: spikes and surges.

Both spikes and surges are overvoltage events: voltage levels higher than the normal voltage levels that come out of the wall socket. Spikes are momentary overvoltages, whereas surges last longer. Both can damage or destroy equipment.

Surge suppressors seem to multiply like rabbits; every store that carries computer equipment offers a huge number of models from different vendors. It's tempting to go with the cheapest model to save a few bucks or buy the most-expensive model (after all, don't you get what you pay for?), but getting the right surge suppressor isn't that easy.

You can make sure you get the right surge suppressor by looking for the following features:

- Make sure you're looking at a true surge suppressor, which has a UL-1449 rating, and not a multiple-outlet strip (UL-1363 transient voltage tap rating). Some stores and product vendors don't adequately mark their products, so it can be easy to mix up these different types of devices.

- The surge suppressor should have a low UL-1449 let-through voltage level (400V AC or less; 330V AC is the lowest available). This might seem high compared to the standard line voltages (115V or 230V), but computer power supplies have been tested to handle up to 500V AC without damage.

Cautions and Warnings

In 1998, Underwriter's Laboratory made significant revisions to its UL-1449 certification tests for surge suppressors. UL-1449 Second Edition tests are much more rigorous than the original tests, but you can't always tell from the packaging or unit markings whether a particular surge suppressor was approved under the original or revised testing procedures. Contact the manufacturer before you buy to make sure you're getting a model that has passed the revised tests.

- A fast response (under 1 nanosecond) to surges helps prevent damage to equipment

- A covered-equipment warranty that includes lightning strikes (one of the biggest causes of surges and spikes).

- A fuse or fail-safe feature that will prevent fatal surges from getting through and will shut down the unit permanently when the unit can no longer provide protection.

- Telephone, fax, and modem protection if your system has a modem or is connected to a telephone or fax—Many users forget that their telephone lines can act as a "back door" to fatal surges, wiping out their modem and sometimes the entire computer.

- Coaxial cable protection if your system is attached to a cable modem—Just as telephone lines can carry damaging surges, so can coaxial cable lines.

- EMI/RFI noise filtration (a form of line conditioning)—This helps prevent electrically "noisy" equipment such as printers from interfering with computers, but it's best to plug laser printers and copiers into a separate outlet (or separate circuit) from your computer.

- Site fault wiring indicator (no ground, reversed polarity warnings)—This can prevent you from using a bad electrical outlet, but is not a substitute for a true outlet tester.

- Most low-cost (under $50) surge suppressors are based on MOV (metal-oxide varistor) technology; MOVs will wear out over time and will self-destruct when exposed to a very high surge. A surge suppressor that uses MOVs should be replaced every couple of years. MOVs also present a potential fire hazard, because they have been known to catch fire when exposed to a high-voltage surge. Better-quality surge suppressors supplement MOVs with other components, but the best (and most expensive) models use non-MOV series designs.

- Metal cases are recommended because the metal case helps minimize the risk of fire if the unit fails and also helps minimize the odds of electrical interference with other devices.

- If you use devices powered by AC/DC converter "brick" style plugs, be sure to use surge suppressors with extra-wide spacing between the plugs.

On the Web

Leading makers of traditional surge suppressors include

- American Power Conversion (APC)—http://www.apc.com
- EFI—http://www.efinet.com
- Panamax—http://www.panamax.com
- Tripp-Lite—http://www.tripplite.com

The following vendors sell the more-expensive series-type surge suppressors:

- Zero Surge, Inc.—http://www.zerosurge.com
- Price Wheeler Corp.—http://brickwall.com

If you use surge suppressors with these features and attach your system to a properly wired outlet, you will minimize system problems caused by power issues.

Battery Backup Systems

While high-quality surge suppressors stop damaging overvoltages, undervoltages and electrical blackouts can also damage your system, and pose even greater risks to your data. If you live or work in an area that is subject to frequent brownouts (voltage under 100V AC compared to normal 115V AC) or blackouts (complete power failure), or if you just don't like surprise power failures, you need to add a battery backup system (also called an uninterruptible power supply or UPS) to your power protection lineup.

Most so-called UPS systems actually provide battery power only when AC power fails and should be called standby power supplies (SPS). However, the term UPS is used for both SPS-type and so-called *true UPS* systems that power the computer from a battery at all times.

Most UPS systems contain integrated surge suppression technology, but vary greatly in how long they'll run your computer. Since a UPS is designed to run your computer only long enough to shut it down without data loss, a runtime of 10–15 minutes is long enough to provide adequate protection.

Fast Track to Success

If you know the wattage or amp requirements of your computer, its peripherals, and your monitor, you can manually calculate the appropriate volt-amp (VA) rating to look for in a battery backup system:

- Multiply total amps by voltage (120V in North America, 230V in Europe and Asia)
- Multiply total wattage by 1.4

However, because it can be difficult to calculate the actual power consumption of your computer and its peripherals, the most convenient (and often more accurate) way to determine the battery backup size you need is to use the vendors' interactive selection tools, available on most UPS vendor Web sites.

The essential features of a battery backup system include

- High-quality integrated surge suppression—In most cases, you should not use a separate surge suppressor with a battery backup unit.

- Appropriate sizing for your system and runtime—The price of a battery backup system goes up significantly as the volt-amp (VA) rating climbs. Buying more than 10 minutes of runtime is usually not necessary unless you frequently run programs you can't shut down until the current process is complete.

- Automatic system shutdown after a power failure has been detected—This requires that your UPS supports the version of Windows that you're using and that you connect the battery backup system to your computer with a compatible serial or USB cable. Windows XP and Windows 2000 have native support for several popular brands, but if you use Windows 9x/Me, you need to install software provided by the vendor. Note that some low-cost UPS systems omit this feature.

- Fast battery recharge, particularly if your area suffers frequent blackouts—Look for systems that recharge in less than 12 hours if you rarely have blackouts, and expect to pay more for recharge times of 6 hours or less.

On the Web

Major vendors of battery backup systems include

- American Power Conversion (APC)—http://www.apc.com
- Tripp-Lite—http://www.tripplite.com
- Invensys (Best Power)—http://www.powerware.com
- Liebert—http://www.liebert.com

Basic or Enhanced Protection? Your Choice, Your Money

All battery backup (UPS) systems will power your system for several minutes during a blackout, most will also protect you against power surges, and many will also shut down your system. However, some are designed to protect you against additional power problems, including

- Undervoltage (brownout)
- EMI/RFI interference (line noise)
- Other power-quality distortions

More expensive battery backup systems typically provide these types of power-conditioning features as well as basic power-outage protection, but you should carefully review the vendors' datasheets to see the differences in features between battery backup systems with similar VA ratings but wide differences in price.

Solving Application Software Problems

CHAPTER **11**

Why Application Software Can Fail

Software applications, the programs you run to balance your checkbook, write the great American novel, digitize your photographic collection, and surf the Internet, cause computer users a lot of grief when they stop working or don't behave as they're expected to. Some of the most common problems you might encounter with broken programs include

- Not being able to run older programs under a newer version of Windows
- Difficulties in updating software because of uncertainties about version numbers
- Difficulties in reinstalling applications
- Problems with automatic software updates
- Programs that stop working after another program is installed

Use the tips in the following sections to help you get your software back on track.

I Can't Run My Program Under a Particular Version of Windows

Unless you replace all your software every year or so with updated versions, you might encounter problems when you try to run older programs with newer versions of Windows. Windows XP is the only version of Windows with a specific tool, the Program Compatibility Wizard, to deal with this problem.

The Program Compatibility Wizard, ideally, fools older Windows programs into thinking it is running under Windows 95, 98, Me, or 2000. Sometimes it works, sometimes it doesn't; this depends primarily on the program in question. You may find that some programs run, but that certain features don't work as they should. Microsoft provides periodic revisions to the Program Compatibility Wizard through Windows Update.

→ *For more details, see "Troubleshooting Programs That Won't Run Under Windows XP," p. 138.*

Most program compatibility issues, however, are caused when running old DOS operating system applications in Windows 2000 and XP.

Although other Windows versions don't have this wizard, you can take manual steps to solve problems, including

- Researching a particular program's compatibility or limitations with your version of Windows

- Configuring program properties sheets to help MS-DOS–compatible programs run under Windows

- Installing service packs for your application to help it run properly under your current version of Windows

In some cases, of course, the only solution is to purchase and install an updated version of the program you want to run. But, if money's tight, or an updated version isn't available, you might be able to convince your old favorite to work by applying these techniques. (Otherwise, you may be out of luck and must either ditch the program or use it on a system running an older, supported, operating system.)

Researching Your Program's Compatibility with Windows

There are three major sources for information on whether your program will work properly with Windows:

- The Microsoft Knowledge Base

- The program vendor's Web site

- Internet search engines such as Google (http://www.google.com)

Because the last option (searching the entire Internet) will usually turn up a lot of useless pages unless you construct your search terms very carefully, I recommend starting with the first two options.

To access the Microsoft Knowledge Base

1. Open your browser (I recommend using Internet Explorer with Microsoft Web sites).

2. Type http://support.microsoft.com into the address window and press ENTER.

3. Enter your search terms. Put quote marks around phrases. For example, to search for Corel Draw, enter "Corel Draw".

Any Microsoft Knowledge Base articles containing the search terms or phrases you entered will be displayed.

If you're having problems getting third-party programs or data to work properly with Microsoft applications, or even problems between Microsoft programs, the Knowledge Base can also help you dig out the answers you need. Just specify both applications in your search.

Fast Track to Success

When you view a Microsoft Knowledge Base article about your application, take a moment to scroll down to the bottom to see the keywords and additional query words listed for the article. You can use these terms to save yourself some typing and find answers faster. Here are a few of the most common search terms you might find useful:

- OFF—Microsoft Office
- PPT—Microsoft PowerPoint
- WORD—Microsoft Word
- PUB—Microsoft Publisher

To search for a particular version, add 97, 2000, 2002, XP, and so on. For example, to search for Office XP, use OFFXP in your search.

If you are having problems with a third-party (non-Microsoft) program, you should also search the technical information provided at the vendor's Web site. Depending upon the site, you might select the application and version, or you might need to query the Web site with the site's own search tool or use Google's Advanced Search.

If you're looking for information regarding a program that is available on multiple platforms and you're getting a lot of answers which don't apply to you, add "Windows" to the search terms you use. This should help screen out Mac or Linux-specific answers that don't apply to Windows systems.

I'm Not Sure What My Exact Program Version Is

In many cases, the solution for compatibility issues between a particular application program and Windows or between two different applications is the installation of a software patch for your application. Some of these patches, also known as service packs, can be very large, and if you have a dial-up modem instead of broadband Internet access, you might prefer to order the patch/service pack on CD-ROM rather than trying to download it.

Because a particular version of a program might undergo small changes from its initial release until its final revision, and because some software patches/service packs are designed to work in sequence with previous patches, you might need to determine exactly what revision of a program you have.

Determining this information can be done in two ways:

- You might need to open the program and click Help, About from the menu bar to display the exact version/revision information
- You might need to search for a particular program file and view its properties sheet in Windows Explorer or My Computer to determine what revision of a program is installed

The software vendor will inform you on its support Web site if you need to use either of these methods to determine an exact software version before you install an update.

Here's an example of using Help, About. If you need to install Service Pack 2 for Corel WordPerfect Office 2000, you need to determine whether you have already installed Service Pack 1. If you haven't, you must download and install it first. Start any major application in the suite; click Help, About from the menu bar; and look for the version number. A version number of 9.0.0.528 in WordPerfect, Quattro Pro, Corel Presentations, CorelCENTRAL, or PerfectFit indicates the original release is installed and must be updated with Service Pack 1. Once Service Pack 1 is installed, the release number changes to 9.0.0.588.

To determine whether you need to install an update using a program file, you'll need to jump through a couple more hoops. For example, some versions of Internet Explorer 4.0 were affected by a problem reported in Microsoft Security Bulletin MS98-013. To determine whether the installed version needs to be updated, you needed to search for the system file mshtml.dll. After the file was located, you needed to right-click on the file, select Properties, and click the Version tab. A version number of less than 4.72.3509.0100 indicated an unpatched system.

I'm Having Problems Removing My Application

If a software patch or service pack doesn't install properly, you might need to remove your application from the system and reinstall it. Normally, this is a simple task:

1. Open the Control Panel.

2. Open the Add/Remove Programs Icon.

3. Select the Change or Remove Programs (Windows XP) or Install/Uninstall tab (other versions).

4. Select the program you want to uninstall.

5. Click Change/Remove or Add/Remove and follow the prompts to start the process.

→ *For more details, see "Add or Remove Programs," p. 470.*

Unfortunately, for various reason, programs don't always uninstall the way they should when following these steps.

If you have manually deleted or moved the folder that contains the main program, deleted folders created in the default Temporary files location (normally the Temp folder beneath the default Windows folder), or misplaced the original program installation CD, you might not be able to run the uninstall program. If the uninstall program is missing (because you removed the folder containing it) or if it can't find information about the program, Windows won't be able to uninstall the program without some help from you. There have also been programs where bugs in the program prevented them from properly uninstalling themselves.

You can still uninstall most programs by using one of these methods:

- Reinstall the program using the same file and folder locations you originally used, then uninstall it—This is probably your best option if you don't have a third-party uninstall program on your system.

- Use a third-party uninstall program such as Norton CleanSweep, Ontrack EasyUninstall, McAfree Uninstaller, or WinCleaner—These programs were very popular when Windows 3.1 was the dominant version of Windows, but are not as popular today as newer versions because of the built-in uninstall support included in Windows 95 and later versions. These programs work best if you use them to track the original installation so they know which files were added, updated, or deleted, and which Registry keys were changed. If you install an uninstall utility only after you installed the application you want to remove, it will need to make some educated assumptions on which files can be safely removed; sometimes, files you really need are deleted.

- If you have Windows XP or Windows Me, you can use the System Restore feature to revert your computer to the condition it was in before the program was installed—This also undoes any other programs you installed after the restore date you select, but doesn't remove any data you created (including installed program files, which you must then remove manually from your system).

→ *For details on System Restore, see "Using System Restore," p. 494.*

- Manually remove the program's registry entries—This is the most difficult way to uninstall a program, and should not be attempted unless you understand how the Windows Registry works, have a backup copy of the Windows Registry, and have a list of the Registry keys you must remove or change.

Contact the software vendor for instructions on how to perform a manual uninstall of the software through changes to the system Registry.

I'm Having Problems Reinstalling My Application

As the previous section suggested, you might need to uninstall and reinstall an application that's stopped working. If you are having problems reinstalling an application, check the following causes and solutions for help:

- Application won't install because it is an upgrade version—Depending upon the application, you might need to provide the serial number for the original version of the program or the installation CD to prove you're entitled to install an upgrade version. Note that some programs don't display the entire serial number in their Help, About display of program information or might create an encoded version of the serial number that can't be translated back into the original.

- Application won't install because you don't have sufficient rights—You need to be the computer administrator (or have administrator status) to install a program on Windows XP (or Windows 2000). If you logged in as Guest or have a guest-level account, the programs you run aren't authorized to make system-level changes to the computer. You'll need to talk to the person "in charge" of the system to get help with this.

- Application CD can't be read—Clean the CD surface and clean the drive and try again. If the application CD's data surface is scratched, you need to repolish the surface to prevent read errors. Check with your favorite computer or electronics store for Skip Doctor, a very popular CD surface repair tool.

On the Web

You can spend as much on software as you do on your computer, or even more. To prevent losing CD-based programs to scratches or dust, check out these vendors:

- CD/DVD Playright—Manufacturer of Trio Plus, a collection of CD/DVD cleaning and protection products. See their Web site at http://www.cdplayright.com/.

- Azuradisc—Manufactures a line of CD scratch removal machines designed for use by dealers and rental stores, and also sells a line of optical media cleaners. See their Web site at http://www.azuradisc.com.

You should also consider making a backup copy of your application CD and store the original in a safe place. While some application CDs are copy-protected (they can be read but not copied without using special software), most are not.

I Can't Use an Existing Program After I Installed Another Program

If you can no longer use an existing program on your system after you installed another program, the most likely reasons include

- The new program has installed versions of certain program files that won't work with your existing program. This problem is sometimes referred to as "breakware" or "DLL Hell" (these files have a .dll extension).

→ For more information about illegal operations and similar errors, see "Troubleshooting Illegal Operations and Other Error Messages," p. 145.

- The new program has replaced the old program—For example, you cannot run Internet Explorer 5.x and 6.x on the same system, even though you might like to for Web site testing or other reasons. Installing IE 6 replaces previous versions of IE.

If you see Illegal Operations or similar types of non-fatal errors when you try to start an existing program after you install a new program, you are probably seeing a case of DLL Hell or breakware.

Note the program name and the exact error message, and search the Microsoft Web site and the software vendor's Web site for answers. Some of the typical solutions you might need to use include

- Upgrading to newer versions of third-party programs—Many third-party programs have been redesigned to install the DLL system files they use into their own folders rather than into a shared folder such as \Windows\System or \Windows\System32.

- Downloading and installing updated system DLL files—This solution might be performed automatically as part of installing application updates, or might require a separate installation. For example, a widespread problem affecting third-party programs after Microsoft Works Suite 99 or other 99-series Microsoft home and home-office products were installed requires the user to download and install the Microsoft Libraries Update, available from the Microsoft Downloads Web site at http://www.microsoft.com/downloads/.

- Manually copying the correct DLL files from the program installation CD to the program's own folder after installing updated system DLL files—If updated system DLL files aren't completely compatible with a particular program, the software vendor might recommend this. For example, after installing the Microsoft Libraries Update, users of WordPerfect 8 were told to copy the mfc42.dll and msvcrt.dll files (which were replaced by the Microsoft Libraries Update) from the WordPerfect CD to the \Corel\Suite8\Programs folder on your hard drive to solve some minor WP8-specific problems.

To help alleviate DLL headaches, Windows XP and Windows 2000 are designed to protect system DLL files from being overwritten by supporting separate versions of the same DLLs. This enables programs that need different versions of a particular DLL file to run on the same system at the same time.

Although many of the examples given in this section are for older applications you might no longer use, the same methods can be used today in case of software component conflicts. While most major commercial programs don't have these issues anymore, you might still need to perform operations like these to cajole some software to work correctly on your system.

Problems with Applications' Default Settings

You might not have any technical problems with your applications, but if you can't use them the way you'd like to, it's still frustrating to work with them.

Some of the typical annoyances you might encounter include

- Menus that show too many or not enough buttons
- Pull-down menus that don't show you all the options at first glance
- Programs that don't use your preferred default document location
- Programs that can't import or export documents in your preferred formats

Fortunately, these and similar problems can usually be solved by using your software's configuration menu.

I Can't Start My Favorite Commands from Menu Buttons

To add buttons or entire toolbars to the default menu or display in your favorite application, you need to locate the Customize or Options menu. Here are a few examples of where to look:

- Microsoft Office—Tools, Customize, Toolbars
- Corel WordPerfect Suite—Tools, Settings, Customize, Toolbars
- CorelDraw—Tools, Options, Customization, Command Bars
- Adobe Photoshop—Window, Show/Hide (various menus)

If you're having problems finding the right menu or understanding how to customize the interface, you should consult the program's Help files or a book dedicated to your specific program.

I Can't See All My Program's Menu Options

Starting with Microsoft Office 2000, and continuing with the latest version of Office, Office XP, Microsoft has used an adaptive menu system for its pull-down menus. If you're accustomed to seeing all the menu options at a glance, adaptive menus (which hide functions that you seldom use) are disturbing.

To change this behavior in Microsoft Office, click Tools, Customize, and uncheck Menus Show Recently Used Commands First. To make hidden options appear without disabling this feature, you should only have to hover the mouse pointer over the opened menu for a few seconds or click a "down arrow" at the bottom of the menu.

I Need to Configure My Program to Use My Default Document Folder

Whether you use the default My Documents folder, which has been with us since Windows 95, or its Windows XP descendent, the \Documents and Settings*username* folder, or use a different folder or drive for your documents, chances are you need to customize your favorite applications to use your preferred document folder.

This can be more complicated than simply specifying a folder for your documents. If your application creates periodic automatic backups, if you use style and document templates, or create custom dictionaries, you should also adjust the default locations of these data types as well to make backups easier.

I recommend that you create a folder beneath your default documents folder for each data type you want to store there. For example, I create a Backup folder inside my default document folder for the timed backups created by Microsoft Word and Corel WordPerfect.

To specify the location for documents and other types of custom data, you need to use the customization or option menu offered by your application. The exact menu location varies by program, but here are a few examples:

- Microsoft Office—Tools, Options, File Locations
- Corel WordPerfect Suite—Tools, Settings, Files
- CorelDraw—Tools, Options, Workspace, Save (for specifying backup file locations; CorelDraw uses the last folder location you opened for its startup default)
- Adobe Photoshop—Tools, Preferences, Plug-ins and Scratch Disks (for plug-ins and temporary files; Photoshop uses the last folder location you opened for its startup default)

I Can't Open a Particular Type of File

While Microsoft Office is the most popular office suite at present, this popularity conceals the fact that there's only partial file-format compatibility between Office 97, Office 2000, and Office XP. And, by default, Microsoft Office doesn't install the necessary import/export filters needed to send data seamlessly between its apps and other popular products such as Corel WordPerfect Suite, Lotus SmartSuite, and older versions of Word, Excel, and Microsoft Office.

To avoid stumbling into the incompatible file-format trap, follow these guidelines:

- Install *all* the file filters for both text and graphics whenever you install any type of program (office suite, graphics, page layout, and so on), particularly if your computers will be used for service bureau or public access work, or if users with different versions of applications bring work to and from the office. Use the Custom installation option to display this choice.
- If you use Microsoft Word XP or Word 2000 and you share files with users of Word 97, use the Tools, Options Save dialog to disable features not used by Word 97.
- If you need to move data files between different applications, test the round-trip process with non-critical files before you rely on it for actual work. Despite improvements in import/export filters, trying to export complex files in another program's file format doesn't always result in a perfect product.
- Don't replace the original copy of the file after you edit it with a different version of a program or with a different application altogether. Save the edited file with a different name in case of problems.
- Use a neutral file format such as .RTF (Rich Text Format) to move documents around whenever possible instead of a more-complex, easier to break format such as Word.

The Unworkable Application

Despite your best efforts, you might discover that you simply can't get a particular application to work with your system. This is particularly likely if you are trying to run an older 16-bit or 32-bit Windows program with Windows XP, or if you are trying to use an orphaned program (a program whose vendor no longer supports the product with technical notes or software patches). Believe it or not, occasionally a publisher will release a program with known serious bugs just to "get it out there." While rare, this most often occurs with gaming titles. In such a case, you're at the mercy of whether or not the developer produces a patch to fix the most serious issues.

The easiest way to avoid problems with your applications is to

- Make sure your application is explicitly supported by your version of Windows

- Install the recommended software patches (if necessary)

- Try the Windows XP Program Compatibility Wizard if you use Windows XP, specifying the Windows version the program is designed to support

- Upgrade to a supported version of the application if the version you use won't work

- Uninstall an application that can't be made to work and replace it with a fully-supported product

While upgrading or replacing a failed application might seem expensive, the costs of possible data loss through computer crashes and the lost time you spend trying to make an old program work on a new system add up quickly. Avoid the pain by refusing to waste time on an old program if it won't respond to the methods provided in this chapter.

Using Windows Diagnostic Tools

Control Panel

The Windows Control Panel (CP) provides access to most of the diagnostic tools supplied with Windows. In Windows XP, the default view of the Control Panel is a task-oriented category view (see Figure A.1).

Clicking an entry in Category view might take you directly to a particular CP icon, such as Add/Remove Programs and User Accounts. It also might only take you to another list of categories from which to choose. Other Category View icons, such as Appearance and Themes, display a submenu of tasks and a list of CP icons (see Figure A.2) in the main window. Related options and troubleshooters appear in the left-hand window. If you choose one of the tasks, Windows opens up the appropriate CP icon and takes you directly to the menu needed to make the change.

If you never used a version of Windows before Windows XP, you might prefer the Category view access method shown in Figures A.1 and A.2. However, people who've used versions of Windows prior to XP will probably miss the "classic" style in which you had direct access to each CP applet. If you prefer direct access to each CP icon (the default in Windows 9x, Me, and 2000), you can click the Switch to Classic View button shown in Figure A.1 to toggle the Classic view shown in Figure A.3. To switch back to Category view, click the Switch to Category View button shown in Figure A.3.

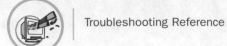

Displays all CP options as icons

FIGURE A.1

The default Category view of the Control Panel in Windows XP.

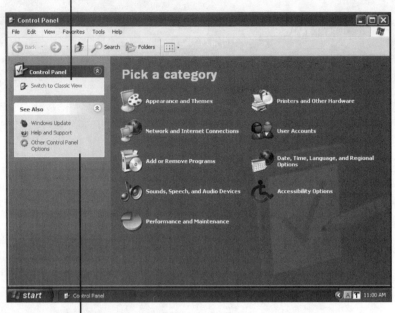

Displays CP icons installed by
third-party hardware or software

Related CP icons or tasks   Tasks

FIGURE A.2

The Appearance and Themes category in Control Panel.

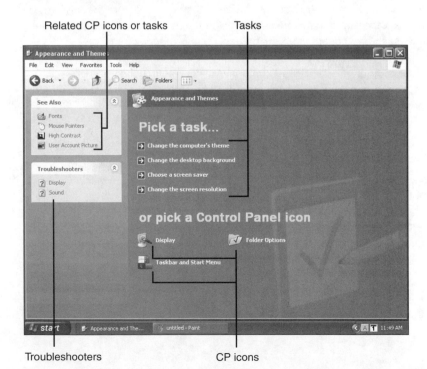

Troubleshooters   CP icons

Reverts to the default display of CP categories

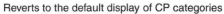

FIGURE A.3
The optional Classic view of the Control Panel in Windows XP.

Table A.1 provides a breakdown of the tasks and CP icons available through each Category View icon in Windows XP. You might find additional options available on your system, depending upon how Windows XP was installed.

TABLE A.1
Category View Access to Tasks and Classic View Icons

Category View	Tasks	CP Icons	See Also	Troubleshooters
Appearance and Themes	Change or Select:	Display	Fonts	Display
	Computer theme	Folder options	Mouse Pointers	Sound
	Background	Taskbar and Start menu	High Contrast	
	Screen saver		User Account Picture	
	Screen resolution			

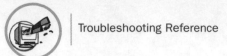

TABLE A.1 (continued)

Category View	Tasks	CP Icons	See Also	Troubleshooters
Printers and Other Hardware	View installed printers or fax printers Add a printer	Game Controllers Keyboard Mouse Phone and Modem Options Printers and Faxes Scanners and Cameras	Add Hardware Display Sounds, Speech, and Audio Devices Power Options System	Hardware Printing Home or Small-Office Networking
Network and Internet Connections	Set up or change Internet connection Create a connection to the network at your workplace (VPN) Set up or change your home or small-office network	Internet Options Network Connections	My Network Places Printers and Other Hardware Phone and Modem Options	Home or Small-Office Networking Internet Explorer Network Diagnostics
User Accounts	Change an account Create a new account Change the way users log off or log on	N/A	N/A	N/A

TABLE A.1 (continued)

Category View	Tasks	CP Icons	See Also	Troubleshooters
Add or Remove Programs	Change or remove programs	N/A	N/A	N/A
	Add new programs			
	Add/remove Windows components			
Date, Time, Language and Regional Options	Change date and time	Date and Time	Scheduled Tasks	N/A
	Change numeric, date, time format	Regional and Language Options		
	Add other languages			
Sounds, Speech, and Audio Devices	Adjust system volume	Sounds and Audio Devices	Accessibility Sound Options	Sound
	Change sound scheme	Speech	Advanced Volume Controls	DVD
	Change speaker settings			
Accessibility Options	Adjust contrast for text and colors	Accessibility Options	Magnifier On-Screen Keyboard	N/A
	Configure Windows to work for vision, hearing, and mobility needs			

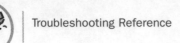

TABLE A.1 (continued)

Category View	Tasks	CP Icons	See Also	Troubleshooters
Performance and Maintenance	See basic computer information	Adminis- trative Tools	File Types System Restore	Startup and Shutdown
	Adjust visual effects	Power Options		
	Free up hard disk space	Scheduled Tasks		
	Rearrange items on hard disk for faster performance (defrag)	System		

As Table A.1 demonstrates, if you prefer to work with CP icons directly, you might prefer to configure CP to use the Classic view. Using the Control Panel in Category view might slow you down because of the extra navigation required. However, if you're not an experienced Windows user, you might prefer the default Category view. It's your choice.

The following sections describe how to use the troubleshooting-oriented Classic view CP icons in Windows XP to perform troubleshooting tasks. Older versions of Windows have similar icons with similar uses.

Accessibility Options

The Accessibility Options properties sheet is designed to help Windows users with physical, sight, or hearing impairments use Windows more easily. If you use the High Contrast display option in Windows, you will need to work with the Display tab.

The Display tab has three functions designed to make using the Windows GUI a bit more comfortable:

- High Contrast
- Cursor Blink Rate
- Cursor Width

The High Contrast option lets you switch back and forth between your normal Windows color scheme and any of about three dozen other normal or high-contrast color schemes, some of which feature large or extra-large text and icons. To switch, press the left ALT, left SHIFT, and PRINT SCREEN keys; if you hit this option accidentally, you can also disable this option from the Settings dialog.

The Cursor Blink Rate and Width use interactive drag controls which provide a real-time preview of your settings.

Shortcut to Success

While older versions of Windows let you select color schemes such as Red, White, and Blue; Brick; or Storm through the normal Display properties sheet, Windows XP offers custom color schemes only through the High Contrast dialog. Use it if you want a fast way to customize your desktop without the effort of selecting all the colors, fonts, and other features manually.

→ *For more information about using High Contrast displays, see "The Text Is Too Small or Too Hard to Read," p. 286.*

Add Hardware

The Add Hardware Wizard in Windows XP has two functions:

- Detects and installs drivers for new hardware
- Enables the user to select a particular hardware device for troubleshooting

To use this wizard to troubleshoot installed hardware, click Next to start the search process. When prompted, click Yes (informing Windows that you have already connected the hardware to your computer), and then click Next. Choose the hardware you want to troubleshoot from the list of installed hardware (see Figure A.4) and click Next to display its current status (see Figure A.5).

FIGURE A.4
Selecting an installed hardware device to troubleshoot.

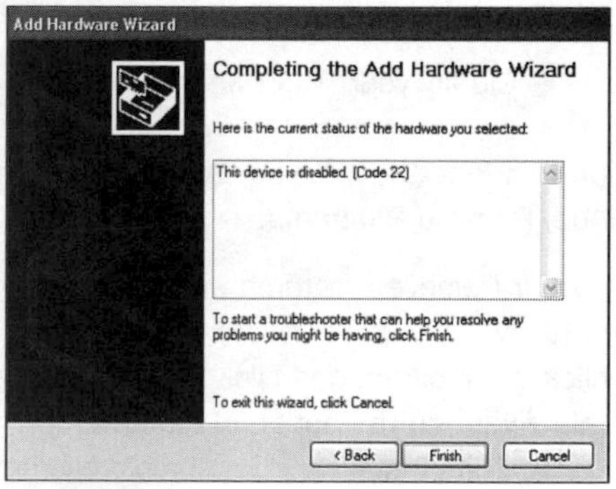

FIGURE A.5
Displaying the status of an installed hardware device.

If the device status box displays an error code or problem as shown in Figure A.5, or if you are having other difficulties with the device, click Finish to open a troubleshooter. This troubleshooter asks you questions based on the type of error Windows has indicated, and provides you with steps you need to take in attempting to fix the problem. If the device is working properly, click Cancel to close the wizard.

Cautions and Warnings

Most hardware used with Windows XP or other recent versions of Windows supports Plug and Play (PnP), the feature which lets Windows automatically detect and install drivers for new hardware when you connect it and start your system. If you're having problems with PnP-compliant hardware, you should try removing the device with Device Manager, restarting your computer, and letting Windows redetect the device and reinstall its drivers. Use Add Hardware to troubleshoot any problems that you might encounter after you use the remove and restart process.

Although Add Hardware works well for non-PnP hardware (hardware which must be manually configured), little of this hardware is still in use.

Add or Remove Programs

If you're having problems with your computer because of a program you just installed, your best option is to remove it. If you want to use a Windows utility discussed in this book but it's not installed yet, you need a way to install it. Either way, you need to use Add or Remove Programs to get the job done.

Use Add or Remove Programs in Windows XP to

- Change the installation of an existing program
- Remove an existing program
- Install a new program
- Modify your Windows installation by adding or removing components

(In Windows 9x/Me, you can also create an emergency startup disk with Add/Remove Programs.)

Add or Remove Programs works along with the install/uninstall program included in virtually every 32-bit Windows application. To change or remove an existing program, click the program and click the Change/Remove button. Depending on the program, this gives you the option of either rerunning the program's installer in order to change or repair its installation, or completely removing the program from your system.

To add or remove Windows components (instead of programs), click the Add/Remove Windows Components icon. This launches the Windows Components Wizard (see Figure A.6), which displays a list of Windows components and services. Checked boxes with a white background indicate all components in the category are installed; blank checkboxes indicate no components in the category are installed. Some categories contain listings of other individual applets that you can choose from. Click the Details button to gain access to check boxes for these programs. If a category that you can open using the Details button contains both checked and unchecked programs, it appears as a gray checked box.

Some components installed
All components installed

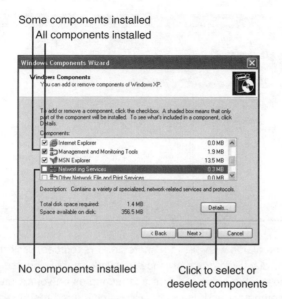

FIGURE A.6
*The Windows
Components Wizard.*

No components installed   Click to select or
                                 deselect components

Fast Track to Success

If you have a "broken" program, use Add or Remove Programs to rerun the program's installer. Depending upon the program's options, you can reinstall the program completely or run a repair option that checks the installed files against the correct versions and replaces damaged files only.

Administrative Tools

Windows XP provides access to six different administrative tools that you can use to manage your computer. The most important of these for home and small-office users are

- Computer Management—Provides access to the Device Manager, hard disk preparation, disk management and defragmentation, and network Shares management.

- Event Viewer—Tracks system events and problems.

- Performance—Displays system performance.

- Services—Displays and manages system services.

For this appendix I've chosen to focus on options that you can find by double-clicking the Computer Management icon (see Figure A.7). If they're not expanded already, click the + icons next to the System Tools and Storage trees on the left side of the window.

FIGURE A.7

The Computer Management display in Windows XP.

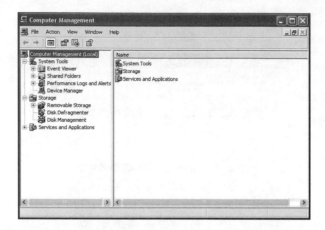

If you're having problems with network shares and resources, click the Shared Folders option to display information about network shares and users. This opens a window that displays the shared folders and resources on your system (Shares), which network computers and users are accessing shared resources (Sessions), and which files are in use across the network (Open Files).

When troubleshooting, knowledge is everything in terms of trying to solve your problem. Sometimes, you can learn more about system problems by using the Event Viewer. Double-click the Event Viewer icon to open, and then select from Application, Security, or System logs to display their contents.

Fast Track to Success

It takes time and expertise to configure Performance Logs and Alerts; unlike Event Viewer, nothing is captured unless you set up the logs and alerts to capture the information you need (check out the Microsoft Knowledge Base article Q310490 to get started). If you're more concerned about real-time performance, press Ctrl+Alt+Del to display the Windows Task Manager. Click the Performance tab for real-time information.

If you use Windows 9x/Me, install System Monitor, Net Watcher, and System Resource Meter to track real-time information.

See "Windows Tools to Keep You Out of Trouble," p. 137 for more information about these tools.

Event Viewer displays three types of events in each of its categories (see Figure A.8):

- Information—Indicates start or completion of a normal operation, signified by a blue i in a white box.

- Warning—Indicates an abnormal event has taken place, signified by a yellow triangle containing an exclamation mark (!).

- Error—A hardware, software, or services error has taken place, signified by a red circle containing a white X.

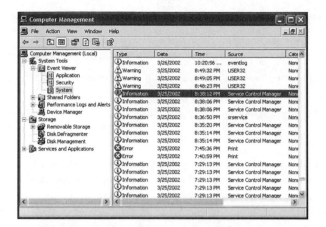

FIGURE A.8
A system log with Information, Warning, and Error entries.

Double-click an entry to see the details of the computer involved, date and time, source of the event, event type, and description (see Figure A.8). Use the scroll buttons shown in Figure A.9 to move to other events.

Scroll buttons

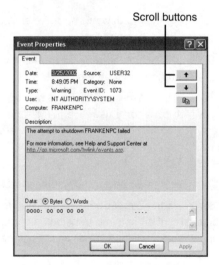

FIGURE A.9
The properties of a Warning event.

On the Web

If you'd like to learn more about a particular event, click the hyperlink listed in the description field. If Microsoft doesn't have specific information about the event, you can use the additional Help and Support Center links to perform your own search online.

Use Performance Logs and Alerts to create and monitor logs and alerts you create yourself.

→ *For details on using Disk Management to configure a new hard disk, see "Preparing an Additional Hard Disk with Windows XP/2000," p. 218.*

If you want access to tools for gathering information and configuring your disk drives, click the Storage icon. This tool has three components:

- Removable Storage—Lists removable-media drives and their contents.

- Disk Defragmenter—Launches the disk defragmenter tool.

- Disk Management—Starts the disk management tool, which replaces FDISK/ FORMAT for preparing hard drives, manages drive letters, and displays disk statistics.

Most of the features found in the Administrative Tools window are for more advanced users. If you're not already familiar with them, you should attempt to use them only for the purposes of gathering information (or seek more knowledge on them from a book dedicated to your version of Windows). If the information they provide is Greek to you, knowing what's there can still be valuable should you have to provide that information to a technical support specialist.

Display

The Display properties sheet in the Windows Control Panel is used to configure and tune your display. It contains the following tabs:

- Themes—Your choice of a coordinated desktop which includes a background image, sounds, icons, and other elements.

- Desktop—Lets you specify a background image or Web page; click Customize Desktop to select which commonly used icons (My Computer, My Network Places, and others) will be placed on the desktop, whether or not to periodically remove unused icons from the desktop, and whether to use a Web page instead of an image on the desktop.

- Screen Saver—Specifies screen saver and settings to use.

- Appearance—Customizes the current desktop's colors, fonts, and spacing. Click Effects to change font smoothing, transition effects, and to enable large icons. Click Advanced if you selected Windows Classic as your theme for additional screen customization.

- Settings—Adjust color depth, adjust resolution, enable or disable multiple monitors (if available), and troubleshoot display problems. Click Advanced to adjust refresh rate, 3D graphics acceleration options, color management, and other options varying by display adapter or monitor (see Figure A.10).

Fast Track to Success

If you're tired of tiny text and fonts onscreen but don't want to spend a lot of time fiddling with the Appearance tab, use these options to customize your desktop quickly and easily:

- Click Appearance, Effects, and click the checkbox to enable large icons.

- Click Settings, Advanced, General and select Large Size (120 DPI) or Custom and specify a larger size than the default 96dpi to increase the size of text onscreen.

FIGURE A.10
The Settings tab in Windows XP.

Folder Options

Double-clicking the Folder Options in Control Panel opens the Folder Options window. This window has three tabs:

- General
- View
- File Types

Click General if you want to switch back to the Windows classic folder view (files and folders only, no tasks), to restore the default task and file/folder view, or to specify folder browsing and file-opening options.

Click View to specify how files and folders will be displayed and to apply current settings to all folders. By default, Windows hides certain pieces of information, such as system files and file extensions. Microsoft elected to "hide" options like these from you because they, quite correctly, feel that most users don't require access to this information. However, sometimes, it can be helpful and even necessary. To change a setting on this tab, just add or remove the checkmark for the selected option.

Fast Track to Success

If you're maintaining or troubleshooting a system, I recommend you make the following changes to the Advanced settings on the View menu:

- Enable Display the Contents of System Folders
- Enable Display the Full Path in the Title Bar
- Disable Hide Extensions for Known (Registered) File Types

- Show Hidden Files and Folders
- Show Control Panel in My Computer

Making these changes will help you navigate faster when you're trying to fix a balky system.

Internet Options

The Control Panel Internet Options icon doubles as the properties sheet for Internet Explorer (IE). It has seven tabs:

- General—Configures your home page, temporary files, history, screen colors, fonts, languages, and accessibility features.

- Security—Configures security zones.

- Privacy—Configures cookie settings.

- Content—Configures the Content Advisor (used to control access to sites based on content ratings or user selections), digital certificates, and personal information used to auto-complete forms or provided to Web sites.

- Connections—Configures dial-up and LAN settings.

- Programs—Selects the default programs to use for Web browsing, email, and other Internet tasks.

- Advanced—Custom settings for many IE features.

Many of the tabs here can become helpful when troubleshooting problems that inhibit your Web browsing. If you can't connect to the Internet, for example, the Connections tab gets you access to the settings associated with your connection. The Privacy, Security, and Content tabs are good for trying to control how your Web browser accesses and filters Web content, but they can also have unintended consequences if restrictions are set too tight. For instance, the Content Advisor might deny you access to a completely innocuous site that, for whatever reason, contains information that *it thinks* you might find objectionable.

Cautions and Warnings

If IE crashes frequently, you should click the General tab and select Delete Files to clear out the disk cache (stored Web content). However, don't click on Delete Cookies if you want easy access to Web sites that require registration; the cookie files that store your registration information will be lost if you delete cookies. To delete certain files only, click Settings, View Files to display the contents of your Temporary Internet Files folder and select only the cookie or other files you want to remove.

Keyboard

The Keyboard dialog has two tabs:

- General—Adjusts repeat delay, repeat rate, and cursor blink rate with sliding controls. Use this dialog if you are having problems with repeating keys or with the cursor being hard to see.

- Hardware—Displays currently installed keyboard(s). Click Properties to view the Keyboard properties sheet. Click Troubleshoot to start the Keyboard troubleshooter.

You might see additional tabs or options if your keyboard uses special software.

Fast Track to Success

You might prefer to use the Accessibility option's Display tab to control the cursor blink rate, because it also offers you the option to adjust the cursor width.

See "Accessibility Options," p. 468 for details.

Mouse

The standard mouse dialog (also used for pointing devices such as trackballs and touchpads) contains three tabs:

- Pointers—Selects from various standard, large, and extra-large mouse pointers. Use this dialog to make the mouse pointer easier to see.

- Buttons—Switches buttons from the default right-hand to left-hand use and adjusts double-click speed. If you find that the mouse buttons are reversed (left-click opens the right-click menu), use this dialog to reset the mouse buttons to their normal behavior.

- Motion—Adjusts pointer speed and acceleration, and enables cursor trails and SmartMove, which moves the mouse pointer to the default button in the current dialog box. Use this dialog to make the mouse pointer easier to control and see, especially for users of notebook computers and LCD display panels. LCD displays have slower response than CRTs, making it easy for the mouse pointer to be "lost" onscreen.

If you install customized mouse-driver software, additional tabs are added to the Mouse dialog. For example, Logitech's MouseWare and Microsoft's IntelliPoint software let you configure your mouse buttons in a variety of ways. For additional mouse troubleshooting, see Chapter 6, "Troubleshooting Input Devices."

On the Web

Even if you're not using a brand-new optical mouse, you can benefit from installing the latest mouse software (Microsoft's drivers might also work with some third-party mice). Here are the Web sites for leading mouse and pointing-device vendors:

- Logitech—http://www.logitech.com
- Microsoft—http://www.microsoft.com/hardware/mouse/download.asp
- IBM—http://www.pc.ibm.com/support/us
- Belkin—http://www.belkin.com
- Kensington—http://www.kensington.com

Network Connections

The Network Connections system folder displays the current network and Internet connections on your system. Right-click a connection to view its properties, repair it, enable or disable it or use it as a bridge to another connection you specify (see Figure A.11).

FIGURE A.11

Using the Network Connections folder in Windows XP to repair a connection.

Fast Track to Success

Figure A.11 shows different types of connections. A Broadband connection requires you to log in and supply a username and password when you connect. A Dial-Up connection uses a dial-up modem and your regular phone line. LAN or High-Speed Internet connections might use Internet Connection Sharing, a router, or a connection to a broadband device that's always on (no login or username/password requirement).

The Network Connections display in Windows XP offers two different ways to fix a broken connection:

- Repair This Connection
- Change Settings of This Connection

Right-click the connection, and select Repair this connection to run the following repair procedures.

The repair option runs a series of commands that are designed to fix common problems with connections that use dynamic IP addresses (as most Internet connections do). You can learn more about what Repair does from Microsoft Knowledge Base article Q289256.

To fix other problems such as an incorrect user-set IP address, or to enable or disable the Internet Connection Firewall, select Properties from the right-click menu or Change Settings of This Connection from the left column. The General tab displays the network components installed. Authentication configures how your connection provides authenticated access to a network. Advanced lets you enable or disable the Internet Connection Firewall.

→ For more information about configuring network components, see "Troubleshooting Network Software Configuration," p. 376.

Power Options

If you need to adjust how and when your computer saves power, use the Power Options dialog:

- Power Schemes—Configures or disables power savings for monitors and hard drives.
- Advanced—Configures options including use of the computer's Sleep button, whether or not to show the Power icon on the taskbar, and whether or not to prompt for a password when the computer comes out of standby.
- Hibernate—Enables or disables hibernation (which stores current program states on the hard disk).
- APM—Enables or disables Advanced Power Management support (not present if computer isn't configured to use APM).
- UPS—Enables or configures battery backup devices.

The power saving features in Windows are nice, but they can also cause problems because they don't always count certain operations as your system being active. Recording to a CD or DVD, for example, can be a time-intensive process that requires no interaction from you. However, if your screen saver or power saving functions kick in mid-burn, it's very likely that the burn will fail.

To prevent your computer from going into standby mode when you stop typing or mousing, increase the time settings on the Power Schemes tab (or disable them, if necessary).

For computers that are run in an interactive kiosk or to display a slide show, select Always On as the power scheme.

If the computer can't go into Hibernate mode, check the required versus available disk space information on the Hibernate menu.

Sounds and Audio Devices

The Sounds and Audio Devices dialog has five tabs:

- Volume—Sets volume controls and speaker configuration; click the Advanced buttons for additional options.

- Sounds—Displays and configures sounds to be played during specified program and system events; your choices can be saved as a sound scheme.

- Audio—Displays and configures devices used for sound playback, recording, and MIDI music playback.

- Voice—Displays and configures devices used for voice playback and recording. Click Test to verify that your hardware works.

- Hardware—Displays hardware devices, drivers and codecs (compression/decompression) programs. Click Troubleshoot to solve sound problems, and Properties to view the properties for the selected item.

→ *To learn more about using the Sounds and Audio Devices dialog to fix sound problems, see "Troubleshooting Sound Problems," p. 311.*

Using Device Manager

One of the most important troubleshooting aids included in every version of Windows is the Device Manager. This tool keeps track of every hardware component in your system, its drivers, and its current state (functional, disabled, and so on). As you've probably noticed, I refer you to this tool quite often throughout this book as an aid in helping diagnose and fix your PC problems.

To open the Device Manger, right-click the My Computer icon (on your desktop or in the Start menu) and choose Properties. On the System Properties sheet that appears, click the Hardware tab and then the Device Manager button. When you open the Device Manager, it displays the device categories found in your computer (computer, disk drives, display, keyboards, and so on) as shown in Figure A.12.

If your computer has devices that are disabled or malfunctioning in a way that Device Manager can detect, they are displayed as soon as you open the Device Manager. For example, in Figure A.12, the Ports (COM and LPT) category displays a malfunctioning port, COM 2, indicated by an exclamation mark (!) in a yellow circle. The parallel printer port, LPT 1, has been disabled, as indicated by a red X. If the malfunctioning or disabled device is an I/O port, such as a serial, parallel, or USB port, any device attached to that port cannot work until the device is working properly.

Malfunctioning Windows device

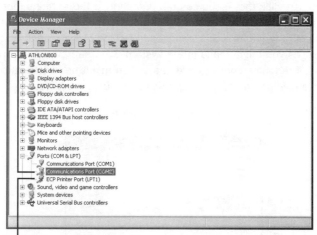

FIGURE A.12
The Windows XP Device Manager with malfunctioning and disabled devices displayed.

Disabled Windows device

Not every problem with a device shows up in Device Manager, but most problems with resource conflicts or drivers are displayed here.

To troubleshoot problems with a device in Device Manager, open its properties sheet by double-clicking on the device. Each device has at least three tabs, including General (displays device status and allows you to enable or disable the device), Driver (displays device driver files and versions and enables you to update the driver), and Resources (displays device's current and alternative settings for IRQ, DMA, I/O port and memory addresses). Some devices also have a fourth tab, Port Settings (displays and allows adjustment of device-specific settings).

➔ *For more information about hardware resources, see "Hardware Resources," p. 117.*

Solving Resource Conflicts with Device Manager

Resource conflicts take place when two or more devices are configured to use the same IRQ (unless they support IRQ sharing), I/O port address, memory address, or DMA channel.

For example, the General tab for the properties sheet of the malfunctioning COM 2 port (see Figure A.13) indicates that the port doesn't have correct IRQ or other resources available.

When you have a malfunctioning device such as the one in Figure A.12, you have several options for resolving the problem:

- Look up the Device Manager code to determine the problem and its solution (see Table A.2).
- Click the Solution button (if any) shown on the device's General properties tab; the button's name and usage depends upon the problem. Table A.2 lists the codes, their meanings, and the solution button (if any).

- Manually change resources—If the nature of the problem is a resource conflict, you can click the Resources tab and change the settings, hopefully eliminating the conflict. Some recent systems that use ACPI power management
don't permit manual resource changes in Device Manager and also override
any changes you might make in the system BIOS setup program. On these
systems, if resource conflicts take place, you might need to disable ACPI
power management before you can solve resource conflicts.

FIGURE A.13

*Windows XP offers a
multipurpose solution
button which can help
you solve the problem
with your device; with
other versions of
Windows, you may
need to use the Device
Manager manually to
solve problems.*

Properties tabs for device

Device Manager code   Solution button

TABLE A.2
Windows XP Device Manager Codes and Solutions

Device Manager Code Number	Problem	Solution Button	Other Steps to the Solution
1	Incorrect device configuration	Update Driver	If Update Driver fails, delete device listing and run Add New Hardware Wizard.
2	Can't determine correct device bus type or can't install driver	Update Driver	If Update Driver fails, delete device listing and run Add New Hardware Wizard.
3	Bad device driver or system resources low	Update Driver	Press Ctrl+Alt+Del (Task Mana-ger) to check system resources; if Update Driver fails, delete device listing and run Add New Hardware Wizard.

TABLE A.2 (continued)

Device Manager Code Number	Problem	Solution Button	Other Steps to the Solution
4	Bad driver or Registry problem	Update Driver	If Update Driver fails, delete device listing and run Add New Hardware Wizard.
5	Bad driver	Update Driver	If Update Driver fails, delete device listing and run Add New Hardware Wizard.
6	Resource conflict with another device	Troubleshoot	If the Troubleshooter cannot resolve the conflict, shut down the computer, change the resources used by the device, and restart.
7	Can't configure device	Reinstall Driver	If Reinstall Driver fails, delete device listing and run Add New Hardware Wizard; obtain an updated driver.
8	Various DevLoader (device loader) problems	(none)	Reinstall Windows to recreate a working VMM32.VXD system file.
		Reinstall Driver	If Reinstall Driver fails, delete device listing and run Add New Hardware Wizard; obtain an updated driver.
		Update Driver	If Update Driver fails, delete device listing and run Add New Hardware Wizard; obtain an updated driver.
9	BIOS enumeration problem	(none)	Delete device listing and run Add New Hardware Wizard; contact vendor for correct registry keys or an updated driver if the problem continues.
10	Device not present, working properly, or other specified problem.	Update Driver	Check physical connection to system (slot connector, cabling, power); restart system. Run Update Driver if Code 10 reappears. If Update Driver fails, delete device listing and run Add New Hardware Wizard.

TABLE A.2 (continued)

Device Manager Code Number	Problem	Solution Button	Other Steps to the Solution
11	N/A	N/A	Windows 9x/Me only.
12	No free hardware resources	Troubleshoot	Follow instructions in troubleshooter; might require removal or reconfiguration of other devices.
13	Device not detected by system	Detect Hardware	If Detect Hardware fails, delete device listing and run Add New Hardware Wizard.
14	Must restart computer before device will work	Restart Computer	Shut down computer and restart to activate device.
15	Resource conflict with another device	Troubleshoot	Follow instructions in troubleshooter to find non-conflicting resources.
16	Some device resources aren't known	(none)	Click Resources tab and manually enter resources required or delete device listing and run Add New Hardware Wizard.
17	Incorrect assignment of resources to multifunctional device	Update Driver	Delete device listing and run Add New Hardware Wizard.
18	Drivers need to be reinstalled	Reinstall Driver	If Reinstall Driver fails, delete device listing and run Add New Hardware Wizard.
19	Possibly bad Registry	Check Registry	Windows will restart and use a previous copy of the Registry; if this fails, start Windows in Safe Mode and use System Restore to return to a working condition.
20	Can't load drivers for device	Update Driver	If Update Driver fails, delete device listing and run Add New Hardware Wizard.
21	Windows is removing specified device	Restart Computer	Shut down Windows and computer; wait a few moments, then restart the computer.

TABLE A.2 (continued)

Device Manager Code Number	Problem	Solution Button	Other Steps to the Solution
22	Device is disabled in Device Manager	Enable Device	Click solution button.
	Device not started	Start Device	Click solution button.
	Device is disabled by driver or program	(none)	Remove device listing and run Add New Hardware Wizard. If the problem persists, use MSCONFIG to disable startup programs (clean boot) and retry; contact the hardware mfr for help if problem continues.
23	Secondary display adapter problems	Properties	Verify primary display adapter works okay.
	Problem with primary display adapter	(none)	Correct problems with primary display adapter and retry.
	Other devices	Update Driver	Click Solution button.
24	Legacy (non-PnP) device was not detected	Detect Hardware	If device still can't be detected, make sure it is properly connected to the system.
	PnP device was not detected	Update Drivers	If device still can't be detected, make sure it is properly connected to the system.
25	Device not completely set up by Windows	Restart Computer	Normally displayed only during first reboots of Windows; if problem persists after Windows is completely installed, you might need to reinstall Windows or remove the device listing and use Add New Hardware.
26	Device not completely set up by Windows	Restart Computer	If problem persists, remove the device listing and use Add New Hardware.
27	Resources can't be specified	(none)	Remove the device listing and use Add New Hardware; obtain updated drivers or help from hardware vendor if problem persists.

TABLE A.2 (continued)

Device Manager Code Number	Problem	Solution Button	Other Steps to the Solution
28	Drivers not installed	Reinstall Driver	If Reinstall Driver fails, delete device listing and run Add New Hardware Wizard. Obtain updated drivers if necessary.
29	No resources provided by BIOS or device disabled in BIOS	(none)	Restart computer, start BIOS setup program, and configure device in BIOS. Save changes and restart the computer.
30	IRQ conflict	(none)	Reconfigure device or conflicting device to use a different IRQ.
31	A specified device is preventing the current device from working	Properties	Reconfigure other device's properties (displayed when you click Solution button) to fix problem; if problem persists, delete device listings and run Add New Hardware Wizard. Obtain updated drivers if necessary.
32	Drivers not available	Restart Computer	Provide installation CD-ROM or log on to network after restarting; if CD-ROM or network doesn't work, resolve its problem so drivers can be accessed.
33	Various hardware errors	(none)	Hardware has failed; replace specified hardware.

On the Web

For more information about the Windows XP Device Manager error codes listed in Table A.2, go to http://support.microsoft.com and search for Knowledge Base article Q310123.

Windows 9x/Me/2000 Device Manager error codes (which vary from those in Table A.2) are explained in Microsoft Knowledge Base article Q125174.

Using Device Manager to Determine Other System Problems

As you saw in Figure A.12, only devices installed in the system will be displayed in the Windows Device Manager. This can also help you determine why you are having problems with a device. For example, if you cannot use a device attached to a Universal Serial Bus (USB) port, and the Universal Serial Bus category isn't listed in Device Manager, you need to enable the USB ports in your system and make sure you are using Windows XP, Windows 2000, Windows Me, or Windows 98SE (other versions of Windows either don't support USB ports and devices or that support is unreliable, at best).

Similarly, if your printer is attached to LPT 2 (a secondary printer port that normally requires an add-on card which may use a software driver), but LPT 2 isn't listed in the Device Manager, the printer won't work until LPT 2 is properly installed and working correctly.

Using the Windows XP Hardware Troubleshooter

In many instances when you're endeavoring to identify a problem, a tool such as Device Manager can automatically take you to a troubleshooter that asks you a series of questions that are intended to identify and fix it.

If you need to manually gain access to a Windows XP troubleshooter, open the Start menu and click Help and Support. On the lower-left section of the Help and Support Center window, click the Fixing a Problem link. This provides you with a list of possible troubleshooting areas. Click the links as appropriate until you arrive at one that opens a troubleshooter associated with your symptoms. (Don't expect to find every PC problem you encounter listed in this utility.) Now, let's take a look at an example of how you can put a troubleshooter to work for you.

If you use a Windows XP troubleshooter, it asks you a series of questions to help you fix problems with your system. For example, the troubleshooter's first question for a problem such as a malfunctioning serial port would be "Is Your Device Installed More than Once?" As Figure A.12 indicates, the answer is "No" in this example. Click Next to continue.

In this example, the troubleshooter suggests that you need to configure one or more devices to use different resources, and the text specifically refers to a disabled device displaying an error Code 12, just as in Figure A.12. Use the troubleshooter's help to reopen the Device Manager, click the properties sheet for your device and click the Resources tab. Click the Set Configuration Manually button to change the settings for the disabled device (see Figure A.14); you might not need to disable another device in spite of the warning listed.

The Set Configuration Manually option is intended for use primarily with ISA devices such as serial and parallel ports, older sound hardware, and ISA cards that can be configured with Plug and Play. Windows and the system BIOS configure PCI devices for you. PCI devices include cards in PCI slots, ATA/IDE host adapters, USB and IEEE-1394a ports, PCI, AGP and onboard video, and newer integrated sound. Depending upon the device and how your computer is configured, you might not be able to alter their configuration settings in Device Manager.

FIGURE A.14

Click the Set Configuration Manually button to set a working configuration for your device.

The Resources tab has a Conflicting Devices list which shows that the I/O port range used by COM 2 is already in use by COM 1 (see Figure A.15). There are three ways to solve such a conflict:

- Select a different, non-conflicting resource for the malfunctioning device (COM 2)
- Select a different, non-conflicting resource for the other device (COM 1)
- Disable the other device (COM 1) to prevent the conflict

FIGURE A.15

The Conflicting Devices list shows the device and the resource setting that conflicts with the malfunctioning device.

Conflicting hardware resource

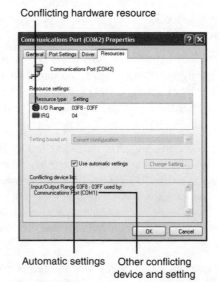

Automatic settings   Other conflicting
                        device and setting

To see whether you can use a different setting, clear the Use Automatic Settings box. In a few cases, you might be able to select the conflicting setting and click Change Setting to select a different resource. However, in most cases, you must click the Setting Based On menu and select a different configuration from those listed. If you can select a non-conflicting setting, the conflicting device will show No Conflicts (see Figure A.16). Click OK. Otherwise, open the properties sheet for the conflicting device and select different settings for it or disable it.

This scroll box lists all basic configuration options Windows has available for a device

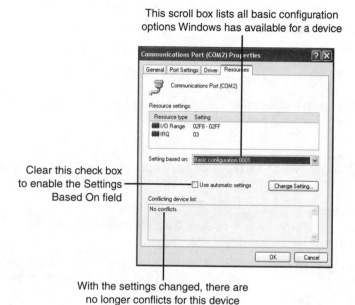

Clear this check box to enable the Settings Based On field

With the settings changed, there are no longer conflicts for this device

FIGURE A.16

Choosing a configuration that uses a different I/O port range solves the problem.

Fast Track to Success

In some cases, you might need to restart the computer and use the system BIOS setup program to correct a hardware conflict involving a built-in port such as a parallel or serial port.

You might also need to restart the computer after some hardware changes; you will be prompted to do so if necessary.

If you are running a Windows XP computer and your IRQs are listed as ACPI IRQs in Device Manager, your computer is using ACPI power management, which also is used to control IRQ allocation. If you have IRQ conflicts you cannot resolve, even after updating drivers for the device, installing the latest Windows updates, and installing the latest system BIOS update, you might want to reconfigure your system as a Standard PC instead of an ACPI PC so you can manually change IRQ settings. To learn more about this process, see the Anandtech.com operating systems FAQ "Why are all my devices using one IRQ in Win2K or WinXP?" available from the FAQ section at http://www.anandtech.com.

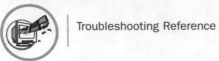

Other Windows Diagnostic, Reporting, and Repair Tools

Windows features a number of other tools you can use to discover and solve system problems, including

- System Information
- File Signature Verification
- DirectX Diagnostics
- Dr Watson
- Backup
- Defrag
- Error-checking (CHKDSK/ScanDisk)
- System Restore
- Program Compatibility Wizard
- Remote Desktop Connection

Table A.3 provides a quick reference to these tools and how to access them in Windows XP and other Windows versions.

TABLE A.3
Starting Other Windows Diagnostic, Reporting, and Repair Tools

Tool	Windows Version	How to Start
System Information	XP, Me, 9x	Click Start, Run, type MSINFO32, click OK
File Signature Verification	XP	Click Start, Run, type SIGVERIF, click OK; or Open System Information, click Tools, click File Signature Verification
DirectX Diagnostics	XP, Me, 9x	Click Start, Run, type DXDIAG, click OK
Dr Watson	XP	Runs automatically; to view, open MSINFO32, click Tools, select from menu; or click Start, Run, type drwtsn32 and click OK
Dr Watson	Me, 98	Click Start, Run, type Drwatson, click OK
Backup	Me, 9x	Open Windows Explorer, right-click drive, click Tools, and select Backup
	XP	Install from the Windows XP Home Edition CD-ROM
Defragment	XP, Me, 9x	Open Windows Explorer, right-click drive, click Properties, click Tools, and select Defragment Drive
CHKDSK	XP	Open Windows Explorer, right-click drive, click Properties, click Tools, and select Check Now
ScanDisk	Me, 9x	Open Windows Explorer, right-click drive, click Properties, click Tools, and select Error-checking
System Restore	XP, Me	Click Start, (All) Programs, Accessories, System Tools, System Restore

TABLE A.3 (continued)

Tool	Windows Version	How to Start
Program Compatibility Wizard	XP	Click Start, (All) Programs, Accessories, Program Compatibility Wizard
Remote Assistance	XP	Click Start, Help and Support Center, Remote Assistance

The following sections discuss the most important of these tools.

Using System Information

Windows' System Information utility provides you with a powerful way to view your system's

- Basic hardware configuration
- Installed hardware
- Installed software
- Current software environment, including startup programs and running services
- Internet settings
- System problems

In addition, the Tools menu enables you to run a variety of additional diagnostic programs, including

- Net Diagnostics—Windows XP only
- System Restore—Windows XP, Me only
- File Signature Verification Tool—Windows XP
- System File Checker—Windows Me, 98—SFC can be run from the command line in Windows XP
- DirectX Diagnostic Tool—Windows XP, Me, 98
- Dr Watson—Windows XP, Me, 98

Windows 98/Me's Tools menu contains several additional tools not used with the Windows XP version. Click Help in those versions of System Information for help with tools not discussed here.

After you start System Information, the System Summary screen appears (see Figure A.17). This displays your operating system version, computer name, motherboard brand and model, processor type and speed, Windows folder, boot drive, username physical and virtual memory, and the location of the pagefile.

Click Hardware Resources and select a subcategory to see the resources (IRQ, DMA, I/O port address, memory) that are used by different devices.

FIGURE A.17

The System Summary screen in the Windows XP version of System Information.

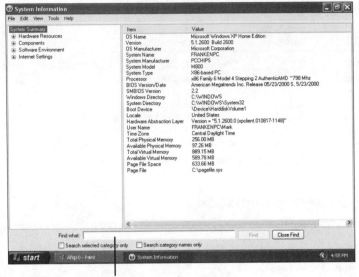

Use Find What to locate specific information about your system

→ *For more information about hardware resources, see "Hardware Resources," p. 117.*

If you see a device listed in the Forced Hardware category, open Device Manager to confirm that it works correctly. If Device Manager reports problems, open the device's properties sheet, click Resources, and click Use Automatic Settings to allow Windows to configure the device. Restart the computer if necessary.

Cautions and Warnings

Forced Hardware is Windows's term for devices that have been manually configured to use particular hardware resources instead of using the device's normal Windows Plug and Play settings. Forced Hardware settings are not recommended because they can cause conflicts with other devices.

To learn more about the devices installed on your computer, click Components to open the category, then navigate through the subcategories and device types to see the name of the device, its driver, its features, and the hardware resources it uses. The exact information provided will vary with the device type. For example, network adapters display IP address and MAC address information, while modems display the AT commands they use to activate major features.

Fast Track to Success

If you're concerned primarily about devices with problems, go directly to Problem Devices to see the device, its PnP Device ID, and a description of its problem.

If all you know about a problem is a single bit of information (IP address, PnP Device ID, and so on), enter that information into the Find What window at the bottom of the System Information display and click Find to locate the device or program in question.

Use the Software Environment categories to determine the software running on your system at startup, details about the driver software used to control hardware, current tasks, and other information. Use Internet Settings to learn how IE and other Internet tools are configured. In many cases, you might find that running System Information is faster than navigating through Computer Management, Internet Explorer or Internet properties settings, Device Manager, and other programs to learn about your system.

To access the tools discussed in the following sections, click Tools and select from the tools listed.

Using Net Diagnostics

Net Diagnostics runs a series of tests on your network, broadband, and dial-up Internet connections to determine whether they are working correctly. Net Diagnostics also checks software configurations for mail and news servers to see if they are properly configured (see Figure A.18). You should start your dial-up or broadband Internet connection before you start Net Diagnostics.

Click the plus (+) sign next to a category to expand it for more information, particularly if it's marked as FAILED. If a failed message appears next to a mail or news server, check the spelling of the name; if the name is incorrectly spelled, Windows can't find the resource. Open your default mail or news reader software (Outlook Express is used by most Windows users) and correct the spelling. If the spelling is correct, the remote server might not be responding.

If you see a FAILED message for hardware such as your network adapter or modem, use Device Manager to diagnose the problem.

Invalid news server name

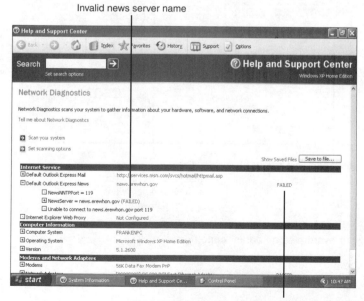

FAILED classification caused by invalid news server name

FIGURE A.18

An incorrect setting for the news server causes this service to fail.

Using System Restore

Available in Windows Me and XP, System Restore enables you to fix problems caused by a defective hardware or software installation by resetting your computer's configuration to the way it was at a specified earlier time. Restore Points can be created by the user with System Restore, and are also created by the system before new hardware or software is installed.

To create a restore point

1. Start System Restore from the System Information Tools menu (see Figure A.19).
2. Click Create a Restore Point and click Next.
3. Enter a descriptive name for the restore point, such as "Before I installed DuzItAll Version 1.0" and click Create.
4. The computer's current hardware and software configuration is stored as a new restore point.

Restores computer to a specified restore point

FIGURE A.19
The main menu of the System Restore program.

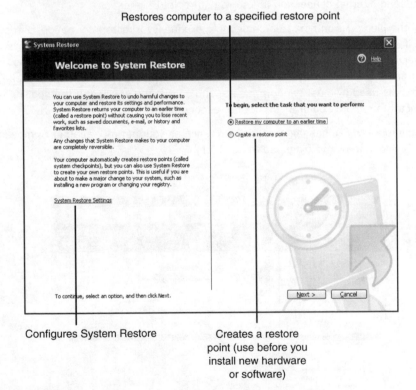

Configures System Restore

Creates a restore point (use before you install new hardware or software)

To restore your system to an earlier condition

1. Start System Restore.
2. Click Restore My Computer to an Earlier Time and click Next.
3. Select a date from the calendar (dates that have restore points are in bold text).

4. Select a restore point and click Next (see Figure A.20).

5. Close any open programs and save your work before you click Next to start the process; Windows will shut down and restart.

6. Click OK to close the System Restore program after the computer restarts.

Cautions and Warnings

You can't lose data by using System Restore, but all programs and hardware installed after a specified restore point must be reinstalled if you restore your system to that point. While the program files remain on the system, Windows can't use them because the registry entries and shortcuts have been removed. Be sure to note the location of the program, and specify the same location when you reinstall the program so that the new installation replaces the old one. This way, you can avoid using up additional disk space by accidentally having the same program files installed twice.

Date with restore point(s) available   Selected restore point

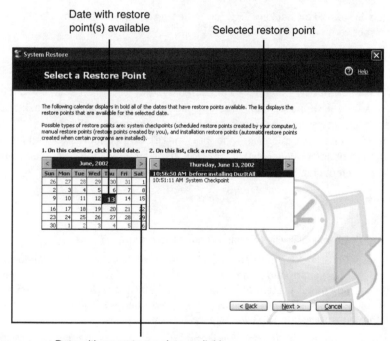

Date with no restore points available

FIGURE A.20
Choosing a restore point.

If System Restore is not available, it might be turned off (or you may not have enough free hard disk space to accommodate it). You can enable System Restore or change the amount of disk space it uses with the System Restore tab on the System properties sheet; click System Restore Settings from the main menu of System Restore to adjust these settings (refer to Figure A.19).

Using File Signature Verification

The default setting for File Signature Verification checks for system files that lack digital signatures. Use this feature to determine whether your Windows installation might be corrupted by the use of out-of-date system files that some older programs may have installed. To determine whether you are using unsigned driver files, click the Advanced button and select Look for Other Files That Are Not Digitally Signed. The use of unsigned drivers isn't necessarily bad (sometimes it's even necessary), but the fact that Microsoft has not certified a hardware device driver leaves the door open that it might cause problems in Windows.

After you configure Advanced options, click OK, and then Start. A status bar informs you of the progress of the scan. Click OK to accept the results of the scan. Click Advanced, Logging, View Log to see detailed results.

To fix problems that could be caused by unsigned files, you can

- Use the Update Driver feature in a device's properties sheet (Device Manager) after you download a digitally signed file (if one is available).
- Run System File Checker (SFC) to replace an unsigned system file with the correct version.

Using System File Checker

SFC is a Windows utility that checks protected system files (files such as .DLL, .SYS, .OCX, and .EXE, as well as some font files used by the Windows desktop) and replaces incorrect versions or missing files with the correct versions. Use SFC to fix problems with Internet Explorer or other built-in Windows programs caused by the installation of obsolete Windows system files, user error, deliberate erasure, virus or Trojan-horse infections, and similar problems.

To run SFC in Windows XP

1. Click Start, Run.
2. Type CMD and click OK to open a command-prompt window.
3. Type SFC /SCANNOW and press ENTER. A status window called Windows File Protection appears and a moving bar notifies you of SFC's progress. If SFC finds an incorrect system file or determines that a system file is missing, a dialog box appears to notify you. If the system file is available in a backup folder on the system, SFC will replace it for you.
4. If the system file is not available in the backup folder (some systems might not have enough disk space to backup all protected files), SFC will prompt you to insert the Windows XP CD-ROM so that the system file(s) can be restored.
5. To close the command window after running SFC, type EXIT and press ENTER. If the computer's backup copies of the system files become corrupted, run the command SFC /PURGECACHE to rebuild the backup folder on the hard disk with correct system files. You can also configure SFC to run at the next startup with SFC /SCANONCE, to run every time the computer is started with SFC /SCANBOOT, and to turn off automatic scanning with SFC /REVERT.

You can run System File Checker in Windows 98/Me from the Tools menu in System Information.

Using DirectX Diagnostics

Use DirectX Diagnostics to determine if DirectX (the software component Windows uses for 3D graphics and sound, game controllers, and multimedia) is working correctly. DirectX Diagnostics has a multiple-tab dialog (see Figure A.21):

- System—A summary of system hardware and Windows version.
- DirectX Files—A listing of files and version numbers and a report of any file problems.
- Display—Information about your displays (multiple-display systems have a tab for each display), a report of any problems detected, and options to test DirectDraw and Direct3D operations.
- Sound—Information about your sound card, a report of any problems found, and an option to test DirectSound.
- Music—Information about MIDI and Wave playback features of your sound hardware, a report of any problems found, and an option to test DirectMusic.
- Input—Information about all input devices and a report of any problems found.
- Network—Information on DirectPlay service providers, a report of any problems found, and an option to test DirectPlay.
- More Help—Options to run the DirectX and Sound troubleshooters, System Information, and to adjust the DirectDraw screen refresh rate.

Menu access tabs   Test buttons

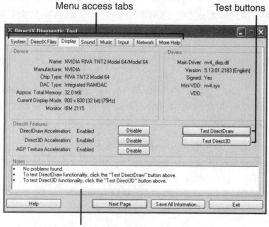

Problem notifications and test advice

FIGURE A.21
Preparing to test DirectDraw features with DirectX Diagnostics.

DirectX Diagnostics can warn you of driver problems and provides you with a way to test your DirectX features. Replace unsigned or defective drivers if you are having problems in DirectX-compatible software (game and multimedia titles). If your computer fails one or more DirectX tests, download and install the latest version of DirectX from Microsoft.

On the Web

Download the latest version of DirectX, get technical help, and learn more about DirectX at the Microsoft DirectX Web site

http://www.microsoft.com/windows/directx/default.asp

Defrag and Error-Checking

➔ See "Maintaining Windows with Drive and Anti-Virus Utilities," p. 152 for details.

Defrag and Error-checking can be run from the Tools tab on the hard disk's properties sheet in My Computer or Windows Explorer. Defrag improves the speed at which your computer can retrieve data from the hard disk (by reorganizing where that data is located on the drive), while Error-checking (known as ScanDisk in Windows 9x/Me and CHKDSK in Windows 2000) detects and corrects disk errors.

Program Compatibility Wizard

➔ See "Trouble-shooting Programs That Won't Run Under Windows XP," p. 138 for details.

This wizard is used to temporarily configure Windows XP to emulate an older version of Windows. This might enable programs which don't work well under Windows XP to run properly. The changes made by the wizard are in effect only while the older program is running.

Remote Assistance in Windows XP

Windows XP's remote assistance feature enables you to ask another Windows XP user for help with your computer, or provide help to another user. To request help, you can start Remote Assistance from the Help and Support menu: Click Invite a Friend to Help You with Remote Assistance, and Invite Someone to Help You.

Using Remote Assistance

To get help using Remote Assistance, click Invite Someone to Help You. You can get help from your Windows Messenger (WM) buddy list or by sending an email to other Windows users (see Figure A.22).

Click Sign In if you want to invite someone on your Windows Messenger (WM) buddy list who is currently online (if you're not already online). If you're already online with WM, click the icon for a buddy list member who can help you, and then click Invite This Person. You can even ask for help from the WM interface; click I Want To…, More, and Ask for Remote Assistance. Select the user from the list to send the invitation.

If you don't use Windows Messenger or all your WM buddies who can help you are offline, type an email address or click the Address Book icon to select an address, and then click Invite This Person.

If you send an email message, specify a maximum length of time for the invitation to be valid (one hour is the default); this helps to prevent unauthorized users from hacking your system (you are, after all, allowing complete access to your PC from a remote computer). You are strongly encouraged, although not required, to set up a password for your helper to use. You must provide the password to the user separately; I recommend that you agree on a password in advance, or call your helper by phone to communicate the password.

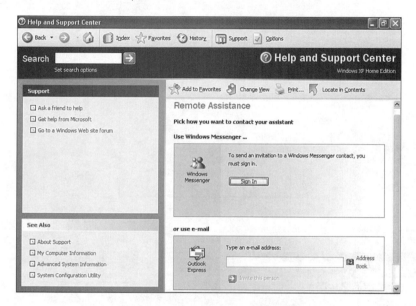

FIGURE A.22

Preparing to invite another user to help you with Remote Assistance.

In either case, once the invitation/offer to help has been sent, the WM Conversation box appears on both sides of the connection. The user who requested help is called the Novice, and the helper is called the Expert. The Expert can click Accept (Alt+A) to start the help process, or Decline (Alt+D) to reject the request for assistance. A similar screen on the Novice side allows the user who asked for help to cancel the request if desired.

During the Remote Assistance process, the Novice controls the process; the Novice must specifically grant permission for the Expert to view the screen and use text chat. A two-column toolbar appears on the Novice's screen during the entire help process; the left column is used for displaying both sides' chat messages; the lower left corner provides a message entry area. The right column contains controls for file transfer, audio chat and quality settings, disconnecting, and stop control, as shown in Figure A.23.

Figure A.24 shows the Expert's view of the requester's screen. The left side shows the chat process, with the lower left corner used for message entry. The larger window shows a scaled or scrollable actual-size view of the requester's display.

Until the Expert clicks the Take Control button, the Novice controls the system; as before, the Novice must specifically permit this to take place. This enables the Expert to watch the Novice try a process, or allow the Expert to take over if necessary. During the process, either side can initiate a file transfer and start or stop voice chat to help solve the problem.

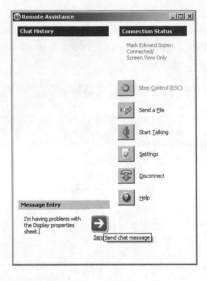

Release/Take Control toggle button

FIGURE A.24
The Expert's control panel during a typical Remote Assistance session. Note the chat window indicates that the Expert has taken control of the system.

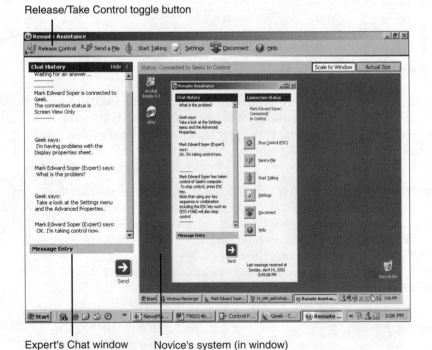

Expert's Chat window   Novice's system (in window)

Whenever desired, the Novice can click Esc to stop remote control of the system. Either side can click Disconnect to stop the process.

Troubleshooting Remote Assistance with Windows XP

If you can't make a connection with Remote Assistance, check to see how both sides are connected to the Internet.

Check the following:

- If both the Novice's and Expert's computers are connected to a type of router that uses a feature called network address translation (NAT) but doesn't support Universal Plug and Play (UPnP), the computers can't connect to each other (check your router's documentation).

- You need to configure your firewall software and your NAT router to allow traffic on TCP port 3389 (the port used by the Remote Desktop Protocol). Check your firewall appliance, firewall software, or router documentation for details.

If your router supports UPnP, but Windows XP doesn't have UPnP installed, and you can't set up a Remote Assistance connection, then you need to install UPnP.

1. Open the Add/Remove Programs icon in Control Panel.

2. Click Add/Remove Windows Components.

3. Scroll down to Networking Services and select it.

4. Click Details.

5. Click Universal Plug and Play.

6. Click OK to install it.

Cautions and Warnings

Installing UPnP creates a significant security risk described in detail in Microsoft Knowledge Base article Q315000.

To prevent UPnP from becoming a way for hostile remote users to take control of your computer, you need to install the patch referred to in Microsoft Security Bulletin MS01-059, "Unchecked Buffer in Universal Plug and Play Can Lead to System Compromise." You can download this patch through Windows Update for Windows XP, or directly from this URL:

http://www.microsoft.com/Downloads/Release.asp?ReleaseID=34951

By default, a patched machine will search only the same subnet or a private IP address for UPnP device descriptions, and only up to four router hops.

Using MSConfig

The Microsoft System Configuration Utility, MSCONFIG, enables you to selectively disable programs and services that run at startup. If your computer is unstable, runs out of system resources very quickly with Windows 98/Me, or has problems starting up or shutting down, using MSConfig can help you determine if a program or service run when the system starts is at fault.

The MSConfig dialog has six tabs in its Windows XP version (see Figure A.25):

- General—Select from Normal, Diagnostic (clean boot), or Selective Startup (you choose which items and services to load); can also be used to manually replace a Windows file (Expand) or start System Restore
- SYSTEM.INI—Selectively or completely disables SYSTEM.INI (legacy hardware) statements
- WIN.INI—Selectively or completely disables WIN.INI (legacy software/configuration) statements; WIN.INI might not be present on some systems
- BOOT.INI—Configures advanced Windows XP startup options
- Services—Selectively or completely disables system services
- Startup—Selectively or completely disables startup programs

The Windows 98 version of MSConfig has Autoexec.bat and Config.sys tabs in place of the Boot.ini and Services tabs.

FIGURE A.25

MSConfig for Windows XP. Click Selective or Diagnostic Startup to stop loading some or all startup programs, optional settings, and optional services.

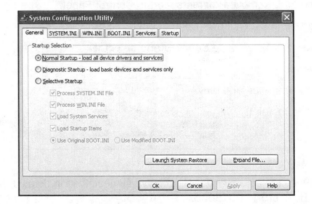

To get started with MSConfig, I recommend you click Help from the General tab and read the Overview of the utility. Scroll down to the bottom and click Create a Clean Environment for Troubleshooting to continue.

Help directs you to select the Diagnostic startup option. After you select this option, click Apply, then OK to restart your system.

Using the Diagnostic startup option disables all startup programs, services, and special options; essentially, you are performing a clean boot of your system.

Cautions and Warnings

Most computers running Windows XP don't have a WIN.INI file (a leftover from Windows 3.1!), so if you select Diagnostic startup on a Windows XP system that doesn't have WIN.INI, MSConfig will choose Selective startup instead with Process WIN.INI as its only option. It's strange, but this bug doesn't cause any problems.

If a startup program is causing your computer to malfunction, but the computer works properly after you restart it with the Diagnostic startup option, one or more of your normal startup programs or processes is at fault. After you restart the computer, reopen MSConfig, click Help, and select The Problem Was Not Reproduced for the next step in the process. Use Help to guide you through using Selective startup to re-enable one part of the startup process at a time.

Fast Track to Success

If you see error messages during startup, open the Help and Support Center, search for Startup Shutdown, and run the Windows XP Startup and Shutdown Troubleshooter. It can also assist you in using MSConfig to find the problem with your system.

Troubleshooting System Resource Shortages in Windows 9x/Me

One of the reasons that Windows XP has become so popular for both home and office use is its stability. Windows XP (and its predecessor, Windows 2000) can manage an almost unlimited number of open windows and programs and can run for long periods of time without requiring a reboot. However, if you use Windows 9x/Me, your ability to open new programs and windows is severely limited by a factor called free system resources, or FSR.

FSR measures the remaining space in a 64KB segment of memory, which the Windows GDI.EXE and USER.EXE programs use. These two programs manage the display and objects that Windows draws onscreen. FSR is reduced with every program, window, and object onscreen, and is *not* affected by the amount of RAM installed in your system; whether you have 128MB, 512MB, or more, only 64KB of memory is used to manage these resources, and every program you open, particularly those that have a lot of windows or other graphical elements, will use up FSR. When you close programs, some of the FSR used by the programs is returned to the system, but because of bugs in program and Windows design, some FSR is lost and can be reclaimed only by restarting the system. Over time, FSR can decline to a level near zero.

Running short of free system resources can cause all sorts of problems, especially when FSR falls below 15%. Any of the following could happen:

- Your computer might run more slowly
- You might not be able to open additional programs or program windows
- Programs already running might crash
- You might lose unsaved data (because of a program crash)
- You might not be able to close programs or shut down your computer

I've seen *every one* of the preceding problems happen on systems running Windows 9x/Me.

On the Web

The Infinisource, Inc. Web site has an excellent article about FSR along with links to related Microsoft Knowledge Base articles. Go to

http://www.infinisource.com/techfiles/win-resources.html

If you use Windows 9x/Me, you should run the optional Resource Meter program to determine whether your computer has enough free system resources (FSRs) to run reliably or allow you to load another program into memory. Resource Meter is an optional program accessed by clicking Start, Programs, Accessories, System Tools, Resource Meter. If it is not already installed on your system, open the Add/Remove Programs icon in Control Panel, click the Windows Setup tab, click System Tools, and then Details to see the program listing. Click Resource Meter to checkmark it and click OK to install it. Provide your Windows CD-ROM if requested to complete the installation.

To run Resource Meter automatically when you start your system with Windows 9x or Windows Me, you can add a shortcut to the Startup folder:

1. Right-click on Start and select Explore.

2. Double-click the Programs folder in the right-hand window to open it.

3. Double-click the Startup folder in the right-hand window.

4. Right-click in the Startup folder window (right-hand window) and select New, Shortcut.

5. Click Browse, navigate to the Windows folder, and select the file called Rsrcmtr.exe (depending on your system settings, you may not see the .exe extension).

6. Click Open to select the file.

7. The Create Shortcut wizard displays the path to the file (see Figure A.26). Click Next in the Create Shortcut wizard to continue.

FIGURE A.26

Creating a shortcut to start the Resource Meter at startup in Windows 98.

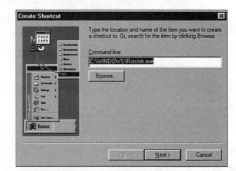

8. Enter a descriptive name (such as Resource Meter).

9. Click Finish to close the Create Shortcut wizard; the next time you start Windows, the Resource Meter will start in your system tray. The indicator changes from green (safe levels) to yellow (marginal levels) to red

(dangerously low levels) as system resources are consumed. To see the details, double-click on the Resource Meter to open it, as in Figure A.27.

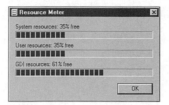

FIGURE A.27
The Windows 98 Resource Meter indicates that free system resources are at 35% on this system.

Depending on the programs you run at startup, the programs you open and close during your computing session, and how many windows your program opens (Web browsers with multiple open windows and programs with floating menus consume FSR very rapidly), you might find that your computer runs short of FSR in a relatively short time period. Unfortunately, adding RAM to a Windows 9x/Me system will *not* help free up FSR. However, closing programs you aren't using helps recover some FSR, and rebooting the system restores FSR to its original startup value.

If you discover that your FSR at startup is under 70%, you might be loading programs you don't need. To determine what programs you can do without, see "Using MSConfig," p. 501.

The Philosophy of Troubleshooting

The Troubleshooting Process

If you don't service computers for a living, it might seem scary to talk about the troubleshooting process. But, believe me, it's worth the effort to follow a process that can find problems in a hurry, whether you earn your living at it or just want to save a few bucks and be the hero of your office or home.

To become a successful troubleshooter, you need to

- Learn as much as you can about what went wrong
- Evaluate the environment where the computer problem took place
- Use testing and reporting software to gather information about the system
- Form a hypothesis about the nature of the problem and how to resolve it (a theory you will try to prove or disprove)
- Use the troubleshooting cycle to isolate and solve the problem

The First Step: Finding Out What Happened

Whether you're troubleshooting your own computers or helping out a co-worker, a friend, your spouse, your kids, or your parents with a computer problem, the first task is to find out *what happened*. Unless you know what was happening when the problem first showed up, you're going to have a very hard time finding and solving the problem.

Here's what you need to find out—or remember:

- What software was being used
- What hardware was being used
- What error messages were displayed
- What the computer user was working on
- What type of environment (electrical and otherwise) was in the work area at the time of the problem

The number one answer you're looking for with all these questions: "What changed since the last time it worked?" I first learned the importance of this question years ago from the writings of long-time *Byte Magazine* columnist Jerry Pournelle (available online at http://www.jerrypournelle.com/ and http://www.byte.com), and it's been endlessly helpful over the years.

Let's look at the first question, what software was being used. You want to find out

- The name of the program and the version—Restart the program and click Help, About to see this information.
- The version of Windows being used—Open the Windows Device Manager and click the General tab to see this information.
- Any other programs that were also in use at the time.

➜ *For more details about software and Windows errors, see "Problems with Programs and Applications," p. 136.*

The second question, what hardware was being used, should reveal what add-on hardware (printer, scanner, CD burner, Internet) was in use.

The third question is simple: What error messages were displayed? You might need to try to reproduce the problem to display a complex error message such as a Blue Screen of Death or Fatal Exception Error.

➜ *For more details about software conflicts, see "I Can't Use an Existing Program After I Installed Another Program," p. 458, and "Troubleshooting Illegal Operations and Other Error Messages," p. 145.*

The fourth question, what was the user working on, is designed to determine the specifics of the task. For example, trying to print a multipage document with lots of graphics to a laser printer is a different task than printing a single page letter to the same printer, or to a different printer. You should also find out what programs the user was running, because some programs might conflict with others running at the same time.

Knowing the amount of time the program was running and what other types of programs were running on the computer at the same time can also be useful, particularly if the user is running Windows 9x or Me. These versions of Windows can run out of resources fairly quickly when some types of programs are being run.

➜ *For more details about system resources, see "Troubleshooting System Resource Shortages in Windows 9x/Me," p. 503.*

Sometimes, after you learn the answers to these questions, the solution to the problem will jump out at you. But sometimes, you'll need to look around your computer space (if it's your problem) or go to the problem's central location and put on your deerstalker cap and play detective.

How to Check Out the Computing Environment

Even if you're trying to solve a problem with your own computer, and especially if you're assisting somebody else, you need to find out some facts about the environment where the computer is located.

What kinds of information are you looking for? Use Table B.1 to provide a quick checklist of what to take with you or what you'll need access to, depending upon what you learned from your initial questions.

TABLE B.1
Troubleshooting Tests and Requirements

Test	Requires
Power	Multimeter, circuit tester
BIOS beep & error codes	List of BIOS codes
Printer self-test	Printer & paper
Windows bootlog	Start Windows with correct option
Hardware resources (IRQ, and so on)	Windows Device Manager

Which test or diagnostic routine is the best one to start with? Before you perform any specific tests, review the clues you got asking the initial questions. For example, if you found out that you could print simple documents to a laser printer with Microsoft Word, but you had problems printing graphics-rich publications with Adobe PageMaker, the problem isn't with Windows (which controls the printer), and probably not with the printer, but it could be with the documents themselves. To learn more about the printer, you should use the printer's self-test.

A laser printer's self test usually indicates the amount of RAM on-board, the emulation (HP or PostScript), and firmware revisions. The amount of RAM on-board is critical, because as is discussed in Chapter 4, laser printers are page printers: The whole page must fit into the laser printer's RAM to be printed.

Thus, there are two variables to this printing problem: the amount of RAM in the printer, and the size of the PageMaker document. If, for example, the self-test reveals the printer has only the standard amount of RAM (2MB) onboard, then it's adequate for text, but an elaborate page can overload it. If a look at the PageMaker document reveals that it has a large amount of graphic content then you're likely to have problems.

There are two easy solutions to this type of problem:

- Add more memory to the printer
- Reduce the graphics resolution

It's easier (and cheaper!) to reduce the graphics resolution to see if the PageMaker documents will print. If this works, you can check with a memory vendor for a printer memory upgrade if you need the full graphics quality, or keep using the printer with the lower graphics quality setting.

➔ *For details about adjusting graphics print quality, see "Accessing the Properties Sheets for Your Printer," p. 268.*

On the other hand, if the problem you're experiencing centers around the computer locking up frequently (and randomly), you'd want to check the electrical power. The first step here is to see if the power the computer uses is good. A low-cost wall outlet analyzer available from Radio Shack or similar stores is a useful tool. This device has signal lights indicating whether the wiring is correct or if there are faults with grounding, reversed polarity, and the like. Random lockups, crashes, and other types of mysterious computer problems can be traced to bad power. If the problem happens only after the

➔ *For details, see "Detecting Overheating and Incorrect Voltage Levels," p. 412.*

computer's been on for awhile, it's time to look at the computer's hardware monitor to check the internal temperature or voltage settings. They system could be overheating.

Conversely, if the system only locks up when you're using a specific application, it's more than likely there's a problem with the application and not your computer. In that case you should check the application vendor's Web site to see if it's a common problem and if there's a patch available to fix it.

Your Diagnostics Toolbox

If you like to be prepared for any computing disaster, it's helpful to have the tools you need ready at all times. Here are the tools I recommend:

- Hex drivers
- Phillips and straight-blade screwdrivers
- Torx drivers
- 3-claw parts retrieval tool
- Hemostat clamps
- Needle-nose pliers
- Eyebrow tweezers
- Penlight and magnifier

For diagnosing power issues and working safely with equipment, I recommend you have

- An AC/DC multimeter with Ohm and Continuity options
- A grounded AC circuit tester
- An anti-static mat and wrist strap

Any set of cleaning and maintenance tools should include

- Compressed air
- Keyboard key puller
- Computer-rated mini-vacuum cleaner
- Wire cutter & stripper
- Extra case, card, and drive screws (salvage or new)
- Extra card slot covers (salvage or new)
- Extra hard disk and motherboard/card jumper blocks (salvage or new)
- Endust for Electronics cleaning wipes and spray

If you think that you might need to reinstall Windows, you'll need

- Your original operating system CD
- Your emergency boot floppy disk (Windows 9x/Me)

Use these tools to help you perform the steps you need to follow during the troubleshooting cycle.

The Troubleshooting Cycle

The troubleshooting cycle is a method that you can use to determine exactly what part of a complex system, such as a computer, is causing the problem.

The first step, as we've seen above, is to determine the most likely source of the problem. The questions you ask the user (or yourself) will help you determine which subsystem is the best place to start in solving the problem. In the previous example, the printing subsystem was the most likely place to start.

To help you focus on the likely cause for a computer problem, use the Symptoms Tables at the front of the book to find your problem and identify which flowchart can help you fix it. Then follow the flowchart for the symptom, and you're on the road to the solution.

Sometimes, you might discover that a particular symptom seems ambiguous: It points to more than one possible solution. In cases like this, it's helpful to realize that any computer is a collection of subsystems. What's a subsystem?

A subsystem is the combination of components designed to a particular task, and it can include both hardware and software components. Use Table B.2 to better understand the nature of the subsystems found in any computer.

TABLE B.2
Computer and Peripheral Subsystems and Their Components

Subsystem	Hardware	Software	Firmware
Printing	Printer, cable, parallel, or serial port	Printer driver in Windows, Application	BIOS configuration of port
Display	Graphics card, monitor, cables, port type, cables, motherboard (integrated video)	Video drivers in Windows	Video BIOS, BIOS configuration of video type, boot priority
Audio	Sound card, speakers, cables, motherboard (integrated audio)	Audio drivers in Windows	BIOS configuration of integrated audio
Mouse and Pointing Device	Mouse or pointing device, serial or mouse port, USB port	Mouse driver in Windows	BIOS port configuration, USB Legacy configuration

TABLE B.2 (continued)

Subsystem	Hardware	Software	Firmware
Keyboard	Keyboard, PS/2 or USB port	Keyboard driver in Windows	BIOS keyboard configuration, USB Legacy configuration
Storage	Drives, data cables, power connectors, USB, IEEE-1394 or SCSI cards, or built-in ports	Storage drivers in Windows	BIOS drive configuration, BIOS configuration of built-in USB or other ports
Power	Power supply, splitters, fans	Power-management software (Windows)	BIOS power-management configuration
CPU	CPU, motherboard	System devices	BIOS cache and CPU configuration
RAM	RAM, motherboard	(none)	BIOS RAM configuration
Network	NIC, motherboard, USB port (for USB devices)	Network configuration files and drivers	BIOS PnP and power management, BIOS configuration of integrated network port or USB port
Modem	Modem, motherboard, or serial port or USB port	Modem drivers, application	BIOS PnP, power management, BIOS port configuration

You can see from this list that virtually every subsystem in the computer has hardware, software, and firmware components. A thorough troubleshooting process will take into account both the subsystem and all of its components.

As you use the Symptoms Tables at the front of this book and the flowcharts, keep the subsystems inside your computer in mind. The flowcharts and chapter writeups are designed to cover the different components of each subsystem. However, in some cases, you might need to check more than one subsystem to find the solutions you're looking for.

Testing a Subsystem

Whether you troubleshoot to save money or to make money, and whether you're operating on your own computer or a friend's, you should take the computer user's version of the Hippocratic oath: "First, do no harm (to the computer)."

Before you change anything, record the current configuration. Depending upon the item, this may include one or more of the following steps:

- Recording jumper or DIP switch settings on the motherboard or an add-in card
- Printing the complete report from the Windows Device Manager
- Printing a complete report from a third-party diagnostic or reporting program such as SiSoftware Sandra
- Recording BIOS configurations

After you have recorded the configuration you are going to change, follow this procedure:

1. Change one hardware component or hardware/software/firmware setting at a time.
2. Try the task the user was performing after a single change and evaluate the results.
3. If the same or similar problem reoccurs, reinstall the original component or reset the software to the original settings and continue with the next item.
4. Repeat until the subsystem performs normally. The last item changed is the problem; repair, replace, or reload it as appropriate to solve the problem.

Best Sources for Replacement Parts

To perform parts exchanges for troubleshooting, you need replacement parts. If you don't have spare parts, it's very tempting to go to the computer store and buy some new components. Instead, if you have one available, take a spare system that's similar to the "sick" computer, make sure that it works, then use it for parts. Why? "New" doesn't mean it works.

A while back, I replaced an alternator on my van with a brand-new, lifetime-warranty alternator that failed in less than a week. Whether it's a cable, a video card, a monitor, or some other component, try use a known-working item as a temporary replacement rather than first forking over good money for a brand-new part. If you have the means, borrow parts from a spare system rather than opening up a working system and taking it out of action. If you have access to a second, working computer, it's easy to borrow parts such as keyboards, mice, and monitors and put them back when you're done. Just be sure to turn off the computer or monitor before you unplug components and leave it off until you reattach the components (except for USB components, which are hot-swappable).

Fast Track to Success

If you're planning to upgrade your hard drive, optical drive, add-on cards, or other components, save the old parts for use as temporary replacements (if they're still working). Make sure you protect these components from environmental damage by putting the old parts into anti-static bags for ESD protection (try bubble wrap or the box the new component came in). As time passes, you'll have a collection of spares you can use for troubleshooting.

If you don't have access to any spare parts to work from while troubleshooting a PC problem, your options become a bit more limited. At this point you may find yourself at the mercy of whomever's technical support department handles your "defective" component. Although, keep in mind that you can find budget versions of most PC components for very low prices. For example, a "cheap-o" mouse or keyboard that you can use for testing and temporary backup shouldn't cost you more than $5 or $10 each.

Where to Start?

As the preceding subsystem list indicates, there's no shortage of places to start in virtually any subsystem. What's the best way to decide whether a hardware, software, or firmware problem is the most likely cause?

Typically, hardware problems come and go, while software and firmware problems are consistent. Why? A hardware problem is often the result of a damaged or loose wire or connection; when the connection is closed, the component works, but when the connection opens, the component fails.

On the other hand, a software or firmware problem will cause a failure under the same circumstances every time.

Another rule of thumb that's useful is known as Occam's Razor, or the least hypothesis. English Philosopher William of Occam suggested centuries ago that the simplest (or least complex) explanation that fits the known facts is usually the accurate one. While TV shows such as the late lamented *X-Files* are enjoyable to watch, their "trust no one" paranoia and incredibly complicated explanations for everything are exactly the wrong approach to take when you're trying to fix a computer problem. Instead, look at the least expensive, easiest-to-replace item first. In most cases, the cable connected to a subsystem is the first place to look for problems. Whether the cable is internal or external, it is almost always the least-expensive part of the subsystem, can easily come loose, and can easily be damaged.

If a cable is loose; has bent pins; or has a dry, brittle, or cracked exterior, replace it. While it may sound overly simplistic, good cables usually look good, and bad cables often look bad.

When new software or new hardware has been introduced to the system and a problem results immediately afterward, that change is often the most likely cause of the problem.

Hardware conflicts such as IRQ, I/O port address, DMA channel, and memory address, or conflicts between the software drivers in the operating system, are typical causes of failure when new hardware is introduced. New software can also cause problems with hardware, because of incompatibilities between software and hardware, or because new software has replaced drivers required by the hardware.

To confirm whether new hardware or software is at the root of a PC problem, you should remove it and reboot your PC. If all functions normally again, then you have your answer (or at least part of it). The System Restore feature in Windows Me and Windows XP is a very useful tool for determining whether the software or hardware you added is at fault; it automates the process of returning your computer to a previous condition before a given software or hardware installation.

→ *For more information about System Restore, see "Using System Restore," p. 494.*

Where to Go for More Information

After you've gathered as much information as possible, you might find that you still need more help. User manuals for components often are discarded, software drivers need to be updated, and some conflicts don't have easy answers. There's one "place" to go to find the information you need: the World Wide Web. Fire up your browser and check out the Web sites suggested in the On the Web sidebars in this book, use search engines such as Google (http://www.google.com) to search for solutions, and also try: manufacturers' Web sites, Cnet's http://download.com.com (for drivers), and online computer magazines such as PCMagazine (http://www.pcmag.com), PCWorld (http://www.pcworld.com), and others.

Keeping Track of Your Solutions

If you hate solving the same problems over and over again (and who wouldn't?), keep detailed notes about the problems you solve. Be sure to note symptoms, underlying problems, workarounds, and final resolutions. Use the copy and paste feature in Windows to store Web site URLs, and use File, Save as Web Archive in Internet Explorer to save useful Web pages and their graphics in the documents you write up.

Summarizing the Troubleshooter's Philosophy

The troubleshooter's philosophy can be summarized as

- Discover what really was happening when trouble happened
- Find out what changed
- Use the troubleshooting cycle to reproduce the problem and discover a solution
- Record the solution in case you need it again

Use this philosophy and the rest of this book to become a troubleshooting hero to your family, friends, and co-workers.

Index

A

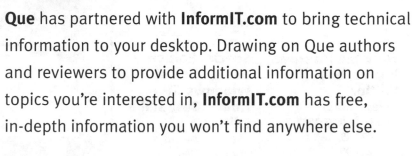

Other Related Titles

PC Fear Factor: The Ultimate PC Disaster Prevention Guide
Alan Luber
ISBN: 0-7897-2825-7
US $24.99, CAN $58.99, UK £17.99

How the Internet Works, 6th Edition
Preston Gralla
ISBN: 0-7897-2582-7
US $29.99, CAN $44.95, UK £21.95

How Networks Work, 6th Edition
Les Freed and Frank Derfler
ISBN: 0-7897-2753-6
US $29.99, CAN $44.95, UK £21.95

Special Edition Using Microsoft Windows XP Home, Best Seller Edition
Robert Coward and Brian Knittel
ISBN: 0-7897-2851-6
US $44.99, CAN $67.95, UK £32.99

Special Edition Using Microsoft Office XP
Ed Bott and Woody Leonhard
ISBN: 0-7897-2513-4
US $39.99, CAN $59.95, UK £28.99

How Computers Work, 6th Edition
Ron White (illustrated by Timothy Edward Downs)
ISBN: 0-7897-2549-5
US $34.99, CAN $52.95, UK £25.50

How to Use Microsoft Windows XP, Bestseller Edition
Walter Glenn
ISBN: 0-7897-2855-9
US $29.99, CAN $44.95, UK £21.95

www.quepublishing.com

All prices are subject to change.